CHURCH AND SECT
IN CANADA

S. D. CLARK

Professor of Sociology
University of Toronto

UNIVERSITY OF TORONTO PRESS

TO
ROSEMARY LANDRY CLARK

Preface

T H I S is not a church history of Canada. Such a history has still to be written. Here the emphasis has been upon the sociological significance of certain general movements of religion in Canadian social development. Much detailed historical material has necessarily been introduced, but much also has been passed over. There has been no attempt to exhaust any of the sources used, nor has there been any attempt to follow through every aspect of Canadian religious development, in however cursory a manner. Had either of these attempts been made, the work would have grown into several volumes. To accomplish the purpose in mind, it was necessary to trace the religious development of Canada over a long stretch of time and for the country as a whole. To others is left the task of detailed studies of particular religious movements in various local areas.

Interest in the religious development of Canada grew out of work on the country's social development. The present study is intended to supplement the author's *Social Development of Canada* (Toronto, 1942) and to pave the way for further studies of other aspects of the same general problem. The author's conviction is that sociology has much to gain from a greater use of historical material. Neglect of developments of the past has limited perspective and led to a narrowing of sociological theory. Sociology has suffered from the failure to bridge the gulf between grand works on the philosophy of history where there has been too little analysis of facts and highly detailed studies of local social groups or communities where there has been too little theoretical interpretation. Use of historical material does not involve abandonment of sociological methods; developments of the past can be examined with as much care as developments of the present. Only through an examination of such past developments can an adequate theory of social change be formulated. The present study, it is hoped, offers some demonstration of the fruitfulness of a sociological historical approach.

I am greatly indebted to Professor H. A. Innis, head of the Department of Political Economy, University of Toronto, for help and encouragement throughout work on the study. My colleagues in sociology, Professor C. W. M. Hart and Miss Jean Burnet, and also Mr. W. E. Mann, Instructor in Sociology, United College, Winnipeg, read the

manuscript or parts of it and provided much useful criticism. Acknowledgment is due my wife for a great deal of assistance. A fellowship from the John Simon Guggenheim Memorial Foundation made possible a year away from the University and greatly facilitated the task of writing.

S. D. CLARK

Antigonish, Nova Scotia
August 1, 1946

Contents

Introduction

In 1775 Nova Scotia found in Henry Alline, Newlight preacher, a great religious prophet. In 1922 a similar prophet emerged in Southern Alberta in the person of William Aberhart, high school principal and bible teacher. The religious movements which these two men initiated were separated in time by a century and a half and in space by over three thousand miles, but they were intimately related in the larger complex of the religious-social development of Canada. The area of the country in which Alline gained his following had been settled for only fifteen years. Aberhart's following was recruited in that section of Alberta which had been settled for almost exactly the same length of time. In the one case, occupation by Acadian French, in the other case, occupation by ranchers delayed earlier settlement, and, when population did move in, it came in a great rush. Alline and Aberhart thus found themselves preaching to much the same sort of people faced with much the same sort of problems. Both movements grew up on the periphery of settled society. They were an expression of the dissatisfactions of a population with the services of a formal religious order.

The social development of Canada has been characterized by a succession of such religious movements of protest. At no time has the religious organization of the Canadian community been wholly stable. The large religious denominations have struggled to secure a dominant position. Some of them have enjoyed the protection and assistance of the state. All of them have had the support of powerful economic and social interests. But in spite of such advantages they have never been able to maintain an undisputed control over the ministration of religious services. Disruption and schism have been more characteristic of the Protestant than of the Roman Catholic Church—and the concern of this study is almost wholly with the former—but neither has escaped movements wreaking havoc upon denominational unity; the chief difference has been that the one Church has tended to cry up, the other to cry down, the effects of religious division. Throughout the development of Canada, from the early settlement of New France to the present day, undercurrents of unrest in religious organization have found expression in the break from established religious authority and in the emergence of new religious forms. The movement towards separation has constituted

a powerful force in resisting any effort to build up in the country a system of ecclesiastical control.

The conflict between forces of order and separation is fundamental in religious development. It is the conflict between the church and the sect forms of religious organization.[1] The church seeks the accommodation of religious organization to the community; the welfare of society is something for which it feels responsible. The sect emphasizes the exclusiveness of religious organization; the worldly society is something evil of no concern to the spiritually minded. While no sharp line can be drawn between the two forms of religious organization (the church always contains some of the attributes of the sect while the sect is never "pure," completely other-worldly in character), within the church the spirit of accommodation tends to dominate, within the sect the spirit of separation. It is the difference in outlook, in attitude of mind, which is so important in setting the one off from the other.

This study is concerned with the conflict between the church and sect forms of religious organization in relation to the changing community structure of Canada. It seeks to offer an explanation of religious change in terms of underlying changes in social conditions.[2] The view set forth here is that the church has been dependent upon a condition of social stability and when such a condition has not been present it has given way to the sect form of religious organization. Thus developments in religious organization, on the one side, in the direction of greater order and union and, on the other side, in the direction of disorder and separation, have been closely related to movements of social order and disorder in the wider community. The church has grown out of the conditions of a mature society; the sect has been a product of what might be called frontier conditions of social life. Within the broad pattern of the social development of Canada, the persistent conflict between these two forms of religious organization takes on meaning.[3]

The study is confined to the period 1760 to 1900. Much could be said for having extended its scope backward to include the religious development of New France and forward to include that of the last half century, but to have done the first would have had little meaning without following through the highly complex subsequent developments of Roman Catholicism, while to have done the second would have involved detailed field studies of a large number of contemporary religious groups

[1]Ernest Troeltsch, *The Social Teaching of the Christian Churches*, translated by Olive Wyon (2 vols., London, 1931).
[2]H. R. Niebuhr, *The Social Sources of Denominationalism* (New York, 1929).
[3]S. D. Clark, *The Social Development of Canada* (Toronto, 1942), introduction.

and movements. The limitation of resources has made necessary the limitation in scope. The present study serves to provide a background for study of the religious organization of the contemporary community. It also serves to broaden the basis of study of the more general social development of Canada.

CHURCH AND SECT IN CANADA

CHAPTER ONE

The Great Awakening in Nova Scotia
1760-1783

T H E conflict of the French and British Empires in America, in terms of religious organization, represented a conflict between church and sect forms of religious control. France employed the church as an instrument of imperial expansion. The close relationship between church and state was evident in the part played by religious leaders in colonial government and in efforts to win the political attachments of the native population. By 1760, the Roman Catholic Church in New France had broken almost completely from the evangelical tradition of Jesuitism and had entrenched itself in the colony as the church of Empire. In New England, on the other hand, religious organization developed in sharp opposition to the interests of Empire. The settlement of Massachusetts had provided an outlet for separatist forces growing up in England, and Congregationalism, closely identified with the local village, offered a strong support in resisting the centralizing demands of an imperialist government. Sectarian tendencies in the organization of the Congregational churches were evident in the development of a closed theocratic system of colonial government in Massachusetts and in a missionary policy based upon the principle that the native population, not being of "the elect," were not qualified to share in the privileges of the white man's religious political order. The religious system of New England stood in sharp contrast with that of New France; it was the religious system of the sect as opposed to that of the church.

The collapse of the French Empire in America in 1760 involved the collapse of the territorial church and the triumph of religious sectarianism. The freeing of the New England frontier from the danger of French encroachments provided a means for the expansion of the sectarian-village system. Growth of settlement along the Atlantic seaboard and in Nova Scotia after 1760 was indicative of the strength of expansive forces within the New England farming and fishing villages and commercial towns. The bitter opposition of New England Protestantism to efforts of the Roman Catholic Church to maintain the attachments of the Acadian and native populations in Nova Scotia was reflected in the insistence upon the evacuation of the Acadians and in the lack

of any sympathetic understanding between the new settlers in Nova Scotia and the natives. The destruction of Roman Catholic influence in Nova Scotia was made complete with the establishment of New England dominance in the Maritime fisheries and with the settlement of New England farmers on the vacated lands of the Acadians. The controls of empire gave way to the controls of the local village, and the religious sect established itself in place of the church.

The rapid expansion of New England during the eighteenth century which was a factor leading to the collapse of the French Empire in America was indicative of the strengths of a system which had developed great flexibility in the organization of religious as of economic life and in methods of waging warfare, but such expansion was secured at the price of increasing conflict with British imperial interests.[1] The destruction of Louisbourg in 1745 was a military undertaking promoted by New England, but the return of Louisbourg to France in 1748 and the founding of Halifax the next year represented efforts of Britain to strengthen the lines of empire. British control in Nova Scotia involved not only the building up of naval and military garrisons but the establishment in the colony of state-supported religious institutions. The organization of the parish of St. Paul's soon after the founding of Halifax and the appointment of a missionary to serve the German settlers in Lunenburg represented efforts to consolidate the British position through the influence of the church. With the growth of settlement after 1760 such efforts were greatly extended.

The impoverished condition of the New England settlers, and the difficulties they faced in recruiting preachers of their own religious persuasion even when the means of financial support were available, encouraged hopes that many of them would abandon the principles of religious nonconformity if the services of the Church of England were provided. The appointment by the Society for the Propagation of the Gospel of an itinerant missionary for the new settlements of Nova Scotia was urged by the Reverend John Breynton, of Halifax, as early as June, 1760. "Of the Utility and Expediency of which," he wrote, "there can be no Doubt when it is considered that there are at this Time no less than eight or ten new Townships in this Colony and all unprovided with Ministers of the Gospel of any Denomination. A pious and prudent Gentleman settled at the Governour's Discretion amongst them in this Time of Poverty and Distress would go a great way to unite them in religious Opinions and reconcile those who dissent

---

[1]H. A. Innis, *The Cod Fisheries: The History of an International Economy* (Toronto and New Haven, 1940), pp. 160-7, 183-213.

from our Doctrines and Liturgy."[2] A confidence that the nonconformists would attach themselves to the Church if only its services were available underlay Breynton's proposal to appoint missionaries to the province. "Altho most of the Settlers are Dissenters," he wrote again in December, 1760, "yet we have reason to believe from their Conduct this year, they would soon be reconciled to the Church of England, provided pious and prudent Missionaries were fixed amongst them."[3]

During the first two years of the settlement of New Englanders, Breynton and his assistant in Halifax, Thomas Wood, undertook missionary tours throughout the new communities. In January, 1762, Jonathan Belcher, lieutenant-governor of the province, urged the appointment of a separate missionary to Kings County:

> The late Considerable increase of our Settlements may require the earliest attention to the Method of supplying them with a Ministry most of the new Townships being without Ministers of any persuasion.
> The first Establishment will be most likely to gain the strongest Attachments, and the Doctrines and Principles of our excellent Church, will be more easily imbibed by them, on the first Impressions of its settled Minister, than it can be after Prejudices from other Teachers settling in the Province.
> I am therefore Sir, by your favor humbly to recommend to the Society, that a Missionary may be appointed for the new Township of Horton; being the County Town, and the most Central of that and the three other Townships called Falmouth, Newport and Cornwallis, in Kings County, and that it may be part of the Instruction to this Missionary that he shall discharge his Function in rotation at these several Townships. A place of Public Worship is much wanted at Horton.[4]

The recommendation of the lieutenant-governor led to the appointment of the Reverend Joseph Bennett as missionary in Kings County in the autumn of 1762. Two years later the Reverend Thomas Wood was transferred from Halifax to Annapolis to serve the new settlements further down the Valley. In Lunenburg a new missionary, the Reverend Robert Vincent, was stationed to minister to the German Lutherans and Swiss Calvinists.

Efforts of the Society for the Propagation of the Gospel to extend missionary work within the new settlements found strong support from the colonial government. "The principal Officers of Government," the Reverend John Breynton wrote in 1767, "are members of the Church of England; Lord Wm. Campbell has upon all occasions encouraged and supported the Established Church. Nor has Lieutenant-

---

[2]Public Archives of Nova Scotia (henceforth cited as P.A.N.S.), Records of the Missionaries of the Society for the Propagation of the Gospel in Nova Scotia, 1760-1786, Halifax, June 24, 1760, John Breynton to Rev. Doctor Bearcroft.
[3]*Ibid.*, Halifax, Dec. 13, 1760, John Breynton and Thomas Wood to Rev. Doctor Bearcroft.
[4]*Ibid.*, Halifax, Jan. 14, 1762, Jonathan Belcher to Rev. Doctor Bearcroft.

Governor Franklin omitted any opportunity of shewing his zeal in the same cause. Mr. Justice Belcher is and always has been indefatigable, and Mr. Secretary Bulkely is our Constant Friend; by their joint Influence and Assiduity a Law has lately passed in Favor of St. Paul's Halifax and all other Parishes that may be hereafter settled."[5] A local missionary or corresponding committee, headed by the lieutenant-governor of the province and made up of prominent officials in Halifax, was organized in 1768 to help direct the activities of the Society for the Propagation of the Gospel in the out-settlements. Although the New Englanders, on settlement in the colony, had been promised freedom of worship, and no direct attempt was made to interfere with this privilege, extension of the influence of the Church of England was urged as a means of securing the loyalty of the inhabitants to the mother country. "I think it my Duty," Franklin, the lieutenant-governor, wrote in 1768, "to represent to your Lordship, that the Providing the Settlement, in their Infancy with Clergymen of the Church of England, is a measure that will be attended with many, and great and good consequences—as the Settlers are generally of various Persuasions, some of whom are replete with Republickan Principles, and unless Government place proper Clergymen among them before they are able to support Teachers of their own, it will be difficult to Inculcate proper Sentiments of Subordination to Government."[6]

So long as an alternative supply of clergymen was not available, the services of the Church of England were accepted, though with little display of enthusiasm. Where, however, the inhabitants were able to secure preachers of their own faith, support of the Church quickly fell off. Both in Lunenburg and in the settlements of New Englanders the missionaries of the Society for the Propagation of the Gospel faced increasing difficulty in holding their congregations together.

The economic impoverishment and cultural isolation of the settlers in Lunenburg favoured for a time the establishment of the services of the Church of England. In April, 1765, the Reverend Robert Vincent wrote "that the Differences in opinion between Lutherans and Calvins appear to be extinct, and seem on both sides, to be perfectly united, they constantly attend divine service and behave with great Diligence and Attention";[7] and, the next year, he wrote "the Germans in

[5]Public Archives of Canada (henceforth cited as P.A.C.), S.P.G., Nova Scotia, vol. B25, 1760-86, Halifax, Oct. 23, 1767, Rev. J. Breynton to Dr. Daniel Burton, London.
[6]P.A.C., Nova Scotia State Papers, vol. A83, Halifax, July 11, 1768, Franklin to Secretary of State.
[7]Records of the Missionaries of the S.P.G. in Nova Scotia, 1760-1786, Lunenburg, Apr. 27, 1763, Robert Vincent to Rev. Dr. Burton.

general attend Divine Service with great Decency, and have no Reason but to believe them sincere as they constantly partake of ye most holy Sacrament."[8] The missionary, however, early faced the competition of Calvinist and Lutheran preachers. "We have a Calvinist amongst us," Vincent wrote in August, 1764, "who hath set up for a Preacher who was always a turbulent Man in his Country, but by the Moderate Conduct and Influence of one Mr. Zouberbuhler our chief Magistrate I believe he will soon desist as he has not above 3 or 4 that appear in ye Cause."[9] Though the attempt to organize a Calvinist church at that time was not successful, it carried threats to the position of the Church of England in the settlement. "The Enthusiast[s] I mentioned in my last," Vincent was able to write in November of the same year "seem at present to be somewhat cool in their proceedings."[10] At the same time, attempts made by the Germans to establish a Lutheran church aroused the concern of the missionary. "With respect to Lunenburg," Vincent wrote in April, 1765, "I am to inform you that the Germans, are now very anxious to introduce a German Minister and are gone so far as to have prepared some timber towards erecting a Meeting House. This is the Result of ye Governments withdrawing their Bountys on ye Produce of their Lands, whilst that lasted they behaved with the greatest seeming Conformity, but now they have nothing more to expect from thence the Mask is thrown off by some, the Young People in general will not adhere to the Scheme."[11] According to Vincent, the Lutherans failed to secure the assistance which they had anticipated from the Germans in Halifax; work upon the meeting-house ceased, and the immediate danger to the position of the Church of England in the community passed. "'Tis the opinion of the considerable part," the missionary wrote in May, 1765, "that 'tis entirely dropt, and what induces me to think so, is, that during the Time it was in Agitation my Congregation diminished considerable but now they come to Church as usual."[12]

Efforts of the inhabitants to secure ministers of their own faith, however, were persisted in and eventually led to the successful establishment of independent religious services. The Swiss Calvinists, failing to secure a regular clergyman from the Dutch Reformed Church in Philadelphia, eventually in 1770 had resort to a preacher ordained by the Congregational Church in Halifax — a Mr. Bruin Romcas

[8]*Ibid.*, Halifax, June 19, 1764, Mr. Vincent to Secretary, S.P.G.
[9]*Ibid.*, Lunenburg, Aug. 15, 1764, Robert Vincent to Secretary, S.P.G.
[10]*Ibid.*, Lunenburg, Nov. 20, 1764, Robert Vincent to Secretary, S.P.G.
[11]*Ibid.*, Halifax, Apr. 29, 1765, Robert Vincent to Secretary, S.P.G.
[12]*Ibid.*, Lunenburg, May 31, 1765, Robert Vincent to Secretary, S.P.G.

Comingo, generally known as Brown.[13] Two years later, the Lutherans succeeded in obtaining the services of a regular German Lutheran minister—the Reverend Frederick Shulz.[14] Support of the Church of England rapidly weakened. In 1771 the Reverend Peter de la Roche, the new missionary in Lunenburg, wrote:

> I am sorry to be obliged to say, that I have found the Church of England in a most deplorable situation here. Her followers are in general bound to her by no other ties than pecuniary interest. They are not obliged to defray the charges of keeping ministers, or to contribute in the least to necessary parochial expenses; and that consideration only supports their attachment to the Church of England: Time must strengthen it; and graft nobler motives on their self-interested hearts. I apprehend you have heard of the Separation of great numbers among the Germans from the Church: They have created two meeting houses; one for the Calvinists, the other for the Lutherans. The first have got a Minister ordained about a twelve month ago for that purpose at Halifax: he is a Hollander, was a mean artificer (a wool-comber) and being very illiterate has no other means for getting a reputation among his hearers than launching out upon the dangerous questions of Predestination, Newlight, etc. The Lutherans, have no regular minister, and whether they will be able to get one at least is uncertain; meanwhile some among them take upon themselves to officiate and to preach. This behaviour howsoever illegal, is prudently winked at: the least attempt at putting a stop to their proceedings would be looked upon and cried up by them, as downright persecution.[15]

Efforts of the Church of England to minister to the New England settlers in the colony were little more successful. For a time the missionary in Kings County, the Reverend Joseph Bennett, was able to boast of the influence of the Church among the inhabitants. "The people here," he wrote six weeks after settling in the County, "are very much divided in their religious sentiments, there are but fue of the established Church, the rest are dissenters of all denominations, yet I hope diligence, moderation and time will bring those who are in Error to a Better way of thinking."[16] By the middle of the next summer Bennett remained equally sanguine as to the prospects of the Church among the settlements of New Englanders. "As the inhabitants of this province," he wrote, "have come from different parts of the World it is But reasonable to Imagine their Religius sentiments must be very different But I make no doubt but the Establish'd Church will

---

[13]Though Brown lacked the educational qualifications for the ministry, failure to secure a more suitable candidate justified the Congregational ministers in performing the act of ordination. "We do not mean that our procedure in this affair," they asserted, "should be made a precedent of, or brought into usage in this infant colony or elsewhere, unless in cases of necessity, as above mentioned." M. B. DesBrisay, *History of the County of Lunenburg* (Toronto, 1895), p. 91.

[14]*Ibid.* Cf. also D. Luther Roth, *Acadie and the Acadians* (Philadelphia, 1890).

[15]S.P.G., Nova Scotia, vol. B25, 1760-86, Lunenburg, Nov. 28, 1771, Peter de la Roche to Secretary of S.P.G.

[16]Records of the Missionaries of the S.P.G. in Nova Scotia, 1760-1786, Fort Edward, Kings County, Jan. 4, 1763, Rev. Mr. Bennett to Secretary of S.P.G.

prevail in some time where there are Missionaries, as the poverty of the inhabitants puts it out of their power to pay Ministers of their own persuasion for some time. . . . I cannot say but I have met with opposition, but it was from people of No weight whose opposition had no Influence."[17] Support of the Church of England, however, quickly fell off with the coming in of ministers from New England or with the establishment of religious services through the use of lay preachers. In June, 1765, Bennett reported to the Society that many of the inhabitants in Kings County were becoming reconciled to the mode and form of worship of the Church of England but "there are some who will attend no regular Clergyman of any persuasion, as they Choose Lay Preachers preferable to any persons properly educated or Legally Authoris'd." He had learned that two clergymen had been ordained in New Haven for Cornwallis and Horton but he was confident that should they come they would not remain "as the people are not as yet in a capacity to pay them, and wou'd much rather attend a Church Minister who wou'd be no expence to them, than a Dissenter whom they must support."[18] Bennett's confidence proved without foundation, and, with the location of a Congregational minister—a Mr. Fuller—in Horton, he received a polite but firm request from the inhabitants to cease holding service in that community. "'Tis their desire," the note from the clerk asserted, "that you wou'd not give yourself the trouble of any longer service among them."[19] Bennett ceased to officiate in Horton, although, as he pointed out to the Society in January, 1766, he would not have done so had there been one family of the Church of England in the community.[20] At Cornwallis, he and Mr. Benaiah Phelps, the new Congregational minister, held alternate services, one in the forenoon and the other in the afternoon, and for a time this arrangement appeared to work satisfactorily. Disagreement between the two ministers, however, eventually led to the separation of the Congregationalists and the organization of a church of their own. The Reverend Mr. Bennett, with only five families claiming allegiance to the Church of England, faced great difficulty in maintaining services, although he boasted that he still had a considerable congregation.[21] In the meantime, the Congregational minister in Horton had been succeeded by a Baptist minister, Ebenezer Moulton, and a new congregational minister had come to Windsor and Falmouth; "I cultivate a good understanding with him," Bennett wrote of the latter, "I do not

[17]*Ibid.*, Falmouth, July 28, 1763, Rev. Mr. Bennett to Secretary, S.P.G.
[18]*Ibid.*, Halifax, June 14, 1765, Rev. Mr. Joseph Bennett to Secretary, S.P.G.
[19]*Ibid.*, Horton, Aug. 10, 1765, Nathan De Wolf, Drs. Clerk to Rev. Mr. Bennett.
[20]*Ibid.*, Windsor, Jan. 27, 1766, Joseph Bennett to Secretary, S.P.G.
[21]*Ibid.*, Windsor, Aug. 22, 1767, Joseph Bennett to Secretary, S.P.G.

find he is a Bigott he is an Irishman."[22] Newlight or Baptist tendencies
in the religion of the New Englanders weakened church order of any
sort, with effects evident in Bennett's efforts to establish the services
of the Church of England. "Numbers of the people in my Mission,"
he wrote, "think but very lightly of the Sacraments either of Baptism
or the Lord's Supper."[23] Throughout the district, the position of
the Church became increasingly unsatisfactory. The Reverend W. Ellis,
who succeeded Bennett in 1775, wrote of the state of the mission
in 1776:

> On my arrival I found the lower orders of the people nearly to a man, Presby-
> terians or Fanatics, many of the better sort indifferent to all Religions, and a few
> Gentlemen's familys well affected to the Church. The too extensive duty of my
> predecessor, had been in part the cause that things were not in a better condition,
> for the people living scattered up and down, and many of them, most of them indeed
> at a great distance from the church, they would not come at the hazard of not finding
> Divine Service, which must be often the case when the Minister was at the distance
> of Cornwallis, they therefore grew indifferent, or else indulged their own whims. . . .
> There was no Clerk, hardly anybody would take the trouble to make a response,
> indeed upon the whole, I believe Almighty God was never elsewhere worshipped,
> in so mean and slovenly a manner.[24]

In other areas settled by New Englanders, the Church of England
made no effective effort to establish the services of religion. In 1764
the Reverend Thomas Wood wrote of his ministrations in Annapolis and
Granville: "There are actually now more than eight hundred souls now
settled in both Townships but have neither a Church nor Minister
among them, and when I told them the truly Venerable Society would
I hoped as soon as possible give their charitable Assistance in endeavoring
to get them supplied with both, & that it was probably I shou'd be
appointed their Missionary & reside among them, their joy was universal
& almost inconceivable."[25] When Wood did locate in Annapolis,
however, he revealed little interest in the religious welfare of the inhabitants but turned increasingly to work among the Micmac Indians and
to a study of the Micmac grammar. Here, as in Cornwallis, the large
body of Congregationalists turned to the support of ministers of their
own faith. By 1776 at least eight or nine regular Congregational ministers
had located within the various settlements: Benaiah Phelps in Cornwallis,
Nehemiah Porter in Yarmouth, Israel Cheever in Liverpool, Samuel

[22]*Ibid.*, Windsor, Feb. 21, 1767, Joseph Bennett to Secretary, S.P.G.
[23]*Ibid.*
[24]S.P.G., Nova Scotia, vol. B25, 1760-1786, Windsor, Sept. 14, 1776, W. Ellis
to Secretary, S.P.G.
[25]Records of Missionaries of the S.P.G. in Nova Scotia, 1760-1786, Halifax,
Oct. 14, 1764, Rev. Mr. Wood to Secretary, S.P.G.

Wood in Barrington and Argyle, John Seccombe in Chester, Jonathan Scott in Chebogue, Asahel Morse in Granville, Seth Noble in Maugerville and Caleb Gannett (until 1771) in Cumberland. In addition, at least one Baptist preacher, Ebenezer Moulton, and one lay preacher, John Frost, were active in church work, the former in Chebogue and Horton and the latter in Argyle.[26]

Efforts of the Church of England to establish itself in the colony threatened the solidarity of the local village settlements and their political and cultural autonomy in relationship to the provincial capital. Episcopalianism was wholly foreign to a population whose cultural values were a product of the closed village-sectarian system of New England; community organization in terms of the village emphasized the importance of the local congregation and the dangers of episcopacy in religious organization. Church functionaries sent in from outside offered a challenge to the village system of proprietory leadership in much the same way as did government surveyors and tax collectors; school teachers appointed by the Society for the Propagation of the Gospel, for instance, threatened to usurp the responsibility for local education. Among the German Lutherans and Swiss Calvinists in Lunenburg, ethnic differences offered an equally strong support in resisting the encroachments of an outside religious authority. The Church of England was the church of empire. Its missionary work represented efforts to strengthen the ties of the colony with the mother country and to integrate more closely the various scattered settlements within a provincial system. Close identification of the interests of the Church with those of the state strengthened the position of the Establishment in the provincial capital—evident, for instance, in the weakness of the Lutheran and Congregational churches in the city—but seriously limited its influence in the out-settlements. Resistance to the Church inevitably developed in relation to the resistance of the out-settlements to the interferences of the colonial government. Strong feelings of local autonomy found support in independent forms of religious organization as a check upon the claims of Church Establishment. This was particularly true of the New England Congregationalists.

The character of the New England settlement in Nova Scotia favoured the establishment of Congregational forms of religious worship. Leadership played a conspicuous part in the promotion of immigration and in the actual carrying out of settlement schemes, and there was less expression than usual as a result of that intense individualism character-

[26]Cf. E. M. Saunders, *History of the Baptists of the Maritime Provinces* (Halifax, 1902); J. B. Brebner, *The Neutral Yankees of Nova Scotia* (New York, 1937); I. F. Mackinnon, *Settlements and Churches in Nova Scotia* (Montreal and Halifax, 1930).

istic of frontier movements of population.[27] The society of the rural
New England village was carried over almost whole to Nova Scotia
in 1760, and local village ties as well as ties with the homeland to some
extent endured within the new settlements. Social organization quickly
established itself, and the common social heritage of the great bulk
of the settlers tended to secure a considerable degree of conformity
to local group controls. The individual fitted himself into a social
system not greatly different from the one of which he had been a part
before migration; if he found himself living among strangers, they were,
for the most part, strangers who had come from one of his neighbouring
villages and were a product of a cultural system not greatly different
from the one which had been his own.[28]

The strength of the local group loyalties of the New England settlers
was apparent in religious life. "The Sabbath," Robinson and Rispin
wrote, "is most religiously observed; none of them will do any business,
or travel, on that day; and all kinds of sports, plays and revels, are
strictly prohibited. They take great care to educate their children in
the fear of the Lord, and early to implant in them a right notion of
religion, and the great duty they owe to God and their parents."[29]
The puritan heritage of the population provided a strong informal
support of religious organization, while religious loyalties found support
in the loyalties to the village group. The town meeting assumed
responsibility for the erection in the new settlement of a place of worship
and lay leaders took the initiative in establishing the services of religion.
Church organization came into being not through the intervention of
an outside religious body but through the act of the local inhabitants in
entering into a church covenant. The record of the founding of the
church of Chebogue reveals the nature of the process of Congregational
church building. The Church Records read:

> In the Year One Thousand Seven Hundred and Sixty-Six, there evidently
> appeared religious Concern on the Minds of some Persons in the Society of Jebogue
> in Yarmouth. Some would embrace the Opportunity of the Sabbath between
> Meetings, and at other Season be speaking of the Things of Religion with Seriousness
> and Attention, to all Appearance.
>
> At this Season of religious Thoughtfulness, Mr. John Frost, Esq. of Argyle, did
> several Times visit the People in Jebogue, and went to their Houses and conversed
> with the People; and being esteemed a serious and good Man, he was much set by
> and esteemed by those that were thoughtful about Religion. Mr. Frost did also,
> about this Time, deliver several Discourses in Publick, as he used to do among
> the People of Argyle; but his Preaching was not very much esteemed by the People
> in general, and could hardly be put up with by some . . . .

---

[27]Brebner, *Neutral Yankees of Nova Scotia*, chaps. II and III; R. H. Akagi, *The Town Proprietors of the New England Colonies* (Philadelphia, 1924).

[28]S. D. Clark, *The Social Development of Canada* (Toronto, 1942), pp. 101-4.

[29]J. Robinson and T Rispin, *A Journey through Nova Scotia* (York, 1774), p. 35.

In the Fall of this Year, (1766) there appeared extraordinary Concern and Engagedness on the Minds of some, and there was a Meeting set up on the Week Time, for Prayer and religious Conference. About this Time also, there was some Persons at Argyle exercised with some serious Concern about the Things of Religion. The People in Jebogue thus seriously inclined, entered into solemn Covenant to walk with God and to watch over one another and to carry on the Concerns of the Redeemer's Kingdom, in about the Space of a Year after their first setting up private Meetings; which Meetings were always held in the Day Time and at the Houses of those that were seriously inclined. The People of Jebogue held meetings on the Lords Day at this Time, tho' they were destitute of a Minister through all the Summer of this Year; Mr. Moulton at this Time being gone to Horton, and Mr. Wood to Barrington; only Mr. Frost was here a few Times this Year, viz 1766.[30]

The Congregational church grew out of the village organization, but religious organization in turn provided a support for village government. The covenant was an expression of the individual's obligations to his neighbours as well as to his church and constituted an explicit declaration of the socially unifying role of religion. As such it served as an instrument for identifying the church with the community and thereby giving to it a tangible basis of organization. Government of the church and village was closely interlocked; the elders of the church and the town proprietors tended to be the same persons. Social distinctions were recognized, and in fact to some extent secured, in religious organization. Status in the local community was associated with the individual's position within the church. At the same time the moral solidarity of the village found support in the harsh puritanical sanctions of Congregationalism.

We do also promise [the inhabitants of Chebogue covenanted] that, by the Grace of God, we will oppose all Sin and Error wherever they appear, both in our selves and others, as far as in us lies; namely, All foolish Talking and Jesting, and Wantonness; All vain Disputings about Words and Things that gender Strife, and doth not edify to more Godliness; Also vain Company-keeping and spending Time idly, at Taverns and Tippling-Houses, or elsewhere; Evil Whispering or Backbiting of any Person; also carnel and unnecessary Discourse about Worldly Things, especially on the Sabbath Day; Unnecessary forsaking the Assembling of our selves together in private convenient Conferences, and also on the Sabbath Day; and all other Sins whatsoever, both of Omission and Commission.[31]

Any act or declaration of the individual which was considered as affecting the welfare of the church was dealt with by means of a public charge within its councils; quarrels between husband and wife, the use of profane language, drunkenness, work on the sabbath, and indulgence in such pastimes as dancing, as well as more serious offences such as adultery, fornication, and sacrilegious utterances, were treated

---

[30]P.A.N.S., Records of the Church of Jebogue in Yarmouth, pp. 9-10.
[31]*Ibid.*, pp. 15-16.

as sins against the church for which public confession and forgiveness were necessary. Through the exercise of such sanctions, the controls of Congregationalism were extended into all spheres of the social life of the local village.

At the same time, Congregationalism closely identified itself with the wider group loyalties—and antagonisms—of the population. The Congregational ministers provided a direct and close tie with the New England home community; the Congregational evangelical tradition provided an indirect but no less enduring connection. On the other side, efforts of the New England settlers to resist encroachments of the Halifax authorities upon the prerogatives of the local village government found their strongest support in the religious separatism of the Congregational Church system. Congregationalism retained many of the characteristics of the religious sect, and these characteristics became particularly pronounced in Nova Scotia in face of the struggle of the out-settlements to avoid absorption into an imperialist-provincial system dominated by Halifax. The strong antagonism of the New England settlers to the colonial government favoured the organization of churches free of political connections of any sort. In competition with the Church of England, Congregationalism was able to capitalize upon the strong separatist spirit within the out-settlements.

In spite of such advantages, however, difficulties were early faced in maintaining the formal organization of the Congregational churches in the province. The Congregational religious tradition constituted a vital force in the pioneer Nova Scotian settlements, but there was lacking within many of the local congregations that harmony of views necessary for the successful maintenance of the machinery of church government. It was far from a united Congregational body which sought to establish organized religion in Nova Scotia after 1760. Far-reaching divisions within the Congregational Church system in New England as a result of the Great Awakening after 1742 inevitably extended into Nova Scotia and affected the establishment of churches there.[32] Many of the New Englanders who settled in Nova Scotia had come under the influence of religious revival, and the conflict between evangelical and non-evangelical elements, which in New England had led to the separation of what were called "New Lights" from "Old Lights," quickly asserted itself.

[32]O. E. Winslow, *Jonathan Edwards, 1703-1758* (New York, 1940); King's Chapel Lectures; *The Religious History of New England* (Cambridge, 1917); A. D. Belden, *George Whitefield, The Awakener: A Modern Study of the Evangelical Revival* (London, 1930); F. G. Beardsley, *The History of American Revivals* (New York, 1912); W. W. Sweet, *The Story of Religions in America* (New York and London, 1930); W. W. Sweet, *Religion in Colonial America* (New York, 1942).

Although no extensive disruption occurred in the organization of Congregationalism in Nova Scotia before 1776—the hold of New England conservatism upon the rural village system was too strong—there were indications very early within some of the churches of serious internal dissensions growing out of fundamental differences in views respecting church government. Conflict tended to develop in particular in relation to the question of the appointment of a minister. The difficulty of securing properly qualified ministers from New England encouraged the employment of lay preachers or the support of preachers of a different faith. When the formal appointment of a minister was undertaken, the Church faced the danger of finding itself divided between those who stressed the importance of orthodoxy and those who were more concerned with maintaining a zeal for the evangelical cause. Where agreement could not be secured under such circumstances, formal separation occurred.

The difficulties encountered in the establishment of a church in Chebogue were illustrative of the sort of problems faced in the organization of Congregationalism in the colony. An early entry in the Chebogue Church Records reads:

December 18, 1767. This Day, the Church of Jebogue in Yarmouth, by a Vote, chose John Frost Esqr. of Argyle, to be their Elder. . . .

Betwixt this Choosing of Mr. Frost, to the Time of his being removed from Argyle to Yarmouth, there was much Consulting among the Brethren of the Church, and various were their Opinions about Mr. Frost: some thought his Gifts and ministerial Accomplishments were not sufficient for the pastoral office, and others thought they were: As for the Congregation, they unanimously rejected Mr. Frost as a Teacher for them.[33]

Because of the dissatisfaction, the brethren asked Frost to release them from their agreement with him, but, stubborn man as he probably was, he insisted that he had been duly elected and refused to accede to the request. Faced with this embarrassing situation, the church met on May 1, 1769, and concluded to ordain him as pastor. The Records continue:

Mr. Frost being come to Yarmouth, he preached but a few Sabbaths before the Congregation manifested much Uneasiness and Disaffection; and their Uneasiness grew to that Degree, that the main Body of the Congregation, with two of the Brethren, separated from the Church, sometime in the Summer of this Year (viz. 1769) and set up a Meeting by themselves on Lord's Days, having Mr. Ebenezer Moulton a baptist Minister for their Leader: and this Separation continued till in the Spring of the year, A.D. 1770. Thus the little Society of Jebogue, consisting of not more than 70 poor Families in all, were divided into two Parties in Opposition

---

[33]Records of the Church of Jebogue in Yarmouth. p. 18.

to each other; at which Time, many hard and bitter Things were vented by both Parties, to the great Dishonour of God, and hurt and wounding of Religion.[34]

As a means of reconciling the two groups, a number of the Society sent a petition to the churches in New England seeking assistance, and, in May, 1770, two ministers were sent to Chebogue.

They were very coldly received by the Church at first: because they being sent for by those who were not looked upon friendly to the revival of Religion among the People, they were ready to conclude that the Ministers were not friendly to the Work and Doctrines of Grace; and so were too much disposed to be shy of and reject them.

But notwithstanding the cold Reception these good Men met with at their Arrival, they sought the Good of the People, both Church and Society; and God so far succeeded their Endeavours, that on the second Sabbath after their Arrival, the Church and Society met in one Place for publick Worship, and the Reverend Ministers preached to the Acceptance of the People, one in the Forenoon and the other in the Afternoon: After which the Church was not so reserve and suspicious of them, being more satisfied respecting their Doctrines and Friendliness to vital Religion.[35]

The ministers advised that both Frost and Moulton cease preaching until choice of a new minister had been decided upon. Frost removed to Argyle and for some time Moulton acceded to the ministerial decision by not preaching on the Sabbath; public worship was led by a lay minister, Mr. Scott. Difficulties, however, soon re-appeared in the organization of the church.

While these Things [the choice of a new minister] were in Agitation, Sometime in the Fall of the Year A.D. 1770; through Misunderstanding and Disagreement among the People, Mr. Moulton was introduced to preach in the Meeting House, which was then the Place of publick Worship: And this Matter was so ordered, that Mr. Scott knew nothing of it, till Mr. Moulton attempted to begin the Publick Worship; upon which Mr. Scott observed to the People, that he knew not that Mr. Moulton was to preach; and as Things were circumstanced, he could not join with them in the Worship at that Time; and then he went away; and some of ye People, both of Church and Society went away with him, and repaired to a private House, where they held their Worship: and Mr. Moulton preacht to ye People that tarried in ye Meeting house.

This Proceeding occasioned a second Separation; most of the Society met by themselves for Divine Worship on Lord's Days, having Mr. Moulton for their Leader: and most of the Church, with some of ye Society met by themselves, having Mr. Scott for their Leader; and this continued all the ensuing Winter; in which Season there was much Talk of setting up a baptist Church, which Mr. Moulton endeavoured to effect at this Time, which if he had succeeded therein, a Foundation would have been laid for a lasting Separation: but Providence ordered otherwise.[36]

---

[34]*Ibid.*, p. 19.
[35]*Ibid.*, pp. 23-4.
[36]*Ibid.*, p. 29. The Reverend Nehemiah Porter of Yarmouth wrote to the Reverend Andrew Elliott in Boston, November 16, 1770, of the situation in the Chebogue

Gradually, the support of Moulton fell off, and when by spring most of the separating members had attached themselves again to the church, the Baptist minister withdrew from the community. By the autumn of 1771 the various parties were in sufficient agreement to call Mr. Scott and have him ordained as minister of the church.

In a number of the other churches similar difficulties were being faced. Mathers Congregational church in Halifax scarcely succeeded in remaining in existence. In Liverpool, dissatisfaction with the Congregational minister, the Reverend Israel Cheever, prompted the lieutenant-governor to propose the establishment of a missionary of the Church of England in the community. "Liverpool is chiefly composed of Dissenters of various Sects," he wrote to the Society for the Propagation of the Gospel, December, 1766, "but there are many people of the Church of England, and many others who profess such moderate Principles, as to attend the Church if any was there Established; they have indeed a Dissenting Minister but as he is much disliked by the people in General, little attention is paid to him, nor are the people as yet in Circumstances to Maintain him."[37] Quarrels between Cheever and members of the congregation continued to weaken the influence of the church.[38] In Cornwallis, the appointment of the Reverend Benaiah Phelps in 1765 was from the beginning not generally well received.[39] In this area of the province, as in Chebogue, Baptist influence made itself felt, and in 1763 Ebenezer Moulton succeeded in organizing for a time a Baptist church in Horton. Probably none of the Congregational churches in Nova Scotia before 1776 were able wholly to escape internal dissension and conflict.

Widespread schismatic movements, however, were held in check by the absence of leaders to give expression to the dissatisfaction within the churches; only where the services of such a preacher as the Reverend Ebenezer Moulton were available did open schism result. Preaching talent was at a premium in the pioneer rural villages in Nova Scotia,

church: "A Congregational Church was gathered here, last September Three Years ago, in which I have to this Day officiated as their Minister—The other Part of the Town settled on a River called Tabogue are less happy than we in Regard of Unity—The Rev'd Messrs Reed & Conant of Bridgewater if I mistake not were here last Spring to assist them to Unity, and so far succeeded as to persuade them to meet in One Assembly, till the last Sabbath, when they parted again, and One Part have Mr Scott a layman among them, & the other Part Mr Moulton a Baptist Minister from Brimfield." "Letters relating to the Congregational Churches of Nova Scotia in 1770," communicated by Samuel A. Green (*Proceedings of the Massachusetts Historical Society*, vol. IV, 2nd series, 1887-9, Boston, 1889, p. 73).

[37]Records of the Missionaries of the S.P.G. in Nova Scotia, 1760-1786, Halifax, Dec. 29, 1766, Michael Francklin, Lieut.-Gov., N.S. to Secretary, S.P.G.

[38]P.A.C., Perkins (Simeon) Diary, Mar. 15, 1775.

[39]A. W. H. Eaton, *The History of King's County, Nova Scotia* (Salem, 1910), pp. 272-3.

and before 1776 the Congregational ministers were faced with no serious challenge to their authority. The social exclusiveness of the small proprietory classes supported the professional exclusiveness of the Congregational ministers. The tie with New England reinforced conservative tendencies in the Nova Scotian rural society. Disaffection among "the masses" within the theocratic social order lacked means of outlet; it expressed itself in sporadic and random defections from Congregational religious controls rather than in any general movement of religious separation. It was not until 1776 that the leadership was secured which made possible any real break with the authority of the established Congregational churches. The Great Awakening of Nova Scotia found its prophet in a local preacher by the name of Henry Alline.

Alline, the son of a New England farmer who had settled in the village of Falmouth in Nova Scotia, began preaching in the summer of 1776 after experiencing a conversion in which he was seized with the conviction that he was called to preach the gospel among his fellow-countrymen. "It being reported at this time," he wrote of these early preaching efforts, "that Henry Alline was turned New-Light preacher, many would come from other towns, even whole boatloads. Some came to hear what the babler had to say; some came with gladness of heart that God had raised up one to speak in his name; and some came to make a scoff, but did not seem to trouble me much; for I trust God was with me to face a frowning world."[40] Thereafter, he quickly extended his field of preaching to the two neighbouring communities of Newport and Cornwallis. By the spring of 1777 he was preaching in settlements as far west as Annapolis.[41] Wherever he went he attracted large followings, and, when the doors of meeting houses were not opened to him, he gathered together those who would attend his preaching in private homes, barns, or open fields. He was constantly on the move, preaching often two sermons a day in two different places,

---

[40]Henry Alline, *The Life and Journal of the Rev. Mr. Henry Alline* (Boston, 1806), p. 47.

[41]The Reverend Joseph Crandall, then a boy apparently living in Chester, wrote of his early acquaintance with the Newlights: "I was born in a place called Triertown, on Rhode Island. My parents, Webber Crandall and Mary Vaughan, emigrated from that country and settled in Nova Scotia about one year before the Revolution. . . . I recollect one day a couple of strangers came to the house where I was living, and talked of a strange man that was preaching in Windsor and Falmouth; that he preached in the night and the people were becoming crazy, and talked about their souls. My father was there at the time, and said they were Newlights, and that they were the people of God, for they were christians. This strange preacher was Henry Allen, and my father said he was right, that no one could go to heaven unless he was converted. Some time after this Mr. John Sargent came to Chester, and he was called a Newlight Preacher; then came Handly Chipman, and then Harris Harding, and there was a great excitement among the people,—numbers professed to be converted. The Vaughan's, the Floyd's, and many other families followed the new preachers." *Christian Visitor*, vol. VI, Apr. 15, 1853.

although when a considerable interest in religion manifested itself in any particular area he concentrated his efforts upon the promotion of a revival. "The work of God," he wrote of a visit to Cornwallis on May 16, 1777, "was so powerful in this town, that I preached sometimes two sermons a day for five or six days together, and the people attended in great numbers. I discoursed of little else but religion night and day."[42]

Alline's influence remained strongest in the rural villages in the Minas Basin and Annapolis Valley, but his ordination by the Newlight church which he had founded in Cornwallis as an itinerant missionary in December, 1778, prompted him to undertake preaching tours throughout the country, and from the spring of 1779 until his death in the summer of 1784 he visited, in many cases on more than one occasion, every important settlement in Nova Scotia and Prince Edward Island. A number of local preachers were attracted to his side, and two of these, John Payzant and Thomas Handly Chipman, quickly gained prominence as Newlight evangelists. Under their preaching, or that of Alline himself, revivals of religion sprang up throughout the country. The growth of revivalist influence in Liverpool was illustrative of the way the movement spread.

Alline visited Liverpool for the first time on December 11, 1781. Of his reception there on this occasion he wrote: "I found a kind people, but in midnight darkness, and vastly given to frolicking, rioting and all manner of levity. When I first preached among them I had but little encouragement."[43] When he returned, however, on December 25, he received a better hearing. "I preached again in different places," he wrote, "and found some little movings among the people."[44] By January 1 he was able to write: "Many were very much awakened; which was such a new thing (neither known nor heard of amongst them) that many did not know what ailed them."[45] The diary of Simeon Perkins provides ample testimony of the growing interest in the evangelical cause.[46] Of Sunday, December 9 (the date did not agree with that given by Alline), Perkins entered into his diary: "Mr. Alline Preached at Mr. Stevenson's in the Evening. A Great Number attended, and in General Approved of his preaching." Of Saturday, January 5, 1782, Perkins wrote: "Warm day. Mr. Alline Preaches this evening at Mr. Smith's House. Many People attend, & generally are pleased with him." Though Alline left the community soon after, the religious interest remained strong, and highly successful meetings

[42]Alline, *Life and Journal of the Rev. Mr. Henry Alline*, p. 53.
[43]*Ibid.*, p. 148.
[44]*Ibid.*, pp. 148-9.
[45]*Ibid.*, p. 150.
[46]Perkins (Simeon) Diary.

were held in private homes under the guidance of local leaders. Of one such meeting, Perkins wrote, February 3, 1782: "A Religious meeting held at my House in the Evening, a large Concourse of People, I believe near 150 Attended, which is till of Late, a Very Strange thing in this Place. Such a meeting having Scarcely been Known in the Place Since the Settlement of it, till Since Mr. Alline was here. what the Event will be God only Knows, but to Appearance many people who have not been remarkable for Religion heretofore, are now under great Concern, and making the Grand inquiry, what they Shall do to be Saved."

When Alline returned to Liverpool in November, 1782, the revival he had promoted the preceding year gathered new strength. He wrote:

When I came to Liverpool, I had the happiness to meet a number of my friends on the wharf, who informed me of the glorious work of God, that had appeared ever since I left them, and was still going on in the place.... Almost all the town assembled together, and some that were lively Christians prayed and exhorted, and God was there with a truth. I preached every day, and sometimes twice a day; and the houses where I went were crowded almost all the time. Many were brought out of darkness and rejoiced, and exhorted in public. And O how affecting it was to see some young people not only exhort their companions but also take their parents by the hand, and entreat them for their soul's sake to rest no longer in their sins, but fly to Jesus Christ while there was hope.... The work of God continued with uncommon power through almost all the place.[47]

As during the winter before, meetings were continued even when the evangelist was not present and his visits only served to intensify the growing religious interest. "I came again to Liverpool," he wrote of December 24, 1782, "where I found the people still vastly engaged in religion, and pressing into the kingdom."[48] Departing on January 1 for Halifax, he returned about ten days later. "O the happy days which I there enjoyed," he wrote of this visit, "not only in my own soul, but to see the kingdom of God flourishing. When I went to preach at the meeting-house, at the hour appointed, the people were crowding to hear; and when the sermon was over, I was obliged to stop many hours in the broad-alley, to discourse with the people; for it seemed as if they could not go away."[49] Entries made by Simeon Perkins in his diary during this winter were suggestive of the strength of religious interests in the town. Even Perkins himself, hard-headed business man though he was, had come very much under the influence of the evangelical preaching.

The work of Alline challenged directly the authority of the Congregational churches in Nova Scotia, and, in the end, the basis of government of the whole Congregational system. The steps leading to

[47]Alline, *Life and Journal of the Rev. Mr. Henry Alline*, pp. 166-7.
[48]*Ibid.*, p. 167.   [49]*Ibid.*, p. 168.

his decision to become a preacher of the gospel revealed clearly the process of disintegration of values underlying the organization of Congregationalism. Through his conversion, Alline received a direct call to preach without the aid of such an intermediary agency as the Church. In responding to this call, he challenged the prerogative of the Church to perform ordination. "Although many (to support the ministry of Antichrist)," he wrote, "will pretend, there is no such thing, as a man's knowing in these days he is called to preach any other way, than his going to the seats of learning to be prepared for the ministry, and then authorized by men: yet blessed be God, there is a knowledge of these things, which an uneducated man knows nothing of. For my own part it.was so clear to me, that I had not the least doubt, but I should preach the gospel."[50] Though accepting the genuineness of the call, Alline at first was inclined to conform to the principle that training was required before entering the ministry. He had not attended school after he was eleven years of age, and as a result considered postponing preaching until he had improved his educational attainments. "The prejudices of education and the strong ties of tradition," he wrote of his troubled state of mind respecting the decision to preach, "so chained me down, that I could not think myself qualified for it, without having a great deal of human learning; and although I sometimes had not the least doubt, but God had called me to the ministry, yet I could not believe, that it was his will, that I should preach, until he had found out some way to get me qualified by human assistance, for I thought I must go, but could not go without learning."[51] The growing conviction, however, that he would not have been "called" to preach the gospel if his training had been considered inadequate eventually led him to reject his early plans to enter a seminary of learning and to embark immediately upon a career of preaching. "About the 13th or 14th of April, 1776," he wrote in justification of his decision, "I began to see that I had all this time been led astray by labouring so much after human learning and wisdom, and had held back from the call of God. One day in my meditation I had such a discovery of Christ's having every thing I needed, and that it was all mine, that I saw I needed nothing to qualify me but Christ."[52]

Acceptance of the "call" implied a revolt from the authority of the Church, and the failure to seek the training necessary to qualify for the ministry involved carrying the revolt one step further. In fact, the authority of the Church was much more seriously threatened by such a failure than by the mere acceptance of the call. The noncon-

[50]*Ibid.*, p. 36.   [52]*Ibid.*, p. 45.
[51]*Ibid.*, p. 41.

formist churches had learned from experience that those who were "called" to preach the gospel usually modified greatly their views during the period of college training and by the time they were ready to preach they had become acceptable candidates for the ministry. It was the person who broke outside the bounds of professional exclusiveness, and who avoided the conservative influence of an academic training, who constituted the chief menace to the traditional authority of the Church. This fact was clearly recognized in the efforts made to bring Alline into conformity with church government. Little attempt was made to persuade him to abandon his intention to preach; all that was required of him was that he postpone preaching until he was duly qualified. This was the position taken by the two Presbyterian ministers, the Reverends Daniel Cock and David Smith, who had been invited to Cornwallis in the summer of 1777 by some of the leading inhabitants to restore order in the Congregational church in face of the enforced withdrawal of the Reverend Benaiah Phelps from the pastorate and the entry upon the scene of Henry Alline. Alline wrote of this episode:

When I came to Cornwallis I heard that there were two ministers come from Cobequid (without my requesting) to inquire into my principles and preaching. They were men I had heard of, but never seen. I went to hear them preach, and had reason to hope that one of them was a minister of Christ, although something sunk into a form without the power. The week following they both came to see me with a number of men, whom I knew to be enemies to the power of religion, which made me suspect, they did not come out of love and tenderness. However, though I had not requested their coming to examine me, I was very ready to discourse with them. I vindicated my principles of religion. They enquired after my right to preach. I told them, finding them much against the power. They asked me for my credentials. I immediately shewed them what I had from the church, which they condemned, because it was not from a society of ministers: which caused a dispute to begin, they affirming that I had no right to preach, without a license from a society of ministers, and I affirming that I had. They likewise thought it next to impossible for a man to be called to preach, who had no college learning. But the chief debate was about the power of ordination . . . when they found I was established in my sentiments and not easily moved, they began to be more moderate, and to advise me, making me an offer of their libraries, and what assistance they could give me, if I would leave off preaching until I was better qualified: I thanked them for their kindness, as I imagined they meant well; but I told them the Lord knew before he called me, how unqualified I was as to human learning and as he had called me, I trusted he would qualify me for whatever he had for me to do. I told them besides, that the work of God was then prospering in my hands and therefore I did not dare to desert it. They told me they looked on me as a stiff young man, and then went away.[53]

The refusal to recognize the right of Alline to preach led to his formal break from Congregational Church authority. The gathering together

[53]*Ibid.*, pp. 55-6.

about him of a body of followers led to a general break from the Congregational membership. Alline's revivalist preaching inevitably involved breaking outside the bounds of institutional religion with its appointed times and places of worship. Alline could not become simply another Congregational minister even if the Church had been willing to accept him. He began where the regular ministers left off, preaching on weekdays as well as on the Sabbath and outside as well as within the meeting house. His movement was a movement within the Church but not subject to its control. He sought to introduce a new spiritual influence into its work, and, as a result, his activities brought him into competition with its ministers. Although the first effect of his preaching was probably that of increasing attendance at the regular religious services through the greatly increased interest in spiritual matters which he aroused, in the end converts, convinced of the ungodliness of the ministers, began to fall away from these services and to meet in groups by themselves. Out of such a separation there emerged a distinctive body of Newlight worshippers and a distinctive Newlight Church.

The first Newlight church was organized in Newport shortly after Alline commenced preaching in 1776. He wrote:

I rode with some of my Christian friends to Newport, in order to gather a visible church, to walk in the order of the Gospel; which I had been some months in agitation. I was chosen to draw the articles, with the assistance of some brethren. Some articles were drawn, and the next day signed by some brethren. I preached a sermon, and the Lord seemed to own us. The reason that we called for no assistance from other churches was, because we did not think the churches in those parts were churches of Christ, but had only a dry form without religion. The Church was gathered both of Baptists and Congregationals; for we did not think that such small non-essentials, as different opinions about water Baptism, were sufficient to break any fellowship, and to obstruct building together among the true citizens of Zion: and the Lord owned and answered us by increasing the gifts, graces and the numbers of the small, feeble band. But the powers of darkness and church of antichrist rose against it from every quarter, both in public and private.

We then returned to Falmouth, where I remained preaching every Sabbath until the 27th of October, when we went over to Newport again, and set apart by ordination two elders: this was done without any assistance from any other church; and these elders came forward to lead the church, as far as their gifts and graces extended.[54]

On July 15, 1778, another Newlight church was organized in Cornwallis, when "there met at the house of Simon Fitch a number of brethren to enter into church covenant, and accordingly signed a church covenant."[55] Here, dissatisfaction with the ministry of the Reverend Benaiah Phelps had already resulted in considerably weakening

[54]*Ibid.*, pp. 48-9.
[55]Quoted Saunders, *History of the Baptists of the Maritime Provinces*, p. 130.

the Congregational church, and the organization of a separate church added to the general confusion. When efforts to restore order through the choice of a new minister failed, a number of the inhabitants joined in inviting Alline to accept the pastoral cares of the community. Though refusing to confine his preaching to Cornwallis, he undertook to give a part of each year to the service of the inhabitants of this place, and, in December of the same year he was ordained by the church as an itinerant missionary. "Was voted," the records of a meeting on December 21 read, "to Give Mr. Henry Allien to be a Pastor and Teacher over us in the Lord; Was Voted to Assist in Setting apart Mr. Henry Allien an Itenerant or Traveling Pastor and Teacher to Preach the Gospel of Jesus Christ and Administer the Ordinances in Christ— Churches wherever the Lord our God in his Providence Shall Call him thereunto—as Soon as Conveniency will allow, which is According to the Best Light and Knowledge we have at present."[56] Strenuous efforts, however, were made by the orthodox Congregationalists to maintain a regular church organization. In June, 1778, they requested the Reverend Jonathan Scott of Chebogue to visit them, and Scott spent the winter of 1778-9 in their midst.[57] The next spring, they appealed again to the church in Chebogue for assistance. "We believe," part of the letter read, "no People's Circumstances ever call'd louder for a faithful and skilful Leader, than what ours hath done for near two Years past. . . . The state of Religion is such among us, notwithstanding the more favourable Appearance at Present, that unless we can obtain your Consent for Mr. Scott to make us another Visit, to carry into Execution what he hath so far brought forward, we think it is more than probable that, through the Influence of a Number that set up for Teachers among us, that our religious Matters will soon get to as bad a Pass as ever."[58] The church in Chebogue, however, was unable to permit Scott to again visit Cornwallis, and further efforts to restore order in the Congregational church failed. In the end, the Glasgow Associate Synod of the Secession Church of Scotland was appealed to, and in 1785 the Presbytery of Edinburgh sent the Reverend Hugh Graham to serve as pastor of the Cornwallis church.[59]

As the Newlight revivals gathered strength, and the movement gained new followers, other Congregational churches suffered a fate similar to that of the church in Cornwallis. The break-up of the churches in Liverpool and Chebogue illustrates the way in which the Newlight

[56]Quoted *ibid.*, p. 130.
[57]Records of the Church of Jebogue in Yarmouth, p. 82.
[58]*Ibid.*, p. 89.
[59]Cf. Eaton, *History of King's County*, pp. 289-90.

movement spread in the village communities and led to division within the Congregational following.

Dissatisfaction with the ministry of the Reverend Israel Cheever had led to a growing state of dissension in the church in Liverpool, and when Alline visited the place he immediately attacked the religious foundations of the Congregational system. "The Lord gave me strength and liberty," he wrote of one of his early meetings in the town, "to declare the truths of the gospel; and I told the elders and members of the church that was gathered there on a form, my mind of their standing, and the Lord shook many of them."[60] By February of 1782, although a church of their own had not yet been organized, the Newlights had separated from the Congregational church and were carrying on religious services independently. "Several People," Perkins wrote under the date February 3, 1782, "not being well Satisfied with Mr. Cheever, & Some in the Church, etc., Meet at Mr. Stephen Smith's, & Carry on Worship, by reading, praying, Singing, etc. Mr. Cheever preaches Very Strenuously against Seperation, & Seems extremely Out of Humour with the People on Account of the Religious Stir there Seems to be. he is Concerned that the people are going out of the way, & Says we are like to be broken up, Etc. Etc."

Cheever, asking for his dismissal from the church with the expectation that he would be urged to remain, was granted it, and, during December of 1782, Alline succeeded in bringing together his followers into a separate Newlight church. "While I was there this last time," he wrote of January 1, 1783, "the Christians gathered together in fellowship, by telling their experiences and getting fellowship one for another; and so joined in a body, separating themselves from the world."[61] The signing of a new covenant, involved in the organization of the Newlight church, led to a break from those Congregationalists who, like Simeon Perkins, while dissatisfied with Cheever and willing to attend the preaching of Alline, were not prepared to support any separatist movement. "A Meeting and Some Consultation," Perkins wrote, January 30, "about Renewing or Coming into a New Covenant. Nathan Tupper, Esq., and Samuel Hunt, Esq., are against it. Stephen Smith, and Benjamin Parker are Leaders for it. there was a great deal Said in the Meeting House upon it, but Nothing Decisive. Mr. Smith Said he was Determined, and Sundry Others Went to his House, where I heard that himself, Benjamin Parker, Isaac Dexter, & Ephriam Hunt, Signed it." As a result of the separation, the Congregationalists

[60]Alline, *Life and Journal of the Rev. Mr. Henry Alline*, pp. 148-9.
[61]*Ibid.*, p. 168.

were left without any minister, and found it necessary to appeal for outside assistance. The Church in Chebogue was appealed to: "As to the particular Circumstances," the brethren of Liverpool wrote, April 9, 1783, "we are under, have not Time to relate; but we are broken to Pieces; although the major Part of the Church holds together."[62] Efforts to restore order, or to unite upon the choice of a minister failed, and, during the next two years, the conflict between the two congregations gathered strength and resulted in the end in open schism. The problem became one of admitting the schismatic party on its terms into the church, and this the adhering members refused to do. "The Proprietors of the Meeting House meet," Perkins noted, March 17, 1784, "to Consult . . . whether the Separate party Shall Come into the Meeting House . . . my Self, for one Declared I would not agree that Mr. Alline, or any of his Adherents, Should ever Carry on the Publick Worship of the Place in that House, & gave my reasons for it, viz:— that Mr. Alline had denied the Fundamental Articles of the Christian Religion." After further negotiations, carried on throughout the summer and late autumn, the church finally refused to accept the Newlight party. "The Separate Party," Perkins wrote, January 7, 1785, "begin to Cut Timber for Building a Meeting House, which they have determined to proceed upon, as I understand, Since the Congregation has refused to Receive them into the Meeting House, on their Terms, which Terms are that they Shall have the whole Rule."

Conflict between the two parties dragged itself out in the course of the next ten years with all attempts to secure a reconciliation failing. Possession of the "Great Meeting House" became a major point of dispute, and the failure of the Congregationalists to obtain a minister from New England placed them in a hopelessly weak position. Congregational services were only occasionally maintained through utilizing the services of visiting clergymen of various persuasions. Eventually all efforts to keep the church in existence were for the time abandoned and those who were not prepared to join with the Newlights attached themselves to other denominations. Only a small nucleus of Congregational supporters remained.

The break-up of the church of Chebogue—which had been so often appealed to by other churches in distress—followed a pattern very much like that followed by the church in Liverpool. In the autumn of 1781 Alline undertook an extensive missionary tour throughout the western end of the province where he preached at Cape Orsue, Argyle, Yarmouth, Barrington, and the settlements at Ragged Islands (Lockeport) and

[62]Records of the Church of Jebogue in Yarmouth, p. 182.

on the Sable River. His arrival in Yarmouth was not welcomed by the Reverend Jonathan Scott who had already witnessed the results of his preaching in Cornwallis. "The minister also at Chebogue," Alline wrote, "came out and raged very high."[63] The painful disintegration of the Chebogue church which followed upon the preaching of Alline was related by Scott in the Church Records. Alline made his first appearance, according to Scott, at the Sunday morning service of the church on October 27, 1781, without having given any previous notice to the minister. Failure of efforts on the part of Scott after the meeting to arouse the concern of the deacons led him to view the situation with anxiety, and he therefore invited Alline to his house for the night where, the next morning, in the presence of one of the brethren, he discussed the whole matter with the Newlight preacher and pointed out the reasons why he could not permit him to preach in the meeting house. Alline preached during the week in private homes, with results which were anything but pleasing to the resident pastor. "By this Time," Scott wrote, "Matters were fomented, so that divers Persons had become warm and zealous in the Cause of Mr. Alline."[64] No separation occurred, however, until the second visit of Alline in February, 1782, when something of a revival of religion occurred through his preaching. "The thirteen Days" Scott recorded, "that Mr. Alline tarried in Yarmouth in this his second Visit, the greatest Part of Mr. Scott's People, both Church and Congregation, but especially the Church, appeared to be under his Influence, and attended him both Night and Day, as he preached much in the Night as well as in the Day-Time. And a considerable Number were religiously impress'd and became very zealous and fervent, and warm in caressing and applauding Mr. Alline; and proportionably cold, shy and disaffected towards Mr. Scott."[65]

A few days after Alline's departure, the Newlight adherents separated from the Congregational church and set up meetings on week-days for religious exercises. These were carried on in spite of the fact that the pastor, seeking to maintain the support of his following, had himself instituted religious meetings during the week. The next month, after a Sabbath service in which Scott attacked the religious principles of the Newlights, a number of the members began holding separate services on Sundays in their own homes, and this situation continued throughout the summer months and until the third visit of Alline in October, when

[63]Alline, *Life and Journal of the Rev. Mr. Henry Alline,* p. 147.
[64]Records of the Church of Jebogue in Yarmouth, p. 135.
[65]*Ibid.,* p. 136.

he was accompanied by Handly Chipman. The day before the evangelists left, highly successful revivalist meetings were held throughout the day and evening, and a number of people were converted. "The Separation greatly increased," Scott wrote, "from this Day and forward, even to near twenty Heads of Families, Men and Women, out of Jebogue, Cape-Forche, and the Little River, with a greater Number of young People and Children."[66]

Although Alline did not again visit Yarmouth, the separation continued and was supported by some of the leading members of the church.

Here, at one View [Scott reviewed the effects of these developments], may be seen the Beginning, or first opening of the Breach between Pastor and People: The Pastor could not receive Mr. Alline, and gave his Reasons for it; The People received and followed him, and justified themselves in so doing, and blamed their Pastor upon this Head, until the Breach became so wide, no Remedy was found. For many of the Congregation joined with the Members of the Church, and were equally warm in vindicating Mr. Alline's Manner of Entrance and Proceeding, and their Right to hear him. And order being now broke down and trampled under Foot, Mr. Chipman, and a Number of other Preachers of the same Stamp with Mr. Alline, soon followed after him, one after another, and secured and established the Conquest which he first made; each one contributing to gain Adherents to the Party.[67]

The separation of the Newlight party led to the rapid disintegration of the Congregational church under the pastorate of the Reverend Mr. Scott. The monthly meetings for prayer and meditation came to be attended by fewer and fewer numbers and ceased altogether by the end of 1786, matters requiring the disciplinary action of the church could not be dealt with because of disagreements among the members, the sacraments were only occasionally attended and on several occasions could not be performed, and acrimonious relationships increasingly developed between the pastor and congregation. Finally, on April 2, 1792, Scott secured his dismissal from the church.[68] Services continued to be carried on intermittently, but for some time no successor to Scott could be secured. "The appearance of things was now," the Church Records read of the situation by 1803-7, "very gloomy & dark. Repeated tryals had been made to obtain a Minister; but all had hitherto failed— the adherents of Mr. Alline, the first cause of the division in the church, who were now become professed New Light Baptists, were endeavouring by every artifice to make inroads upon them and to draw off the members of the Church to their party, some of which, and several of the Congregation, they had actually preverted."[69] In 1807 there was something

[66] *Ibid.*, p. 143.
[67] *Ibid.*, p. 149.
[68] *Ibid.*, pp. 153-5.
[69] *Ibid.*, p. 211.

of a revival of interest in the Congregational cause, and articles in
that year were entered into by the church and congregation to secure
and support a new minister. Difficulties remained, however, in maintaining the organization of the church.

By the time of Alline's death, scarcely any of the Congregational
churches in the Maritimes had escaped the disrupting effect of the
Newlight evangelical crusade. On July 29, 1779, the church of Maugerville appealed to the church of Chebogue for assistance. "We are sorry
to acquaint you," part of the letter of appeal read, "that, after a Manifestation of God's Goodness, by a visible Out-pouring of his Spirit in
this Place, there hath Division and Contention arisen among us, issuing
to an open Separation and setting up an independent Church on a different
System. . . . It was in or about the Month of May, 1779, that Henry
Alline visited the River St. John in Character of a Preacher, and in
July following 1779, he had torn this poor Church of Maugerville
(the only Church of Christ on this River at this Time) to Pieces, and
set up a separate and 'independent Church upon a different System,'
for himself, or under his Influence."[70] By 1785 order had broken down
completely in the church of Maugerville. The church of Chebogue
was again appealed to:

> We suppose you are no Strangers to the Jars and Di putes which happened among
> us some Years ago, which terminated in an open Separation and Division of the
> Church in this Place: And also that we have for a long Time been destitute of the
> preached Gospel, and the Ordinances. But what has rendered our Case yet more
> melancholy and distressing, is, Differences that has of late arose among those of
> the Church who for a long Time had been united: So that two of our principal
> Members being offended and aggrieved, have declined assisting us in our publick
> Meetings on the Sabbath. In short, we are so confused and unsettled at present,
> as not to be in a Capacity to settle a Minister, or even unitedly to labour after
> one.[71]

In 1783, the church of Granville broke up, and its pastor—the
Reverend A. Morse—was dismissed in face of the organization of a
Newlight church. The churches in Annapolis and Wilmot suffered a
similar fate. The church in Chester continued still for some years under
the charge of the Reverend John Seccombe but it also, with the appointment of the Reverend Joseph Dimock as pastor, passed outside the
control of Congregationalism. Within some of the churches in the more
remote settlements division was avoided, but these likewise as a result
of the difficulty of securing ministers gradually ceased to be Congregational in attachment.[72] Only one or two churches, through later

[70]*Ibid.*, pp. 99-100.
[71]*Ibid.*, p. 186.
[72]On October 24, 1814, the church of Sheffield wrote the London Missionary

assistance from the London Missionary Society, were able to reorganize and remain in existence. As a denomination, Congregationalism virtually disappeared in the colony.

The rise of the Newlight movement, and the disintegration of Congregationalism, reflected underlying problems of social organization in the rural settlements of Nova Scotia. So long as the village system remained stable, and the tie with New England endured, the position of the Congregational churches was relatively secure, but forces quickly asserted themselves within the Nova Scotian settlements which weakened the village system and the New England tie. Though the character of the movement of population to Nova Scotia made for a considerable degree of social continuity, frontier influences were too strong to make possible the establishment of social order without serious strain.

In spite of the controls secured through the proprietory system of village government, a degree of individualism early developed among the New England settlers in Nova Scotia. Decisions with respect to the location of lots, for instance, were not always accepted by individual settlers who preferred to rely upon their own judgment and initiative in locating land in the new frontier. The weakness of the proprietory system in the distribution of land extended into the whole field of local government; settlement in a new land tended to encourage individual initiative and to weaken attachments to the village group. The weakening of village attachments was accompanied by the weakening of ties to New England. For many the move to Nova Scotia offered an opportunity to break free from the heavy controls of the New England rural society. The new frontier of Nova Scotia tended to recruit its settlers from those elements of the New England population which were least stable, least a part of the New England cultural system. Thus many of the Nova Scotian pioneers resented an attempt to introduce methods of control which they had not been too prepared to accept even in their homeland. Settlement in Nova Scotia represented a further step in the

---

Society: "We whose names are hereunto subscribed are a small society of protestant Dissenters who have the most of us been educated in the Congregationalist profession, a church of that denomination having existed in this place for more than forty years who have (when we have not had preaching which has been but a small part of the time) regularly kept up the worship of God on the Lords day by praying and reading sermons and singing and although our members are now small, many having departed this life and we have reason to believe have joined the church triumphant. Some have joined the Baptist and others the Methodist society late in the Rev. Mr. Wesley connection, yet we have reason to hope with a little assistance at first to be fully able to support an able and faithful gospel minister. There are other destitute societies in this province, particularly one about thirty miles distant from us, who are in connexion with us; Indeed there is a very large field open for Evangelical preaching in this province, but laborers are very few." "Documents of the Congregational Church at Maugerville" (*Collections of the New Brunswick Historical Society*, vol. I, Saint John, N.B., 1894, pp. 147-8).

movement out of the frontier. It was from what had recently been frontier areas that many of the settlers came, and even when they were from one of the older communities of New England they were likely to be persons least attached to the traditional cultural group. The village institutional system which established itself in Nova Scotia depended upon a leadership which conformed to the traditional mores of the New England society. Such leadership in the new frontier area rested upon a less solid foundation than that upon which it had rested in New England. The "folk" of the New England village tended to give way to the "masses" of the Nova Scotian frontier. To the extent that this was the case the whole social system of the rural village broke down.

The weakness of village authority was accentuated by the strained relationship with provincial authority. Limitations upon the controls of the proprietory system owing to the resistance of the local settlers were increased through the resistance of governmental authorities in Halifax. Unwillingness of local settlers to accept decisions with respect to the distribution of land was encouraged by a provincial government jealous of the land granting authority of town proprietors.[73] Efforts of Halifax to build the province economically and culturally about itself involved inevitably serious challenges to the ties of the out-settlements with New England and to the principle of autonomy of the local village. The policy of government encouraged an intensification of individualism in the rural settlements by challenging the cultural controls of the rural village system.

These social strains within the rural Nova Scotian settlements were considerably intensified with the outbreak of the American revolutionary war.[74] The restlessness of the New England population in Nova Scotia with British colonial policy was reflected in attitudes of dislike to governmental authority, and the suspicion of governmental authorities that the population was not loyal widened the breach between government and people. Political dissatisfactions entered into and became closely tied up with social dissatisfactions. Many of the leading men in the rural villages, conscious of their weak position, leaned over backwards in showing deference to the colonial government, and such abasement lost for them the respect of many of the more independently minded settlers. On the other hand, other leading men, with greater zeal than judgment, threw in their lot with the rebelling colonists and

[73]D. C. Harvey, 'The Struggle for the New England Form of Township Government in Nova Scotia" (*Report of the Canadian Historical Association*, 1933, Ottawa, 1933). See also, Brebner, *Neutral Yankees of Nova Scotia*, pp. 211-19.

[74]Cf. Brebner, *Neutral Yankees of Nova Scotia*, chap. X.

the advantage of their leadership was completely lost in the rural villages. The revolution in itself, touching Nova Scotia very closely, resulted in far reaching adjustments in the rural village hierarchy; it very greatly hastened the process of individualization, of the breakdown of rural village authority.

The economic effects of the war combined with the political effects to weaken the rural village cultural system. Trade restrictions led to great economic hardships, and, at the same time, offered opportunities for profiteering by hoarding and smuggling. Speculation increased, and traditional primary group relationships gave way to pecuniary relationships. The trader emerged in the rural village as in the larger town, and commercial success tended to replace land proprietorship as the social basis of prestige. Nova Scotia, with the growth of trade from war, entered into the first phase of a commercial revolution, and here, as in New England itself, the effect was to sharpen the break with the old traditional social order based upon a rural village system.

Congregationalism very quickly felt the effects of these changes within the community structure of Nova Scotia. In the first place, the weakening of village control over settlement, and the pushing of population into remote areas of the country, intensified very greatly the problem of providing religious services. The Congregational Church grew up within the village, and no effective machinery had been developed to extend the teachings of religion beyond village boundaries; Congregational ministers did not itinerate and no central organization existed to support a body of special missionaries. So long as the regularly organized churches could be supplied with ministers, the failure to serve the outlying sections of the population led to no serious weakening of the Congregationalist position, but with the outbreak of the American Revolution increasing difficulty was faced in accomplishing even this. There were lacking facilities within the province to train men for the ministry, and the Revolution cut off a supply from New England. For the seven years of war no new Congregational ministers were recruited to provide for the needs of a steadily growing population. Nova Scotia lost rather than gained ministers during this period. Many of those ministers in the country—Samuel Wood in Barrington, Seth Noble in Maugerville, Benaiah Phelps in Cornwallis, and probably some others—left with the outbreak of war and returned to the revolutionary colonies. Their churches were left unsupplied.

The result was that an increasingly large proportion of the population of the country was left destitute of the religious services of Congregationalism; in his journal Alline repeatedly referred to areas which

had not been visited for years by a minister of religion.[75] Where this was the case, the inherited loyalties to Congregationalism gradually weakened and died; to some extent, there was a shift away entirely from religious values. In the older village settlements, the weaknesses of Congregationalism likewise were partly the result of the failure to maintain Congregational religious services.[76] Dissatisfaction with the ministry of Cheever in Liverpool, Phelps in Cornwallis, and Scott in Chebogue resulted in division because of the impossibility of securing ministers to take their place; when these ministers were finally dismissed, the churches remained unsupplied. The emphasis upon high educational qualifications for the ministry, of course, prevented the building up of a body of local preachers in the country. In the end, such a body of local preachers was raised up outside rather than within the church organization.

Even where religious services were provided, however, difficulty was faced in maintaining the loyalty of adherents. Congregationalism in New England, in face of the Great Awakening which had set in during the seventeen-forties and which had led to the organization of a number of separate Newlight churches, had tended to swing in a conservative direction in reaction to the radicalism of the evangelists. An increasing emphasis upon formalism led to a weakening of the spiritual influence of the Church. Congregationalism shifted steadily away from the position of the religious sect in becoming a worldly church. The shift was evident in the character of many of the supporters of the Church, in the growing interest in secular affairs, and in the weakening of attitudes of devoutness and piety. It was also evident in the character of many of the Congregational ministers, in their lack of spiritual zeal, and in their emphasis upon such ministerial qualifications as education and social standing. These tendencies within Congregationalism early asserted themselves in Nova Scotia. The great majority of the settlers probably retained a strong attachment to evangelical religion, either as faithful members of the Congregational Church or as converts to the Newlight cause, but most of those who were active in founding the churches in the Nova Scotia villages represented the more conservative

[75]This was particularly true of the western parts of the province where the difficulties of transportation led to the extreme isolation of the various settlements. "I went to Sable river," Alline wrote of one of these settlements, "where I found a very dark people. . . . There were many on that shore, that had not heard a sermon for fourteen years preached unto them. Only sometimes one of their readers would come along and read a sermon to them." Alline, *Life and Journal of the Rev. Mr. Henry Alline*, p. 148.

[76]Respecting the difficulty in paying the salary of Congregational ministers, see the petition of the Cornwallis congregation to the New England clergy, *Proceedings of the Massachusetts Historical Society*, vol. IV, 2nd series, 1887-9, pp. 67-9.

element within the Congregational membership; they were the substantial classes within the community. Likewise, most of the ministers who were recruited from New England in the years before 1776 tended to be the upholders of religious orthodoxy. They were graduates of the best schools, and sought to maintain in the new pioneer settlements the strict standards in the form of religious service which had been established in the churches in New England. Their ministry emphasized the importance of correct theological doctrine but was characterized in many cases by little spirituality.

The effects of the conflict of formalistic and evangelistic tendencies within Congregationalism were early evident in problems of church government in Chebogue. The growing current of unrest in many of the other churches resulted from the play of very similar opposing forces. It was not the formalism of Congregationalism as such, but the conflict within Congregationalism of the church and sect idea of religious organization which led to the strains in government. The break from Congregationalism resulted from the rise of the revivalist spirit not outside but within the Church. Strong evangelistic elements within the membership became increasingly restless with the services of a church which made no effort to appeal to evangelical interests. On the other hand, the emphasis upon form found support from the more influential of the Church's members; they were the ones who became identified with Congregationalism when the break from the Church took place. "I have reason to believe," Alline wrote of his home town of Falmouth in 1776, "there were no more than five or six Christians in the whole town and they sunk into death and formality: there was nothing of the power of religion, the travail of the soul: and conviction and conversion were scarcely mentioned; only externals, and duties, and commands, and different principles, etc."[77] What Alline had to say about a number of other Congregational churches was very similar; if his view gave expression to the bias of the revivalist, it was with this bias, very prevalently held, that Congregationalism had to reckon. Its failure was very largely a failure to capitalize upon the strong core of evangelistic sentiment within its membership body.

Problems of religious conflict within Congregationalism reflected problems of social conflict within the village organization. Congregationalism had grown out of the proprietory system of village government inherited from New England, and declined with the weakening of proprietory interests in the new frontier settlements. The disintegration of values of social worth setting off the Gentlemen and Esquires from the great

[77]Alline, *Life and Journal of the Rev. Mr. Henry Alline*, p. 20.

mass of the population affected inevitably the status of the leading members of the Congregational churches. These developments gained significance in relationship to the declining importance of spiritual values within Congregationalism. So long as there was no threat to the social influence of the churches, the lack of spiritual influence was not seriously felt. What was lost in religious interest was gained in the interest to maintain respectability; status in the community implied membership in the Church. With the loss, however, of social status of the ministers and of those upon whom the Church depended chiefly for support, the effect of the decline of the Church in terms of spiritual leadership increasingly made itself felt. The restlessness of many members of the Church was a restlessness growing out of a condition of disorganization in relation to the cultural values of the village community.

Such a condition of disorganization was greatly accentuated with the outbreak of revolution in the American colonies. Congregationalism lost the support of the cultural and political tie with New England. The close identification of the Congregational churches in New England with the revolutionary cause intensified the difficulties faced by the Congregational churches in Nova Scotia in adjusting to the new political situation. Some of the Congregational ministers in the province immediately joined the revolutionary forces. The Reverend Samuel Wood of Barrington became a chaplain in the revolutionary army,[78] and his revolutionary sympathies led the Reverend Seth Noble in Maugerville to return to New England.[79] Others, though remaining in the province, became involved with the British authorities. The Reverend Benaiah Phelps in Cornwallis, according to his son, "got into trouble with the Government" which led to his sudden departure from the province in 1778.[80] Seccombe, in Chester, in December, 1776, was taken before the Provincial Council charged with having preached a seditious sermon, and, in January of the next year, he was again brought before the Council, when an affidavit was produced that he had prayed for the success of the "rebels"; he was ordered to find security for good behaviour in the sum of £500, and to cease preaching until he signed a recantation.[81] Political disaffection spread beyond the ministry to include a number of prominent members, and, although most of the New Englanders in Nova Scotia refrained from any overt expression of sympathy for the cause of their compatriots, Congregationalism became suspect in

[78]E. A. Crowell, *A History of Barrington Township and Vicinity* (Yarmouth, about 1832), p. 166.
[79]*Collections of the New Brunswick Historical Society*, vol. I, pp. 74-8.
[80]Eaton, *History of King's County*, p. 273.
[81]DesBrisay, *History of the County of Lunenburg*, p. 280.

the eyes of colonial officials. "I take upon me to tell your Lordship," Major-General Massey wrote to Germain, in 1776, "that until Presbytery is drove out of His Majesty's Dominion, Rebellion will ever continue, nor will that set ever submit to the Laws of Old England."[82] The roots of Congregationalism were imbedded deeply in the culture of New England, and revolution in New England inevitably affected the political status of the churches in Nova Scotia. As a result of the stigma of disloyalty they could not entirely shake off, they lost the prestige and claim to respectability which had been among the chief forces holding them together.

Ecological, cultural, and political forces combined in weakening the position of Congregationalism within the rural village settlements of Nova Scotia. Such tendencies towards the disintegration of the Congregationalist system had set in well before 1776, but it was only after the outbreak of the American Revolution that they became conspicuously evident. War and revolution imposed greatly increased strains upon the rural village society. The growing weakness of cultural supports, with the break from New England and the development of trade, placed new demands upon religious leadership at the very time Congregationalism was least able to meet them. The failure of Congregationalism was a failure to provide a new basis of social solidarity when the traditional basis of the rural village system broke down. The Congregational Church organization was deeply implanted within the traditional organization of the village, and when the one disintegrated the other did likewise. The population, left without the social supports of the village system, was also left without the social supports of Congregationalism.

In contrast, the Newlight movement, through the flexibility of its organization and the attraction of its evangelical appeal, was able to make religion a powerful social reorganizing influence in the community. The willingness of Alline and his fellow preachers to break through the bounds of professional exclusiveness which made the Congregational churches dependent upon college trained clergymen, offered a means of overcoming the problem of supplying religious services when Nova Scotia became cut off from contacts with New England. The direct call to preach the gospel served to short-circuit the tedious process of raising up men for the ministry. Furthermore, the Newlight preachers secured a maximum of results from their efforts by holding meetings during week-days as well as on Sundays and by constantly going from one place to another. No systematic itinerant organization was developed

[82]Nova Scotia State Papers, vol. A96, Halifax, Nov. 22, 1776. Massey to Germain.

—like the Congregational churches, the Newlights lacked a central directing body—but the ordination of Alline as an itinerant missionary was a recognition of the need of pushing gospel preaching into areas in which church organization could not be supported. The result was that, as the population of the rural village spread out into the open country, the Newlight organization was sufficiently expansive to provide for the religious needs of the scattered inhabitants. The new religious forms conformed to the ecological patterns of the changing community structure.

At the same time, the new religious appeal met basic social needs of the population. Newlight preaching was directed against the cold, formal services which had come to be characteristic of the respectably minded Congregational churches and against the emphasis upon "good works" of the Calvinistic Congregational ministers. Newlightism was a religion of inspiration and feeling; the appeal was to the emotions rather than to reason. Thus religion was given a new meaning in the life of the community. Its close functional relationship to the community structure was re-established, and it became again, as it had once been within Congregationalism, a support of a sense of social solidarity.

This was most evident in the emphasis upon sin in Newlight religious teachings. The Newlight movement did not grow—as some of its early leaders tended to suggest[83]—out of a state of "gross immorality" in society, but it did grow out of a condition of ecclesiastical organization in which the concern for worldly affairs was weakening the sectarian spirit of asceticism. The increasing urge towards respectability within Congregationalism had checked the uncompromising exercise of the moral sanctions of the Church. The Newlight preachers recognized none of the claims of the gentleman in waging their war upon sin. The crude conception of sin in their evangelical preaching provided a faithful expression of the moral outlook of the rural society; the asceticism of the religious sect offered a means of asserting the solidarity of the rural social group threatened by increasing social mobility and the weakening of such rural virtues as work and frugality. It was directed against the ne'er-do-well within the pioneer society, the irresponsible settler who spent his time in drinking, card-playing, and dancing. It was also directed against the prospering business or professional man who could afford a life of ease and luxury. In this way it gained importance as a means of resisting changes in the village society resulting from the increasing acceptance of the social conventions of that new class which was attaining a position of social influence through success

[83]See, for instance, Alline, *Life and Journal of the Rev. Mr. Henry Alline*, p. 60.

in trade or through closer ties with the governing or military groups in the provincial capital.

Thus the social significance of the emphasis upon sin in Newlight teaching lay in its effect in securing the sharp separation of the simple folk of the rural village from other elements of the population. Conversion undoubtedly had some influence in bringing about a moral reformation of the individual who was converted, but its chief influence was in setting off the virtuous from the sinful—that is, the saved from the unsaved—and in securing a sense of solidarity among the former. Outward manifestations of morality may have been strengthened, but the shift from a life of vice to one of virtue, like the shift from a state of godlessness to one of faith, had most meaning within the psychological experience of conversion. The Newlight movement, generally speaking, did not make people more virtuous but made them think that they were. In that way, differences were emphasized which set the Newlight converts off from other people.

Closely allied to the spiritual and ascetic appeal of the Newlight movement, the cultural appeal offered a means of interpretation of the social situation to the individual when political and class ties tended to disintegrate.The break of the New Englanders from their homeland, and the weakening of class and village loyalties within the Nova Scotian communities, tended to a feeling of social detachment. The primary attachments of the folk and the secondary attachments of the nation weakened in face of the pressures of war and trade. The Newlight movement cut through the traditional political and cultural patterns of group life to organize the population in terms of a hierarchy of religious piety. Man's relationship to God rather than to his fellowmen came to constitute the measure of social worth. The concept of "the elect" had restored to it its full theological significance. Thus the social effect of Newlight teaching, on the one hand, was one of extreme individualization—all that mattered was the state of the individual's soul, while, on the other hand, it was one of social unification—the individual gained significance through his identification with the invisible church. This dual appeal of individualization and socialization reflected strong social tendencies in the rural villages of Nova Scotia at this time. In the intense emotional experience of conversion the individual gained a new consciousness of his own worth and of his relationship to his fellowmen.

The Newlight movement represented, therefore, something of an adjustment in the village society of New Englanders in Nova Scotia forced on it by revolution in the homeland and the development of a

trading economy in the new land. That is not to say that there was to be found a class doctrine in Newlight teaching, much less a concrete social programme. Alline and his fellow evangelists preached a primitive Christianity which recognized a sharp distinction between things of the world and things of the spirit. The social and political significance of the Newlight religious teaching emerged from within the religious appeal. As a result, the Newlight churches were able to avoid the political controversies which were forced upon the Congregational churches with the outbreak of the American Revolution. Though his journal covered almost exactly the period of the revolution, Alline referred to it only twice and then quite incidentally. This complete indifference to war or politics was not a cloak which he wore to shelter him from the criticism of his enemies but was the essence of the religion he taught. War or politics were of no concern to him or to his following; they belonged to the realm of the profane as distinguished from that of the sacred. Thus, through the insistence upon the spiritual, the Newlight movement shifted attention from the issues of the Revolution and contributed to the reorganization of a society severely strained by its influences.[84] The Newlight preaching canalized in a religious direction strong undercurrents of dissatisfaction in the political, economic, and social organization of Nova Scotia and was able to capitalize therefore upon social tensions which precipitated revolution in the other colonies (where, perhaps significantly, revivalist movements had exhausted themselves well before 1776).

In a somewhat similar manner, the Newlight movement avoided the political issue of Church Establishment and was able, as a result, to appeal in a way that Congregationalism could not to strong feelings of hostility to political interference in religion. The Congregational churches, though denied political privileges in Nova Scotia, had developed strong vested interests in Church Establishment in New England and consequently lacked the philosophy to champion effectively the cause of non-Establishment in Nova Scotia in opposition to the claims of the Church of England. Within the Newlight movement, in contrast, the complete indifference to ecclesiastical forms and the emphasis upon spiritual values of religious association produced an attitude of mind—and a social philosophy—which undermined the whole position of Church Establishment.

The effect of the Newlight movement in weakening the cause of Church Establishment had significance in terms of the regional as

[84]See Maurice W. Armstrong, "Neutrality and Religion in Revolutionary Nova Scotia" (*New England Quarterly*, Mar., 1946).

well as the ecclesiastical organization of Nova Scotia. Geography had
isolated the village settlements and emphasized their dependence upon
outside ties; the break from New England with the American Revolution
left them without any solid social supports. Efforts of Halifax to
strengthen political controls in hinterland areas were paralleled by
efforts of the Church of England to strengthen religious controls. The
local community base, even if it had been stable, was too narrow to
maintain the organization of religion, and the divorce from New
England left the Congregational churches in an exposed position.
The Church of England threatened to seize the advantage afforded by
organization in terms of the wider provincial structure and the imperial
tie. This tendency was arrested by the rise of the Newlight movement
which, because of its lack of dependence upon formal ecclesiastical
machinery, could draw support from evangelical movements in the
American colonies without violating codes of political neutrality.
The self-ordained prophet provided means of contact with outside
religious influences by virtue of the very fact that he had no appointment
from an ecclesiastical body. The sect spirit provided the flexibility in
religious organization which smuggling and tax evasion did in economic
life. In this way, it served greatly to stiffen resistance to centralizing
forces growing out of war and commercial expansion.

The conflict between Church Establishment and religious sectarianism
which had found expression in the bitter opposition of New England
to any sort of Roman Catholic control in Nova Scotia and which had
led to the complete collapse of Catholicism and to the serious weakening
of the Church of England in this area also made itself felt in the struggle
for possession of the St. Lawrence Valley region. The military battles
fought in the interior of the continent and the final campaign launched
against Quebec were the culmination in many respects of a prolonged
and deep-rooted conflict between the New England way of life, represented on the religious side by Congregationalism, and the French-
Canadian way of life, represented on the religious side by Roman
Catholicism—a conflict fundamentally between the sect and church
forms of religious organization. The capitulation of Quebec in 1759
and the Royal Proclamation of 1763 represented the triumph of New
England commercialism and, religiously, of Protestant sectarianism.
The invitation to the old colonies to send merchants to the colony[85]
and the formal disestablishment of the Roman Catholic Church marked
the end on paper of the feudal ecclesiastical system which had grown
up in the valley of the St. Lawrence.

[85]See A. L. Burt, *The Old Province of Quebec* (Minneapolis and Toronto, 1933),
pp. 103-5.

But, in sharp contrast with Nova Scotia where geography favoured the expansion of New England commercialism and placed sharp limitations upon any form of centralization, the continental expanse of Quebec favoured military control and sharply limited the expansion of trade. Only a few hundred merchants located in the colony, and, while the Quebec fisheries and the north-western fur trade offered opportunities for a growing trade, conditions before 1776 were too unsettled to encourage any great investment in mercantile pursuits. Provisioning the army provided immediately the most certain form of profit, and such a trade emphasized the subordination of commercialism to militarism. The army acquired a dominant position in the political life of Quebec, as the navy never could in Nova Scotia, and army dominance assured the dominance of the church form of religious organization.

Most of the merchants almost certainly were Presbyterians or Congregationalists, but they were too few in numbers to exert any influence upon the religious life of the colony. Instructions to the local governor made it clear that the Protestant religious services which were to be established were those of the Church of England.[86] Church Establishment was viewed here as in Nova Scotia as the means of securing the ties of the colony to the mother country, and the hope was entertained that not only the old Protestant subjects but the new Catholic subjects as well could be prevailed upon to change their religious attachments in the Church's favour. With this purpose in mind, French-speaking missionaries were sent out to the colony and located in Quebec, Montreal, and Three Rivers: the established Church of England formally assumed the role which had been played by the Roman Catholic Church during the French regime.[87]

Establishment of the Church of England effectively checked the development of religious sectarian movements. After 1763, no new immigration to the colony took place and until 1776 the interests of empire and church remained dominant. The bitter hostility which developed between the merchants and the French-Canadian population and between the merchants and the army,[88] reflected the opposition of the nonconformist religious group to Roman Catholicism and Church Establishment, but this group did not succeed in securing either the evacuation of the Catholic population as it had been evacuated in Nova Scotia or the dis-establishment of the Church of England. The lack of outside support and of official support within the colony isolated

---

[86]Adam Shortt and Arthur G. Doughty, *Documents Relating to the Constitutional History of Canada, 1759-1791* (Ottawa, 1918), part I, pp. 191-3.
[87]See H. C. Stuart, *The Church of England in Canada, 1759-1793* (Montreal, 1893).
[88]Burt, *Old Province of Quebec*, chap. VI.

the "sectaries" and left them without the means of developing independent religious institutions.

On the other hand, the attempt to substitute the influence of the Church of England for that of the Roman Catholic Church was far from successful. The French Canadians did not change their religious along with their political allegiances, and this failure of the Church of England to gain any support from among the new subjects emphasized the importance of the policy of the local governors—Murray and Carleton—in supporting the claims of the Catholic Church. The latter Church's concern with maintaining the conditions of a stable peasant society secured for it the favour of the governors, hostile to the demands of the military group as well as to the demands of the "rabble of unprincipled traders" in Montreal, and through an evasive compliance with instructions from the home government, those privileges were conceded to the Church which it considered essential to its continued existence. By the Quebec Act of 1774, concessions granted the Church were given formal recognition. A hierarchical system of church government was re-established, the right to collect tithes secured, and provision made for the recruitment of clergy.

Dependence upon the native population for a supply of priests was reflected in lowered standards of education for admission into the priesthood but it strengthened the hold of the Church upon the rural inhabitants. The local curé became increasingly the channel of communication with the outside world, and economic self-sufficiency and cultural homogeneity supported the isolation of the rural parish. Thus as Roman Catholicism in the new world had escaped the challenge of the Reformation through the highly centralized controls of the French imperial system which had made possible the exclusion of Huguenot Protestant influences, it was able to escape the challenge of the French Revolution through the only slightly less highly centralized controls of the British imperial system which led to the exclusion of French rationalist influences.[89] When the isolation of the colony finally broke down after 1790 the Counter Reformation was complete, and outside religious and philosophical influences had little effect upon the position of the Church.

With the re-establishment of the Roman Catholic Church, efforts of the Church of England to appeal to the French-Canadian population failed completely while such efforts weakened the influence of the Church among the Protestant population. In 1774 an English-speaking

[89]See R. Flenley, "The French Revolution and French Canada" (in *Essays in Canadian History*, ed. by R. Flenley, Toronto, 1939, pp. 45-67); also H. A. Innis, foreword to *Marketing Organization and Technique*, ed. by Jane McKee (Toronto, 1940).

missionary was sent out to Sorel but, arriving at the outbreak of the American Revolution, he returned after a year in Quebec City to England where he continued to receive for ten years £200 a year as the holder of a Canadian benefice.[90] The inability of the missionaries within the colony to conduct services properly in the English language, and their somewhat questionable reputation as private persons, antagonized the Protestant elements. In none of the three centres of Quebec, Montreal, and Three Rivers, where the English-speaking people were located, was the Church able to command any considerable support. A Memorial in 1786 *On the Present State of the Church of England and its Clergy in Canada* read:

At Quebec, the only clergyman o the Church of England is a very old Swedish gentleman who cannot speak one word of plain English—in consequence of which and his unpopular private conduct the English inhabitants at Quebec (which are numerous and very respectable) are deprived of Divine Service and the minister an object of contempt and ridicule.

At Montreal the case is the same—the clergyman is also a foreigner, and speaks English so very unintelligibly that our Church is totally neglected, notwithstanding the English inhabitants here are very numerous and respectable but not having a proper minister of their own Church are under the necessity of encouraging Presbyterian and other sects, who taking advantage of the neglected state of our religious affairs in this country, are now crowding in from all quarters of the United States, and, of course, sowing the seeds of that disaffection to our Church and constitution which contributed not a little to the loss of our other colonies.

At Three Rivers, the situation of our Church is still more unfortunate, and may be justly called *shameful*, for in addition to the inability of the other gentlemen (in the performance of Divine Service with decency and propriety) their clergyman here is that kind of character that would disgrace the meanest profession. He speaks English worse (if possible) than the other two, and was expelled (for some flagitious acts) from a community of Friars to which he belonged, prior to his conversion to our religion.

This is the true and melancholy state of the Church of England in Canada, and which (if permitted to continue so) it needs no great share of penetration to foresee must soon be followed by the most unhappy political consequences—laying all moral considerations out of the question.[91]

While the charges against the clergy were considered in official circles as greatly exaggerated, there was no denial that they contained a considerable element of truth. The Church of England lacked any foundation of local support in the colony, and the worst abuses of its system of clerical appointments were perpetuated without any means of check from the pressure of local interests. Establishment in effect existed only on paper, and the Church offered no effective leadership

[90]Stuart, *Church of England in Canada*, p. 38.
[91]Quoted *ibid.*, pp. 81-2.

in reorganizing the Protestant religious community, and in building up a sense of social solidarity.

After 1776 as before, however, there was lacking any other source of Protestant religious leadership in the colony. The outbreak of the revolutionary war prevented the movement of American preachers—as well as of settlers—into the Province of Quebec, and new religious currents running strongly within the rebellious colonies did not extend across the border to the north. Unlike in Nova Scotia, where the cultural heritage of the population lent strong support to the spread of evangelical religious movements in spite of the severance of political ties with the American Colonies, in Quebec there was lacking any point of contact with religious developments to the south. The Revolution completely isolated the rural and trading society in the St. Lawrence Valley, and the policy of the local governors of relying upon close co-operation with the Roman Catholic Church was justified by the failure of the invasion of American forces. The Church, if not all the inhabitants, rallied to the support of the British cause, and the increased emphasis upon military strategy furthered efforts to maintain the feudal-peasant system. At the same time, the forces which promoted the close identification of imperialist with Roman Catholic ecclesiastical interests served to strengthen commercial interests when control of the fur trade shifted from Albany to Montreal, and the growth of large-scale commercial organization under Scottish leadership led to the increasing restriction of the area of free enterprise. Trading monopoly became a faithful ally of church and state. Thus the isolation of the rural society through the Roman Catholic Church was paralleled by the isolation of the trading group through the Church of Scotland. The challenge to the rural-commercial feudal order awaited mass immigration and the pressure of free-hold land settlement. The development of powerful evangelical religious movements came with the extension of American frontier settlement in Canada.

CHAPTER TWO

The Great Revival in the Maritime Provinces

1783-1832

T H E religious development of Nova Scotia before 1783 emphasized
the close connection with New England and the weaknesses of forces
of centralization in the economic, political, and social life of the colony.
The strong spirit of local independence in the outlying fishing and farming
village settlements made its effects felt in the efforts during the revolution to maintain trading relationships with New England, in the
indifferent military support of the war against the rebellious colonies,
in the failure of the Church of England to supplant the nonconformist
religious denominations and in the rise of new sectarian movements
when the formal organization of religion represented by Congregationalism offered an inadequate support of local village autonomy. The sect
form of religious organization, inherited from New England, rooted
itself deeply in the culture of Nova Scotia. The Newlight Church
emerged during the revolutionary years as one of the most dynamic
forces of social reorganization within the out-settlements.

Conclusion of the American revolutionary war in 1783, however,
led to a considerable strengthening of centralizing influences within
the Maritime colony. The political connection with the old American
colonies was finally and completely broken, and British naval supremacy
and settlement in the colony of large numbers of United Empire Loyalists
and, later, of Highland Scots emphasized the strength of the imperial
tie. Closer relationships with Britain offered advantages to the overseas
churches which had established themselves in the colony. Many of the
Loyalist settlers were attached to the Church of England: some of
them, indeed, had been clergymen in the old colonies and took up
appointments as missionaries in the new.[1] The Highland Scots were
either Presbyterians or Roman Catholics. Indirectly, as well as directly,
the overseas churches found support in developments which took place
after 1783. The growth of trade with the West Indies, and the cutting

[1]A. W. H. Eaton, *The Church of England in Nova Scotia and the Tory Clergy of the
Revolution* (Salem, 1910), pp. 155-90.

off of commercial relationships with New England, greatly strengthened
the position of Halifax in the Nova Scotian economy at the expense
of the out-settlements, and this change in the economic balance was
reflected in the greatly increased political influence of those interests in
the colony closely identified with the provincial capital and the imperial
connection. Trade lent support to the more insistent demands of loyalty,
and loyalty provided an effective instrument in furthering the claims
of Church Establishment.

Yet the organization of the separate provinces of New Brunswick,
Prince Edward Island, and Cape Breton, and the growing opposition
of the outports to the dominance of Halifax in trade and politics, were
indicative of the persistence of strong decentralizing influences in the
Maritime society. As a result of the revolutionary war, Nova Scotia
was cut off from New England and brought into much closer contact
with Britain, but, if the maritime expansion of New England was
arrested by the war, the continental expansion of the new American
Republic was not. The settlement of New Brunswick represented,
in a sense, another stage in the extension outwards of the American
frontier. The frontier movement of population after 1783 was not one
simply into the West; indeed, it was not until after 1795 that the great
western migrations really began. The movement between 1783 and
1795 was one largely directed towards the south and the north; the
peopling of New Brunswick was closely related to the peopling of the
outer New England states—Vermont, New Hampshire, and Maine.
The new farming—and lumbering—communities which grew up beyond
the Chignecto Isthmus were continental as well as maritime in their ties.

The new continental ties of Maritime society after 1783 made their
effects strongly felt upon religious organization. The American frontier
was an area of religious experimentation. In Kentucky, West Virginia,
upper New York State, and Maine new religious forms emerged with
the advance of the frontiersman. Inevitably, the religious influence of
the American frontier extended across the border into the Maritime
Provinces. The sect spirit, which had gained its early strength in Nova
Scotia through the connection with New England, found new strength
through the connection with the American West. Extension of sectarian
influence was evident in the expansion of the Newlight movement
and, even more, in the rise of the Methodist movement.

The death of Henry Alline in 1784 marked a sharp break in the
development of the Newlight movement, but the loss with his passing
was more than offset by the rise of new evangelical preachers. Some
preachers came into the country from outside; among the Loyalists

were a number of Baptists and at least one Baptist preacher, the
Negro, David George. More important, however, was that body of
preachers raised up out of the ranks. John Payzant and Thomas Handly
Chipman had secured prominence before Alline's death; after 1784,
a number of other preachers appeared upon the scene—Harris Harding,
Joseph Dimock, Edward Manning, James Manning, Theodore S.
Harding, Joseph Crandall, and many more. All of these men underwent
the same sort of emotional experience before turning to a career of
preaching; conversion and the acceptance of a direct "call" to preach
characterized the manner of their induction into the ministry of the
gospel.[2] None of them had any training; all of them were possessed of
great zeal.

The area of greatest Newlight influence continued to be found in
those communities settled by people from New England; it remained
for some time after 1783 essentially a movement among the Congregationalists. In Liverpool, the work begun by Alline was carried on
by a succession of preachers who visited the place; Perkins referred
in his diary to visits from, among others, Harris Harding, Handly
Chipman, John Payzant, Joseph Dimock, and David George.[3] A steady
growth in the strength of the Newlight cause was evident, while
periodically revivals broke forth which resulted in sudden outbreaks
of religious feelings. The effects of revivalist influences in religious
meetings were occasionally noted by Perkins. On June 11, 1786, he
wrote: "a Very Great Crying out at the New Light meeting. Miss
Jedidah Tracy Screamed very Loud, & was Said to be in fits at times."
On March 29, 1791, he wrote: "a New Light meeting also this Evening,
where I understand, Charles Murray, Polly Murray, and Patience,
or Hope Freeman, Cryed out. there Seems a great Stir among the
People, what the event will be, I will not pretend to say." On April 10
of the same year Perkins again wrote: "a great Stur at the Newlight
meeting." On February 9, 1794, Perkins made reference to a Newlight
meeting at the "Great Meeting House" in which three preachers
participated. "They are from," he wrote, "some part of the Bay of
Fundy. their Names are Martin, Johnson, and Harriss. Martin was
here last summer, in Company with one Mr. Perason [Pierson?] an
Elderly man, a Baptist's preacher. I attended their Meeting in the
Evening at Capt. Bangs House. Johnson began the Exercise with
Singing. prayed, & sang again, then took his Text in the 3d Chapter

---

[2] Cf. E. M. Saunders, *History of the Baptists of the Maritime Provinces* (Halifax,
1902), chap. III.

[3] P.A.C., Perkins (Simeon) Diary.

of Collosions, first Verse. he spoke Sometime when Mr. Harriss Spoke, & then Mr. Martin. they appear very much engaged, and Some people were moved during Mr. Martin's exercise." On December 20, 1795, appeared the brief note in Perkins's diary: "I understand there was much Stir among the New Light people, at ye Meeting-House, between meetings." Harris Harding wrote of a meeting in Liverpool when he visited there in July, 1792: "I think I had not spoke but a few minutes before numbers rejoiced, and cried so loud that my voice could not be heard. And while most of the old Christians stood by wondering, or silently weeping and looking on, these professed young converts were some of them shouting for joy. Others in such distress seemingly for sinners, that one or two would be employed holding them: whilst others again would seem so overcome by redeeming love as to be almost motionless, as if their breath was gone."[4]

In other areas settled by New Englanders, Newlight influence also continued strongly. Of Barrington and Argyle, Harding wrote, September 17, 1791: "I was a week at Barrington; where there was a great moving in the minds of the people. I left a number there crying for mercy, and some to all appearances near the kingdom. I had only two meetings at Argyle; where a general shaking appeared among the dry bones, and a shouting was heard among the Israelites."[5] During the winter, Harding preached in Yarmouth where he was able again to report successful revivals of religion. "There is some appearance," he wrote, January 27, 1792. "of a reformation in this place. People flock in great numbers to hear the everlasting Gospel. Several seem moved by the Holy Ghost. Doors are almost everywhere open for meetings, and prejudices are abundantly removed from people's minds."[6] Joseph Dimock wrote from Granville in the summer of 1791:

I can tell you that all I have ever seen before is small in comparison with what I have seen here . . . . Many meetings continue till almost midnight, sinners crying aloud for mercy, Christians bowels yearning over poor souls on the brink of eternal ruin. Some meetings have continued all night; and O, the heavy, heartrending cries would answer each other, enough to pierce the stoutest heart . . . .

The work prospered. The people thronged to meeting sometimes from fifteen to twenty miles distant. Often have I known young females to come twelve miles on foot on Lord's day morning before we had breakfast.[7]

Among at least one element of the new Loyalist population, a revivalist movement grew up after 1783 in close relationship to the Newlight.

---

[4]Quoted J. Davis, *Life and Times of Rev. Harris Harding* (Charlottetown, 1866), p. 30.
[5]*Ibid.*, p. 229.
[6]*Ibid.*, p. 58.
[7]Quoted Saunders, *History of the Baptists of the Maritime Provinces*, p. 36.

The Loyalist migration brought to the Maritimes a considerable number of Negroes, and most of these Negroes and some of the poorer Whites among the Loyalists held to the Baptist faith. Organization of churches was soon undertaken under the leadership of the Negro preacher, David George. George had arrived in Halifax in 1784 with a party of Negro and White Loyalists, and the next summer he moved to Shelburne. Here he set himself up as a Baptist preacher.

Numbers of my own colour were here, [George related of his early preaching in Shelburne] but I found the white people were against me. I began to sing at first in the woods, at a camp, for there were no houses then built. They were just clearing and preparing to erect a town. The black people came from far and near; it was so new to them. I kept on so every night in the week, and appointed a meeting for the first Lord's Day, in a valley between two hills, close by the river, and a great number of white and black people came; and I was so overjoyed with having an opportunity once more of. preaching the Word of God, that after I had given out the hymn, I could not speak for tears. In the afternoon we met again, in the same place, and I had great liberty from the Lord.[8]

Harris Harding wrote of attending a meeting of George's followers: "Yesterday morning I attended David's meeting; where, as soon as I came, I found twenty or thirty made white in the blood of the Lamb . . . . Several of them were frequently obliged to stop and rejoice. Soon after David began in prayer; but was so overcome with joy he likewise was obliged to stop, and turned to me with many tears, . . . desiring me to call upon that worthy name that was like ointment poured down upon the assembly."[9]

A meeting house was built, and a church organized on the principle of adult baptism by immersion. George's account continued: "The first time I baptized here was a little before Christmas, in the creek which ran through my lot. I preached to a great number of people on the occasion, who behaved very well. I now formed the Church with us six, and administered the Lord's. Supper in the meeting-house, before it was finished. They went on with the building, and we appointed a time every other week to hear experiences. A few months after, I baptized nine more, and the congregation very much increased."[10]

The next summer George visited Liverpool. Of this visit, Simeon Perkins entered in his diary, June 18, 1786: "a Black man, from Shelburne, Said to be a Baptist Teacher, holds forth at the New Light Meeting House. he Speaks Very Loud, and the people of that meeting,

[8]Quoted I. E. Bill, *Fifty Years with the Baptist Ministers and Churches of the Maritime Provinces* (Saint John, 1880), p. 20.
[9]Quoted Davis, *Life and Times of Rev. Harris Harding,* p. 35.
[10]Quoted Bill, *Fifty Years with the Baptist Ministers and Churches of the Maritime Provinces,* p. 21.

I understand, like him Very well." During the next year or two George preached in either Shelburne or the neighbouring Negro settlement of Birchtown, or made short excursions to outlying areas such as Ragged Islands. In the winter of 1791-2 he crossed the Bay of Fundy and preached in the Loyalist settlements in the St. John valley. "Part of the first Saturday I was there," he related, "was spent in hearing the experiences of the black people; four were approved, some of whom had been converted in Virginia. A fortnight after I baptized them in the river, on the Lord's Day. Numerous spectators, white and black, were present, who behaved very well."[11] Leaving a local convert to exhort among the population, George returned to Shelburne and from there sent one of his elders to look after the affairs of the church in Saint John. When a number had been converted, George returned to conduct the baptismal service, going by way of Halifax and Horton, where in the latter place he engaged for some time in preaching. Returning to Shelburne once more, he visited Preston, near Halifax, and in the autumn of 1792 he joined the party of Negroes sent to Sierra Leone.[12] While most of the churches he had formed broke up, small nuclei of Baptist converts were left behind in Shelburne, Birchtown, Saint John, Jones' Harbour, Ragged Islands, Preston and Halifax.

Growth of the Newlight cause after the turn of the century followed much the same pattern as that of the early years of the movement's development. Revivals of religion periodically broke out here and there, and at times waves of mass religious hysteria swept the country-side. When religious feelings grew strong, meetings went on for days and weeks; the whole church—indeed, almost the whole community— gave itself up to the cause of religious salvation. During such periods of revival, all work and worldly matters in the community were suspended. The rising tide of emotional excitement left few of those participating in the meetings unaffected; the more sensitive were completely carried away in the grip of strong psychological forces. Success of the revival was measured in terms of the number of people converted.

Some of these revivals appear to have been spontaneous occurrences, without apparent cause, but most of them developed as a result of extraordinary efforts on the part of the Newlight preachers. The constant travelling of the preachers from one place to another served as a means of arousing an interest in religious revival within the various churches. The visit of an outside preacher offered the occasion for the holding of special religious meetings and for a drive to secure new members. In 1798 the Reverend Joseph Dimock undertook an extensive tour

[11]Quoted *ibid.*, p. 23.
[12]*Ibid.*, pp. 24-5.

throughout Nova Scotia, and he entered in his diary an account of the successful revivalist meetings which he held:

Chester Dec'r 8th (1798). I have not wrote for some time & now have not that to write that I could wish but would here Stand amazed at the Goodness of God to me & my ungrateful returns for Such goodness the Season past hath not been Such as I have seen yet there hath been some reviveing season & in some place verry powerful ones in May with my companion I went to Newport to See my Friends preached on my passage at Hallifax without much effect yet an unusual attention at Newport I preached 3 Sabbath besides frequent Lectures people flocked in abundance to here the word & many seamed verry Serious Christians Hungering & thirsting after Righteousness & Some Sinners destressed about Eternal things. went to Horton & Cornwallis where I found God had done great things for his own cause & many Souls were born to God & Sat under the droping[?] of his sanctuary & his name was Sat on high in their Souls Hundreds were added to the Millitant Family many Old Christians woke up & are following the Lord in his Institutions more than a 100 have been Baptized there in a Short time here I met the Ministers in Association & received a request to assist in organizeing a Church & ordaining a Minister at St. Mary's Bay which was accomplished at the Lower end of Granville preached in Nictox on my journey here the Lord hath wrought the greatest change have yet seen where but two or three Evidenced a change when I was here last now there is about 40 communicants & many more that give evidence of a renewed Heart.[13]

The revival of religion in Nictaux which developed in the autumn of 1798 under the influence of Dimock's preaching continued throughout the winter months. A Betsy Parker wrote from there to the Reverend Edward Manning of its effects, March 4, 1799:

With satisfaction I take my pen to write a Few Lines to let you know that the Lord is Caring on his work and Blesed be god our lives is falin in pleasant places is and we have a good Leheritage. Mr. Chipman preached at John Gates is after Sermon Aline Chipman prayed and John Gates Spack and Nathaniel Poby Dodge was very very much Distress He cudent speke for anour and Frelove was in Drietful Distress and Samuel likewise and Charles was very happy in his mind and tacked very Solmon Frelove caled uppon his father to se the torments of hell and it was a sight to Behold A father and Five Children all in the hands of a just god the Sunday folowing Mr. Fellers and his wife and John Chipman and Nathe and Aline Chipman came up and monday eving severl of us went up to my Brothers Nathaniel and god was there for I felt him in my Soul I saugh the windows of heaven open Henry Prayed and the next eving there was a meting at Obedience Morses and there there was a wonderfull meting and i had such a pitte for poor Siners I cud forgit myself but I cudent for get poor sinners when i see where they stood Peter morse ten years old was converted and Nane Chipman com out and her god and rejoiced in the god of her Salvation Alin Chipman shouted and rejoiced Siners I was crying out for mersy and Santys rejoicing . . . a monday eving after meting Samuel dodge come out and rejoiced in the god of his Salvation Samuel Gates is Converted and Henry

[13]Acadia University, Baptist Historical Collection, Joseph Dimock's Diary, pp. 132-3.

Baker and Sevrel more and I have giving you a short account of the wonderful power of god amonest us but we see and here every day of some being convicted and convert'd.[14]

In Dimock's own church in Chester revivalist influences developed strongly during the summer of 1806. From here the Reverend James Manning wrote his wife, June 14:

Dear Janey with delight I Emprove these few moments to let you I am well I have been getting better Sence I left home. The Lord has conducted my Steps to this place for good I have no dubt but in my mind but our Coming to Chesster Will be had in eternal remembrances There was a Church meeting on Satterday and the Lord was very preasent with many it was a time of Refreshment from the Gloriosys Lord likewise on Lords day I think it was one of the best Sabaths I Ever Saw in my life Mr. Chipman Preached in the forenoon and I Strove to preach in the afternoon Mr. Chipman Spoke Very Well the People ware much affected and in the intermishon the Saints of God at least some of them felt there souls deliver'd You could Scarce See a dry eye in all the house and so in the afternoon and in Sacrament time the Lord appear'd at his own table and people stay'd all most till night at the meetin house it was hard to get any Sleep a tall a monday a very grate audance attended and the people ware very Sollom but no grate appearance of any thing very Extraordinary but after business was over the fire broke oute on every side Saints Rejoiced indeed and poor sinners all in tears and Some backsliders with sorry and joye enterwoven in all there Countannances I think it was one off the best days I Ever saw not I was so much Engadged but to see and hear the the fathers & mothers in Isreal praying and adoring God for the many blessing they ware bless'd with and Young men and women they kept it up till night I have Concluded to stay here three Sabaths and Mr. Demock will Come in my rome.[15]

In the older-settled areas of the country the promotion of revivals of religion served to strengthen the organization of the churches and to secure additions to membership. In the newer-settled areas, or in areas far remote from the chief centres of population, revivalist preaching

[14]Acadia University, Baptist Historical Collection, Correspondence of Rev. Edward Manning, Nictaux, Mar. 4, 1799, Betsy Parker to Rev. Edward Manning.

[15]*Ibid.*, Chester, June 14, 1806, James Manning to his wife. The next year Dimock wrote of the state of religion in Chester:"Sept. 4th 1807 Chester I am about to make a few remarks on the fears on that is past as it respects the work of God it hath been a low time here for some but there appear an Increasing Desire for the Salvation of Souls & gods people many of them have Spoke with Great ashureance of better & more Glorious Days but at length the time to favor Zion came & about the month of August the Lord made a Glorious Descent on the Earth against the strong holds of Sin & Satan & caused an immortal Shakeing among the Dry bones & bone came to his Bone to that the Sabbath after that the work broke out was concluded with Great Shout among the Saints and a Great out cry among Sinners for mercy Monday Evening was the most Noisy meet I have seen in Chester both German & English My Companion to Night broke her chains & for the first time told the world what the Lord had done for her Soul—& blessed God for bringing her from her fathers house to hear his powerful voice—numbers were brought to bow to the Septre of Glorious Christ & I Baptized 3 persons last Lord's Day the work of God Still goes on an increases our meeting are large for people throng in Great abundance from every Quarter to hear & were much affected & many power-fully wrought upon 7 Savingly converted." Joseph Dimock's Diary, pp. 161-2.

constituted the means of extending Newlight influence and of bringing into being new Newlight churches. After 1800 many of the more enterprising of the Newlight preachers engaged upon missionary tours in various parts of the country. In 1800, for instance, the Reverend Joseph Crandall, after having promoted an extensive revival in Westmoreland and Albert counties in New Brunswick and the organization of a church in Sackville, visited, in company with the Reverend George Harding, the St. John Valley, and under his and Harding's preaching revivalist influences spread up the valley as far as Fredericton. Harding wrote from·Saint John to the Reverend James Manning, February 17, 1802:

> Dear Brother I at last imbrace the opertunity of writing a few lines to you to give you some account of the progress of the Gospel on the River St. John last monday was a week since Mr. Lewis was ordained my Sister polly was at the ordination and she says that She never saw half such good meeting in her life as they had there Mr Harding Mr Brooks Mr Crandle and Mr Harris attended the occasion and Mr Harding has not Been to town yet Mr Crandle I believe by accounts is attended with the Spirit of Elijah and power of the holy Ghost boldly says that when he stood before the Congregation to preach his Countenance imitated immortality and his tears that Roled Down his Cheeks Discovered the Desire of his soul and he had Scarcely began to speak when the house was filled with Cries and tears and praises to God and when Mr harding Bore testimony to the Gospel he stood in such power that it was observed by some that they Believed that the very heavens assembled. But you are Judg of such trembling heavens Mr harding and Mr Crandle went from the ordination up to fred'ricktown where there is a Great Deal of a work amongst the people the Gentry that had a play house there have opened it for a preaching house and last Sabath there was to be some people Baptized in freddrickton I have a Great Deal to write but time fails me at present.[16]

Still more typical perhaps of the effort of the Newlight preachers to spread the message of the gospel was the preaching of Peter Crandell in the isolated fishing community on Brier Island. His letter to the Reverend Edward Manning, January 10, 1810, was revealing of the way the influence of religion was extended to a population largely cut off from contacts with civilization. The letter read in part:

> Revn'd and Dear brother in the Kingdom and Patience of our Dear Lord I gladly Embrace this oppertunity to inform you of the happy revival of Religion in one of the Islands of the Sea Called Brier Island with about twenty families on it as God Did By his Love and tender Compassion in time of Old Sweetly Draw a Number of poor fishermen to be his followers has in few months past Chosen a few on this Island and has Established their feet on a rock and has put a new Song in their mouths Even praise to the Lord being Convinced that God had had Commanded

---

[16]Correspondence of Rev. Edward Manning, Saint John, Feb. 17, 1802, George Harding to James Manning. A full account of his missionary labours in New Brunswick was provided by the Reverend Joseph Crandall in the *Christian Visitor*, vol. VI, June 10, 1853.

me to go and blow the Gospel trumpet on that Island I obeyed the heavenly Command the eleventh Day of august last I landed on the Island But O the Cutting pangs of Soul my tongue Cannot express to See the abominations that was prevalent in that Small place which then made me Cry out Lord who is eduquate to the task Lord I am willing to be the instrument but thou Can Do the Work. the First meeting we had their was one young woman Cried out for the Lord to have mercy on her and a Number more Struck under Conviction I was made to believe that the Lord had begun a great work on this Island. I tarried here Several Days the people seemed to be very anxious to hear preaching their was Some Crying for mercy almost every meeting .... the Seventeenth of October I returned to the Island again their seemed to be Some Labouring under the weight of Sin the first meetting their was a young lad about fifteen years old Cried out for mercy I believe the Lord was with us of a truth the next meeting was in the evening the Congregation seemed to be very Solemn During the Sermon but the Lord was pleased to Smile upon Several young people and Cause them to rejoice in their blessed redeemer While number of others was Struck under Conviction and was forced [?] to Crie out for mercy O it was enough to melt the flinty rock to hear the Cries of those under Conviction and the prayers and praises of them just brought into Liberty they continued most of the night before morning the Lord was Pleased to bring Several more into Liberty numbers in a few Days and Since has become made to rejoice in god their redeemer and was very anxious to be formed into a Church agreeable to the Gospel plan of Salvation it being a remote place I thought fit to Call assistance from Sissiboo Church and batitize them into that Church .... I staid on the Island about ten Days and was made to believe that the Lord was still carrying on his Work to the Converting of many Souls on that Island but being Constrained to leave them for Some but Still bearing them in mind at the throne of Grace being anxious to visit them again Still found the work of God prospering with as great power as I most ever saw.[17]

Journals, diaries, private correspondence, reminiscences, and official reports provide some indication of the way in which the Newlight movement spread in the years after 1800. In Argyle and Yarmouth a revival of religion was reported in 1806-7 by Enoch Towner, T. H. Chipman, and Harris Harding.[18] During the winter of 1807-8 the Reverends Isaac Case and Henry Hale from the state of Maine visited Horton, Falmouth, Granville, Cornwallis, Rawdon, Onslow, and parts of Cumberland County; revivals of religion resulted from their preaching.[19] In Liverpool "a most extraordinary awakening among the people" was reported in 1807.[20] In 1809 there were fifteen churches belonging to the recently organized Baptist Association with membership as follows: Argyle, 123; Yarmouth, 250; Digby, 68; Granville, 70; Annapolis, 146; Cornwallis, 65; Horton, 276; Chester, 122; Newport, 90; Prince William, 30; Waterborough, 30; Sackville, 52; Petitcodiac branch

[17]Correspondence of Rev. Edward Manning, Jan. 10, 1810, Peter Crandell apparently to Edward Manning.
[18]See Saunders, *History of the Baptists of the Maritime Provinces*, pp. 144-6; Davis, *Life and Times of Rev. Harris Harding*, pp. 84-93.
[19]Saunders, *History of the Baptists of the Maritime Provinces*, pp. 146-7.
[20]*Ibid.*, p. 155.

of Sackville church, 40; Onslow, 33; and Amherst, 15.[21] In addition, there were many other churches or loosely organized religious bodies in charge of local preachers. The real strength of the Newlight movement could not be measured in number of members.

In the meantime, among the Yorkshire English Methodists in Cumberland County, another revivalist movement had grown up after 1783. Many of the Yorkshire English had been followers of John Wesley before settling in Nova Scotia, but the outbreak of revolution in 1775 prevented Wesley from sending missionaries to the colony, and evangelical religious interests languished during the early years of the war. The appointment of a Church of England missionary, the Reverend J. Eagleson, to this area represented an effort to restore the attachments of the inhabitants to Church Establishment. "The whole district of Cumberland," Franklin, the lieutenant-governor, wrote in October, 1767, "in which are already upwards of eleven hundred souls, are without a Clergyman or teacher of any sort, and we do expect the number of Inhabitants will soon be greatly augmented in that neighbourhood, even the ensuing year; so that the sooner a Missionary is placed among them the better as they will supply themselves with Teachers of various sects, as soon as they are able to support them."[22] The ministrations of Eagleson probably did something to maintain religious interests among the population, but it was not until the Methodist cause was revived that religion became a powerful socially reorganizing force within the pioneer settlements.

The arousal of an interest in evangelical religion may have owed something to the influence of the Newlight preachers; Alline visited the Cumberland settlements in 1781, and, during the next year or two, he and his fellow-evangelist, Thomas Handly Chipman, held revivalist meetings among the Yorkshire English Methodists as well as among the New England Congregationalists in this area. But it was not outside leadership, but leadership developed from within the local group itself, which led to the rise of the Methodist movement. In 1779 an attempt was made in Amherst to reorganize the Methodist societies. Groups gathered together in various homes to engage in religious discussions and to strengthen religious interests. One of the young people who actively supported these endeavours was William Black, the son of a local settler. Under the influence of the revival which took place Black was converted, and, receiving the "call" to preach, he undertook to lead the local societies and to engage in exhortation. Out of these

[21]*Ibid.*, p. 125.
[22]P.A.N.S., Records of the Missionaries of the S.P.G. in Nova Scotia, 1760-1786, Halifax, Oct. 22, 1767, Michl. Franklin to S.P.G.

early preaching efforts, he emerged as the prophet of Methodism in Nova Scotia.[23]

Black began evangelical preaching in his family circle in 1779. In the summer of 1780 he undertook preaching assignments within his home community of Amherst and in the neighbouring settlements of Prospect and Fort Lawrence. During the winter he visited Tantramar and, in the spring of 1781, the settlers on the Petitcodiac River. In November of this year, having reached the age of twenty-one, he embarked upon a career of full-time preaching. The winter was spent in constant preaching within the Yorkshire English settlements; after about five weeks in his home communities of Amherst, Fort Lawrence, Prospect, and Tantramar, he set off after the new year to visit again the settlers on the Petitcodiac River. In the Spring he visited Alline's field of labour, preaching in Cornwallis, Horton, Falmouth, Windsor, and Newport, and, after preaching in Halifax, he set out for Annapolis, holding meetings at Horton, Cornwallis, and Granville on the way. Returning to Amherst in the middle of the summer, and reviving his work there and in Sackville, he once more set out on an extended missionary tour in the autumn, visiting Windsor, Horton, Cornwallis, Granville, Annapolis, and Halifax.[24]

The winter was spent in Cumberland County, and in the spring of 1783 he sailed for the towns along the south shore. In Liverpool, where by this time Alline had aroused considerable interest in evangelical religion, Black's success was conspicuous. He wrote:

Sunday, June 1st.—The Rev. Mr. Frazer preached in the meeting house twice, and I once. At noon a multitude of persons followed me to Mr. Smith's; the house, was pretty well filled, and the Lord was in the midst of us. Many were deeply convinced of sin, and many were exceedingly happy, praising the Lord.—On Monday I preached on the east side of the river; and oh! what a meeting. The power of the Lord was eminently present . . . . I think there were about fourteen crying out in great anguish of soul; while others were shouting for joy. Such affecting heart-piercing cries as were uttered by one, my ears never heard . . . . After the meeting some wanted me to go this way, and some that; their entreaties were so importunate, and yet so opposite, that I was involved in much perplexity. I concluded to go over the river to brother Dean's. We kneeled on the shore, prayed and parted with those who could not accompany us. Those who conveniently could, went over the river with us, to whom I proposed that we should spend part of the night in prayer. The power of God descended upon the people; cries, groans, or rejoicing were on every hand. Thus it continued till about one o'clock in the morning, soon after which we retired.[25]

[23]Cf. T. Watson Smith, *History of the Methodist Church of Eastern British America* (Halifax, 1877), vol. 1, pp. 88-95.
[24]Matthew Richey, *A Memoir of the Late William Black, Wesleyan Minister* (Halifax, 1839), p. 58-75.
[25]*Ibid.*, pp. 103-4.

Of this visit of Black to Liverpool, Perkins made the following entries in his diary:

"Wednesday, May 28th,—Mr. Black, a Methodist Newlight preacher, belonging some where up the Bay of Fundy, Arrives from Halifax, and Preaches at the Meeting House at Evening. . . .

"Thursday, May 29th,—Mr. Black preaches in the day, & evening. the People that followed Mr. Alline, Seem very fond of him. . . .

"Tuesday, June 3d,—Mr. Black Continues to Preach Day & Night. Very extraordinary Stir among his hearers. great Cryings out, etc."

By the spring of 1784 Black had visited almost the whole of Nova Scotia and Prince Edward Island. Although his most intensive preaching had been carried on in the Yorkshire English settlements, where a number of Methodist societies were revived or organized for the first time, the movement quickly assumed under his leadership the character of a general evangelical crusade. Black secured a considerable following among the New England Congregationalists, and, with the coming of the Loyalists, the field of his preaching was still further widened. Though most of the Loyalists were nominal adherents of the Church of England, many of them had formed Methodist attachments or at any rate had come in contact with Methodist teachings in the old colonies, and their settlement in the Maritimes held out the promise of adding considerably to the following of the Methodist movement.

With the growth of population, the number of Methodist preachers in the country increased. Among the Loyalist settlers were some Methodists who had served as local preachers in the American colonies or who at least had undergone the experience of religious conversion, and many of these turned to a preaching career after settling in the Maritimes. John and James Mann, William Grandin, Thomas Whitehead, and John Cooper were some of the early local preachers who secured prominence in the Methodist movement in Nova Scotia.[26] In New Brunswick, the emergence of Duncan McColl as a Methodist preacher was typical of the way religiously minded Loyalist settlers turned to a career of preaching. While serving in the Argyleshire Regiment during the American revolutionary war, McColl had come in contact with some Methodists and had become increasingly concerned about his religious state. Arriving in Halifax after the revolution, business connections led him to settle at St. Stephen, New Brunswick, and here he soon began to exercise what gifts he had as a preacher. He wrote:

I found a mixed multitude of people from many parts of the world, without any

---

[26]Cf. Smith, *History of the Methodist Church of Eastern British America*, vol. I, chaps. V and VI.

form of religion. There was a man who professed to be a Baptist, but the people would not hear him because of his immoral character. I inquired after him, and found him very full of visions and dreams. I had charity to hope he meant well. The first Sunday after I got to St. Stephens, six of our neighbours came to our house; I read and had prayer with them, and it did appear as if God was with us. The next Sunday we had upwards of sixty people, to whom I read and expounded the word, exhorted them to turn to God, and dismissed them with prayer. The time was very encouraging, and the people crowded out every Sunday . . . . I had nothing in view but to do good to the people. I had no idea of preaching; nevertheless my whole soul was taken up in the work, and many experienced the pardoning love of God in so clear a manner as is seldom seen in our days. All at once the thoughts of my own situation, a multitude attending, sinners converted, and no minister to take charge of them, and I was joined to no connexion. I fasted, and prayed, and laid our case before the Lord. And the prophecies of Jeremiah xx.8, 11, came with such force to my soul as to remove all scruple, and I was sure that the Lord called me to the ministry. I never from that time scrupled my call, Jeremiah's case suited mine exactly. I was deeply sensible of my want of suitable talents for the ministry; but God added spiritual help, adding daily to my gifts, and to him all the praise.

My house was now like a public house . . . . I then called the believers together, and joined them together as near the Methodist plan as I knew and was able . . . . I gave up all worldly business, took to the study of the word, to preach and exhort on all occasions.[27]

McColl for some time remained entirely on his own. "I was not," he wrote of about 1790, "in connexion with the Methodists yet, neither did I ever see any of their preachers. Some Baptists came through the country, but unfortunately they did not turn out to be moral men. My object was to find a people whose experience, doctrine, and practice, came up exactly to the Scriptures."[28] In 1791 he journeyed to Halifax in the hope of meeting with Mr. Black, but Black at this time was in Newfoundland and instead he made the acquaintance of John Regan, a newly arrived American preacher. From then on he considered himself in connection with the Methodists, and in 1795, as the other local preachers had done, including Black himself, he visited the United States to secure ordination.

The rise of a number of local preachers strengthened greatly the resources of Methodism within particular areas of the country, but the expansion of the movement depended upon the work of travelling evangelists going from settlement to settlement, and the building up of such a body required outside assistance. Realizing the hopelessness of obtaining sufficient Wesleyan missionaries to serve the needs of the country, Black turned to the United States for a supply. The appointment in the early spring of 1785 by the General Conference of

[27]"Memoir of the Rev. Duncan M'Coll" (*British North American Wesleyan Methodist Magazine for the Year 1841*, Saint John, vol. I, pp. 299-300).
[28]*Ibid.*, p. 301.

the Methodist Episcopal Church of two evangelists for Nova Scotia—Freeborn Garrettson and James Oliver Cromwell—marked the beginnings of efforts to supply the Maritime field from the United States. In 1787 Garrettson and Cromwell returned to their homeland but another missionary was sent to take their place. At the New York Conference in 1791 six preachers were appointed for work in the Maritimes; in addition, in 1788, the first Wesleyan missionary made an appearance in the colony.[29]

With the increase in the number of preachers, Methodist evangelistic efforts were greatly strengthened. In Horton a revival took place during the winter of 1786-7 under the preaching of Black and Garrettson. "We had some very happy times," Black wrote, "during the winter, especially at Horton, where there was a powerful awakening among the people."[30] Garrettson was equally cheered. "My time this winter," he wrote Wesley, March 10, 1787, "has been spent mostly in Horton, Windsor, and Cornwallis. In the former there has been a divine display; many convinced and converted to God. A few months ago the place was famous for the works of the devil—now for singing, praying, and hearing the word. If the work continue much longer as it has done, the greater part of the people will be brought in."[31]

In Liverpool, the Methodist preachers were even more successful. In the winter of 1786-7 a revival took place here as well as in Horton. On February 24, 1787, Perkins wrote: "At Evening I attend meeting with the Methodist Society at Mr. William Smith's. Many Young people are praising God for Pardoning mercy. I understand Near Ten persons have professed that they have Recd Manifestations of the pardon of their Sin, & acceptance. this week 6 or 7 of them in one Night, and many more are under Conviction, a most Remarkable time with the people."[32] The next day appeared the entry: "I attend meeting at Mr. Mann's in the evening. Mr. Wells, the Shoe-maker, Professed to receive Great Comfort, & was praising God." On February 27, Perkins again referred to the lively interest in religion among the Methodists in the town: "I attend Meeting in the Evening at Mr. Mann's. After the Service was over, there was a very great Rejoicing among the Young people that profess Lately to have received a Change of Heart, & pardon of their Sins." Black wrote of this revival in Liverpool to John Wesley in England: "At Liverpool there has been an astonishing

[29]Cf. Smith, *History of the Methodist Church of Eastern British America*, vol. I, chaps. VII-VIII.
[30]Richey, *A Memoir of the Late William Black*, p. 164.
[31]Nathan Bangs, *The Life of the Rev. Freeborn Garrettson* (New York, 1829), p. 171.
[32]Perkins (Simeon) Diary.

outpouring of the spirit. Nine were set a liberty at one meeting. Of forty who joined society in a few weeks, seventeen profess faith. I do not know any part of the province in which the work of God has gone on, as in this place, with so little declension for six years or more. The manners of the people are entirely changed. If the work spreads as rapidly as it has done, much longer, almost all in the place will be brought in. Brother John Mann has been with them all this winter. The people seem all on fire for God, especially the young people, and exhort all they see to make their peace with God."[33]

In 1796 another revival took place in Liverpool. Perkins wrote, December 20, 1795: "a Meeting at Mr. Joshua Newton's. a Considerable stir among the people. Some rejoicing, & others distressed." On January 17 he again wrote: "at Evening Mr. Frank Newton Preaches at his Brother's. A Lively time among the people after Meeting. two that had professed to be converted Some time ago, were in a wonderful extisay. Mrs. Fraser is Supposed to have experienced a Change. Hetty Draper, that Lives in my Family, was in great distress, & Seemed in a Manner to Swoon, & remained in that State a long time. She was not Able to git home." In the early part of February, the revival had gathered force. "There has for Some time passed," Perkins wrote, February 7, "been a remarkable Stir, & Religious Concern among the people." During the remainder of February, meetings were held with great frequency, and were characterized by a high state of religious excitement and a large number of conversions. The following entry made by Perkins on February 8 is typical of several he made during the month:

Last Evening I was at Meeting at Mr. Newton's when, after the preaching was Over, there was an Extraordinary Stir among the Young people, principally the Females. Sally Slocombe Said to be converted, many Others in distress. Priscilla Page was Continually Exhorting, while her Strength held out. She would appear to Swoon, and as Soon as recovered a little, she would begin again. Several of the young converts appeared to be in Exticies, & Raptures of Joy. I observe the Operation, both when under Conviction & after being Set at Liberty, has Seemed to be Stronger, & attended with Swoonings, & Exticies, to a greater degree than I have usually observed in persons under Such Operations in times passed. God grant that their future Lives, & deportment may be Answerable to their profession. great allowances must be made for the Tender frames of Young Females, and different Constitutions of Different persons in making up a Judgement about Such extraordinary Appearances. we cannot prescribe measures to the Spirit of God. He works on the Hearts, & minds of men as Seemeth Good to him.

Extravagances in some of the meetings led the preacher in charge to urge the need for order and moderation and to lay down certain rules

[33]Richey, *A Memoir of the Late William Black*, p. 187.

to be observed. Though some of the recent converts were offended, and the enthusiasm of the revival cooled, a strong interest in matters of religion continued during the next few months. In June the local gaol, where one of the Methodist stalwarts was confined as a debtor, became the chief centre of revivalist meetings. "A Very extraordinary Meeting," Perkins wrote June 20, "at the Jail this Evening. it was a Class meeting. their Singing, & Crying was heard to my House, & all about the point." The influence of the revival extended into areas neighbouring Liverpool. "The Revd. James Mann," Perkins wrote August 12, "Returns from Port Mutton, Port Jolly, & Port Hebere, where he has been preaching, and Says he finds the people doing well in the ways of Religion. There is a wonderfull Change in the people in them Settlements."

After 1800, under the preaching of Wesleyan missionaries and local preachers, a high state of religious excitement continued to characterize Methodist meetings in Liverpool, and revivals of religion continued to occur. "A prayer Meeting," Perkins wrote, June 24, 1801, "at Richard Thomas House. Mr. Cooper, & Mr. Bennett attended. Mr. Cooper gave a word of Exhortation in a Very Moving Manner, which Seemed to effect the hearers Very Sencibly. Several Females Cryed out a Loud for Mercy, and the House Seemed to be in a great Commotion." On June 18, 1802, Perkins noted: "Mr. Black preaches at the Chapel in the Evening. Some woman made a noise as in distress. the people Stayed Sometime after the last prayer. They Sang, & Several prayed." On Sunday, May 12, 1805, an increase in religious interest was again evident among the Methodists in Liverpool. Perkins wrote: "Mr. Sutcliffe preached three times. as Soon as the third meeting was dismissed, before the people got out, a young woman, I learned afterwards it was Jane Cotman, Cried out, Either in distress, or rejoicing. Mrs. Ward Soon Joined her, & I believe, Some others, Jane Hunt, who was Christnd this day, I believe, was one. there was a great adue for Sometime." The next year, under the ministry of the Reverend William Sutcliffe, a Wesleyan missionary, an extensive revival took place in the settlement among the Methodists as well as among the Newlights.[34]

Farther down the south shore, where New Englanders likewise predominated among the population, the influence of Methodism also gained strength. "God is carrying on his work," James Mann wrote Garrettson during the winter of 1786-7, "in a glorious manner in Barrington; the people flock from every quarter to hear the word: many have been convinced, and about fourteen have been set at liberty,

[34]Smith, *History of the Methodist Church of Eastern British America*, vol. I, pp. 403-5.

some of whom were famous for all manner of wickedness."[35] On March 28, 1792, Perkins wrote in his diary: "Mr. Boyd has a Letter from Mr. Barrey, Informing that there is a very great Religious work at Barrington. Seventy persons Said to be Converted, & many others under Concern. *a Wonderful Work indeed!*"

In 1801 the cause of Methodism was revived in the Yorkshire English settlements with the establishment of the Westmorland mission in charge of the Reverend Joshua Marsden, Wesleyan missionary. Marsden adhered to a strict two weeks itinerant schedule in carrying out his preaching engagements. On Sunday he preached at Pointe de Bute, Monday at Fort Lawrence, Tuesday at Amherst, Wednesday at Nappan River, Thursday at the home of a local magistrate in another part of the mission, and on Friday he returned to Pointe de Bute. Saturday was spent in crossing the marsh to Sackville where he preached on the second Sunday, and on Monday he set off through the woods to Memramcook, or Dorchester, the western extremity of his mission, and, in this settlement he preached during the week "in one place and sometimes another, to meet the scattered state of the inhabitants."[36] What time Marsden had free after his preaching engagements was spent in visiting from house to house.[37]

The next year Marsden was transferred from the Westmorland mission to the St. John Valley, and here he put into effect the same rigorous plan of organization. "I found in the city [of Saint John]," he wrote of his arrival upon the mission, "a lively and united little church, and entered upon my labours among them with much comfort. They were few in number, but warm-hearted, and zealous. . . . Besides the whites in society, we had a number of free blacks, some of whom, were truly pious, and greatly helped me by their prayers."[38] As soon as travel was possible he proceeded up the river, and undertook to revive societies which had been formed earlier. "During this visit," he wrote, "I preached with much profit at Sheffield, where we have a chapel. . . . I also visited Majorville, Nash-Walk, St. Anns, or Fredericktown; together with the Grand Lake, and several other places. . . . At St. Anns, we had a good chapel, but the town being the residence of the governor, and others connected with the government, we did little good. At Sheffield, and lower down the river, religion had been greatly revived, under the ministry of Mr. Bennet."[39] Under Marsden's

[35]Bangs, *Life of the Rev. Freeborn Garrettson*, p. 171.

[36]Joshua Marsden, *The Narrative of a Mission, to Nova Scotia, New Brunswick, and the Somers Islands* (2nd ed., London, 1827), pp. 43-5.

[37]*Ibid.*, p. 50.

[38]*Ibid.*, p. 134.

[39]*Ibid.*, p. 148.

preaching during the next few years Methodist influence was greatly increased throughout the St. John Valley. "During this winter, 1804-5," he wrote, "I laboured in St. John, and along the banks of the river, with visible success, and much satisfaction. Old differences in the society were composed, and the contending parties reconciled. Among the town's people, prejudices seemed to lose ground. There was a manifest increase of christian affection and simplicity among the society."[40] In the autumn of 1806, while Marsden was engaged in another part of the mission, a revival of religion broke out in Saint John, and, when he returned, it quickly gathered force. "Such a stir in religion," he wrote, "was quite a new thing in Saint John; some wondered whereunto it would grow; others condemned the whole as enthusiasm and delusion."[41] In a letter to a fellow minister, Marsden wrote in March of the effects of the revival:

The magistrates and principal inhabitants cannot deny that there is a great change in the place for the better, as many of the young people who are subjects of this work, were once both loose in their principles, and irregular in their practices, but they are now new creatures; and one can hardly go through the street of this little city without hearing the voice of praise, or seeing the young men assembling together for prayer . . . .

Our little chapel is so crowded, that you can scarcely see any thing but human heads; and the meetings are solemn beyond any thing seen in this place for a long time. Often, towards the conclusion, a cry for mercy begins which spreads from one to another, till the union of the voices of those who are either praying, crying, or rejoicing, forms what worldly people call confusion . . . . Our meetings are become the common topic of conversation. Some wonder, some mock, some acknowledge the power of God, and several not in society defend the cause to the utmost of their power. But, as yet, none of the rulers have believed on Him. The good that is done is chiefly among the poor and middling classes of people.[42]

The rise of the Methodist movement strengthened greatly sectarian religious forces in the Maritime Provinces which had earlier found expression in the Newlight movement. In many areas, such as Liverpool, Methodism combined with Newlightism to establish firmly the evangelistic religious cause. In some other areas, the Methodist evangelists were able to reach people who had not come under the influence of the Newlight preachers. In New Brunswick, in particular, the Methodist cause gained great strength after the turn of the century. It was here that the influence of the Great Revival of the West made itself most felt.

The Great Awakening of the revolutionary period established the sectarian tradition in the religious life of Nova Scotia, and under its

[40]*Ibid.*, p. 169.
[41]*Ibid.*, p. 208.
[42]*Ibid.*, pp. 216-17.

impact the Congregational churches were forced to give way to churches organized on the Newlight plan. The Great Revival of the later period extended the influence of the sectarian tradition and completed the disruption of the formal institutions of religion. Few of the Congregational churches which had survived the break-up before the turn of the century were able to escape the effects of the later religious disturbances. Of the other religious bodies in the community, the Church of England was most affected by the spread of the spirit of religious revival.

In many areas of the country after 1783 the Church barely succeeded in maintaining religious services. "The Church here," Bishop Inglis wrote in his journal, of Cornwallis, July 22, 1788, "is small and unfinished. The settlement very extensive, and populous; yet few Church people. The inhabitants divided into many sects and carried away by a variety of enthusiasts that undertake to preach to them. This is also the case at Horton."[43] The missionary himself wrote of the state of his mission, in 1792: "Mr. Twining, Missionary at Cornwallis," the abstract of his letter read, "has visited the most distant settlements upon the Bay of Fundy, near 20 miles from his place of residence, and he preached at some one of them every other Sunday during the summer season, when travel is practicable; and he hopes that it has given some check to the spirit of Fanaticism, which very much prevails among the lower class of people."[44] The mission of Newport and Windsor was in an even less satisfactory state than the one of Cornwallis and Horton. Inglis wrote, July 31, 1791: "The Church of England has declined and the Methodists have gained ground in Newport, chiefly through Mr. Ellis' inattention, neglect and unclerical behaviour."[45] Little more satisfactory was the mission of Wilmot and Aylesford. "Preached today at Aylesford," Inglis wrote, August 7, 1791, "to about 60 people . . . . An enthusiastic Sect, called New Lights are active in disseminating their tracts here. They are Anabaptists. One of their Teachers from Cornwallis, boasted that in a late excursion he had *converted* five people in Aylesford and Wilmot."[46]

Farther down the valley towards Annapolis the proportion of Loyalist settlers in the population increased and the Church gained somewhat greater support, but it faced many difficulties here also. "Few dissenters in this place," Inglis wrote of Annapolis, July 27, 1788, "and the inhabi-

[43]P.A.N.S., Bishop Charles Inglis Journal, 1785-1810.
[44]*Abstract of the Proceedings of the Society for the Propagation of the Gospel*, 1793 (London, 1794), p. 45.
[45]Bishop Charles Inglis Journal, 1785-1810.
[46]*Ibid.*

tants appear to be the most decent and regular I have yet seen in the province."[47] In Granville, however, the influence of the evangelical movements had made itself felt. "The state of Granville is peculiar," Inglis wrote the Society, October 16, 1789, "and calls for more than ordinary attention. . . . A set of enthusiastic Anabaptists, called here by the name of New Lights, have got footing among them, and threatened to subvert all order and rational religion. The people having Divine service solemnized, and a sermon preached only four Sundays in the whole year by Mr. Bailey, can hear no other than those fanatics the rest of the year. The youth especially having no regular place of worship, run after them or spend Sunday in taverns."[48] The failure of the missionary in Annapolis to visit Granville regularly led to the establishment of a separate mission.[49] The evangelical denominations continued to interfere with the work of the Church. "The Methodists, and an enthusiastic Sect called New Lights," Inglis wrote the Society again, November 9, 1791, "are very troublesome here [Granville] and at Annapolis."[50]

In Digby, where Loyalist settlers were predominant, the influence of the evangelical sects was not felt for some time. "The party-spirit which was so violent formerly," Inglis wrote in his journal, of Digby, September 9, 1791, "has entirely subsided, and the people live in great harmony. They discouraged the New Lights and Methodists Teachers from coming among them."[51] In a letter to the Society in 1791, Mr. Viets, the missionary at Digby, wrote "That there is no other sort of publick worship in his Mission, or in the vicinity, and all other Denominations become more and more reconciled to the Church. That the Methodists and New Lights, who have created much confusion in the neighbouring Missions, have made but little progress in his, except among the Blacks and the lowest of the Whites."[52] In 1801 Viets again wrote that "He is happy to say, that though the New Lights and other Enthusiasts are very troublesome in the skirts of his Mission, Digby and its vicinity are still uninfected by them. Indeed the poor ignorant people, in the outparts, who have been excited to the highest enthusiasm, had so far neglected their temporal concerns to follow these rambling preachers, that they had become much dis-

[47]*Ibid.*
[48]P.A.C., Letters and Journals of Two Nova Scotia Bishops, Halifax, Oct. 16, 1789, Bishop Inglis to Secretary, S.P.G.
[49]*Proceedings, S.P.G.*, 1790, p. 37.
[50]Letters and Journals of Two Nova Scotia Bishops, Halifax, Nov. 9, 1791, Bishop Inglis to Secretary, S.P.G.
[51]Bishop Charles Inglis Journal, 1785-1810.
[52]*Proceedings, S.P.G.*, 1792, p. 44.

tressed for the bare necessaries of life, which seems at length to have cooled their zeal, and abated their frenzy."[53] By 1805, however, the Society missionary was becoming more concerned respecting the inroads of the evangelical movements. In that year, the abstract of his letter to the Society read in part: "That the New Lights encrease in the vicinity of Digby, and although they have made but little, if any impression there, yet at Clements, Sissaboo, and other places, they have occasioned much confusion. Their paroxysms of enthusiastic zeal and madness exceed all that he has ever heard or read of."[54]

In Yarmouth, Barrington, and neighbouring communities, early settlements of New Englanders, the Church of England secured little influence. The Reverend Mr. Viets visited this part of the province in the autumn of 1796. The abstract of this letter read: "He preached there three Sundays and on several Week-days. They have no Minister of any denomination, except Itinerant New Light Exhorters."[55] Inglis wrote in his journal, July 28, 1790:

> The number of families in the township of Barrington is 120, of whom 60 reside at the harbour. The people much led away by Methodist teachers and New Lights . . . . In Argyle township are between 60 and 70 English families, besides about 40 Acadian families, who are occasionally visited by a Romish Priest. The largest settlement of English families is at Franklin, on the head of the Tusket River. Their number is about 20 families, chiefly Loyalists. The Methodists have not been here . . . .
> Yarmouth is a flourishing settlement—from 150 to 200 families, chiefly Dissenters. They have lately erected a meeting house, but have no Minister. They have been visited by Methodists and New Lights and expect a Minister from New England.
> The number of families professing the Church of England at Barrington is 6. At Argyle, about 20 families; at Yarmouth, about 12 families.[56]

The situation respecting the Church of England in other parts of Nova Scotia was generally unsatisfactory, although here and there some support was secured. The Reverend Mr. Norris, missionary at Chester, wrote the Society in 1798 that "Many who are called New Lights attend his preaching; and he trusts their prejudices will in time wear away, as they have not been visited lately by any of their fanatic teachers."[57] In Lunenburg, dissatisfaction with the Society missionary —the Reverend Mr. Money—encouraged the growth of the evangelical sects. "His congregation encreases but slowly," the abstract of a letter he had written the Society in 1793 read. "That the New Light Preachers had come among them, and a Sect who term themselves Tolerated

[53]*Ibid.*, 1801, p. 33.
[54]*Ibid.*, 1805, p. 41.
[55]*Ibid.*, 1789, p. 39.
[56]Bishop Charles Inglis Journal, 1785-1810.
[57]*Proceedings, S.P.G.*, 1799, p. 48.

Anabaptists. One of their practices is to new dip those who have been baptised already. At present they have gained most ground among the Lutherans and Calvinists."[58] Even in Halifax, the capital of the province, the support of the Church of England fell off. Inglis wrote the Archbishop of Canterbury, December 26, 1787:

> The congregation of Halifax has considerably declined of late. The causes which are assigned for this are—two popular preachers in town, one a Roman Catholic, the other a Presbyterian, each of which has had a place of worship built; besides a Methodist meeting house lately erected—the neglect of building another church about the year 1783, when a large accession of church people came to Halifax. Mr. Weeks, whom Dr. Breynton left as his curate, though much liked as a man, is disliked as a preacher. I have been repeatedly assured that if I had not come over in autumn, half the remaining church people would have joined other communions . . . . Certain it is that the Church here is in a disagreeable situation.[59]

In Cape Breton, though the evangelical sects were not particularly active, they constituted a threat to the Church of England. A Methodist preacher—Oliphant—was settled at the North West Arm, but, a Wesleyan from England, he recognized the superior position of the Church of England, and refrained from baptizing, administering the sacraments, or marrying, and his followers usually attended the services of the Church in addition to the Methodist meetings. In Sydney, however, a local preacher, a shoe-maker by the name of Miller, was less inclined to recognize the tie of the Methodists to the Church of England.[60] Dissatisfaction with a clergyman of the Church of England, the Reverend Mr. Cossit, had resulted in lowering considerably the prestige of the Church.[61] In Prince Edward Island also the position of the Church of England was not satisfactory. "I may affirm," Walter Johnstone wrote of the state of religion there in 1820, "that the Episcopal has succeeded the worst of any form of church order adopted upon the Island. Those who might be expected to be its warmest friends and supporters, I mean emigrants from England, are some of its worst enemies."[62]

In New Brunswick, where the population was largely Loyalist, the Church of England secured a stronger foot-hold, but even ·here the evangelical sects gained considerable support. "The people of this house," Inglis wrote of the place he stayed over-night on his way up the St. John River, July 17, 1792, "complained that Mr. Scovil had not visited this part of his parish for upwards of a twelvemonth, of

[58]*Ibid.*, 1794, p. 43.
[59]Letters and Journals of Two Nova Scotia Bishops, Halifax, Dec. 26, 1787, Bishop Inglis to Archbishop of Canterbury.
[60]Bishop Charles Inglis Journal, 1785-1810, July 8, 1805.
[61]*Ibid.*, July 7, 1805.
[62]W. Johnstone, *Travels in Prince Edward Island in the Years 1820-1* (Edinburgh, 1823), p. 110.

which neglect the Methodists had availed themselves, and were very assiduous in making proselytes. Church People offended at Mr. Scovil's neglect and officiousness of the Methodists, who do much injury to the country."[63] The same year the missionary reported to the Society in London: "Mr. Scovil Missionary of Kingston," the abstract of his letter reads, "extends his spiritual offices, for about half his time, to the remote parts of that parish, and to the adjacent ones of Westfield and Springfield, which is attended with much fatigue, but chearfully undertaken, in hopes of keeping up a due sense of religion, and preventing the people from being misled by the wild enthusiasm of strolling Teachers, or sinking into profaneness and immorality, from the want of religious worship and instruction."[64] The missionary at Maugerville, the Reverend Mr. Beardsley, in a letter to the Society in 1794, reported "That the state of his Mission is nearly the same, but he has had some trouble to keep the weak and wavering from running after strolling enthusiastic Teachers."[65] Eight years later the missionary in Maugerville, now the Reverend James Bisset, reported that "The adjacent Parishes are filled with the wildness of enthusiasm, but Maugerville is comparatively free from the infatuation."[66] The Reverend Mr. Andrews, missionary at St. Andrews, wrote, 1797, that "as it is the largest County in the Province, and he can only attend once or twice in the year at the distant parts, the people are much exposed to the influence of Enthusiastic Teachers."[67] Two years later a letter from the same missionary "assures the Society of his constant attention to his Mission, and wishes he could add, that a regard for Religion improved more than it does: but while an ignorant, distracted herd of unsent Teachers infest the extremity of his Mission, gaiety and inconsideration prevail in the interior parts."[68] The Reverend Oliver Arnold of Sussex Vale reported in 1797 that "the work of the Church goes on slowly."[69] In 1802 Arnold informed the Society "that for a year past, the intemperate zeal of the New Light and Baptist Teachers, (who on their way from Nova Scotia to the river St. John had given much disturbance in his Mission) had abated, their numbers decreased, and many of his parishioners, who appeared to be unsettled in their principles, are now returning to a serious and sober sense of Religion, and of their duty."[70] The Reverend Mr. Millidge, missionary at Westmorland, reported to the Society that

[63]Bishop Charles Inglis Journal, 1785-1810.
[64]*Proceedings, S.P.G.*, 1793, p. 55.
[65]*Ibid.*, 1795, p. 45.
[66]*Ibid.*, 1803, p. 49.
[67]*Ibid.*, 1798, p. 41.
[68]*Ibid.*, 1800, p. 39.
[69]*Ibid.*, 1798, p. 43.
[70]*Ibid.*, 1803, p. 50.

"The Newlights seem to be losing ground."[71] Similarly, the Reverend Mr. Clarke, missionary at Gagetown, was able to report in 1798 that "the wild, enthusiastic principles propagated by a set of Visionary Teachers, seem to be declining."[72] The situation here continued to remain satisfactory. "Mr. Clarke, Missionary at Gage Town," the Society reported in 1802, "in his letters to the Society, assures them of the religious disposition of his parishioners, untainted by that fanaticism which so abounds in the country, from strolling teachers of various denominations."[73]

The missionaries if possible tended to paint the bright side of the picture since they were dependent for their jobs upon convincing the Society that promising opportunities in the colonies were faced by the Church. On the other hand, it should be recognized, complaints of defections to the evangelistic sects often had reference to the shift of attachments of people who had always been nonconformists. Efforts of the Church of England to capture the support of the nonconformist population brought it much more sharply into competition with the evangelistic sects than if it had been content to rely upon the support of those who were its regular adherents. Probably not a great number of Church of England members as such joined the Newlight or Methodist followings. The weakness of these movements in Shelburne and in centres where military garrisons were stationed was a reflection of their failure to gain any great support for the evangelistic cause among those attached to the Established Church. Wide social differences separated members of the Church of England from the great mass of the population and this cultural isolation of the Church of England membership tended to shelter it from the influence of evangelistic movements growing up among the masses.

If the Church of England, however, did not experience any great loss of adherents to the revivalist sects, the rise of these sects rendered almost wholly ineffectual the efforts of the Church to extend its influence beyond its own membership. The Church gained little from the denominational chaos resulting from the break-up of the Congregational churches or from the fact that the settlement of Yorkshire English brought to the colony a group of people who, while attached to Wesleyanism, remained nominally in connection with Establishment. It is true, some of the Congregationalists joined the Church of England in face of the disintegration of their own churches, but they were of the upper classes of the rural village society who sought by this means to improve

[71]*Ibid.*, 1798, p. 40.
[72]*Ibid.*, 1799, p. 51.
[73]*Ibid.*, 1802, p. 43.

their social position; their number represented an insignificant proportion of the total Congregationalist population.[74] The great majority of the Congregationalists shifted over to the support of the Newlight churches or of the other nonconformist churches in the country. Similarly, few if any of the Methodists were won back into the fold of the Church; the rise of the Methodist movement in the colony completed the break which had begun in Yorkshire through the preaching of John Wesley and in New York State (among those who became Loyalists) through the preaching of Philip Embury, Captain Thomas Webb, and others. Unlike the Congregational Churches which were virtually destroyed by the evangelistic revival, the Church of England maintained without any difficulty its separate religious identity, but it was driven back to rely almost wholly upon the support of those people who because of their background had a distinct preference for its form of religious service. Claims of the Church to the privileges of Establishment were seriously weakened as a result.

The Presbyterian Church did not wholly escape the effects of the revivalist influence although it experienced fewer losses than those suffered by the Church of England. The support given to Presbyterianism by many Congregationalists who were not able to maintain services of their own and who were not prepared to join with the Newlights led to some strengthening of the Presbyterian cause in the older-settled areas of the colony, while the persistence of clan loyalties among the Scottish settlers tended to the preservation generally of Presbyterian attachments. Nevertheless, the Church generally was considerably weakened by the growth of the spirit of revivalism. In the newer settlements in New Brunswick, in particular, many isolated Presbyterian families attached themselves to one of the evangelical religious sects.[75] In Truro, Halifax, and even in Pictou County, while attachments were more secure, the support of Presbyterians could not always be relied upon. Newlight and Methodist evangelists became increasingly active in carrying on religious services within the Scottish settlements in the colony after the turn of the century. Not only were the strongholds of Presbyterianism invaded but the strongholds of Roman Catholicism as well. Some success attended these labours.

In terms of the needs of the local Maritime society, the evangelistic religious sects enjoyed many advantages in competing with the formal

[74]A. W. H. Eaton, *The History of King's County, Nova Scotia* (Salem, 1910), p. 251.
[75]See J. Robertson, *History of the Mission of the Secession Church to Nova Scotia and Prince Edward Island* (London, 1847), pp. 196-9; and G. Patterson, *Memoir of the Rev. James MacGregor, Pictou, N.S. and of the Social and Religious Condition of the Early Settlers* (Philadelphia, 1859), pp. 350-1.

institutions of religion. That was particularly true with respect to the Church of England. It was about this time that the Church was at its weakest both at home and abroad, and nowhere perhaps were the effects of mis-government—and, indeed, of petty corruption—more felt than in the Maritime Provinces.[76] All those abuses which had grown up within the organization of the Church in Britain in the eighteenth century made their appearance within the colony. Because conditions were very different in the new land the effects of such abuses were much greater. Scarcely in any particular did the Church make an effort to adapt itself to the new environment.

Much the most serious cause of weakness in the Church resulted from its failure to recruit clergy suitable for service in the colony. At home many of the men who entered upon clerical office in the Church had little competence for the tasks they assumed, and it was usually the least competent who accepted missionary appointments abroad. Willingness to serve in a distant land indicated very often a failure to secure preferment in an appointment to a home parish rather than a desire to spread the teachings of the gospel. There was little zeal for missionary work either among the Church's leaders or among its clergy. The effect of such lack of zeal was evident in the failure of the Society missionaries to gain any great support from the colonial inhabitants.

Inglis, the new bishop in the colony, anxious to reform the Church, was unsparing in his criticism of the missionaries who had been sent out; most of them he described as thoroughly incompetent, hopelessly lazy, lacking in any understanding of the problems of the population, and, at times, even given to such vices as intemperance. "In this province," he wrote the Archbishop of Canterbury, December 18, 1788, "the Society now have *eleven* missionaries. Of these, *four* are diligent, useful clergymen—*three* are indifferent, neither doing much good or harm, and as for the remaining *four*, it would be happy for the Church, if they were not in their orders. I mention no names, because no injury is intended, and they have all shewed a proper attention to me. The evil is the more to be lamented, as it scarcely admits of a remedy, but from the slow hand of time."[77] In his private journal, Inglis was even less reserved in his criticisms of some of the missionaries in the province. Of Twining, the missionary at Cornwallis and Horton, he wrote: "He is a decent young man in his appearance, but rather too fond—as I have been informed—of amusement."[78] The unorthodox manner of

[76]Elie Halèvy, *A History of the English People in 1815* (London, 1924), book III, chap. I.
[77]Letters and Journals of Two Nova Scotia Bishops, Halifax, Dec. 18, 1788, Bishop Inglis to Archbishop Canterbury.
[78]Bishop Charles Inglis Journal, 1785-1810, Sept. 14, 1789.

dress of the missionary offended the tastes of the bishop. "Mr. Twining came this morning to Church," he wrote, September 27, 1789, "in his boots and coat. I took notice of this and he seemed to think he was justified in it because some clergymen in England did the same. This neglect in waring his habit had given offence to the people of Cornwallis."[79] Of Jacob Bailey in Annapolis, Inglis wrote: "He appears to be a meek, inoffensive man."[80] The Reverend John Wiswell, spelled Wiswall by the Bishop, missionary at Granville, was much less satisfactory. "I learned that the people of Granville," Inglis wrote in his journal, September 18, 1879, "were strongly prejudiced against Mr. Wiswall, and that he would by no means answer this mission."[81] Two years later, the bishop wrote: "Wiswall is an infirm man, and rather incapable of that exertion which the state of the country requires. Like too many of the Clergy here, he does not seem to have such notions of order, conformity to the Rubrics and subordination as I could wish; nor of the necessity of vigorous exertions in the Clergy, where the country is overrun with Sectaries who are indefatigable and where the people are extremely ignorant."[82] The next year, the bishop had cause for further annoyance with Mr. Wiswell. "I was sorry to hear," he wrote, July 4, 1792, "that discontents prevailed on account of Mr. Wiswall's remissness in his duty. He had lately fixed a Sunday for administering the Sacraments at Wilmot, but did not attend because a small shower of rain fell that morning. He misses his turn frequently at Aylesford, and observes no regular order in the Sundays he attends."[83] The conduct of the missionary did not improve in later years. In a letter dated August 4, 1796, Inglis strongly reproved him for his persistent failure to conduct services in Aylesford, and, in a letter to the secretary of the Society for the Propagation of the Gospel the next month, the bishop complained bitterly of the missionary's negligence.[84]

The missionary in Windsor and Newport was equally unsatisfactory, and the bishop found it necessary to take disciplinary action. He wrote in his journal, August 1, 1791:

Sent for Mr. Ellis to confer with him on the state of his mission. I mentioned his disrespectful neglect in not attending my visitation, and not answering my questions, or even writing to me. He alleged his inability to ride or write, to which I replied that a person who was unable to do either was utterly unfit for the duties of a mission.

---

[79] *Ibid.*
[80] *Ibid*, July 27, 1788.
[81] *Ibid.*
[82] *Ibid.*, Aug. 14, 1791.
[83] *Ibid.*
[84] Letters and Journals of Two Nova Scotia Bishops, Halifax, Aug. 14, 1796, Bishop Inglis to Mr. Wiswall; and Halifax, Sept. 3, 1796, Bishop Inglis to Dr. Morice.

I then proceeded to mention the ruinous state of his mission—that he had abandoned two thirds of his charge, Newport and Falmouth; that he was scarcely on speaking terms with any person at Windsor; that his behaviour in general, and particularly on Easter Eve, when after burying a corpse, he pulled off a man's hat in a rage and struck him with it, had given such universal disgust that the Church of England was in danger of being totally ruined in these parts. that it would be better to have no Clergyman here, than to have things remain in their present state. that duty to God and the Church obliged me to interfere, though it was exceedingly painful to me to speak to him in this manner, and that something must be speedily done to retrieve the state of the Mission.[85]

In Lunenburg, dissatisfaction with the missionary led to the disintegration of the Church, and in 1790 the bishop undertook to investigate the situation to determine the cause. He wrote in his journal, August 18, 1790, after his inquiry:

None of the Vestry alleged any neglect of duty against Mr. Money, and the truth is that this is not the charge, that has been alleged against him; but the following particulars—1st, want of temper. 2nd, outrageous and abusive language, such as calling one man *a rogue*, another *a rascal*, the body of the people at Lunenburgh, *a parcel of Dutch Scoundrels*, etc. 3rd, intermeddling in family matters and promoting discord between neighbours, propagating injurious reports concerning individuals, such as reporting men in trade to be bankrupt, etc. etc. 4th, that he is intemperate, sometimes to intoxication; does not pay a due regard to Sunday, usually has large companies to dine with him on that day, and even on Good Friday. These are the charges, but what truth may be in them I cannot certainly determine. That he is unguarded in his language, and has not a due command of his temper is too true.[86]

From Shelburne, the bishop was also the recipient of complaints relating to the character of the resident clergyman, Mr. Rowland. "We lament the Necessity for informing you," four justices of the peace wrote, April 18, 1803, "that the Situation of the Church of England in this Place is truly alarming and Distressing to us. We forbear to be particular at present—hoping, that you, Right Reverend Sir, will soon visit the Church here; but if unfortunately your Health should not permit a Voyage to this Town, we request, that you will please to direct a Clergyman (of *Experience*) to Visit us—to learn *whatsoever* is *true* respecting our Church."[87] In later communications, the justices were more specific in their criticism of Mr. Rowland, and, although the bishop contended that the objections were the result of personal animosity, the exchange of correspondence revealed the failure of the clergyman to command the loyalty of his followers.[88]

[85]Bishop Charles Inglis Journal, 1785-1810.
[86]*Ibid.*
[87]P.A.N.S., White Collection, vol. VII, Shelburne, Apr. 18, 1803, copy of letters of four Justices of the Peace to Bishop of Nova Scotia.
[88]*Ibid.* In particular, letter of Bishop Inglis to Justices, June 24, 1803 and reply of one of the Magistrates, July 5, 1803.

In Cape Breton, also, lack of harmonious relationships between the missionary and the members weakened the influence of the Church, and eventually, in 1805, led to. the missionary's removal. Inglis wrote: "It appears that Mr. Cossit did not catechise children at Church and it appears indispensibly necessary that he should be removed from this Mission. All the officers of Government and people of any property and distinction are violently prejudiced against him. Nor can it be otherwise; for he wages incessant war against them. Were he continued here, the Church of England would probably sink entirely."[89]

New Brunswick secured on the whole a better class of missionaries than Nova Scotia, largely as a result of the stronger Loyalist influence in this province. "They are a worthy, respectable body of men," Inglis wrote on the occasion of a visitation in Fredericton, August 18, 1798 "—of good moral and exemplary lives, diligent in the discharge of their clerical duty, and beloved and respected by their congregations."[90] Yet not all of them were satisfactory, a fact evident from comments made by Inglis himself in his journal. Many of the refugee clergy, none too competent when they arrived in America from England, had acquired habits and attitudes from their participation in the American revolutionary war which unsuited them for clerical office, particularly in communities made up of non-Loyalist inhabitants. The refugee clergy hardened tory tendencies within the Church.

Realization of the price paid by the Church in maintaining missionaries in the Maritimes who were unsuited to the needs of the communities they served, led Inglis to urge more careful methods of selection. "I take the liberty to inform your Grace," he wrote the Archbishop of Canterbury, November 20, 1788, "—that in this country more than in any other, the support of religion and growth of the Church depend on the personal qualities of the Clergy—that in Halifax, the capital of this province, the rector will be connected with all descriptions of people from the highest to the lowest, strangers that resort here in great numbers, and therefore he should be affable, prudent, good tempered, and able to support the dignity of his office."[91] In another letter to the Archbishop the next month, after pointing out the unsatisfactory character of the missionaries, Inglis wrote:

This will account for the earnestness with which I entreated your Grace in my last to prevent any Missionaries from being sent over, who are not *well known* to the Society, and *known to be fit for the office.* In this country the address, persuasion,

[89]Bishop Charles Inglis Journal, 1785-1810, July 7, 1805.
[90]*Ibid.*
[91]Letters and Journals of Two Nova Scotia Bishops, Halifax, Nov. 20, 1788, Bishop Inglis to Archbishop Canterbury.

exemplary conduct and exertions of the clergy must affect what in Europe is done through habit, usage and by virtue of established laws and supply their place. Judge then what must be the condition of religion in a congregation where the clergyman possesses none of those qualities! Yet the useless missionary, however unqualified, is as expensive to the Society as the most diligent and best qualified; and although he retards, instead of forwarding the growth of religion, yet he enjoys his portion of the bounty which was given for propagating the Gospel . . . .

Were this Diocese once supplied with a set of respectable, active Clergymen, we should have few Dissenters in a little time.[92]

Failure to provide the colony with more suitable missionaries resulted in a strengthening of attitudes of antagonism to the Church. Inherited suspicions of a nonconformist population were sharpened through contacts with the missionaries. There was little attempt to adapt the services of the Church to the tastes of the population. Rather, the missionaries seem at times to have gone out of their way in passing derogatory remarks respecting the illiteracy of the colonial population and its lack of any appreciation of cultural values. In this respect, they made little distinction between adherents and non-adherents of the Church.

[92]*Ibid.*, Halifax, Dec. 18, 1788, Bishop Inglis to Archbishop Canterbury. Establishment of a seminary in Nova Scotia to train young men for the Church offered a more promising means of securing clergy suited to the needs of the country, and Inglis devoted much of his energy to the promotion of such an institution. The bishop, anxious to obtain the funds from England for the support of the seminary, was probably inclined to exaggerate its immediately beneficial results, but through its establishment the foundation was laid for the raising up of a native clergy.
"Ten years have now elapsed," Inglis wrote the secretary of the Society for the Propagation of the Gospel, November 15, 1797, "since my arrival in this diocese. . . . Although the state of this diocese is far from being what I aimed at, and what, with the blessing of God, is attainable in a little time, especially if peace should be restored; yet I have reason to be thankful that so much has been done. Through the liberality of Government a seminary has been established, which has already supplied the Church with some very promising young Clergymen, and will probably supply still more. How much an Institution was wanting for this purpose you must be sensible on recollecting how difficult it was to prevail on Clergymen of character to leave England for this country; and what trouble we had to procure some of the Society's former Missionaries from the Revolted Colonies, and yet our attempts were all fruitless. The Church in this Diocese would not be in so good a state as it is at present, were it not for the assistance derived from this Seminary." *Ibid.*, Halifax, Nov. 15, 1797, Bishop Inglis to Secretary, S.P.G.
W. S. Moorsom wrote of the problem of securing suitable Church of England clergymen in 1830:
"The general effect of this recruiting system is bad; not that the principle is defective, but that the execution is improperly conducted. Many of the Missionaries we have seen arrive in the province, are persons of a description ill suited to the country and to the office they have to fulfil. . . .
"In this country, the personal qualities of the minister have far greater effect upon the number and improvement of his congregation than is the case at home. . . . Yet we have found those whose qualifications do not admit of their entering into orders in England, receiving an episcopal benediction for this province; and again, we find the few who have regularly passed through the University courses, bringing with them, and maintaining, ideas, demeanour, and habits, but little calculated to conciliate their parishioners in this country." W. S. Moorsom, *Letters from Nova Scotia* (London, 1830), pp. 134-5.

The character of the clergy not only accounted for the antagonism to the Church in those areas where its services were provided but also accounted, at least in part, for its failure to supply religious services to large sections of the country. The tendency on the part of the missionaries to treat rather lightly their responsibility to the people they were paid to serve resulted in the frequent neglect of part of their missions. Convenience rather than need often determined the places where services were held, and interference on the part of the bishop with the irresponsible arrangements made by the missionaries was strongly resented. When Wiswell, for instance, neglected to serve Granville, which was part of his mission, reproof from the bishop secured little result. "In short," Inglis wrote, "he used very improper, disrespectful language and talked like one whose intellect had suffered a derangement. He seemed to think that a Bishop had very little to do with the Clergy."[93] The problem reflected a general weakness in the organization of the colonial church. The missionaries owed their appointment to the Society in London and their salaries were paid partly by the Society and partly by the Government; their relationship to the colonial bishop was never too clear. Certainly, the bishop lacked those means of discipline which gave to the Methodist Conferences such effective control over the Methodist preachers. Many of the reforms which Inglis recognized as clearly needed could only be secured by means of supplication to the authorities at home. The ambiguous position of the bishop resulted inevitably in a failure to develop an *esprit de corps* among the missionaries. Morale suffered through the weakness of local authority. Thus, while in principle the Church was authoritarian in character, in practice the centralization of control in England meant that the individual missionaries in the colonies were free of almost any control.

This fact accounted in part for the failure of the Church to develop an itinerant system in the Maritimes. In theory, the missionaries—that is, those clergy not attached to parishes—were itinerants, but an effective itinerant system implied close centralized control and the adherence upon the part of individual missionaries to a strict preaching schedule. The lack of centralized control, and the lack of a spirit of resourcefulness among the missionaries, meant in effect that each missionary confined his activities very largely to his place of residence. Certainly none of them pushed into new areas of settlement, and few of them visited all those settlements within their missions which had been specifically assigned to their care. The result was that fringe areas were almost

[93]Bishop Charles Inglis Journal, 1785-1810, Sept. 7, 1789.

wholly neglected, and the work was very imperfectly organized within older-settled communities. The lack of travelling missionaries for the country as a whole meant, furthermore, that when vacancies occurred in already established churches there were no means available by which services could be maintained. Inglis wrote to the secretary of the Society for the Propagation of the Gospel, March 22, 1805:

Permit me now to advert to a subject, which is a source of great anxiety and uneasiness to me, and is of the utmost consequence. I refer to the great number of vacant churches in this Diocese. Besides Cumberland there are no less than five churches which were built since my arrival in this Province,—namely those of Parrsborough, Preston, Chester, Clemens and Weymouth, which are now destitute of a resident Clergyman. Through the infirmities of the incumbents, those of Annapolis and Wilmot are in almost as bad a shape . . . . You may easily conceive what unfortunate circumstances present to the Methodist and New Light teachers, among people with many of whom vociferation and violent gestures, and certain Sectarian phrases, are in higher estimation than literary qualifications, regular ordination, or the decent order of our church. Those teachers abound in every district and avail themselves of the above circumstances; and they are also dispersed in various populous settlements where no missions have been yet established.[94]

Abuses in government which led to the failure to develop an effective missionary organization were partly responsible for the weakness of the Church in the Maritime rural society, but even if its work had been prosecuted more vigorously it would not have gained very much greater support. The religious services of the Church were such as to make little appeal to a population of strong nonconformist background. Among some of the clergy, after 1812, it is true, there were efforts to bring the teachings of the Church more in line with the dispositions of the people being served. Evangelical movements, taking their rise within the Church in England, extended into the Maritime Provinces and strengthened considerably these efforts. A growing evangelical interest among some of the students in King's College reflected currents of sentiment which were particularly pronounced in congregations within the larger towns. In Halifax, the preaching of the Reverend John T. Twining served to crystallize the views of the evangelical party, and there grew up among a section of the parishioners the practice of meeting together in private homes to engage in religious exercises. In Sydney, also, tendencies towards the emergence of a distinct evangelical party were evident. Though lacking such concrete expression, evangelical sentiments were probably even more prevalent among followers of the Church in New Brunswick; the settlement in this province of many Irish Episcopalians lent support to the spread

[94]Letters and Journals of Two Nova Scotia Bishops, Windsor, Mar. 22, 1805, Bishop Inglis to Secretary, S.P.G.

of such sentiments. The colonial hierarchy of the Church, however, stiffly resisted the introduction of innovations involving a shift to a more evangelical position. When the parishioners in Halifax sought to secure, upon the retirement of the incumbent, the appointment of Twining as rector of St. Paul's, their wishes were disregarded in a manner which appeared an arbitrary exercise of ecclesiastical authority. Failure of the Church to recognize the evangelical church founded by the separating party led to the defection of the leaders of the movement to the Baptists. Throughout the country, the Church authorities failed to avail themselves of the opportunity of capitalizing upon the strengthening evangelical interests of many of the members; such interests were suppressed or found expression through defections to the more evangelical denominations. The rise of the tractarian or Oxford movement within the Church in England, as a reaction against the growing evangelical movement, strengthened reactionary forces within the Church in the Maritime Provinces. The Church, officially, became more formalistic than ever, emphasizing its distinctive claims to apostolic succession and its distinctive rites and ceremonies. The conflict between the Bishop of New Brunswick and the evangelical party was indicative of efforts to emphasize the claim of the Church to the title of "Catholic" rather than to the title of "Protestant."[95] Among Loyalist and English elements of the population, and particularly among those anxious to maintain upper-class status in the community, the shift to a "high church" position provided the Church with distinct advantages. Throughout the country as a whole, however, sentiment favoured the introduction of simplicity in religious services and afforded little support to claims of any denomination to an exclusive right to administer religious ordinances. The prevailing religious philosophy was essentially American in origin.

Claims of the Church to an exclusive right to administer religious ordinances were closely related to its claims to the privileges of Church Establishment. Loyalty was employed as an instrument to secure the extension of church influence. Religious nonconformity, in whatever guise, assumed in the eyes of the Church, and in the eyes of the colonial authorities, the character of a threat to the imperial connection and to monarchical political institutions. Support of the Church by the state reflected the conservatism of governmental parties in reaction to the American — and, later, the French—Revolutions. Church Establishment was viewed as a means of strengthening the foundations

[95]See W. O. Ketchum, *The Life and Work of the Most Reverend John Medley* (Saint John, 1893), pp. 64-5.

of the Second Empire growing out of the wreckage of the first. Bishop Inglis wrote the Duke of Kent, July 26, 1800:

> The province contains at present many subjects who are truly loyal; but at the same time it must be lamented that levelling, Republican principles—the epedemic evil and disorder of the times—are prevalent among great numbers. Particularly among an enthusiastic sect called New Lights, in the western and middle districts; and in some of the eastern parts, among a sect of Dissenters from the Church of Scotland, known here by the name of Seceders and in Europe by that of Antiburghers, if my memory does not fail. Unfortunately both these are numerous, and have much increased lately. The events that have taken place in Europe and America within our memory, clearly evince that we cannot be too much on our guard against those principles; as they are calculated to produce, and have actually produced the greatest evils to Society.[96]

The next year Wentworth, the lieutenant-governor, wrote the Secretary of State:

> He [the Bishop of Nova Scotia] fully concurs with me, in opinion that every exertion should be made to provide for constant performance of public worship according to the Church of England, both in Halifax, and in other parts of this Province, where it is certain Missionarys are most seriously wanted to preserve the poor dispersed settlers from the dangerous fanatical assiduity of mendicant, migratory new light teachers, who are generally as badly disposed to the duty's of loyalty as they are to our religious establishment. Nor have I doubt that among them are artful people, acting under the wicked influence of democratic, foreign, Anarchists. Their mischief can only be counteracted, and His Majesty's subjects best preserved from civil and religious distractions, by the establishment of additional Missionarys in several parts of the Province—Five or Six might be employed immediately with the highest usefulness—Their salary's not less than one hundred pounds sterling per Annum would be infinitely compensated by the advantage— From Halifax to the remotest bounds of the Province on the Gulf of St. Lawrence, there is but one Missionary of the Church of England—It was happily observed that in his Parish the people were peaceable orderly, sober and without itinerant Teachers—I found the contrary without exception on all the rest of my progress, and could trace it to the mischievous pursuits of Itinerants, unchecked by any regular Church establishment—Their arts are so exerted, and toward such a dispersed various people, that the Laws do not reach the evil, nor is it at at all times prudent to afford opportunity to such persons to misrepresent the proceedings of law, as the influence of persecution and intolerance.[97]

The support of the state, if it provided certain advantages, proved in the end a source of great weakness to the Church. In the first place, it affected the hold of the Church upon its own adherents. Though an attempt was made to encourage voluntary financial contributions from

[96]Letters and Journals of Two Nova Scotia Bishops, Windsor, July 26, 1800, Bishop Inglis to Duke of Kent.
[97]Nova Scotia State Papers, vol. A133, Halifax, July 27, 1801, Wentworth to Secretary of State.

the colonial population, the knowledge that financial support was forthcoming from the homeland led to an attitude of indifference to the Church's financial needs. Church leaders sought quite deliberately to promote a feeling of dependence upon the homeland; such a feeling seemed the best guarantee of preserving the imperial connection. "I never wish the clergy," Bishop Inglis frankly admitted, "to be wholly independent of the parent state—a moderate salary from home will always act as a tie, and be a bond of union; and a regular clergy here will ever have a considerable share of influence on the people."[98] What church leaders failed to recognize was that the strength of the Church depended upon the active participation of the population and that such participation developed slowly when the responsibility for the financial support of religious services was not assumed. In its very great concern to strengthen the loyalty of the colonial population to the Empire, the Church failed to develop means of preserving the loyalty of that population to itself.

In the second place, of course, the close identification of the Church with the state weakened its position among the large nonconformist population in the country. The atmosphere of thought in the pioneer communities of the Maritime Provinces favoured the sharp divorce of church and state; the population was distrustful of any interference in religion on the part of the state. Efforts of the Church to promote religious controls through resort to state sanctions weakened inevitably its religious influence. In the end, it was forced into politics as a means of maintaining its tie with the state.

A political intolerance on the part of the Church was accompanied, not in any way paradoxically, by a theological tolerance. To maintain its exclusive political position it was prepared to include people with widely divergent doctrinal views. There was a vagueness about the teachings of the Church which reflected its shift away from any fundamentalist religious position. Some of the clergy—even in the Maritimes—had become sceptics so far as literal interpretations of the bible were concerned. Certainly, the more prominent members of the Church tended to represent the least religiously minded of the colonial population. Philosophically— or theologically—the Church had become very tolerant, tolerant of new ideas and of new theological interpretations, and this tolerance, this willingness to recognize wide differences in people's views of the nature of the divinity and of man's relationship to such a divinity, constituted a serious weakness in the pioneer com-

[98]Letters and Journals of Two Nova Scotia Bishops, "State of the Church of England in the Three Provinces of Quebec, New Brunswick and Nova Scotia," to Mr. Granville, Sept. 8, 1790.

munities of the Maritime Provinces towards the close of the eighteenth century. The unlearned, simple-living fisherman or farmer wanted a straight-forward, literal interpretation of the bible, and tended to be suspicious of the free and easy manner of life and the expression of advanced theological doctrines of the clergymen of the Church of England. The evangelical religious sects were reactionary—they denounced resort to reason and the tendency to treat as equally valid alternative theological interpretations—and it was this sort of appeal to simple, unchanging truths which the population demanded.

It would be quite unfair to conclude that the Church of England exerted no important religious influence in the colonial society of the Maritime Provinces. Among those people who belonged to what can be called the colonial upper class, the Church certainly maintained a dominant position as an agency for the dissemination of religious teachings and as a focus of social and cultural life. A sense of group solidarity—a consciousness of social class—was secured in part at least through membership within the Church. The bishop's palace, together with Government House, served as a centre and symbol of the upper class.

Within the rural settlements, also, the Church had a very real meaning to considerable numbers of the inhabitants. Those people brought up within the Church sought to maintain their ties with the past—their traditional loyalties and faiths—through a close identification with its work and teachings. Where the demands of the new society were not so great as to severely shake these traditional loyalties and faiths, attachments to the Church were successfully preserved. A great many of the Loyalists in New Brunswick, for instance, were able, partly through geographical segregation, to maintain a sense of group distinctiveness, and among them the influence of the Church continued to remain strong.

It was among those sections of the population which became detached from a traditional group life and which had to work out new social attachments that the Church of England exerted little influence. The Church acted strongly in preserving traditional loyalties, but conspicuously failed to develop new loyalties where traditional loyalties weakened. It was an effective instrument of cultural preservation but not of social reorganization. The really important function of religious leadership within the pioneer communities of the Maritime Provinces was the function of developing a new sense of group solidarity. Folk and class loyalties had disintegrated, in face of settlement in the new land, and the Church of England failed to take a lead in developing new ones to take their place.

What was true of the Church of England was true to some extent of the Presbyterian Church as well. The failure of the Scottish churches to send out sufficient missionaries left large areas populated by a scattering of Presbyterians or by people who might have turned to Presbyterianism unsupplied. Dependence upon congregational "calls" tended to a timidity among Presbyterian ministers which favoured their location in Scotland, and there was lacking a strong missionary organization to come to the support of clergy seeking an opening overseas. The result was that few Scottish clergy volunteered for service abroad. A petition of the inhabitants of Douglas in 1802 read, in part:

We cannot help expressing our sincerest grief at the continued backwardness of young preachers to come out to this country. There are four petitions from the neighbourhood lying before you for seven years, and some of them much more, still unanswered. How many of the young generation are growing up in these congregations without God, without Christ, without hope, insensible of their sin and danger, who might, if they were under the charge of faithful ministers, be an ornament to the gospel profession! . . . We are without the means of grace—we have no ministers, few books, little knowledge. Unlearned and unordained men sometimes offer their assistance to teach us; but we think we may as well offer to teach them, though we cannot discern between right and wrong, good and evil . . . . Such has been the cry of these people, and we are persuaded that it would have been answered long ago, if the young preachers under your inspection had either the spirit of Isaiah —('Here am I, send me,')—or the zeal of Roman Catholic priests; for, permit us to tell you, that the Papists in this part of the world can more easily get out priests than we ministers.[99]

The Reverend James MacGregor wrote of the state of Presbyterianism in the country to the *Christian Magazine*, October 31, 1805:

If we had more ministers, our church would flourish much more than it does. Prince Edward Island is still unprovided for. Several of our congregations will in a few years need to be divided into two. Merigomish, near Pictou, will take a minister as soon as he comes. This summer I made a tour of a considerable part of the Province of New Brunswick. I went about three hundred miles from home. I saw many settlements in a very destitute situation. In general they were so thinly peopled, that they could not support the gospel in their present lukewarmness . . . . When I reached my journey's end, where I set down one foot of the compass where I was, and extend the other two hundred miles, and describe a circle, I fear it would not include two real gospel ministers. There are a few Church of England ministers on the river, (with whom I had not an opportunity of personal acquaintance,) but I was informed that the people left them, when they became concerned about their souls . . . . When I went among them, I found that many of them never saw or heard a Presbyterian minister. They heard of them and thought them all good. They heard me with apparent eagerness and pleasure. Had we a few ministers in that Province I suppose they might unite with us.[100]

---

[99]Robertson, *History of the Mission of the Secession Church*, pp. 198-9.
[100]Patterson, *Memoir of the Rev. James MacGregor*, pp. 350-1.

Adherence to the strict Calvinist discipline and to the system of congregational calls provided rigidities in the organization of Presbyterianism which weakened it as a missionary church. Though individual ministers occasionally itinerated, there was no systematic effort to introduce Presbyterian services into areas where regular services had not been established. In communities which were predominantly Presbyterian, the Church successfully maintained the attachments of the population, but it failed to exert any considerable influence outside Presbyterian strongholds. It served, like the Church of England, as an agent of cultural preservation but not of cultural reorganization. Where cultural values persisted, Presbyterianism maintained its hold; where those values disintegrated in face of new conditions, it provided little effective leadership.

What both the Church of England and the Presbyterian Church lacked were means of exploiting the religious resources of the rural pioneer society. This was particularly evident in their failure to employ the services of local preachers. Religion in areas of new settlement depended upon such services. Among a frontier population there were always men of strong religious convictions anxious to set themselves forward as teachers of the gospel. Employment of such men as preachers involved no great financial obligation. Furthermore, it was such preachers who were able to go furthest in adapting the religious service to the tastes of the population; without education or social standing, tradition exercised no hold upon their thinking or behaviour. They were the religious radicals of the frontier. It was the genius of the religious sect that it exploited to the full the services of local preachers, while it was one of the fundamental failures of the traditional Church that it did not in any way avail itself of such services. The emphasis within the Church was upon a professional ministry—the very nature of the Church made such an emphasis necessary—while the frontier social situation demanded a break from professional standards, in medicine and law as well as in religion. In neither the Church of England nor the Presbyterian Church was there any indication of a willingness to depart from the practice of employing only properly trained clergymen. Such an unwillingness was a reflection of a general failure to adapt to new social conditions.

The weaknesses of the traditional churches, and particularly of the Church of England, stood in sharp contrast to the strengths of the evangelical religious sects. Whereas the traditional churches failed to adapt themselves to new social conditions, the sects were essentially a product of these conditions. That was evident with respect to both

the Newlights and Methodists. As a religious movement of the outlying fishing and farming settlements, there was little that was new within the Newlight movement after 1783. In terms of organization and appeal, it continued to serve as an effective agency for the dissemination of religious teachings in those areas of society where the formal organization of religion gained little hold. In much the same manner, the Methodist movement after 1783 succeeded in meeting those needs of the population which were not being met by the traditional churches.

Within Methodism the problem of supplying religious services to a growing and scattered population was taken care of through the raising up of local preachers, through the support of the Methodist Episcopal Church which sent missionaries to the country, and through the putting into operation, in a very modified form, of the itinerant system developed by Wesley in England. With respect to forms of organization as such, the Methodist movement possessed distinct advantages over the Newlight. Centralization had developed as an accepted principle of church government, and centralized control made possible the development of an extremely effective itinerant system. The missionaries in the Maritimes attended the General Conferences of the Church in the United States, and, from 1786 on, annual conferences were held within the country itself. Responsibility for appointments to the various circuits was assumed by the annual conference, while, after 1787, a superintendent was appointed to assume general direction of the work. Although itinerant practices were not closely adhered to, and the number of missionaries was inadequate, considerable success was nevertheless achieved in extending the teachings of Methodism throughout the scattered Maritime settlements.

In the methods used in appealing to the population there was little difference between the Methodist and Newlight movements. Where the English Wesleyan influence remained strong, the Methodist appeal was probably more restrained in character, but generally there was the same reliance upon revivalist techniques. Perkins in Liverpool found the meetings of the Newlights and the Methodists very similar. Techniques of conversion, developed out of experiences of Methodist revivals in the American colonies, were employed by the preachers in the Maritimes. William Black from the beginning, though lacking the fanatical zeal of Alline, employed a highly emotional appeal, placing a considerable emphasis upon the arousal of a state of religious excitement and upon the conversion of sinners.[101] The American Methodist preachers were even more inclined to rely upon an emotional appeal. "Blessed

[101]Richey, *A Memoir of the Late William Black*, pp. 49-50.

be God," Garrettson wrote Wesley from Shelburne in 1786, "there have been many as clear and as powerful conversions in this township, as I have seen in any part of the States."[102] Though extreme physical manifestations of religious excitement, such as barking, jerking, or rolling on the ground, did not occur in Methodist revivalist meetings in the Maritimes, there was nevertheless an emphasis upon outward, visible signs of regeneration. "The things that appeared most out of the ordinary way," Marsden wrote of the revival in Saint John in 1806, "were praising God aloud, crying for mercy, children exhorting, several praying at the same time, and holding the meetings till twelve o'clock at night, nay, upon a few occasions, till two or three in the morning: although I generally dismissed them myself about ten o'clock."[103] Women, youth, and children were particularly influenced by the emotional appeal of the revival. "One little girl," Black wrote of a meeting he held in Tantramar, "about seven or eight years of age, got up on a form, and told, in a wonderful manner, what Jesus had done for her soul."[104] "The children," Marsden continued of the revival in Saint John, "were much and unusually wrought upon, they prayed much for their parents and relations, and several of them stood up, and at the prayer-meetings, they exhorted others, to the admiration of all that heard them."[105] Generally speaking, within the Methodist revivals, the problem of the preacher was not so much that of promoting but of controlling outbursts of religious excitement. Strong revivalist sentiments among the population sought means of expression within religious organizations. The Methodist movement was prepared to capitalize in a way that the traditional churches were not, upon such sentiments, to exploit them in strengthening attachments to the Methodist body.

Similarly, the asceticism of Methodism, like that of Newlightism, was a faithful expression of a strong moral sense within the rural Maritime community. The notion of man's sinful state, and the conception of a God of wrath exacting vengeance upon the unfaithful, occupied central places in Methodist teachings. Methodist preachers in the Maritimes waged a relentless war upon all activities of a frivolous or pleasure seeking character. "Mr. Black preaches in the Afternoon," Perkins wrote in his diary, October 28, 1787, "is very pointed against Dancing." On April 21, 1791, Perkins wrote: "Mr. Grandine preaches a Severe Sermon to Back Sliders, Drunkards, Swarers, Lyars, etc."

[102]Bangs, *Life of the Rev. Freeborn Garrettson*, p. 174.
[103]Marsden, *Narrative of a Mission*, p. 208.
[104]Richey, *A Memoir of the Late William Black*, p. 50.
[105]Marsden, *Narrative of a Mission*, p. 212.

Duncan McColl entered into his journal, referring to the winter of 1796-7: "I have in public and private insisted upon it, that there is nothing in practice but what has a tendency to promote good or evil— consequently, I set my face against all such diversions as cannot be used in the name of the Lord Jesus; such as gambling, dancing, &c."[106] Sermons emphasizing the moral dangers of such forms of behaviour as dancing and card playing developed among the Methodists a distinctive attitude of mind. Asceticism became a part of the social creed of the group. It served to support a sense of group solidarity. This was particularly so because it was directed against those forms of behaviour associated with classes outside the rural community. Marsden wrote of his work in Saint John in 1805:

> As the Spring opened my trials increased; I was led to deal very faithfully with my congregations, but the more faithfully I discharged my conscience, the more the old serpent and his brood of vipers hissed upon me. I had to preach against sabbath breaking, and the magistrates thought I reflected upon their conduct, because during the herring, salmon, and shad season, they allowed the people to fish upon the Lord's day, and assigned as a reason, that fish ran more abundantly on that day than any other. But they were merchants, and bought the fish, and sordid interest will never want a plea for breaking in upon the most sacred duties. Dancing and revelling prevailed in an unusual degree: I had to take notice of these, hence some of the gay ones, who occasionally came to the chapel, thought themselves implicated, and came no more. Conscience and duty required me to preach against drunkenness, and as this was the besetting sin in the place, "master by so saying thou condemnest us," was felt by a number of delinquents. I had to animadvert upon smuggling, and this came home to the very doors of the church of God; an official brother, possessing some property, and more influence, would hardly speak of me with charity, or treat me with common civility.[107]

The asceticism of Methodism was closely related to its social or class appeal in the community. Because of the highly emotional and ascetic content of its teachings, it tended to antagonize "respectable" elements of the population. The Methodist movement, like the Newlight, gained its chief support from humble fishermen and farmers; it secured large numbers of converts among the Negroes about Shelburne and in the St. John Valley. On the other hand, it made little headway among governmental officials, army officers, well-to-do merchants, and the landed gentry. The conversion of Colonel Bayard in Annapolis called for special comment by practically every Methodist writer. "Alas, sire," Marsden wrote of Bayard's conversion, "we can seldom on our missions boast of such converts to the power of religion, nor do our labours in general derive much benefit from the support of men in

[106]"Memoir of the Rev. Duncan McColl" (*British North American Wesleyan Methodist Magazine for the Year 1841*, vol. I, p. 458).
[107]Marsden, *Narrative of a Mission*, pp. 173-4.

power and authority. But perhaps, this is rather a blessing to us than otherwise; in the splendour of great names and great patronage, we might lose the simplicity of religion."[108] Of the revival in Saint John, Marsden wrote: "In this revival, none of the rich and great received the truth."[109] This reliance upon the support of the "lower orders" inevitably influenced the character of the movement and accounted for much of its strength. Though no clear-cut class ideology emerged, the bias in Methodist teaching tended to an association of virtue with the way of life of the ordinary folk and of sin with the habits and values of the privileged classes. The implications of such an appeal with respect to the class structure were indirect but far-reaching. Immediately, and very directly, the Methodist movement, together with the Newlight movement, offered to the masses a means of securing status and social recognition which were denied to them within the traditional institutional structure of the community.

The Newlight and Methodist movements combined to exert a powerful religious influence within the Maritime Provinces during the last quarter of the eighteenth and early part of the nineteenth century. In the final analysis, the number of people who actually changed their denominational allegiances through conversion by evangelical preachers was probably not large if the shift from Congregationalism to Newlightism is excepted. Adherents were gained among those who were brought up in the faith (as, for instance, among the New England Newlights or the Yorkshire English Methodists) or from among those who were lacking in denominational attachments of any sort. It was more a matter of the evangelical sects gaining new adherents to religion than a matter of the traditional churches losing members to the evangelical sects. This fact implies the very great extension in the influence of religion, both in terms of the number of people whose interest was aroused and in terms of the intensity of such interest. At a time when little support could be found for rational methods of thought, the evangelical movements restored to religion its significance as an explanation of man's relationship to that which was outside himself. Religion was made a vital force in the community.

The role of the evangelical movements determined the range and limitations of their influence. Developments in the Maritime Provinces growing out of the American Revolution, and the expansion of agriculture, fishing, trade, and ship-building, tended in the direction of increased interdependence and the breaking down of barriers of social isolation. The folk gave way to the masses, and free economic enterprise

[108]*Ibid.*, p. 188.
[109]*Ibid*, p. 213.

weakened the supports of a society based upon feudal arrangements and class privilege. Emancipation frcm traditional social attachments involved painful adjustments upon the part of the individual and the population as a whole. The disintegration of group loyalties led to a feeling of detachment, of not being part of something outside one's self. Individualization and emancipation extended furthest among those people who had inherited institutional systems lacking solid supports within the traditional culture and who were most exposed to new social conditions. It was the New Englanders and Loyalists who were most subject to these influences. Neither of these groups brought with them upon settlement a strong cultural tradition; secular and religious developments in New England before 1760 were weakening the village congregationalist system transplanted to Nova Scotia, while the outbreak of revolution in 1776 destroyed much of that social system which the Loyalists sought to preserve in the new homeland. Both of these groups, on the other hand, were fully involved in the new developments taking place in the Maritime region—in the fisheries, agriculture, trade, and ship-building. In contrast, the Highland Scots in eastern Nova Scotia inherited a cultural organization resting upon strong ties of an ethnic and religious character, and isolation upon the fringe of settlement sheltered them to a considerable extent fom the influence of new developments and made possible the preservation of a folk culture. Thus it was among the New Englanders and Loyalists rather than among the Highland Scots that social and religious disorganization was most extensive, and it was among these groups that the evangelical sects exerted the greatest influence.

The evangelical movements were essentially movements of social reorganization or social unification. They offered a means of interpretation of the individual's relationship to his society. The fact that the interpretation was religious in character gave to it no less a social significance. Directly, evangelical movements strengthened bonds of fellowship in revivalist meetings, prayer meetings, confessional gatherings and religious conferences. The emotional excitement aroused by evangelical preaching, the exhortation of laymen, and the recitation of private experiences broke down the reserve of the individual and led to the establishment of intimate social relationships. That these meetings occurred almost daily and lasted until the late hours of the night was indicative of the importance of their function in developing social fellowship. Indirectly, also, the evangelical movements, through their religious appeal, served to break down the feeling of isolation of the individual and to develop a sense of identification with something

outside himself. The sect's emphasis upon separation from the world developed among those who separated a strong feeling of social solidarity. The sect comprised those of faith as distinguished from those of no faith; it was a community of the saints. Instead of feeling isolated and detached, the convert was made to feel that he was one of a very privileged group; the person unconverted was the abandoned wretch, leading a solitary existence without the benefit of faith. Conversion secured the status of those who lacked status in the traditional culture. By "giving themselves up to God" they became one of the elect. It was this role of securing a re-integration or strengthening of the social organism which accounted for the development of evangelical movements. The strength of the Newlight and Methodist movements in the Maritime Provinces reflected extensive changes in social relationships and social attachments. The effects of these movements upon general social organization, and in particular upon the organization of religion, were evident in areas of social life where demands of new conditions imposed heavy strains upon the traditional culture.

CHAPTER THREE

The Great Revival in Canada

1783-1832

T H E American Revolution and the Indian war in the West checked any extensive movement of population into the interior of the continent during the thirty years after the British conquest with the result that in Quebec the old rural-ecclesiastical order of the French régime was successfully re-established without the interference of any seriously disturbing influence from outside. After 1795, geographical and ethnic barriers to communication and the retention of the seigniorial system of land holding, had the effect of preserving the isolation of the French-Canadian society in face of the sudden expansion of population into the West, and the supremacy of Roman Catholicism continued to receive no serious challenge. The Constitutional Act of 1791 strictly defined the borders of the new province of Lower Canada to exclude the Indian lands of the West, and within these borders, with the exception of the area which became known as the Eastern Townships, the population remained predominantly Roman Catholic in attachment, and conditions of social life favoured the sort of controls which Roman Catholicism sought to maintain. Religious separatism—the spirit of the religious sect—was completely stifled by the weight of an elaborate ecclesiasticism.

Outside of what became the province of Lower Canada, however, the isolation of the continental interior suddenly and completely broke down after 1795, and the mass movement of population into the West gave rise to a vast new "open frontier" which included the recently organized province of Upper Canada. Throughout this whole area—the new American West—the issue of the form of religious organization came quickly to the fore as religious bodies struggled to gain a footing, and the Great Revival which swept through the Western American settlements between 1795 and 1812 was indicative of the strength of religious sectarian forces in the frontier social situation. In Canada, the vast majority of the population, in social background and experience, was little different from the population pouring into the American West, and social conditions were much the same on both sides of the border.

But Canada was a British colony with a government anxious to maintain the underlying conditions of British order, and religious forces which developed virtually unchecked in the American West came into sharp conflict with political forces in the new Canadian West. Here the issue of the imperial connection, and of an aristocratic form of government, was brought into close relation with the issue of Church Establishment, and efforts to maintain a political and social *status quo* led to a vigorous attempt to push the claims of the Established Church. The resources of empire were brought to the support of the church form of religious organization. Lieutenant-Governor Simcoe wrote in 1791:

The State Propriety of some form of public Worship, politically considered, arises from the necessity there is of preventing enthusiastick & fanatick Teachers from acquiring that superstitious hold of the minds of the multitude which Persons of such a description may pervert & are generally inclined to pervert to the Establishment of their own undue consequence in the State & often meditate & not unfrequently to turn such an Ascendancy to its injury & destruction, & this prescribed form of Worship becomes more or less necessary as the minds of the People are more or less susceptible of superstitious Impressions, & as attempts to turn them from the national Form of church Government are more or less prevalent. Those who shall be bred in solitude and seclusion which the first settlers must necessarily be, & to whom perhaps the stated periods of public Worship are the only ones in which in their meetings & associations they shall become acquainted & sympathize with each other. Such a Description of men will become the fittest instruments for the mischief making Enthusiasm of the Sectaries to work upon and this at a Period when we know that all Men read & only one description of People write; & when the Aim of the Sectaries is avowedly to destroy the national establishment.[1]

Although the overwhelming majority of the new settlers were dissenters, the hope was entertained, in Canada as earlier in Nova Scotia, that if the Church of England were early in the field, most of the population could be won over to its support. New religious movements in America had resulted in multiplying the number of religious denominations in the country and in making religious affiliation in many cases a matter of momentary interest, and, since migration to Canada took place from those areas where these movements had developed their greatest strength, the new Canadian population tended to represent a great diversity of religious groupings. The Canadian as well as American frontier became an area of shifting religious attachments, and this floating character of denominational membership afforded some reason for the aggressive claims of the Church of England. "Of the settlers in Upper Canada," the Bishop of Quebec wrote in 1794,

[1]Major-General Cruickshank (ed.), *Simcoe Papers* (5 vols., Ontario Historical Society, 1923-6), vol. I, pp. 31-2.

"the majority is composed of Dissenters of various descriptions: But I have the strongest reason to believe that if a proper number of ministers of the Church of England be sent amongst them, before each sect shall become able to provide ministers of its own, they will to a man conform to that Church."[2] Lieutenant-Governor Simcoe shared the same hope:

> The great body of Puritans in America, however misrepresented, draw their Origin from the Church of England, and are nearer to it in their religious Beliefs and Customs, than they are to any other sects, or religious Descriptions; the state of Poverty in which they must for some time remain after their Emigration will naturally prevent them from the possibility of supporting their Ministers by public subscription; in the mean while, the Government has it in its Power immediately to provide for any Protestant Clergyman, in the separate Townships, by giving him a reasonable landed property, in perpetuity, for himself and family, and entrusting him with the care of that Seventh which is to be reserved for the Protestant Clergy.[3]

The assumption of responsibility by the colonial government for the payment of a portion of the salaries of missionaries appointed to charges in the country eased the financial strain upon the Society for the Propagation of the Gospel and made it possible to establish the services of the Church without depending upon the local population to take the initiative. Appointment of missionaries at Kingston, Ernestown, and Niagara shortly after 1790 extended the work of the Church beyond the province of Lower Canada where missionaries by this time were located at Quebec, Montreal, Three Rivers, and St. Henry, and episcopal control passed from the bishop of Nova Scotia to the new bishop of Quebec. Additional missionaries were recruited as the population grew, and by 1821 there were fifteen missionaries of the Church stationed in Lower Canada and seventeen in Upper Canada.

Government support, and the strong British sentiment of some of the earlier and more influential of the settlers, favoured the establishment of a Canadian state church. Settlement after 1783 had brought to the country a body of Highland Scots, many of them disbanded soldiers, who retained a strong sense of group solidarity; their attachment to the Church of Scotland lent support to the cause of Church Establishment. Some of the United Empire Loyalists, and most of the few English settlers in the country, belonged to the Church of England, and their anxiety to maintain their separate group identity tended to strengthen their church attachment. Even more important, in terms of its general social influence, was the large standing army during the early years of settlement. Military control supported, and found support in, Church

[2]*Ibid.*, vol. III, p. 43.
[3]*Ibid.*, vol. I, p. 252.

Establishment; the strength of the Church of England in centres where military interests dominated was indicative of the close relationship between the religious functions of the Church and the policing functions of the army.

In the rapidly growing farm settlements, however, the Church of England had little claim upon the attachments of the population, and the strong feeling of political separateness which was characteristic of the thinking of this frontier population combined with a feeling of religious separateness to produce movements of religion directed against church establishment. The sect spirit of sharp separation of religious matters from worldly affairs found expression in forms of religious organization which had grown up on the American frontier and which quickly spread across the border with the extension of settlement into the Canadian frontier. The Great Revival in Canada followed upon the Great Revival in the American West. The growth of Methodist influence in the country after 1795, in particular, was phenomenal. In the end, the effect was to prevent any successful establishment of a state church in the colony.

The strength of the Methodist movement in the American frontier favoured its rapid growth in the new frontier of Canada. How many of the Loyalists and Americans in Canada had belonged to the Methodist connection before leaving the United States is difficult to estimate, but a considerable number must have been brought in contact with Methodist teachings since it was from those areas of greatest Methodist growth that most of the early settlers came. Whatever the total numbers, here and there, throughout the new Canadian settlements, there were to be found single individuals or members of small groups who had experienced the emotional ecstasy of Methodist conversion, and these people formed the nuclei for the organization of societies and served to build up a body of exhorters and preachers. Disbanded soldier settlers, converted to Methodism in the army or before enlisting, local farmers who had come in contact with Methodism before their arrival in the country, and Methodist teachers from the United States with no other licence to preach than that of their conviction that they had been called undertook evangelical work in Canada and organized the first local societies. Thus, in 1780, Tuffy, a commissary of the Forty-fourth Regiment and Methodist local preacher, preached in Quebec while his Regiment remained there; in 1785, the Hecks, some of the Emburys, and John Lawrence, settlers in Augusta, held a class meeting among themselves; in 1788 Colonel Neale preached and formed a class near Niagara; and Lyons, an exhorter from the United States, and McCarty, a converted Irishman and Whitefield Methodist, held meetings in the

Bay of Quinte district.[4] These pioneer efforts of isolated individuals prepared the ground for the more systematic evangelical work carried out by itinerant preachers assigned to the Canadian field by the Methodist Episcopal Church in the United States.

The first regular Methodist preacher, William Losee, entered the country in 1790, crossing the St. Lawrence River and preaching throughout the Bay of Quinte district in Kingston, Ernestown, Fredericksburg, and Adolphustown. The first Methodist class in Canada was formed by Losee in February, 1791, and an extensive revival took place under his preaching during the summer of this year.[5] The next year two circuits were established by the New York Conference in Canada, *Cataraqui*, embracing the Kingston and Bay of Quinte settlements, and *Oswegatchie*, embracing the townships of Elizabethtown, Augusta, Edwardsburg, Matilda, Williamsburgh, Osnabruck, and Cornwall; Darius Dunham joined Losee in the work. Thereafter Methodist preaching was steadily extended throughout the Canadian settlements. The number of preachers increased to four in 1796, five in 1798, seven in 1800, ten in 1802, seventeen in 1806, and twenty-one in 1811, and new circuits were organized as the field of preaching was widened—Niagara in 1796, Ottawa in 1800, Montreal in 1803, Yonge Street and Smith's Creek in 1805, Long Point, St. Lawrence, Quebec, and Stanstead in 1806, Ancaster in 1808, and Detroit, Three Rivers, and St. Francis River in 1810. Direction of the work fell under the complete control of the Methodist Episcopal Church, governing by means of a general conference meeting every three years and a number of regional conferences meeting annually. The Genesee Annual Conference assumed responsibility for the work in the district of Upper Canada and the New York Conference for the work in the district of Lower Canada; Stanstead circuit was organized separately under the control of the New England Conference.

Rapid extension of Methodist organization, reflected in the increase in the number of preachers and circuits, resulted in the rapid growth of Methodist influence. Recruits were won to the movement through evangelical preaching, and gains in membership represented largely accessions of people who previously lacked strong denominational attachments. Methodism was a movement of religious expansion, depending little upon traditional loyalties for its strength and influence. Thus reliance upon evangelization as a means of establishing Methodist societies emphasized the importance of religious revivals. Successful revivals in various parts of the country were recorded by the preachers

[4]John Carroll, *Case and His Cotemporaries, or the Canadian Itinerants' Memorial* (Toronto, 1867-77), vol. I, pp. 6-7.

[5]G. F. Playter, *The History of Methodism in Canada* (Toronto, 1862), p. 24.

:n the field at different times. In 1801, for instance, a revival took place in the Niagara district, extending from Niagara to the head of Lake Ontario and westward to Long Point on Lake Erie; other revivals occurred the same year on the Bay of Quinte and Oswegatchie circuits.[6] As settlement pushed farther into the interior, the work of individual Methodist preachers led to the extension of revivalist influence. In 1802 Nathan Bangs succeeded in promoting revivals in a number of remote settlements reaching from Burford to Oxford. "The good work quickly spread," Bangs wrote, "through the neighbourhood, sweeping all before it. In this way the revival prevailed in both these places, so that large and flourishing societies were established, and no less than six preachers were raised up."[7] In later years, Methodist preachers pushed westward as far as settlements along the Thames River and Lake St. Clair.

In 1810 an entensive revival occurred in these western settlements under the preaching of William Case. On his arrival, Case found a people, long cut off from the influence of religion, whose moral standards generally had disintegrated. "The country, perhaps," he wrote to Bishop Asbury, "is the most wicked and dissipated of any part of America." The amusements of the population, he related, were horse-racing, dancing, and gambling, which, together with the destructive practice of excessive drinking, had prevented the prosperity of the country. The holy Sabbath had no preference over any other day, except that it was chosen "as a day of wicked amusements, visiting in parties, often dancing, hunting, fishing, etc." Few of the people knew anything of the bible, having never learned to read, and some of those who could read had no bible in their homes. "Nor did they think they needed any," the Methodist itinerant asserted, "for some have openly blasphemed the name of the Lord Jesus, and spoke of the Virgin Mary in a manner too shocking to repeat." Opposition to Methodist preaching quickly asserted itself. Case's life was threatened, if his own testimony be accepted, some of the magistrates forbade the people to permit meetings to be held in their homes on pain of a heavy fine, and one "rough fellow" came to the Methodist meeting with a rope, declaring he would hang the preacher if he did not preach to suit him. Nevertheless Case was able to secure a hearing, and in some parts of the district he was cordially received. His greatest success was achieved in what was called the Lower Settlement, and here a general revival of religion broke out under his preaching. His letter to Asbury continued:

The first sermon I preached in this place was attended with almost a general weeping; the sermon produced among some of the wildest of them a visible alteration.

---

[6]Abel Stevens, *Life and Times of Nathan Bangs* (New York, 1863), p. 77.
[7]*Ibid.*, p. 85.

They began to hang around, as if loath to leave the place, and, accounting me no longer their enemy, appeared to wish for an opportunity to speak with me, which I embraced, and spoke to them one by one . . . .

While they mourned, I rejoiced, and pursued them by exhortation and prayer with redoubled zeal and courage; and the Lord Jesus, in his mighty Spirit's power, was present at every meeting, so that a general enquiry, "what shall I do to be saved?" was heard almost through the settlement for 15 miles . . . .

Dear Sir, you would have been truly delighted to see this people, without being previously instructed, or having ever been in any revival, fall into the very same spirit and manner of the revivals in the States and elsewhere, crying amain for mercy, even as they went along their road home; while some did the same in the barns, and others in the woods, till the groves rang again with the cries of penitents, and soon with the joyful notes of glory and praise to Jesus Christ for his redeeming love.

The revival gradually spread throughout the settlements on the Thames River and into the neighbouring districts. Societies were organized, and instruction given to the population on the form of the Methodist discipline. "When I came away," Case concluded in his report to Asbury, "the work was still spreading."[8] The next year the Conference reported a return of 134 members on the Detroit circuit.[9] Growth of Methodist membership in the country generally reflected the influence of religious revivals. Greatest progress was evident in those areas first settled in Upper Canada; Augusta returned 450 members, Bay of Quinte 655, Smith's Creek 120, Yonge Street 95, Niagara 527, and Ancaster and Long Point 569. Methodist growth in Lower Canada before 1812, however, was also significant, particularly in the Eastern Townships; Dunham returned 335 members and Stanstead 200. Ottawa circuit had 116 members, Quebec 26, Montreal 35, St. Francis River 47, and Three Rivers 18.[10] The distribution of Methodist membership reflected the close relation between the growth of the movement in the country and the settlement of Loyalists and Americans. Methodist preachers followed closely upon the heels of the frontiersmen in the new American West and in the new settlements opening up in Canada.

The War of 1812-14 checked the growth of the Methodist movement in the country. Many of the preachers returned to the United States, classes were broken up through the lack of preaching services and the enlistment of local leaders, and religious interests weakened as the war came increasingly to occupy the attention of the population. Yet within many of the local communities, and among the military forces on the front, efforts were made to maintain means of religious

[8]Carroll, *Case and His Cotemporaries*, vol. I, pp. 182-6. See also, Public Archives of Ontario (henceforth cited as P.A.O.), Journal of William Case, pp. 43-52.
[9]Playter, *History of Methodism in Canada*, p. 105.
[10]*Ibid.*

fellowship. Soldiers converted on the field of battle carried the message of the gospel to the civilian population behind the lines, while the more devout members of the local societies undertook to lead meetings for exhortation and prayer in the absence of those more qualified for or more unequivocally called to the task. When the war came to an end, the regular work generally was resumed. Preachers from the United States returned to their appointments or new preachers accepted the call of evangelization, and societies which had broken down were quickly reorganized.

The holding of the Genesee Conference at Elizabethtown in June, 1817, resulted in an extensive revival and in a large number of new members. The revival began in Elizabethtown during the sitting of the Conference, and some one hundred persons were converted. Societies in the neighbouring townships were affected and the revival spread throughout the Augusta circuit. "At a quarterly meeting in Augusta," William Case wrote, "the divine power was gloriously manifest; and among the hundreds from whose eyes the tears of gratitude and joy were falling, were 8 persons above the age of 60, who had lately obtained mercy."[11] Although the revival did not spread east into the St. Lawrence and Cornwall circuits, it swept rapidly westward. The way it began in Fredericksburg, in the Bay of Quinte circuit, on August 17 was thus described:

For some time previous to the awakening, the young people of the neighbourhood had manifested less desire for public amusements, and had obtained leave of Brother Cain to meet at his house for the purpose of learning to sing; after which they joined with the pious, in the solemnities of public worship. At one of these meetings, a youth was present who had lately found peace with God . . . . He arose and addressed the meeting on the subject of his late conversion, and invited them all to taste the joys of this great salvation . . . . The meeting continued several hours. Six young persons found peace with God before the close. The news of the meeting brought numbers together; and the meetings grew so large, that no house in the settlement could hold the people, so that they went into the field, and spent the time in preaching and praying for the distressed. At every meeting, numbers were converted. Like a devouring fire, the revival spread through the neighbourhood; thence it travelled east; thence north, through the German settlement, around the head of Hay Bay, and so on to the Napanee river—sweeping in its irresistable course almost all the families in the way. From Brother Cain's it also took a westerly direction, and spread the entire width of the peninsula of Adolphustown, leaving a blessing in most of the families as it passed along.[12]

Within fourteen months, according to Playter, more than three hundred persons were converted on the Bay of Quinte circuit; the quarterly meetings were attended by so many people that the chapels

[11]*Ibid.*, p. 163.
[12]Quoted *ibid.*, pp. 160-1.

would not contain the assemblies, and the presiding elder would stand at the door and preach to those inside and outside at the same time, or the preaching would be done by two persons.[13] The revival extended to the Hallowell circuit and later spread as far as the Niagara circuit. George Ferguson, preaching in the Niagara district, wrote of the religious enthusiasm which was aroused: "The work here seemed as remarkable as any yet described. While standing and singing, the converts would fall like a log of wood. Sometimes on or across a form or bench until one might suppose they would have been injured. But I never knew of one receiving any hurts in those times."[14] About four hundred were converted on the Niagara circuit in the course of the year. The total increase of membership, according to Playter, resulting directly and indirectly from the revival was about fourteen hundred.[15]

Recruitment of preachers from Ireland as well as from the United States and from among the local population made possible the rapid expansion of Methodist work after 1815. In 1818 a meeting for the first time was held in York, and a circuit was organized comprising the town and vicinity. In 1821 two preachers were appointed by the Missionary Society of the Methodist Episcopal Church to travel in the new settlements north-west of York in the townships of Toronto, Trafalgar, Chinguacousy, Esquesing, and Erin. By 1824 the new settlements had been organized as a mission circuit with the addition of the townships of Nassagawaya, Eramosa, and Caledon. "In a circuit of three hundred miles, through new and incomplete settlements," the Reverend Thomas Demorest wrote of the work of himself and assistant, Brother R. Heyland, in this circuit in 1824, "it cannot be expected that we should have in every place large congregations. At one appointment our congregation is made up of two families, seven in number; and to reach them, we rode a considerable distance."[16] East of York, areas, earlier neglected or unsettled, were included in the field of Methodist preaching. In 1824 Methodism was introduced into Port Hope in the Smith's Creek circuit. "This afternoon, by previous arrangement," the Reverend Anson Green wrote of November 30, 1824, "I delivered what I was informed was the *first sermon* preached in Port Hope by a Wesleyan minister—it was certainly the first appointment in our circuit work there. I had a shoemaker's shop for my church,

[13]*Ibid.*, p. 162.

[14]University of Toronto, Victoria University Library, Journal of the Rev. George Ferguson. A Minister of the W. Methodist Church in Canada, copied from the original, p. 93.

[15]Playter, *History of Methodism in Canada*, p. 163.

[16]*Ibid.*, pp. 231-2.

his shoe-bench for a pulpit, and six persons for a congregation."[17] In the meantime, the first of the second tier of ciruits had come into being with the establishment of the Rideau circuit in 1820, and the northward push of settlement resulted in the creation of a second circuit, that of Perth, in 1821. Revivals periodically swept through the backwoods communities with the extension of preaching appointments leaving in their wake a large body of new converts. If backslidings reduced the numbers on the rolls of the Methodist societies, religious interests among the population generally were nevertheless greatly strengthened. "Blessed be the Lord," William Case wrote of the state of religion in the western part of Upper Canada, "we are prospering finely in this country. . . . Churches are crowded with hearers. Youth and children, instead of wandering in the fields, or loitering in the streets, are, in many places, thronging to the [Sabbath] schools, books in hand, and learning to read the book of God."[18] The area of Methodist religious teachings was steadily extended with the extension of settlement. Growth of membership was in part indicative of the success with which Methodism pushed into new areas of community life, but Methodist influence reached beyond those called into its ranks. There were many settlers who did not join its societies but whose only contact with religious teaching was with that of its preachers. Methodist services, at one time or another, were held in almost every area of new settlement in the country. "The fruits of the labours of the Methodists," Stuart wrote in 1820, "are striking in Upper Canada. . . . They have evidently been (and in a very extensive degree) the ministers of God to the people for good. They pervade, more or less, almost every part of the province."[19] The Reverend William Proudfoot, twelve years later, likewise conceded that the Methodists were chiefly responsible for the carrying on of religious services in the pioneer settlements. "The evil is in part remedied now," he wrote regarding the extent of religious destitution in the country, "by Methodist preachers, who have spread themselves over all the province, and who, owing to the efficiency of their mode of operation, have penetrated into almost every township."[20] On another occasion, Proudfoot wrote: "Mr. Bell, my neighbor, called tonight, and we had a great deal of talk on the religious wants of the West. He told me that all along the shore of Lake Erie there are

[17]*The Life and Times of the Rev. Anson Green, Written by Himself* (Toronto, 1877), pp. 57-8.
[18]Quoted Playter, *History of Methodism in Canada*, p. 208.
[19]C. Stuart, *The Emigrant's Guide to Upper Canada* (London, 1820), pp. 113-14.
[20]"Journal of the Rev. Wm. Proudfoot" (*Transactions*, London and Middlesex Historical Society, 1914, p. 72).

not any ministers except Methodists."[21] By 1830 there were in the country 11,348 members attached to the Canada Conference, served by sixty-two itinerant and a great number of local preachers.

The Methodist was the dominant evangelical religious movement which developed out of the Great Revival in Canada after 1790, but a number of other movements grew up to lend it support. Of these, the American Presbyterian and Baptist were the more important. The connection of the American Presbyterian to the Methodist movement was particularly close.

Presbyterianism on the American frontier had developed techniques of organization not unlike those which had been developed by Methodism— Presbyterian as well as Methodist preachers participated in the first camp meeting in Kentucky—and, while the American Presbyterian Church never built up a highly centralized missionary organization like the Methodist Church and therein lost out in the end as a frontier religious denomination, many of its individual preachers displayed a resourcefulness and zealousness in extending the message of the gospel into new areas of settlement equal to that of the Methodist preachers. Two of these preachers, the Reverends Jabez Collver and Daniel Ward Eastman crossed the Niagara River into Canada, the first in 1793 and the second in 1801.[22] Neither had any extensive theological training—Collver had little education of any sort—but they had undergone the intense emotional experience of conversion and turned to preaching the gospel under "a call of God." Together with the Reverend Lewis Williams, a native of Wales who came to Canada in 1808, Collver and Eastman carried on missionary tours throughout the Niagara peninsula. Rather than waiting as under the regular system of Presbyterian church government for congregations to organize themselves, they struck out into unexplored territory and held services wherever as many as two or three people could be brought together. Churches were organized independent of presbyterial supervision, and in many cases the work of the Church was transacted by direct congregational vote without the supervision of elders. Flexibility of organization made possible the extension of Presbyterian services into areas where the number of Presbyterians was not sufficient to support a regularly formed church, and revivals promoted by the American Presbyterian preachers led to a general strengthening of religious interests.

The War of 1812-14 checked the growth of the American Presbyterian movement in the country as it did the Methodist movement, but, unlike

---

[21] *Ibid.*, p. 48.
[22] W. Gregg, *The History of the Presbyterian Church in Canada* (Toronto, 1885), p. 187.

the Methodist, the American Presbyterian work did not quickly recover. Most of the preachers were lost to the movement and it was not until 1830 that Presbyterian revivalist preaching was resumed. In that year, a revival of religion in western New York State led to a considerable strengthening of the Presbyterian evangelical cause, and rapid growth of the movement here led to its growth across the border. In 1831 the Reverends A. K. Buell and Edward Marsh arrived in Canada from New York State, and revivals under the influence of their preaching spread throughout the western peninsula.[23] In May, 1833, the Niagara Presbytery was organized to supervise the work, and several more preachers made an appearance in immediately succeeding years. By 1837 there were ten ministers and five missionaries of the American Presbyterian Church in the country and the movement had grown to become a dominant religious influence in many of the rural settlements stretching westward from Niagara.

Baptist work in Canada assumed little importance until after 1815. The number of early Baptist settlers in the country was small—most of the American Baptists had identified themselves with the revolutionary cause and remained in the United States—but, even where adherents had settled, the Baptist denomination revealed little capacity before 1815 to provide religious leadership. By the turn of the century the old Baptist churches on the Atlantic seaboard had moved far in a conservative direction—formalism and an emphasis upon doctrine tended to take the place of evangelical teaching—and, as a result, the great revivalist movements which swept into the American West drew little Baptist support; leadership was taken almost wholly by the Methodists and Presbyterians.[24] Although a few Baptist or "Newlight" preachers found their way into Canada, the movement was one confined almost wholly to the activities of isolated individuals and groups.

After 1815, however, the Baptist cause was greatly strengthened. American Baptists in increasing numbers settled in the Eastern Townships and in Upper Canada, while overseas immigration led to the settlement of many Scotch Baptists in the Ottawa Valley and in Oxford County. Although the New England Baptist churches (with the exception of those of the Freewill Order) continued to neglect evangelical work, local Baptist preachers who had come in contact with the Great Revival in the American West found their way across the border of Canada and undertook evangelical preaching and the organization of churches. In western Upper Canada in particular, where the American frontier influence was strong, the Baptist cause

[23]See Harry E. Parker, "Early Presbyterianism in Western Ontario" (*Transactions*, London and Middlesex Historical Society, 1930).
[24]See F. G. Beardsley, *The History of American Revivals* (New York, 1912).

grew rapidly. "The Baptists are making progress in this quarter," the Reverend William Proudfoot wrote of the London district, February 9, 1836, "principally I believe by the restless activity of some of that persuasion and aided by the ignorance of those on whom they operate, and this all helped by the distance which the people live from one another which leaves them at the disposal of those who go about to make proselytes."[25] When the Reverend F. A. Cox visited Canada in 1835 he found from sixty to seventy Baptist churches and forty Baptist ministers in Upper Canada, from fifteen to twenty Baptist churches in Lower Canada, and, in addition, a number of Freewill Baptist churches in the Eastern Townships.[26]

American Presbyterian and Baptist preaching supported the general movement of religious reorganization of the Canadian frontier settlements secured through Methodist influence. Religious revivalism cut across traditional lines of social class and denominational attachment to produce a new sense of spiritual fellowship. The religious sect emerged to take the place of the church. Although the effects of the revival in Canada were less dramatically evident than in Nova Scotia where the Great Awakening resulted, in the case of Congregationalism, in the almost complete breakdown of the formal organization of religion, it made its influence, nevertheless, directly felt upon church life in the country. Growth of revivalist influence led particularly to a serious weakening in the position of the Church of England.

As 'early as 1792, the Reverend John Langhorn, missionary at Ernestown and Fredericksburg, complained of disaffections within his congregations to the Methodists. "The Methodist teacher," he reported in that year, "who has been settled there some time, went out to the Rebel Colonies in the Summer and is returned with (as he expects it will prove) a rod for his own back, an Associate, who takes upon him to baptize, marry, and administer the Lord's Supper; but as he is only a newcomer, cannot pretend to tell what luck he will have."[27] In 1802 Langhorn wrote: "Ernest-Town is a sore refractory town against the Church of England: and one of Capt. Hawley's sons seems setting up for a Methodist preacher: but Capt. Hawley himself appears still to stick close to the Church of England."[28] Two years later he again

[25]"Proudfoot Papers" (*Papers and Records*, Ontario Historical Society, vol. XXX, 1934, p. 128).
[26]F. A. Cox and J. Hoby, *The Baptists in America. A Narrative of the Deputation from the Baptist Union in England to the United States and Canada* (London, 1836), pp. 227-8.
[27]A. H. Young, "The Revd. John Langhorn, Church of England Missionary, at Fredericksburgh and Ernesttown, 1787-1813" (*Papers and Records*, Ontario Historical Society, vol. XXIII, 1926, p. 26).
[28]A. H. Young, "More Langhorn Letters" (*Papers and Records*, Ontario Historical Society, vol. XXIX, 1933, p. 54).

wrote: "In the compass of last year I only baptized four children from Ernest-Town; it being a very disaffected place to the Church of England and still continues so. They want to have God-fathers and God-mothers discontinued at baptism; me to associate with their preachers, and to respect them, their preachers to be allowed to preach in the Church of England Churches; and that I shall not mutter in the pulpit against their religions, nor even out of it."[29] In 1805 he wrote: "I was not asked to administer the Lord's Supper last winter at St. Luke's, Fredericks-burg; and I did not go to Hallawell last Winter, because those that have been formerly Communicants of the Church of England there do not seem now to want my Company; nor did any of them come to see me last winter."[30] He did not perceive, however, Langhorn went on to say, that he and his party had grown any weaker "to make any account of." The attempt of the Methodists upon St. Warburg's was likely to come off but poorly; "In all appearance," he maintained, "they would have liked to have got me turned away from a house there that I lodged at: but I believe they will fail." In 1810 Langhorn again made reference to the work of the Methodists in his mission. "Presbyterians, and Methodists," his terse statement read, "making all opposition, that ever they can."[31]

It was about Ernestown and Fredericksburg, where Langhorn endeavoured to establish the services of the Church of England, that the Methodists gained one of the largest of their early followings; this area from the beginning had constituted the chief stamping ground of Methodist evangelists from across the line. In a number of other areas, however, the Church of England missionaries also faced difficulty in maintaining a following as a result of the competition of the Methodists. In the Sandwich mission, the Reverend Richard Pollard had reason to be concerned respecting the state of the Church. "He is sorry to say," a report from him in 1809 read, "that, for want of regular Clergy, The Methodists are gaining converts."[32] The next year he reported that, "having reason to think that the Methodists had made great progress by means of the most illiterate teachers," he had distributed sermons explaining the orthodox faith of the Church, on faith and work and on divine grace.[33] Of a missionary visit he made to the settlements on the River Thames in 1823, he wrote: "The Methodist minister baptized the children and he is fearful the practice will continue unless

[29]*Ibid.*, p. 55.
[30]*Ibid.*, p. 58.
[31]*Ibid.*, p. 64.
[32]A. H. Young, "The Revd. Richard Pollard, 1752-1824" (*Papers and Records,* Ontario Historical Society, vol. XXV, 1929, p. 466).
[33]*Ibid.*

a clergyman of the Church of England is sent there."[34] In the old
settlements of Elizabethtown and Augusta, the Reverend John Bethune
reported in a similar vein regarding the work of the Methodists. "The
country adjoining his Mission," he wrote in 1815, "has been settled
nearly 30 years. The population is numerous and in general wealthy,
but from the want of Established Clergymen Fanaticism has been
very much diffused among the people by a number of Methodist Teachers,
who previous to the declaration of war successively visited the Country
from the neighbouring states."[35] From York, the Reverend John
Strachan wrote, November 10, 1817: "The Sectaries are gaining ground
in many parts of the Province. A large importation of English Methodist
Clergymen have arrived. A competition has been raised between them
and their brethren from the United States—new zeal has been excited,
and converts multiplied. The Church finds much the same enmity in
each. The Anabaptists begin to make their appearance."[36] Even in
Kingston, where the position of the Church was least unsatisfactory,
the influence of the evangelical sects made itself felt. "The people are
very anxious," the Reverend G. O. Stuart wrote from here, December
6, 1825, "to have frequent preaching—opposed by the Methodists and
Baptists, whose prejudices, however, are fast wearing away."[37]

The situation after 1814 led to some improvement in the position
of the Church in the colony. The War of 1812-14 had revealed the
military dependence of Canada upon the mother country, and the
development of the timber trade asserted its economic dependence upon
the British market. Military and economic interests combined to
strengthen greatly the force of patriotism in Canadian life, evident,
for instance, in the increasing British consciousness of the United
Empire Loyalists. The growth of imperial sentiment reflected itself
directly in the strengthening of Church Establishment; religion combined
with economic and military interests as a force promoting colonial
dependency. At the same time, overseas immigration vastly enlarged
the Church's constituency in the colony, and, while not all of the new
settlers were its adherents, the hope was entertained that with aggressive
church leadership their support could be gained. The Reverend John

[34]*Ibid.*, p. 477.
[35]A. H. Young "The Bethunes" (*Papers and Records,* Ontario Historical Society,
vol. XXVII, 1931, p. 562). "The War," Bethune pointed out, however, "has put a
stop to the visit of the Methodist Preachers, one or two are settled in the neighbourhood but their influence appears to be on the decline."
[36]G. W. Spragge, *The John Strachan Letter Book, 1812-1834* (Toronto, 1946),
p. 141.
[37]A. H. Young, "The Revd. George Okill Stuart, Second Rector of York and of
Kingston" (*Papers and Records,* Ontario Historical Society, vol. XXIV, 1927, p. 532).

Strachan set forth this view, in a memorandum on the state of religion in Upper Canada drawn up in 1820:

> That a Considerable number of the Inhabitants of this Province are not particularly attached to any denomination of Christians
>
> That those belonging to the Established Church are much more numerous than those belonging to any other Denomination . . .
>
> That by allowing matters to remain as they are the majority of those who have not yet joined any denomination will attach themselves to the Established Church
>
> That the greater portion of Lutherans Presbyterians &c will gradually conform as Clergymen multiply . . .
>
> That should Gov't support the Clergy of the different denominations the favourable disposition towards the Established Church which at present exists would disappear and religious animosity be fostered
>
> from all which it appears that if no prospect be held out to support their Clergy at the Expence of Gov't the greater portion of the Different denominations will in a few years Conform.[36]

A considerable increase in the following of the Church was evident after 1820, but serious losses of membership to the evangelical sects continued to be experienced. The travelling missionaries of the Society for Converting and Civilizing the Indians, and Propagating the Gospel among the Destitute Settlers in Upper Canada, appointed first in 1832, found reason to be greatly concerned respecting the position of the Church, particularly in outlying settlements. "It is to be regretted," the Reverend Adam Elliott wrote of the Home District, November, 1834, "that many persons who originally belonged to our communion have joined other persuasions."[39] The Reverend W. F. S. Harpur, in the Midland District, noted in his journal several instances of the loss of members to the sects. "The Episcopalians," he wrote of a service he had at the Marmora House near the Marmora Iron Works, December 26, 1834, "formed the most considerable part of the congregation, but in this township, like most others in the province, the members of the church having so long been destitute of her ministrations, many of them have been compelled, as it were, to join other persuasions in search of that instruction which they have no means of obtaining from their own."[40] The next month Harpur visited West Loughborough. "There is, perhaps, no township in the province," he wrote, "where the ill effects of the want of a regular ministry is more lamentably apparent than in this, for the unfortunate Settlers being, in a great measure, if not indeed wholly destitute of sound religious instruction,

[38]Spragge, *John Strachan Letter Book*, pp. 199-201.
[39]W. J. D. Waddilove (ed.), *The Stewart Missions* (London, 1838), p. 61.
[40]*Ibid.*, p. 112.

are consequently, literally tossed to and fro with every kind of doctrine that may chance to come in among them."[41] Of Marmora Township, he wrote in January, 1835: "The majority of the Settlers in this part of the township have joined the Methodist Society, but have been originally Church people."[42] In a general submission on the state of the Church in his district, Harpur emphasized the seriousness of the loss of members to other religious bodies. "The number of Episcopalians, scattered through the district," he wrote, "far exceeded my expectations; they are numerous in most of the townships, and in some are decidedly the majority. In several parts of the district, numbers of them have been induced to leave our communion, and to join other denominations, solely from being unable to obtain the ministrations of their own."[43] The Reverend Thomas Green in the London District, found much the same situation respecting the Church. "In many places," he wrote, October 21, 1836, "it is observable that, from the total want of sound and evangelical teaching, the most fanciful and extravagant theories in religion readily find disciples."[44] Of the Irish settlement near Walpole, he wrote in his journal: "The families settled in this place were all originally members of the Church, but in the absence of her ministrations joined themselves to the Methodists."[45] In more general terms, he commented: "I perceive that many of those who are now connected with Dissenters, have joined that connection from necessity; they were originally attached to the ordinances of the Church, but the same pious feeling which produced that attachment, made them feel more deeply the entire absence of her religious ministrations, and led naturally to that result."[46]

The Scottish Presbyterian Church, relying heavily upon the support of the Scottish population and making little effort to extend its services to those not of the Presbyterian faith, felt less directly the effects of the competition of the evangelical sects. Nevertheless, some inroads were made upon the Presbyterian membership. The Reverend William Proudfoot in London found many old Scottish Presbyterians who had abandoned their faith and joined themselves with the Methodists. "Was told," he wrote in his journal, November 7, 1832, "that many of the Scotch who have settled in Lobo have turned to Methodism."[47] Of a congregation to which he preached in Dumfries, near Brantford,

---

[41]*Ibid.*, p. 112.
[42]*Ibid.*, p. 115.
[43]*Ibid.*, p. 123.
[44]*Ibid.*, p. 155.
[45]*Ibid.*, p. 206.
[46]*Ibid.*, p. 199.
[47]"Journal of the Rev. Wm. Proudfoot" (*Transactions*, London and Middlesex Historical Society, 1914, p. 63).

January 29, 1833, Proudfoot wrote: "Some of them were Presbyterians, most of them Methodists. A good many of the Methodists had been Presbyterians in the old country."[48] The next day he wrote of the country about Galt: "The people in this district are almost all Presbyterians. Some of them have turned Methodists."[49] In a general comment on the state of his own district of London, August 18, 1833, Proudfoot observed: "Methodism is increasing in this part of the country, principally by means of Camp meetings and such strong stimulants."[50] The Reverend William Fraser, who joined Proudfoot in missionary work in western Upper Canada also found reason to be concerned with the shift of Presbyterians to the Methodist cause. "The Methodists," he wrote in his diary, March 30, 1835, of his visit to West Gwillimbury, Tecumseth and Essa, "are making inroads in the place. I have understood that among some Scotch folk to the west of the Nottawasaga river in the township of Essa they had established a sufficient footing to have a class formed."[51] The Reverend George Ferguson, Methodist preacher, boasted of his work in Beverly, in the Dumfries circuit, 1841-2: "Some members of the families, of the Scotch Presbyterians were converted."[52]

A number of other religious bodies in the country also suffered some loss of support through the drawing off of members by the evangelical religious movements. Many Lutherans, Congregationalists, and Quakers found their way into the Methodist camp, and some Roman Catholics were converted if the claims of Methodist and Baptist preachers are to be accepted. Even the smaller exclusive sects, lacking the evangelical aggressiveness of the Methodists and Baptists, experienced heavy losses of membership in those areas where geographical isolation could not be maintained.

Failure of the traditional institutions of religion to adapt to new social conditions accounted for the weakening of their influence within the Canadian community. The fundamental problem of religious organization in Canada was the problem of meeting the needs of a scattered backwoods population. Within the new backwoods settlements, the traditional attachments of the old world—ties of folk and class— broke down in face of powerful forces of individualization, and new attachments had to be established in terms of a new sense of social

[48]"Proudfoot Papers" (*ibid*, 1922, p. 51).
[49]*Ibid.*, p. 52.
[50]"Proudfoot Papers" (*Papers and Records*, Ontario Historical Society, vol. XXVI, 1930, p. 570).
[51]"Diary of the Rev. Wm. Fraser" (*Transactions*, London and Middlesex Historical Society, 1930, p. 125).
[52]Journal of the Rev. George Ferguson, p. 171.

purpose. It was the failure of the traditional churches that they offered
no effective support of forces of social reorganization in the Canadian
backwoods society. The traditional organization of religion weakened
with the weakening of the traditional social organization in general.

Weaknesses in the organization of the Church of England early
became apparent in Canada. In spite of government support, and
the advantage of being first in the field, the Church from the beginning was unable to provide with the services of religion more than a
small proportion of the growing Canadian population. Unlike Nova
Scotia, where most of the missionaries after 1783 were recruited from
the old colonies, missionaries for Canada had to be supplied almost
entirely from overseas; it was not for some time that the Protestant
Episcopal Church in the United States recovered sufficiently from
the shock of the War of Independence to interest itself in foreign
missions. Difficulties of transportation and communication provided
obstacles to the recruitment of clergymen from overseas which were
not readily overcome by a church lacking a strong missionary spirit.
Missionary work in Canada was looked upon as that of providing
for an outpost of empire, of assuring the supremacy of the established
church within the imperial system, and the rank and file of the clergy
in England shared in this lack of any real interest in spreading religious
teachings. Considerations of a comfortable livelihood and of social
prestige, and an emphasis upon the ministry as a career, discouraged
emigration to a frontier area which held out little in the way of material
reward.

Realization of the difficulty of securing clergy from overseas early
led to proposals favouring a greater reliance upon local recruits for the
ministry. "Few men of ability," Strachan pointed out in a report to
the Chief Justice on the state of religion in Upper Canada, March 1,
1815, "will be found willing to leave England for so distant a Colony—
much dependence ought not therefore to be placed on this source of
supply."[53] There was lacking within the colony, however, any large
local reservoir of supply from which to call up workers; the recruiting
methods and training programme of the Church were too rigid to
permit the ordination of those whose only qualification was their desire
to preach the gospel. "Of the persons born in the country," the Bishop
of Quebec had written in 1800, "I need not inform your Grace that few
indeed have been so educated as to give them any decent pretension
to instruct others, and among the persons who come to settle here,
there is less probability of finding proper subjects. Your Grace, I am

[53]Spragge, *John Strachan Letter Book,* p. 74.

sure would be very far from recommending it to me to open the Sacred Profession for the reception of such adventurers, as disappointed speculations may have disposed to enter it."[54] Institutional impediments to safeguard the ministerial profession might have broken down if a greater number of the local inhabitants had insisted upon organizing Church of England congregations with local, untrained preachers in charge, but the membership of the Church in the colony was confined to the "respectable" portions of the population, and there was lacking favourable soil for the breeding of the religious prophet. Orthodoxy in clerical qualifications was maintained at the price of failing to secure a sufficient supply of ministers.

The result was that new settlements grew up and no clergymen were available to provide religious services. The Bishop of Quebec wrote in 1794 on the completion of a visitation of his diocese:

With respect to Religious instruction the state of these settlers is for the most part truly deplorable. From Montreal to Kingston, a distance of 200 miles, there is not one Clergyman of the Church of England: nor any house of religious worship except one small Chapel belonging to the Lutherans, & one, or perhaps two, belonging to the Presbyterians. The public worship of God is entirely suspended, or performed in a manner which can neither tend to improve the people in Religious Truth, nor to render them useful members of society. The Presbyterian and the Lutheran Clergymen are, I believe, men of good character, but their influence is necessarily limited to their own little congregations. The great bulk of the people have, and can have no instruction, but such as they receive occasionally from itinerant & mendicant Methodists; a set of ignorant enthusiasts whose preaching is calculated only to perplex the understanding, & corrupt the morals; to relax the nerves of industry, & dissolve the bonds of society.[55]

Missionaries at Kingston, Ernestown, and Niagara, the bishop went on to point out, served considerable congregations but were not able to supply the needs of the rapidly growing population in the western part of the province, while in Lower Canada the state of the Church remained unsatisfactory although some improvement had been secured. Increase in the number of missionaries after 1800 made possible the extension of the services of the Church but many areas were left unsupplied. "It is really painful," the Reverend Richard Pollard, missionary at Sandwich, wrote in 1807, "to see such a fine extensive country with a population of 10,000 people, & only six of the regular Clergy for their instruction. In his District on the River Thames are 500 souls without a Minister, Church, or School. On Lake Erie, another settlement in the same

[54]P.A.C., Series Q, vol. 85, Quebec, Aug. 20, 1800, Bishop of Quebec to Duke of Portland.
[55]Cruickshank, *Simcoe Papers*, vol. III, pp. 91-3.

predicament."[56] In 1820 C. Stuart wrote of the general state of the Church in Upper Canada:

> Although some recent improvements have been made, the church of Christ has deplorably languished, and still deplorably languishes in Upper Canada . . . .
> There are at present in Upper Canada, twelve or fifteen clergymen of the established church, and not quite so many churches . . . . I need not add (stationary as they are, or at least confined to narrow circuits) how totally insufficient such a provision must be, for the spiritual wants of a secluded population, scattered over a frontier of nearly one thousand miles. To the mass of the people, it is almost as nothing.[57]

After 1820, with rapid growth of overseas immigration and the pushing of settlement into the backwoods areas, the problem of providing the population with the services of religion became even more difficult. It is true, the number of Church of England missionaries in the colony greatly increased; reforms within the Church tended to produce a more zealous missionary spirit on the part of the hierarchy and of the clergy, while social influences acted to increase the number of those willing to accept service abroad. Clergymen were drawn increasingly from distressed agricultural areas in England and, later, Ireland; the same forces led to their emigration as to the general emigration from these areas after the Napoleonic War. The impact of the depression upon the old country rural society was reflected in the settlement in Canada of people drawn from the upper as well as lower social levels, and this broadening of the social effects of the depression had considerable to do with bringing about a greater willingness on the part of Anglican clergymen to leave their homeland for colonial missionary work. But while the number of missionaries in the country increased after 1820, the Church failed to make the most effective use of their services. Clergymen brought out from England tended to establish themselves as quickly as possible in the larger centres of population, and this reliance upon a stationary ministry involved a failure to serve the large, and growing, backwoods population which could only be reached by a clergy employing itinerant methods.

Some of the missionaries, it is true, did conduct services outside the community in which they were stationed. "For the last three months," a letter from the Reverend John Bethune, in 1816, read, "he has performed evining service every other Sunday in the back settlement 6 miles distant from the Church in Augusta and he Has the satisfaction to find that it has been the means of adding a Tolerably numerous and

---

[56]Young, "The Revd. Richard Pollard, 1752-1824" (*Papers and Records*, Ontario Historical Society, vol. XXV, 1929, p. 464).
[57]Stuart, *Emigrant's Guide to Upper Canada*, pp. 110-11.

very respectable congregation to the Church."[58] Mrs. Stewart, living in Douro, north of Peterborough, wrote in 1824 of the hardships involved through isolation. "Being as far back as we are has great disadvantages and we have felt many of them. The want of a place of worship and a clergyman is the greatest." The district, however, was not completely unsupplied. "Mr. Thompson, the clergyman of Cavan township," Mrs. Stewart continued, "preaches occasionally about 5 miles from here. He comes every month that has five Sundays in it; but I have never yet been able to find out the hour in time to be present."[59] In Kingston, the Reverend G. O. Stuart recognized the need of going out beyond the bounds of the town. "He contemplates," a letter from him, December 18, 1828, read, "when his health is better, extending his Preaching frequently throughout the Mission being aware that united to the Sacraments of our Church, it is productive of much benefit to the enlargement & interests of the Church of England in a country where Dissenters and Sectaries abound."[60]

Such efforts to reach out beyond regular centres represented some adjustment to the needs of the scattered backwoods settlements, but they were only in the way of supplying adjoining neighbourhoods. The area served by these casual visits was limited by the distance from the mission station, and usually some sort of church building was constructed before the visits were made, at any rate with regularity. Numbers of adherents of the Church were too far removed from centres of population to be within reach of even the most casual visits of the missionaries or parish clergy, and to serve these the Church lacked a body of clergy truly itinerant in character. "I know of no part of Canada," the Reverend Henry Pope, Wesleyan missionary, wrote from Shipton in the Eastern Townships, October 28, 1821, "that stands in more need of the Gospel ministry . . . than this Circuit and some townships adjoining it. . . . Two of the Townships between this and Stanstead, where Br. Hick is stationed, a distance of forty-five miles, have an Episcopal minister in each of them; but the townships are from twelve to fifteen miles square, and those ministers do not itinerate."[61] Mac-Grath, though a member of the Church of England, recognized that much of the weakness of the Church was a result of the lack of itinerant preachers. "The Methodist dissenters," he wrote, "have obtained an

[58]Young, "The Bethunes" (*Papers and Records,* Ontario Historical Society, vol. XXVII, 1931, p. 567).

[59]E. S. Dunlop (ed.), *Our Forest Home: Being Extracts from the Correspondence of the Late Frances Stewart* (Montreal, 1902), p. 57.

[60]Young, "The Revd. George Okill Stuart" (*Papers and Records,* Ontario Historical Society, vol. XXIV, 1927, p. 534).

[61]Carroll, *Case and His Cotemporaries,* vol. II, p. 389.

ascendancy over our infant population. Their habits of domiciliary visitation, their acquaintance with the tastes and peculiarities of the Canadians, their readiness to take long and fatiguing rides, in the discharge of their self-imposed labours, renders them formidable rivals to our more *easy going* clergy."[62]

Realization of the need of strengthening the organization of the Church in the rural settlements led Strachan in 1829 to urge upon the Bishop "the expediency of employing a travelling Missionary in each District or one or two for each Archdeaconry" and "the expediency of allowing it in your Lordships power a Missionary to read the morning Service occasionally at stations where it is not in his power to attend in the early part of the day."[63] Strickland, deploring the generally weakened state of the Church, advocated the full adoption of an itinerant system:

Much good would result from the clergymen of our establishment itinerating from place to place, taking up their abode in private houses, where they would always be honoured guests, and preaching and reading prayers during their so-journ. A real necessity exists for their performing such charitable missions, till the scattered villages get churches and ministers of their own. To show the need of such itineration, I need only state that my own county of Peterborough, containing eighteen townships (of which Douro, in which I reside, is one) possesses only three churches, to supply the wants of a population, which, at the last census, numbered more than twenty-seven thousand souls, and which now would amount, from emigration and increase, to nearly thirty thousand.[64]

With the organization in 1830 of the Society for Converting and Civilizing the Indians, and Propagating the Gospel among the Destitute Settlers in Upper Canada the Church of England for the first time obtained a body of itinerant clergymen. Three, and later four, travelling missionaries were placed under the charge of the Society, one in the Home District, one in the Midland District, one in the London District, and one in the District of Quebec. The Society did something to extend the ministrations of the Church into isolated areas of settlement,[65] but the number of its missionaries was far from adequate. Three or four clergymen could scarcely do more than pay an occasional visit to those communities easily accessible to the traveller from outside. Regular services in the backwoods were impossible, and large areas

[62]T. W. Magrath, *Authentic Letters from Upper Canada*, ed. by T. Radcliff (Dublin, 1833), pp. 194-5.
[63]P.A.O., Strachan Letter Book, 1827-1839, York, Apr. 27, 1829, Strachan to Bishop of Quebec, p. 39.
[64]Major Samuel Strickland, *Twenty-Seven Years in Canada West* (London, 1853), vol. II, pp. 325-6.
[65]See J. J. Talman, "Church of England Missionary Effort in Upper Canada, 1815-1840" (*Papers and Records*, Ontario Historical Society, vol. XXV, 1929).

were left unprovided with services of any sort. "The society in Toronto," wrote the author of an anonymous pamphlet in 1836 urging reform in the Church, ". . . has done faithfully what its means have enabled it to do. . . . Its missionaries are unwearied; their fields are far too large; their visits to each section of the country far too unfrequent; yet still whole districts abounding with church people, have in no way benefitted by their exertions."[66] As late as 1840 many areas which by then had been settled for some time were still not being served by the Church. "There is no church," James Logan wrote in 1838, "for many miles around my brother's residence [twelve miles beyond Dundas], and many of the settlers rarely hear a sermon above twice a year."[67]

The immediate result of the failure of the Church to serve more effectively the backwoods communities was to weaken the religious interests of its adherents. The extent to which the absence of means of religious worship was responsible for the religious indifference of the population was open to question—the extent of the religious indifference in itself was a matter upon which there was no general agreement—but the break in habits resulting from the failure to main-tain the conditions of religious fellowship inevitably led to a shift away from religious systems of thought. "Another want in these Townships," the Reverend Charles Stewart wrote of the situation in the Eastern Townships in 1817, "and that of a most serious nature, is their destitute state with regard to the supply of ministers of the Gospel. . . . The deficient and dangerous state in which the people are situated with regard to knowing and fulfilling their duties . . . while they are left without the aid of any regular ministry of the Gospel, needs not to be represented. Were they long to continue in this state, they would degenerate into barbarism."[68] The concern expressed by Stewart was shared by a number of other observers. "It is evident," Howison wrote in 1821, "that the deficiency in the number of religious establishments must have a fatal effect upon the principles of the people; for the Sabbath, presenting no routine of duties to their recollection, gradually approxi-mates to a week day. They spend the day in idleness and amusement, either strolling among the woods, or shooting game, or wandering between their neighbours' houses."[69] J. R. Godley, much later, made a

[66]*Thoughts of the Present State and Future Prospects of the Church of England in Canada.* By a Presbyter of the Diocese of Quebec (1836), p. 5.

[67]James Logan, *Notes of a Journey through Canada, the United States of America and the West Indies* (Edinburgh, 1838), pp. 52-3.

[68]Hon. and Rev. Charles Stewart, *A Short View of the Present State of the Eastern Townships in the Province of Lower Canada* (printed in Montreal, reprinted in London, 1817), p. 17.

[69]John Howison, *Sketches of Upper Canada* (Edinburgh, 1821), pp. 157-8.

similar assertion. "There is much to lament," he wrote, "in the religious condition of most of the rural districts, as must always be the case where the population is much scattered, and allowed to outgrow the supply of ecclesiastical ministration. From never having the subject forced upon them they begin to forget it, gradually neglect the observance of the Lord's Day, or else employ it as a day simply of bodily relaxation and amusement, omit to have their children baptized, and end by living as though they had no religion at all."[70] The missionaries of the Society for Propagating the Gospel among the Destitute Settlers in Upper Canada found considerable evidence of the growth of attitudes of religious indifference as a result of the failure of the Church to serve the backwoods population. "It is, however, deeply to be regretted," the Reverend Thomas Green, in the London District, wrote, October 21, 1836, "that in many places there is a total disregard of the Sabbath, but this may be traced entirely to the total want of stated services and Sunday schools."[71] In his journal, Green returned to the subject of Sabbath observance; "it is deeply to be deplored," he wrote, "how soon the poor Emigrant in the absence of any state Momentor, forgets how the Sabbath ought to be passed, and falls quickly and generally into the loose habits of his American neighbours, many of whom appear entirely to disregard the sacredness of that day which the Lord Jehovah hallowed."[72] Conditions found by the Reverend Hervey Vachell among Church adherents in a tour of English-speaking settlements in Lower Canada were of an even less favourable character. "Short as my tour has been," he wrote, January, 1837, "since I left Grosse Isle, I have seen enough to say 'darkness covers the earth, and gross darkness the people.' I have personally visited about 120 families, scattered about in the bush, these are not considered the worst off, for in one settlement a Minister is supposed to attend *once* in a month, whilst all the others have the *benefit of a sermon twice a year.*" Of the first settlement visited he wrote: "In about three families only did I find the common observance of family devotion, all alike lamentably ignorant of the word of God, about two or three children only that understood any thing of the Scriptures." Of the second settlement he visited, he wrote: "In only two families did I discern any vestige of religion." The remainder of the tour revealed a similar state of religious destitution. "At the next place I visited," Vachell continued, "I found many things to discourage and cast down. . . . In this settlement I did not find *above two or three*

[70]J. R. Godley, *Letters from America* (London, 1844), vol. I, p. 174.
[71]Waddilove, *Stewart Missions*, p. 155.
[72]*Ibid.*, p. 206.

children possessing even a shadow of religious knowledge. . . . The next settlement was pretty much like it."[73]

Where a weakening of religious interests did not result, the adherents of the Church were forced to turn to other denominations in search of means of carrying on public worship.[74] While many of those who left the Church returned to it again as soon as an opportunity was provided for participating in its services, when a considerable interval elapsed before such an opportunity was provided, the loyalties of adherents were often permanently broken. Among the second generation in particular considerable difficulty was faced in re-establishing traditional attachments. "In every township in this Province," Archdeacon Strachan wrote in his journal of visitation, September 2, 1828, "the travelling missionary discovers here and there scattered episcopal families; sometimes one or two, sometimes a more considerable number, who are entirely deprived of the ministrations of the Church. Their children are growing up ignorant of our church, and wandering from her communion."[75] The travelling missionaries were equally aware that the chief threat to the position of the Church was the loss of the support of the second generation. "I am persuaded," the Reverend Adam Elliott wrote, "that it would be easy at present, for clergymen adequate to the undertaking, to organize a congregation in every neighbourhood of the Home District. But it is to be apprehended that this will not long be the case if the number of our Missionaries be not speedily augmented. The present generation of Episcopalians having passed away, their posterity cannot be expected to inherit their attachment to the Church, if they be suffered to grow up uninstructed in her principles, and unacquainted with her form of worship."[76] The Reverend W. F. S. Harpur expressed a similar fear. After pointing out that many adherents of the Church who had joined other denominations rejoiced at the opportunity of again participating in Anglican services, he went on to say: "These persons of whom I speak were Europeans, who have been brought up in the bosom of the Church; their children, however, can scarcely be expected to retain the same affection and attachment; indeed, under existing circumstances, it would be folly to look for it—how can they love that which they have not seen, and of which they know nothing."[77]

Failure of the Church to serve more effectively the Canadian backwoods population emphasized shortcomings resulting from its overseas heritage. Reliance upon a traditional parish system led to a considerable

[73]*Ibid.*, pp. 211-12.   [74]*Ibid.*, pp. 61, 112, 123, 155, 199.
[75]E. Hawkins, *Annals of the Diocese of Toronto* (London, 1848), p. 118.
[76]Waddilove, *Stewart Missions*, p. 61.   [77]*Ibid.*, p. 123.

weakening of the Church in Britain itself in face of population movements with the revolution in agriculture and industry, and a reluctance
to depart completely from parish principles in Canada led to a similar
weakening in face of population movements with the expansion of
agricultural settlement. The failure to build up an adequate body
of itinerant missionaries and to integrate an itinerant system into the
regular organization of the Church, were simply obvious limitations
in the methods employed in the Canadian situation. The inherent
weakness of the Church lay in its general failure to depart from principles
of church government which had developed out of very different
circumstances.

Defections from the Church were an inevitable result of its failure to
provide the population with religious services. Yet in Canada, as in
the Maritime Provinces, there is little reason to suppose that the Church
would have been a great deal more successful if its services had been
made available to the population. The effects of its weaknesses in
the loss of membership were to some extent exaggerated by spokesmen of the Church itself by virtue of the very fact that its interests
were closely identified with the imperial connection. Reports from
missionaries in Canada were intended to provide information on the
state of religion in the mission fields but they were also intended as
propaganda to encourage subscriptions to missionary funds. The
British population was urged to support missionary work as a means
of extending the influence of the Church and thereby strengthening
the imperial connection, and, to arouse a favourable response to such
pleas for additional support, it was necessary to emphasize the seriousness
of the losses suffered by the Church through not having sufficient
missionaries in the field. The imperialistic interests of the Church
inevitably led to the deliberate misleading of people in Great Britain
as to the true religious conditions in the colonies: at times, appointments of additional clergy were urged to serve communities which, in
terms of the number of adherents, actually had an oversupply. Where
other religious denominations enjoyed the advantage of having a
greater number of ministers—and of adherents—the effects of the shortcomings of the Church were likely to be particularly stressed. Representatives of the Church clung to the illusion that many of the Canadian
settlers could be won from other religious persuasions if only an opportunity were presented to them to participate in Anglican services.

"We only want Clergymen," Strachan argued in 1818, "to have a
decided majority in our favour, but as I have already said in a former
letter we must strain every nerve and outpreach, and outpractice our

opponents."[78] That condition was scarcely met by the Church which established itself in Canada. Although the Canadian missionaries were chosen with somewhat greater regard for the particular conditions under which they were to labour than those who had located in Nova Scotia, there were nevertheless many missionaries sent to the country who had few of the qualities required for success in a new world frontier. The concern early expressed by Lieutenant-Governor Simcoe respecting the importance of sending out missionaries acceptable to the inhabitants was indicative of a realization of the inadequacies of some of the clergymen already in the country:

> I only refer to your Lordship's slight experience of the habits and manners of the American Settlers to say, how very different they are from those of Great Britain, and how unlikely it is for Clergymen educated in England, with English families and propensities, habituated in every situation to a greater degree of refinement and comfort than can be found in a New Country, or possibly anywhere without the precincts of Great Britain, How unlikely it is that such persons could obtain that Influence with their Parishioners which may essentially promote the objects of their Mission . . . .
>
> On the other hand I am persuaded, if at the outset a few pious, learned men of just zeal and primitive manners, shall be sent out to this Country with sufficient inducement to make them support this honorable banishment with Cheerfulness, and that in the first instance Your Lordship shall not too strenuously insist upon *Learning* as a qualification for Ordination, where there are evident marks of religious disposition and proofs of Morality, I am confident the *rising Generation* will be brought up competently learned and properly embued with Religion and Loyalty.[79]

Charges that some of the missionaries settled in the country were indolent and even immoral were not free from bias, but the fact that such charges were constantly being made were indicative at least of what large sections of the population thought. "There were no preachers of the gospel near us," Nathan Bangs, Methodist preacher, wrote of the Niagara District in 1800, "except the poor drunken card-playing minister of the Church of England, whom I sometimes heard mumble over his form of prayer so fast that I could scarcely understand a word of it, and then read his short manuscript sermon with the same indifference and haste."[80] William Case, another Methodist preacher, wrote of the settlements along the Thames River in 1810: "They have no preaching save the Roman Catholic's, and some of the Church of England, whose priests, I understand, have frequently, after service, joined their congregations at dancing and playing at cards, which

[78]Spragge, *John Strachan Letter Book*, p. 156.
[79]Cruickshank, *Simcoe Papers*, vol. III, p. 350.
[80]Stevens, *Life and Times of Nathan Bangs*, p. 42.

renders them very popular, especially in the higher circle."[81] George
Ferguson, who became active as a Methodist preacher after the War
of 1812-14, made a similar charge respecting the worldliness of the
Anglican clergy. "There was, however," he wrote of his arrival with
his regiment in Sorel in May, 1815, "an English Episcopal Church n
the village—the clergyman was aged and decrepid—wicked and profane.
I saw him frequently at Major Davis' in company with officers, engaged
at the card-table."[82]

An improvement in what might be called the moral character of the
Anglican clergy was evident after 1820; reforms within the Church at
home which involved raising the standards of those admitted to
clerical orders were reflected in the higher standards of missionaries
sent out to Canada. The clergy gained in social respectability, but there
was less evidence of any gain in zealousness or preaching talent. Higher
standards for ordination within the Church did not imply the building
up of a body of preachers with a strong evangelical interest; if anything,
it implied the very opposite. Missionaries were expected to observe
more carefully the refinements within the Church of England service,
and those who were the most punctilious in this regard were often
the least successful in winning the favour of the rural inhabitants.
"He [Mr. Chadwick] told me," Proudfoot wrote of the Reverend
Mark Burnham in St. Thomas, March 31, 1833, "that there is a great
want of the gospel in the place; that the Episcopal clergyman is not
worth the having which I fancy is true."[83] Other observers, with less
reason for bias, remarked in similar fashion respecting Church of England
clergy. "I have little to say," Bigsby wrote, "respecting the Quebec
clergy. They were personally amiable. They worked the outward
machinery of the Church of England with professional accuracy, but
I fear they did little more than visit and relieve the sick when called
upon."[84] Of the clergy in the Eastern Townships, Henry Taylor wrote:
"If a more frequent service were performed by the Ministers of the
Church of England, and especially, if another thing which I consider
of great weight, . . . namely, that Eloquence in these Ministers should
determine their appointment to these country places; I should conceive
that many dissenters would return to the Bosom of the Church they
had seceded from."[85] The concern shown by Archdeacon Mountain,

[81]Carroll, *Case and His Cotemporaries*, vol. I, p. 181.
[82]Journal of the Rev. George Ferguson, p. 67.
[83]"Proudfoot Papers" (*Papers and Records*, Ontario Historical Society, vol. XXVI, 1930, p. 507).
[84]J. J. Bigsby, *The Shoe and Canoe or Pictures of Travel in the Canadas* (London, 1850), vol. I, p. 28.
[85]Henry Taylor, *Journal of a Tour from Montreal to the Eastern Townships* (Quebec, 1840), pp. 35-6.

in his journal of visitation, July 4, 1830, respecting the qualifications required in the clergy in Canada was indicative of a realization that some of those already in the field were not wholly satisfactory.

A clergyman established as the pastor of these people [he wrote] must first win them to attend diligently upon his ministrations by his acceptableness in his public performances and the personal respect which he acquires among them, and may then succeed in teaching them a right knowledge and a just value of the church and her ordinances. It is a great point if he is an able preacher, or, as some of them express it, a smart speaker, but it is of more importance still that he should be discreet, circumspect, spiritual, zealous and laborious. The Americans expect a great deal in a clergyman, and it is useless for a man to go among them in that capacity who will not seem to be truly a man of God. A hypocrite may sometimes succeed with them. A careless worldly clergyman never can. A sincerely devout and exemplary pastor will seldom fail to build up the church among them, and gain the respect and goodwill of those who conform but partially or not at all. Upon the whole, however, it must be plainly confessed that the difficulties of the ministry are great in the missions of this diocese.[86]

To some extent the lack of adequate supervision accounted for the failure to develop a more zealous ministry. As settlement extended into the interior, the various missionaries or parish clergymen became increasingly separated from one another, and no agency existed within the Church to bring them together to discuss common problems and to inspire one another. Centralization of authority discouraged a spirit of individual initiative, while the failure of the bishop or of the missionary society to properly supervise much of the work in outlying missions resulted in some of the clergy falling into lax habits of behaviour. "It is quite evident," Strachan wrote in 1831, in advocating regular annual convocations within the Church much like the synods of the Church of Scotland, "that we cannot proceed successfully if we continue scattered & without Union. . . . At present we have no Gov't at all. We have no unity of action. Everything depends upon the will of a single person who may be swayed by motives altogether indefensible. . . . There is moreover no vigilant inspection over the Clergy in their respective Missions to see whether they are lukewarm or active & zealous."[87] Failure to develop effective techniques of control accentuated weaknesses in the character of the clergy which derived originally from the policy of recruitment. The conservatism of the Church generally with respect to the form of its religious appeal tended to become accentuated as a result of the isolation of the missionaries from outside liberalizing influences.

[86]A. W. Mountain, *A Memoir of G. J. Mountain, Late Bishop of Quebec* (Montreal, 1866), p. 139.
[87]P.A.O., Strachan Letter Book, 1827-1839, York, June 27, 1831, Strachan to Rev. Robert Cartwright, pp. 144-5.

The character of the clergy serving within the Canadian colony reflected the failure of the Church of England to make any real effort to adapt its organization or form of appeal to the needs of a crude frontier society. Conditions within the Canadian rural communities tended to weaken formal habits of devotion and interest in elaborate theological systems, and even among adherents of the Church there was a tendency to neglect the performance of the more exacting duties of the religious service. Receiving the sacraments involved an individual effort which was not readily made by the self-conscious pioneer who was much more comfortable when worshipping in a crowd. "He finds it a difficult task," Mr. Rudd, missionary at Cornwall, wrote, August 2, 1802, "to establish the custom of Churching."[88] The Reverend G. O. Stuart, missionary at York, reported in the same year that "notwithstanding the prejudices of those, who nominally dissent from the Church of England, he has the satisfaction of seeing a numerous congregation at Church on Sundays, but Communicants are very few."[89] Two years later a letter from the same missionary was read "assuring the society of his continuing to discharge his duty, and tho' sensible that religious impressions have been made upon several of his Congregation, yet he has cause to lament the general reluctance of the people to receive the sacrament, tho' he has urged in his discourses the obligation, necessity, the beneficial effects of observing that Institution of Love: which he rather attributes to ignorance than to prejudice & mistaken scruples."[90]

If a disinclination was evident among adherents of the Church to accept its sacramental obligations, such a disinclination was even more pronounced among those not brought up accustomed to its form of service. There was little patience among the population generally for a religious appeal which seemed to sacrifice meaning to form and which aroused little in the way of an emotional response. Few of the pioneer farmers possessed sufficient aesthetic sense to appreciate the beauties of the Church's ritual and still fewer had the theological understanding necessary for acceptance of the Church's claim to apostolic origin. In terms of ecclesiastical authority, all religions tended to be treated as of equal validity; the worth of a particular church was measured by the results it secured rather than by its form of service or system of government. "The great objection," Langhorn wrote from Ernestown

[88]A. H. Young, "The Mission of Cornwall, 1784-1812" (*Papers and Records*, Ontario Historical Society, vol. XXV, 1929, p. 491).
[89]Young, "The Revd. George Okill Stuart" (*Papers and Records*, Ontario Historical Society, vol. XXIV, 1927, p. 520).
[90]*Ibid.*, p. 521.

in 1806, "people here have against me is, that I will not model my religion to their fancy, but adhere to the Church of England."[91]

Among some of the clergy by about 1830 there were indications of an attempt to modify the form of service of the Church to make it more attractive to the rural population. Efforts to meet the competition of the evangelical churches led to the adoption of some of their techniques. "He appears to be anxious," Proudfoot wrote in his diary of the Reverend Mr. Luggan, missionary of the New England Society to the Indians on the Grand River, "to do good not only to the Indians but to the white people of Brantford, but his mode of doing good is in the style of the high churchman, consequently he is not a match for the Methodists, who underwork him and work around him."[92] The next day, however, after talking with the missionary about the problem of Methodist competition, Proudfoot was more favourable in his comment. "He feels sadly annoyed by them," the entry in the diary read, "and has some design of fighting against them with their own weapons, particularly by calling more frequently into activity the influence of the Indians and by giving them some say in the affairs of the church. Much to my surprise I found him rather favourable to revivals and he spoke of adopting some parts of the system, such as calling young communicants before the church some time before admitting them into its fellowship and speaking to them and praying for them."[93] The Reverend John Ryerson, no friend of the Church of England, had much to say in praise of the Anglican clergyman in Sandwich. "Here I had the pleasure," he wrote of a visit to Sandwich, February, 1830, "of being introduced to a minister of the Church of England, who promises great usefulness to the people of his charge. Through his worthy example, his zealous and faithful administration of the word of life, together with his urbanity of manners, he has raised the church, of which he is a minister, and the standard of public morals, to a degree of influence and respectability, to which they had never attained through the instrumentality of any of his predecessors."[94] The growing influence of the Episcopalian Church in the United States upon the Church n Canada, evident, for instance, in the arrival in the country of missionaries of the New England Society, and the coming in during the eighteen-thirties of a number of clergy from Ireland—"driven out . . by the violence of those who refuse to pay the church tithes"—promised to

[91]Young, "More Langhorn Letters" (*Papers and Records,* Ontario Historical Society, vol. XXIX, 1933, p. 62).
[92]"Proudfoot Papers" (*Transactions,* London and Middlesex Historical Society, 1922, pp. 54-5).
[93]*Ibid.,* p. 56. [94]*Christian Guardian,* Mar. 13, 1830.

introduce a more evangelical spirit into the Canadian work. "I met one of this description," the Reverend George Mortimer wrote of one of the newly arrived Irish clergymen, November 8, 1832, "the other evening at the bishop's, a warm-hearted and spiritually minded Irishman."[95]

The strengthening evangelical influence within the Church of England made itself felt in Canada through ties with the United States and Ireland and directly through the connection with England. The growing Irish immigration, in particular after 1830, but also the immigration of the poorer classes from England, tended to force the teachings of the Church in Canada into evangelical channels. The vested interests of ecclesiastical authority, however supported by the large body of settlers of upper class English origin, strenuously resisted innovations which threatened the purity of the Anglican rites. Unorthodoxy in the conduct of the clergy or in the performance of the religious service was severely frowned upon. The determination to preserve the distinctive forms of the Church led inevitably to the discouragement of evangelical tendencies, evident in the opposition to the arrival of the Irish clergy.

With the exception of one Clerical Gentleman introduced to me by Your Grace [Strachan wrote to the Archbishop of Dublin, April 28, 1836], the Clergymen who came to this country from Ireland are strangely Calvinistic in their Sermons—& go much farther than those who are called Evangelical in England. Some of them have also a foolish fancy of Preaching without rites—they brandish a little bible in their hand fastened with brass clasps and open it from time to time to read their quotations . . . . These persons are so wide in their doctrines & unguarded in their statements that I am really afraid to allow them to preach for they seem never to have known the distinctive principles of the Church of England or to have thrown them away on the voyage.[96]

The rise of the Oxford movement in England strengthened tendencies towards formalism and ritualism within the Church in Canada. Among certain elements of the Church, evangelical sentiments continued to gain in strength, and efforts to establish a new episcopal paper in Montreal were indicative of a growing dissatisfaction with ecclesiastical policy,[97] but the hierarchy tended to become increasingly high church in outlook. "I quite tremble," the Reverend George Mortimer wrote his sister in 1840, "when I think of the probable results of the present wide spread of tractarian notions. . . . These principles are exerting no

[95]Rev. John Armstrong, *The Life and Letters of the Rev. George Mortimer* (London, 1847), p. 191.
[96]P.A.O., Strachan Letter Book, 1827-1839, Toronto, Apr. 28, 1836, Strachan to Archbishop of Dublin, p. 243.
[97]See *The Register*, vol. I, Nov. 23, 1842.

small degree of influence in our province."[98] Bigsby wrote of the leaders
of the Canadian Church in 1850: "Many of them are laborious and
useful men, but others again are deeply tainted with Puseyism (so
worshipful of bishops), and are doing no little harm by frowning down
evangelical religion—oppressing it, I ought to say—and encouraging
formalism, which is sure to end in Popery."[99] High Church leadership
effectively checked efforts to bring the teachings of the Church more
in line with those of the evangelical denominations, and emphasis
upon the distinctive claims of the Church to apostolical succession
intensified the conflict with nonconformity. The editor of the *Christian
Guardian* wrote, December 14, 1842: "Nothing is more evident in
Canada as in England, than that there is struggle between Protestantism
and Puseyism, which is Popery in its minority, daily adding to its age
and strength: nothing is more evident than that the Episcopalian
Church in Canada is Puseyitic in its spirit, pretensions, and unceasing
enmity to all other Churches, more especially the Wesleyan Methodist
Church. . . . The proofs of what we now assert are to be found in the
Church paper, and in the designs, declarations, and doings of the
Ministers of the Episcopal Church throughout the country."[100]

The movement towards increased formalism and a more intolerant
attitude to the nonconformist religious groups lost to the Church the
sympathy of many of those who favoured a more evangelical type of
religious appeal. It is true, on the other hand that it probably resulted in
strengthening the attachments of many adherents through the development of an increasing consciousness of the distinctive principles of the
Church. Much of the weakness of the Church could be accounted for by
the fact that its adherents, unlike the adherents of the evangelical
denominations, were lacking strong convictions in support of their
attachments. Few Episcopalians, in spite of the claim of the Church to
apostolical succession, possessed the unshakable confidence in the
validity of the teachings of their Church which was characteristic
of the Methodists with respect to the teachings of Methodism. The

[98]Armstrong, *Life and Letters of the Rev. George Mortimer*, p. 234. Mortimer himself
was accused, possibly unfairly, of being a High Churchman. "Not long since," the
editor of the *Christian Guardian* wrote, May 12, 1841, "so we are told, Mr. Mortimer
became a lecturer somewhere within the bounds of his so-called parish, and made
remarks so tinctured with Puseyite sentiment that some of his best hearers were
offended by their stringency."
[99]Bigsby, *Pictures of Travel in the Canadas*, vol. I, p. 345.
[100]*Christian Guardian*, Dec. 14, 1842. See the *Church*, Nov. 1, 1844, for a typical
statement of the High Church position. See, also, *A View of the State of the Church
in the Canadas, in a Letter to the Society from the Bishop of Montreal* (London, 1836);
I.K., *The Church and the Wesleyans* (Cobourg, U.C., 1838); *Ten Letters on the Church
and Church Establishments*. By an Anglo-Canadian (Toronto, 1839).

Oxford movement, therefore, by emphasizing the distinctive principles of the Church, did result in a strengthening of the Church's denominational supports. Strachan wrote of the work of the Reverend Mark Burnham in St. Thomas, upon his visitation there in September, 1842:

> It is gratifying to state the very prosperous condition in which I found this parish, owing to the zealous and judicious exertions of its exemplary clergyman. The success attendant upon his labours, latterly so very marked and striking, he ascribes, under the Divine blessing, to a more clear and earnest development on his part of the distinctive principles of the Church, the bringing her claims more fully, plainly, and decidedly before his people, as the depository of Divine truth, and the channel of heavenly grace. While he performed his duty conscientiously, with all calmness and zeal, as a minister of Christ, but without bringing forward prominently the government, order, and peculiar excellences of the Church, the necessity of communion with her, by those who expect the privileges and blessings of the Redeemer's sacrifice; his people were decent and discreet in their Christian walk, but they seemed scarcely conscious of any difference between themselves and the sectaries around them. It was not till he pointed out distinctly and emphatically, the nature and privileges of the Church, her close resemblance to the apostolic pattern, the many important and decided differences between her and other "Protestant denominations," that his congregation began to feel that they were a distinct and privileged people.[101]

The increasing acceptance of the duties of the Church by its adherents did not mean, however, that it came to exert any powerful religious influence within the community. Such acceptance was more a matter of social obligation than a result of deep religious conviction. "At Wardsville," the Reverend E. Sallows, Wesleyan missionary, wrote in his journal, June 22, 1848, ". . . the Bishop of Toronto was attending a confirmation service. I was told that several young persons were confirmed, & the Bishop told them they had received the Holy Ghost. What blasphemy! Some of the persons were wicked indifferent characters."[102] The increase in the number of upper class overseas people who had strongly favoured in the homeland the highly ritualistic Anglican service furthered the tendency for the duties of the Church to become a matter of habit divorced from any strong feeling respecting religion. The sophisticated outlook of the upper class Englishman tended to a subsuming of rationalistic attitudes behind an outward display of conformity to pious teachings. Religious services were faithfully attended, and family obligations in religious worship were respected, but religious values were not permitted to interfere with rational systems of thought. Not all of the adherents of the Church had attained

---

[101]*A Journal of Visitation to the Western Portion of His Diocese by the Lord Bishop of Toronto in the Autumn of 1842* (London, 1846), pp. 34-5.

[102]University of Toronto, Victoria University Library, Journal of Rev. E. Sallows, 1848-1849.

such a degree of intellectual sophistication, but those members with the least conviction in religious matters tended to be the most influential in church councils. Efforts upon the part of the Church to maintain the support of the more sophisticated section of its following led to a failure to develop a type of religious appeal which would have extended its influence out among the more general rural population. This population, denied the advantages of education, the comforts of an old world society, or the opportunities for stimulating intellectual contacts characteristic of a mature cultural order, sought in religion for an interpretation of pressing social and emotional needs, or it rejected religion entirely in favour of more immediately satisfying social experiences. The Church of England had little to offer in meeting such needs. Its form of appeal assumed a richer cultural heritage than that possessed by the Canadian rural society.

The weaknesses of the Church of England's religious appeal were closely related to its position within the colonial class structure. To some extent the identification of the Church with social privilege was a consequence of its failure to capture the support of the backwoods farming population; to some extent, on the other hand it was responsible for such a failure. Modifications in the form of service, or recruitment of the clergy from the lower ranks of society, were resisted by those elements of the population which disliked the levelling influence of an evangelical religious appeal, and reluctance of the Church to lose the support of "respectable" social groups checked efforts to strengthen its position among other groups. The highly formal character of the sermon, the emphasis upon ritual in the service, and the practice of holding worship only in properly dedicated church buildings, assured to the Church its claim to respectability; that which was vulgar, such as sensationalism in the exhortations of the preacher or an emotional display in the public worship of the congregation, was discouraged. Seating arrangements within the church served to emphasize the recognition of class status. "They have raised a contribution," the Reverend G. O. Stuart reported from York in 1809, "for the erection of a gallery at the west end of the Church to accommodate the soldiers of the garrison near York, and for many of the poor inhabitants, as the pews have been purchased by persons of rank."[103] Much later, Buckingham, in contrasting religious service in the United States with a service of the Church of England in Toronto which he attended, was struck with the close identification of ecclesiastical arrangements with class divisions:

[103]Young, "The Reverend George Okill Stuart" (*Papers and Records*, Ontario Historical Society, vol. XXIV, 1927, p. 524).

In the United States, scarcely any distinction is seen, either in the size of the pews, their furniture and decoration, or in the apparel of the persons who occupy them; all the seats are equally large, and equally well fitted, and all the congregation are so well dressed, that it would be difficult to determine, by any external appearance, the relative rank, wealth, or condition, of any of the individuals or families present. Here, on the contrary, the distinction was very marked: some of the pews were large and elegantly furnished, others were small, without any furniture at all in them; some of the persons were elegantly dressed, others were in very homely, though always decent apparel.[104]

The emphasis within the Church upon class distinctions had the effect of strengthening its position among the upper classes of the colonial society. There were definite social advantages to belonging to the Church, a fact which its spokesmen were not slow to point out. "You may assure the people," a local catechist in the Township of Leeds, Lower Canada, was instructed in face of the threat of a visit from some Methodist preachers in 1838, "that in a short time the Bishop will send them a clergyman to live and labour among them, if they choose to receive him; and that a church or two will consequently be built, in a great measure, at the Bishop's expense, who has funds for that purpose; and point out to them the impossibility of having a clergyman of any other denomination unless they are able to support him; and how much it would increase the respectability of the settlement, and the value of property, to have a respectable clergyman resident among them."[105] Throughout the rural communities settled by people from overseas, and in the larger towns, the Church gained the support of persons of property, governmental officials and army officers. The "respectable" of the community tended to adhere to the church with an unquestioned claim to respectability. "There is an Episcopal Church," Proudfoot wrote of Forty Mile Creek, October 29, 1832, "which, here as in other places, contains the gentility."[106] "What might be deemed," Senator John Macdonald wrote of the Church in Toronto, in the early eighteen forties, "the aristocratic portion of the city attended the Cathedral. Several of the important of those days were of Imperial appointment, such, for example, as that of the Receiver-General, which office was filled by the Honourable John Henry Dunn, who with his family attended the Cathedral. There also were to be found the chief justice, the judges, with few exceptions, bankers, the members of the legal and medical professions, merchants, government officers; in fact, it was the fashionable congregation of the city."[107]

[104]J. S. Buckingham, *Canada, Nova Scotia, New Brunswick* (London, 1843), p. 17.
[105]Quoted in the *Christian Guardian*, Oct. 24, 1838.
[106]"Journal of the Rev. Wm. Proudfoot" (*Transactions*, London and Middlesex Historical Society, 1914, p. 51).
[107]Hon. Senator Macdonald. "Recollections of British Wesleyanism in Toronto" (*Methodist Magazine*, vol. XXIX, Jan. to June, 1889, Toronto and Halifax, p. 149).

The emphasis upon class distinctions within the Church led inevitably to the weakening of the support of those who had no pretensions to upper class status. The frontier destroyed status relationships, and emphasized values of individual worth and equality, and where the frontier influence was strong, as a result, the social foundations of the Church disintegrated. In becoming the church of the colonial upper class, the Church weakened its influence among the large rural population. "To give the preponderance to the Church of England establishment," Strickland wrote, "that church in Canada, which at present is only that of a rising aristocracy, must become also the church of the poor."[108] The failure of the Church to liberalize its social appeal resulted largely from its failure to adopt a more democratic principle in the selection of candidates for clerical orders.

Reared in an English upper class setting, sharp cultural differences set the Church of England clergy off from the backwoods farmers, particularly the backwoods farmers of American origin. Such a clergy could have little appreciation of the manner of life and peculiar problems of a pioneer farm population, and, as a result often locked with distaste upon forms of behaviour which were an inevitable feature of pioneer society. The rural population, on its part, had equally little appreciation of the manners and training of the Anglican clergy and often disliked that which was in the old world society an acceptable form of clerical behaviour. Thus differences in the cultural background of the clergy and population became exaggerated into issues of moral worth; the feeling of mutual distrust and antagonism, based upon a failure to understand each other, created a situation unfavourable to the acceptance of the ministrations of the Church. "It seems to me," J. J. Bigsby wrote, "that the Episcopal clergy are taken from too high a class for colonial service. They are usually so dissimilar from their flocks in tastes, habits, and prejudices, that they might come from another planet. Their early nurture has been too nice, and their education too academic, to admit of that familiarity, combined with true respect on the part of the people, which gives such well-earned influence to the Roman Catholic clergy in certain parts of Europe, and to the Wesleyan in Britain."[109] Not only in their social contacts, but in their work in the pulpit, the class prejudices of the Anglican clergymen handicapped them in winning the support of the rural population. "That missionary zeal can scarcely be," the Reverend James Beaven wrote in 1846, "whilst the clergy are only men educated as gentlemen; whilst their mental condition and ordinary habits keep them involuntarily from

---

[108]Strickland, *Twenty-Seven Years in Canada West,* vol. II, pp. 326-7.
[109]Bigsby, *Pictures of Travel in the Canadas,* vol. I. pp. 343-4.

familiar intercourse with the lower classes; whilst the gradations of clergy extend themselves to all the upper classes of society, but do not ramify through the lower."[110]

The identification of the Church with the colonial upper class inevitably became closely related to its identification with British imperial interests and, in the end, with the cause of ecclesiastical establishment. The Church remained English as well as upper class in outlook, and, while such a disposition strengthened its hold upon the population of overseas origin, it weakened its influence among those of American origin and among those coming increasingly to think of themselves as Canadian in attachment. Failure of the Episcopalian Church in the United States to take any lead in the work in Canada inevitably led to the dependence upon leadership from England and to the dependence upon clergymen of English origin, and such clergymen of an old world background could not win the sympathy of people with a new world, American background. In 1815 Strachan, aware of this weakness, had written respecting the advantages of training men for the Church within the colony itself. "If brought up and educated in this Province," he pointed out, "the Clergy will be more useful among the people, and more happy themselves; and care may be taken that they be equally Loyal, and attached to the Mother Country."[111] Twenty-one years later the same view was urged by the author of the anonymous pamphlet urging reform within the Church. "Without depreciating in the least," he wrote, "the valuable services of the clergy from England and Ireland, to whom the church owes much of its improvement, within the last ten years, I think that all will acknowledge, that young men, educated in the country, habituated to the manners and customs of the people, endeared to the fatigues and privations attendant upon a missionary's life in new countries, and accustomed to the climate, from which many strangers suffer severely, are, *caerteris paribus*, better suited for supplying our wants than those educated in Europe."[112] The problem of the Church was one, as the anonymous author went on to point out, of building up in the country institutions for the training of men for the ministry. Unlike the evangelical churches, the Church of England was unwilling to recruit men without such training and, indeed, without in addition a thorough scholastic education; the establishment of theological schools which would admit young men with scarcely any education and in six months or a year would equip them for the ministry was

[110]James Beaven, *Recreations of a Long Vacation: Or a Visit to Indian Missions in Upper Canada* (London and Toronto, 1846), p. 163.
[111]Spragge, *John Strachan Letter Book*, p. 74.
[112]*Thoughts on the Present State and Future Prospects of the Church of England in Canada. By a Presbyter of the Diocese of Quebec*, pp. 7-8.

something which the Church was never prepared to undertake. The result was that the Church only very slowly built up a Canadian ministry in the country.

The Church of England failed to become a Canadian church because its interests in maintaining the privileges of Establishment made it dependent upon the imperial tie. Any move to introduce a greater measure of autonomy within the Church carried the threat of weakening the relationship of the Church to the state. The Church could not become a Canadian church without becoming a "free" church. Vested interests of ecclesiastical Establishment, therefore, led inevitably to the identification of the Church with the tory cause in the colony. Imperial interests, on their part, sought within a system of Church Establishment to build up a body of sentiment within the colony favourable to the perpetuation' of the imperial relationship. The interests of state and the interests of church became closely allied in maintaining ecclesiastical pr'vileges and in discouraging the development of nonconformist religious denominations.

Regulations favouring the Church of England in the performance of such services as that of marriage and burial gradually were modified and eventually disappeared altogether[113] but not until they had given rise to deep feelings of bitterness which made themselves felt in the growing movement directed against Church Establishment. Privileges of the Church with respect to education even more came to arouse resentment from spokesmen of other religious bodies in the colony. Government grants and patronage assured the Church considerable influence in the supervision of education even where more direct means of control were not secured. "Things continued in this state," the Reverend William Bell, Presbyterian minister, wrote of a school he started in Perth in 1817 to which the government granted £50 a year to pay his salary, "till the end of 1819, when an episcopal clergyman came here to settle, who kindly agreed to take the school off my hands without my consent. Against this measure the inhabitants unanimously petitioned, but without effect." Bell was assured by the deputy quartermaster-general that his work was perfectly satisfactory but that "he thought it right that a clergyman of the Church of England ought to have a situation under government in preference to any one else."[114] The condition of affairs in Perth at this time, where a military form of local government was established, was somewhat peculiar, but the intervention here of official authority in support of the claims of the

---

[113]See William Canniff, *History of the Settlement of Upper Canada* (Toronto, 1869).
[114]Rev. Wm. Bell, *Hints to Emigrants, in a Series of Letters from Upper Canada* (Edinburgh, 1824), p. 125.

Church of England to control education reflected a general policy of the colonial administration. "The true foundation of the prosperity of our Establishment," Strachan admitted in writing in 1821, "must be laid in the Education of Youth the command and direction of which must as far as possible be concentrated in our Clergy. This has hitherto been the silent policy of all the measures taken for the Education of Youth adopted in this Province."[115]

The close alliance between church and state strengthened the position of the Church among the official and privileged classes within the colony, but it weakened its position among the great body of rural farmers. "Where a new Government is to be formed," Richard Cartwright had predicted as early as 1793, "as in the present case, among a people composed of every religious denomination, and nineteen-twentieths of whom are of persuasions different from the Church of England to attempt to give that Church the same exclusive political advantages that it possessed in Great Britain, and which are even there the cause of so much clamour, appears to me to be as impolitic as it is unjust."[116] However justified governmental and ecclesiastical authorities felt themselves to be in promoting Establishment as a means of strengthening imperial bonds, the general body of inhabitants were not prepared to accept the pretensions of the Church to superiority as a spiritual agency. Two centuries of frontier experience, particularly in the middle Atlantic colonies, had broken down the old world conception of the relationship of church and state, and, even in those areas such as New England where theocratic systems persisted, aggressive evangelical movements had forced a considerable degree of religious liberty. In the new western American frontier, the secularization of political and social life had become almost complete, and it was this area which produced the greater proportion of early Canadian settlers. Religion to the frontier farmer was something purely personal; it was something for which he felt he should not have to pay. Ecclesiastical taxation was disliked as strongly as other forms of taxation.

Thus efforts of the Church to maintain the privileges of Establishment led increasingly to the participation of its hierarchy and even of many of its clergy in colonial politics. "This attack," Strachan wrote the Bishop of Quebec in 1817, in seeking for himself an appointment to the Legislative Council, "on the Clergy sevenths and the failure of the bill for educating young men for holy orders twice successively in the Upper House point out the necessity for strengthening the establishment and the time is come when the Church ought to have in the Legislative

[115] Spragge, *John Strachan Letter Book*, p. 212.
[116] Cruickshank, *Simcoe Papers*, vol. II, p. 88.

Council several Friends judiciously alive to her Interests."[117] So long as the position of the Family Compact in the colony was secure, representation of the Church in the Legislative Council afforded a considerable measure of protection, but the growth of the Reform party after 1830 offered a threat to the influence of the narrow ruling class and forced the Church, as well as governmental officials, to participate actively in politics. Anglican clergymen, whether they liked it or not, found it necessary to become something of politicians. "Everybody wholly occupied with the approaching elections," Proudfoot entered in his diary, June 23, 1836, "party spirit runs high. Parson Cronyn has been all over the township electioneering—bah!"[118]

Participation of the Church in politics led directly to the weakening of its influence among those sections of the population identified with the reform cause. Indirectly, but even more significantly, such participation weakened the Church as a spiritual agency. The Church assumed increasingly the role of a secular institution; its functionaries became men of affairs, concerned with questions of state policy and with problems of secondary religious importance such as education. Some of the clergy themselves realized that their concern with matters relating to politics interfered with their work as teachers of religion. "I cannot express to you," Archdeacon G. J. Mountain wrote his father, the Bishop of Quebec, from England where he had been sent in the interests of the Church, 1825, "how much I should desire to have done for ever with public men and public offices, and to hold some charge in God's church which might leave me independent of the favour or frowns of political power, and unconnected with any engines of government."[119] The vested interests of the state church led inevitably to the intrusion of political questions into ecclesiastical councils. This secularization of the Church's outlook would have constituted no great weakness in a community where the population had been largely emancipated from religious values; the Church in such a situation would have been looked upon simply as a social institution engaged in "good works." In the Canadian backwoods settlements, however, there was no such sophisticated view of the functions of ecclesiastical Establishment; the strength of the evangelical sects was indicative of the strong interest in purely religious values. The political activities of the Church of England, and the worldly attitude of its clergy, as a result, sharpened its divorce from the great mass of the population.

The weakness of the Church of England in Canada was a weakness

[117]Spragge, *John Strachan Letter Book,* p. 131.
[118]"Proudfoot Papers" (*Papers and Records,* Ontario Historical Society, vol. XXX, 1934, p. 134).
[119]Mountain, *Memoir of G. J. Mountain,* p. 85.

which derived from its position as an outside religious body which lacked any basis of support in the mores and sentiments of the Canadian frontier population. Settlement on the frontier emphasized the unimportance of political boundaries and of symbols of political sovereignty; even the Loyalists who moved to Canada were more attracted by the opportunity to secure cheap land than by the opportunity to enjoy the privilege of British citizenship. The Church of England depended almost wholly for its influence upon the fact that it was the church of empire. Where vested interests secured imperial attachments the attachments to the Church persisted, but where such interests did not exist the Church possessed no means of making its influence felt. In the final analysis, it failed to capture the support of the unattached masses of the Canadian backwoods settlements because it was a church. Dependent upon the support of people with social status, it could make no effective appeal to those people without social status.

The Scottish Presbyterian churches were little more able than the Church of England to provide effective religious leadership in the Canadian backwoods settlements. Before 1812 the number of Presbyterians in the country was not sufficiently great to give rise to any serious problem in the way of supplying Presbyterian religious services but after 1815 the growing immigration of Scots and northern Irish led to a considerable increase in the Presbyterian population, and limitations in the organization of the Church became evident. The recruitment of ministers lagged far behind the growth of population, and many areas of Presbyterian settlement were left without any provision for religious services. "We have often most deeply lamented," an address of a committee appointed by the United Presbytery of Upper Canada in 1830 read, "the wide spread desolations that here present themselves to view in the Church of God, and we have felt our own insufficiency, from want of funds and of Ministers, to occupy vast fields of Missionary labour in this country. We have hitherto been unable from our own resources, to supply the increasing and destitute settlements in the Province, with the administration of the ordinances of religion."[120] The Reverend Andrew Bell was appointed by the United Presbytery to make a missionary tour through the western parts of Upper Canada in order to ascertain the needs of the Presbyterian inhabitants. "In the Western District," he wrote to the editor of the *Christian Guardian*, November 27, 1830, "there are but very few Presbyterians, and indeed there is not a very great number of inhabitants

---

[120]*Minutes of the Synod of the Presbyterian Church in Canada in Connection with the Church of Scotland; Together with the Acts and Proceedings of the Synod, 1830-1865.* 28 pamphlets in one vol. *Meeting of Presbytery, 1830, p. 6.*

altogether; but, in the Gore, London and Niagara Districts, the Presbyterians are considerably numerous, and in several places, there are
large congregations, anxious to obtain ministers, and both able and
willing to give them a moderate support."[121] About two years later,
the Reverend William Proudfoot wrote of the state of the United
Synod:

> The Synod has congregations at wide intervals from Cornwall, fifty miles below
> Prescott, to London, in the Western Territory; and from York to Lake Simcoe.
> The number of ministers is fifteen, but some of these have as many as six congregations
> under their charge. Indeed, I know of only two or three ministers who preach statedly
> on Sabbath in one place. Many of these congregations, which were nice missionary
> stations, and perhaps are so still, have so grown in numbers and worldly circumstances
> as to be able to support each a minister at a moderate stipend. But the Synod has
> not ministers to send to them; and consequently there is reason to fear that some of
> these congregations will go over to those churches that can afford them a regular
> ministry, if the Synod receive not help from the United Associate Synod, or from
> Ireland, whence they have hitherto drawn their chief supply of preachers. Within
> the bounds of the Synod there are very many townships where small congregations
> might be collected, which the ministers have never visited, and which they cannot
> visit . . . .
> That part of the country that is without the limi's of the United Synod is very
> extensive, and very destitute of preaching. There are places in which the people
> have not heard a sermon for a year.[122]

Lack of a missionary spirit within the Presbyterian churches to some
extent accounted for the failure to extend the area of religious services.
The Scottish clergy, in particular, were reluctant to leave their homeland
for work in a distant colony; the system of promotions within the
Church favoured the acceptance of a call from a congregation in Scotland
itself even though immediately it offered little in the way of material
reward. "In the meantime," Proudfoot wrote in his diary, February
26, 1835, "our great want is the want of preachers—without these we
can neither extend the church nor even keep the ground which we
have occupied, and where preachers are to be got we cannot tell for
those at home are too timid or too selfish to come hither. At least it
appears so."[123] At the same time, conditions of work within the Canadian
colony discouraged the immigration of Presbyterian ministers. The
system of ministerial appointments, by which the minister's location
depended upon a congregational call, though gradually modified as
the missionary organization of Presbyterianism was strengthened,
served to make difficult the recruitment of ministers from abroad.

[121]*Christian Guardian,* Dec. 18, 1830.
[122]"Journal of the Rev. Wm. Proudfoot" (*Transactions,* London and Middlesex
Historical Society, 1914, pp. 70-2).
[123]"Proudfoot Papers" (*Papers and Records,* Ontario Historical Society, vol.
XXVIII, 1932, p. 102).

Ministers were reluctant to face the trials of seeking out a suitable location in a distant land and the uncertainty of steady employment after having become established. Furthermore, the lack of adequate financial support of missionary work left the ministers dependent to a considerable degree upon the casual contributions of local congregations. "From him, I learned," Proudfoot remarked of a conversation he had with a minister in Brantford, "that the Canadians are not willing to pay anything to their minister at all like a competence, and that if they are spoken to on the subject they will run off to other denominations and pronounce the man who asks what may make him live, a selfish, greedy, money-loving man—altogether unlike the Apostles who wrought with their hands that they might make the gospel free of charge. Such is the prospect for ministers in Canada."[124] With respect to his own situation in London, Proudfoot had much to say regarding the problem of financial contributions. "I must have a poor account to give to the Synod," he wrote, November 6, 1833, of a meeting called in Westminster to raise a stipend for him. "Most of the people in this quarter belonged to that beggarly thing, the establishment, and have no notion of making any effort and do not know even that it is their duty."[125]

Strengthening of missionary organizations in Scotland did something to encourage the volunteering of ministers for colonial service and to provide means of financial support for the work. The organization in 1830 of the Glasgow Colonial Society led to more vigorous efforts upon the part of the Church of Scotland to extend its influence in Canada, while the missionary activities of the United Associate Synod strengthened greatly the position of the Secessionist Church. At the same time, the work of the Presbyterian Church of the United States and of the Associate Synod in the United States was extended in Canada; organization of the presbyteries of Niagara and Stamford reflected the growing influence of American Presbyterianism in the country.

The problem, however, in the case of the Presbyterian Church as of the Church of England, was only in part one of supplying a greater number of ministers to serve the country. The isolation of the backwoods settlements made difficult the bringing together in any one place of sufficient Presbyterian adherents to organize a congregation. "The population," Proudfoot wrote, September 19, 1832, "is scattered in a struggling kind of way along the road sides, and it must require a

[124]"Journal of the Rev. Wm. Proudfoot" (*Transactions*, London and Middlesex Historical Society, 1914, pp. 53-4).
[125]"Proudfoot Papers" (*Papers and Records*, Ontario Historical Society, vol. XXVII, 1931, p. 447).

long journey for many of them to meet together in such numbers as
to form a church able to support half sermons. There seems, as far as
I have travelled, to be fully as many preachers as the people are able to
support. Ministers must either be supported from other sources or
they must undergo a very great deal of fatigue in preaching to different
little churches to raise as much as will support them."[126] Because of
his family responsibilities, Proudfoot felt at times that he was not
the sort of person who should have come out; conditions within the
Canadian society made it desirable to have preachers willing to endure
the hardships of constant travel in the backwoods. Presbyterianism
did not succeed in developing the itinerant system in its missionary
work in Canada. The strength of the congregational principle in church
government, if nothing else, limited the extent to which itinerant
practices could be put into operation. Occasionally, individual preachers
undertook missionary tours throughout the country—Proudfoot made
a number of such tours before settling down in London—but no body
of travelling missionaries was built up by the Church. Matthew Miller,
who preached throughout the Home, Newcastle, Midland, and Bathurst
districts in 1832 as a missionary of the Glasgow Colonial Society urged
the greater adoption of the practice of appointing travelling missionaries
for work in Canada. "I would now take the liberty," he wrote to the
Society in November, 1832, "of impressing upon you again the importance of sending out travelling missionaries in preference to ministers
appointed to particular places. This would be much more satisfactory
to the people, and I am persuaded, to the missionaries themselves."[127]

The strength of the principle of congregational autonomy within
Scottish Presbyterianism, while it weakened the missionary organization
of the Church, did provide a support of denominational loyalty which
was conspicuously lacking in the Church of England. Where two or
three Presbyterian families were settled together, attachments tended
to be maintained even if services of the Church were not available.
Furthermore, the group solidarity of Presbyterians which derived
partly from the strength of congregational loyalties tended to lead
to their segregation in new areas of settlement, and such segregation in
turn made less difficult the maintenance of group solidarity. This was
particularly true of the Scots among whom clan loyalties combined
with denominational loyalties to favour their settlement as isolated
groups in the community. Where such isolation was secured, the
congregational machinery of Presbyterianism was transferred almost

---

[126]"Journal of the Rev. Wm. Proudfoot" (*Transactions*, London and Middlesex
Historical Society, 1914, p. 37).
[127]Gregg, *History of the Presbyterian Church in Canada*, p. 463.

intact to the new community. The Presbyterian system depended upon the maintenance of the conditions of the "closed frontier," and the fact that the chief support of the Church in Canada came from the Scots who had in effect avoided the open frontier upon settlement accounted for much of the strength of Presbyterianism in spite of its form of organization.

Where the "open frontier" emerged, however, Scottish Presbyterianism lacked the means of maintaining the form of church government. The Presbyterian cause was weakened where settlement took place of individual families and there was little segregation of people of similar religious faith. The population outside the limited area in which the traditional Presbyterian organization operated was almost wholly dependent upon the services of other religious denominations. Backwoods settlement implied a steady expansion of the area of community life, and, while Presbyterianism had developed highly effective techniques to secure the consolidation of its position, it lacked means of expansion. By failing to extend its ministrations to people of other religious faiths, it failed to maintain the support of its own adherents on the outer margins of the rural society.

If this was evident in the organization of Presbyterianism, it was also evident in its religious appeal. Scottish Presbyerianism set itself solidly against the use of revivalist methods in gaining recruits for the Church. Reliance was placed entirely upon the ordinary means of religious propagation. "There has been no movement in any of our Churches," the York Presbytery reported to the United Synod of Upper Canada in 1833, "of a very extraordinary or marked character. But there has been a steady increase in all of them. . . . We have never sanctioned the use of any means of a suspicious or doubtful character for the purpose of producing excitement in our flocks; but, in the faithful discharge of duty, in the use of the means of grace evidently of Divine appointment, we have looked for the Divine blessing which can alone make rich."[128] The missionaries of the United Associate Synod, though less conservative, joined with the representatives of the Church of Scotland in resisting revivalist influences. The methods employed by the American Presbyterian preachers attached to the Niagara Presbytery aroused strong criticism from Proudfoot. "Read today," he wrote, December 11, 1832, "in the *Presbyterian* many complaints of the mischief done by revival men. . . . I shall endeavour to collect all the information I can get on the subject, and endeavor to let my countrymen know it,

---

[128]*Minutes of the Synod of the Presbyterian Church in Canada.* 28 pamphlets in one vol. *Extracts from the Minutes of the United Synod of Upper Canada at their Meeting in Prescott, Tuesday 4th June, 1833* (York, 1833), p. 6.

that they may be disabused of this infection."[129] On another occasion, after pointing out that the American Presbyterians had adopted revivalist methods in order to keep ahead of the Methodists, Proudfoot wrote: "This may be an unjust supposition, but it is well supported by what I have heard in the way in which revivals are conducted, and does tend in no small degree to confirm my dislike of this newfangled manner of making Christians. I have seen so many evidences of the carnal policy of men in them that the farther I carry my enquiries I feel the stronger dislike."[130]

Where the American ties of Presbyterianism were strong revivalism made its influence felt upon its teachings. The American Presbyterian Church was the most evangelical of the various branches of Presbyterianism, but evangelistic tendencies were also evident in some of the other Presbyterian churches. A secession of Americans from the St. Gabriel Street church in Montreal resulted in the organization of a separate congregation with the support of Congregationalists, and, under the preaching of a Reverend Mr. Christmas, revivals of religion occasionally occurred among members of the new church.[131] In other areas, close to the United States, revivalist influences were also evident in Presbyterian preaching. The Reverend Mr. Smart, the Presbyterian minister in Brockville, gave to the *Christian Guardian* an account of a four-day protracted meeting held in the winter of 1831 in the Presbyterian church in Brockville,[132] while further west, American Presbyterians and Congregationalists again joined forces in promoting the establishment of a number of churches, some of which tended towards an evangelical appeal. "Called at John Wilkes," Proudfoot wrote, January 30, 1834, while at Brantford, "where I was informed there had been a Protracted Meeting at Brantford which lasted, I think, 11 days, the result of which was that there has been formed a church of 50 members. The church is to be Independent but is to be called Presbyterian. This is a stroke of Wilke's who is a Congregationalist and has tacked to the name in order to catch the Presbyterians. In this there is more policy than piety."[133]

Scottish Presbyterianism, however, remained completely uninfluenced by American revivalist practices. Where a number of Americans were settled splits tended to occur between them and the Scottish Presby-

[129]"Proudfoot Papers" (*Transactions*, London and Middlesex Historical Society, 1922, p. 10).
[130]*Ibid.*, p. 29.
[131]Rev. John Wood, *Memoir of Henry Wilkes* (Montreal and London, 1887), p. 40.
[132]*Christian Guardian*, Jan. 11, 1832.
[133]"Proudfoot Papers" (*Papers and Records*, Ontario Historical Society, vol. XXVII, 1931, p. 461).

terians. Fraser, in the course of a missionary tour, had occasion to
refer to the divisive effects in Puslinch of the work of the Anti-burgher
or Associate Synod of the United States,[134] and Proudfoot in various
places came into contact with its competitive influence. "Received
from him," he wrote of a conversation he had with the Reverend Andrew
Bell in York, December 10, 1832 "an account of the violent manner
in which the Anti-burghers from the States act when they come over to
Canada. From his statements it would appear that their conduct is
anything but handsome."[135] Of the Anti-burgher element in Galt,
he wrote, January 30, 1833; "A nest of as violent Antiburghers as ever
existed in any part of Scotland."[136] In his own district of London,
Proudfoot did not escape the influence of the rival secessionist party.
"During the time I was at the English settlement," he wrote, June 2,
1833 "there was much talk about the Antiburgher cession, i.e., the
cession of 4 or 6 families to the Antiburghers—all of those who spoke
of it regretted it—for the sake of the interests of religion, for the sake of
their social intercourse, but none expected them to return and none
seemed to desire it, as the Antiburgher party have since their separation
acquired a very disputatious turn—a self-conceitedness—an anti-social
tendency. This is always the effect of religious division."[137]

The failure of the Scottish Presbyterian churches to capitalize upon
revivalist religious sentiment in the Canadian backwoods communities
was offset to some extent by the preaching power of their ministers.
Presbyterianism had developed a high standard of oratory in the pulpit,
and among the Secessionist ministers in particular such standards were
fairly successfully maintained. Proudfoot, for instance, revealed his
awareness of the importance of making his sermons attractive to the
sort of people he served. "To keep myself from wearying," he wrote
on one occasion, "I have employed myself in working a new service
to-day. It has occurred to me that there is a simplicity in teaching
here required more than at home, and I wish to give my sermons less
of a literary and more of a plain cast in the hope that they may be
more useful, for I do wish to be useful."[138] Evidence of at least a willingness to listen to Proudfoot was suggested by the remark in his diary,
June 1, 1834, "I did not give an evening sermon,—lest I should weary

[134]"Diary of the Rev. Wm. Fraser" (*Transactions*, London and Middlesex Historical
Society, 1930, p. 137).
[135]"Proudfoot Papers" (*ibid.*, 1922, p. 9).
[136]*Ibid.*, p. 52.
[137]"Proudfoot Papers" (*Papers and Records*, Ontario Historical Society, vol.
XXVI, 1930, p. 551).
[138]"Proudfoot Papers" (*Transactions*, London and Middlesex Historical Society,
1922, p. 11).

the people, I had already spoken for six hours," [139] although his complaint on an earlier occasion—"Still some Methodistical practices, such as persons rising up in the time of the sermon and going out"[140]—might be taken to indicate that some of his congregation were at times wearied of listening to him. The ministers of the Church of Scotland, more like those of the Church of England, were often lacking in the qualities required for service in the Canadian rural society.

> One great evil which is observable, [J. B. Brown wrote in 1844] in all the churches of Canada, and mostly, I feel in truth constrained to observe, in the Church of Scotland as it existed—has been that men of indifferent abilities have usually fallen to the lot of the colonists. This is, without question, the effect of the natural principle (from the influence of which not even ministers of the Gospel are exempted), that the lower the rate of worldly encouragement the more indifferent the description of ability presents itself in the field which calls for occupation . . . . The consequence has been that, where it was of material importance the labourers should be powerful and skilful, the field has been all too much occupied in a manner most unfortunately calculated to aggravate the evils.[141]

Realization that some of the ministers in the country were not wholly satisfactory, led the Reverend Matthew Miller to urge upon the Glasgow Colonial Society in 1832 more careful methods of selection: "Great as the want of preachers is, they had better not come at all than come with low qualifications; unless their preaching be acceptable they cannot possibly obtain congregations. This is eminently a country for mind to display itself; in all departments there is free scope for talent and exertions, and according to these will be each man's success. This is as strikingly true in the department of the Gospel ministry as any other: a man must be qualified for the office in order to succeed at all; and according to the measure of his qualifications will be that of his success. It may be added that reading sermons is peculiarly unpopular here."[142]

The effect of the failure of Presbyterianism to develop a more evangelical religious appeal was evident in the decline, to some extent, of religious interests among its adherents and in the limitations of its influence outside the closed Presbyterian group. Complaints of the Presbyterian ministers of a lack of any strong religious interest among the people they served were seldom qualified by references to an expression of strong religious feelings. The remarks of the Reverend John

[139]"Proudfoot Papers" (*Papers and Records*, Ontario Historical Society, vol. XXVII, 1931, p. 481).
[140]*Ibid.*, vol. XXVI, 1930, p. 565.
[141]*Views of Canada and the Colonists, by a Four Years' Resident* (Edinburgh, 1844), p. 244.
[142]Gregg, *History of the Presbyterian Church in Canada*, p. 464.

Machar, the minister of the Church of Scotland in Kingston, in his correspondence home, were for the most part typical. "Alas," he wrote in 1831, "there is much practical indifference at present; few seem to have ears to hear what the Spirit saith unto the Churches!"[143] Four years later he wrote: "Here we grow in number, and in some cases also, I trust, in faith and love of the Saviour, but the barrenness that prevails around us is very great. The church does not seem in these days to be reviving anywhere."[144] Proudfoot, in his diary, in a very large number of entries, deplored the religious indifference of the Scottish Presbyterian population. "Went to the Scotch Kirk this forenoon," he wrote of his visit to York in December, 1832, "and heard Mr. Rentoul preach. . . . I could not help noticing that the behaviour of his congregation was quite Scotch. There was the same apparent listlessness, the same seeming idle, unthinking appearance, the same gazing about during prayer and the same want of interest in the Psalmody."[145] To some extent, the lack of expression of any strong religious feeling upon the part of Presbyterians in Canada was a general characteristic of Scottish Presbyterianism; Presbyterianism in Scotland had grown not so much through the agency of religious revival as through the exercise of a strict religious discipline, and, in Canada, as a consequence, the indifference of the Scottish settlers to outward religious forms was not wholly indicative of a lack of religious interest. Discipline in the Church weakened, however, with the increasing tendency towards formalism, and the religious attachments of adherents were often founded more upon prejudice than upon any lively sense of spiritual values. This was perhaps more true of the Church of Scotland than of the Secessionist Church, but even within Secessionism the emphasis was largely upon the peculiar religious ethos of the Presbyterian population. Thus Presbyterianism maintained the support of its strict adherents but developed little capacity to provide leadership to those elements of the population lacking the strong denominational ties which preserved a sense of group identity.

Limitations of Scottish Presbyterianism in the Canadian situation of a more general character were also evident. The close identification of the Church with the Scottish ethnic group in itself weakened its influence as a religious agency. The Scots tended to think of themselves—and

[143]*Memorials of the Life and Ministry of the Rev. John Machar, Late Minister of St. Andrew's Church, Kingston, edited by members of his family* (Toronto, 1873), p. 46.
[144]*Ibid.*, p. 58.
[145]"Proudfoot Papers" (*Transactions*, London and Middlesex Historical Society, 1922, pp. 19-20).

of the Church—as a closed social group, and little tolerance was displayed towards members of other national groups. "Matters," Proudfoot wrote of the state of the Church in the London District, October 26, 1833, "do not wear so promising an appearance in the Proof Line as they did a while ago. The cause is that the Scotch and Irish do not like one another. The Irish would be the most active and the Scotch, who will do nothing, are jealous of them."[146] Class differences also tended to intrude themselves into the Scottish Presbyterian following and to weaken the religious influence of the Church. This was particularly true of the Church of Scotland.[147] It was the church of the substantial—if not aristocratic—classes of the community, and this identification with the upper classes, as in the case of the Church of England, weakened its influence among the backwoods farming population. Senator John Macdonald wrote of the Church in Toronto:

The congregation of St. Andrew's Church might be said to be made up of well-to-do people, men of push, energy and substance, who had made their influence felt in giving direction to many of the enterprises of the young city. There Judge McLean, with his fine, manly bearing, could be seen with his handsome family. Nearly the whole of the prominent business men of the day were to be seen at St. Andrew's: Isaac Buchanan; Mr. Ross, of Ross & McLeod, afterwards Ross, Mitchell, Leslie & McGlashan; John Robertson, Isaac Gilmour, and others, who were the leaders in the wholesale dry goods of that day. And then as to the retail dry goods trade, all the great houses of the day were there represented: Walter McFarlane, of the Victoria House; Bryce & McMurrich, Shaw & Turnbull. Of bankers, there were John Cameron, Peter Patterson, of the Commercial Bank; Mr. Wilson of the Bank of Montreal, Dr. Telfer and Dr. Primrose. Leading physicians; old Mr. Campbell, of the North American, the Carfreys, the Arthurs; with the leading builders and mechanics of the city—a good gathering of that substantial element which goes to make up all that is implied in a prosperous and well-ordered city. The leading grocers of the city were there also. The Sutherlands, Duncan McDonnell, the McKays, Badenach; Ogilvie and Mackie, McIntosh, Cameron, John Thompson, Joseph Rogers, the hatter; the Holts; Hugh Scobie, the editor of the *British Colonist*, and John Balfour. Of lawyers, R. P. Crooks, Angus Morrison, and Joseph (afterwards Hon. Judge) Morrison; John Bell, Oliver Mowat, now Honourable Attorney-General; also Captain Dick, Robert Hay, John Sproule. There, too, could be seen occasionally the McNabb, dressed in the tartan of his clan; there, too, was John Ross, the undertaker. . . ; Colonel E. Thomson, Professor Murray, with old Mr. McLean as the minister's man, with many others who have faded from my memory, consti-

---

[146]"Proudfoot Papers" (*Papers and Records*, Ontario Historical Society, vol. XXVII, 1931, p. 445).

[147]On the whole, the Secessionist Church seems to have been the church of the poor Scottish and Irish Presbyterian farmers. "I am satisfied," Proudfoot complained in 1844, "that our church and Mission have suffered much from the want of an ordinary acquaintance with the manners of good society. The want of those accomplishments which are common amongst the polite class has confined our influence wholly to the lower classes, which have the least influence and are the most difficult to manage." *Ibid.*, vol. XXXII, 1937, p. 99.

tuting a congregation not surpassed in the city for a combination of intelligence, substance, energy and worth.[148]

The close identification of the Church of Scotland with the upper classes in the Canadian colonial society, again like the Church of England, was closely related to its support of the principle of Church Establishment. Reliance upon the tie with the state weakened the Church in Scotland and weakened it in Canada as well. The Secessionist Church, on the other hand, was uncompromisingly liberal in outlook, and ministers like William Proudfoot in London took a lead not only in opposing any sort of alliance between church and state but in opposing anything in the way of political privilege; even when the reform cause was popularly discredited with the abortive rebellion of 1837 Proudfoot remained·faithful (unlike some of the leading Methodist preachers) to the cause. The liberalism of the Secessionist Church won for it many friends, but was not in the end of decisive importance in extending its influence among the backwoods population. The backwoods community did not provide a fertile field for the dissemination of the principles of liberalism; the liberal movement developed only with the increasing commercialization of agricultural enterprise. The reaction of the backwoodsman to state religion tended to find expression in evangelical religion; a religion without a social or political philosophy. Scottish Presbyterianism, particularly as represented within the Secessionist Church, made ultimate contributions of vast importance to the development of social thought in Canada, but immediately, within the backwoods society, social reorganization tended to proceed on a lower level and was secured more successfully through the leadership of the evangelical churches.

The various other churches or religious groups which had developed a traditional outlook by the time they established themselves in Canada displayed weaknesses very similar to those displayed by the Church of England or the Scottish Presbyterian churches. Very early, Lutheran preachers made an appearance in the country, and Lutheranism continued to command the support of large elements of the German population but it exerted little influence outside this ethnic group. Congregationalism, lacking an effective missionary organization, developed only in isolated parts of the country, and the shift of many Congregationalists to the support of Presbyterianism was indicative of its failure to establish any strong cause. Congregationalism had lost most of its evangelical force while it still retained many of the attributes

---

[148]Macdonald, "Recollections of British Wesleyanism in Toronto" (*Methodist Magazine*, vol. XXIX, Jan. to June, 1889, pp. 149-50).

of the religious sect, and it lacked, therefore, both the strength of the evangelical movement in pushing into new areas of religious influence and the strength of the religious denomination in consolidating its position among its own adherents. In many respects, the same weaknesses were evident within the Society of Friends.

Quaker settlement took place in Canada very soon after the American revolutionary war, and by 1812 sizable Quaker communities were to be found about the eastern end of Lake Ontario, in the Niagara District, on the north shore of Lake Erie, and north on Yonge Street.[149] Direction in the location of settlement, and sectarian and family ties, resulted immediately in the considerable segregation of the Quaker population. Continuity with the past was thereby maintained, and little difficulty was faced in instituting religious services in the new homeland. Reliance upon lay preachers simplified the problem of setting in motion the machinery of the sect, and the work of the specially appointed itinerant preachers—a few of whom early visited the Quakers in Canada— reawakened an interest in religious values and strengthened the sense of group solidarity. The rigorous but autonomously administered discipline of the Quaker societies maintained a high standard of moral conduct; religious beliefs were deeply imbedded in the culture of the sect, and group identity as a result found support in cultural as well as religious values.

So long as segregation was possible, frontier settlement in Canada offered little threat to such group identity. The pioneer stage of development favoured the directed settlement of ethnic and sectarian groups. After 1812, however, the rapid growth of population, and the emergence of the backwoods community, tended to make the isolation of such groups increasingly difficult, and this was particularly true of the Quakers. New settlers invaded the area in which Quakers were settled, while, on the other hand, many Quaker families moved into the backwoods where they became cut off from the larger group. Schisms within the sect, and defections to Methodism, were the result of the failure to adjust to such conditions of population mobility. Like all pietist sects, the Quakers had failed to develop effective means of proselytization, and failure to extend the services of the Society beyond the body of adherents involved inevitably a weakening of its influence in face of the inroads of more aggressive religious groups. The pietist sect as a form of religious fellowship was essentially adapted to the conditions of the pioneer community; it thrived so long as isolation rather than

[149]See A. G. Dorland, *A History of the Society of Friends (Quakers) in Canada* (Toronto, 1927).

growth was the dominant characteristic of the society. With the passing of the pioneer phase of development, however, the sect tended to disintegrate if it failed to build up denominational supports. That was what happened to the Quaker cause in Canada. Without a strong central body, it had no means of professionalizing its ministry or of developing, even, a ministry which was itinerant in character. At the same time, its pietistic tradition checked the development of a vigorous evangelical appeal. Lacking effective means of recruiting new members, Quakerism became more and more dependent upon passing down its teachings from generation to generation. It became increasingly an ethical—and educational—society, commanding the respect of the more enlightened sections of the population, but at the price of exerting any powerful religious influence within the society of the backwoods.

The other pietist religious sects in the country—the Moravians and Mennonites—faced much the same sort of problems as the Quakers with the increasing mobility of the population following upon more rapid frontier development.[150] Schisms within the Mennonite sect, and the emergence of a more evangelistic Mennonite movement, were indicative of internal strains in face of this situation. In contrast with the Quakers, however, the isolation of the Moravians and Mennonites was supported by ethnic as well as sectarian differences. Language was employed as an effective means of maintaining segregation from the outside world. Thus the process of sectarian disintegration operated much more slowly. Efforts of the evangelical churches to break into the following of these sects were almost completely unsuccessful. Secular influences, in the end, rather than evangelical religious influences, were to lead to a weakening of their close group controls.

The stability of some of the smaller sects, and of the Roman Catholic Church, in face of movements of population resulting from frontier, backwoods settlement in Canada suggests that, given certain conditions, religious organization was able to adapt itself to changing social demands without such disruption as that evident in the rise of new religious movements. The reason for this lay largely in the fact that any expansion of community life involved the·emergence of what might be called the "closed frontier" side by side with the "open frontier." Individuals, as individuals, pushed into new areas of social life; their movements were dictated solely by personal interests, such as the desire to secure cheap land, to move as far as possible beyond the reach of the law, or simply to enjoy freedom from all social restraints. Where such development

---

[150]See L. J. Burkholder, *A Brief History of the Mennonites in Ontario* (Toronto, 1935).

took place, the problem of religious organization—as of social organization generally—was that of meeting, without much possibility of controlling, the kinds of demands for social fellowship which emerged. Where, however, it was not individuals but groups which moved into new areas of social life, the problem of social control was very different. Group settlement implied direction from the beginning, and, where such direction could be maintained, demands for social fellowship were canalized within existing systems of social organization. It was the weakness of the Society of Friends, that the control which had characterized early Quaker settlement in the country could not be maintained in face of the emergence of open frontier conditions. Among the Mennonites, on the other hand, ethnic differences supported the social isolation secured through the controls of the sect. In somewhat similar fashion, ethnic and doctrinal differences supported the isolation of the Roman Catholic population secured through the elaborate denominational controls of the Church. In sharp contrast to the Church of England which exercised little control over the movements of the Protestant population, the migration of Roman Catholics tended to be a migration into a closed frontier area; the Church moved with its following, and to some degree directed the whole process of population movement. Religious—and social—stability was maintained by maintaining the conditions of the inherited religious and social system.

It was in the open frontier that the most complete breakdown of the traditional organization of religion occurred. Conditions of backwoods settlement in Canada led generally to a very considerable emphasis upon individual enterprise in economic and social life. Religious interests weakened with the weakening of social interests generally. The frontier society represented a break away from traditional systems of thought and traditional means of control. Folk ties disintegrated in face of the unsettling effects of frontier life, and class ties broke down in face of powerful levelling forces in the frontier community. Folk and class gave way to the social masses.

Such tendencies made inevitable a weakening of the basis of religious organization, but they made almost equally inevitable the emergence of new religious forms within the frontier society. The break from a traditional religious order was accompanied by a break from a traditional social order in general. Individualization weakened a sense of collective life and made difficult the building up of new forms of social organization. In Canada, as in the Maritime Provinces, secular interests were not sufficiently strong to support a vigorous group consciousness, and support of such a consciousness

had to come in the end from religious interests deeply imbedded in the culture of the new frontier population.

The strength of religious interests among the population accounted for the strength of new religious movements. The traditional churches weakened not because they lacked the support of strong religious interests but because they failed to capitalize upon such support. Too strong religious interests endangered the denominational ties of the Church, and, as a result, it tended to discourage any strong manifestation of religious feelings. The evangelistic religious movement, on the other hand, grew directly out of the expression of such religious feelings. Its forms of organization and appeal were determined by the needs of the population it served. Its strength lay in the close identification with a frontier people which had no strong social ties and group attachments. The strengths of the evangelistic religious movement were particularly evident in the case of Methodism.

The rapid growth of Methodist influence was owing to the success with which it met the peculiar needs of the Canadian frontier society. Its growth was in terms of the support of those people who stood on the margin of the Canadian community, geographically and socially— the backwoods farmers. The American—and overseas—heritage of the Methodist movement was essentially a frontier heritage. The movement had developed in both countries out of a social situation resulting from the migration of population. It had grown up to meet the needs of marginal social groups within the community. However different the particular circumstances may have been, the problem of religious organization presented by frontier settlement in Canada was fundamentally the same problem of religious organization out of which had grown the Methodist movements in England and the United States.

That problem, in the first place, was one of providing a population cut off from the traditional social organization of the community with the services of religion. With their American and British experience, the Methodists were familiar with the sort of techniques required in extending the teachings of religion to people who were beyond the reach of the ordinary means of carrying on religious services. The success with which the movement recruited preachers for the work in the rapidly growing Canadian settlements was in itself an important factor in the extension of its influence. The system of apprenticeship by which young men with a desire to preach the gospel started out as local exhorters or as class leaders and went on to assume more responsible tasks provided an easy means of recruiting—and training—a body of Methodist preachers. Qualifications were such as to encourage the enlistment of

large numbers of zealous persons who seized upon a career of preaching when more inviting careers were lacking in a pioneer society or required greater training than that which such persons possessed.

Few of the early Methodist preachers in Canada could boast of an extensive education and many of them had received no formal education whatsoever. What little Carroll, the Methodist biographer, had to say respecting the educational qualifications of the preachers with whom he dealt provides evidence of this fact. Samuel Coate "was immeasureably above the rest in personal appearance, natural eloquence, and in educational and polite accomplishments" and "he was no doubt an accomplished English scholar." Sylvanus Keeler "had no advantages of education in early life; and when he first began to speak in public, it is said, he could scarcely read his hymn." Nathan Bangs "received a good New England common-school education, although his father failed in his project of giving him a classical one." James Coleman "grew up in ignorance and sin." Joseph Sawyer "had received a fair English education, and had evidently seen good society in early life, by which his manners were polished into the old fashioned style of politeness." Andrew Prindle "received his education in Canada, when there were no schools and no books." John Reynolds, born in Canada, "had received a fair education for the day and country,"[151] Unfortunately, the biographical records of many of the early evangelical preachers provide no information with respect to educational attainments, the only fact considered important being the conversion experience of the young prophet. Failure, however, to indicate what education the preacher had received can be accepted in most cases as evidence that it was not very extensive; when a preacher had received a very good education stress was usually placed upon the fact. Such a view is supported by records of the occupational background of the preachers. Of those Methodist preachers in Canada before 1828 for whom Carroll indicates the previous occupation, nine had been school-teachers (an occupation requiring no considerable education at that time), four trained in some branch of physics or medicine, three farmers, two blacksmiths, two carpenters, two engaged in the clothing trade, one a boxer, one a pedlar, one a surveyor, one a soldier, and one a sailor. Some probably turned to preaching as a result of failure in an earlier occupation and others as a means of avoiding more strenuous ways of making a living, but it is probably only fair to assume that the great majority were motivated by the genuine conviction that they had been "called." Most of the recruits into Methodist preaching ranks

[151]Carroll, *Case and His Cotemporaries*, vol. I, pp. 19-21, 27, 41, 119, 133, 159.

were young men starting out upon a career who might under ordinary circumstances have become farmers, small tradesmen, or school-teachers; their lack of opportunities for educational advancement made it impossible for them to enter one of the professions. It was the genius of Methodism, in a frontier community where institutions of education were largely lacking, that it availed itself of the services of this large number of ambitious young men rather than restricting itself to the employment of only those who had been properly trained. Thus it faced little difficulty in gaining recruits for the ministry at the very time when the traditional churches were dependent upon a limited outside supply.

The spirit of self-sacrifice which was characteristic of many of those who became Methodist preachers made possible their employment without imposing upon the population a heavy burden in their support. Strict limitations were placed upon the pay of the Methodist itinerants, and the great part of this pay was rendered in goods and services rather than in money. The living standards of the itinerants, as a result, tended to be no higher than those of the pioneer farm people whom they served. "We patched up an old house," George Ferguson wrote of his work on the Burford circuit in 1821-2, "that had been lying untenanted for a long time, to stay in. We took flax, wool, provisions, and whatever the people had, and felt disposed to give us as Quarterage. . . . We received this year, in all, $125—a small sum to feed and clothe a family."[152] The local Methodist preachers, who did not travel but accepted responsibility for carrying on stated services in their home community, were even less of a financial burden upon the people whom they served. Depending upon farming as their chief means of livelihood, the Methodist Church could afford to license an almost unlimited number of such preachers, and the result was that here and there throughout the Canadian rural communities local Methodist preachers were to be found who carried on the day-by-day work of the Church, preaching, leading prayer meetings, conducting funerals, and visiting the members in their homes.

The itinerant system made possible, in a way that no other system could, the establishment of religious services in the Canadian backwoods settlements. The strength of the system derived largely from the centralization of control in the Methodist Conference. Preachers were sent where they were most needed without any regard to their wishes or the wishes of particular congregations, and in this way the wastes of preaching talent resulting from the concentration of workers in

[152]Journal of the Rev. George Ferguson, p. 108.

those areas where conditions of life were most pleasant and where the congregations were most able to make their voices heard were avoided. The rule that the itinerants must remain unmarried until they had travelled for at least four years served to maintain a ministry with a high degree of mobility; [153] without sacrificing the strengths of a married clergy closely identified with local communities through family ties, Methodism was able, by setting the itinerants apart from the body of local and located preachers, to build up in a manner similar to the Jesuit Order an army of celibate evangelical workers free from social obligations which interfered with mobility. Strict supervision through the conferences maintained a high level of efficiency among the preachers. Centralization of authority, however, was not extended to the point where it discouraged a spirit of initiative on the part of the preachers. The success of the itinerant system depended upon the nice balance of centralized authority which took care that no area was neglected through overlapping of services and which secured a ministry enjoying sufficient freedom of action to establish preaching appointments wherever opportunities presented themselves. Settlement grew steadily in the country, and the development of the Methodist movement was partly a matter of making contacts. Preaching in many areas could only take place whenever and wherever people could be got together, and sometimes several months would elapse between the visit of one preacher and that of another. With the growth of population, visits were made more frequently and eventually the work was organized in terms of regular preaching appointments. By the careful arrangement of such appointments, one or two preachers could cover a very large area and nevertheless provide services every two weeks or every month. "I have now preached," Anson Green wrote of his work, in co-operation with another preacher, on Smith's Creek circuit in 1824-5, "in all the regular appointments, and find we have enough to do. We preach in twelve townships, have thirty-three appointments each for every twenty-eight days, lead all the classes after public service, preach funeral sermons, and attend as many prayer-meetings as possible. Our circuit . . . requires a ride of 400 miles to get around it, which we performed, winter and summer, on horseback."[154] Willingness of the preachers to adhere to such a strenuous preaching schedule, and the flexibility of the Methodist economy in the employment of any sort of place for the holding of religious services, made possible the development of an effective itinerant system. Methodism, in a literal sense,

[153] *The Minutes of the Annual Conferences of the Wesleyan-Methodist Church of Canada, from 1824 to 1845 Inclusive* (Toronto, 1846), p. 20.
[154] *The Life and Times of the Rev. Anson Green, Written by Himself*, p. 56.

was brought to the population. The scattered settlers were searched out, and preaching appointments arranged within a short distance of their home; often, the practice of prayer was introduced by the preacher into the home itself.

Camp meetings served to complement the work of the itinerant preachers. The time for holding them ordinarily was so arranged that a number of preachers drawn from different circuits could co-operate. Thus, like later fall fairs, they moved from one part of the country to another during those seasons of the year favourable for their holding. Announcements in the *Christian Guardian*, after 1829, served to keep the faithful informed as to the places where meetings were being held at any particular time. As a means of bringing together people scattered over a great area, such gatherings were highly effective. Families travelled several miles over bush roads to join in these mass meetings of worship; regular encampments were made and most of the people who attended remained on the grounds until, at the end of a week or ten days, the meeting broke up.[155] The size of such gatherings varied greatly, and many of the smaller ones probably did not attract more than one hundred people, but in providing an opportunity for the settlers to get together they proved a highly effective instrument of religious propaganda in a community where great distances were a serious obstacle to participation in other forms of group fellowship.

In religious appeal as in form of organization, the Methodist movement served as an effective socially reorganizing influence in the Canadian backwoods settlements. The strength of that appeal lay largely in the fact that it was directed towards the emotions and feelings and relied little upon reason. The close American connection of the movement in Canada inevitably determined the highly emotional character of its appeal. It is true that such forms of mass hysteria as barking and jerking, typical of religious meetings in the western and southern states, did not emerge. "Except in a few instances," William Case wrote of the revival on the Thames River in 1810, "the whole progress is gradual, and but little of that wild and boisterous spirit, which is sometimes seen in real revivals of true religion. There are some instances of persons falling down, but these are few."[156] Nevertheless, Methodist meetings in Canada as in the United States (and much more than in the Maritime Provinces) were characterized by a high degree of religious excitement. "When I arose to follow him [Sawyer]," Nathan Bangs wrote of his first experience as an exhorter, "I shook in

---

[155]See Patrick Shirreff, *A Tour through North America* (Edinburgh, 1835), pp. 183-8.
[156]Carroll, *Case and His Cotemporaries*, vol. I, p. 186.

every limb, my lips stiffened, and I could hardly speak; but soon they were loosed, and the power of the spirit descended on the assembly in such a manner that some sobbed aloud, some praised God audibly, and others fell to the floor as if shot dead."[157] Case recorded in his journal the success which attended his preaching in 1808 and 1809. "Here at brother VanNatters," he wrote of a meeting in what was called "the New Purchase," "the Lord was with us in a most glorious manner. . . . My soul was full of joy for the Lord attended the word to the conscience of the people so that many cried out. . . . After a season meeting was closed but the people continued praising the Lord in shouts of glory until ten o'clock at night, about seven hours without intermission, or very little."[158] At a quarterly meeting on Yonge Street, Case was equally successful in arousing a strong religious concern. "Many," he wrote, "seemed to feel the effects of the gospel. On Saturday while I was preaching on Jacob's vow a woman appeared greatly troubled, she wept and cried aloud for mercy and in the evening prayer meeting professed to find deliverence from her trouble by faith in the Savior. At the table also it was a melting time. I then spoke in Deut. 6 and 7, at the close of the ceremony the people were greatly moved, many both young and aged wept through the congregation."[159] At another quarterly meeting which began on September 9, he recorded: "Preached at eight o'clock but so great was the power of the spirit among the people that I could hardly finish my sermon, at the close of which in the time of Sacrament, several sinners cried aloud for mercy and professed to find the Savior."[160] On occasion, the preacher found it necessary to discourage too strong expression of feelings. "On Sunday 9th July [1809]," he wrote, "preached three times in different places and a universal attention, and concern among the people but their applauses are too much and causes me many painful emotions."[161]

George Ferguson, an Irishman who entered upon a career of preaching as a soldier during the War of 1812, was greatly struck by the methods employed by the Methodist preachers in Canada. "When I had concluded," he wrote of a meeting in the Niagara District in 1813 which he shared with the Reverend T. Harmon, a travelling preacher from the United States, "he [Harmon] exhorted the people. I listened with amazement. His voice, I think, might have been heard a mile. He uncovered the depravity of the human heart, and thundered the terrors

---

[157]Stevens, *Life and Times of Nathan Bangs*, pp. 63-4.
[158]Journal of William Case, pp. 16-17.
[159]*Ibid.*, p. 20.
[160]*Ibid.*, p. 24.
[161]*Ibid.*, p. 45.

of sin. . . . There was a shaking among the people."[162] The next Sunday Ferguson again shared a meeting with Harmon. "While preaching that evening," he wrote, "he fell, and laid as one dead, for some time. I had never seen a preacher fall before.—Several of the members fell in prayer-meeting, and also a man named Green, belonging to the incorporated Militia, above six feet high, fell, and professed religion."[163] Ferguson, himself, was not slow to exploit the methods of revivalism. "The Lord poured his spirit upon the people," he wrote of a series of meetings he held at Warner's Chapel during the summer of 1814, while his regiment was stationed at Fort Niagara, "—a spirit of seriousness and enquiry was awakened in the neighbourhood, and a number of conversions took place. Some, during the meetings, would fall to the floor under the power of God,—others in trying escape from the house, were arrested by the Spirit's influence and brought to the ground."[164] Various stratagems were adopted by different preachers to give effect to their message; Ferguson, in begging sinners to seek salvation, resorted very often to dropping on his knees while exhorting. A state of excitement was more easily aroused if the preacher himself appeared to be in the grip of strong, unseen forces.

In some respects, the early Methodist preachers were highly skilful exhibitionists; they put on a good show because they knew it got results. But for the most part, they were simple, honest, upright men, intent only on doing good. Their piety, zealousness, and straight-forward manner of speaking made a strong appeal to the sort of people to whom they ministered. The emotional character of their preaching, while to some extent deliberately developed, was an expression of their temperament. Many of the preachers were highly unstable emotionally— such emotional instability accounted in the first place for their enlistment in the preaching ranks—and this instability led naturally to a highly emotional type of preaching. The fact that some of the early preachers were suffering from tuberculosis and that others, after a highly successful career of evangelization, encountered mental breakdowns, was not without significance. The role of the religious prophet called for exceptional qualities. The unusual methods employed in revivalist preaching in part resulted from, and in part promoted, a distinctive type of religious propagandist.

The emotional appeal of the Methodist preachers became highly effective in arousing a state of religious excitement when large numbers of people were brought together. The feelings of the preacher combined

[162]Journal of the Rev. George Ferguson, p. 45.
[163]*Ibid.*
[164]*Ibid.*, p. 58.

with the feelings of the crowd to generate a general state of emotional hysteria. The excitement aroused by revivalist preaching reached a particularly high pitch at camp meetings. The crowds assembled on such occasions, the variety of preaching talent, and the constant reiteration of the same message day after day, resulted in the producing of a mental fatigue among the listeners which led easily to mass outbursts of emotional feelings. The description by Nathan Bangs of the camp meeting held near Adolphustown in 1804 affords some indication of the character of these religious meetings.[165] Services began the first day Bangs was present with singing, prayer, and a short sermon, and, after an intermission of about twenty minutes, another sermon was delivered; "some lively exhortations followed, and the Spirit of the Lord seemed to move among the people." After an interruption of an hour and a half, a prayer meeting was held, and towards its close "the power of God descended on the assembly, and songs of victory and praise resounded through the forest." Exercises continued with preaching, exhorting, and singing until midnight when the people retired to their booths; during this day six persons were converted. The next morning at five o'clock a prayer meeting was held, and at ten o'clock a sermon was preached. By this time the congregation had increased to about 2,500, and the "people of God" were seated together on logs near the stand, while a crowd was standing in a semi-circle around them. During the sermon there occurred one of those spontaneous outbursts of religious excitement which it was the object of these large gatherings to promote. Bangs wrote:

I felt an unusual sense of the divine presence and thought I could see a cloud of divine glory resting upon the congregation. The circle of spectators unconsciously fell back, step by step, until quite a space was opened between them and those who were seated. At length I sprung from my seat to my feet. The preacher stopped and said, "Take it and go on." "No," I replied, "I rise not to preach." I immediately descended from the stand among the hearers; the rest of the preachers all spontaneously followed me, and we went among the people, exhorting the impenitent and comforting the distressed; for while Christians were filled with "joy unspeakable and full of glory," many a sinner was weeping and praying in the surrounding crowd. These were collected together in little groups, and exhorted God's people to join in prayer for them, and not to leave them until he should save their souls. O what a scene of tears and prayer was this! I suppose that not less than a dozen little praying circles were thus formed in the course of a few minutes. It was truly affecting to see parents weeping over their children, neighbors exhorting their unconverted neighbors to repent, while all, old and young, were awestruck. The wicked looked on with silent amazement while they beheld some of their companions struck down by the mighty power of God, and heard his people pray for them. The mingled

---

[165]Stevens, *Life and Times of Nathan Bangs*, pp. 151-5.

voices of prayer and praise were heard afar off, and produced a solemn awe apparently upon all minds. As the sun was setting, struck by the grandeur of the spectacle and the religious interest of the crowd, a preacher mounted the stand and proclaimed for his text, "Behold, He cometh with clouds, and every eye shall see Him." The meeting continued all night, and few, I think, slept that night. During this time some forty persons were converted or sanctified.

The next morning, Sunday, a love-feast was held, and, afterwards, the interest and excitement were so great and the crowd so large that while some assembled around the stand, a preacher mounted a wagon at a distance and addressed a separate congregation. A feeling of religious enthusiasm was general, and praying groups were to be found in almost every tent. At noon the Lord's supper was administered, and, after the sacrament, a young woman, "of fashionable and high position in Society," was "smitten down" and with sobs entreated the prayers of the people. Her sister forced her away, but a preacher followed and brought them back at the head of a procession of their friends and a circle gathered about them and sang and prayed—"the unawakened sister was soon upon her knees praying in agony, and was first converted; the other quickly after received the peace of God, and they wept and rejoiced together." A back-slider, "who had become a maniac, and was in despair," was brought to the camp. It required several strong men to hold him while prayer was offered for him. The Lord was besought to restore his faculties, "which was done," and he then prayed for himself and before the close of the meeting, he was converted. The final night of the camp meeting marked a grand crescendo of religious enthusiasm. Bangs wrote:

All the neighboring forest seemed vocal with the echoes of hymns. Turn our attention whichever way we could, we heard the voice of prayer or praise. As it was the last night, every moment seemed precious; parents were praying for their children or children for their parents, brothers and sisters for one another, neighbors for neighbors, all anxious that before they left the consecrated ground they should be "sealed" as the "heirs of salvation." I will not attempt to describe the parting scene, for it was indescribable. The preachers, about to disperse to their distant and hard fields of labour, hung upon each other's necks weeping and yet rejoicing. Christians from remote settlements . . . wept, prayed, sang, shouted aloud, and had at last to break away from one another as by force. As the hosts marched off in different directions the songs of victory rolled along the highways. Great was the good that followed. A general revival of religion spread around the circuits, especially that of the Bay of Quinte, on which this meeting was held. I returned to Augusta circuit and renewed my labors, somewhat worn, but full of faith and the holy ghost.

William Case, in recording in his journal the camp meetings he attended during the summer of 1808, emphasized their importance as agencies of religious revival. "On Friday morning," he wrote of some

time in May, 1808, "I came on C[amp] ground in Clinton where I
met with brothers Sawyer, Ryan, Smith, Reynolds, Whitehead, Holmes,
etc. Here we spent three days on the ground with the multitude
preaching, praying and singing etc. and to many it was a glorious time
and a great means of awakening to many poor sinners, some of whom,
were brought by the grace of God to rejoice in his pardoning love."[166]
Later in the summer, Case attended another camp meeting. "On Friday
19th August," he wrote, "our C. M. began and continued till Monday
10 o'clock during which time we had a peaceable, agreeable, convicting,
joyful, glorious time. Very many, according to the number professed
to find religion most youth."[167] The next month a camp meeting was
held in Niagara; "the meeting," Case wrote, "was lively, especially
in the latter part which was a glorious melting time."[168] The last camp
meeting recorded by Case began on October 7 at Long Point on Lake
Erie. "Our C. M. began and continued three days," he wrote, "and J
think the most peaceable meeting of its kind that I was ever in, during
the whole time there was no disturbance made by any person but all
seemed attention, desirous to know of these things, and happy for
many who were greatly strengthened in the Grace of God, and some
few converted and many left the ground apparently under concern,
convinced of sin, although part of the time it was wet and raining,
yet with great diligence the people continued their exercise."[169]

Camp meetings came to be increasingly relied upon as agencies in
the promotion of religious revivals. Particular efforts were made at
such meetings to gain the attention of those lacking in religious faith
and to secure striking conversions. The novelty of such meetings led
to the attendance of people of different religious persuasions, and of
people with few religious convictions of any sort, and while much
disorder often resulted from this mixing together of the faithful and
the sceptical it offered an opportunity of reaching beyond the closed
Methodist group. Published reports of various camp meetings tended to
play up stories of persons, often fashionably dressed, who attended for
no other reason than to see the curious exhibitions of religious feelings
but who themselves fell victims to the spiritual power of the gathering.
However much such stories may have been exaggerated, outside testimony would support the conclusion that camp meetings were highly
effective instruments in gaining the support of those who were not
regularly attached to Methodism. The psychological force of suggestion

[166]Journal of William Case, p. 8.
[167]*Ibid.*, p. 22.
[168]*Ibid.*, p. 27.
[169]*Ibid.*

at work in such meetings made it difficult for any one to attend them without being affected.[170] The camp meeting, therefore, more than any other form of religious fellowship, was an agent of religious expansion. It provided a means of carrying the religious message to those sections of the population which had no strong religious attachments. "Many people," the editor of the *Christian Guardian* wrote, "attend such meetings who will not go to any other. At every place where we have been lately holding them, not more than fifty persons usually meet to hear the word; and we have found the average attendance to be nearly four hundred."[171] Though not favourably inclined towards the camp meeting as such, the Wesleyan missionaries found it necessary to develop what they called field meetings as a means of attracting the attention of the population outside the Methodist fold. Benjamin Slight wrote in his journal, May 23, 1836:

> Yesterday (Sabbath) & today we have been holding a field meeting . . . .
> Being fully convinced that the efforts of Xtn Ministers must not be confined within the walls of the sanctuary, for howsoever efficacious a preached Gospel may be, none can derive direct benefit but those who hear it; & what then is to become of the tens of thousands who stand aloof from its services. It therefore behooves every minister to seize every opportunity of warning sinners to flee from the wrath to come. This meeting was therefore appointed in hopes of drawing some coloured people & Indians, together with french & other whites, who never or rarely ever attend any place of worship.[172]

Camp meetings were equally important in strengthening the religious interests of members of the Methodist group and in building up a distinctive group consciousness. However much the attention may have been directed towards sinners from outside, the greatest impression was made upon those already the most religiously minded. The emotional experience was of a character to impress upon the members of the assembled multitude a strong feeling of group rapport. The camp meeting, in a way no smaller gathering could, provided a convincing spectacle of the strength of the Methodist body. The hundreds of worshippers brought together for several days in succession became a closed social group, each participant vitally concerned about the welfare of the others. The practice, carefully promoted by those in charge of the meeting, of having numbers of people pray for the salvation of

[170]See Susanna Moodie, *Life in the Clearings Versus the Bush* (London, 1853), pp. 149-59.
[171]*Christian Guardian*, Oct. 6, 1841.
[172]University of Toronto, Victoria University Library, The Journal of Benjamin Slight, Missionary, Appointed by the Wesleyan Missionary Committee, London, to Upper Canada, 1834-1857, vol. I, pp. 109-11.

particular individuals fostered a sense of group responsibility. It was in this way that the camp meeting served to strengthen the solidarity of the Methodist group while at the same time serving as an instrument of Methodist expansion.

Protracted meetings came to complement the work of camp meetings. Introduced into the country in 1831, such meetings immediately proved an effective means of arousing an interest in religion. "We have heard," the *Christian Guardian* wrote of the first meeting in Canada, "of an extraordinary religious meeting held in Grimsby, at Smithsville, Niagara District, which, though it had continued *twelve* days at the time of our latest intelligence, had no appearance yet of drawing to a close. . . . It is said to be altogether the most extraordinary religious meeting that was ever held in Canada."[173] Frequent reports of the results attained in protracted meetings, which appeared in the *Christian Guardian* and in other religious publications, offered evidence of the general use which was made of them and of their importance in the dissemination of Methodist teachings. The report of Benjamin Nankevill of a meeting in Matilda chapel which commenced January 1, 1841, might be considered typical:

This meeting is still progressing, and night after night the altar is crowded with penitents, with heart-rending sighs and tears flowing amain, declaring that they never would give up their suit until they should know that God had power on earth to save such hell-deserving sinners. O, sir, to see the chapel covered with the spiritually slain, what a blessed sight it is. Husbands and wives, parents and children, all in a kind of regular confusion, weeping, exhorting, praying, and rejoicing alternately with and for each other; So graciously has God engaged the hearts of the people, in quest of salvation, that at times I have had much to do to prevail on them to disperse and go home.[174]

The protracted meeting never became quite as spectacular in character as the camp meeting; the fact that it was held indoors and usually only in the evenings meant that it did not subject people to as great a mental strain as the camp meeting. Nevertheless, it served effectively to arouse among those attending night after night strong emotional feelings which often found expression in some overt act associated with conversion. The emphasis of the preachers in charge was upon sustained efforts prolonged until resistance was broken. The length of the protracted meeting was often determined by the length of time it took to secure a minimum number of converts. Thus such meetings, as revivalist techniques, were greatly superior to the ordinary religious

[173]*Christian Guardian,* Aug. 27, 1831.
[174]*Ibid.,* Feb. 10, 1841.

meeting occurring only at regular intervals. Their peculiar advantages were well stated by the editor of the *Christian Guardian*:

> Protracted meetings are naturally calculated, when properly conducted, to make deep and serious impressions, and excite a high tone of religious feeling. Impressions made by a single sermon are frequently, we might add generally, effaced by the destroyer of the good seed, by the influence of worldly society and the natural volatility and carnal enmity of the unregenerate mind. Even the impressions of the faithful instructions of a whole Sabbath are often obliterated and forgotten in the multitude business and pleasures of the week.—But when service succeeds service; when sermon follows sermon; when demonstration is added to argument; persuasion to demonstration; entreaty to persuasion; and these exercises are continued from day to day, to the exclusion, in a great degree, of other employments, the judgment of the at first, perhaps, thoughtless hearer at length yields to the accumulated force of truth.[175]

Other types of religious appeal developed by the Methodists served to reinforce the influence exerted through camp and protracted meetings and through the more regular evangelical work of the travelling and local preachers. An emphasis upon the conversion of children, characteristic of most evangelical movements, was to be found in Methodist revivalist efforts. The emotional exercises of the revivalist meeting made a deep impression upon the child who through parental instruction had been made conscious at an early age of the need of a religious experience. Children, on occasion, caught in the grip of strong psychological forces, undertook to exhort their elders to seek salvation, and, more often, they joined with their elders in confessing in public what they considered were their sins, or, if converted, in relating the experience of gaining faith. Such juvenile exhibitions had a highly suggestive influence upon the adults present at revivalist meetings, and consequently revivalist promoters tended to encourage them in the indulgence of the most extreme forms of religious expression. Conversion at an early age was regarded as the most desirable since it gave greatest assurance of the maintenance of faith; furthermore, it usually could be most readily secured. The growth of the evangelical movement, indeed, depended to a very considerable extent upon work among the young.

The strength of the Methodist religious appeal lay simply in the fact that it was able to attract the attention of people outside the boundaries of the closed religious group. The camp meeting provided the most effective means of accomplishing this object, but other techniques employed tended to secure the same sort of results. The capacity of the Methodist preacher to raise his voice in such a way

[175]*Ibid.*, Feb. 8, 1832.

that it was heard for great distances, and the noise of revivalist meetings, had, in attracting the attention of the neighbourhood, effects which may not have been wholly unintended. Whenever Methodists gathered together, a somewhat spectacular scene was enacted, while the curious manner of dress and conduct of the Methodist parson travelling about the country could not but secure the attention of the unfaithful as well as the faithful. Many people, it is true, were antagonized by the exhibitionism of the Methodist preachers and followers, and sharp religious division emerged, but many others were won over to the cause by those very methods which appeared so objectionable to some. Methodism had all the vitality of the exclusive religious sect while it avoided the weakness of the exclusive sect in shutting itself off without means of recruiting to its ranks. Strong in-group feelings promoted the solidarity of the Methodist body, but these feelings were combined with a strong evangelical zeal which led to an urge to extend as far as possible the teachings of the Church. The Methodist convert sought to justify his conversion, not by excluding himself from his fellow converts, but by gaining new converts. It was this continual drive to reach out in search of the "lost soul" which accounted for the rapid growth of the Methodist movement in the Canadian backwoods society.

The asceticism of Methodism was closely related to its religious appeal. The Methodist preachers, in Canada as in the Maritime Provinces, waged a continuous and unrelenting war upon sin. Drinking, card playing, dancing, and ostentatious dress were denounced as forms of behaviour unbecoming a Christian, and no effort was spared to bring Methodist principles to the attention of offenders of whatever station in society. The Methodist preacher assumed the role of the guardian of the community's morals. William Case wrote of his work in Canada during the summer of 1809:

Excessive drinking greatly prevails in many places. Many of the high as well a[s] low, the rich as well as poor followed this pernicious practise. Several in the highe[r] walks in life I have conversed with in plainess on the subject, especially Esqrs. B. and N. members of the Parliament. To them I bore my testimony against these several practises which they it seems were guilty of. Drinking, dancing, and card playing. They seemed to think there was no harm in the two latter as their Church priests practised them. The brethren have been very kind to me and still discover great affection, so that whatever I enforce from the Scripture they seemed anxious to attend to. Some had falled into a mode of dress, according to the sain practice and spirit of the world but in general have given up the Babylonish garment and golden weago.[176]

---

[176]Journal of William Case, p. 40.

Exclusion from the membership of the Methodist society operated as a powerful sanction in securing conformity among those who were adherents. George Ferguson wrote of his work on the Ottawa circuit in 1816: "My experience in Church-government was extremely limited.— In this, however, I was strict, as far as my knowledge extended—dwelt much on plainness of dress in our members—a regular attendance on duty,—prayer, private, family, and public. I tried to enforce the reading of the Scriptures—the duty of reproving sin, and of watching 'over one another in love'."[177]

In 1835, the Reverend Benjamin Slight wrote of the moral influence of the Methodist movement, in speaking of his work among the people of Amherstburg and Sandwich: "Methodism will do much good where it does not gain Members. It will & does do it here. It exerts an influence on Society, & is a check to fashionable follies. There is none here to bear a testimony against Balls, cards &c but myself. The Episcopalian Minister is silent on the subject, & the Presbyterian Minister attends them. I have lately been lifting up my voice against them, & have excited (as I have heard) many thoughts & reflections in their minds."[178]

Methodism was the religion of pioneer farmers, and pioneer farmers had little money and little leisure time. Extravagance and dissipation had no place in their way of life. Thus asceticism was essentially the expression of the philosophy of a social class. It was a protest against the manner of life of the privileged social classes in the community. It was also a protest against the irresponsibility and thriftlessness of an immigrant farm population which had little incentive to raise its standards of living. The lack of outside markets tended to weaken the economic drives within the rural frontier society, and asceticism served as something of a substitute for the profit motive. Its effect was to develop a disciplined farm working population. It met a real— and vitally important—need of the pioneer rural society by providing a strict code of conduct grounded in religious belief.

In terms of its more general cultural appeal, Methodism was likewise closely adapted to the needs of the Canadian frontier communities. Before 1832, the Canadian population was predominantly of American origin, and the close American connection of the Methodist movement gave it a great advantage in winning the support of the people it sought to serve. Most of the early Methodist preachers were drawn from the United States; those who were not tended to have something of an American outlook. Methodism grew up in Canada as a distinctively American movement.

[177]Journal of the Rev. George Ferguson, pp. 79-80.
[178]Journal of Benjamin Slight, vol. I, pp. 73-4.

At the same time, it was a rural movement. Although Wesley gained most of his support in England from the industrial working class population, Methodism in the United States grew in terms of the support of a frontier farm population. Most of the preachers were of rural background, and the form of organization which Methodism developed emphasized its close connection with the rural community. The rural outlook of the movement strengthened its divorce from a traditional class system. Methodism was not, strictly speaking, lower class in its appeal; it lacked any identification with class symbols, whether lower or upper. The sect ideal in Methodist teachings of a spiritual elect offered a substitute for feelings of class identification. It was in this way that Methodism gained its strength as a social force in the Canadian backwoods society. The backwoods farm population had no strong sense of social status, and membership in the Methodist movement involved no break from already established social ties. Social ties were secured within the movement itself.

The limitations of rural leadership emphasized the importance of such a religious movement as Methodism in providing a basis for the social reorganization of the community. With all their shortcomings in terms of education and experience, the Methodist preachers assumed the role of leaders in the rural society. That is not to say that they interested themselves in problems of community welfare or political reform; the itinerants had a singleness of purpose from which they never veered. Their message was a spiritual message and the leadership they offered was a spiritual leadership. But it was through this single emphasis upon the spiritual that they gained their enormous social influence. In a community where the population was drawn from various kinds of background and, isolated, had little sense of common interest, organization in terms of a social appeal presented enormous difficulties. Conversion emphasized the break from a social past and secured a sense of collective solidarity through identification with spiritual values.

The Methodist was by far the most successful of the religious movements which developed in Canada before 1832 but the American Presbyterian and Baptist movements possessed advantages similar to it. Though lacking the highly centralized denominational organization of Methodism, American Presbyterianism was little different in organization and appeal. Similar methods were employed in the recruitment of preachers, and, although a strict itinerant system was not adhered to, most of the preachers itinerated rather than located in particular centres. The fullest use was made of revivalist techniques. Because of the small number of preachers in the country, no camp meetings were held,

but protracted meetings were extensively employed as means of arousing strong religious feelings. The Reverend William Proudfoot's account in his journal of a four-day meeting which he attended in January, 1833, at the Presbyterian church of Barton, near Hamilton, provides a picture of a religious gathering which might as easily have been Methodist as Presbyterian.[179] With respect to their attitude to such questions as drinking, also, the American Presbyterians were much closer to the Methodists than to the Scottish Presbyterians.

In the case of the Baptists, the strength of the movement depended upon the strength of the local church. Reliance was placed almost wholly upon the work of local preachers, and willingness to accept almost anyone who had a desire to preach the gospel meant that little difficulty was experienced in the organization of religious services. Wherever a group of Baptists had settled, there emerged a Baptist preacher and a Baptist church.[180]

Although some of the early Baptist preachers had no great interest in evangelical religion, many of them in their manner of preaching were little different from the Methodist preachers. Baptist revivalist meetings, perhaps, tended to be more orderly than those of the Methodists, but there was the same intense religious excitement resulting in the overt expression of feelings and emotions. "When I was in the West," Proudfoot wrote December 5, 1832, while in York, "I heard

[179]See "Proudfoot Papers" (*Transactions*, London and Middlesex Historical Society, 1922, pp. 34-45). The Reverend W. F. Curry, visiting Canada from the United States, wrote more generally of the protracted meetings among the Presbyterians in Western Upper Canada, December 25, 1833:

"More than two years since the first protracted meeting amongst the Presbyterians in this province, was held in one of these churches. I was present. The meeting was blessed not only to the church, but also to about 70 others, who hopefully gave themselves to Christ. About 50, if I am not mistaken, were then received into the church—some of whom have fallen back, we fear to perdition; but the most of them appear well compared with other professors. About two weeks after this meeting, another was held in another church. I was also present there. About 70 were supposed also at this meeting to have been converted and between 30 and 50 were received into the church. These also appear, as far as I can learn, much like the others. Another meeting was soon held in a third church; this also was signally blessed. I was not at this meeting; but a few weeks after I came, at the request of brother Edwards Marsh, (Who had just organized a Presbyterian church in this place,) to assist him in a special effort. We commenced in Barton, two miles and a half from the village, in an ungodly neighbourhood, where some of the people had voted for a protracted meeting for sport. There was not a professor amongst them when we began, but in five days we numbered about fifty as interesting converts as I ever saw, who from that day to this have maintained a closer walk with God than any persons I ever knew under like circumstances." *Christian Guardian*, Feb. 19, 1833. Quoted from the *New York Evangelist*.

[180]See "Principles and Practices of the Early Baptists in the Ottawa Region" (*Minutes of the Ottawa Baptist Association*, 1865, pp. 38-40). Also Zella M. Hotson, *Pioneer Baptist Work in Oxford County* (Woodstock, Ont., n.d.); B. F. Rice, "Sketches of Baptist Life in Canada West, 1800-1860," Master of Arts thesis, McMaster University.

of the people of Lobo that there are many Methodists and Baptists amongst them, and that the Baptists are throughout the community as wild as the Methodists, a piece of information for which I was not prepared, as I had been accustomed to think the Baptists a very excellent class of Christians."[181] Later experience was to confirm in Proudfoot's mind the impression which he had received of the Baptists. He wrote, January 4, 1834, in London: "The Baptists in this neighbourhood are of the Freewill order and maintain the most absurd notions. The leader of them is one Huckins, a joiner, who seems to be an artful, vulgar person. The Baptists are in the habit of holding class meetings in the neighbourhood of those they wish to gain over to their way of thinking and then invite them to attend and this they do till they gain their point. It is impossible to resist these people for their work is all done in secret and they hang on till they have taken the victims of their delusions across the Rubicon and then they set out upon some other poor ignorant victims."[182]

The protracted meeting was introduced among the Baptists in Canada some time during the eighteen-thirties and soon became extensively used as a means of promoting religious revivals. In contrast with the camp meeting, it was closely adapted to the economy of the local Baptist church; ordinarily, it was the resident preacher who undertook to hold a protracted meeting, and the only outside help necessary was that of a travelling missionary or of a preacher from a neighbouring church. Reports of such meetings in various Baptist journals provide some indication of the growing reliance placed upon them in the propagation of Baptist religious principles and in the promotion of revivals.[183]

Growing out of the protracted meeting, there developed among the Baptists a form of religious fellowship much like the Methodist camp meeting but which might more properly be described as a "field meeting." Although such meetings never became common, or at any rate were never often referred to, they were probably used to good effect in the promotion of religious revivals in the more scattered areas of settlement. One of these meetings was held in Eaton, in the Eastern Townships, in 1842.[184]

However important extra efforts on the part of the Baptists may

[181]"Proudfoot Papers" (*Transactions*, London and Middlesex Historical Society, 1922, p. 6).

[182]"Proudfoot Papers" (*Papers and Records*, Ontario Historical Society, vol. XXVII, 1931, p. 455).

[183]See, for instance, the *Canadian Baptist Magazine*, vol. IV, Feb., 1841; *The Register*, vol. II, Dec. 21, 1843.

[184]*The Register*, vol. I, Nov. 23, 1842.

have been, the strength of the Baptist religious appeal depended upon the exertions of the local preachers and the members of the various local churches. The Baptists could not rival the Methodists in the staging of spectacular religious meetings which commanded the attention of the whole country-side; nor were the Baptists, even those of the Free Will order, able or inclined to appeal so strongly to, the emotions and feelings that a general state of religious excitement swept through the community to the exclusion of all other interests. The Baptists, on the whole, were quiet while the Methodists were noisy; the very fact of their quietness limited greatly the range of their evangelical influence. Yet the Baptist movement, like the Methodist, was a movement of the social masses. If the Baptists strained towards a folk appeal—and the Methodists towards a mass appeal—their support came nevertheless from those elements of the population cut off from the traditional social order and left—on the margin of the community— without strong social attachments. The Baptist churches became, that is to say, the churches of the backwoods population.

The evangelical religious movement grew by extending the teachings of religion to that large section of the Canadian rural population which stood on the margin of Protestant religious society. Support was gained from people outside the traditional religious system. Such people to a very large extent were outside the traditional social system as well. Ecologically, the evangelical following tended to be found on the outer rims of the community—or, in other words, in the backwoods community. In terms of its location within the moral, cultural, and political order, the evangelical following also tended to be marginal in character. The type of organization of the evangelical religious movement which enabled it to extend the teachings of religion into isolated areas of settlement, the character of its religious appeal which placed primary emphasis upon an emotional response, the strong emphasis upon asceticism in a situation which demanded relentless work and frugality, the almost complete disregard of the conventions of polite society where frontier settlement had weakened relationships of social status, and the tendency to avoid all concern for worldly affairs in the appeal to a population which had few secular interests provided distinct advantages in gaining the support of marginal elements of the population or what might otherwise be described as the "social masses." The evangelical religious movement in Canada was a product of the frontier social situation. It was in the character of the needs of this social situation that the explanation of its rapid growth at the expense of the traditional Protestant denominations was to be found.

Growth of population associated with the development of a frontier agricultural area, and the character of the settlement which took place, imposed demands upon religious organization in Canada which required fundamental adjustments in techniques and methods. Population grew in an area which hitherto had been completely unsettled and lacked therefore any sort of social organization. Settlement in Canada after 1783 did not constitute an extension of the boundaries of the agricultural community which had much earlier been established in the valley of the St. Lawrence; French Canada, geographically and ethnically, remained largely isolated from the new frontier opening up. As a result, the French-Canadian rural society contributed little in meeting the problem of social organization within the English-speaking communities in the Eastern Townships and Upper Canada. The establishment of religious institutions was part of the general problem of the erection of a social order, and, with the exception of some work carried on by the Roman Catholic Church of French Canada among the Highland Scots, such institutions had to be brought in from outside. The problem of religious organization was essentially a problem of breaking into a new field of development.

In meeting this problem, geography greatly favoured those churches with headquarters in the United States. The difficulty of securing ministers from overseas, particularly before there was any great overseas migration of people, was evident in contrast with the ease of recruiting them from the United States. Preachers could be sent across the border on short notice and for short intervals of time, and many ventured on their own accord when the journey did not involve any long absence from home or friends. Missionary organizations, developed to meet the needs of the advancing American frontier, were available for the direction of work in Canada. Within the new Canadian communities, ties with the American churches were sufficiently strong to encourage the emergence of local preachers who identified themselves with religious institutions across the border. The considerable dependence upon American direction and reliance upon American preachers emphasized the frontier relationship of Canada to the United States. That relationship was closest in the western sections of Upper Canada but throughout the settlements which had come into being after 1783 the lines of communication tended to run in the direction of the neighbour to the south. On the other hand, the failure of the overseas churches to provide missionaries except to the larger centres of population emphasized the fact that the Canadian colony was little more than an outpost in the British imperial system. It was this conception of the relationship of

Canada to Britain which determined the early missionary policy of the overseas churches; the interests of empire secured the establishment of missionaries at strategical points, but the small number of overseas settlers in the colony limited the area which was served.

These considerations suggest that the American connection was decisive in determining the form taken by religious organization in Canada during the early period of settlement. When advantages secured through an evangelical tradition were combined with advantages of geography, the American religious movement was placed in a particularly strong position. Principles of organization developed within the Methodist movement in England under the leadership of Wesley and in the United States under the leadership of Asbury proved highly effective in meeting the problem of erecting a religious order within the Canadian pioneer community. The success achieved by the evangelical movement in Canada in providing religious services was largely a success in terms of the recruitment of preachers. The evangelical principle of relying simply upon a "call" to the ministry rather than upon educational qualifications—or qualifications of social class—eased the problem, already greatly facilitated through close geographical ties, of building up in the country an effective preaching force.

Efforts to provide the rapidly growing Canadian rural communities with religious services emphasized the importance of techniques of organization in the recruitment of personnel and in the effective employment of available resources. To some considerable extent the problem of maintaining a religious interest was a problem of religious organization. Where opportunities for participating in religious services were lacking, a general state of religious indifference resulted; an interest in spiritual things was closely related to the interest in human fellowship and weakened when left without the support of the social interest. On the other hand, a strengthening of religious interests followed directly upon the strengthening of religious organization, and this was particularly the case when there were few other outlets for the expression of the need for fellowship and for the acceptance of social responsibilities. Vested interests of religious organization prompted efforts to extend the facilities of worship into areas where such facilities were denied, and these efforts were rewarded by the canalization of the population's social interests into religious channels. A religious heritage facilitated the establishment of religious forms, but the presence or absence of this heritage was not decisive in determining the success of religious organization; religious values deteriorated even though the religious heritage was strong if organization was absent, while, on the other hand, religious values asserted themselves if religious organization

was strong though the population may not have inherited any strong religious attachments. This fact suggests that nothing more was necessary than organization for the establishment of the religious interest if alternative means of social fellowship were lacking, and to some extent this was the case in the Canadian frontier settlements. Attachments of the population tended to be determined by the availability of agencies of social fellowship, and the overwhelming dominance of institutions of religious propaganda favoured the establishment of religious attachments. The tendency of many frontier settlers to shift from one religious persuasion to another, differing at times very widely in doctrine and form of church government, reflected the impermanency of religious organization and the willingness of the individual to participate in whatever religious service was available. The successful establishment of any particular religious denomination involved its putting more men in the field than did its competitors. The strength of the evangelical movement in the Canadian backwoods communities was partly a result of competitive advantages in this regard.

The problem changed in character, however, when the community developed to the point where it was provided with alternative forms of religious organization. The nature of the service became increasingly important, and emphasis shifted from the mobilization of a sales staff to the improvement of the art of salesmanship. The necessity for such a shift in emphasis became increasingly evident in Canada with the extension of the religious services of various denominations. Denominational attachments became a matter of competitive advantages in the religious appeal. Rapid growth of the evangelical religious movement, and the resulting weakening of such denominations as the Church of England, must partly be accounted for in terms of advantages in this regard enjoyed by the former.

To what extent the growth of these new religious movements in the Canadian rural society was responsible for a general strengthening of religious interests can only be conjectured. The vested interests of the evangelist inevitably led to an exaggeration of the results secured through evangelical preaching. The population was never as indifferent to religious values as the promoter of a revival tried to make out; on the other hand, the religious enthusiasm which apparently resulted from the revival was to some considerable extent an enthusiasm of the stalwarts and, indeed, of the preacher himself. Nevertheless, there would seem little doubt that religious values gained in strength with the strengthening of the evangelical religious movement. Many of the early settlers in Canada had inherited no strong attachment to a religious way of life. The American Revolution had led to a considerable weaken-

ing of the religious ethos among the American population,[185] while the French Revolution, the Napoleonic wars and the rise of the liberal movement had had similar effects upon religious thought in Great Britain. Conditions of life within the Canadian pioneer society tended to accentuate this break from a religious tradition. The struggle to make a living was unfavourable to religious values. The testimony of general observers would support the conclusion that religion at least was not a dominant influence in the life of a very large number of the early pioneer farmers.

The task of extending the influence of religion into the new frontier settlements and of gaining the support of those large sections of the population which had stood outside the area of religious teaching was one performed largely by the evangelical religious movement. Growth of the evangelical movement in the country, it is true, resulted in part from the settlement of people who had previously been adherents —without such support the evangelical religious movement could hardly have taken its rise—but many of those who came to be included among the evangelical following were drawn from outside. The evangelical religious movement owed its claim to the title of evangelical, to its capacity to gain recruits from among those who previously lacked any strong interest in matters of religion. It grew through the growth in strength of the religious interest. Inevitably, as a result, the strengthening of the evangelical religious cause tended to a weakening of the traditional religious order. The traditional religious denominations depended upon a nice balance between religious and secular interests. In the frontier settlement, where secular interests broke down, with the emergence of the evangelical religious movement there was a growing tendency to think exclusively in terms of religious ends. The other-worldliness of the evangelical religious appeal had the effect of developing an intolerance towards religious institutions which had accommodated themselves to the demands of the secular world. The convert of the religious revival was one who denied himself the privilege of compromise. The result was that those who came under the influence of religious revivals tended to break completely from the traditional religious order and to seek fellowship within the evangelical sect.

A crude manifestation of religious feelings amounting at times to an exhibitionism distasteful to people of reserved manners inevitably characterized to some extent the religious appeal of the revivalist movement. If evangelical religious meetings in Canada escaped some of the excesses of such meetings in the United States, there was still

[185]See Thomas C. Hall, *The Religious Background of American Culture* (Boston, 1930).

much in their character which struck the person accustomed to the dignity and ritual beauty of the traditional religious service as ugly, uncouth, and, indeed, degrading to human nature. Evangelical religion, theologically reactionary, involved a reversion to a system of thought based upon elementary passions and primitive superstitions. It was this character of evangelical teaching, however, which constituted its great strength. If it was deplored by the liberal philosopher who looked upon it as directly opposed to rationalist teachings, it served nevertheless to meet a real need in the rural frontier society. The crudeness of the evangelical religious appeal reflected the crudeness of frontier life. There was in the backwoods community little to support the paraphernalia of a mature, highly developed social system. The social losses accompanying frontier settlement inevitably involved the emergence of a society considerably more backward than those societies with which it was originally connected, and this social retardation was reflected in the reversion to a lower form of religious life.[186] "Here, without means of instruction, of social amusement, of healthy and innocent excitements," Mrs. Jameson wrote, "—can we wonder that whisky and camp-meetings assume their place, and 'season toil' which is unseasoned by anything better? Nothing, believe me, that you have heard or read of the frantic disorders of these Methodist love-feasts and camp-meetings in Upper Canada can exceed the truth; and yet it is no less a truth that the Methodists are in most parts the only religious teachers, and that without them the people were utterly abandoned."[187] The evangelical religious movement rapidly spread at the expense of traditional religious systems, not only because its religious teachings were available, but because it offered something which could be comprehended by a backwoods population, largely illiterate and cut off from any stimulating contacts with the world of knowledge. The evangelical movement brought the religious message down to the level of intelligence of the population.

The evangelical religious appeal provided, in a way much more effectively than the traditional religious appeal, the backwoods population with a meaningful interpretation of its relationship to the larger social cosmos. The close identification of the aspirations of the convert with the idea of salvation took on a social significance within the more general religious context. The experience of faith resulting from conversion was very closely related to initiation into the social fraternity of believers. The religious interest took on meaning only to the extent

---

[186]See Arnold J. Toynbee, *A Study of History* (London, 1934), vol. III, pp. 136-7.
[187]Anna Jameson, *Winter Studies and Summer Rambles* (new ed., Toronto, 1923), pp. 183-4.

that it was supported by the social interest. The conception of religion in those terms, of course, was farthest from the thoughts of those who undertook its propagation or of those who accepted its teachings; the evangelical appeal gained social significance by the very fact that it was divorced from worldly interests and worldly systems of thought. In this way, the evangelical group freed itself from the inhibitions and restraints of the traditional social order and developed a form of fellowship in which a population cut off from traditional ties could freely participate.

It was in those areas, and among those people most cut off from traditional ties that the evangelical movement gained its greatest strength. Thus it was not simply the fact that the early movements in Canada originated in the United States that accounted for their success chiefly among the settlers of American background. The heritage of the frontier had provided that population which crossed the border into Canada with few cultural ties to support efforts to erect a society within the new frontier environment. For the most part, it was a second-generation frontier people which came from the United States to Canada, and such a people, cut off from the social heritage of the first generation, had not yet developed a rich heritage of its own. An extreme individualization, as a result, tended to characterize the American settlers in the country, and the effects of such individualization, or emancipation from traditional controls, were evident in a weakened sense of group consciousness. Concern was largely with immediate interests—clearing the land, planting the crop, caring for the livestock, transporting produce to market, and seeking such means of relaxation as those provided by the cross-roads tavern or neighbourhood group. Few points of collective interest emerged which served to focus attention upon some definite purpose or goal lying outside the individual's immediate range of activity. The mobility of the frontier had destroyed among the American settlers any sense of being a distinctive "folk"; on the other hand, lack of means of communication checked the development of any sense of belonging to "a public." It would be expected, therefore, that the evangelical religious appeal, as an agent in social unification, would exert its greatest influence among the American settlers; they had, of the various groups within the Canadian rural community, the fewest materials out of which to develop a cultural system.

The evangelical religious movement, however, spread beyond the population of American origin and made a strong appeal to the economically impoverished overseas immigrants settling in Canada after 1815. To some extent, it is true, the richer cultural heritage of the British settlers made them less inclined to the support of an evangelical religion;

letters from friends and relatives in Great Britain, the cherished hope of
returning eventually to the homeland, and the strong patriotism of
the Britisher living abroad served to maintain among the immigrants
from overseas a feeling of belonging to something outside the range of
the individual's immediate interests. Such forms of social identification,
however, provided no sense of intimate fellowship or even any sense of
relationship to vital needs. Cultural attachments of the overseas settlers
which had any real meaning were broken through the movement into
a strange environment. The character of the new environment made
such a break with a cultural past inevitable. The overseas settlers found
themselves isolated within the backwoods community. Bush farms
provided the only means by which the poorer English, Scottish, and
Irish immigrants could establish themselves on the land, and speculative
prices and incompetency in management eventually drove many of
those with capital into the backwoods as well. Tendencies towards
individualization inherent in the conditions of frontier life were
accentuated in the case of the overseas settlers by a cultural heritage
which emphasized dependence upon secondary institutions rather than
upon the family or neighbourhood group; failure readily to adjust
to this situation where many of the tasks normally performed by
agencies of the formal social order were performed by the family or
by informal social groups left the individual with virtually no cultural
supports. Inherited class distinctions which had little relationship
to the needs of a frontier society checked further the development
of means of social intercourse among the overseas settlers and intensified
the isolation of the individual. A detachment from traditional systems
of thought and patterns of conduct proceeded rapidly among such
people who found within their cultural heritage few means of adjustment to the strange frontier environment, and alternative forms of
social fellowship developed slowly without the aid of outside agencies.
The extreme loneliness of the upper class overseas settler, resulting on
occasion in personal disorganization, was indicative of a failure to
secure enduring social attachments without breaking outside a traditional class system. Among the large mass of overseas immigrants,
free of the inhibitions of a social class system, the sudden break
from old world cultural systems was more often followed by a strong
reaction against traditional restraints of all sorts and the acceptance of
new social supports such as those offered within evangelical religion.
The highly emotional experience of the evangelical religious revival
served, among the overseas settlers, as a means of personal re-organization and, on the social plane, as a means of securing new cultural ties.
    The importance of the evangelical religious appeal in developing

among the backwoods population a sense of belonging to something, of being a part of a social entity reaching beyond the horizon of the individual's immediate world, suggests a close relationship between the teachings of the evangelical religious movement and the moral and cultural values of the community. While the evangelical religious appeal gained its social significance from within itself, more general social characteristics of the movement promoted the social influence of the religious appeal. Even more, on the other hand, the social characteristics of traditional religious institutions weakened their religious appeal as an instrument in the development of a group consciousness among the rural population. The religious institution inevitably was made up of people with certain social interests and with a certain social standing in the community; the character of the institution in this regard was closely related not only to its purely religious appeal but to its attitude towards such problems as morals, education, nationalist ideologies, and politics. The social teachings of the evangelical sect supported its religious teachings in strengthening its position of leadership within the Canadian frontier settlements. The frontier emphasized self-sufficiency within the family and neighbourhood groups, and specialized skills were of less value than the general capacity to provide for the basic human needs. Non-specialization was evident in the organization of social institutions as in the organization of the labour force, and the success of religious institutions depended largely upon the degree of their integration within the community or neighbourhood structure. Denominational, sectarian, or class divisions restricted greatly the effectiveness of religious organization, and those churches were most influential which appealed to all religious, cultural and political groups within the community. The doctrine of salvation by faith propounded by the evangelical preachers offered no obstacle to the inclusion of people with a wide variety of beliefs. Only the smaller pietistic sects which had succeeded in maintaining the geographical segregation of their following could afford the luxury of adhering to the dictinctive beliefs of a particular social group. Such religious denominations as the Church of England and Presbyterian Church, by failing to develop a more inclusive social philosophy, became inevitably class churches or churches dependent upon the support of particular ethnic groups in the community. The task of organizing the masses in terms of the wider community relationship was one assumed very largely by the evangelical sect.

CHAPTER FOUR

The Break with American Sectarianism
1783-1832

R A P I D growth of the Newlight and Methodist revivalist movements in the Maritime Provinces emphasized the importance of religious sectarianism as a socially unifying force in the community. The evangelical message of salvation served to draw people together and to create a common interest based upon experience of faith. Spiritual values replaced denominational vested interests as the basis of religious organization. The serious weakening of the traditional churches in the Maritime community toward the close of the eighteenth century was an indication of the strength of an elementary religious appeal which cut across denominational and doctrinal lines to emphasize the common interest of man in the cause of religious salvation. The co-operation of Newlights and Baptists, in those areas such as Horton and Yarmouth where Baptists had settled alongside of Congregationalists, and of Newlights and Methodists in those areas where evangelists of the two movements engaged in preaching activities, served to create to some extent a common evangelistic front during the early period of rapid growth of the Newlight and Methodist movements. Preachers of the different sects joined together in the holding of religious meetings; the rank and file were even less inclined to distinguish between religious evangelists of one faith and another. In Liverpool, Simeon Perkins for some time attended the meetings of both the Newlights and Methodists, his choice on the particular occasion depending upon what preacher happened to be in town. Many others were equally casual in the formation of their religious attachments. The disintegration of denominational ties resulting from the revival of religion produced among the evangelical following an almost complete indifference to matters of organization and to doctrinal peculiarities.

So long as the experience of faith was the one dominant interest of those people belonging to the evangelical sects, harmony was successfully maintained. Differences of views were subordinated to the larger cause of salvation. Very quickly, however, within both the Newlight and Methodist movements, points of conflict emerged which gradually

increased in intensity as problems of organization and doctrinal teachings forced themselves upon the attention of evangelical church leaders and of the evangelical church following. Failure to reconcile differences led in some cases to open division and to a serious weakening of influence. The evangelical religious movement faced the danger of breaking up into innumerable fragments, each claiming to represent the true teachings of the movement.

This growing tendency towards division was in part a consequence of efforts to strengthen the denominational organization of the evangelical religious movement. On the other hand, the development of such organization offered the only means of arresting the tendency towards division. The Newlight and Methodist movements, after the first flush of revivalist excitement, moved steadily in the direction of establishing greater church order in matters of organization and doctrine. They moved, that is to say, in the direction of the church form of religious fellowship away from that of the sect. Out of the early Newlight and Methodist evangelical movements there appeared by 1800 the beginnings of the Baptist and Wesleyan Methodist Churches of the Maritime Provinces. Such a development reflected fundamental undercurrents of unrest, dissatisfaction, and conflict which forced an adjustment in the viewpoint of evangelical church leaders and, in the end, of the evangelical following.

Growth of the Newlight movement in Nova Scotia from the beginning was secured with the support of Baptists as well as Congregationalists, and, with his complete unconcern for theological principles, Alline failed to take any lead in reconciling the doctrinal differences of the two groups. He himself continued to accept the fundamental theological teachings and principles of church organization of Congregationalism, but he accepted without question converts of different religious beliefs. His was a religion of feeling rather than of doctrine, and, while he stubbornly refused to recognize as Christians those who had not emotionally experienced faith, he offered no other obstacles to membership in the fellowship of Christ. In spite of his attitude, however, doctrinal questions pressed to the fore when Newlight church organization included people of the Baptist faith.

On October 29, 1778, Alline organized a church in Horton out of the remnants of the early Baptist church formed by Ebenezer Moulton, and here doctrinal differences immediately threatened the unity of the new ecclesiastical body. "O may the time come," Alline complained, "when Ephraim shall no more vex Judah, nor Judah envy Ephraim, and that there might never more be any disputes about such nonessentials, as water baptism; the sprinkling of infants, or baptising of

adults by immersion; but every one enjoy liberty of conscience."[1] Two
years later, the doctrinal dispute threatened to break up the church
in Horton. Alline wrote in his journal:

> November the 28th [1780], I went with a number of the Brethren from Cornwallis
> to Horton to meet the churches of Horton and Falmouth there, in order to settle
> some matters in dispute, to heal breaches, and make up divisions. There seemed to
> be a desire for unity in many; but some were so stiff in non-essentials, that they
> were not willing to walk with those that differed from them in those matters. O that
> christians would bear and forbear! And what forbearance is there if we cannot
> walk with those that differ with us in some non-essential points. For my own part
> I have always been very positive ever since I knew the difference between the form
> and powers of religion, not to receive or walk with any christians that had not known
> a work of grace in their souls; for which I have often been called censorious and
> uncharitable; but I desire no charity without grounds. But as for any difference in
> non-essential matters or the externals of religion, they never were, or I hope, ever
> will be any bar to me in walking or communing with those I believe to be followers
> of the Lamb in Sincerity and in truth; and have the life of religion, although they
> might differ from me in many small matters.[2]

In Cornwallis, where the Newlight church was largely under the
care of Alline himself, doctrinal disputes also made their appearance.
The Records of a church meeting on July 5, 1780, reveal the character
of the strained relationships between the Congregationalists and
Baptists: "The Church met at Mr. Dewey's, for procedure in Matters
before them, some accusations were brought against the Rev. Henry
Alline for what he had delivered concerning water Baptism, whereby
some of the brethren were offended—he readily acknowledged that
he had spoken too rash on the matter & made satisfaction therefor to
the offended Brethren, but still held of the same mind respecting
the Nature of water Baptism & could by no means retract his sentiments
which he had delivered."[3] Of the situation in the church, Alline wrote
respecting a visit to Cornwallis in the winter of 1780-1: "I preached
often there among the people, and found many of the christians very
lively in religion, but there remained still some disputes between the
baptists and congregationals about water baptism. Many hours were
very unprofitably spent by some of the christians, contending about it."[4]

The doctrinal dispute weakened the Newlight movement, particularly
by making difficult the development of co-operation between the
churches, but so long as Alline lived there was no complete break
between the Congregationalists and Baptists. The Baptists, or those

---

[1] Henry Alline, *The Life and Journal of the Rev. Mr. Henry Alline* (Boston, 1806),
p. 67.
[2] *Ibid*, pp. 97-8.
[3] Quoted E. M. Saunders, *History of the Baptists of the Maritime Provinces* (Halifax,
1902), p. 131.
[4] Alline, *Life and Journal of the Rev. Mr. Henry Alline*, p. 101.

with Baptist leanings, lacked leaders, and were dependent upon lay preachers who possessed little talent for evangelization. In Horton, for instance, the Baptists, to quote Alline, "made choice of one N. Person, (who was not endowed with a great gift in the word) for their elder; intending to put him forward, until God gave them some better one, or brought him out more in the liberty of the gospel; after which he was ordained."[5] Alline remained alone the prophet of the evangelical movement, and, under his leadership it remained a movement within Congregationalism. In Nova Scotia his role in the Congregational churches was similar, if on a smaller scale, to the one being played at the same time by Wesley in England in the Church of England; both men identified themselves with the teachings and theological principles of the denomination in which they had been reared, and only sought to bring into it a greater spiritual drive. The fact that Alline set up churches of his own did not mean a break from Congregationalism; it meant only a break from those Congregational churches already in existence. Reliance upon the principle of congregational autonomy and the absence of any central organization made possible in effect schisms from individual churches without schism from the Church as a whole. Only the Baptists among Alline's followers looked upon the movement as supporting a separate religious denomination.

After 1783 the preaching of David George lent considerable support to the Baptist cause within the Newlight movement, and doctrinal differences which had emerged in Alline's time became increasingly pronounced. Influences reaching into Nova Scotia from the Southern American States growing out of Baptist developments were reinforced by influences from New England where many of the Newlight Congregationalists passed over to the Baptist Church. Division within the Newlight movement in Nova Scotia steadily grew as some of the Newlights clung to Congregationalist beliefs and others shifted to Baptist beliefs. The leadership in such a shift was taken by many of the Newlight preachers themselves. There was no sudden change in doctrine, but rather a gradual change in the views of individual preachers, with the result that there was increasingly lacking any doctrinal uniformity in Newlight teaching as a whole. "The Revnd Mr. Chipman is here," Perkins wrote, August 13, 1797, "& preaches at the New Light Meeting. I understand he Seems to Advance doctrines Very different from Mr. Harding."[6] Inevitably, as many of the preachers undertook to organize their churches along Baptist lines, bitter conflicts

[5]*Ibid.*, p. 67.
[6]P.A.C., Perkins (Simeon) Diary.

emerged between them and some of the members of their congregation. In Horton, where many Baptists from New England had settled and Ebenezer Moulton had carried on preaching for a time, the Newlight church from the beginning, under the pastorate of Piersons, had adopted the Baptist close communion plan. The opposition of one of the deacons, however, led to its abandonment, and it was not until much later, under the ministry of Theodore S. Harding, that the church was again organized as Baptist. The Newport church continued, with Daniel Dimock as preacher, upon the open communion plan until the end of the century though identifying itself with Baptist principles. In Cornwallis, the care of the church with the death of Henry Alline passed to John Payzant, his brother-in-law, a Congregational minister of the Newlight connection. He was succeeded by Edward Manning who soon accepted the doctrine of adult immersion, and undertook to organize the church as Baptist. Such efforts were strongly resisted by the Newlight members of whom a John Pineo was the leader, and in the end, in 1807, Manning was forced to withdraw with his Baptist adherents and form a new church alongside the Newlight.[7] In Chester, the church remained until 1793 in charge of the Reverend John Seccombe, a Congregational minister; it then passed to the care of the Reverend Joseph Dimock, a Baptist. Dimock, attempting to organize his church along Baptist lines, was faced with increasing difficulty in trying to maintain harmony between the Newlights and Baptists. In 1807 he wrote in his diary:

a little Jealousy among our peado Baptist Friends because of the growing Kingdom & Interest of our Baptised Lord but I hope god will in mercy ever grant a meekness to practice his command & to distinguish between my Erring Brethren & their Errors to love the one & despise the other—
but as there was still some of the old leaven in our Houses it caused Great uneasiness which began with Small Jealousy among the peadobaptist especially when the Order & Ordinances of God's house was preached us then they would oppose which would cause the Baptist by degrees to examin whither we stood on Gospel Ground a few at length withdrew from our Communion because they could not commune with unbaptized persons I found numbers were runing into sinful Excesses & found no way of bringing them to an account in our present state for we had but one divine rule to deal with offenders & that was a Sharp Sword with two Edges which if it began to be applyed I found would cut off all that did not come up to the Gospel Standard & after many prayers Fastings and church meetings we at length adopted Baptist Articles & all that could not adopt them were left where they were; more Baptist were Droped & could not go forward & renew covenant for what was then called close communion plan than peadoes God seemed to own us with at least Supporting grace & an establishment in the truth & for my part I can Say it was a

---

[7]See Saunders, *History of the Baptists of the Maritime Provinces*, pp. 131-41.

day I longed for & I did not count all the trials that led on to the Day as too heavy to bear in some measure could Say I remembere i my Sorrow no more.[8]

In Onslow, likewise, conflict between Newlights and Baptists made difficult the re-organization of the church on a Baptist basis.[9] In 1798 one of the deacons of the church—Joshua Higgins—raised objections to Harris Harding and Edward Manning "as labourers in the Gospel," and, failing to secure satisfaction, he withdrew as a member. In 1804 the church attempted to regulate the question of baptism. "Voted that New Articles," the Church Records read, "should be wrote containing Singly of the Faith & Practice adopted by the Baptist Church for the Church (or Such of them as are so deposed) in Onslow to sign proposing at the same time that the Church in future should be governed by the Baptist order with the reason that where as there is Some of the members of Said Church that has not come forward to Baptism by Amerson that they still hold their own place and priviledge in the Church as usual but their be no more taken into the Church but by the Baptism order." Four years later, in face of opposition, the regulations were modified; "Voted that all that were in Covenant as well as those who were Baptised as those who were not to stand in Regular order & standing in the Church exactly with same rights and priviledges vis . . . without Discrimation." The next year, however, the views of the Baptists prevailed and, under the ministry of Cleveland, the church was organized under the close communion plan. Thereupon, in 1814, the rival faction obtained a preacher of its own, and a separate church was organized on the principle "that the Door of the Church in future Shall be open for every meet members to be admitted whether he or they be baptised by Amersion or otherwise provided that the Church is satisfied of the work of Grace in their hearts & that they outwardly walk agreeable to their professes." Threats to the church in 1817, however, with the arrival of a Presbyterian clergyman forced a recon-ciliation between the two parties and an agreement was reached in the choice of a new minister.

In a number of the other churches, reorganization in terms of Baptist doctrines also came about very slowly. In Argyle, the church formed by Alline disappeared, to be later, in 1807, succeeded by one of the Baptist denomination.[10] Liverpool, which had been visited on several occasions by preachers who adopted the Baptist method of baptizing, eventually received a Newlight preacher, the Reverend John Payzant,

---

[8]Acadia University, Baptist Historical Collection, Joseph Dimock's Diary' pp. 164-6.
[9]Acadia University Library, Onslow, N.S. Baptist Church Record Book, 1791-1869.
[10]J. Davis, The Life and Times of the Rev. Harris Harding (Charlottetown, 1866), pp. 91-3.

who kept the church faithful to Congregational principles. The churches in Yarmouth, Nova Scotia, and King's Clear, New Brunswick, clung to the Newlight position. In other churches, though the Baptist mode of baptism may have been adopted, Newlight principles persisted in the organization of the church. The Reverend Joseph Dimock wrote of the church in Sackville, in 1807:

They were formerly a very flighty people in their Sentiments most of them carried away by what was called New-Dispensation Scheme—holding the Doctrine of predestination in such a light as to render all striveing against sin resisting temptation praying without feeling the Spirit of God as useless Hypocrisy that is no worse to 'act out their Darkness' as they call it, 'than to feel it' that Christians are not accountable for any of their Sins because it is their Flesh that Sins & Baptism & the Lords Supper have had their Day & are of no more obligation in the Church of God—Duties & commands are not congenial to a State of Gospel Liberty— & they have got beyond them.[11]

The shift within most of the Newlight churches to Baptist doctrines was accompanied by the development of a form of central organization which involved a still further break from Congregationalism. The churches formed by Alline accepted the congregational principle of organization; there was no attempt to establish a central directing body. As the various churches, however, became organized along Baptist lines, the need for some sort of general association became increasingly felt. Doctrinal chaos threatened not only to break up individual churches but to separate sharply one church from another. The first general meeting of the Newlight-Baptist preachers took the form of a conference at Cornwallis in 1797, and it was there agreed that there should be held an annual meeting of the representatives of the various churches. At the meeting the next year, concern for the doctrinal divisions and the dangerous doctrinal tendencies within the churches was evident. "The ministers discoursed largely," the minutes record, "on the necessity of order and discipline in the churches and continued until midnight in observing the dangerous tendency of erroneous principles and practices, and lamenting the unhappy consequences in our churches."[12] Harris Harding was reproved by the meeting as an apologist for the "New Dispensationers" and for having treated lightly "the ordinances of God's house," and he was only received into the conference after making written acknowledgment of his offences. There was no attempt at this conference to secure doctrinal uniformity within the churches; Newlight as well as Baptist preachers were represented, and the term association was avoided as suggesting a form of ecclesiastical organization. By the next year, however, the shift to Baptist principles had

[11]Joseph Dimock's Diary, pp. 172-3.
[12]Quoted Saunders, *History of the Baptists of the Maritime Provinces*, p. 85.

gone so far that the meeting could be called "The Baptist and Congregational Association." In 1800 the name "The Baptist Association of Nova Scotia" was adopted, and the change in name made complete the separation between the Baptist and Newlight churches. John Payzant's name, representing the church in Liverpool, was dropped from the minutes of the Association and the churches in Yarmouth, Argyle, and Chester in Nova Scotia, and in King's Clear in New Brunswick, though leaning to the Baptist form, withdrew from the Association since their membership included people who had not been baptized by immersion. Henceforth, only those churches which conformed to the strict Baptist system were admitted into the Association.

The problem of reconciling opposing religious interests early made its appearance within the Methodist as within the Newlight movement and similarly led in the end to the establishment of a distinctive denominational organization. One of the earliest of such sources of conflict resulted from the intrusion of preachers from England attached to Lady Huntingdon's Society, a Calvinist Methodist group which had broken away from Wesley's leadership. In the late summer of 1783 one of these preachers—William Fermage by name—turned up in Liverpool, and his preaching here during the winter added to the general religious confusion in this south shore town.[13] Another of these preachers was active in Shelburne. "A Negro man by the name of Morant," Garrettson wrote Wesley in April, 1786, "lately from England, who says he was sent by Lady Huntingdon, has done much hurt in society among the blacks at Burch town. I believe that Satan sent him. Before he came there was a glorious work going on among these poor creatures, now (brother Cromwell not being able to attend) there is much confusion."[14] In 1788 two missionaries from England, James and Milton, sent out by Lady Huntingdon, arrived in Maugerville where they were warmly welcomed; the next year James became the settled minister.[15] Unfamiliarity of the Methodists in Nova Scotia with differences which had developed in the movement in England left them open to be served by any preacher who came along bearing the Methodist name. Only the difficulties of transportation checked a greater incursion of such "heretical" Methodist preachers from overseas.

[13]See Perkins (Simeon) Diary; Also T. Watson Smith, *History of the Methodist Church of Eastern British America* (Halifax, 1877), vol. I, p. 174.

[14]Nathan Bangs, *The Life of the Rev. Freeborn Garrettson* (New York, 1829), pp. 167-8. By autumn, however, Methodist influence was re-established. "My hope revives for Shelburne," Garrettson wrote Wesley in September; "there has been an addition, and the society has become more lively. . . . Most of the coloured people whom Morant drew off have returned." *Ibid.*, p. 174.

[15]*Collections of the New Brunswick Historical Society* (Saint John, N.B., 1894), vol. I, p. 86.

Much more serious and widespread was the conflict which grew up within the Methodist movement between Wesleyan and Newlight influences. The movement had grown up in the first instance as a result of a revival of religion among the Yorkshire English Wesleyans but it quickly gathered support from among Newlight elements of the population. The term "New Light" was often used to apply to the followers of William Black as well as to those of Henry Alline. No clear distinction between the two groups was at first made by the leaders themselves. The work of Alline among the Yorkshire English Wesleyans and of Black among the New England Congregationalists was looked upon as contributing to the general cause of religious revival.

As Black, however, sought to establish societies in conformity with the Methodist pattern he quickly found that the work of the Newlight evangelists was a seriously disturbing influence. Co-operation between the leaders of the two groups gave way to bitter conflict. In the spring of 1781 Alline visited the Yorkshire English settlements in Cumberland and shortly thereafter he was followed by Thomas Handly Chipman. The result was to introduce division within the Methodist societies. Black wrote of Chipman's visit:

About two hundred met regularly in the class, and God was eminently with us. Of these, one hundred and thirty or more professed faith in Christ. Shortly after Mr. C [hipman] paid us a visit at Mr. Alline's request . . . and a flood of antinomianism; mingled with mysticism, was soon poured forth. Several of the friends talked with him, but to no purpose. Ten of the principal friends wrote to him, pointing out the impropriety of his conduct, and informing him that if he persisted in preaching such doctrines, they could not continue to hear him. But before the letter reached his hands he had left Amherst and never returned. Though he was gone, his doctrines took root, and presently caused a division.[16]

By autumn, the effects of the Newlight influence upon the Methodist societies were pronounced. Black wrote, November 28, 1781:

I now continued my labours, visiting the friends at Amherst, Fort Lawrence, Prospect, and Tantramar, for about five weeks; and sorely grieved was I, to see the enemy likely to obtain a great advantage by antinomian doctrine, which made many oppose that precious word of God which was once as the food of their souls; and inveigh against their brethren, because they warned them of their danger. Under pretence of avoiding legality, the commandments of God, than fine gold more precious, were dressed up as scarecrows; and to enforce them on the conscience was looked upon as a mark of our ignorance, if not of our being total strangers to the Gospel of Jesus. This was peculiarly afflictive to me. Even some of my own children rose up against me.[17]

---

[16]Matthew Richey, *A Memoir of the Late William Black, Wesleyan Minister* (Halifax, 1839), pp. 44-5.
[17]*Ibid.*, p. 51.

In the spring Alline was again preaching in Amherst. "Since I left this [place]" Black wrote July 14, 1782, "Mr. Alline has paid a second visit—completed a separation—drawn about seventy of the members of society away from us—thrown all into confusion—broken up the classes; and introduced a flood of contention, the consequences of which I dread."[18] In other settlements the Newlight influence also resulted in division. "About fifty," Black wrote of the society at Fort Lawrence, August 26, "seemed desirous to continue in the Methodist connection; nine or ten of whom had joined Mr. Alline, but now saw cause to return to the way in which God had first called them. These, together with those at Petitcodiać, made about eighty. Many stood aloof, and did not unite with either society as formerly."[19] On November 20 of the same year he wrote: "I rode over to Tantramar, where I am sorry to find mysticism and antinomianism spreading like fire; and their deadly effects already manifest.—The people are informed publicly that they have nothing to do with the law of God—that David was a man after God's own heart when wallowing in adultery and murder—that it was only his body that sinned, that his soul never sinned at all."[20]

In Cumberland, the doctrines of Alline probably exerted the greatest influence in the thinking of those New Englanders who had settled alongside the Yorkshire English and arrested efforts of Black to extend Methodist teachings beyond the Wesleyan population, but the close proximity of the two groups resulted inevitably in the acceptance of Newlight views by many of the original Wesleyans as well. On the other hand, the preaching of Black in the settlements of New Englanders in the Annapolis Valley and along the south shore meant that Alline's efforts to reorganize the Congregational churches along Newlight lines were interfered with. Though Black was at first accepted within these Newlight strongholds, opposition quickly manifested itself. "Several of Mr. Alline's friends were present," Black wrote of his visit to Falmouth. "They rejoiced greatly, declaring, it was the very Gospel which they had heard, . . . but afterwards, when Mr. Alline returned from Cumberland, and they found that I had opposed his (peculiar) doctrines, as well as his design to set aside the Methodist discipline, their course was changed."[21] In Liverpool, also, the Newlights and Methodists for a time co-operated, but soon a division took place between the two parties, and some of the less fanatical of the supporters of evangelical religion, like Simeon Perkins, joined the ranks of the

[18]*Ibid.*, pp. 77-8.
[19]*Ibid.*, p. 81.
[20]*Ibid.*, pp. 90-1.
[21]*Ibid*, p. 67.

Methodists in opposition to the Newlights. The extreme position taken by the Newlight preachers led inevitably to a reaction among those people less evangelically minded and competition between the two became keen. "Allen's small party oppose us warmly," Garrettson wrote of the Methodist society here in 1786; [22] possession of the "Great Meeting House" constituted the main issue of dispute between the two parties. In Barrington, also, Garrettson met with Newlight opposition. "When I first made my entrance among the people at Barrington," he wrote, September, 1786, "Satan strove in every possible way to hinder. . . . There was a party of those they call New Lights, who stood in opposition, and a preacher of that denomination warned the people against me, telling them I was legal and destitute of faith."[23]

In the St. John Valley, efforts to extend Methodist influence encountered the resistance of large numbers who had earlier become caught up in the Newlight movement. During the winter of 1791, under the preaching of Mr. Abraham Bishop, a Methodist revival occurred in the St. John Valley largely among people who had come under the influence of Henry Alline's preaching. While many attached themselves to the Methodists, others, as the revival progressed, engaged in forms of religious exercise which threatened the order of the Methodist meetings. McColl, who joined Bishop in the revival, wrote: "They separated from the rest, and became extravagant indeed. They soon undertook to prophecy, and to speak with new tongues, and to work miracles. They called multitudes together to hear their new language, and to see the miracles about to be wrought by a Mr. H—, and John L—. By the time I got up they were fully engaged. They sometimes broke into our public meetings, and scattered the congregations."[24]

In the spring Black visited the Valley and, in Saint John and Fredericton, was encouraged with the results of the revival. In Sheffield, however, the effects of Newlight influence among the population were evident. "Among these," he wrote, "there are many Newlights, or more properly *Allinites*—much wild fire, and many wrong opinions."[25] Lack of sufficient preachers made impossible the maintenance of regular Methodist services in the St. John Valley, and the Newlight movement remained strong and checked the establishment of stable Methodist societies. During the winter of 1798-9 McColl again visited this area,

---

[22]Bangs, *Life of the Rev. Freeborn Garrettson*, p. 167.
[23]*Ibid.*, p. 173.
[24]"Memoir of the Rev. Duncan M'Coll" (*British North American Wesleyan Methodist Magazine for the Year 1841*, Saint John, N.B., vol. I, p. 333).
[25]Richey, *A Memoir of the Late William Black*, pp. 285-6.

and met the competition of Newlight preaching. "The word seemed to take hold, and the baptisms were very solemn," he wrote of a meeting in Saint John; "but no sooner was I done, than an Antinomian preacher, who attended with some of his friends, spoke up and denounced me to hell. Some of his friends stood by him, and seconded his charges; others also began to oppose."[26] Later Methodist preachers in the Valley also encountered the disrupting effects of the Newlight influence. "It pains me to the heart," Marsden wrote to a fellow-minister after the revival in Saint John in 1806, "that I have not books to distribute among the young converts, as many of them will be in danger from seducing spirits, and that doctrine of evils, antinomianism."[27]

In areas bordering on the United States the problem of maintaining order within the Methodist societies was particularly great as a result of the intrusion of Newlight influences. McColl in St. Stephen found his work constantly interfered with by wandering Newlight preachers. In the autumn of 1805 a preacher from the St. John Valley arrived in St. Stephen, and his preaching, in the words of McColl, "blew up the coals of the old new-light business." "They carried on," McColl continued, "as they always do, extravagantly enough. They boasted of converting thirty people at Milltown, in St. Stephen's, and of breaking up this Church. They came in a body for that purpose—screaming and falling into fits, &c, running into the water to be baptized."[28] Other preachers, from across the line, exerted an even more disturbing influence among McColl's followers.

Efforts of the Methodists to appeal to the New England Congregationalists brought them into close competition with the Newlights, and failure to emphasize the distinctive principles of Methodism involved the danger of its following becoming absorbed within the Newlight movement. The early dependence upon American preachers, and particularly preachers from New England, strengthened the tendency to minimize differences between Methodism and other evangelical sects. Many congregational principles of organization, such as the election of elders and deacons to control the affairs of local church bodies, were taken over by the Methodists in the Maritimes, reflecting the close tie with New England Congregationalism. The movement which had grown out of a Wesleyan revival among the Yorkshire English tended increasingly to become an evangelical movement among

[26]*British North American Wesleyan Methodist Magazine for the Year 1841*, vol. I, p. 460.
[27]Joshua Marsden, *The Narrative of a Mission to Nova Scotia, New Brunswick, and the Somers Islands* (2nd ed., London, 1827), p. 127.
[28]*British North American Wesleyan Methodist Magazine for the Year 1841*, vol. I, pp. 491-2.

the New England settlers in the country and, as a result, it was very considerably affected by influences similar to those which produced the Newlight revival among the Congregationalists.

With the growing influence of the Loyalists within the movement, however, Methodism tended to draw away from the Congregational tradition, and as local Loyalist preachers—such as McColl in St. Stephen —gained prominence in the preaching ranks the distinctive principles of Methodism secured increasing emphasis. The influence of the local Loyalist preachers found support in the influence of Wesleyan preachers sent out from England, and the growing reaction against the American Methodist preachers reflected the increasing self-consciousness of the movement. The shift in sentiment paved the way for the break from the Methodist Episcopal Church in 1800. Increasing dissatisfaction with the leadership provided by the Methodist Conference in the United States led William Black in this year to seek a connection with the Wesleyan Conference in England. Although a Wesleyan missionary had been sent to Nova Scotia in 1788, and he had been replaced by another in 1791, the English Wesleyan Conference had left the chief responsibility for managing Methodist affairs in the Maritime field to the American Church. The acceptance by the Conference in 1800 of Black's invitation to take up the work in the Maritimes, and the appointment of a number of missionaries to serve in the country, marked a complete shift in the outside relationships of the local Methodist movement.

It also marked a very fundamental shift in the relationships of the movement to other religious groups within the country. So long as Methodism depended largely upon the support of New Englanders, the separation from the Church of England was emphasized but difficulties were faced in distinguishing its appeal from that of the Newlight-Congregationalists. The shift to a greater emphasis upon the distinctive principles of Wesleyan teachings sharpened the lines marking off Methodism from Newlightism and drew Methodism closer to the Church of England. Features of organization which had been borrowed from Congregationalism, such as the office of deacon, were abandoned, and an effort was made to re-establish the principle that Methodism was an evangelical society rather than a separate denomination. Deferential attitudes to the Church of England were characteristic of the outlook of the Wesleyan missionaries, and some of these missionaries refrained from holding services at the same time as the Church. This shift towards the view of the Church of England as the "mother church" arrested to some extent developments leading to the erection of an independent Methodist Church but it made possible the immediate creation of a

powerful missionary organization. Establishment of the Wesleyan tie signified the beginnings of the break of the Methodist movement from the position of the religious sect. Out of this break there eventually emerged the Wesleyan Methodist Church in the country. Significantly enough, the shift within Methodism from its tie with New England Newlightism to its tie with English Wesleyanism took place the same year—1800—as the break of the Baptist Church from its Newlight origin.

Growing conflict within the Newlight and Methodist movements, and efforts on the part of Newlight and Methodist church leaders to establish more enduring denominational ties, reflected problems of religious organization growing out of underlying changes in the community structure of the Maritime Provinces after 1783. The development of trade, the rise of towns, and improvements in farming techniques and transportation facilities marked the growth of Maritime society beyond a frontier stage of development, and such a growth resulted in placing new kinds of demands upon religious organization. In the old-settled parts of the country substantial town and farm homes made their appearance, new institutions serving recreational and cultural needs developed, and the local community here generally assumed an increasing air of prosperity and well-being. Introduction of capitalist forms of organization of economic enterprise involved the steady shift from traditional relationships within the primary group to pecuniary relationships within the secondary group; the conventions of trade replaced the values of the inherited culture and the mores of the village folk. Sophisticated ways of thinking crept into the culture of the rural as well as the town population.

Cultural maturity offered threats to the narrow sectarian organization and the naive teachings of evangelical religious bodies depending upon the supports of a more simple social system. In the pioneer community religious teachings and controls served as substitutes for secular influences; in the older settled community they came in sharp conflict with such influences. Adjustment of the evangelical religious movement to a condition where its teachings were no longer the sole unifying force in society involved fundamental changes in organization and appeal, and efforts to bring about such changes led to serious internal dissensions and to open conflict. In the end, adjustment meant the elaboration of a more complex denominational machinery and the break from the sect ideal of religious fellowship. The evangelical movement was forced to become a part of the community, and, in becoming such, it lost much of its narrow sectarianism in organization and appeal. It accommodated itself to the secular by ceasing to concentrate upon the religious.

Weaknesses within the Newlight movement which resulted in growing conflict with the Baptists and which led to the eventual acceptance of the Baptist system early made themselves felt. The movement had grown up as a religious revival among the Congregationalists, and considerable success rewarded the efforts of the Newlight evangelists in breaking down traditional cultural ties and loyalties and in arousing a favourable response to the evangelical appeal for salvation by faith. The movement expanded with the disintegration of the rural village community and offered a means of social reorganization outside the traditional culture. With the spread of the movement, however, and the organization of Newlight churches, the evangelical appeal came increasingly into conflict with the mores and cultural sentiments of the wider community. Efforts to extend Newlight teachings into areas of society where traditional ties and loyalties persisted resulted in rebuffs to the movement which eventually forced a modification in appeal.

Alline early faced difficulty in gaining a hearing in certain parts of Nova Scotia. In those areas where military interests predominated, or where sophisticated ways of living influenced thought, his evangelical message failed to arouse a sympathetic response. In April, 1779, he crossed the Bay of Fundy and engaged in preaching in the settlements in the St. John River Valley. In the town, where the military garrison was stationed, little success attended his preaching. "Although it was a dark place and the King's garrison," he wrote, "yet I must acknowledge there appeared some movings of the spirit among them; especially among some of the soldiers. But O the darkness of the place. The greatest part of the people conducted as if they were to die like beasts. I suppose there were upwards of 200 people there come to the years of maturity, and I saw no signs of any Christian excepting one soldier."[29] In the winter of 1780 he visited Halifax to secure the publication of some of his writings, and here he was even less successful in promoting the evangelical cause. "O the trials I went through there," he recorded, "to see the darkness and death of that great throng of people, and no door to proclaim the gospel, as my soul longed to do it."[30] The spring of 1781 found him once again in Halifax. The entries in his journal for March 21 and 22 gave expression to the discouragement which he experienced:

21st. This was an unhappy day to me; for although I had success in getting a book from the press, yet not seeing an opportunity to preach the gospel, as I longed to do; and having no religious society (though I found two or three christians there) almost made ready to sink. O that I could always live with God in the world.

---

[29]Alline, *Life and Journal of the Rev. Mr. Henry Alline*, p. 73.
[30]*Ibid.*, p. 98.

22nd. I remained in the town till the evening. O what a land of darkness it is. Who could believe by the conduct of the crowd, when passing through the place, that they were bound for an eternity, each one having an immortal soul of more value than millions of worlds. O how it grieved my soul, when there appeared no desire no room for the gospel.[31]

From Halifax he went to Windsor where he preached for the first time in the town on April 1, and again he met much opposition to his message. "There appeared something of an hearing ear," he wrote; "but at the same time the devil was raging, and the great men of the place very much opposing."[32] Later in the month he returned to preach at Windsor. "The Lord blessed his word by me," he wrote on April 29, "and there appeared an attention with hunger here and there. One began to make enquiry about that, which is so much undervalued by the generality of mankind." The next day held out equally promising prospects: "altho," he wrote, "many of the great men oppose the gospel, and my preaching here; yet there appeared more and more doors opened for me to preach."[33] By the next day, however, he had stirred up such emotional enthusiasm among his followers that many people became offended. "The evening raged," he wrote, "to that degree that I was threatened by some of the leading men of the government to be silenced, and put on board a man of war."[34] When he returned to Windsor two months later the opposition which had been aroused on his previous visit gathered force. He was assaulted one day by an officer on the street, and two ruffians, as he described them, with drawn swords went to his house threatening his life. The next day about twenty men gathered around the door of the house in which he was staying and threatened that if he did not leave the place or cease preaching his life would be taken; characteristically he refused to go until duty called him. Later, another party gathered outside the house, mocking and hooting, and the next day they came to the house where he was preaching—cursing, swearing, and threatening his life.[35] In many other parts of the country Alline met with similar opposition to his preaching. When he went to Cobequid to preach in August, 1782, for instance, the ill-feeling towards him was so strong that he had considerable difficulty in securing lodging accommodation.[36] Even in his home community of Falmouth he did not escape violent attacks from those opposed to his teachings.

[31]*Ibid.*, pp. 117-18.
[32]*Ibid.*, p. 119.
[33]*Ibid.*, p. 123.
[34]*Ibid.*, p. 123.
[35]*Ibid.*, pp. 131-3.
[36]*Ibid.*, pp. 160-1.

With the growth of the Loyalist population in the country after 1783 the opposition to the highly evangelical Newlight appeal greatly increased. The difficulties faced by the Newlight preachers in gaining any hearing in Shelburne, a wholly Loyalist town, were an indication of the general dislike by many Loyalists of Newlight teachings. When Harris Harding visited Shelburne, in 1791, the evangelistic appeal held little attraction for the inhabitants. "Many attend our meetings in this place," he wrote, "at different times, with great opposition."[37] On another occasion, he wrote: "I am now in one of the darkest places in the Province, There is no appearance of reformation, unless it is in their unspeakable opposition against the everlasting Gospel."[38] Still later, in a letter dated August 25, 1791, he wrote: "Last night, while I was crying, 'Behold the Bridegroom cometh!' to an assembly in this place, numbers gathered about the door. Their countenances spoke their opposition to the Gospel. They railed and raged in a fearful manner. . . . So I . . . dismissed the meeting and went peaceably home. Satan's kingdom being disturbed, and the Holy Ghost giving me some utterance in speaking, are the only signs I see of Christ's kingdom coming among these strangers."[39]

Opposition to the Newlight evangelical appeal found strongest expression among the Loyalist tories but many other elements of the population came increasingly to dislike certain features of that appeal. The gradual shift of Perkins in Liverpool from a position of supporting the Newlight preachers to one of opposing them was indicative of a general change in sentiments which was taking place among the more "respectable" classes of the village communities. Opposition to Newlight teachings strengthened throughout the country as tendencies within those teachings led to an increasing emphasis upon emotionalism and to a stirring up of religious excitement.

The Congregational doctrine of salvation by faith depended upon the strict disciplinary controls of the congregational system, and, when those controls were weakened through evangelical revivals, the literal interpretation of the doctrine led to an antinomianism which discredited the whole evangelical appeal. Such a tendency towards extravagances had been evident in the Newlight movement in New England and it quickly became evident in the movement in Nova Scotia as well.

Alline's emphasis upon faith and his condemnation of "good works" as a means of salvation led inevitably to antinomian views among many

[37]Quoted Davis, *Life and Times of Rev. Harris Harding*, p. 32.
[38]*Ibid.*, p. 32.
[39]*Ibid.*, pp. 32-3.

of his followers. "A number of anti-Christian ministers," Alline wrote, "are labouring night and day to prove that a feeling knowledge of redemption in the soul is not to be attained, and that all such pretensions are a vain imagination and delusion; and tell their hearers, if they do so and so, and are baptized, join the church, come to the Lord's table, and do their best in those outward things, all will be well."[40] So long as "good works" were considered as consisting of baptism, attendance upon the sacraments, and the observance of the sabbath, and faith as involving a reformation of the individual's habits of life as well as a belief in God, the effect was to strengthen rather than weaken moral standards. Yet the literal interpretation of "good works" as conformity to external values and "faith" as simply a belief in the presence of God, was not absent in Alline's teaching. "When those " he wrote, "that are brought from a life of debauchery, declare what they have found, what they enjoy of God, and what they think of the moralists (as young converts are very apt to do) how hard is it for the moralists to believe them, who have been so long members of churches, and are advocates in the externals of religion."[41] It was this emphasis which made possible the tremendous influence of evangelical religion among the "socially disgraced" who were considered outcasts by the respectable religious denominations, but such influence was gained at the risk of attracting those who sought a means of rationalization of their moral conduct through religious faith.

Alline himself stood too close to Calvinist teachings to apply too literally his interpretation of the doctrine of faith, but among some of his disciples—Payzant and Pineo, for instance—the whole attention of evangelical preaching tended to be given to arousing a state of high emotional excitement and no attention to improving moral behaviour or ways of living. Those who were saved through conversion felt themselves freed from the moral shackles of the unregenerate, and justified in looking with scorn upon their right-living neighbours who had not experienced the healing grace of faith in God. The result was that irregularities became increasingly prevalent within Newlight meetings, and many of the Newlight converts—and some of the Newlight preachers —indulged in forms of behaviour which shocked the moral sense of the more conservative members of the community. Of Harris Harding, who was believed to be the father of an illegitimate child, Perkins wrote, April 18, 1797: "I am Sorry for the Honor, and reputation of the Town, that a man of his Character, & principles should be So much encouraged to preach, and I am Mistaken if it has not a Tendency to disturb the

---

[40] Alline, *Life and Journal of the Rev. Mr. Henry Alline*, pp. 89-90.
[41] *Ibid.*, p. 142.

peace, & quiate of the Settlement, and will in the end, break the New Light Society to pieces."[42] The Reverend John Brown, with the bias of a Presbyterian minister, wrote of the Newlights in a letter to a fellow-minister in Scotland, November 5, 1798:

> It is difficult for me to give you an account of the peculiar principles of this sect, as these are both numerous and very remarkable. They seem to have got the name which they bear from those visions or light which they pretend to see. In general they are ignorant of the true Gospel of Jesus Christ.—The great body of them deny the imputation of the righteousness of Christ for justification. They think it absurd to depend upon a Christ without them, but hold a righteousness in their own hearts as the foundation of their own hope. There are some of them who deny the resurrection of the same body, and say that if Thomas had reached forth his hand and endeavoured to have thrust it in the Redeemer's side, he would have felt nothing. They speak of extraordinary communications of the Spirit, whatever their own heated imaginations suggest they take it for a divine emanation. They talk of voices which they hear from Heaven, and of strange lights which they behold. They have great convictions at or before their conversion, and often fall into fainting fits.[43]

It was this tendency towards extravagances within the Newlight movement which threatened to cùt it off increasingly from the support of the more respectable elements of the population and which led in the end to the shift of many of the leaders within the movement to a Baptist position. The Baptists within the movement from the beginning reacted strongly against antinomian views, and, as these views became more pronounced among the fanatical Newlights, the conservative minded Newlights joined with the Baptists in a move away from the Newlight position. Formation of the Baptist Association in 1800 offered itself as a solution of the problem of accommodating evangelical religious teachings to the mores of the wider community. The Baptist system provided instruments of church and doctrinal control which secured the carrying out of moral obligations and which served as an effective check to tendencies to religious hysteria; emphasis in the Baptist order was placed upon the discipline of the local church and upon the strict Calvinist interpretation of the doctrine of good works and faith. The objective of religious organization shifted from the development of techniques of conversion to the development of techniques of control.

Weaknesses within the Methodist movement as a result of changing social conditions after 1783 were of a somewhat more general character but their effect in the end was much the same in forcing a greater accommodation with the secular community. The eventual acceptance

---

[42]Perkins (Simeon) Diary.
[43]*Presbyterian Witness,* Halifax, Dec. 27, 1862.

of English Wesleyan leadership was an indication of the need to acquire more enduring denominational supports if the movement was to continue to make progress.

One of the first problems faced by Methodism was that of supplying the growing population after 1783 with religious services. The lack of a formal tie with the Methodist Episcopal Church in the United States weakened the movement in the Maritimes in its missionary efforts. The fact that only those American preachers who volunteered were sent to the Maritimes resulted in a failure to recruit from outside a sufficient number of workers; only for a brief period after 1791 were there ever more than one or two American preachers in the country at any one time. Visits of William Black to the General Conference failed to arouse a greater interest in the Maritime field; the energies of American Methodism were being directed into the work in the new American West. Local preachers had to be largely relied upon in carrying on the work in the Maritimes.

Reliance upon local preachers led to a failure to develop an effective itinerant system. Such preachers, often engaged in some other occupation as well as preaching, were reluctant to serve in areas far removed from their home community. They were particularly reluctant to move from one area to another at frequent intervals. This was even true of Black who, while undertaking extensive missionary tours, tended to concentrate his efforts in that community in which his family was settled. Preachers like McColl in St. Stephen never departed, except on short visits, from their home community. Introduction of the system of annual conferences in 1786 served to provide a greater degree of central direction in the work of the preachers, but the Methodist practice of conference appointments without reference to the wishes of the preachers could not be fully adopted. The appointment by Wesley of an English missionary—James Wray—as the first superintendent of the work in Nova Scotia represented an effort to strengthen the circuit system, but the difficulties faced by Wray in dealing with the local preachers and his resignation as superintendent and appointment of Black in his place were indicative of the opposition to any considerable centralized control. The failure of Wesley to organize the work of the Maritimes along strictly Methodist lines was paralleled by a similar failure on the part of the Methodist Episcopal Church in the United States. The American preachers who entered the country were itinerants, but the moment they left the United States they ceased to be subject to the control of the American conferences. Their appointments were arranged in terms of the much more loosely organized circuit system of the Nova Scotia conferences.

The lack of sufficient preachers or of an effective itinerant system left many areas unsupplied or supplied only occasionally. "To Cumberland, Annapolis, Digby, and the whole province of New Brunswick," Black wrote Wesley, April 27, 1787, "we can at present give no assistance, for want of Preachers."[44] Limitations in numbers made impossible regular services throughout the various settlements, and interest in religion tended to weaken in areas which had not been visited by any of the preachers for some considerable time. Cumberland County, in spite of the fact that it was here that the Methodist movement first developed, was one of the areas most neglected by the Methodist preachers. "There is little of the life of God among the people here in comparison of what there once was," Black wrote in June, 1784.[45] In Halifax, also, the preachers had difficulty in keeping alive Methodist societies. "When I came to Halifax," Black wrote in August, 1786, "I found the little society I had left here in the fall, almost all scattered. They had but little preaching during the winter, for it was not in our power to supply all the places."[46] The Reverend Joshua Marsden wrote of the state of religion in Windsor in 1800: "Formerly, religion flourished in this town, and much good was done, but of late, whether from want of missionaries, or some other cause, the lovely plant seemed on the decline, and great indifference, gaiety, and fashion prevailed in its place; for though there was a church and a small Methodist chapel, I saw little vital christianity."[47]

Establishment of a connection with the English Wesleyan Conference in 1800 represented an effort on the part of such local preachers as Black to secure a stronger support of the work of the movement. The Wesleyan Conference had built up a powerful missionary organization, and its acceptance of responsibility for providing the Maritimes with preachers offered a means of meeting the problem of supplying religious services to a steadily growing population. As a result of the change, the Methodist movement became something of a missionary church.

The need for additional preachers was the most important single influence leading Black to approach the English Wesleyan Conference in 1800. Other influences of a more general sort, however, acted to secure the same result. Like the Newlight movement, the Methodist movement grew up within a fairly close ethnic-religious group and its expansion beyond the area in which it first developed brought it into conflict with the cultural values and mores of the wider community. Black early encountered, in a way similar to Alline, considerable

[44]Richey, *A Memoir of the Late William Black*, p. 188.
[45]*Ibid.*, p. 132.
[46]*Ibid.*, p. 156.
[47]Marsden, *Narrative of a Mission*, p. 32.

indifference to the evangelical message in the capital city of Halifax. "Tuesday, 11th," he wrote of June, 1782, "and on the two following days, preached at Halifax to a stupid set of people. Few seemed to care about their souls. O what a town for wickedness is this. Satan has here many faithful and steady servants."[48] Garrettson, later, met with an even more unfavourable reception in Halifax where he was severely stoned by a mob when attempting to hold revivalist services.[49] About the same time, Black, although meeting with no violence, was effectively prevented by the authorities of the city from preaching when he visited Saint John.[50] It was in the purely Loyalist settlements, however, that the greatest opposition was met with. The Methodist preachers were little more successful than the Newlights in gaining a hearing in the loyalist town of Shelburne. Black wrote of a meeting here in June, 1783:

> While I was praying, a person came up in the garb of a gentleman, cursing and swearing that what I said was a d——d lie: and threatening if I did not cease to knock me down . . . . He went away, and in a short time returned with two servants of the devil, more sturdy than himself. They came on like the mad bulls of Bashan; their mouths were full of blasphemies and awful imprecations. Their object was to tear me down, but the people would not suffer them to touch me.   One of them, swearing he could preach as well as I, mounted the stump of a tree, and poured forth a flood of oaths . . . . During the sermon, one man from the skirts of the congregation, threw a stone at me with great force, which had it struck me, would probably have carried death with it.[51]

The character of Methodist preachers and of Methodist preaching weakened the influence of the movement among certain elements of the population. As dependence increasingly came to be placed after 1790 upon preachers from the United States, antagonism to these preachers because of their American background became more pronounced. "I made bold to open matters to Mr. Wesley," Garrettson wrote to Asbury in 1786, "and begged of him to send one preacher from England, as a number of people would prefer an Englishman to an American. Many have refused hearing me on this account."[52] Methodism felt the effects of the change of attitudes resulting from the growing British feeling in the country after the American revolutionary war and during the early years of the war with France. The Yorkshire English, though nursing many of the dissatisfactions of a neglected colonial population, were deeply loyal in outlook, while the United

[48]Richey, *A Memoir of the Late William Black*, p. 69.
[49]Bangs, *Life of the Rev. Freeborn Garrettson*, pp. 156-7.
[50]T. Watson Smith, *History of the Methodist Church of Eastern British America* (Halifax, 1877), vol. I, pp. 225-6.
[51]Richey, *A Memoir of the Late William Black*, pp. 105-6.
[52]Bangs, *Life of the Rev. Freeborn Garrettson*, p. 178.

Empire Loyalists were aggressively so; upon these two groups the Methodist movement depended heavily for leadership and support. The growing importance of nationalist sentiments in the determination of religious attachments was an indication of the failure of the movement to adhere to the strict sectarian position of remaining indifferent to matters of political loyalty. The demands of British patriotism weakened the movement so long as the connection with the Methodist Episcopal Church was continued, and led in 1800 to the break of that connection and to the establishment of the tie with the English Wesleyan Conference.

Growing dissatisfaction with the American connection of the Methodist movement was closely related to a dislike among large sections of the population of the highly evangelical Methodist appeal. It was the Americans such as Freeborn Garrettson who were the most evangelical of the Methodist preachers and who were the least concerned about building up permanent loyalties and denominational attachments. They were evangelists whose one interest was to arouse a feeling of intense excitement; success was measured in terms of the number of converts rather than in terms of the strengthening of the regular church following. The result was that revivals tended to create momentarily an outburst of religious enthusiasm but to be followed by a reaction against all religious—and moral—principles of conduct. The unreliability of many Methodist converts gave rise to a feeling of distrust of Methodist revivals. Perkins wrote in his diary, January 12, 1797, of the religious state of the Methodist society in Liverpool after the revival the preceding winter:

> Contrast between the last winter, and this—then, both young and old, Gentle & Simple, were attending Religious Meetings, and their principal concern appeared to be: *what must we do to be Saved.* but how is the *Gold* becom dim, & the *find Gold* changed. Is not Religion the same now as it was last winter, is not Salvation of the Same Importance as it was then. Surely it is. what then has produced this change. is it because the people have had a taste of Religion and do not like it, or is it because they fancy themselves Safe, and have nothing more to do, but Like the Rich fool in the Gospel having much goods laid up for many years, they will take their ease eat drink, & be merry.

With the growth of Loyalist influence in the Methodist movement opposition to the use of a highly emotional appeal in revivalist meetings stiffened. The attitude of Duncan McColl in St. Stephen to religious extravagances was probably typical of that of Methodist preachers with a Loyalist background. McColl consistently strove to prevent excesses of religious excitement among the people to whom he ministered. "I do not encourage a noise, or crying out in meetings," he wrote of a meeting

on January 22, 1797; "yet, in cases where convictions are very strong &
terror great, it is difficult to restrain it."[53] In the winter of 1798-9
McColl was invited by Black to visit Annapolis where a revival was
in progress under John Cooper, a local preacher. "I immediately set
out," he wrote, "and found, on my arrival at Annapolis the next day,
this noisy work going on under the preaching of J.C.; but I felt sorry
that I could not altogether approve of the work."[54] Reliance upon
highly evangelical methods reflected the close connection of the
Methodist with the Newlight movement, and the growing reaction
against the use of such methods was indicative of a breaking from this
connection and of an increasing emphasis upon the traditional connection
with the Church of England. The American preachers, like Garrettson
from New England, and many of the local preachers were strongly
"New Light" in outlook even though they came in conflict with the
Newlight preachers; that was inevitably so where the American connection of the movement in the Maritimes was primarily with New
England Methodism. The break with the Methodist Episcopal Church
thus constituted something of a break from Newlightism and a reversion
to the early tie with Yorkshire Wesleyanism. The demand in 1800 for
the services of Wesleyan missionaries was a demand for preachers
who would keep the Methodist appeal more in line with the tradition
of a movement which had grown out of, and had not sharply separated
itself from, the Church of England. In appeal, as in form of organization,
establishment of the English Wesleyan tie signified the beginnings in
the Methodist movement of a shift away from the position of the
religious sect and the emergence of the church form of religious
organization.

Formation of the Baptist Association and establishment of the
English Wesleyan tie were a product of forces at work within the
Newlight and Methodist movements which were compelling a strengthening of denominational supports. By 1800 neither of these movements
could rely upon the sectarian principle of separating off from the world
and remaining indifferent to the mores and sentiments of the community
outside. Rapid changes in social relationships, resulting from war,
the development of trade, and the growth of wealth, led to the
intrusion of new values among the evangelical followings. Newlight
and Methodist leaders were given the choice of exercising very much
more ruthlessly the sectarian powers of excommunication and finding
themselves with a very considerably reduced following or of making

[53]*British North American Wesleyan Methodist Magazine for the Year 1841*, vol. I,
p. 458.
[54]*Ibid.*, p. 461.

their peace with some of the more insistent demands of the secular community and finding themselves with an increased but very much more worldly following. Vested interests of office almost inevitably determined that the latter choice would be made. The Newlight and Methodist movements in the first instance had grown out of demands within the community structure which placed primary insistence upon the sectarian attribute of separatism. With the change in nature of those demands, the will to exist led naturally—even though painfully— to the shift away from a separatist position and to a greater acceptance of the obligations of a church existing in close relationship to the community.

In Canada, as in the Maritime Provinces, the evangelical religious sect developed as the dominant form of religious organization within the new areas of settlement. Influenced by American frontier religious experience, the revival became the chief means of extending religious teachings and of gaining adherents to the religious cause. Churches which clung to a traditional approach found their influence seriously weakened in face of the growth of movements relying upon a more elementary religious appeal. Religious sectarianism led to a break away from religious forms and to an almost exclusive emphasis upon the experience of religious faith. Denominational lines were obscured with concentration upon the cause of religious salvation.

As in the Maritime Provinces, however, the spirit of harmony which characterized the evangelical crusade soon came to an end. Differences which at first were subordinated to the grand cause of religious salvation increasingly asserted themselves, and movements towards division within the evangelical following forced increasing attention to such matters as organization and doctrinal order. The sect inevitably had to grow into the church if it were to avoid the prospect of disintegration. In the Maritime Provinces, internal differences within the Newlight movement led to the shift to Baptist doctrines and to the organization of the Baptist Association and within the Methodist movement to the break of the tie with the Church in the United States and to the establishment of the connection with the English Wesleyan Conference. In Canada, internal differences within the evangelical movements led to very similar developments.

Before 1812 the close tie with the United States made possible the development of Methodism in Canada under the complete control of the Methodist Episcopal Church. The dominance of this Church in the American frontier settlements went unchallenged, and that dominance was readily extended into Canada. The General Conference made no distinction between the work on the two sides of the

border; appointments and the organization of circuits were determined in terms simply of Methodist interests. The demands of the frontier were decisive in moulding the general character of the movement.

After 1815, however, the Canadian society ceased to be simply a projection of the American frontier; population increasingly was drawn from older-settled areas of the United States, and from Great Britain, and new channels of communication developed. Conservative influences evident in the development of Methodism in the eastern United States and in England made themselves felt in the development of Methodism in Canada. The reaction to the narrow religious sectarianism bred on the frontier led to the intrusion of new Methodist movements which had departed a considerable distance from the highly evangelistic position of the Methodist Episcopal Church.

The growing importance of New England in the development of Canada was reflected in the spread of New England Methodist influence into the country. The Great Awakening in New England had run its course long before the rise of the Methodist movement under the leadership of Asbury, and the Methodist societies organized in the area, never enjoying any great strength, tended to resist the absolute dominance of the Methodist Episcopal General Conference.[55] Out of this dissatisfaction with the religious dictatorship of the frontier a number of new Methodist movements grew up in New England and some of them extended their influence across the border into Canada. In 1816, for instance, a group of Canadian Methodists in the fourth Concesssion of Ernestown, influenced by the Reformed Methodist Secession in New England, broke from the Episcopal Church and organized what they called the new "Reformed" Church.[56] Later, the American Protestant Church spread across from New England into the Eastern Townships where, by 1838, it had a sizeable following.[57] Though neither of these movements had any far-reaching effects upon the development of Methodism in the country, they were significant as indicating a growing revolt from the frontier religious tradition.

Much more far-reaching and permanent in its effects was the introduction of Wesleyan Methodist influences from England. Unlike Nova Scotia, where the early adherents of the Methodist movement had been Wesleyans from England, Wesleyanism had no following in Canada before 1812. Missionary work was left entirely to the American

[55]See Herbert Asbury, *A Methodist Saint: The Life of Bishop Asbury* (New York, 1927).
[56]John Carroll, *Case and His Cotemporaries, or the Canadian Itinerants' Memorial* (Toronto, 1867-77), vol. II, p. 48.
[57]See the *Methodist New Connexion Magazine and Evangelical Repository for the year 1838.*

Methodists. With the outbreak of war between Canada and the United States, and the withdrawal of most of the American preachers, the field was left open to Wesleyan missionary efforts. The immediate demands of patriotism growing out of the war situation, and the later demands of religious loyalty resulting from the settlement of a number of English Wesleyans in the country, led the English Wesleyan Conference to embark upon an ambitious missionary programme in Canada. The first Wesleyan missionaries arrived in 1816.

Wesleyanism seriously cut into the following of the American Methodist preachers who undertook to re-organize their work in Canada on the conclusion of the War of 1812. The effects of their competition were immediately felt in such places as Montreal where the British tie was strong. "The society in Montreal," Ferguson wrote of the early part of 1816, "was now divided, and . . . our people were chiefly poor, and had to hire a house to preach in. . . . The P. Elder had employed a Local Preacher, for the town."[58] During the year 1817-18 the American society increased by only one member. "We opine," Carroll wrote, "the current ran strongly towards the British Society. They had gone up to 80."[59] By the end of the year 1818, in the words of the Methodist historian, "the American Section of Methodism in that city was so reduced by the presence and the influence of the British brethren, that then and for several years before, and even after, till 1820, when they finally removed, as there was no missionary fund to fall back on, the place was forced to receive a single man, who, however, was usually ordained to deacon's orders at least."[60]

In other centres, where the British Wesleyans became established, the American Methodists lost support. "In this place also," Ferguson wrote of the work in Johnstown in 1817, "the unhappy differences occasioned by the interference of the English Missionaries, exerted an unhappy influence. A demand was made by one of the Missionaries, Mr. Henry Pope, upon our preachers, to go into the interior and leave the frontiers to the English, etc."[61] On the Cornwall circuit, the American Society lost in members during the year 1817-18. "So much for the effects," Carroll wrote, "of the 'Missionary war!' The British brethren were evidently fast crowding the first occupants to the wall on this ground."[62] The next year the American preacher, Nathaniel Reeder,

[58]University of Toronto, Victoria University Library, Journal of the Rev. George Ferguson, A Minister of the W. Methodist Church in Canada, copied from the original, p. 70.

[59]Carroll, *Case and His Cotemporaries*, vol. II, p. 132.

[60]*Ibid.*, p. 185.

[61]Journal of the Rev. George Ferguson, p. 87.

[62]Carroll, *Case and His Contemporaries*, vol II, p. 133.

appointed to the circuit, faced increasing difficulty in holding the Society together. "The British missionaries," Carroll wrote, "two in number, and very able and industrious men, had taken possession of the ground, and appealed strongly to the loyalty of the people of that region, while he [Reeder] was very American, both in his speech and manners; and, with all his piety, vastly inferior in ministerial qualifications to his European rivals. Hence, notwithstanding his proverbial laboriousness, he only returned an addition of four to the members of the previous year."[63]

The competition of the rival groups in Niagara was even more keen and bitter. "Mr. Pope, the English Missionary," Ferguson wrote of his work on this circuit in 1817, "commenced the unenviable work of setting up other altars, in opposition to ours. . . . Mr. Pope used every means to prejudice the minds of the people against us. He preached 'Loyalty' 'British Authority,' etc. He succeeded in drawing a few away. But his adherents were, chiefly, persons who had been shorn of their spirituality by politics and war. In some places, where he reared his standard in our society—the 'wild fire,' as he called it, burned him out."[64] The success of the British missionaries during the year 1817-18 was evident in the enrolment of seventy members while Ferguson and his fellow-worker, Smith, lost a greater number.[65] In the Augusta circuit, the American preachers reported a loss of thirty-eight members in the year 1819-20 while the British missionaries had a gain of fifty.[66]

By this time Wesleyanism had established itself in the town of York with effects felt by the American Society. "Despite the liveliness of the York Society meetings," Carroll wrote, "Mr. Belton returned at the end of the year [1819-20] only 43 members, against the 65 of the previous year. Some of these may have been lost by the 'alteration of boundaries,' but I am inclined to think that it arose entirely from several of the old country members transferring themselves to the society which was formed during this Conference year, under the auspices of the British missionaries."[67] During the year 1820 the Reverend Henry Pope preached in York. "His preaching," Carroll wrote, "was very acceptable to the better educated, and drew a sizeable congregation. He collected, also, a very considerable Society. Some of these were respectable Wesleyans from the Old Country—both English and Irish. There were the Coates, and Hutchinsons, and Woodalls, and Bosfields, and Bulls, and others gathered in from the town. A

[63]*Ibid.*, pp. 179-80.
[64]Journal of the Rev. George Ferguson, pp. 93-4.
[65]Carroll, *Case and His Cotemporaries*, vol. II, p. 216.
[66]*Ibid.*, p. 246.
[67]*Ibid.*, p. 227.

number of the Society from the wooden meeting-house on King Street, left and joined them: such as the Levers', and some others."[68] The membership of the American Society dropped to twenty-two while that of the British Society reached thirty.[69]

The agreement of 1818 between the Methodist Episcopal Church in the United States and the Wesleyan Conference in England by which the former abandoned the work in Lower Canada and the latter the work in Upper Canada with the exception of Kingston was an attempt to put an end to the bitter conflict developing between the two bodies in the Canadian field. The solution, however, was only in part successful. The formal withdrawal of the Methodist Episcopal preachers from Lower Canada constituted for the most part a recognition of a situation which had already become established. By 1820 the American Society in Montreal had reached a precarious state of existence, where worship was carried on in an upper room of an old building. Nevertheless, while many of the members after the agreement transferred their allegiance to the Wesleyan Society, others joined with a number of American Presbyterians in the organization of an American Presbyterian Church.[70] In Upper Canada, the strains involved · in the re-organization were considerably greater; many of the supporters of Wesleyanism did not readily shift their support to the Methodist Episcopal societies.

As prejudice had been increased against the preachers to whom the country was to be given up, by controversy, they [the members of the Wesleyan societies] were slow to put themselves under their care. Some of them never did so at all, but either joined other communions—and were lost to Methodism—or they failed to join any Church, and were lost to God and religion. Thus in Toronto, while the Bosfields, and Levers, and Lackeys, and Bulls—some later, some later—united with the so-called "American" preachers; the Coates', and Hutchinsons, and Fentons never did. Mr. Coates and some others held a separate meeting, to the writer's certain knowledge, at least for four years afterwards.[71]

The Episcopal Methodists were little more successful in re-establishing their cause in Niagara. Here, according to Carroll, relying on the testimony of the Reverend Mr. Brady, "very few of the British members joined the other Society after the Missionaries left."[72] In other areas, also, the Methodist Episcopal preachers met with resistance from people of overseas origin; "some of them, however," the Reverend Richard Jones wrote of the Methodists in the Perth settlement who

[68]*Ibid.*, p. 342.
[69]*Ibid.*, p. 227.
[70]*Ibid.*, p. 335.
[71]*Ibid.*, p. 345.
[72]*Ibid.*, p. 340.

had participated in a revival under his preaching, "had been members in Ireland, and were greatly prejudiced against American Methodism."[73]

The agreement of 1818 shut out the Wesleyan missionaries from Upper Canada but opposition to the Methodist Episcopal preachers, many of them Americans, remained strong. Organization in 1824 of an annual conference in Canada to control Methodist work in the country was part of a general move to free Canadian Methodism from American control. In 1828 the Canada Conference was formed and the Methodist Church in Canada became completely independent of the Methodist Episcopal Church in the United States.

The drive to secure an independent Canadian Methodist Church, however, had not proceeded sufficiently rapidly to prevent a schism within the movement of a number of Irish Methodists under the leadership of Elder Henry Ryan. Ryan had taken a strong stand against the American tie of Methodism and his protests had much to do with the establishment of the Canada Conference; he broke from the Church the very year the Conference came into being. The schism constituted a protest of the more conservative Irish Methodists against the strong American frontier influence in Canadian Methodism.

The limitations of Ryan as a church leader served to check any rapid growth of the religious movement he promoted, but its rise carried threats to the position of the main Methodist body, particularly among the Irish population. Organizing what he called the Wesleyan Primitive Methodist Church, Ryan soon attracted fellow-preachers to his side, and societies were successfully organized in many parts of the country. Gains in membership cut into the following of the regular Methodist societies. "My removal to Hallowell," Ferguson wrote of the year 1828, "was still more distressing to me. Mr. Ryan had commenced his career. He was zealous, and talented withal. Loyalty was his catch-word, and he constantly denounced the ministers of the Canada Conference as disloyal. Hallowell was one of his strongholds."[74] Before the end of the conference year, James Jackson withdrew from the Canada Conference and began the organization of rival societies in this circuit.[75] From Cobourg, William Case wrote, November 17, 1828: "I again write you to say that information is received by Bro. Evens who has just come up to his circuit that Mr. Ryan is again proceeding in his work of stirring up the feelings of the people to discontent and division."[76] The next year Carroll and David Wright

[73]*Ibid.*, p. 435.
[74]Journal of the Rev. George Ferguson, p. 125.
[75]Carroll, *Case and His Cotemporaries*, vol. III, pp. 234-5.
[76]Quoted C. B. Sissons, *Egerton Ryerson; His Life and Letters* (Toronto, 1937), vol. 1, p. 92.

were appointed to the Cobourg circuit. "We found the upper part of the Circuit," Carroll wrote, "much torn to pieces by the Ryan-Jackson division. There was only one small class at the Back Chapel, and no organized class in Cobourg."[77] In other areas, as well, the party led by Ryan made headway. "The young preacher on the Cavan Circuit," Carroll wrote, "had his own anxieties. His inexperience had to cope with the hostility engendered against the Conference and the Church, by a strong sympathy among our Irish friends in that region for Mr. Ryan. Mr. Moses Blackstock, who was very influential among his neighbors, withdrew, and was several years outside of central Methodism, in the Province, and many others went also."[78] In his reminiscences, Anson Green wrote of May 9, 1830: "This day I preached in Niagara, where a bold and lion-like effort had been made to drive us from our church and congregation. Last Sabbath evening when my colleague went to the church he was surprised to see our old friend, Mr. Ryan, in the pulpit; but before he recovered from his surprise, he was still more astounded to see Mr. R. stand up, without saying a word to him, and preach at his appointment, to his congregation, and in his presence! And then, with his characteristic modesty, give out another appointment for this evening, at my hour!"[79] The clash of John Ryerson with the Ryanites in Emily, in the Cavan circuit, in 1833, was an indication of the continuation of bitterness between the rival groups.[80]

The defection of Irish Wesleyans under the leadership of Ryan indicated very clearly the growing instability of the Methodist movement in Canada. The Canadian Methodists found it increasingly difficult to capture the support of the British Wesleyans settling in the country, and this division within the Methodist body afforded a justification to the English Wesleyan Conference in disregarding the agreement of 1818 and in deciding upon the resumption of missionary work in Upper Canada. In 1832 Alder, who had presided at the District meeting of Lower Canada that year, suddenly appeared in York accompanied by three other Wesleyan ministers; services were carried on in the Upper Canadian capital in direct competition with services held by two Methodist Episcopal preachers. "Now," in the words of Carroll, "the Metropolitan school-house, under the direction of the Archdeacon of York himself, is thrown open to the newly-arrived Wesleyan ministers!"[81]

[77]Carroll, *Case and His Cotemporaries*, vol. III, p. 267.

[78]*Ibid.*, p. 237. The English in Cavan circuit, however, Carroll pointed out, did not support the Ryanite party.

[79]*The Life and Times of the Rev. Anson Green, Written by Himself* (Toronto, 1877), p. 137.

[80]See, *Christian Guardian*, May 1, 1833.

[81]Carroll, *Case and His Cotemporaries*, vol. III, pp. 351-2.

Inquiries elicited the discomforting information that the English Wesleyan Conference proposed to provide missionaries to all the English Wesleyan settlements in Upper Canada. Union of the Canadian and English Conferences offered itself as the only means of preventing the complete division of Methodist forces in the country. From such union there emerged the Wesleyan Methodist Church in Canada.

The Baptist movement in Canada never enjoyed the unity which was characteristic of the early development of Methodism under the control of the Methodist Episcopal Church of the United States. The failure of the American Baptist churches to develop any centralized missionary organization during the early years of the nineteenth century left the Baptist work in frontier areas of settlement entirely under the direction of individual congregations. Churches were formed wherever preachers were available, and little concern was shown whether the preachers were of the Regular or Free Will Baptist order. A great variety of doctrinal views found expression in the early Canadian Baptist churches; any attempt to have introduced greater order would have been jealously resisted by the different congregations.

Yet in terms of the general character of the Baptist movement as it developed in Canada before 1830 a semblance of unity was evident. The movement was distinctively American in origin. If the American Baptist churches had no strong ties with the frontier, the Baptist churches in Canada were nevertheless considerably influenced by frontier religious practices. This was particularly true in Upper Canada. Here most of the Baptist settlers were people who had been a part of the American frontier movement of population. Their religious thinking had been formed out of experiences of the Great Revival of the American West. The preachers they recruited during the early years of church building were likewise men who had secured their early religious training under the influence of the evangelical revivals of the American frontier. An intense sectarianism was characteristic of all the early Baptist churches of Upper Canada.

Overseas immigration after 1820 brought to the country an increasing number of English Baptists, and by 1837 sizeable groups of such Baptists were to be found in the Eastern Townships, Montreal, and in various parts of Upper Canada, particularly in the area north of Peterborough. Settlement of English Baptists led to demands for the services of English Baptist preachers, and out of such demands there emerged in 1837 the Canada Baptist Missionary Society to recruit missionaries from overseas. The rapid increase in the number of English Baptist missionaries during the next five years led to the consolidation of English influence, and organization of the Canada Baptist Union

in 1843 marked the culmination of efforts to secure centralized control of the Canadian movement through the establishment of strong ties with the English Church. Out of the union of the individual Baptist churches there emerged something of an integrated Baptist denomination in the country.

Divisive forces also made themselves felt in the development of the American Presbyterian movement. The War of 1812-14 almost destroyed the movement in Canada. Most of the preachers were lost to the United States, and overseas influences within Presbyterianism were strengthened greatly with the growth in the number of Scottish people in the country. The revival of the American Presbyterian cause in the eighteen-thirties was a reflection of the continued strength of the American frontier tie in the western parts of Upper Canada, but the rebellion of 1837 led to a weakening of that tie and to the complete disintegration of the American Presbyterian movement.[82] Most of the American Presbyterian preachers were considered disloyal by a population threatened with punitive expeditions from the United States, and churches which before 1837 had prospered through separation from Scottish Presbyterianism suddenly faced the necessity of accepting Scottish Presbyterian leadership. American Presbyterianism as a distinctive evangelical movement disappeared in Canada.

The Methodist, American Presbyterian, and Baptist evangelistic religious movements had grown out of the social situation in Canada produced by the expansion of the American agricultural frontier into the country and the emergence of the backwoods community. Development of the timber trade, overseas immigration, and the construction of public works and the shift from mixed to specialized wheat farming led gradually to fundamental changes in social conditions evident in the growth of towns, the strengthening of class lines, the growth of a powerful merchant class, and the increasing cultural maturity of the older-settled agricultural areas which called for far-reaching adjustments within the organization of religion. Techniques developed to meet the needs of backwoods settlement, where population was socially and culturally isolated, proved increasingly inadequate when the chief problem of religious organization became one of serving communities which were economically and culturally mature. Efforts of the evangelistic religious movements to adjust to this changing situation led to bitter internal conflicts and eventually, through the support of ties with overseas churches, to the breaking away from a sectarian religious position and to organization along denominational lines.

[82]H. E. Parker, "Early Presbyterianism in Western Ontario" (*Transactions*, London and Middlesex Historical Society, 1930, pp. 10-79).

The failure of Canadian Methodism to meet the competition of English Wesleyanism, which led to the necessity for union in 1832, was an indication of weaknesses within the movement growing out of changes in the community structure after 1815. Methodism had developed in terms of the needs of isolated frontier settlements peopled largely from the United States, and the problem of adjusting to the conditions of a more mature society forced changes in organization and appeal which could only be brought about through English Wesleyan leadership. Union was the price paid to overcome the strong resistance of sectarian influences which persisted within the Canadian Methodist movement.

One of the most immediate problems of adjustment faced by the Methodist movement after 1815 was that of providing religious services to a rapidly growing population resulting from overseas immigration. Growth of population called for an increasing number of recruits to the ministry at the very time the Methodist movement was threatened with a reduction in its preaching ranks through the dying off of the old preachers. By 1820 Methodism in Canada had ceased to be a first-generation movement. The Great Revival which had swept over the western United States and Upper Canada between 1791 and 1806 had raised up hundreds of preachers to carry on the work of Methodist evangelization. Case and Bangs were two of those preachers who had played a prominent part in the spread of Methodism in Canada. As the movement became older, however, reliance upon the revival as a means of recruiting preachers became increasingly precarious. The "call" to the ministry became less compelling as other occupational opportunities presented themselves.

The drying up of the sources of ministerial supply became evident in Canada immediately upon the close of the War of 1812-14. Most of the American preachers left the country on the outbreak of hostilities and considerable difficulty was faced in recruiting a new supply after the war. By the eighteen-twenties Canadian Methodism was forced to think in terms of relying upon preachers raised up within the country. Difficulties in making this adjustment came during the period of the rapid influx of overseas immigrants. By the time of the union with the English Conference, several areas settled by Methodists in Canada were being inadequately supplied with religious services. A correspondent wrote in the *Christian Guardian* in 1832: "Many of those who first entered the itinerant field in Canada are worn or nearly worn out, and some have gone from labour to rest and reward. Most of the circuits are very large, for want of preachers to supply the work. Now this

excess of labour is wearing out those who are still efficient, and will probably hurry many of them into an untimely grave."[83]

The problem faced by the Church became one of replacing those who were gradually retiring from the field and, at the same time, of securing additions to take care of the increase of population. Among the reasons for its failure to meet this problem, the correspondent to the *Christian Guardian* emphasized two in particular.

> But the great deficiency in the temporal support of the Itinerant labourers in our Church, and the want of a permanent provision for the future subsistence of those who are worn-out in the service of the Church, is another cause, inasmuch as it prevents (it is to be feared) many from entering, and drives others from the field. There are probably not more than one third of our preachers who receive their full disciplinary allowance, and many who do not receive much more than one half of it, which exposes them oftentimes (especially if they have families) to pinching want . . . .
>
> Another cause is the general want of accommodations for preachers' families. This in many, and I may say in almost every part of the Province, is not only a source of grief and temptation to Preachers, but a disgrace to the Methodist Church.

The problem of Methodism after 1820 was not simply one of increasing the number of workers in the field. Fundamental weaknesses in the Methodist organization became apparent with the extension of its work into the towns and into the older-settled communities. The yearly rotation of the Methodist preachers, and reliance upon the itinerant system, weakened the cause in those areas where the building up of the church depended upon more permanent contacts. Within the rural communities, the local preachers working in co-operation with the itinerants, performed this role of maintaining permanent contacts between the church and the members, but conditions were unfavourable to the development of a body of local preachers in the more culturally mature communities. In such communities, without the services of permanently located ministers, the population was dependent upon the infrequent visits of itinerants. The *Christian Guardian* wrote editorially, April 9, 1834:

> Methodism, like the agricultural improvements of the Province, is in an imperfect state; it is pure in its doctrines and principles, but imperfect in its degree. Its ordinances are in general but partially enjoyed, and some of its rules are little more than a dead letter. This arises from the circumstances of the work. For example, how *many hundred* places are there in which there ought to be preaching *every* Sabbath, instead of once a *fortnight*, as is now generally the case, and sometimes only once in four weeks? And how many hundred places are there in which there ought to be *Sabbath*, instead of *week-day* preaching? It is well known that in all the circuits,

---

[83] *Christian Guardian*, Aug. 1, 1832.

except a few towns and villages, the people enjoy circuit preaching only once a fortnight; in many cases not so often.[84]

The consequences, the editor went on to point out, were evident in the generally weakened state of the Methodist societies. Where congregations had no access to books and were entirely dependent upon preaching for correct views on points of faith and practice, they were governed more in their views and actions by their feelings than by their judgments and were therefore liable to many inconsistencies and frequent backslidings and were blown about by every wind of doctrine. Those of the congregations who were not members of the societies, having the preached word but half or not half of the sabbaths, did not form a habit of regular attendance, and in the intervals they attended other places of worship and in some instances became regular hearers there or, as was more generally the case, they became indifferent to sabbath observance and eventually attended no public worship at all. "But this is not all," the editor continued. "In these long intervals, factionists and wolves, with various forms of sheep's clothing, creep in, and not unfrequently divide, destroy and devour. The teacher and shepherd is absent. Queries are proposed that the partially informed cannot solve; objections are started that the unskilful cannot answer; representations and appeals are made, calculated to disquiet, agitate, and inflame." Finally, for want of visiting from house to house, family religion was neglected, while Methodist children were sometimes brought up without being taught the principles of religion.

Methodism increasingly faced the problem characteristic of the religious sect which relied in its early development upon self-appointed prophets but which was forced to become dependent upon a professional ministry. Attitudes of the sectarian among the Methodist following checked the provision of those conditions necessary for the making of the ministry professionally attractive. Efforts to establish a Methodist college were indicative of a realization that ministers in the future could only be secured the hard way; but colleges—and increased salaries to ministers—cost money, and Canadian Methodists were little inclined to make financial contributions to the Church. Union with the English Wesleyan Conference offered itself as the only practicable solution to the problem of meeting the growing overhead costs of denominational organization. English Wesleyanism had all the advantages of. the territorial church while Canadian Methodism clung to the narrow separateness of the religious sect. The English Wesleyan Conference had built up a powerful missionary organization, and the growing imperialist

[84]*Ibid.,* **Apr. 9, 1834.**

interests of the Wesleyan membership in Britain led to a willingness to make heavy financial contributions towards colonial missionary activities. Union made it possible for Canadian Methodist leaders to share in the financial resources of an imperialist church even though by doing so it meant destroying the sectarian basis of the Canadian Methodist movement.

The problem of recruiting more preachers, and building up a professional ministry, was not the only one faced by Canadian Methodism after 1815. The weakening of the movement derived in part from its continued reliance upon a highly evangelistic religious appeal. Whereas such an appeal had been a means of strengthening the cause in the rural backwoods society, it came increasingly to lose its effectiveness with the passing of backwoods conditions of life. Strengthening of secular interests within the community reflected the richer cultural heritage of the British immigrants and the accumulating social experience of the older settlers and was reflected in the strengthening of secular organizations. The general state of ignorance, characteristic of the earlier frontier stage, was passing with the passing of the frontier, and improvements in the cultural arts had weakening effects upon a religious movement relying upon a primitive religious appeal. Changes in educational standards of the population and in its cultural values and tastes led to growing dissatisfaction with the revivalist preaching of the Canadian Methodists.

Criticism of the Methodist religious appeal came naturally from those who had the least appreciation of the evangelical tradition. "Meetings are held," Howison wrote about 1820 respecting Methodists in the district of St. Catharines, "at different houses, three or four times a week. At some of these I have seen degrees of fanaticism and extravagance exhibited, both by the Preachers and congregation, which were degrading to human nature."[85] Proudfoot, with the prejudices of a Scottish Presbyterian, was severe in his condemnation of the Methodist religious influence. On one occasion, while visiting a Scottish farmer in the district of London, the conversation turned to the subject of the Methodists. "The extravagances of Methodism," part of the entry in the diary reads, "were often referred to. These people are certainly honoured to do a great deal of good and yet they are chargeable with as many follies as one could well suppose attachable to men who do so much from, as they say, the fear of God."[86]

Camp meetings, held under conditions where order was difficult

[85] John Howison, *Sketches of Upper Canada* (Edinburgh, 1821), p. 150.
[86] "Proudfoot **Papers**" (*Transactions*, London and Middlesex Historical Society, 1922, p. 65).

to maintain, were particularly exposed to outside criticism. Edward Talbot, unfriendly to everything American, had nothing favourable to say of such meetings:

Regular encampments are formed and whole families relinquish the pleasures of home for the enviable lot of sitting for a week or ten days under the continual sound and thunder of the American Gospel,—I should rather say, for the felicity of seeing promiscuous thousands exhibit the wildest specimens of the wildest fanaticism; while some are displaying a burlesque or caricature of religion, and others are admiring the piquancy of the design, the remainder take advantage of the general confusion, to delineate in all shades of fraud, and vice, and debauchery, and profaneness, a most accurate picture of impiety.[87]

Proudfoot wrote, December 13, 1833, of the effects of a camp meeting in the London District: "Was told by Mr. McFarlane that some who made a great show at the late camp meeting on the Proof Line have in consequence of over exertion in shouting been in bad health ever since, and that one man has died and that another is speechless. It is a horrible delusion."[88] On another occasion, speaking of the Methodists, he wrote: "Every person of Scottish origin is shocked at the absurdities and unpieties of their camp meetings."[89]

Efforts to defend the camp meeting suggest the recognition, even on the part of Methodists themselves, that irregularities sometimes occurred. "Exceptions have been taken to Camp meetings," Ferguson wrote in his journal, "because of the frequent disorder, and vice perpetrated by the lawless and unprincipled. The assembling together such a vast number of persons of all characters, cannot fail to produce crime and disorder, it is said, however vigilant and careful the friends may be. Still, it cannot be denied that incalculable good has attended them. The wicked lay hold of every opportunity to do evil, and they would, perhaps, do none the less crime if Camp meetings were not held."[90] Wilkie, though inclined to defend the camp meeting, was prepared likewise to admit that irregularities occurred as a result of the attendance of people who were not religiously-minded. "I may observe here, that whatever contradictory statements have been promulgated regarding the religious meetings that take place in the woods, I cannot help believing that the indecencies are not part and portion of the transactions sanctioned by those who lead the devotions of the assembly. It would be injustice to lay to the charge of those who assemble for

[87]E. A. Talbot, *Five Years' Residence in the Canadas* (London, 1824), vol. II, pp. 157-8.
[88]"Proudfoot Papers" (*Papers and Records*, Ontario Historical Society, vol. XXVII, 1931, p. 451).
[89]"Proudfoot Papers" (*Transactions*, London and Middlesex Historical Society, 1922, p. 65).
[90]Journal of the Rev. George Ferguson, pp. 137-8.

sacred purposes, all the sins that are committed by idlers, who choose to spend their time in licentiousness, and seize the opportunity to do so, while others come together for the exercise of their faith and religion."[91]

The *Christian Guardian*, similarly, insisted that the disorder occurring at camp meetings resulted from the intrusion of those who were opposed to the purposes of such meetings:

Much has recently been said by one description of press in the Province against religious revivals, and meetings well adapted to promote them. Some of the meetings have been represented as designed to encourage the most disgraceful and pernicious vices . . . . Careful observation warrants us in the remark, that persons who speak reproachfully of meetings, the primary and sole object of which is to suppress vice and encourage virtue, are the disorderly culprits, who, in defiance of the published and diligently enforced regulations of such meetings, attempt to perpetrate the very immoralities which they profess to exclaim lustily against in others.[92]

Claims of Methodist apologists that the rowdyism of camp meetings was caused by outsiders contained an element of truth, but such an explanation overlooked the obvious fact that it was the very purpose of such meetings to attract the unattached and the irreligious. The camp meeting could not operate successfully as a closed group. Thus it was inevitably exposed to the charge that it provided a meeting place for the rowdies of the community. Efforts to maintain order through the appointment of special constables, and the adoption of the practice of erecting a fence around the grounds and admitting people only through properly appointed gates, met with some success, but there was a limit to the extent to which people could be excluded because they were considered undesirable. Expulsion rather than exclusion became the chief means employed to put an end to irregularities within the camp meetings.[93]

[91]D. Wilkie, *Sketches of a Summer Trip to New York and the Canadas* (Edinburgh, 1837), p. 225.
[92]*Christian Guardian*, July 30, 1831.
[93]That such means proved fairly effective was indicated by the emphasis in reports of various camp meetings upon the fact that little disorder occurred. "No instances of disorderly conduct," a correspondent wrote of a camp meeting on Long Point circuit, "occurred on the encampment, although the general Training was held within a half mile of the meeting" (*Christian Guardian*, June 25, 1831). Of a camp meeting on Ancaster circuit, the report read: "The good order of the vast assemblage was unexampled in that part of the province. But one or two instances of disorderly conduct occurred during the whole four days" (*ibid.*, June 25, 1831). A meeting on the Toronto circuit was equally free from irregularities. "The order of the meeting," a correspondent signing himself "A Labourer" wrote, "throughout was undisturbed, except in one or two instances. A magistrate in Toronto (Esq. B) kindly offered to swear in a number of special constables, to maintain the observance of the rules of the meeting; but such was the orderly and respectful conduct of those who attended on the occasion, that the official services of constables were not required" (*ibid.*, July 16, 1831). Another correspondent wrote of a camp meeting on the Waterloo circuit: "During the whole encampment there was not a single instance of either rabble or tumult on the outside of the camp. All were quiet, all

The charge of irregularities associated with the camp meeting was only one of the criticisms levelled against this form of religious fellowship. In the end, it was not the rowdyism of the irreligious but the emotional excitement of the religious which was objected to most. The camp meeting in this respect appeared particularly objectionable because it was so open to public view. Publicity had been the means of establishing the popularity of the camp meeting, but publicity was also the means of discrediting it among large sections of the population. Reports of extraordinary conversions which took place within such gatherings aroused a feeling of disgust on the part of those people who disliked revivalist methods. "As to excitement of feelings," the *Christian Guardian* wrote in answer to the criticism that camp meetings encouraged fanatical forms of religious expression, "we know of nothing more there to produce an improper one than at other places. The truth is preached with plainness and boldness, warm exhortations are given, and fervent prayers offered up for the conviction and conversion of sinners and sanctification of believers; and what religious person, especially a Methodist, can disapprove of feelings proceeding from these causes, even though they should rise in an agony of supplication, or extacy in rejoicing and praise."[94]

The increasing space which the *Christian Guardian* devoted to answering such attacks upon the camp meeting was perhaps the best indication of their growing seriousness. So long as the opposition to the Methodist evangelical appeal came from spokesmen of such religious bodies as the Church of England it aroused no concern; one more proof was offered that the Church of England was given up to formalism and had no real interest in religious salvation. When the opposition, however, came from sections of the population to which the Methodists were anxious to appeal, it carried threats to the whole Methodist

---

were peaceable; insomuch that we were under no necessity of shutting the gates day or night, or of having a guard" (*ibid.*, July 25, 1832). The *Christian Guardian* wrote editorially respecting the generally good order maintained in camp meetings, July 3, 1833:

"As to disorder, we are bold to say, from what we have known of these meetings for several years, there is no just ground for the charge. The meeting is begun, conducted, and ended, with the most scrupulous regard to order. With a view to this, the ground is enclosed with a compact barrier of timber and brush, having a main gate for entrance, another to the watering place, and two others for private retirement—the men's on one side, the women's on the other, with the most positive and repeated injunctions against intruding on each other.

"During preaching, the men and women sit apart on seats prepared for them, and the same order is observed in the prayer-meetings. A vigilant watch, of from 10 to 20 persons, selected each day for that service, is kept up night and day, and the ground is well illuminated at night with blazing fires on stands erected for the purpose."

[94]*Christian Guardian*, July 3, 1833.

position. That became the case with the growth of the Wesleyan population in the country. Wesleyanism in England had lost much of the evangelical zeal which had been characteristic of the movement in the time of Wesley and Whitefield, and the English Wesleyans settling in Canada in increasing numbers after 1820 were little attracted by the highly evangelical appeal which was characteristic of Canadian Methodism.

This was most evident in the opposition of the Wesleyans to the camp meeting. Indications were not lacking that Wesleyan leaders hoped, with the union with the Canadian Conference in 1832, to abolish completely the holding of such meetings in Canada.[95] When such an object appeared impossible of accomplishment, grudging support was given to these meetings but it was made clear that they should be considered as only temporarily expedient. "From all I have been able to learn," W. M. Harvard, the President of the Wesleyan-Methodist Conference wrote in the *Christian Guardian*, "it appears to me that Camp Meetings were certainly more necessary in former days, when the country was more thinly settled, and places of worship but few in number. And there can be no doubt they have often been rendered signally useful in the conversion of sinners to God. Now it is conceived Protracted Meetings will very generally supercede them in many places."[96]

The attitude of the Wesleyans to camp meetings reflected their attitude in general to revivalist methods. Every effort was made by Wesleyan missionaries in conducting revivalist services to discourage any strong expression of religious feelings. "I trust this revival," the Reverend Benjamin Slight, Wesleyan missionary, wrote of a revival on one of his appointments in Eramossa in January, 1841, "is of somewhat better character than those in general seen in the country. There is too much effort to produce excitement. They are too often 'got up.' In consequence of this the greater part *fall away*, & a general deadness ensues. On this account they tend to bring religion into disrespect."[97] Later, in the Eastern Townships, Slight found that one of the reasons for the weakness of the Methodist cause was the love for excitement of the members. "Something new," he wrote in support of this claim, "is the constant object of enquiry. The most absurd & enormous statements are swallowed with greediness: wild & erratic

[95]See Sissons, *Egerton Ryerson*, vol. I, p. 156.
[96]*Christian Guardian*, July 11, 1838.
[97]University of Toronto, Victoria University Library, The Journal of Benjamin Slight, Missionary, Appointed by the Wesleyan Missionary Committee, London, to Upper Canada, 1834-1857, vol. II, p. 2.

theories are cherished."[98] Other Wesleyan missionaries were equally opposed to revivalist methods. "He was not what one would call a revivalist," Senator John Macdonald wrote of John P. Hetherington, the second superintendent of the Wesleyan St. George Street church in Toronto after the dissolution of the union, "and objected to the holding of special services, unless special reasons were manifest for these."[99]

Opposition of the Wesleyan missionaries to revivalist methods afforded them considerable advantages in meeting the competition of Canadian Methodist preachers in areas settled predominantly by old-country people. It was the leaders rather than the following of the Canadian Methodist movement who were most sensitive to trends in social thinking away from elementary religious conceptions. These leaders themselves had become increasingly sophisticated in regard to religious matters and readily turned to union in 1832 as a means of retaining the support of the more sophisticated section of the Methodist population. Union constituted a formal, if not wholly realizable, abandonment of the highly evangelistic religious appeal introduced into the country by the American itinerant preachers.

The break from a highly evangelistic religious appeal was inevitable in terms of the changing character of the Methodist movement. Devout Methodists became prosperous, partly because of their devoutness, and the movement which had grown up through the support of the masses found itself more and more dependent upon the support of the classes. The intrusion of class values in the thinking of the Methodist following—and Methodist leadership—became particularly evident with the rapid growth of the Wesleyan population in the country. Conflict between Canadian Methodism and English Wesleyanism reflected increasing strains in the movement resulting from the strengthening of class lines within the Methodist membership.

Methodism had grown up in Canada in terms of the support of a rural backwoods population which had no vested interests in a system of class distinctions. The character of the early American itinerant preachers reflected the social character of the movement generally. The itinerant preacher was something of a rustic serving a rustic population. His limited educational qualifications and his humble social background constituted little handicap in a society where education had made little progress and where the great majority of the rural families had been drawn from an American frontier which had been

___

[98]*Ibid.*, vol. II, no pag.
[99]Senator John Macdonald, "Recollections of British Wesleyanism in Toronto" (*Methodist Magazine*, vol. XXIX, Jan. to June, 1889, p. 526).

characterized by the almost complete absence of class distinctions. With the growth, however, of towns, the increase of wealth, and the immigration from overseas of people of education and social standing, the limitations of a movement depending upon uneducated preachers became increasingly more evident. Such preachers experienced difficulty in ministering to a population which had some appreciation of learning and which also had an understanding of theological principles. "Although my want of knowledge and information," Ferguson admitted, "often embarrassed me in the more intelligent circles, I invariably experienced their good will and kindness, as well as from the people generally."[100] The homely style of preaching of the Methodist itinerants, and their lack of any great philosophical or theological understanding of the problems with which they dealt, while no handicap in the country districts, placed them at a disadvantage in the towns where they came in competition with ministers who set a high standard of pulpit oratory. "The sermon," Proudfoot wrote of a service of a Methodist local preacher which he attended in Brantford, "was a very poor production, unfit for the purposes (so far as I could see) of either instruction or piety. I marvelled that such a man could have ever fancied that he was born to be an instructor."[101]

[100]Journal of the Rev. George Ferguson, p. 107.

[101]"Proudfoot Papers" (*Transactions*, London and Middlesex Historical Society, 1922, p. 51). Mrs. Moodie wrote of a backwoods local preacher who was probably connected with the Methodists:

"Old Thomas was a very ambitious man in his way. Though he did not know A from B, he took it into his head that he had received a call from Heaven to convert the heathen in the wilderness; and every Sunday he held a meeting in our loggers' shanty, for the purpose of awakening sinners, and bringing over 'Injun pagans' to the true faith. His method of accomplishing this object was very ingenious. He got his wife, Peggy—or 'my Paggy,' as he called her—to read aloud to him a text from the Bible, until he knew it by heart; and he had, as he said truly, 'a good remembrancer,' and never heard a striking sermon but he retained the most important passages, and retailed them second-hand to his bush audience." Susanna Moodie, *Roughing It in the Bush* (new ed., Toronto, 1913), p. 345.

With reference to the influence of evangelical preachers, Methodists and Baptists, in the townships of Malahide, Bayham, Dereham, Middletown, Houghton, Walsingham, Charlotteville, Woodhouse, Walpole, Townsend, Windham, Norwich, Southwold, and Yarmouth, the Reverend Daniel Allan, missionary within the bounds of the Presbytery of Hamilton, wrote in 1838:

"The character of the people generally as to religious knowledge, ordinances and duties, may easily be inferred from that of the greater number of those who profess to be their teachers.—These are generally speaking, a set of well-meaning, *perhaps*, but very illiterate men, under the influence of the wildest fanaticism, incapable of enlarged or consistent views of any religious system, and whose knowledge can scarcely be said to extend beyond a few peculiarities, either in doctrine or in discipline, by which their particular party happens to be distinguished.—The necessary consequence of which is, that the great bulk of their followers have but very few just or rational ideas of religion. It is a melancholy fact that the greater number of those of them who make pretensions to superior piety, are really no better than a set of mere visionaries, who appear to take it for granted that reason, common sense, and even common decency, ought to have as little as possible to do with religious duties. . . . Many of them are so ignorant, or so unsettled in their religious opinions

Recognition of the costs of a ministry not properly equipped to serve town populations led to efforts to provide a programme of study for young preachers entering the field[102] and to efforts to choose suitable preachers for the town stations. Thus, as an instance of the latter, two very different types of preachers, W. H. Williams and James Richardson, were appointed in 1824 to the Yonge Street and York circuit which consisted of the town and surrounding country districts. Williams, according to Carroll, was very popular in the country parts of the circuit but objection was taken to him in the town because "he was at times very boisterous, and not always very clear in his expositions." Richardson, on the other hand, "was very respectably connected; he had been better educated than the most of that day; he had moved in good society, and was of genteel manners; he had borne a commission in the navy, and carried the mark of his loyalty and valor, in the absence of his left arm; he had since been in his Majesty's commission of the peace; and though he had a family to support, he had private resources of his own, by which to supplement the lack of disciplinary allowances." The result was, Carroll went on to say, "his residence in the town gave the society a social status and an amount of pastoral attention which it had never possessed and enjoyed before."[103] Two years later, in the making of the circuit appointments, attention was again given to the special demands of York by stationing there William Ryerson, at that time one of the most effective of Methodist preachers in the country. "William's preaching" Carroll wrote, "was the great attraction to the York chapel; and the augmented congregation necessitated the enlargement of the church, which was effected in his time and paid for. Now, for the first time, the writer began to notice some of the old aristocratic families in the congregation on Sunday evenings."[104]

More careful disposition of the preaching force probably did something to strengthen the position of the evangelical church in those areas where the cultural standards of the society were unfavourable to the services of ill-trained and uneducated preachers, but such adjustments could not be carried very far so long as sectarian principles dominated among the evangelical following. The character of the Methodist movement was typified by the local preacher. Education

---

that I know not what absurdity, be it ever so monstrous, they may not by a little tact and management, be induced to assent to and receive." Quoted in *Christian Guardian,* May 30, 1838, from the April number of the *Canadian Christian Examiner and Presbyterian Review.*

[102]See G. F. Playter, *The History of Methodism in Canada* (Toronto, 1862), pp. 258-60.

[103]Carroll, *Case and His Cotemporaries,* vol. III, pp. 16-17.

[104]*Ibid.,* p. 109.

was considered detrimental to evangelical religion. "Everybody here," Proudfoot wrote in his diary, February 16, 1833, "still speaks of the Methodists. M₁. Donaldson told me a good thing. A Methodist minister was declaiming against ministers being learned, said that it was never intended that they should get human learning, and that human learning rendered them useless."[105] The *Christian Guardian* wrote, March 19, 1834:

> In no one thing are the Methodists as a body more deficient than a due and practical attention to the importance and advantages of a *solid and liberal Education*, both in the Ministry and Laity of the Church . . . .
> We are compelled to confess that education does not receive that attention and encouragement among us as a body, which its great importance to the permanent prosperity of the church, the interests of religion, and the welfare of the Province demands . . . .
> We know it has been said that Methodism prospered at an early period of the Province without education, why not now? As well might it be said, the early settlers had no other vehicles of conveyance but ox-waggons, carts, and sleds, why are any others used now? . . .
> It may also be remarked, that as the same description of mechanics who found abundant employment thirty years ago, would not receive equal encouragement now . . .; so must the Ministry and Church advance with the advancing state of society, or be compelled to retire from the'high and important station they now occupy, and sink into comparative insignificance and uselessness.[106]

The education and social status of the Wesleyan missionaries provided them with a distinct advantage in appealing to the overseas settlers in the Canadian community. Wesleyanism had developed a high standard of oratory in the pulpit, and the English missionaries in Canada quickly proved more than the equal of the American rivals in preaching power. "We might observe," Carroll remarked, referring to the Wesleyans in the year 1821-2, "that the Missionaries were considered the very best preachers the country possessed, and drew troops of persons from all the churches to hear them on Sunday evenings."[107] Advantages enjoyed by the Wesleyan missionaries in appealing to the higher social classes of the colonial society early became evident. In Quebec, Montreal, Kingston, and York, the Wesleyan missionaries gained a considerable following made up of the more "respectable" members of the community. "Our richest members are tradesmen in the middle class," the Reverend Mr. Williams wrote of the society in Quebec City in 1816.[108] In Montreal "several wealthy gentlemen" came to the support of the Wesleyan cause in promising to assist in

---

[105]"Proudfoot Papers" (*Transactions*, London and Middlesex Historical Society, 1922, p. 67).
[106]*Christian Guardian*, Mar. 19, 1834.
[107]Carroll, *Case and His Cotemporaries*, vol. II, p. 385.
[108]*Ibid*, p. 23.

the building of a new chapel in 1818.[109] In York, as Carroll indicated, the Wesleyan preaching quickly proved acceptable to the better educated of the town's population.[110] In the Fort Wellington circuit, the Wesleyan missionary, Thomas Catterick, was able to boast that the more respectable Methodists supported the British missionaries.[111] To some considerable extent, a division of the field of work took place between the rival bodies. Wesleyanism tended to dominate in the towns, and particularly among the trading classes, while American Methodism maintained its supremacy in the rural districts of Upper Canada. Thus the claims of the British missionaries that their influence was gained in areas neglected by the preachers from the United States were more justified than their rivals were willing to concede. Conflict in particular centres resulted as much from the extension of the boundaries of American Methodism as from the intrusion of British Wesleyanism.

Wesleyanism constituted a serious challenge to the American Methodist movement for the simple reason that this movement was becoming increasingly "respectable" in character. The saddle-bag preacher was giving way to the preacher with some learning and of polished manners, and the practice of holding religious services in any sort of place was gradually being abandoned as permanent places of worship were erected. Methodism, in short, was adjusting itself, if slowly, to the new conditions of Canadian society where the older-settled communities were becoming mature and greater attention was being given to such matters as education and the amenities of home life. It was the gains from such adjustments which were threatened by Wesleyan missionary activities. The claim to respectability, just within the grasp of Methodism, was sharply denied by the emergence of a rival movement with an indubitable claim to respectability. To some extent, the conflict between the rival groups can be interpreted as a struggle for the control of the new *bourgeoisie* in Canadian colonial society. There was nothing remarkable in the fact, therefore, that it was those Canadian Methodist ministers who had abandoned most completely the crude manners of the saddle-bag preachers who took the lead in bringing about the union of the Canadian and English Conferences. Efforts of the Canadian leaders to raise the social standing of the Methodist movement found support in the alliance with the British missionaries. The union secured to the Church the support of those respectable elements of the population which had owed attachment to

[109]*Ibid.*, p. 126.
[110]*Ibid.*, p. 342.
[111]*Ibid.*, pp. 279-80.

the Wesleyan cause in England or which were attracted to the Wesleyan services within the colony.

The change forced upon Methodism in its relationship to the colonial class structure was closely related to the change forced upon it in its relationship to politics. The movement had relied in its early development upon the philosophy of the religious sect which maintained that the message of the gospel was in no way connected with national or political interests. With perhaps a few exceptions, the Methodist preachers who entered the country from the United States were perfectly honest in their claim to a position of national and political neutrality. They had no interest in promoting the cause of American national expansion or in propagating American republican ideas. They were other-worldly in the message which they brought to the people. Before 1812 the rural Canadian population tended to favour a religious doctrine which had no relationship to national sentiments or political views. The frontiersman himself was other-worldly in a sense; he felt no strong attachment to any particular state or to any political party—he simply wanted to be left alone. After the War of 1812-14, however, national and political issues became much more clearly defined in Canadian society. The War had done much to develop among the United Empire Loyalists a sense, hitherto lacking, of being a distinctive nationalist group, and the colonial self-consciousness of the Loyalists combined with the imperial patriotism of the British settlers, steadily increasing in numbers after 1815, to create within the Canadian society a body of sentiment unfavourable to the acceptance of things American. At the same time the war, and developments which took place afterwards, raised up new problems of an economic and political character which sharpened the lines between conservatism and radicalism. Tory views hardened as the radical cause gained strength, and political divisions became closely related to the conflict between British and American influences. Such tendencies challenged the position of the religious sect, with its boast of neutrality with respect to matters of national loyalty and politics, and favoured the shift to the conception of the territorial church. The weakening of the supports of the sect type of religious association was first evident within the Methodist movement in the conflict which developed between American and British national sentiments.

The strengthening of imperial sentiment in the country after the War of 1812, and the emergence of feelings of strong antagonism to the United States, led directly to the invitation to the Wesleyan Conference in England to send out missionaries to serve the Methodist settlers in the colony. The invitation was extended, in the words of

the Reverend George Ferguson, by those members who "were more national than Christian, in their feelings, and who contended more about politics, than 'for the faith once delivered to the Saints'."[112] The bitterness of feeling aroused by the war favoured the shift to the support of Wesleyanism on the part of many of the Loyalists in the country as well as on the part of the British immigrants. "The Methodist brethren from the United States," the Reverend Henry Pope, one of the Wesleyan missionaries, wrote from Fort George, May 28, 1818, "scarcely make an attempt in many of the most populous and important places on the frontier, as the resentment which was kindled in our people by the injuries received by the enemy was not extinguished by the termination of the war. . . . But in the interior of the country they are more acceptable, and in many places very useful."[113] Some of the American preachers were prepared to admit that their connection with the United States limited their influence. The Reverend Fitch Reed wrote of his work in York in 1820-1: "A general prejudice existed against the Society—really, no doubt, because of their simple-hearted, earnest piety, and the obscurity of their social position; but ostensibly because they were subject to a foreign ecclesiastical jurisdiction, and their ministers mostly foreign. This prejudice indeed extended to all our Societies in the Province, and our ministers and people suffered many annoyances by reason of this foreign element. We felt it more, perhaps, at the centre of government influence, than elsewhere."[114]

Establishment of a Canadian annual conference in 1824, and the complete separation of Canadian Methodism from the Methodist Episcopal Church of the United States in 1828, were efforts to meet the growing criticism of the movement because of its American connection. At the same time, some attempt was made to appoint old-country preachers in districts settled by old-country people; in 1819, for instance, an Englishman, James G. Peale, was appointed to the Cornwall circuit as a means of meeting the competition of the British missionaries with a consequent increase in the membership of the American society.[115] Recruitment of an increasing number of Canadians, and some English and Irish, into the preaching ranks made it less difficult to provide preachers who were of the same nationality as the population which they served, and weakened the charge that the Methodists were "foreign agitators," teaching doctrines contrary to the principles of the British government. "Much has recently been said,"

112Journal of the Rev. George Ferguson, p. 66.
113Carroll, *Case and His Cotemporaries*, vol. II, p. 213.
114*Ibid.*, p. 231.
115*Ibid.*, p. 243.

the *Christian Guardian* wrote editorially, January 1, 1831, "in some of the U.C. Journals about *American* Preachers, &c. &c. . . . There are now *sixty one* Itinerant Ministers of the M.E. Church in Canada, of whom *twelve* were born in the United States; *four* were born in the British Colonies; *twenty-seven* were born and educated in Upper Canada; *three* were born in Nova Scotia; *three* were born and educated in England; and *thirteen* were born and educated in Ireland."[116]

By 1831 Methodism had progressed very far in the direction of becoming a Canadian movement. The shift, however, did not bring an end to the conflict within the Methodist body which had emerged after the War of 1812. In abandoning the principle of the sect—of separation from the world—and accepting the principle of the territorial church, Methodism moved one step closer to the position of Wesleyanism; but the territorial identification of the one body was with that of the Canadian community, the territorial identification of the other with that of the Empire. The Canadianism of Methodism came into sharp conflict with the Imperialism of Wesleyanism. The conflict was accentuated by the sharp political differences between the two groups. Canadianism tended to become associated with radicalism, imperialism with toryism.

The increasing participation of the Canadian Methodists in politics resulted, in the first instance, from the conflict with the Church of England. Egerton Ryerson's entry into the arena of pamphlet warfare in answering charges against the Methodist movement which had been made by John Strachan marked a sharp break from the evangelical tradition. The philosophy of the religious sect, of ignoring other religious denominations and concentrating upon the single object of saving souls (taking pride, in fact, in the progress of the evangelical cause in face of persecution and constitutional disabilities) was abandoned, and efforts now came to be made to secure for Methodism equal rights with other denominations. Inevitably, as a result, Methodist leaders and the Methodist religious journal, the *Christian Guardian*, became caught up in political issues. The privileges enjoyed by the Church of England were political privileges, and in attacking them Methodism found itself aligned with the reform cause within the colony. Championship of Methodist rights by William Lyon Mackenzie brought welcome support to the movement, but left it open to the charge that it was promoting sedition and the break of the imperial tie. Political discussion tended to crowd out religious discussion in the columns of the *Christian Guardian*. Although most of the local preachers and many of the itiner-

[116]*Christian Guardian*, Jan. 1, 1831.

ants remained true to the principles of the evangelical sect, the hierarchy, more and more dominated by men such as Egerton Ryerson, became increasingly concerned with matters of politics to the exclusion, at times, of religious interests. "It cannot be denied," Carroll admitted, "that as the Methodists, in common with all other religious bodies not of the so-called Church of England, had received the assistance of the Liberal politicians and editors of papers in obtaining their religious rights, so these political men expected the assistance of Methodists in obtaining their political rights or objects. It led to a fraternization between the two, which caused the Methodists, in many cases, to become too much interested in mere political partizanship."[117] The effect of such tendencies within the Church was to strengthen its denominational position—if not its religious influence—among radical elements of the population but at the price of seriously weakening its position in appealing to the growing English Wesleyan population in the country. That the danger of Wesleyan competition was very real because of the political ties of Canadian Methodism was made evident in a letter written by Strachan apparently to a Wesleyan official in England, December 13, 1831, urging that the Wesleyan Conference resume missionary work in Upper Canada. The letter read in part:

It may sound very well as a flourish of Speech that Methodists are the same all over the World but I cannot hardly conceive any two Christian denominations who differ more widely in practice than the Methodists in England & those of the United States. In regard the Episcopal Methodists in this Province their rancour against the Church of England and all the Colonial institutions and all persons in authority & Methodist Preachers from England are too notorious to require any additional proof at my hand.

A file of their Newspaper called the Christian Guardian edited by two Preachers and regularly circulated by all their Clergy Itinerant and Local and forced into their band and class meeting &c. will sufficiently indicate the spirit which directs them & were any farther corroboration wanting it would be found in their allowing their Chapels to be used for seditious Meetings.

It ought however to be carefully kept in mind that the greater part of their people are still inclined to be quiet & peaceable and that many have actually withdrawn from the connexion seeking religion & not rancorous politics—the corruption is to be attributed to a few bad men who have acquired the direction of the Society.

The Settlers belonging to your denomination [that is, the Wesleyans] have more need than the Indians that your Preachers should be sent among them.[118]

The arrival of the Wesleyan missionaries in Upper Canada in 1832 held out the threat of drawing off from the Canadian Church the

---

[117]Carroll, *Case and His Cotemporaries*, vol. III, p. 428.
[118]P.A.O., Strachan Letter Book, 1827-39, p. 179.

support of the large Conservative element within the Methodist membership. Union constituted an effort to neutralize Methodism politically. It was a bid not only for the support of the more politically conservative Wesleyans but for the support of that increasingly large body of Canadian Methodists who were shifting to Conservative views. Nowhere was that shift more evident than in the Canadian Methodist leadership, but the sharp break of Egerton Ryerson, and his brother John, with the Radical party reflected underlying changes which were taking place in the political thinking of many Canadian Methodists. Ryerson's "Impressions of England," published in the *Christian Guardian*, prepared the ground for the sharp about face which came with the union with Wesleyan conservatism. Union offered a support of the position taken by the Canadian Methodist leaders in throwing their weight on the side of the tories. John Ryerson wrote his brother, Egerton, November 7, 1833, of the effect of the "Impressions":

I have some times thought you had better not have writen the article, particularly at this time, yet I have long been of the opinion that we had (both with regard to measures & men) leaned to much towards *Radicleism* & that it would be absolutely necessary sooner or later to disengage ourselves from them *entirely* . . . . Uppon the whole I am glad of its apperrence, & I hope whenever you have occation to speak of the Government, etc., will do it in terms of high respect. But at the present the less said about Polliticks or Political men the better; yet I am ankeous to obtain the confidence of the government & entirely disconnect ourselves with that tribe of villans with whom we have been too intimate & who are at any time ready to turn around and rend us when we don't please them. I fear Wm. is so much attached to those men & their measures that he will injure us & himself too. But perhaps he will come over after a little.[119]

Forces compelling a greater accommodation of the Methodist movement to the wider community made themselves increasingly felt after 1815. The need of developing a professional ministry, of moderating the evangelical appeal, of building up educational institutions, and of breaking the close identification with Americanism and radicalism could only be met by broadening considerably the denominational basis of the movement. Had Methodist leadership remained firmly faithful to the principles of the primitive evangelical church a means of adjustment would have been sought through a shift to a greater exclusiveness. Methodism could have sheltered itself from the demands of the outside community by becoming more other-worldly; in doing so, it would have lost tremendously in following but would have retained the support of the truly faithful. Vested interests of leadership, however, almost inevitably forced an adjustment in the opposite direction.

[119]Quoted Sissons, *Egerton Ryerson*, vol. I, p. 190.

Faced with the choice of developing into an exclusive religious sect or into a church, the latter course was followed. Union with the English Wesleyan Conference constituted a very considerable abandonment of the principles of evangelical sectarianism. Such union afforded an easy means of erecting new denominational supports of the Church.

A similar set of influences operated to force the Canadian Baptist churches to accept the leadership of English Baptist missionary organizations. Overseas immigration, and changes in the Canadian community structure, made necessary adjustments in church organization and religious appeal which could only be secured through the support of the English Baptists, and in the end, such adjustments involved, as in the case of Methodism, a departure from the evangelistic position of the religious sect. Dominance of English Baptist influence was indicative of weaknesses of the separatist religious sect in competition with the territorial evangelical church.

Points of strain very quickly emerged within the Baptist movement in Canada in face of developments which took place after about 1820. The growing tendency for Baptists to settle as individuals or single families throughout the rural areas raised problems of providing religious services, particularly among the American but also among the Scotch Baptists, and these problems became considerably accentuated with the increasing immigration of Baptists from England. Factors of strength in the early organization of the Baptist churches became factors of weakness as the problem became one of supplying with religious services a very greatly increased Baptist population. Failure to develop techniques to carry Baptist teachings beyond adherents to people of other denominational attachments resulted in the end in a failure to maintain religious services among adherents.

The autonomy of the individual Baptist church made organization possible immediately upon the settlement of any considerable number of Baptists in one district, and the lack of any centralized authority meant that each church strove independently to secure the services of a preacher. The number of preachers in the country was not sufficiently great to meet such demands. Failure to pay adequate salaries meant that most preachers offered their services on a part-time basis. Many churches were left unsupplied, while the close tie of the preacher with the local community in which he made a living, usually by farming, checked the development of itinerant practices. "Our friends at home," the travelling missionaries, Topping and Bosworth, wrote of the Baptists in the Eastern Townships in 1840, "have little idea of the hardships some of the ministers in the Townships endure. Many of them are obliged to be actually engaged in manual labor through the week for

their support, and on the sabbath day are called upon to preach two or three times."[120] Of the Freewill Baptists in the Eastern Townships, Topping and Bosworth wrote: "Although their ministers are very poor, and receive very little support from their people, and are obliged to labour with their hands to supply the necessaries of life, they strive industriously for the salvation of souls; some of them performing five days' hard labour each week, and preaching from five to eight times, which, from the distance between their appointments, is attended with much toil."[121] Employment of untrained, part-time preachers made possible more rapid growth of the Baptist cause but had weakening effects upon the organization of the individual churches.[122] The lack of any central authority to build up a body of itinerant preachers separate from the local preachers accentuated the dependence upon the local preacher.

> Now we want for our Baptist Churches in this Province [Wm. Freeman wrote in the *Christian Observer* in 1851], a modifyed system of itinerancy. First that all our efficient brethren in the ministry, should have an opening to exercise their proper gift from Christ. And secondly, that no Church may be entirely destitute of their own ministers . . . . Until the Churches in this Province, become so consolidated as to be able to sustain their respective pastors, until the members shall have increased from 12 to 20 to 50 and 60. When instead of contributing 20 to 30 dollars for the support of the gospel; they will be able to sustain their minister, with even a tolerable support. Till then, let those weaker Churches be supplied with a minister; once a fortnight, or once a month.[123]

The failure to develop any sort of effective missionary organization, and the weakness before 1837 of outside support of missionary activity, left large sections of the Baptist population without religious services. "There are, in the Upper Province," the editor of the *Canada Baptist Magazine and Missionary Register*, pointed out, June, 1837, "about fifty Baptist Churches: some of them flourishing, others stationary, and a few, we fear, declining. In the Lower Province the number is not so great; but the influx of English Baptists last year into the Eastern Townships would give great facility to the formation of new ones, if

---

[120]*Canadian Baptist Magazine and Missionary Register*, vol. IV, Oct., 1840, p. 100.
[121]*Ibid.*
[122]The diary of the Reverend William Marsh in Whitby brings out the difficulties faced by the preacher dependent upon the farm for a livelihood. Marsh found himself again and again in embarrassing relationships with his creditors. While attempting to maintain the respect of his congregation, he was treated by outsiders as a "debtor." McMaster University, Baptist Historical Collection, Diary of Wm. Marsh, March, 1843—January, 1845.
[123]*Christian Observer*, vol. I, May, 1851, p. 74. "These hints," Freeman was careful to go on to say, "are in no way intended to interfere with the independence of the Churches; which is our glory, and our boast, we do not, we cannot, recognize any ecclesiastical body, that would dare to rule over Gods heritage."

there were but preachers to instruct and organize them."[124] A missionary tour of the Eastern Townships conducted by Topping and Bosworth during the months of July and August, 1840, revealed a great need for additional preachers. The church in Eaton, consisting of sixty members, had no other public service than that provided once in every two months by a minister who came from forty to sixty miles to administer the ordinances of the Lord's Supper; a small Baptist church, of fourteen members, in the township of Clifton had no regular preaching; a recently organized church in Barford was served by a preacher dependent upon the very inadequate and uncertain financial support of the Vermont Baptist Convention; the church at Barnston was the largest in the Townships but there was need of preaching around the neighbourhood; in Compton there was a small Baptist church which was very seldom supplied with preaching; on Beebee Plains a church had been recently organized but it had only a temporary supply for one sabbath in the month; the state of things in the Georgeville church was encouraging, but the field was too large to be taken care of through the exertions of one preacher. "Out of thirteen churches," the missionaries summarized their findings, "situated in a tract of country containing 200 square miles, there are but five supplied with pastors, and they are inadequately supported and over-worked."[125] A missionary tour by the Reverend John Edwards in Upper Canada the next year revealed much the same situation; the church in Toronto, though divided, was regularly provided with preaching; the one in Markham had been long without a pastor and was in a languishing state; the two churches in Whitby were taken care of, one very inadequately, by a single preacher; a number of Baptists in Clarke were anxious for the visit of a missionary; the church in Peterborough was regularly supplied; the preacher in Hamilton conducted services in a small church in the township and in the courthouse of the town and also itinerated fourteen miles farther north where a considerable number attended; the churches in Haldimand and Cramahe each had a pastor but neither was in a satisfactory state; the church in Murray was without a pastor, but those in Rawdon and Sydney were regularly supplied; the church in Thurlow had no pastor and was compelled to share in the labours of the pastor of Sydney; the recently formed church in Kingston was without its regular pastor but was supplied with preaching; the church in Augusta had no pastor and was in a declining state; the church at Farmersville had recently been revived but was without a pastor; the church in Bastard was without a pastor although it numbered fifty

[124]*Canada Baptist Magazine and Missionary Register*, vol. I, June, 1837, p. 17.
[125]*Ibid.*, vol. IV, Oct., 1840, pp. 99-100.

members who were in circumstances, had they been alive to their duty, to support one.[126]

Effects of the failure of the Baptist denomination to provide more fully the population with religious services were evident in the high mortality of Baptist churches and in the weakening of religious interests generally. In those areas particularly where services could only be provided infrequently by preachers from neighbouring churches, the religious enthusiasm of the members cooled in the long intervals between visits. William Marsh, the preacher in Whitby, wrote in his diary:

> Wednesday, Oct. 14, 1843. started for Marypossa . . . in the evening preached at Br. McAdoos to a Crowded assembly enjoyed some freedom the people seemed verry attentive and much affected. I fully believe if these people Could have regular and frequent preaching much might be done for the Cause but I feel satisfied that my labors there are nearly wasted my appointments are so far apart that but little good is effected—often when I go there and stay a few days I get my expectations raised with the idea that a reformation is about to breake out . . . but alas when I go again all these impresians seems to be worn off . . . and I find it more difficult to raise the excitement than before . . . . but I still have hopes that something pleasing will take place my hopes are like the tide rising and falling untill I am satisfied that I had better Confine my labors to narrower limits and preach more frequent in the same place—that when favorable symptons appear follow up the means—but the way I now manage and have all the season past wearing myself out fast by so much travel—while my visits are so seldom in any one place being able to get around but once a month that but little is effected.[127]

The problem of supplying the Baptist churches with preachers was the single most decisive influence bringing about the intrusion of English missionary organizations. The Baptist churches in Canada lacked the financial resources to recruit preachers from outside, and they lacked the means within the country to raise up a supply. Without union, there was no way of securing co-ordination in the prosecution of missionary work or in undertaking such ventures as that of establishing a denominational college. In addition, the narrow sectarianism of the local Baptist population made impossible any programme which called for extensive financial contributions. As in the case of Methodism, the Canadian Baptist movement sought the means of strengthening its denominational supports through a tie with the financially powerful English Baptist movement. Formation of the Canada Baptist Missionary Society in 1837, the establishment of a Baptist college in Montreal the next year, and the extensive undertaking of missionary work and the training of Baptist preachers in the country were indicative of some of the gains from English Baptist leadership.

[126]*Ibid.*, vol. V, Dec., 1841, pp. 138-9.
[127]Diary of Wm. Marsh, March, 1843—January, 1845.

Other weaknesses which became evident in the Baptist movement after 1820 tended to strengthen tendencies forcing a closer connection with the English Baptist movement. Like the Methodists, the Baptists faced increasing criticism from those opposed to a highly emotional religious appeal, and such criticism assumed a serious aspect with the growing settlement of English Baptists in the country. The English Baptist, like the English Wesleyan, missionaries were strongly opposed to the use of those crude revivalist techniques which had been developed by American frontier sects, and their opposition found increasing support in the community with the changing values of the population. The intense excitement aroused in protracted meetings was particularly disliked by the English Baptists. "I find much prejudice in many places," the Reverend George Wilson wrote from St. Catharines, December 6, 1844, "against protracted meetings, which I think has arisen partly from imprudence in managing those meetings, and partly from the unwise course pursued after the meeting has closed. The animal passions are often too much excited in these meetings, and the understanding left uninformed, and not care enough manifest in receiving members into the church."[128] Another correspondent in Dumfries, writing January 22, 1844, expressed similar views. "In reference to these revival meetings," part of his letter read, "it appears to me (and I know many others who hold the same opinion) that there is in them too much effort to create excitement, by violent appeals to the mere feelings of the audience; and it is evident that under the influence of that excitement many persons come forward to 'the anxious seat,' and ultimately are received into the church, who very soon fall away, and bring disgrace on the cause which they had professed to espouse."[129] A more general statement, from a correspondent in Blenheim, set forward the English Baptist attitude to the use of protracted meetings:

> Protracted meetings are often held with a view to promote revivals of religion, and in many cases they have been wonderfully blessed. But it is to be feared that in many instances, owing to the manner in which they have been conducted, they have excited feeling rather than promoted that solid and substantial piety which is founded upon the word of God. Hence we have often seen after such a meeting has ended, that the people have fallen into a worse state than they were in before. All excitement has subsided, and their religion having too much consisted in this, is gone too. Converts have been hurried into the church upon the strength of strong feeling, without sufficient care in examining the grounds of their piety, and instructing them in the true principles of the religion they are about to profess; when the meeting has passed, they find themselves unsupported by the real principles of Christianity,

---

[128] *The Register*, vol. IV, Jan. 9, 1845.
[129] *Ibid.*, vol. II, Feb. 8, 1844.

and soon fall off to their old habits and companions. Religion is too much regarded by some as consisting in some extraordinary feeling or impulse of the mind, which takes place, or is supposed to take place, in a moment, instead of being viewed as a radical change of the affections of the heart. And too many professors of religion think they can never pray nor take any part in religious exercises, except they feel just in such a frame of mind. And thus when the protracted meeting is gone by, family altars are forsaken, and the house of God left empty on the Sabbath, as well as at the appointments for prayer.[130]

Intrusion of English Baptist influence meant a break from a highly evangelistic religious appeal. The conservatism of the English Baptist preachers was most evident in the character of the religious service of the Montreal Baptist church; here there was little to distinguish the Baptist appeal from that of the Congregational or Presbyterian. In the country generally, however, the influence of the English Baptist missionaries tended to a moderation in the evangelical appeal. The exhortations of the local preacher gave way increasingly to the polished sermons of the missionary.

Changes forced upon the Baptist movement in the character of its religious appeal implied changes which were being forced upon it in the character of its ministry. People of little education, and thereby inclined towards elementary forms of religious expression, had predominated in the Baptist membership before 1837, and the lack of education in the membership body was reflected in the lack of education in the local Baptist preachers. Without training schools, and without the financial means of paying full-time qualified ministers, the Baptists were dependent upon the services of preachers who were often scarcely able to read and write and who had few of the manners of the polished gentleman. Proudfoot wrote of the Baptist preacher in York, December 5, 1832: "Was considerably disappointed to-day in Mr. Stewart (the Baptist preacher). I have been now several times in his house, but never heard anything that could indicate his possessing a literary turn. He is always working as a labourer, covered with mud and lime. His manners are the manners of a man of work, and forwardness and conceit supply in him the place of ease."[131]

---

[130] *Ibid.*, vol. I, Dec. 7, 1842. Some of the local Baptist preachers were little more favourably inclined towards a highly emotional appeal. The Baptist preacher in Whitby and Markham, Wm. Marsh, wrote in his diary, October 6, 1844: "11 o'clock found the Chapel well filled heard Mr. Bliss [a student from Hamilton Baptist College] preach though he preached too much terror to be profitable—I don't believe in scaring folks to heaven—so much about hell and Damnation sometimes Creates excitement—but the Gospel of the grace of God is more likely to win the heart—there appears evidently to be an excitement in the minds of some what it will amount to I cannot tell my mind is much distressed." Diary of Wm. Marsh, March, 1843—January, 1845.

[131] "Proudfoot Papers" (*Transactions*, London and Middlesex Historical Society, 1922, p. 5).

The limitations in the character of the Baptist preachers made their effects felt with the growth of towns, the increasing social maturity of the older-settled communities, and the growth in the number of English Baptists in the country. The Reverend F. A. Cox, in reporting upon the state of the Canadian Baptist churches in 1835, found the lack of education of the preachers a seriously weakening factor.[132] Difficulties faced in maintaining the Baptist cause in Toronto were indicative of the effects of relying upon preachers who could make no appeal to a town population. The Reverend R. A. Fyfe wrote of the early development of the Baptist Church in the capital: "These early prospects were blighted by a succession of laborers, who were defective either in character, or talent, and therefore failed to bring in and keep united the elements of which a church of Christ is composed. The members, one after another, retired to other denominations, or formed themselves into lesser divisions, either with or without a ministry, their usefulness being restricted thereby almost to themselves."[133]

The growing realization of the inadequacies of untrained preachers led the Eastern Baptist Association in 1838 to resolve "that we feel the circumstances of the times demand that the Ministers of the Gospel should be better educated, possessed of more extensive acquirements, and of more cultivated minds, than their predecessors; qualified to teach Congregations of growing intelligence; to supply that quenchless thirst for knowledge which has been excited in all classes, as well as to meet the various forms under which error may present itself; and to repel the attacks which may be made, either by the rationalist or infidel."[134] The support of English Baptist missionary organizations offered itself as the most effective means of securing the trained ministers—and the training schools—necessary for raising the educational standing of the Baptist group in the community. The overseas missionaries who took up work in the country were men of education and of cultural attainment. They were not only able immediately to raise the social standing of the churches they served, but they also provided the leadership which was necessary for the establishment of Baptist educational institutions. The Baptist college in Montreal brought prestige to the movement in Canada, and its work in training preachers in the country laid the foundations for the building up of a local professional ministry. Outside Montreal, the Canadian Baptist churches remained long

[132]The Reverend F. A. Cox and the Reverend J. Hoby, *The Baptists in America; A Narrative of the Deputation from the Baptist Union in England, to the United States and Canada* (New York, 1836), pp. 227-8.
[133]Quoted J. E. Wells, *Life and Labors of Robert Alex. Fyfe* (Toronto, n.d.), p. 159.
[134]*Minutes of the Nineteenth Anniversary of the Upper Canada Eastern Baptist Association,* held with the Church at Beamsville, on the 6th and 7th of June, 1838.

after 1840 predominantly rural in character, but English Baptist influence resulted in drawing in, at least to some extent, Baptist support from the new *bourgeoisie* classes growing up in the towns.

In terms also of the changing political demands on Baptist leadership, establishment of the English Baptist tie was probably of considerable significance. Baptist Church leaders—and the Baptist following—never became as entangled as the Methodists in colonial politics, but politics nevertheless intruded in Baptist thinking. The American heritage of the Baptist population in Upper Canada favoured a close identification with the Reform party; many of the Baptists openly supported republican principles of government.[135] With the settlement of English Baptists in the country sharp differences in political views emerged; most of the English Baptists aligned themselves on the side of the conservative cause. Acceptance of English leadership, in the Baptist as in the Methodist movement, offered a means of bringing about a break from Canadian radicalism.

Within its more limited sphere of operations, the American Presbyterian movement faced problems in organization and appeal similar to those faced by the Methodist and Baptist movements. In face of the rapid growth of population in the country during the eighteen-thirties, American Presbyterianism had not developed to the point where it could rely upon local recruits to the ministry. The preachers attached to the Niagara Presbytery had come from upper New York State. When these preachers left the country after the Rebellion of 1837, the movement was left without the means of maintaining religious services. The evangelical appeal of American Presbyterianism also proved something of a weakening factor as the movement became more dependent upon the support of a population which had left behind backwoods conditions of life. Finally, patriotism operated increasingly as a force favouring Scottish Presbyterianism at the expense of a Presbyterianism closely identified with the American republic. The sharp reaction following the rebellion against things American and against radical ideas of government created an atmosphere of thought in which American Presbyterianism could not survive. In contrast with the Methodist and Baptist movements, the Presbyterian evangelical movement could not turn to an overseas evangelical church for the support it needed in accommodating itself to the new conditions of Canadian community life, and the movement perished.

Close contacts of Canada with the United States and later with Great Britain favoured the rapid spread into the country of evangelical

[135]See, for instance, Diary of Wm. Marsh, March, 1843—January, 1845.

religious movements. The bulk of the new Canadian settlers came from sections of these two countries where religious fundamentalism had the strongest hold. The break from traditional systems of religion tended to take place in areas of high population mobility, in the United States and in Britain, and these areas contributed most to the settlement of Canada. The effect was to shelter the new Canadian rural society from what might be called metropolitan as distinguished from frontier influences upon religion. The character of community life within the country strengthened influences favouring an untraditional form of religious expression. Backwoods settlement implied extreme isolation of the individual and social group, and such isolation effectively checked the introduction of movements of intellectual enlightenment. Conditions unfavourable to rational systems of thought proved favourable to a religious frame of mind, and the evangelical religious movement grew rapidly at the expense of more complex forms of social fellowship.

Contacts of Canada with the outside world, however, were not solely confined to those areas which provided the bulk of her rural settlers. Immigration also took place of people drawn from the professional and entrepreneurial classes, and these classes were located chiefly in the towns or cities of the United States or Great Britain where religious fundamentalism tended to be much weaker. At the same time, movements of intellectual enlightenment gaining strength in the larger American or old-country centres made their influence felt in Canada with improvements in printing and the introduction of cheaper postal rates. Within the country itself, the opening up of markets led to an increasing emphasis upon agricultural production for export and the development of trade, and the growth of towns and the general raising of material standards in the older-settled rural communities were reflected in the strengthening of new currents of thought. The emergence of the public meeting as a forum of discussion, and the increasing importance of the platform speaker, had far-reaching effects upon religious organization. The authority of the pulpit was challenged by prophets from outside, while prophets from within wrecked new havoc upon the unity of "the church" by employment of the new tools of propaganda. Rapid growth of secular movements took place which weakened the integrating influence of the evangelical appeal. Backwoods settlement, in the first instance, had emphasized the disunity of the social structure—the backwoods settler, figuratively speaking, lived apart from his fellow-men; the role of the evangelical religious movement was that of bringing about within such a situation a sense of social solidarity. With the shift away from backwoods settlement, and the rise of new economic interests in the towns, new points

of disunity emerged and this disunity was reflected in the breakup of the evangelical religious movement.

Influences resulting in Canada in a growing conflict within evangelical religious movements and between these movements and non-religious currents of thought came largely from outside. The Wesleyan revival in England and the Great Revival in the United States had given rise to powerful religious autocracies which led to movements of revolt within the field of religious organization; the break from the evangelical position within the Wesleyan movement in England was paralleled by breaks from the control of the Methodist Episcopal Church in the United States. At the same time, the spirit of intolerance generated by these revivals to any form of thought opposed to the religious interpretation resulted eventually in a strong reaction to religious teachings and the strengthening of movements finding support in the new developments of science. The wide variety of forms of social organization which emerged reflected the growing cultural complexity of urban society and the increasing division of labour in face of economic developments associated with commercial and, in England, industrial capitalism. Canada stood on the periphery of the new metropolitan social order, and movements running strongly in England and the United States made their influence only slowly felt in the country. Weakening of the unity of the evangelical religious movements, however, was indicative of a failure to wholly escape the disintegrating effects of such influence.

It was in no way remarkable that the most conspicuous effects of disintegration should be evident in the growth of conflict within the evangelical religious movements themselves. Disturbing cultural influences were the most easily communicated within a religious universe of discourse, and the vested interests of the religious community as a whole emphasized the advantages of seeking means of adjustment within the organization of religion. Secular influences, if left to work their effects out without denominational interference, would have led to defections from all forms of religious organization. Politics intruded itself into church councils through the effort to resolve conflicts in religious values without damage to the cause of religion. The effect of the growing rationalist movement was to strengthen religious denominationalism. New currents of thought antagonistic to a fundamentalist religious type of thinking made their influence felt in the older evangelical strongholds; the break from an evangelistic position and an emphasis upon denominational organization, through the establishment of ties with the English evangelical churches, were in effect desperate efforts to repair the breaches.

CHAPTER FIVE

Conflict of Church and Sect

1832-1860

W I T H the strengthening of their denominational organization, the Baptist and Methodist movements were in a position after 1800 to take a lead in extending the influence of religion into new fields which were opening up in Nova Scotia, New Brunswick, and Prince Edward Island. These movements developed into powerful mission churches, and their growth was largely a growth in terms of a strengthening missionary organization.

The expansion of Baptist missionary undertakings was particularly striking. Reliance ceased to be placed upon the random preaching activities of individual preachers as means of pushing Baptist influence into new areas of settlement. Organization of the Home Missionary Society for Nova Scotia was a recognition of the need for some sort of central agency to direct the work in distant areas and to maintain order and regularity in outlying churches. Gradually, as funds accumulated, a number of preachers came to be employed as full-time Baptist missionaries.

In 1820, for instance, the Reverend David Nutter, originally from England, was employed on a number of missionary tours, and Baptist influence through his preaching was extended into isolated settlements in eastern Nova Scotia. Preaching first at Truro, Nutter proceeded east to Pictou, Antigonish, and then on to Guysborough and Canso in the autumn of 1820. The next spring he returned to this part of the country and held preaching services in isolated fishing villages along the east coast and on islands in the Gulf of St. Lawrence; churches were formed at Antigonish, Canso, Guysborough, and Tracadie, the latter made up of coloured folk.[1] In the summer of 1821 Nutter undertook a missionary tour along the south shore, preaching and forming churches at Liverpool, Port Medway, and Ragged Islands. In Liverpool, the religious meetings which he held were particularly successful.[2]

[1]See I. E. Bill, *Fifty Years with the Baptist Ministers and Churches of the Maritime Provinces* (Saint John, N.B., 1880), pp. 237-9, and E. M. Saunders, *History of the Baptists of the Maritime Provinces* (Halifax, 1902), pp. 156-7.
[2]Saunders, *History of the Baptists of the Maritime Provinces*, pp. 157-8.

Other preachers also engaged in missionary work throughout the Maritimes. In 1822 Joseph Dimock was engaged by the Missionary Board to preach in the western part of Nova Scotia. Missionary work in Cumberland County resulted in the organization of a church at River Philip in 1818 and one at Little Forks a few years later. In 1825 Dimock organized a church at Sydney, Cape Breton. In the same year the Reverend Charles Tupper was sent on a short missionary tour of Prince Edward Island; his was the first visit of a regular Baptist preacher to the Island. "My reception," he wrote, "on first reaching the Island did not seem propitious; but the prospect soon brightened. The attendance and the seriousness evinced were highly encouraging. On one of the Sabbaths, when the meetings were held at a considerable distance apart, quite a number of young persons, who did not profess religion, travelled, in going and returning, about thirty miles. It was manifest that some of them were deeply concerned."[3] In 1826 Elder Joseph Crandall and Elder T. S. Harding visited the Island, the former preaching at Tryon, Cape Traverse, Crapand, North River, West River, Charlottetown, Cross Road, and on the road to St. Peter's and the latter at Tryon, Crapand, Cape Traverse, and Bedeque.[4] The next year Tupper again was engaged as a missionary on the island, and in 1830 Elder Samuel McCully visited the settlements on the south side.

Organization of a separate association for New Brunswick in 1821 was indicative of the growing demands placed upon the Baptist Church with the extension of settlement. The Baptist Association of New Brunswick, upon its formation, was made up of thirteen churches— Germain Street (Saint John), Sackville, Salisbury, Waterborough, Prince William, Wakefield, Fredericton, St. Mary, Stellarton, Norton, Miramichi, and Hopewell—with six ministers and five hundred and six members.[5] Missionary labours of preachers sent over to New Brunswick in 1826 and 1827 by the Baptist Missionary Society of Massachusetts resulted in the extension of Baptist influence into outlying settlements and in the establishment of new churches. In 1826 Elder David James performed an extensive mission in the Miramichi valley, visiting settlements at the mouth of the river and along various branches. "There are a great many inhabitants scattered in this wilderness," he wrote of settlements along the south-west Miramichi, "who are altogether destitute of the means of grace. The morals of the people are very corrupt."[6] Revivalist preaching resulted in a number of converts to

[3]Bill, *Fifty Years with the Baptist Ministers and Churches of the Maritime Provinces,* pp. 663-4.
[4]*Ibid.,* pp. 664-5.
[5]*Ibid.,* p. 573.
[6]*Ibid.,* pp. 574-5.

the Baptist cause throughout the area. In the same year Elder William Sears preached at Buctouche and in other settlements along the east shore. Elder William Johnson from Maine engaged in missionary work in Charlotte County during the year 1826 and in the early part of the next year he performed a four weeks' mission in the settlements of Red Head, Black River, and Loch Lomond and a two weeks' mission at Magaguadavic. Elder John Masters undertook a missionary tour up the Grand Lake. Local preachers were also engaged in missionary work. In 1827 the Missionary Board of New Brunswick appointed Elder David Harris on a four weeks' mission up the Oromocto River and at Rushagonish, and the Reverend Francis Pickle preached in the New Jerusalem Settlement, up the St. John River, and at Long Reach, and later visited the settlements on Grand Lake and Cumberland Bay.[7] Subscriptions to the Baptist Domestic Missionary Society made possible the support of increasingly extensive missionary work in succeeding years.

Extension of Baptist influence throughout the Maritime field after 1828 was indicative of the effectiveness of Baptist missionary organizations. Between 1827 and 1840 the number of churches in Nova Scotia grew from twenty-nine to seventy, the number of ordained ministers from seventeen to thirty-nine, and the number of members from 1,711 to 6,097. In the same period the number of churches in New Brunswick grew from twenty-eight to forty-six, the number of ordained ministers from fifteen to twenty-one, and the number of members from 1,347 to 2,944. Growth was also evident in Prince Edward Island; in 1834 there were seven Baptist churches and three ordained ministers. The strengthening of home missionary organizations, and the development, particularly among the women of the various congregations, of such associational activities as mite societies, provided the churches with greater financial resources and with greater lay support. Associations within the various churches replaced to some extent the preachers as instruments for the promotion of Baptist interests.

The growth of Methodist influence after 1800 was little less striking. Establishment of the connection with the Wesleyan Conference resulted immediately in a considerable increase in the number of Methodist preachers in the country, and offered some assurance of a steady supply for the future. Financial responsibility for the work was assumed by the Wesleyan Conference, and the growing interest of the English Wesleyans in missionary activities abroad provided solid support for the expansion of the movement in the Maritime Provinces. Formation

[7]*Ibid.*, pp. 577-8.

of the General Wesleyan Methodist Missionary Society in England in 1817 secured a central agency for the promotion of missionary activities, and the work in the Maritimes passed almost entirely under the control of the English body. Revivalist techniques still continued to be relied on, but as Methodism extended beyond the area of Newlight influence into areas populated by Loyalists, and as it came to depend more and more upon Wesleyan missionaries from England, it lost something of its original evangelical drive. The evangelical appeal became caught up, as in the Baptist Church, within institutional systems. Regularly paid missionaries took the place of self-appointed prophets. The influence of evangelical preaching was extended and strengthened, but such preaching became a function of a denomination rather than the dynamic of a religious movement. The greater emphasis upon pastoral visiting, and the adherence to a strict itinerant schedule, were indicative of the growing importance of denominational claims within the movement. Local preachers remained within the organization, but the activities of most of them were gradually brought in line with centralized controls. The transfer by Duncan McColl in 1826 of the church property in St. Stephen to the Society was indicative of the passing of control of the movement out of the hands of the local preachers. "I have offered to the Committee [in London]," he wrote, "all the assistance in my power, consistent with my situation; and desiring them to view me always as one of them, although it is not in my power to travel according to their rules."[8] McColl was one of the last to cling to a position of independence in the Methodist organization. From 1825 onwards all appointments within the country were made by the English Society, and the various missionaries were required to submit to it an annual report of their work. In some of the more remote areas of settlement, it is true, efforts to secure a centralization of the work were not wholly successful. Local or lay preachers continued to carry on without recognizing any close connection with the formal Wesleyan body. Such preachers depended upon no outside financial assistance—what their flock did not contribute to their support, they secured through their own labour—and in their teaching there was often considerable divergence doctrinally from the accepted Methodist position. In some cases, only the name denoted any connection with the larger movement. Thus, as late as 1846, strange preachers calling themselves Methodists but without any connection with the Society held religious services in Campbelltown and Dalhousie in Restigouche

[8]"Memoir of the Rev. Duncan M'Coll," (*British North American Wesleyan Methodist Magazine for the Year 1841*, Saint John, N.B., vol. I, p. 577).

County.[9] These detached groups were of considerable significance in that they staked out claims for the future advance of the cause and kept alive to some extent the evangelical spirit in teaching, but they represented only random ripples within the main Methodist current which was directed steadily towards a greater integration and systematization in methods and organization.

Centralized control of missionary activities, though it checked in the end the building up of a strong local denominational organization, made possible the considerable extension of Methodist influence with the growth of population and the opening up of new areas of settlement. The contrast of the Methodist movement with the Baptist in this regard was striking where the latter had to build up a home missionary organization through the co-operation of individual churches highly jealous of their local autonomy. Methodism in the prosecution of missionary work had none of the characteristics of the sect; it was a mission church, operating, in the eyes of its Wesleyan leaders, scarcely outside the boundaries of the Church of England. This exclusive interest, as far as the direction of the work was concerned, in the extension of religious influence, provided the Methodist movement with considerable advantages in outlying parts of the country. The elaborate organization developed by Wesley in England proved highly effective in the establishment of Methodist influence in the growing communities in the Maritime Provinces.

Methodist societies in the province of Nova Scotia were considerably strengthened and increased in numbers through the extension of missionary preaching and the promotion of revivals. Wesleyan immigrants from England added to the support of Methodism in the colony, and the followings in old centres of Methodist influence were strengthened and new followings were secured. Areas such as Liverpool continued as important centres of preaching and for the holding of revivalist meetings; in 1820, in co-operation with the "open communion" section of the Baptists (that is, the Newlights), an extensive revival took place in Liverpool. In the western part of Nova Scotia, particularly in the Barrington district, the Methodist movement also remained strong, and new gains were secured in Yarmouth through the support of an English shipbuilder, Captain Anthony Landers.[10] Enlistment of a German school-teacher as a Methodist preacher made possible in 1815 for the first time the extension of the work into the Lunenburg district. In Cape Breton the early efforts of lay preachers paved the way for the

[9]*British North American Wesleyan Methodist Magazine for the Year 1846-47*, vol. V, p. 115.
[10]P.A.N.S., manuscript by Frank A. Doane, Methodism in Barrington.

later organization of societies in Sydney and in outlying fishing settlements through the support of Channel Island fishing interests; Peter
de Lisle, a Jersey merchant, was influential in the organization of a
church in Sydney in 1829, and an agent of a Guernsey firm assiste'd
in the building of a church at Ship Harbour in 1828.[11] Missionary work
in Guysborough and Canso between 1819 and 1821 led to the organization of a number of societies in this area. The work in the Annapolis
Valley and Cumberland district was successfully maintained, and in
Halifax the early foot-hold of Methodism was strengthened. Extensive
revivals took place in the capital in 1832 and again in 1841.[12]

Extension of Methodist influence in Prince Edward Island was secured
through the visits of missionaries from the mainland and through the
work of local preachers; effective missionary work began here in 1816.
Walter Johnstone, sent out from Scotland to establish Sabbath schools
and to investigate the religious state of the country, was impressed
with the work of the Methodists on the Island. In addition to a number
of local preachers, two missionaries were regularly stationed. "They
have so many excellent local preachers," Johnstone wrote, "that they
seldom want sermon in all their regular places of worship; and it must
be acknowledged that wherever the Methodists abound, vice and
immorality is made to a great measure to hide their head, and every
man and woman is taught to pray."[13] The predominance of overseas
elements in the population of Prince Edward Island accounted for the
following of English Wesleyanism in the province. Lay leaders among
the settlers from Britain played a prominent part in the organization of
the first societies, while the work of the regular missionaries served
to extend Methodist influence into areas where societies had not been
organized hitherto.[14]

Division of the Maritime field in 1825 into the Nova Scotia and
Prince Edward Island District and the New Brunswick District, the
latter including the Annapolis valley and a section of the township
of Cornwallis, reflected the growing importance of Methodist work in
New Brunswick. Settlement of large numbers of English and Irish
Wesleyans in the province brought new sources of strength to the
movement, and lay leaders connected with the Wesleyan movement

[11]T. Watson Smith, *History of the Methodist Church of Eastern British America*
(Halifax, 1877), vol. II, pp. 195-200.
[12]See *Nova Scotia and New Brunswick Wesleyan Methodist Magazine*, vol. I, no. 1,
March, 1832, p. 56 and the *British North American Wesleyan Methodist Magazine,
for the Year 1841*, vol. I, pp. 400-1.
[13]W. Johnstone, *Travels in Prince Edward Island in the Years 1820-1* (Edinburgh,
1823), p. 115.
[14]*Nova Scotia and New Brunswick Wesleyan Methodist Magazine*, vol. I, no. 1,
Mar., 1832, p. 59.

in the homeland formed the nuclei for the organization of Methodist societies in the new settlements. As settlement pushed into the interior of the province missionary activity was extended. A missionary was appointed to the settlements on the Miramichi River in 1830, in 1832 preaching services were provided at Richibucto, Bathurst, and Wood-stock, and in 1838 monthly visits of a preacher at Buctouche were secured. The organization of new societies and revivals of religion were reported by missionaries in the field. "The gracious revival of religion in Miramichi," the Reverend S. McMarsters wrote March 29, 1841, "of which you have no doubt heard, has extended almost through every part of the Circuit. On the South West there are added to our societies, including those who are still on trial, about seventy-six persons. In Boies Town we have a very promising society of 28 members, and in Price's settlement a class of eleven. The good work is still going on."[15] Prospects on the Bathurst circuit were less promising. "The state of religion in Bathurst," the missionary here wrote, December 13, 1843, "is sad enough, the members hold on, and that is all, no additions to society, no conversions.—I have commenced a fresh effort to save some from Hell if possible. At other places the societies are doing well."[16] A visit of the missionary to the county of Restigouche, where he held preaching services at Dalhousie and Campbellton, resulted in the strengthening of the religious loyalties of the few Methodists in the area. The missionary in Woodstock reported a highly successful revival during the year 1842.[17]

New techniques of evangelization were introduced by the Methodist preachers in the Maritime field to meet the religious needs resulting from changing social conditions, although Wesleyan conservatism checked radical innovations. Camp meetings, developed on the American frontier and employed extensively by the Methodists in their work in Canada, did not become established in the Maritime Provinces, but a form of meeting similar in character early made its appearance and later there developed what became known as protracted meetings. Without apparent plan, a great religious meeting was held on Nictaux Plains on the last Sunday and Monday of September, 1817, through the co-operation of Methodist and Baptist preachers. During the first day, when about fifteen hundred people attended, five Methodist ministers, two Baptist ministers, two Methodist local preachers, and two Baptist exhorters carried on the religious services; the next day

[15]*British North American Wesleyan Methodist Magazine for the Year 1841*, vol. I, p. 403.
[16]Supplement to the *British North American Wesleyan Methodist Magazine for the Year 1843*, vol. III, p. 21.
[17]*Ibid.*, p. 16.

two other Methodist preachers joined those taking part. In 1818 another such meeting, lasting for three days, was held at Granville when services were carried on by five Methodist ministers and one Baptist minister in addition to a number of local preachers; about two thousand people attended. In 1819 Nictaux Plains was again the site of a meeting much like those of the two preceding years.

This was the last of these early meetings carried on through the co-operation of Baptist and Methodist preachers. The whole idea was foreign to the Baptist system with its reliance upon individual churches enjoying a considerable measure of congregational autonomy. Few Baptists attended the three meetings which were held, and their management was left almost entirely in the hands of the Methodist preachers; the one or two Baptist preachers who took part assumed the role of visiting lecturers. The idea was equally foreign to the Wesleyan system, and it quickly met with opposition from those Wesleyan representatives in the country who were anxious to rid the Methodist movement of practices introduced from the United States. In 1820 the holding of these gatherings was virtually prohibited when, at the annual meeting of the ministers in Liverpool that year, a resolution was passed that "no more great meetings, so called, be held by our preachers without the previous consent of the district meeting."[18] The increasing control exercised by the Wesleyan Missionary Society after 1820 effectively checked the introduction of forms of religious service which had their origin in American frontier practice. No further meetings of such a nature were held in the Maritime Provinces.

The communication in 1835 of the secretary of the Wesleyan Missionary Society to the chairmen of the Nova Scotia and New Brunswick districts suggesting the holding of "protracted meetings" represented a radical change of policy in the English body resulting from the serious inroads of schismatic Methodist movements which had introduced into England the American camp meeting.[19] Protracted meetings became increasingly used in the Maritimes after 1835 as a means of promoting religious revivals. The influence of Wesleyan missionaries who had served for a time in Canada and there been forced to develop such meetings to offset the competitive advantages enjoyed by the American Methodists through their use of camp meetings contributed to their introduction in the Maritimes. "Protracted meetings," the Reverend William Croscombe wrote in 1840, "once of comparatively rare occurrence in these Provinces . . . may be of great utility to our people generally. Before my appointment to Canada I had strong

[18]Smith, *History of the Methodist Church*, vol. II, p. 91.
[19]See Henry W. Clark, *History of English Noncomformity* (London, 1913), vol. II.

prejudices against such meetings, or at least, strong doubts as to their scriptural character and authenticity. Conviction of their importance and reality was, however, forced upon my mind while resident in the City of Montreal, where I had the happiness to see hundreds of precious souls brought to God as the result of a protracted meeting."[20]

Communications from various missionaries to the *British North American Wesleyan Methodist Magazine* indicate the general use of protracted meetings. In December, 1840, Croscombe reported a highly successful meeting at Kennetcook, on the Newport circuit, commencing on October 2 and lasting for a week.[21] Another meeting on the same circuit was held at Kempt, commencing January 8, 1841. "The regular protracted meeting," Croscombe wrote of it, "continued for just *one week*, and I have the happiness to state that about eighty persons profess to have been made happy in the Lord! As to the subjects of this gracious work I may remark, that a great proportion of the men are mariners— masters of vessels, with their mates and crews, have all been made happy."[22] A three-day protracted meeting was reported by the Reverend Mr. McNutt from Miramichi, January 20-3, which had been followed for the next four weeks by religious services every evening.[23] From Bridgetown, the Reverend J. S. Hennigar reported the holding of a meeting which began on Hanly Mountain in the latter part of February and proved so successful that it was continued on the mountain and at Wilmot for three weeks.[24] The Wesleyan missionary, C. Churchill, strongly supported the principle of the protracted meeting in describing one which he had attended at Kennetcook in 1839:

> I was, on this occasion, made fully sensible where the peculiar advantages of such meetings lie. There is a combination both of talent and of faith brought to bear on a given point, by the employment of different persons, both ministers and laymen, each succeeding the other in exhortation and prayer. Each meeting is commenced, generally, with a short sermon; some remark forms a subject for enlargement by a following speaker; new ideas are thrown out; new light is poured upon the subject; appeals are forced home, and desires are awakened; above all, the Spirit of God, working above all, through all, and in all, gives efficiency to the means.[25]

Protracted meetings gained in popularity not only among Methodists but among members of other religious groups, and in the latter part of 1841 one was held in Newport where the population was made up predominantly of Episcopalians, Baptists, and Campbellites. Two

[20]*British North American Wesleyan Methodist Magazine for the Year 1841*, vol. I, p. 236.
[21]*Ibid.*, p. 149.
[22]*Ibid.*, p. 315.
[23]*Ibid.*, p. 278.
[24]*Ibid.*, p. 403.
[25]*Memorials of Missionary Life in Nova Scotia* (London, 1845), pp. 78-9.

Methodist preachers conducted the services, and, although the opening congregation was small, the numbers increased steadily in succeeding days. "It was truly delightful," one of the preachers in attendance wrote, "to see the eagerness with which the people flocked to the house of God. In whatever direction you might turn your eye, whether along the public roads or across the open fields, you would see some on foot, some on horseback, and some in two-wheel and four-wheel carriages, loaded to the full, all bending their course to the place in which God's honour dwelleth."[26] The meeting lasted ten days and resulted in the formation of a Methodist society and also in additions to the Baptist church in the district.

The protracted meetings of this time differed from the earlier "great meetings" which had been held at Nictaux Plains and Granville in that they were carried on entirely indoors. The earlier gatherings, which had grown up without any definite idea as to their arrangement, would almost inevitably have developed in a manner similar to that of camp meetings. At the meeting at Granville in 1818, for instance, the services began within the chapel but the crowds were so large that a lay preacher gathered together a number outside and commenced to carry on a second service. Lack of control on the part of those responsible for those gatherings resulted in considerable disorder among the masses of people which congregated together, and the occurrence of serious irregularities probably had something to do with discrediting this form of service in the eyes of the Wesleyan ministers. The later introduction of protracted meetings represented a sharp break from developments tending to the building up of what would almost certainly have become camp meetings. They were much more orderly in character and, held indoors, they attracted much fewer numbers. They developed out of the tradition of English Wesleyanism rather than American Methodism.

The protracted meeting illustrates perhaps as well as anything the kind of techniques developed by the evangelical church in the elaboration of its missionary organization. By the eighteen-thirties neither the Baptists nor Methodists relied upon the undisciplined religious evangelist to carry the message of salvation to the scattered settlers in isolated parts of the country. Emphasis was placed upon order in the organization of the work and in the religious service. Within this system of order the evangelical drive was sufficiently strong to lead to a continuous effort to widen the influence of the church. In the missionary work of both the Baptists and Methodists there was kept alive something of the spirit of the religious sect.

[26]*British North American Wesleyan Methodist Magazine for the Year 1842*, vol. II, p. 36.

Increasingly after 1800, however, the sectarian spirit within the Baptist and Methodist movements in the Maritime Provinces weakened in face of the social demands of the older, culturally mature, communities. The growth of trade, the rise of towns, the increase of wealth, the improvement of means of communication and transportation, and the development of public educational facilities greatly strengthened secular agencies of social organization, evident in the spread of liberal attitudes of thought and the growing importance of the secular press, and secular interests came increasingly in conflict with the narrow religious interests of the sect. Problems of evangelical church leadership which had made their appearance before 1800 became very much more pressing in later years. Efforts on the part of the evangelical churches to maintain their followings in the older-settled parts of the country emphasized the weaknesses of the sectarian form of religious organization and forced adjustments involving a greater accommodation to the secular community. The problem of reconciling the opposing influences of worldliness and other-worldliness became the fundamental problem of evangelical church organization.

Problems of church government, resulting from the conflict between the church and sect idea of religious organization, were particularly apparent in the development of the Baptist movement after 1800. That which revealed perhaps most clearly the pressing character of the problem was the increasing defection of Baptists to religious denominations commanding greater prestige and making fewer demands with respect to private conduct. Such defections took place largely in terms of single individuals. Members dropped away from the church, engaged in "bacchanalian" diversions like dancing and card-playing, joined perhaps the Freemasons, and, in the end, through social or business connections became affiliated with the Church of England or the Presbyterian Church. No records of changes in denominational affiliations were made by the church clerks, but stray remarks in the journals and correspondence of Baptist preachers provide convincing evidence of their occurrence. The growth of towns and of trade tended to an increasing sophistication in social relationships, and new class distinctions developed on the basis of wealth and political influence. Occupational, political, and class lines cut through the sectarian lines separating off the religious group from the community. Baptists became caught up increasingly in associations which involved acceptance of values opposed to the values of the religious sect. The Baptist denomination found itself an integral part of the community before it had developed forms of religious organization to secure its distinctive position in the

communal institutional structure. Defections to more socially accommodated religious denominations represented efforts of the individual to secure adjustments which had failed to be secured on the institutional level.

Standards of the sect weakened as the pressure of worldly interests made itself felt. On the other hand, principles of the sect persisted sufficiently strongly to check the development of denominational supports of religious organization. The Reverend Edward Manning referred constantly in his journal to difficulties that he faced in managing the affairs of his church in Cornwallis. In particular, he deplored the attitude of his congregation to church attendance, conference duties, and private worship. The failure of anyone to attend religious services because of a rainstorm led to an outburst of annoyance in his journal, October 16, 1814: "The aged are stupefied and irreligious, and the rising generation who have been neglected by their irreligious parents are profane, ignorant, heady, high minded, Sabbath-breakers, debauched, gay and dissolute, and are, in fact, unfit for civil or decent society."[27] A similar circumstance during the next winter led Manning to make the following entry in his journal, January 15, 1815: "It is melancholy to think of the woeful stupidity that prevails among the people." Two weeks later Manning returned to the subject of the lack of support from his congregation. "Much cruelty has been exercised," he wrote, "much neglect, much fraud, much pride, much self-will, much worldly-mindedness, much uncleanness, much narrow-heartedness, much hyprocricy, much drunkenness, much profanity, much Sabbath-breaking, much neglect of duty." Under the date of November 4, 1817, he wrote out in the form of a memorandum some of the things which distressed him in relationships with his congregation. In addition to other evils, he found: first, a neglect of prayer; secondly, an irregular way of attending to the public ordinances of religion; thirdly, a disinclination to support the gospel, any debt being paid sooner than a gospel debt and these debts being paid with that which they could not turn into money to pay other persons; fourthly, a failure to attend conference meetings many of the most wealthy and the best accommodated not coming until late and making such excuses about the hurry of business that the hearts of the pious and especially of the minister were wounded; fifthly, a neglect of reading the scriptures and other good books so that they did not know when the truth was preached and when not in many points; sixthly, an itching of ears to hear strange preachers, and, not

[27]Acadia University, Baptist Historical Collection, Rev. Edward Manning's Journal, vol. I, 1778-1821.

being well instructed by reading, a tendency to be imposed upon by a man of gift and zeal who was not a sound evangelical minister; seventhly, a neglect of discipline, a man under censure for open immorality remaining in the church for nine years; eighthly, a willingness to believe reports against their minister, contrary to scripture; ninthly, the minister being obliged to do business such as buying land, hiring money, selling, building, and collecting and being censured for attempting to collect a debt which was unjustly kept back for five years; tenthly, their not making the meeting house comfortable when it was in their power, much to their own inconvenience and discredit, and much to the injury of the minister's health; and, eleventhly, their neglecting family government and letting their children talk saucily to their parents and others in their presence, letting them go abroad at nights to parties, cards, frolics, etc., so that such precedents were very demoralizing and the minister found it very difficult to keep order in his family and his children in subjection. Much later in his journal Manning referred again to the problem of maintaining an interest in religion among his followers. "I am much depressed in my mind," he wrote, January 11, 1821, "about the state of Religion in this place. I fear there is something of an alienation in the minds of some professors, that does not appear as yet, that may yet prove hurtful to the progress of this Church. The want of energy in leading characters, and an undue attachment to worldly things, I fear, prevails too much."

Some of the other Baptist preachers complained in similar fashion respecting the conduct of their congregations. The effect of the evangelical appeal was to weaken among the Baptist membership any sense of denominational attachment. Its effect was also to weaken any sense of belonging to a secular public. The church, as such, with its elaborate organization and its formal ritual of service, was in the eyes of the convert a worldly society. The half-way covenant of Congregationalism had been a recognition of the dependence of the religious denomination upon the worldly interests of its members. Within the Newlight-Baptist movement, the spiritual basis of membership in the religious society was restored; members were not born into the sect but joined it by virtue of their religious experience. It was this principle of religious fellowship which provided the powerful dynamic in the expansion of the evangelical sect, but it also provided the basis for division and schism; where large numbers were brought together with nothing more in common than the experience of religious conversion, the unity of the religious body inevitably rested upon a precarious foundation. With no strong sense of denominational loyalty, the members joined in whatever meeting was held in the local community

if it offered something in the way of religious excitement, and defections
from one group to another constituted a constant threat to the organization of religion. "As there is so much shifting among professors," Joseph
Dimock wrote in his diary, December 11, 1822, after a revivalist meeting
at Lewis Head, "I insisted much that those who fear the Lord Should
be as Mount Zion immoveable always abounding in the word of the
Lord. This appears to be a very important stand where they are visited
by Men who can change as often as the chemelion."[28] Elder David
Harris wrote of his congregation in Sackville to Edward Manning,
October 5, 1817:

> The greatest difficulties is the want of Church members that is rooted and grounded
> In the Doctrine of Christ but for the want of that there is But little grounds to hope
> that there will ever be A regular Gosel Church in this place they have Drank so
> Deep into Eroes that never will be physck'd off I am afraid Some may Say what
> are these errors brother you know one is neglect of Family worship another is Tatling
> and Backbiting some spends time at Taverns and gets entoxicated others neglects
> coming to Church meetings Forget to Support the preacher you know it is easier to
> Sign a paper Than to pay an other eror A falling back from what they Voted Which
> brings Such triall on me that I know not to bear The burden.[29]

Weaknesses of the Baptist Church through the persistence of the
sect spirit in the management of local affairs were most evident in the
difficulties faced by the preachers in securing proper pay for their
services. Manning complained again and again in his journal that his
congregation refused to pay him sufficient to maintain his family and
forced him to accept many indignities in collecting what little was
coming to him. The view that the preacher should serve without pay,
depending upon his own labour and voluntary contributions as means
of support, persisted strongly in the thinking of members of the Baptist
churches. Any sort of contractual obligation to pay the minister a
stipulated amount was considered a violation of the spirit of the primitive
church; it implied that the minister would only preach the message
of the gospel in return for a professional fee corresponding in character
to fees charged by other professional people. Efforts to secure improvements in conditions of pay, as a result, met with stiff resistance, and
the salaries of Baptist ministers throughout the country remained low.
Manning provided an estimate of the income of a number of Baptist
preachers about 1820; Thomas Handly Chipman, of Wilmot, had a farm,
laboured hard to support his family, and received from the people
about $150 a year; Thomas Ansley, of Granville, having left a valuable
property in Sussex, New Brunswick, received about $300 a year from

[28]Acadia University, Baptist Historical Collection, Joseph Dimock's Diary. p. 189.
[29]Acadia University, Baptist Historical Collection, Correspondence of Rev. Edward
Manning, vol. I, 1778-1817.

his church; Peter Crandall, of Digby Neck, received $200 a year from his people; Enoch Towner, of Sissiboo, was in low circumstances, having a small family which was supported mostly by his people; Harris Harding, of Yarmouth, was in low circumstances; John Craig, of Ragged Islands, received a little from his church but very little as his people were poor; James Manning, of Lower Granville, had a small farm and received but a small salary; Joseph Crandall, of Sussex, New Brunswick, received but a small support from his people; Elijah Estabrook, of Waterborough, New Brunswick, had a good farm, a large family, laboured hard, and received but very little from his people; Lathrop Hammond, of Kings Clear, New Brunswick, had a good landed property and received but little from his church toward his support; Abadiah Newcomb, of Hopewell, New Brunswick, had a handsome property and received $160 a year from the people; T. S. Harding was in easy circumstances, having received property by his wife, and he also had a moderate support from his church.[30] The large number of local, unordained preachers throughout the country received even less in the way of salary than the regular ministers; they invariably depended upon some other occupation as their chief means of support.

Failure to pay more adequate salaries led to an increasingly serious problem in recruiting new ministers. The preachers raised up by the Newlight revival—Chipman, the two Mannings, Harris Harding, Theodore S. Harding, and a few others—were passing beyond middle age, and the church offered few attractions to younger men. "One thing affected me much," the Reverend Irah Chase wrote in the *Massachusetts Baptist Magazine* in 1827, on his return from a visit to the Maritime Provinces, "—most of the ministers seemed to be far advanced in life; and I could hear of very few young men or middle-aged brethren that were ready to fill the places of those who must soon be called away from their labours."[31] The effect of the lack of sufficient preachers was particularly evident in the failure to supply with regular ministers those churches formed through missionary work. Extension of Baptist influence through evangelical preaching and revivals secured little strength to the Baptist cause when the churches which were organized were often left for several years without ministerial guidance. "When . . . it was considered," the Reverend David Nutter wrote of the problem of organizing a church in Liverpool in 1821, "that the new body would likely be left without a minister to strengthen and feed them, we hesitated before taking this step."[32] Disintegration of

[30]Saunders, *History of the Baptists of the Maritime Provinces*, pp. 215-16.
[31]Quoted *ibid.*, p. 215.
[32]Quoted *ibid.*, p. 158.

the church in Liverpool, making necessary its reorganization in 1829, suggests that Nutter's concern was not without foundation. A number of other churches experienced similar difficulties in maintaining religious organization while lacking a minister.

The problem of recruiting a sufficient supply of ministers reflected a more general problem of religious organization. The Baptist Church was steadily losing those attributes of the evangelical sect which had accounted for its early rapid growth, while it had acquired too few of the attributes of the denomination to maintain its position through ties with strong vested interests. The claims of secular interests—trade, politics, and recreational or cultural activities—drew off the less evangelical-minded of its membership, while the stubborn adherence to principles cf the sect prevented the infusion of secular interests into church affairs to the point where worldly activities would have offered a support of religion. Failure to pay the ministers salaries sufficient to maintain decent standards of living checked improvements in the status of the ministers and of the Church generally. The membership clung to the prerogatives of the sectarian while becoming increasingly less willing to accept the obligations implied in such forms of religious fellowship. Conflicts between the ministers and their congregations reflected underlying conflicts between the sect and church type of religious organization.

Accommodation of the Baptist Church to the community at large could come only through the development of a greater interest in activities which brought the Church as a whole as well as individual members into closer contact with outside social groups. Such a development involved the creation of a Baptist public out of the Baptist religious group. It meant in the end the abandonment of the sectarian principle of separation from the world and acceptance of a denominational responsibility for the problems of the secular society. Formation of the Baptist Association and the organization of missionary societies had constituted first steps in the process of denominational accommodation. Increased denominational accommodation proceeded along the lines of developing Baptist institutions outside the church organization which served the function of drawing the church closer to the life of the community. Of such developments, the building up of Baptist educational institutions and the promotion of temperance reform and Sabbath observance were the most significant.

Though the Baptists inherited from Congregationalism a tradition favourable to education, the condition of the Newlight revival resulted in discrediting a reliance upon an educated ministry and the effect of this was to weaken an interest in education in general. Evangelical

religion implied a reaction against intellectualism in the pulpit and rationalism in everyday affairs. It became a matter of principle that the educated minister was one lacking in zeal and the educated layman was one whose mind was distracted from the elementary problem of salvation. As a consequence the Baptist churches grew up with a ministry almost wholly untrained and with the support of people who were largely illiterate. By 1820, the lack of an educated ministry and of a literate membership had come to constitute a distinct handicap. It checked the professionalization of the ministry, and it checked efforts to make the Church a more respectable body. "The Baptists," Dr. E. A. Crawley wrote of this period, "enjoyed but a small amount of public favour, especially in Halifax, and were regarded as occupying the lowest rank in religious estimation—were in fact despised as an ignorant and deluded sect."[33] Ambitious young men in Baptist families trained themselves for one of the secular professions—or secured ordination within the Church of England! Missionary work in new communities suffered through lack of a sufficient supply of preachers and the position of the churches in old communities weakened through lack of the support of influential sections of the population.

Some of the older Baptist preachers—Edward Manning for one— recognized the need of promoting educational institutions, but the great body of members and many of the preachers remained indifferent. Leadership came from outside rather than from within the Baptist churches. Efforts of Dr. Thomas McCulloch, Presbyterian minister in Pictou, to promote the cause of education led him to seek the support of the Baptists. McCulloch was interested in developing institutions of higher education which would serve a constituency larger than that of the Presbyterian religious group; he had hopes that Baptists would find their way into Pictou Academy. He was also concerned, as a nonconformist, in raising the social status of the nonconformist ministry generally. "In thinking upon the state of religion in the Province," he wrote to the Reverend Edward Manning, "it has occurred to me that the clergy, both Baptists and Presbyterian, are subjected to hardships which they ought not to feel, and one consequence of this is, that when Presbyterian clergy, on the one hand, pride themselves upon their learning as a qualification for preaching the gospel, on the other, the pulpits of Baptist churches have been perhaps too much open to persons who were more willing than qualified to preach; and this has deprived other Baptist clergymen of that respect and support to which they are justly entitled."[34] The example set by the Presbyterians, and

---

[33]Quoted *ibid.*, p. 181.
[34]Quoted *ibid.*, p. 176.

the influence of McCulloch upon some of the Baptist preachers such as Manning, undoubtedly did much to arouse an interest in education among the Baptists. The influence of Presbyterian educational leaders was limited, however, by denominational barriers to social intercourse. Vested interests within the Baptist churches resisted movements to support educational undertakings promoted by other religious groups.

It was from the Church of England rather than from the Presbyterian Church that the Baptists derived the leadership which resulted in the eventual establishment of extensive Baptist educational institutions. The evangelical preaching in Halifax of the Reverend John T. Twining, curate of St. Paul's church, which had given rise to differences with the bishop, had led the curate and his followers to separate and to form a church of their own; when ecclesiastical recognition of the new church was not forthcoming most of the dissentients including the pastor returned to St. Paul's, but a small group remained and carried on as an independent church body. Eventually, in 1827, the church was organized as Baptist by the Reverend Irah Chase, professor of theology in Newton Theological Institution, and Alexis Caswell, professor of Columbian College, Washington, and the next year it was admitted into the Association. The defection brought into the Baptist Church a number of the prominent citizens of Halifax: James W. Johnston and E. A. Crawley were lawyers, the former at the head of the bar, and J. W. Nutting was prothonotary of the Supreme Court; others, such as S. N. Binney, John Pryor, Charles Twining, and John Ferguson were also men of education and social standing. Organization of their church with the aid of Baptist educational leaders invited from the United States was indicative of the reluctance of the new converts to identify themselves too closely with churches in the country depending upon an uneducated ministry. The Granville Street church immediately assumed the leadership in promoting the cause of education in Baptist ranks. "We feel a growing conviction," the Reverend Alexis Caswell, who was appointed pastor of the church, wrote Manning, April 7, 1828, "of the importance of establishing a Seminary of Learning under the patronage of the Baptists."[35] At the meeting of the Association in 1828 Crawley presented a prospectus of the Nova Scotia Baptist Education Society the purpose of which was to found such a seminary of learning and, although some opposition was met particularly from the Reverend Robert Davis, a preacher who had built up a following among the poor of Halifax, the Association endorsed the scheme of the Granville Street brethren. Out of such action there emerged Horton Academy and eventually Acadia University. A somewhat similar course of events

[35]Quoted *ibid.*, p. 197.

in New Brunswick led to the initiation of an educational movement there which resulted in the founding of a seminary in Fredericton in 1836.[36]

The shift to an interest in education represented a fundamental change in the character of the Baptist denomination. With means of training provided, the ministry gained in prestige and attracted into its ranks young men interested in professional advancement; it also attracted men trained in theological schools outside the country. At the same time, educational institutions came to serve increasingly as centres of recruitment to the Baptist membership; a number of revivals after 1829 originated among the students in Horton Academy and, later, in Acadia University. Thus, with respect to both functionaries and followers, there was secured a means of maintaining the continuity of the denomination. Reliance shifted from conversion to education as a technique of recruitment. In contrast with the sect which depended largely upon proselytization as a means of continued existence (the younger people often not inheriting the sectarian loyalties of their parents), the Baptist denomination became an institutional system of religion provided with means of perpetuating itself from generation to generation. Such a development involved an important step in the direction of denominational accommodation. The Baptist churches became more concerned with preserving the support of the young people growing up within the fold than with winning the support of people outside. Baptism by adult immersion lost much of its importance as a mechanism of recruitment. Competition between denominations came to operate much more powerfully within Sunday schools and within educational establishments. The strengthening of techniques by which it could participate in such competition implied the shift on the part of the Baptists away from the isolation of the religious sect.

The development of educational institutions led to a raising of the cultural standards of the community at large as well as of the pro-

[36]See Mrs. F. Beavan, *Sketches and Tales Illustrative of Life in the Backwoods of New Brunswick* (London, 1845), pp. 60-3. "The different opinions expressed regarding this," Mrs. Beaven wrote of a discussion about education at a meeting of the New Brunswick Baptist Association which she attended, "finely developed the progress of mind throughout the land. Some whiteheaded fathers of the sect, old refugees, who had left the bounds of civilization before they had received any education, yet who had been gifted in the primitive days of the colony to lead souls from sin, sternly declaimed against the education system, declaring that grace, and grace alone, was what formed the teachers. All else was of the earth earthy, and had nought to do with heavenly things. One said that when he commenced preaching he could not read the bible—he could do little more now, and yet throughout the country many a soul owned its sickness to have been healed through him. Another then rose and answered him—a native of the province, and of his own persuasion, but who drank from the springing fountains of science and holiness. . . . He pleaded, as such should, for extended education, and his mighty words had power, and won the day."

fessional standards of Baptist preachers. Education was a social problem of general concern. It contributed to the welfare of the community rather than to the separateness of a particular religious group. The exclusiveness of the sect, with its emphasis upon the salvation of the elect, broke down with the development of denominational educational institutions which quickly assumed a strong sense of responsibility to the community at large.

In another way, also, the promotion of educational institutions led to the greater integration of the Baptist churches into the life of the community. Efforts to found a denominational college forced Baptist church leaders into the arena of politics, and the extremely controversial political issue which developed led to a growing interest among the Baptist membership generally in public affairs. J. W. Johnston emerged as the acknowledged political leader of the Baptists in Nova Scotia as E. A. Crawley had become their acknowledged educational leader. Dependence upon Baptist leaders in Halifax led to the identification with the Conservative cause; Howe's opposition to the founding of Acadia University strengthened the ties of the Baptists to the Tory party. Alignment with the Conservatives resulted in raising considerably the social status of the denomination. In a more general way, the increasing participation of the Baptists in politics had the effect of raising their relationships with other religious groups from the plane of sectarian conflict to that of political conflict. The denominational school, on the one side, and the political party on the other, became powerful agencies for the support of church interests. The shift was particularly significant in the new role of the preachers. They emerged as strong influences in the lives of the young people in the community; they also secured considerable influence as local political "bosses." Growth of democracy promoted the party spirit with effects evident in religious organization, and particularly in the organization of the Baptist churches. The establishment of strong stakes in the field of politics provided the Baptists with denominational supports which had been lacking so long as reliance was placed upon the sect type of religious organization.

The promotion of temperance reform paralleled, and in many respects was closely related to, the promotion of educational institutions. The temperance movement among the Baptists developed out of leadership provided from the United States. It quickly gained the support of the more worldly-minded of the Baptist preachers, and developed as a prominent interest of the various individual churches and of the Baptist associations. As early as 1830 the Nova Scotia Association was urging upon the churches the need of forming local temperance societies.

By 1832 the Association was able to report considerable success in promoting the movement. Active societies were in existence in Newport, Nictaux, Lunenburg, Horton, Wilmot, Chester, Yarmouth, Aylesford, and New Albany; some of these societies comprised as many as eight hundred members.[37] Reports of later years indicate the steady growth of the temperance movement throughout the Maritime Provinces, and, although some of the Baptist churches hesitated for a time before endorsing the movement, the great majority came to identify closely the cause of religion with the cause of temperance. Efforts of the churches to secure temperance pledges from the members lent support to recruiting efforts of the temperance societies, while the Baptist associations officially endorsed the cause by calling upon the membership to abstain from the use of intoxicating liquors and to do all in their power to further temperance societies.[38]

Promotion of temperance constituted a further break of the Baptist churches from the tradition of the sect. The moral behaviour of its members, it is true, had been from the beginning a matter of vital concern to the Baptist religious group; techniques of moral control developed by Congregationalism were inherited by the Baptist churches. Members guilty of drunkenness, playing cards, dancing, sacrilegious utterances, and more serious misdemeanours such as fornication were charged before the meeting of the church and, if cause for forgiveness was lacking, they were excluded from the church body. So long as the various Baptist churches preserved the close group identity of the religious sect, moral sanctions were imposed with a high degree of effectiveness; excommunication strengthened the moral solidarity of the group and maintained ascetic standards of behaviour among the members. The increasing shift from primary to secondary relationships within the membership, however, imposed strains upon the moral machinery of the churches. People only casually acquainted were reluctant to inquire into one another's private conduct. As standards of respectability developed they interfered with the maintenance of standards of moral conformity; the successful merchant resented an examination which involved the laying bare of facts of his private life before his lowly townsmen. Discrimination in terms of class differences inevitably entered into the judgments of the church courts.

[37] *Minutes of the Nova Scotia Baptist Association, Held at Cornwallis, 25th, 26th, and 27th June, 1832, Together with Their Circular and Corresponding Letters* (Halifax, N.S., 1832).

[38] See *Minutes of the Nova Scotia Baptist Association, Held at Onslow, Colchester County, on the 21st, 22nd, and 23rd June, 1841* (Halifax, 1841) and *Minutes of the Fifty First Session of the Nova Scotia Baptist Association, Held at Nictaux, from June 22nd to June 26, 1850, Inclusive* (Halifax, 1850).

As a result, the moral controls of the churches tended to become increasingly formal in character. Their weakening was indicative of the passing within the Baptist denomination of the attributes of the sect.

Developments within the wider community gave rise to conditions unfavourable to the continued reliance upon the moral sanctions of the sect. On the other hand, these conditions favoured the promotion of such moral movements as temperance reform. Drinking became more prevalent while at the same time the economic supports of the rum trade weakened. The increasing emphasis upon economic enterprise, and the operation of the profit motive, led to a growing concern with the economic costs of drinking. The development of agricultural societies reflected the growing commercial interest in the promotion of the agricultural industry, but drunkenness contributed, along with inefficient farming methods, to the backward nature of the industry. At the same time, the development of the ship-building industry, and the shift to capitalist forms of economic organization in the fisheries, increased the importance of wage-labour, and drinking became an increasingly important problem in the mobilization of an efficient working force. Capitalism which had grown in part out of the rum trade came increasingly to depend upon the virtues of sobriety and industry. Where taboos upon drinking had earlier secured the support of only the less respectable members of the community, they came now to be endorsed by some of the most influential people. Temperance reform meant in effect the building of temperate working-class habits; the sect's taboo upon drinking had been a means of sheltering the brethren from the sophisticated habits of the upper classes.

The shift in the Baptist denomination from reliance upon the moral sanctions of the sect to promotion of movements of moral reform was indicative of fundamental changes which were taking place in class affiliations within the Baptist membership. It was also indicative of the strengthening of ties with the wider community. Like education, temperance was a social cause which implied in its promotion an acceptance of responsibility for the welfare of the community at large. Temperance reform affected the total population, not simply the members of an exclusive religious sect. Participation of Baptists in the movement involved their working with members of other religious denominations and with secular leaders. Recruitment of temperance supporters was therefore only indirectly related to efforts to recruit church followers. Substitution of these indirect means of strengthening denominational following in place of more direct means eased the conflict between

religious groups and contributed to denominational and wider community accommodation. Baptist preachers and lay leaders came increasingly to depend upon work on temperance committees (and boards of education) as means of furthering the interests of the denomination.

The temperance cause, like that of college education, eventually passed into the realm of politics, and its support involved increasing participation in party organizations. It contributed, therefore, to the arousal among the Baptist membership of an interest in public affairs and strengthened considerably the political influence of the preachers. Efforts to secure prohibitory liquor legislation furthered the shift of the evangelical religious groups away from liberal principles. Temperance lobbyists and propagandists became increasingly influential in pressure politics and took a lead in the strengthening of the churches as political pressure groups.

The Sabbath observance movement developed somewhat later than the temperance movement, though, like drinking, the desecration of the Sabbath had occupied from the beginning the attention of the individual Baptist churches. The movement as such grew up outside the organization of individual churches and of particular religious denominations; it was a movement promoted by church leaders concerned with the interests of religion in general. It came to command the full support of the Baptist churches. Baptist preachers undertook to arouse a local interest in the cause, and the Baptist associations set up special committees to support the movement in its propagandist and, later, lobbying activities. Annual resolutions and special reports served to call the attention of the membership body to what were considered glaring abuses of the Sabbath such as travelling or the delivering of the mails on that day.[39]

Efforts to secure greater observance of the Sabbath, like temperance reform, grew out of conditions of the new capitalistic order. The growth of business, and the development of new modes of communication and transportation, imposed increasing strains upon the moral machinery of the churches in dealing with the problem of Sabbath desecration. The problem became an impersonal rather than personal one, and the religious group found itself helpless in its reliance upon the sectarian weapon of excommunication. The Baptist churches could scarcely excommunicate large business enterprises or the government itself! The shift to propaganda and lobbying represented an adjustment of the churches to the problem of controlling the impersonal forces of a

[39]See *Minutes of the Fifty First Session of the Nova Scotia Baptist Association, Held at Nictaux, from June 22nd to June 26, 1850, Inclusive.*

capitalistic order. On the other side, it represented efforts to secure greater order within the competitive system. Sunday labour had raised no problems of unfair competition in an economic order of individual enterprise in farming and the fishing industry, but the increasing importance of the profit motive in the organization of business forced the question to the front as an economic issue. Observance of the Sabbath, like temperance reform, became a problem in the building up of a rational working-force and of a rational business system; its promotion secured, therefore, the support of powerful economic interests. Endorsement of the cause by the Baptist churches was indicative of the increasing infusion of *bourgeois* values into the Baptist religious philosophy.

In terms of religious organization, support of the cause of Sabbath observance furthered tendencies towards denominational accommodation and the integration of the Baptist churches into the life of the community. Organization of Sabbath alliances paralleled the organization of temperance leagues, and Baptist preachers and lay readers became involved increasingly in associational activities outside denominational boundaries. Vested interests in the community, and in the field of politics, secured new supports for the Baptist denomination, but at the price of recognizing more fully vested interests of other religious groups.

By 1850 the Baptist Church had become engaged in a wide range of social activities in the Maritime Provinces which had gone far to break down the narrow exclusiveness which had earlier characterized it. It would not be true to maintain that the Church had broken completely from its sectarian origin—the spirit of congregational autonomy served to preserve something of the sect ideal in religious organization—but out of the earlier evangelical movement there had emerged a powerful evangelical church. Much of the leadership in the drive to strengthen the denominational machinery of the Church was taken by the preachers; they had much to gain from the raising of standards of organization and appeal. But increasingly, lay support offered itself in bringing about a greater consciousness within the Baptist denomination of its obligations to the wider community. Baptists shared in the commercial prosperity enjoyed by the Maritime Provinces during the first half of the nineteenth century. The impact of the commercial revolution was felt in the changing character of the Baptist Church.

Points of disturbance in the organization of the Baptist churches were not wholly removed with the development of outside denominational activities. Secular interests continued to grow in strength and imposed pressures on religious loyalties which were only partly allayed by efforts to broaden denominational interests. Influences from overseas

and from the United States strengthened rationalist tendencies in social thought, evident, for instance, in the growing interest in such questions as biological evolution, and rationalism involved to a certain extent a complete break from the religious ethos. Although movements of the enlightenment made greatest progress among the upper social classes of the Maritime community upon which the Baptist denomination was still not greatly dependent for support, they spread out into areas which had been strongholds of the denomination. Paradoxically as it may have seemed, evangelical religious teachings actually contributed to the cause of the enlightenment. By weakening the hold of traditional systems of religious thought, the shift to non-religious beliefs came about easily when a break from evangelical religious teachings took place.

In terms of denominational adjustment to the social conditions of culturally mature communities, the sect ideal exerted much less influence in Methodist than in Baptist religious organization. The Baptist churches grew out of the highly autonomous congregational organization of Congregationalism while the Methodist societies grew out of the highly centralized missionary organization of Wesleyanism. In its early development, therefore, the Methodist movement possessed a much stronger denominational organization than the Baptist movement. As the movement developed, however, its control through the Wesleyan Missionary Society situated outside the country checked adjustments in denominational organization. In the promotion of education, temperance reform, and other community objectives, the Methodists lagged behind the Baptists. It is true that the development of such activities was not as essential to the progress of the Methodist as of the Baptist movement; the Methodist ministry generally, through the fact that most of the preachers came from England, had a much better training than the Baptist ministry, and the considerable emphasis in Methodist preaching upon such moral problems as drinking meant that less dependence was placed upon the moral machinery of the individual churches and therefore that less need was felt for such techniques of control as temperance reform. Nevertheless, the increasing pressure of secular influences resulted in a considerable weakening of Methodist organization particularly in areas most exposed to such influences and emphasized the need for the development of stronger denominational supports.

The establishment of a Methodist college, the promotion of temperance reform, and the publication of a religious journal constituted means of strengthening the organization of the Methodist movement and securing greater accommodation in the wider community, and

these undertkaings met with the stiff resistance of the leaders of the movement in England and of many of the Wesleyan missionaries. In contrast with the other religious denominations, there was lacking among the preachers in the country any group prepared to take the lead in establishing a college, while the English Wesleyan Society took the view that training schools in England were adequate in preparing missionaries for work in the colonies. Early proposals to found such a college, as a result, received little support. In the case of temperance reform, indifference gave way to determined opposition on the part of the Wesleyan Society, and the view of the parent body was shared by most of the Wesleyan missionaries. Temperance reform was essentially an American movement and was looked upon by the Wesleyans as another form of religious fanaticism. A number of Methodist preachers in the country did support the temperance cause but their support constituted a defiance of the authority of the Wesleyan Society. Religious leadership in the movement was taken almost completely by the Baptists. Efforts to found a religious journal met with even more determined opposition from the Committee in London anxious to maintain the circulation of its own missionary journal. Only four issues of a journal, started in 1832, appeared and, while a journal founded in 1840 enjoyed a longer career, its publication also was eventually terminated. The Wesleyan Society sought to maintain the organization of the work in the Maritime Provinces upon a missionary basis. Such organization had proved highly successful in pushing Methodist influence into new areas of settlement. It left the Methodist movement weak, however, in the older and more fully developed communities.

The establishment of a college in 1843 and of a regular religious journal in 1849, and the shift towards a more friendly attitude to the cause of temperance reform, reflected the growing strength of provincial interests in the Methodist organization. Dissatisfaction with the authoritarian control exercised by the Wesleyan Society in England found expression in the promotion of activities in terms of the needs of the local community and in efforts to secure a greater measure of independence in the control of the local Methodist organization. Discrimination against colonial preachers in favour of the overseas missionaries discouraged recruitment of local men into the ministry and increased the bitterness of local leaders towards the English body. The establishment in 1855 of the Eastern British American Conference was a culmination of developments directed towards the strengthening of the denominational supports of the Methodist movement. The considerable measure of independence enjoyed by the early Methodist preachers had reflected

the essentially local character of the movement as it had grown up under the leadership of William Black. Failure of the Church in the United States to assume more active leadership in the movement led to the increasing control through the Wesleyan Society in England when the rapid growth of settlement particularly in New Brunswick after 1812 called for the vigorous prosecution of missionary work. During the period from 1812 to about 1830 the Methodist movement, because of its strong outside supports, enjoyed distinct advantages over the Baptist movement. With the end of rapid expansion, however, and the emergence, on the one side, of economically and culturally mature local communities and, on the other side, of areas of economic depression and depopulation, the Methodist movement required for its continued existence a strong provincial organization integrated more fully into the life of the wider community. Outside control of the movement checked such development, and full denominational accommodation only came with the break from the English body and the organization of a distinctively Maritime Church.

The promotion within the Baptist and Methodist churches of activities which brought them into closer relationship to the general social life of the community led to a fundamental change in their relationship to the traditional churches in the country. The shift from the sect to the church type of religious organization involved a shift from a conflicting to an accommodative position. There developed increasingly among Baptist and Methodist preachers a willingness to accept the ministers of other churches as fellow-teachers of the gospel. They found themselves working with these other ministers on boards and in various community activities, and tendencies towards inter-denominational co-operation were already becoming evident.

The traditional religious denominations, on their part, became much more accommodated to the evangelical churches. The implications of this tendency were particularly significant with respect to the Church of England. Abandonment of the position of the sect of separation from the world was accompanied by the abandonment of the position of the Established Church of the enjoyment of an exclusive monopoly of religious ordinances. The sect church and the territorial church both tended to give way to the free church. Modifications in the law permitting clergy of the various denominations to perform the marriage ceremony were indicative of the development of accommodative techniques. Retreat of the Church of England from the position of attempting to monopolize educational institutions, though involving prolonged controversy, served in the end to improve greatly its relationships with the other religious denominations. Instead of relying upon

state privileges and the claim to apostolic succession, a greater effort was made to strengthen the positive appeals of the Church. The introduction in Halifax in 1835 by both the Church of England and the Presbyterian Church of the practice, employed from the beginning by the Methodists, of holding services on Sunday evenings as well as on Sunday mornings was illustrative of the manner in which the traditional churches sought to compete with the evangelical churches on the same level.[40] The vigorous prosecution of Sunday school activities constituted another means employed by the Church of England and the Presbyterian Church of strengthening their competitive position.

By 1850 tendencies in religious organization in the older-settled parts of the Maritime region were running strongly away from any considerable emphasis upon evangelical methods and revivalist techniques. What might be described as the general evangelical movement—or "Great Awakening"—which had taken its rise with the preaching of Henry Alline and William Black had run its course. Institutionalization of the early Newlight-Baptist and Methodist movements had set up vested interests which favoured the closer integration of the evangelical denominations into the life of the wider community. Persistence of sectarian principles in the thinking of many of the members of the evangelical churches checked denominational adjustments involving greater accommodation to other religious institutions, but social conditions within the Maritime community generally favoured the disintegration of the sect type of religious organization and the dominance of the "free church" principle. Improvements in means of transportation and communication, the general raising of standards of living, the introduction of social and cultural amenities, the establishment of provincial educational systems, and the growing interest of the population generally in affairs of the local community and of the province at large imposed new strains upon religious organization and led to efforts to strengthen religious influence through the support of secular interests. The shift of the evangelical churches from "other-worldly" to worldly interests was indicative of the increasing limitations of a purely religious appeal. The great proportion of the inhabitants in the older communities by 1850 had become fully incorporated into the society of which they were a part. They had secured social status, and were no longer dependent upon membership in the evangelical sect as a means of securing a stake in society. The result was an increasing reluctance to sacrifice other interests to the exclusive interest of religion. If the evangelical denominations were to survive they had to abandon the conflict position of the sect, intent upon setting up a sharp separation

[40]Smith, *History of the Methodist Church*, vol. II, p. 212.

between the interests of the elect and the interests of the worldly, and accept a more accommodating position. Baptists and Methodists achieved success in business; they became respectable and in many cases recognized leaders in their local communities. Maintenance of the support of such "worldly" members compelled the Baptist and Methodist churches to seek status and supports in the wider community. In doing so, they gradually abandoned the integrative function of the religious sect in areas of society where secular interests were not sufficiently strong to support social organization.

The break of the Methodist and Baptist movements in Canada from their American connection and the establishment of ties with English religious bodies was an indication of the effects of changes taking place in the Canadian, as in the Maritime, community structure which made necessary a greater accommodation on the part of religious organization to the secular order. The English tie provided an important support in the transition from the sect to the church form of religious organization. Out of developments which took place after 1832, the Wesleyan Methodist Church and the Canada Baptist Union emerged as distinctive religious denominations in the community.

Increasing social accommodation of the Methodist movement after 1832 was evident in the greater reliance upon a professional ministry, in the shift away from an evangelical appeal, in the weakening of ascetic standards of behaviour, in the growing identification with the upper social classes in the community and in the increasing alignment with Conservative political forces. In securing such accommodation, English Wesleyan leadership played an important role, but significant support was drawn from local leaders and local members. Union with the English Conference was as much an outgrowth as a cause of the growing denominational consciousness of the Canadian Methodist movement.

By 1832 Methodism had almost completely ceased to be a movement which relied upon "the call" as the sole qualification of the preachers it employed. The agreement of 1832 with the English Conference sharply limited the influence of the local preachers in Methodist organization, and henceforth leadership was assumed by those who had undergone a systematic training for the ministry and had held regular appointments in the Church. The Wesleyan missionaries came out to the country with the advantages of a thorough theological training; the Canadian preachers turned increasingly to Methodist theological institutions in the United States and quickly developed their own theological school in Canada. With greater training, the preachers could demand more comforts and higher pay, and the saddle-bag

itinerant gave way to the stationed minister with a regular salary. The increase in the importance of the town station was accompanied by a decline in the importance of the country circuit. The building of churches—or chapels as they were called by the Wesleyans—was indicative of the establishment of deeper stakes in the settled community.

This change in the character of the Methodist ministry was closely related to the change in the character of the Methodist religious appeal. The highly evangelistic preaching of early Methodism was largely the work of the local preachers, and as the ministry became increasingly professionalized Methodist preaching became more moderate in character. The revival became less important as a means of extending the influence of the Church.

The decline in the importance of the camp meeting was the most significant indication of the extent of the shift within Methodism away from an evangelistic position after the union with English Wesleyanism in 1832. The camp meeting attained its fullest development in Canada during the eighteen-twenties and by the next decade it was coming to be less used as an agency of religious revival. The decline was evident in the fewer numbers of such meetings, in the falling off of attendance, and in the weakening of the religious fervour of those who did attend. Under the heading, "Who is for the camp?," the editor of the *Christian Guardian* wrote in July, 1841: "Sometime before Conference we ventured to direct the attention of our ministers and people to the subject of Camp Meetings, and entertained a high expectation that many would be held this summer. As yet we have heard of only six or seven throughout our extensive Methodist field. How is this? Have we churches and school-houses to accommodate all the people that will assemble to hear the word of God?—or are they disinclined to worship in the grove? Neither is the case."[41]

The next year the editor returned to the subject in a lengthy article in which he deplored in particular the growing tendency on the part of the members to attend only the Sunday services rather than to arrive at the beginning of the camp meeting and to remain on the grounds for all the services.[42] Advertisements of camp meetings in the pages of the *Christian Guardian* suggest something of the change which was taking place. Such meetings came to be more carefully arranged, more formal, and very much more confined to special seasons of the year. They no longer assumed the character of mass outbursts of religious feelings.

[41]*Christian Guardian*, July 28, 1841.
[42]*Ibid.*, Aug. 17, 1842.

Some of the reasons for the abandonment of camp meetings were suggested in a communication to the editor of the *Christian Guardian* by a correspondent signing himself Horace Dean.

When I commenced this I only intended to send you a few thoughts on the propriety of keeping up Camp Meetings. I am convinced they are on the wane . . . . Several causes may have brought about such a state of things . . . . It is said that Protracted Meetings have superseded the necessity of Camp Meetings . . . . It is said that the time and expense of getting up a Camp Meeting are reasons against them . . . . It is said that a greater amount of good is accomplished with the same labour and expense at a Protracted Meeting than at a Camp Meeting . . . . It is said that, owing to many causes beyond our control, Camp Meetings often prove a failure.[43]

In arguing for the retention of such meetings, the editor of the *Christian Guardian* was forced to concede their unpopularity among certain sections of the population. "We have no alliance," he wrote, April 21, 1841, "—nor do we wish or intend to have—with those persons who say, the religious knowledge and habits of the colonists, are so matured, and their intellectual refinement so palpable, Camp-meetings are superseded by the ordinary means of grace, and forbidden as vulgar and rustic by the usages of respectable life, and the dictates of good taste."[44] However much their decline was deplored by some Methodist leaders, camp meetings became steadily less useful as agencies of religious propaganda. They lost their distinctive advantage as the population became less scattered and more able to attend regular places of worship. Furthermore, they ran counter to the commercial *mores* of the time. With the increasing emphasis upon the profit motive, in the agricultural industry as in other economic pursuits, the loss of time in attending camp meetings came to be considered wasteful; thus the growing practice of holding them only in certain seasons of the year and the even more prevalent practice of attending only the Sunday services. The camp meeting passed with the passing of those frontier conditions where the absence of outside markets placed considerable limitations upon economic effort. "It is found," the Reverend George Poole wrote of the population of settlements which were old and rich, "that not many of these have time to attend [camp meetings], or if they do come, they cannot come with preparation to occupy tents; and they do not feel at home, or if they do feel exactly at home, some are burdened above measure in sustaining the meeting."[45]

The decline of the camp meeting was not an isolated phenomenon in the progress of Methodism; it was symptomatic of fundamental changes

[43]*Ibid.*, July 26, 1843.
[44]*Ibid.*, Apr. 21, 1841.
[45]*Ibid.*, July 7, 1841.

taking place in the character of the Methodist religious appeal. The town pulpit gained in prestige at the expense of the rural station, and the more conservative type of religious sermon as exemplified in the preaching of Egerton Ryerson in Toronto became increasingly more acceptable than the rambling exhortations of the local backwoods preacher who often memorized his text because of his lack of ability to read. The shift to a reliance upon the preaching of professional evangelists as a means of promoting religious revivals was the most significant indication of the changing character of the Methodist movement. Although it was not until about 1880 that the professional evangelist became the chief agent within the Methodist Church in the promotion of "extraordinary" movements in religion, the tendency to rely upon such preachers had developed well before 1860. In 1840, the Reverend James Caughey, an evangelist of the Methodist Episcopal Church in the United States, visited Canada and held a number of revivalist meetings in St. John's, Quebec, Montreal, and other centres in Lower Canada before proceeding to England to engage upon a revivalist campaign.[46] In 1851 he returned to Canada, and highly successful revivalist meetings were held in the city of Toronto.[47] It would not be true to assume that the Methodist Church had lost the power, except through calling in outside help, to promote revivals of religion, but the number of preachers within the Church who possessed the talents required to arouse strong convictions of the need for salvation steadily became smaller.

The weakening of the zeal of the preachers was accompanied by the weakening of the evangelical interest of the followers. The decline in the importance of the class meeting in the Methodist system as a result of the growing reluctance of members to enquire closely into the private affairs of one another was an indication of the passing of one of the basic supports of the sect policy. "We are backward," the editor of the *Christian Guardian* complained, "in telling to another plainly and lovingly what we think wrong in him or her."[48] With the passing of the close group sanctions of the sect, the religious solidarity of the body weakened. A communication to the *Christian Guardian* in 1840 deplored the fact that no longer was the rule observed of Methodists giving a preference to other Methodists, by employing them, buying from them, or helping them in business.[49] As indicative of the same general tendency,

---

[46]*Methodism in Earnest: The History of the Revival in Great Britain . . . in Connection with the Labors of the Rev. James Caughey. With an introduction by Thos. D. Summers* (Richmond, Va., 1851).

[47]J. E. Sanderson, *The First Century of Methodism in Canada* (Toronto, 1910), vol. II, pp. 79-80.

[48]*Christian Guardian*, May 29, 1833.

[49]*Ibid.*, Feb. 12, 1840.

the practice of Methodists of dressing simply and plainly gradually disappeared as the sense of being a distinctive body weakened and values of individual worth and advancement became increasingly prevalent.[50]

Changing conditions of Canadian society after about 1830 forced upon Methodism an adjustment not only in its religious but in its moral appeal. New forms of social behaviour, associated largely with the increasing use of money in the rural community and with the growth of towns, led gradually to the deterioration of the moral virtues of pioneer society, and the increasing urgency of moral problems called for a fundamental adjustment in the attitude of the evangelical church. Reliance upon the inquisitorial system of the class meeting and the sanctions of the local church worked so long as the problem of moral behaviour was simply one of minor infractions of the moral code. Few of the members of the local community were likely to be completely innocent of such forms of misconduct as profanity, working on the Sabbath, or indulging in frivolous pastimes. The confessions of the class meeting, therefore, tended to emphasize the fact that all were sinners alike. This, however, came increasingly to be less true with the growing complexity of society. Moral problems assumed a more serious character and came to threaten the welfare of the community in general. Furthermore, such problems came increasingly to be associated with particular groups within the community, and groups which for the most part remained outside of the Church. If the miscreant did not attend Methodist class meetings he could hardly be admonished through such channels for his sins. New weapons were essential for the promotion of the religious war upon sin. Development of the temperance movement was the most obvious example of the sort of adjustment forced upon Methodism through the changing conditions within the moral order. The temperance reformer took his place at the side of the professional evangelist; both of these persons stood slightly outside the religious organization but became increasingly important in the promotion of the religious cause. Other instruments of moral control also developed to cope with particular problems demanding attention. The emergence of the Sabbath observance movement reflected the increasing effect of commercial enterprise upon rural mores built up around the sacredness of the seventh day.

The activity which came to be displayed generally in the promotion of movements having as their object the raising of moral standards suggests a considerable strengthening of puritan attitudes within the

[50]See *ibid.*, Feb. 17, 1841.

community. Much of the asceticism of the religious sect was incorporated into the ethic of the new commercial capitalism; the new economic leaders of society favoured the maintenance of virtues which had been cultivated within the evangelical religious group. Puritanism became a force directed against the conduct of the (commercially) unsuccessful farmer and the undisciplined worker. Virtues of frugality and enterprise were vitally important in the building up of a progressive agricultural class and a steady, industrious working class. The result was that Methodism, in attempting to adjust to the changing conditions of society, was compelled to introduce a class bias into its moral appeal. In ceasing to give expression to the attitudes of a backwoods population, it came to champion the moral point of view of the new *bourgeoisie*.

That, of course, was inevitable as a result of the change which was taking place in the social basis of the Methodist membership. The Methodist Church was coming to be the church of the successful of both the town and the country. The Wesleyan tie offered a strong support in raising the social standing of Methodism in the community; the Wesleyan missionaries appealed particularly to the more respectable elements of the population. "I am certainly much amazed," the Reverend Benjamin Slight wrote in his journal, October 26, 1834, "at our Congregation at Amherstburgh. The most respectable people in the town attend, and *all* the most respectable & they attend regularly Sabbath after Sabbath; they also hear with deep and fixed attention. I am given to understand they have not been accustomed to do so in times past."[51] The growing concern of leaders of the Church after 1832 with such problems as that of education was indicative of a realization

[51]University of Toronto, Victoria University Library, The Journal of Benjamin Slight, vol. I, pp. 55-6. Senator John Macdonald wrote of the Wesleyan congregation in Toronto in the early eighteen-forties:
"The congregation of the George Street Methodist Church was somewhat different from either of these [of the Church of England or the Church of Scotland]. No professional man, either physician or lawyer, was found among its worshippers. It had several who were engaged in business, but none whose business was large enough to be remarkable. . . .
"The George Street congregation had a monopoly of the merchant tailors and master shoemakers of the city, among the former of these was George Bilton, Richard Score, Charles and William Walker; among the latter, John Sterling, Nixon, Simpson, Sheppard, Duyrea, Morgan, not to forget an old coloured man, whose name was Truss. . . . Then of builders there were Richard Woodsworth, Thomas Storm, Mr. Harborn, James Price, old Mr. Purkiss, the boatbuilder . . . ; Alexander Hamilton the painter, Samuel Shaw the cutler; John Bowes . . . one of the leading wholesale merchants; John Eastwood in the dry goods trade . . . ; old Mr. Brown, the bookbinder . . . ; Mr. Mason . . . ; Mr. Mathews, father of the Messrs. Mathews, the picture-dealers, Yonge Street; John Rogers . . . who kept a second-hand book stall in the market . . . ; Mr. Watson, a tinsmith . . . and others." Senator John Macdonald, "Recollections of British Wesleyanism in Toronto" (*The Methodist Magazine*, vol. XXIX, Jan. to June, 1889, Toronto and Halifax, pp. 150-1).

that the future progress of the movement depended upon reaching out and gaining the support of the upper class of the colonial society. This was made very clear by a remark of the editor of the *Christian Guardian* in 1837—a remark which would have saddened the early prophets of Methodism. "If we are to maintain that stand," the editor wrote, "among the Churches which Providence seems to have designed us to fill, and which the good of the respectable portion of society seems to demand, it must be, under the blessing of God, by enabling our Ministers themselves to feel that such are their opportunities of literary improvement, and such their appearance and station in civil society, that they can mingle without fear in those circles whose education and standing may make them, when brought under the influence of Divine grace, useful members of civil and religious society."[52] This straining within the movement toward securing the support of the socially influential classes of the growing towns was inevitable in terms of the developments taking place within the colonial society. The commercial revolution provided vast new opportunities for acquiring wealth, and Methodists participated actively in trade. The Church gained immensely in the way of financial support and prestige but at the price of conforming much more to the demands and the tastes of the socially respectable. It ceased to be primarily the church of the socially humble.

The changing class affiliations of Methodism hardened changes taking place in its political affiliations. The shift of Canadian Methodism to a conservative position was greatly hastened with the union with English Wesleyanism. Wesleyanism, conservative in England—a fact well recognized by George Ryerson in urging the view that union with them should not be contemplated[53]—was even more conservative in Canada where the growing radical movement appeared to threaten the imperial connection. Outwardly, the immediate result of the Wesleyan influence was to strengthen the evangelical principle that religious teachings had nothing whatever to do with politics. The resolution of the Conference in 1834 that the *Christian Guardian* should not discuss matters of politics but "shall be properly and truly a religious and literary Journal,"[54] was indicative of efforts to establish an attitude of political neutrality. Actually, however, the Wesleyan policy involved not so much a break from politics as a shift from the support of the radical to the conservative cause. To refrain from attacking social

[52]*Christian Guardian*, May 17, 1837.
[53]C. B. Sissons, *Egerton Ryerson, His Life and Letters* (Toronto, 1937), vol. I, pp. 137-40, 163-4.
[54]*Christian Guardian*, June 25, 1834.

privileges, and particularly the privileges of the Church of England, meant in effect supporting the Conservative view.

The Wesleyan influence within the Church increasingly asserted itself as the union settlement worked itself out. "The correctness of your views & statements," John Ryerson was able to write his brother, Egerton, from Hallowell, February 16, 1836, "are now universally acknowledged & your defamers distested by all candid men. Political things in this country are working very favourably at the present time; the Radical party are going down hedlong; & may a gracious Providence speed them on their journey."[55] A by-election in Belleville in the spring of 1836 found John Ryerson and the Wesleyan Methodists aligned on the side of the tory candidate who was successful. "This riding you will recollect," John wrote his brother Egerton, May 4, 1836, "is the stronghold of Episcopal Radicalism. The Episcopals, so called, & the Roman Catholicks joined together & as many more children of devel as they could press into their service. . . . Every Wesleyan Methodist in Bellville was on the right side & so they were from the country with 8 or 10 exceptions."[56] In the events leading up to the general election of 1836, and in the election itself, Methodist leadership indicated clearly that it was in favour of the party supporting the lieutenant-governor, Sir Francis Bond Head. In a series of letters to the London *Times*, Egerton Ryerson, then in England, expressed views strongly favouring the conservative cause in the Canadian colony,[57] and the Conference meeting that year protested its strong attachment to the British constitution and its loyalty to the British Crown.[58] No definite stand was taken during the election, but an editorial in the *Christian Guardian*, June 15, 1836, undertook to advise Methodists how to vote in a way which left no doubt as to the sympathies of the editor. The clergy reserves, it was pointed out, might have been settled if it had not been for the unreasonable demands of irresponsible parties, while the demand for responsible government, the editor argued, really meant a demand for a republican system of government—the government of the colony already was responsible to a considerable degree. When the election was over, John Ryerson was able to boast of the influence exerted by the Wesleyan Methodists in bringing about the defeat of the Reformers. "Not one Radical," he wrote from Toronto, September 25, 1836, "was returned from the bounds of the Bay of Quinty District. The preachers & I laboured to the utmost extent of our ability to keep every scamp

[55]Quoted Sissons, *Egerton Ryerson*, vol. 1, p. 287.
[56]Quoted *ibid.*, pp. 332-3.
[57]See *ibid.*, pp. 339-45.
[58]*Ibid.*, pp. 346-7.

ɔf them out & we succeeded. And had the preachers of done their duty in every place, not a *ninny* of them would have been returned to this parliament."[59]

During the next year, with the increase in political bitterness, resulting in the end in the outbreak of rebellion, the tory alignments of Methodist leadership were strengthened. In a communication to the *Christian Guardian*, April, 1837, a correspondent signing himself "A Wesleyan Methodist" indicated the lines which were to be followed in arguing that Methodists were increasingly learning to comport themselves as those "whose kingdom is not of this world," and that they were becoming less than ever disposed to unite with those "who are given to change."[60] The remarks of the Reverend Benjamin Slight in his journal relating the events of the rebellion in which he gave expression to strong feelings against the rebels—"the party of that vile man McKenzie"—represented probably fairly accurately the views held by the English Wesleyans.[61] The rebellion brought to a head the issue of the imperial relationship, and hardened the conservative position of the Wesleyan controlled Methodist Church. In the shift from sectarian separatism to alignment with the Conservative political cause, Methodism had gone a long way in becoming accommodated to the politics of the Canadian community.

The accommodation of Methodism to politics was simply one aspect of an accommodation to the secular institutions of the community at large. Such accommodation by 1850 was far from complete—it required another thirty-five years to bring the various branches of Methodism together in one united church—but it had advanced sufficiently to indicate fairly clearly the future lines of denominational development. Influences tending to a shift away from the evangelical position increasingly asserted themselves from 1820 onwards. Methodism in Canada had grown out of the situation created through the settlement of the backwoods. It was essentially an evangelical movement of the rural frontier. By 1840 the rural frontier had ceased to exist in the lake shore areas of central Canada. Well settled rural communities oriented about country towns had taken the place of scattered backwoods settlements with no definite centre, and, at the same time, the larger town, or city, had made its appearance. Successful business men and well-to-do farmers became the social leaders of the new commercial-agricultural society, and these classes contributed very largely to the support of Methodism. Persistence of Methodist attachments among people finding themselves in a very different kind of social setting

[59]Quoted *ibid.*, p. 361.
[60]*Christian Guardian*, Apr. 5, 1837.
[61]The Journal of Benjamin Slight, vol. I, pp. 146-50.

resulted inevitably in far-reaching adjustments in the character of the Methodist movement. The new society based upon agricultural special- ization and commercialism was essentially a secular society. Religious values remained strong—devoutness was a distinctive characteristic of the successful business man—but they were subordinated to the values of secular life. Religion could no longer remain an exclusive concern of the populace.

This fact was evident among the Methodists in the shift from a sectarian point of view. Members and preachers alike became increas- ingly concerned about external evidences of denominational prosperity— the size of the church building, the prestige of the minister in the pulpit, and the respectability of the local church leaders. In many respects, the social standing of the church in the community became closely related to the social standing of its members; the business man found it desirable to belong to the best clubs, to send his children to the best schools, and to bring his family to the best church. Defections of members from the Methodist Church to the Church of England were inevitable in face of such social pressures, but many of the most success- ful of Methodist members remained within the Church with effects evident in the increasing accommodation of Methodism to secular values and interests. Acceptance of the values of the successful class involved the abandonment of a position in which emphasis was placed exclusively upon religion. Preoccupation with matters of religion was largely characteristic of the unsuccessful. As Methodism became increas- ingly the church of the successful, emphasis inevitably shifted and attention came to be given to matters of worldly interest. This was most evident in the field of politics, but it was also evident with respect to the changing character of the religious appeal, the emergence of the temperance reform movement, and the growing concern for matters of education. Methodism found itself more and more promoting interests which related to the community at large.   In doing so, it gained greatly in denominational strength and assured its future position as one of the important churches in the Canadian Dominion. Such gains, however, were achieved at the price of abandoning its claim of being the evan- gelical church of the social masses.

The accommodation of the Baptist Church in Canada to the secular community never became as complete as that of the Methodist Church. The sect spirit which found support in the principle of local church auton- omy remained too strong to permit any extensive absorption of religious interests in the denominational organization of the Church. Aloofness from politics was rigidly maintained in undertakings in which the Church was involved, and centralization of control within the denomina-

tion itself and the building up of a body of church office holders were checked through the strong pressure exerted by local congregations. Even the most worldly minded of the English Baptists retained strong attachments to the long sectarian tradition of the Church.

Accommodation to the secular community was carried sufficiently far, however, in those areas where the English Baptist influence made itself felt, to enable the Baptist movement to profit from the commercial revolution which took place in Canada during the quarter of a century after the formation of the Canada Baptist Union. Increasingly after 1840 immigration from overseas consisted of Irish workers and of English business men, and many of the latter were Baptists. The support of the new Canadian merchant class was essential to the future prosperity of the Baptist Church. In a very real sense, therefore, the tie with the English Baptist Church constituted an effort on the part of the Baptist movement in Canada to adjust itself to the new commerical revolution. It was in Montreal, where the English Baptist influence secured the strongest hold, and where the effects of the commercial revolution were most fully felt, that the denominational accommodation of the Baptist Church was carried furthest.

By 1850 forces in the older-settled areas of Canada as in the Maritime Provinces were running strongly against sectarian forms of religious organization. The population in these areas was one which had gained social status. Economic, cultural, nationalist, and political interests crowded out the religious interest as the basis of social organization. The religious interest, to survive, had to become integrated within this larger complex of social interests. The Methodist or Baptist who became an enterprising business man, Orangeman, Britisher, and tory could no longer remain other-worldly in interest or outlook. To retain the support of such a member, the Church had to abandon its other-worldly position. Lacking support within a narrow, exclusive interest in religion, it was forced to establish stakes within the wider secular society. Efforts to bring about such an accommodation met with strong resistance from within the membership body—sectarian principles persisted strongly in the thinking of large elements of the evangelical following— and the evangelical church leadership had been forced to seek outside means of support. Establishment of a connection with the English evangelical churches provided the Canadian Methodist and Baptist church leaders with the backing of powerful ecclesiastical organizations in forcing the evangelical following into line. Failure of the American Presbyterians to establish such a connection made impossible sufficiently rapid accommodation and the movement disappeared as a separate religious force.

CHAPTER SIX

New Frontiers and New Sects
1832-1860

E F F O R T S of Baptist and Methodist church leaders in the Maritime Provinces after 1800 were increasingly directed towards checking the expression of the sect spirit in religious organization. That such efforts were successful was evident in the development of an elaborate denominational machinery as a support of religious activities and in the broadening conception of the role of the church in the affairs of the community. By 1850 the disturbing influence of local preachers within the Baptist and Wesleyan Methodist churches had been almost wholly removed, and these churches had gone far in establishing for themselves a position of respect and prestige.

The break of the Baptists and Methodists from their sectarian origin, however, was no sooner accomplished than new sectarian movements grew up outside the regularly organized church bodies. The sect spirit, stifled in religious denominationalism, found expression in movements which constituted a break from denominationalism. The rise of these new movements coincided almost exactly in time—about 1820—with the passing of control out of the hands of the local preachers within the Baptist and Methodist churches. It was as a protest against the growing influence of a professional ministry that their development gained significance. They were an expression of the dissatisfactions of local preachers denied means of recognition within the formally organized denominations.

The Baptist Church, with its strong tradition of congregational autonomy, was particularly exposed to sectarian influences growing up outside the control of the denominational organization. Establishment of the Baptist Association in 1800 had constituted a means of bringing dissident groups into line, but tendencies towards nonconformity remained in places where Newlight influences persisted strong or in outlying areas of the country which were seldom visited by Baptist missionaries; in many parts of New Brunswick religious sects grew up with no other names than that of the local preacher in charge.[1] In some

[1] "In Sheffield and Waterborough," Walter Bates, sheriff of King's County, wrote of a visit to Maugerville shortly after the arrival of the Loyalists, "the people were

cases the problem created was simply one of reconciling within the Baptist church body the opposing views of different religious groups; in several communities the Newlights persisted as a sectarian influence even though they had disappeared as a sectarian party. In other cases, however, the problem became one of meeting the competition of self-appointed evangelists who sought to maintain a separate church organization. As late as 1820 a number of Newlight preachers remained active in the country. One such preacher was a John Hull in Sydney; another, Harris Harding in Yarmouth.[2] In Cornwallis, also, Newlight preachers continued to carry on evangelical work long after the break with the Baptists in 1807.

Here John Pineo, who before 1807 had taken the lead in resisting the shift to Baptist principles, remained in charge of the Newlight church, and through his preaching or that of visiting evangelists the regular Baptist church under the pastorate of the Reverend Edward Manning was faced with a serious threat to its security. Entries by Manning in his journal provide some indication of the concern which he felt at the inroads made by the Newlights upon his church.

Difficulties in New Canaan with the Newlight party led Manning to engage in preaching there on November 26, 1814. "The congregation (for the place)," he wrote in his journal, "large and very attentive. But Mr. William Blenkhorn from Cumberland County, who is in the habit of speaking in public but a vile enthusiast, arose and contradicted the plain truth of the Gospel."[3] In September, 1817, John Payzant, the Newlight minister in Liverpool, visited Cornwallis and engaged in evangelical preaching. "Went with Mr. Payzant and Mrs. Manning and Mrs. John Eaton to Mr. David Eaton's," Manning wrote of the second day of Payzant's visit, September 29, "and spent the evening. . . .

---

divided into three sects named after their own preachers, namely, Hartites, Brookites and Hammonites. Each sect preached their own doctrine, but were annually inspired by two travelling preachers from Nova Scotia." Quoted in foot-note W. O. Raymond, (ed.), *Winslow Papers* (Saint John, N.B., 1901), p. 392.

[2]The Reverend R. Alder, Wesleyan missionary, wrote of Harding's following in Yarmouth when he visited there in 1817: "There was no *public* teacher in the place, except one called a New Light Preacher. Antinomianism and Mysticism had been disseminated among the people for the doctrine of the cross. They had been told that they were not *moral agents*; that they could do nothing respecting spiritual and eternal things; that they had nothing to do; that it was in vain for them to pray till they were born again; and after they were born again they could not finally perish. . . . Many of them treated with much inattention the written word of God, and were guided by the feeling of the mind, and their pretended revelations." Quoted J. Davis, *Life and Times of Rev. Harris Harding* (Charlottetown, 1866), p. 195.

[3]Acadia University, Baptist Historical Collection, Rev. Edward Manning's Journal, vol. I, 1778-1821.

Mr. John Eaton seems to think as if I was afraid of him taking the Baptists, which he calls ducks, and making them chickens, but I told him he was at full liberty to make them all if he could." Two years later something of a revival of the Newlight cause in Cornwallis occurred when William Payzant, presumably the son of John Payzant, became active as an evangelical preacher. "Hear of Mr. William Payzant's preaching," Manning wrote, February 18, 1819, "or speaking for he can hardly Preach, being successful in Habitant in calling the attention of the People, and that he is going to be Baptized by Mr. John Pineo, a man of unsound Principles and immoral conduct, and not Baptized himself." During the succeeding month Payzant engaged in revivalist preaching throughout the district. Manning wrote in his journal of one of those meetings which he attended.

March 16, 1819 . . . . Went to hear Mr. William Payzant. He appeared solemn, tender and zealous, but much confusion and ignorance. Mr. John Pineo, spoke and he is to. Mrs. Stokes spoke, and then Sullivan, the Irishman, I then spoke a few sentences to show the Way of Salvation and its effects, and then Mrs. Stokes again and others, but there was some confusion. I recommended Order, that one should speak at a time. Bro. Danl. Sanford was speaking moderately & rational, and according to the Word of the Lord, and he was interrupted, and I came away. General remarks upon this stir. There is an attention to the things of religion, but there is a Party Spirit and anger with some, much ignorance with all generally, and I fear the event. They may be some converted, but they will suffer for the want of able teachers.

The revival resulted in the organization of a Newlight church much to the discomfiture of Mr. Manning. "To Day the Habitant People," he wrote, March 27, "are to meet for church meeting. O how little they know what they are about." Some of Manning's followers came under the influence of the revival. "Several called this afternoon," he wrote May 15. "Among the rest Levi Rand, a subject of the late work of Grace, (I hope), in Habitant. Talks innocently, simply, mistically, and in rather a deranged strain, but not in any way outrageous. There seems to be something among some in that stir that appears to be not of a sound mind, owing, I think, to the confused sentiments, of those that affect to teach among them and the bad management in their meetings &c." On a later occasion Manning wrote of another convert to the Newlight cause: 'Sept. 3, 1820, . . . Had much talk with Samuel Lowden, who is a Christian but entangled with the New Light system, and joined the Pineo party. Appears tender and as candid as I could expect, considering his natural turn, and the doctrine he hears, and the people he associates with. Lamentable indeed is the

state of that people. Some converts there are among them, but alas, what confusion."[4]

In Cornwallis, under Manning's leadership, the Baptists had become the dominant party, and the Newlights assumed the character of a dissident sect. In Liverpool, however, the Newlight church, under the pastorate of the Reverend John Payzant, maintained its supremacy and Baptist influence here was exerted entirely from outside. In the spring of 1821 the Reverend David Nutter organized a Baptist church in Liverpool but opposition was met with from the Newlights. "We had many conversations," he wrote, "on the subject of arranging a church at Liverpool. There were objections arising from two sources. On the one hand many of these who had been baptized had friends in the Newlight Congregational Church, and were desirous of remaining there. On the other hand, we knew that the members of that church were strongly opposed to such a measure, and our few Baptist brethern in the town and vicinity were intimately connected with them and their minister."[5] In the autumn of 1821 Manning visited Liverpool. The highly emotional response of the people to religious services discouraged the prospect of establishing regular church order in religious affairs. He wrote of a religious meeting on September 2, in charge of Mr. Payzant and Harris Harding:

I returned to the Meeting-house and the communion was over, but the communicants were sitting at the Table and I, unwilling to hurt their feelings, went into the Gallery. No sooner was I seated than a young Woman whom I knew not, screamed out, and a number below, all females, a melancholy sound to me, because I thought there was such an extravagancy of Voice, and such uncommon gesticulations, leaving their seats, running round the broad Isle, Swinging their Arms, bowing their heads to the Ground, Stretching their hands out right and left, then stretching them up as high as they could while the head was bowed down to the floor almost. I hope

---

[4]The Reverend David Nutter wrote of the influence of the Newlight party in Falmouth, about 1826: "I also had lectures frequently in Falmouth. . . . There were in Falmouth many of the old New Lights. . . . As I was now located near the seat and centre of operations of this remarkable sect of Christians, it will not be out of place if I pause to notice them. As to their genuine Christianity, I have no cause to dispute it. As to my labouring amongst them, I did not find them the most difficult people in the world to deal with. They had more experience than doctrine—more imagination than judgment—more spiritualism than spirituality—more of the ideal than the substantial. At the time to which I allude they had no ordinances, no creed, no discipline. They paid little or nothing to support religion, either at home or abroad. To pay money for religion was with them one of the greatest abominations the sun ever shone upon. But they believed in regeneration by the Spirit, in Christ as a Saviour, and in heaven and hell. But they were not uniform, or at all agreed in what they did believe. Their religion was all feeling. Every thing in the Bible, in the Old or New Testament, was but allegorical, and was what all Christians experience." Quoted Davis, *Life and Times of Rev. Harris Harding*, p. 184.
[5]Quoted E. M. Saunders, *History of the Baptists of the Maritime Provinces* (Halifax, 1902), p. 158.

they are good, but I truly wish they were more orderly. The young woman up in the gallery came directly to me with an awfully disfigured face, screeching verry loud indeed, calling me brother, O my brother! O my brother! O my brother! until she was exhausted and then she turned away. I hope they were all good and their exercises good intentionally, but surely I would freeze to death before that would warm me.[6]

Two days later Manning and Isaac Dexter, one of the local Baptists in Liverpool, conducted a religious meeting at Port Medway. Here, also, the religious fanaticism of the people appeared disconcerting to the Baptist preacher. Manning wrote:

Went to the School House. A crowded auditory. Preached to them . . . . Old Brother Dexter spoke and prayed well. While he was Speaking a young woman screamed out and continued to screech for some time. What a pity that pious people are not better instructed than to think that God Almighty is pleased, or his people edified, or sinners benefitted by Ravings of poor mistaken, tho' sincere Christians. O how much I esteem the Solemn devotions of the truly pious, and well informed Christian assemblies I have seen. I decidedly prefer the Solemn exercises of the pious in Cornwallis to the uncommon Vociferations of these Persons in and about Liverpool. They seem to know no better than that they are never in the liberty of the Gospel but when they are all agitated and their Voices extended so that you can hear them a Mile. O for a clearer Ministry.

The impression formed by Manning of the religious state of Liverpool was not encouraging with respect to the future prospects of the church formed by Nutter in the spring. "This place," he wrote, "is lamentably destitute of proper Religious Instruction, and where Allinism is not, Methodism is the prevailing System. They are wonderfully charitable to all denominations as they say, but the Chapels are shut up against all denominations and they are undermining them as fast as they can, the Episcopal Church not excepted." Rapid disintegration of the Baptist church in Liverpool was indicative of the strength of the Newlight influence.

In the end, however, the Newlights as a separate religious party offered no great threat to the Baptist churches. They lacked any sort of denominational organization to hold the various churches together. Thus by virtue of the very fact that the movement did not develop the church type of organization it failed to maintain its influence as a distinctive religious sect. Few new preachers were raised up, and complete reliance upon the principle of congregational autonomy made impossible any sort of concerted action in providing preaching services to a following scattered throughout the country. Churches in charge of local preachers in isolated areas lacked means of outside support, and when Baptist preachers made their appearance considerable

[6]Rev. Edward Manning's Journal, vol. I, 1778-1821.

advantages were offered in organizing along Baptist lines. Thus the local Newlight preacher in Sydney, John Hull, though maintaining his independence for years, eventually changed his views and became a Baptist, and when the Reverend Joseph Dimock visited Sydney in 1825 the church was reorganized as Baptist.[7] Even the churches in the older-settled communities faced difficulties in maintaining organization, and in fact only remained in existence so long as those preachers who had been followers of Henry Alline were still alive. The church in Liverpool depended upon the zealous leadership of John Payzant, and disappeared with his passing. The church in Cornwallis steadily lost in strength after 1820 and was absorbed by the Baptist denomination or by new religious movements. Harris Harding in Yarmouth abandoned his Newlight principles to eventually connect himself with the Baptists. Organization of missionary societies provided the Baptist denomination with a powerful weapon to force recalcitrant religious groups into line with the general movement, and the Newlights lacked the leadership necessary to withstand such denominational pressures.

The Newlight movement had secured its chief following in western Nova Scotia and in central parts of New Brunswick where the tradition of New England Congregationalism remained strong; disintegration of the movement reflected the final disappearance of the old order of local village organization in Maritime society. The Newlight appeal was one to the past, to the spirit of pre-revolutionary New England.

In Prince Edward Island social isolation of a similar sort led to the emergence of a similar type of intensely separatist religious sectarian movement. Here the population was predominantly of overseas origin, and the influence of Scotland and Cornwall was evident in the religious development of the colony. Among the Baptists the most serious challenge to denominational solidarity came from the religious group known as Scotch Baptists, members of the religious sect founded by the Haldane brothers in Scotland.[8]

A number of Scotch Baptists had settled in Prince Edward Island after the turn of the century, and in 1814 Alexander Crawford, who had studied in Haldane's school in Edinburgh and who had for a time preached in western Nova Scotia, settled among them and immediately undertook the organization of churches.[9] Churches were formed at Tryon, where Crawford resided, Bedeque, and at a number of other centres of settlement. Extension of Baptist missionary work into Prince

[7]See Saunders, *History of the Baptists of the Maritime Provinces*, pp. 158-9.
[8]See Rev. John Cunningham, *The Church History of Scotland* (Edinburgh, 1859), vol. II, pp. 570-7.
[9]See the *Christian Visitor*, Jan. 12, 1848; also W. Johnstone, *Travels in Prince Edward Island in the Years 1820-21* (Edinburgh, 1823), pp. 115-16.

Edward Island in 1825 brought the regular Baptist preachers into contact with Crawford, and efforts to gain the support of the Scotch Baptists raised sharp points of conflict between the sect and church type of religious organization.

The close group controls exercised by the Scotch Baptist churches constituted both a strength and a weakness. Reliance was placed upon lay preachers who were not expected to receive pay for their services, strict disciplinary controls were exerted by the group over the private conduct of the members, religious services were extremely simple and were not accompanied by music, and brethren were excommunicated if they married outside the church. The strong personal influence exerted by Crawford took the place of any denominational machinery in holding the group together.

So long as social isolation continued the religious separateness of the Scotch Baptists was successfully maintained, but as such isolation broke down group solidarity weakened and dissatisfaction with Crawford's autocratic leadership developed among the membership body. The Reverend Charles Tupper had written in 1825 of the limitations of Crawford as a church leader:

Some of his peculiarities, however, seemed to me to diminish the usefulness o his labours. He could not conscientiously receive any support as a minister, though he would not refuse a present as a poor man from a person out of his church, nor would he allow one to set the tunes at his meetings. He also maintained that every member who married outside of the church must be excluded. In consequence of these views, he had less time to devote himself to ministerial labour. In some instances he had no singing in public worship, and was led in different cases to such interference in matrimonial alliances as subjected him to much disaffection and censure. The church which he had gathered at Tryon and Bedeque, containing some who were Baptists before, had become wholly disorganized, and he saw no prospect of getting it into order again.[10]

Extension of the work of the Baptist Missionary Board in Prince Edward Island placed the Scotch Baptist churches increasingly at a disadvantage and, in 1832, a meeting was held between the two groups to discuss conditions of union. On most points of difference except the matter of members marrying outside the church the Scotch Baptists were prepared to give way; while not finally committing the Association, it was agreed that in this one particular the distinctive principles of the Scotch Baptist churches should be retained. The next year two of the Scotch Baptist churches, those of Three Rivers and East Point, joined the Association. Other churches were forced to follow suit as difficulties of maintaining an independent existence became greater.

[10]Quoted Saunders, *History of the Baptists of the Maritime Provinces*, pp. 160-1.

In 1842 the church at Lot 49, in 1843 the church at Cavendish, in 1844 the church at York and Elliot River, and in 1845 the church at Tryon became parts of the Association.[11] The Scotch Baptist movement virtually disappeared as a separate religious group in Prince Edward Island.

A much more serious threat than that of either the Newlight or Scotch Baptist movements to the position of the Baptist Church in the Maritime Provinces made its appearance after 1820 with the rise of the Free Will or Free Christian Baptist movement. The movement had grown out of a break in New Hampshire from Whitefield Calvinism in 1780 under the leadership of a Benjamin Randall; Randall had been a Baptist preacher but was excluded from Baptist fellowship for his anti-Calvinist views. He formed a church of his own called Free Will Baptist, and his following rapidly grew; by 1808, the year of his death, over one hundred churches had been organized. The movement represented a sharp break in New England from the increasing tendency within the Baptist Church towards formalism and centralized control; it was a product of the New England frontier, gaining its greatest strength in the State of Maine.

In 1816 Asa McGray, who had been a Methodist preacher in Maine but was ordained by the Free Will Baptists in 1814, came to Windsor, Nova Scotia, and the next year engaged in evangelical preaching in Cape Sable Island. A church was organized here in 1821. McGray was joined in the work in Nova Scotia in 1818 by Jacob Norton who had been ordained by the "Church of Christ" in Swansville, Maine, in 1814; Norton, calling himself a "Christian," preached throughout Shelburne and Yarmouth counties and organized a church at Argyle in 1819. Extensive religious revivals took place under the preaching of the Free Baptist preachers, and the movement quickly made its influence felt upon the work of the regular Baptist churches.

In 1820 Norton visited Manning's field of labour in Cornwallis and his preaching led to serious disturbances within the Baptist church. "The new preachers," Manning wrote in his journal August 18, 1820, "that are coming from the United States of the freewill order, or Christian Band as I hear they fondly call themselves, occasions some uneasiness."[12] Five days later, Manning attended a meeting held by Norton. "Great many attended from Horton and almost all parts of Cornwallis," he wrote, "and he addressed them from 3rd John and last verse with much vociferation. Is a man of some ability, but an unsound man. . . .".

[11]See I. E. Bill, *Fifty Years with the Baptist Ministers and Churches of the Maritime Provinces* (Saint John, N.B., 1880), pp. 667-9.
[12]Rev. Edward Manning's Journal, vol. I, 1778-1821.

Appears uncommonly zealous, but I am jealous that he is an impostor."
On September 3 Manning again heard Norton preach. "Feel tried
today," he wrote, "about the meeting of Mr. Norton. . . . Just heard
Mr. Norton preach a very rousing but corrupt sermon, I think much
false zeal and error mingled with some truth and many striking things.
. . . Much people taken with these free-willers." The next day Manning
wrote: "In the morning felt a weight on my spirits concerning the new
minister, new doctrines. My fears renewed. I am still jealous that the
foundation is rotten, the zeal not according to knowledge and that
the people are taken with the extraordinary operations of nature
mechanically put in motion, instead of the real operations of the Spirit
of the Lord, and yet I feel how to conduct." Norton's preaching weakened
ties of church membership. "Went to conference meeting," Manning
made the entry, September 9. "A good meeting. A number that are
taken with the doctrine and the wonderful Norton attended and renewed
covenant, but I fear they are not sincere, for as soon as they could get
away they went to Norton's meeting. But the members generally
seemed to stand firm." The next spring Norton was again preaching
in the district with results disastrous to the Baptist church in Horton.
"Great meeting today in Horton," Manning wrote, March 10, 1821,
"called by Mr. J. Norton who calls himself a *Christian*, to distinguish
from all other Sects, and means to pull them down and establish his
own denomination on their ruins. . . . May the Lord appear for the
support of Bro. D. Harris." On March 27 Manning wrote: "I feel
gloomy. Mr. Norton the American Gentleman who is so famous for
making divisions, and hath made Such an inroad in the Horton Church,
is going to preach at Mr. David Chipman's this afternoon, but I think
I will not hear him, and think I am clear that it is my duty to have
nothing to do with him, more nor less. But in this I will be Sensured
by those that are disaffected to Truth, and verry much given to change."
By the next year the influence of the Free Baptists had spread throughout the Cornwallis district. "The impostor N——n," Manning wrote of
Billtown, north-west of Cornwallis, February 1, 1822, "is operating
in that and all the districts in this Vacinity, and all the disaffected
of all denominations follow him, notwithstanding the Scandalous
Character he bears, and the unquestionable proofs that are brought
against him. Such are the prejudices that exist in the minds of the
People of this place, that is, a number of them." The settlement in
1823 of the Free Baptist evangelist at Horton, significantly one of the
early centres of conflict between Newlight and Baptist influences,
led to a considerable strengthening of the cause in this area. Probably
a large proportion of Pineo's Newlight followers shifted their support to

Norton's church with the disintegration of the separate Newlight organization.

Growth of the Free Baptist movement in the Cornwallis area was paralleled by its growth in other parts of the country. As the movement spread it gathered support from a number of local preachers in western Nova Scotia and in New Brunswick who had never accepted the Calvinist doctrine of predestination and who had carried on preaching activities without entering into any connection with the Baptist Association. Lacking any means of fellowship among themselves, they welcomed the opportunity of associating with the Free Baptist movement. In Nova Scotia, Thomas Crowell, a native of Barrington and convert of Henry Alline, who had engaged in revivalist preaching in his home community independently of the Baptist Association, in 1821 organized a Free Baptist Church, and Harris Harding, the Newlight preacher in Yarmouth, whose church was not admitted into the Association until 1827, entered into connection with the Free Baptist movement. In New Brunswick a great number of travelling evangelists, vaguely describing themselves as Newlights or Baptists but operating independently of the Baptist Association, found themselves eventually associated with the Free Baptists. Thus Robert Colpitts, who had come as a child with his family to the settlement on the Petitcodiac River began to preach in 1810 and for twenty years consistently refused to join himself with any church while carrying on evangelical work in various parts of New Brunswick; in 1830 he was baptized by a Free Baptist preacher at Mill Stream, Kings County, and two years later secured ordination in the church.[13] Similarly, Samuel Hartt, ordained as a Free Baptist preacher in 1831, had carried on evangelical preaching throughout the St. John Valley from the time of his conversion in 1825 without connecting himself with any denomination.[14] A number of other local preachers in New Brunswick had a history much the same, such as Daniel Shaw at Mill Stream, Kings County, Charles McMullin at Andover and Perth, in Victoria County, Samuel Weyman at Sussex, Kings County, and William E. Pennington at Queensbury, York County. All of these preachers were located in outlying areas of the country and for that reason were able to maintain their independence in face of efforts of the Baptist Association to build up centralized control. Connection with the Free Baptist movement provided a means of securing support for local church organization while preserving much of the sect spirit of separation from outside direction.

[13]Saunders, *History of the Baptists of the Maritime Provinces*, pp. 415-16.
[14]*Ibid.*, pp. 416-18.

As the work spread through the activities of local preachers, new preachers were recruited from across the line. In 1830 Samuel Nutt who was a minister of the "Christian Church" in Maine was induced to visit New Brunswick, and extensive revivals resulted from his preaching in Queensbury, York County; the Bear Island church was organized by him. In 1835 Samuel Wormwood, a Free Will Baptist minister in Maine, carried on preaching in Lower Brighton, Carleton County, and in 1839, in company with another preacher, he made a second visit. A number of other preachers from the United States also took up work in New Brunswick or in Nova Scotia. The effect of the growth of the Free Baptist movement was evident in the continued falling off of support of the regular Baptist churches. In February, 1838, Manning wrote to the *Christian Messenger* of the state of the Baptist cause in New Brunswick:

> Since I wrote you last I have preached the gospel in five different counties, viz: York, Sunbury, Queens, Kings and St. John, and in thirteen different parishes. There have been Baptist churches organized in some of these, but they are lamentably neglected, and some of them have nearly, if not quite, lost their visibility; and another denomination called 'Free-willers' have taken the ground. They style themselves, 'The Christian Church'. Many of the Baptist churches have broken covenant with their more regular brethren. O! this is distressing, to see those little hills of Zion neglected and given up to a lamentable sterility.[15]

The Free Baptist movement grew by attracting the support of all those dissenting Baptist groups which had not been prepared to attach themselves to the Association. It was this which constituted its great strength as a movement of religious expansion. Among the early Free Baptist evangelists were men who had come out of different schismatic churches in Maine; thus a variety of names were used in describing themselves — "Christians," "Free Christian Baptists," "Freewill Baptists," or simply "Free Baptists." Some of the local preachers, like Harris Harding in Yarmouth, though connecting themselves with the movement, seem to have assumed no definite name. All the Free Baptists were in protest against the Association, and particularly the strict Calvinism of the churches attached to the Association. It was this, and the interest in evangelization, which bound them together.

As the movement grew, however, organization became increasingly necessary, and the establishment of such organization sharpened the break with the regular Baptist Association. In 1832 the "New Brunswick Christian Conference" was formed as a result of a meeting of Free Baptist preachers in Wakefield, Carleton County, and five years later

[15]Quoted *ibid.*, p. 424.

the "Free Christian Baptist Conference" was formed in Nova Scotia. Eventual union of the two bodies brought into being a powerful evangelical church in competition with the regular church.

The Methodists were little more fortunate than the Baptists in escaping the disrupting effects of new sectarian movements after 1820. Growth of the Free Baptist movement in the country had some effect in weakening Methodist solidarity. A number of Free Baptist evangelists were recruited from the ranks of Methodist local preachers. Thomas Brady, for instance, an Irish local preacher at Petite Rivière, withdrew from the Methodist Church about 1821 and became a Free Will Baptist preacher,[16] and James Melvin, who had been sent out to the colony as a missionary by Lady Huntingdon and who had been engaged as a Methodist preacher in the Liverpool circuit and in Prince Edward Island, in 1829 settled in Queen's County and shifted his allegiance to the Free Will Baptists though he ultimately ended up as a Congregational pastor in Liverpool.[17] Edward Reynolds in north Queen's County, ordained in 1825 as a Free Baptist preacher, also came out of the ranks of the Methodists.

The defection of Methodist preachers was inevitably accompanied by the defection of many members. In areas bordering Maine in particular, Methodist work was interfered with by evangelists who entered the country and carried on vigorous proselytization activities. The Reverend Duncan McColl in St. Stephen found reason to complain of the activities not only of Newlight but of Free Baptist preachers. "It is singular to say, ' he wrote of the state of the Methodist society in 1817, "that no sooner (generally speaking) doth an awakening begin, than these noisy fanatical Antinomians are sure to come to disturb the work. Now some of them crowd in from the westward, and A— is also blowing the coals of delusion among children and weak and foolish women in Calais. . . . There is no intrigue but what they use in order to draw disciples after them."[18] On occasion, the Methodist meetings were actually invaded by these outside preachers. "On the 17th of January [1818]," McColl again wrote, "while we were at our class at Mill Town, on cometh one of our noisy neighbours from the States— a stranger to me. I whispered to him, telling him that this was a private meeting of our friends, where we did not admit any but members. He then commenced his untoward harangue."[19] Of the next summer

---

[16]T. Watson Smith, *History of the Methodist Church of Eastern British America* (Halifax, 1877), vol. II, p. 94.
[17]*Ibid.*, p. 189.
[18]"Memoir of the Rev. Duncan M'Coll" (*British North American Wesleyan Methodist Magazine for the Year 1842*, Saint John, N.B., vol. II, p. 9).
[19]*Ibid.*, p. 9.

McColl wrote: "We have of late many travelling men preaching through the country. Some from the United States, and several from Ireland, but alas they are not such as we want, and therefore we see no good following them."[20]

Other sects which had grown out of schisms from Methodism in the United States or in Great Britain established themselves in the Maritime Provinces after 1820. Dissatisfaction of a number of Methodists in Saint John with the dismissal for drunkenness in 1825 of their popular minister, James Priestley, led to a separation from the church and the holding of independent services with the support of some Irish Primitive Wesleyans in the city. The seceding religious group, calling itself the "United Primitive Methodists," succeeded for a time in maintaining services in a new chapel which they built, but an unfortunate choice of an Irish Primitive Wesleyan preacher led to difficulties, and the chapel in 1830 passed into the hands of William W. Ashley, a follower of Alexander Campbell.[21] In Halifax, the arrival in the latter part of 1832 of a preacher from Virginia, William Jackson, belonging to the Protestant Methodist Church, which had been formed in 1829 as a result of a schism from the Methodist Episcopal Church, led to the formation of an independent church. Jackson, preaching in the market square, attracted a considerable following, and, when he was refused permission to use the Methodist chapel, he commenced holding services in a public hall and the next spring secured the construction of a place of worship of his own which was named "Ebenezer Methodist Protestant Church." Jackson was succeeded by Thomas Taylor who had been a Wesleyan missionary in the province but had met with the disfavour of the Committee in

[20]*Ibid.*, p. 47. That conditions remained disturbed in Methodist work in the border community of St. Stephen was evident when in 1844 a schism occurred in the Milltown church, fifteen members, many of them socially prominent, withdrawing from the regular body and forming an independent Methodist church under a pastor from the United States; later they joined with the Congregationalists in the town. (Smith, *History of the Methodist Church*, vol. II, pp. 341-2). The Reverend R. Cooney, who was stationed in St. Stephen as a Wesleyan missionary in 1852, wrote of the schism in Milltown: "Methodism here was never in a very healthy or sound condition. The community, generally speaking, never adopted it. . . . This is very generally the case on border circuits, both in New Brunswick and Canada. The peculiarities of Methodism are rather distasteful to many of the people. The doctrines are received in almost every instance, but the administration is regarded with suspicion and aversion. It is too particular; a little too stringent; it has not enoug h of the democratic element in it.

"A few years ago, a considerable secession took place here among the Methodists. The promoters of this schism alleged that our discipline was too strict; that the Conference had too much power; and that 'the Poll Deed' was an artful contrivance to establish and perpetuate an ecclesiastical domination. That these separatists were but partially acquainted with Methodism, and that they were but slightly attached to it, may be inferred from the fact, that they became the nucleus of a Congregational church, of which they are now the main pillars and supporters." *The Autobiography of a Wesleyan Methodist Missionary* (Montreal, 1856), pp. 160-1.
[21]Smith, *History of the Methodist Church*, vol. II, pp. 122-6.

London and in 1838 the church passed into the charge of a Wesleyan Reform missionary from Manchester, England, Robinson Beare. Eventually it was taken over by the Presbyterians in the city.[22] In 1845 another Methodist schism occurred in Halifax when, on the refusal of the superintendent of the church to permit a West Indian local preacher to use the pulpit, the coloured members withdrew and carried on services independently, securing on the departure of the West Indian local preacher a minister from the Zion Methodist Episcopal Church of the United States.[23]

Much more significant in terms of the break from the Wesleyan Methodist connection was the introduction into Prince Edward Island of the Bible Christian Connexion, or "Bryanites" as they were sometimes called, a Methodist sect which had grown up in Cornwall after 1815 through a schism from the Wesleyan Conference caused by the introduction of the American camp meeting by a number of local preachers.[24] Through the close trade connections between Prince Edward Island and the west ports of England a number of Bible Christians had settled in the province and succeeded in organizing a church under the charge of a local preacher. In 1831 a missionary, Francis Metherall, was sent out by the Bible Christian Conference in England and the cause rapidly strengthened. Metherall began his work among the settlers on the Union Road but soon extended it to include the settlers on Princetown Road as well; appointments were also taken up at Little York, Covehead Road, and Mill River.[25] In 1834 a second missionary, Philip James, was secured, and the work in the Island spread out in various directions, Metherall taking charge in the area east of the Hillsborough River and James in the area west of Charlottetown, from Union Road to New London. Preaching was extended to Sturgeon, Beers near Montague, Gallas Point near Vernon River, and Rustico Road; in all, thirty-six different places were served by the two preachers. By 1840, in addition to the missionaries, there were at least seven local preachers in charge of churches[26] and, in October, 1842, there began what became known as the "Great Revival" which resulted in the considerable strengthening of the movement throughout the province during the next two years. In 1844 two more missionaries arrived from England.

[22]*Ibid.*, pp. 209-11.
[23]*Ibid.*, p. 316.
[24]Henry W. Clark, *History of English Nonconformity* (London, 1913), vol. II, pp. 333-4.
[25]John Harris, *The Life of the Rev. Francis Metherall, and the History of the Bible Christian Church in Prince Edward Island* (London, 1883), pp. 11-12.
[26]*Ibid.*, pp. 41-2.

Efforts of Wesleyan missionaries to extend Methodist teachings into Prince Edward Island led to sharp conflicts between the two groups. Many of the areas in which Wesleyan societies had been organized were invaded by Bible Christian preachers, and the organization of Bible Christian churches resulted in defections from the Wesleyan membership. At Three Rivers and Murray Harbour the Wesleyans were forced to give way in face of the revival of 1843 which swept almost the whole Methodist population into the Bible Christian church.[27] In other areas, the existence of strong Bible Christian churches effectively prevented the Wesleyan missionaries from establishing religious services.

Strong local supports of the Bible Christian movement gave it a considerable advantage in meeting the competition of the highly centralized Wesleyan missionary organization. It possessed all the strengths of the local religious sect which identified itself with the needs of an isolated rural population while English Wesleyanism, like absentee landlordship, constituted a system being imposed from outside. Within Methodism, the Bible Christians gave expression to the spirit of independence from denominational control which found expression in the Baptist movement among the Scotch Baptists. The two movements, sharply separated on ethnic grounds, were closely related in terms of religious sentiments and ideals. Both, significantly, in Britain, had developed in isolated areas of the country, and both grew up in Prince Edward Island in similarly isolated areas.

A number of other religious sectarian movements grew up in the Maritime Provinces after 1820 to give support to the anti-denominational influence exerted by the new Baptist and Methodist sects. The Campbellites, later known as Disciples of Christ, entered the country about 1830 and apparently gained a considerable following especially in New Brunswick. It was a Campbellite preacher who assumed control of the church in Saint John when it passed out of the hands of the Primitive Methodists. Campbellite evangelists were active further up the St. John Valley and in the Miramichi Valley, and some of them probably made an appearance in western Nova Scotia as well. In Prince Edward Island the strong sectarian spirit of the population found expression not only in Baptist and Methodist religious movements but in movements which grew out of Presbyterianism. One such movement was that known as the "McDonaldites."

The McDonaldites were a Presbyterian group which broke from the Church of Scotland under the leadership of a Reverend Donald

[27]*Ibid.*, pp. 50-2. Also Smith, *History of the Methodist Church*, vol. II, p. 344.

McDonald. McDonald had been a missionary in Scotland but, given to intoxication, he resigned his mission and came out to Cape Breton in 1824. After something of a moral reformation, he moved over to Prince Edward Island in 1826, where he commenced preaching among the Scottish inhabitants. His methods were those of the evangelist. Preaching on week days as well as Sundays, in private houses, school houses, barns, and on hillsides, his parish soon extended a distance of ninety miles from Richmond Bay to Murray Harbor.[28] In 1830 Elder Samuel McCully of the Baptist Church, during his visit to the Island, had occasion to take notice of the work of McDonald at this time.

Brother McCully mentions [the Report of the Home Mission Board read] an extraordinary excitement among many of the people on Prince Edward Island, especially those that speak the Gaelic language, under the ministry of Rev. Donald McDonald, of the established Church of Scotland. This man professes to have recently experienced a change of heart, and now preaches in a very alarming manner. Great numbers attend his preaching; and the effects produced on many are unusual. They are seized with convulsive affections, and their bodies and limbs are distorted in a wonderful manner. Mr. McDonald informed Brother McCully that upwards of three hundred had been the subjects of these unusual bodily affections; and he stated that he judged about one hundred and forty of these had been savingly converted.[29]

McDonald's influence steadily grew through the use of revivalist methods and when the Reverend Norman MacLeod of the Church of Scotland visited Prince Edward Island in 1845 the movement had assumed considerable proportions. MacLeod had occasion to meet McDonald, and preached in his church. He wrote:

There was a man, McDonald, a missionary some twenty years ago, in the braes of Glen Garry. I believe, chiefly from his having been given to intoxication, he was obliged to resign his mission, and came to Cape Breton, and staid for a year or two. After suffering great mental distress, he became a perfectly sober and steady man. He began preaching among the Highlanders. His preaching had great effect. He separated himself from the other clergy, because he thought them careless and bad. His sect, became stronger and stronger. Many wild extravagancies attended the "revivals" under him, crying out and screaming—fits of hysteria, which were attributed to extraordinary influences. The result, however, has been that three thousand people, including fifteen hundred communicants, adhere to him; he has eight churches built and twenty-one prayer-meetings established; no lay-preaching; elders in all the churches; sacraments administered. He keeps all a-going, and has never received more than £50 a-year, on an average. He is laughed at by some, ridiculed by others, avoided by the clergy; but all admit that he has changed, or been

---

[28]Rev. John MacLeod, *History of Presbyterianism on Prince Edward Island* (Chicago, 1904), pp. 154-8.
[29]Quoted Bill, *Fifty Years with the Baptist Ministers and Churches of the Maritime Provinces*, pp. 667-8.

the means of changing, a thousand lawless, drunken people into sober, decent godly livers.[30]

The Reverend John MacLeod estimated that McDonald's following reached a total of five thousand persons and that he had about a hundred elders working under him. His churches were scattered all over the Island.[31]

Although the influence of the McDonaldites never extended beyond Prince Edward Island, it gained significance as indicative of the religious temper of the Island population. Regular church work was undertaken late on the Island—for several years the only religious teacher was a clergyman of the Church of England—and in many areas sects under the leadership of local preachers had become firmly established before regular church ministers put in an appearance. "I find nothing so much wanted," Walter Johnstone had written of conditions in 1822, "as money and good ministers."[32] Disintegration of the separatist sect in some cases followed upon the entry of regular ministers but in other cases the sect persisted in maintaining an independent existence and efforts to establish some sort of denominational order failed. Isolationism operated as a powerful factor in support of religious separatism.

The new religious sects which took their rise in the Maritimes after 1820 constituted a sharp challenge to the growing claims of denominationalism in the religious organization of the community. Altogether, it is true, the number of people who attached themselves to these sects was not impressively large; denominational vested interests had become too powerful to be easily shaken by sectarian protests, and by far the greater proportion of the population remained faithful to the older churches. Yet the rise of new movements assumed considerable significance in indicating the limitations of the church form of religious

---

[30]Rev. Donald MacLeod, *Memoir of Norman MacLeod* (New York, 1876), vol. I ' pp. 243-4.

[31]The Reverend John MacLeod, saw something of the religious services of the McDonaldites which were characterized by violent bodily exercises. He wrote in his *History of Presbyterianism on Prince Edward Island*: "As noticed by the writer, it generally commences with a sort of spasmodic motion or jerk of the head, accompanied by a peculiar sound. As the truths spoken or sung operated upon the intellect and feelings the action becomes more marked and the sound louder and more definite, until the subject springs to his or her feet and gives vent to the feelings by violent motions or by words, or by both, either calling for mercy or giving utterance to feelings of praise and gratitude for mercies received. The motions made, it is worthy of remark, are always either backwards or forwards with the head to and from the speaker, or up and down, on the feet, but never, so far as we noticed, from side to side. We have seen as many as thirty or forty at a communion table, all at once leaping up and clapping their hands, crying out, 'Glory, glory be to God on high' " (pp. 158-9).

[32]Macleod, *History of Presbyterianism on Prince Edward Island*, pp. 159-63.

[32]Walter Johnstone, *A Series of Letters Descriptive of Prince Edward Island* (Dumfries, 1822), p. 16.

organization in a community which was still subject to disturbing social changes. Sectarianism was a measure of the continued strength of the frontier influence in Maritime society after 1820.

Although developments in the Maritime Provinces from 1820 onwards were overwhelmingly in the direction of strengthening the supports of a culturally mature and traditional society, evident in the growth of wealth and the increase in influence of the commercial classes, developments also took place which led to the emergence of new frontier societies sharply cut off from traditional influences and controls. In New Brunswick, new farm settlements grew up along the river valleys lacking any sort of centres or clearly defined boundaries; they became communities without depth but extending indefinitely in length. In Prince Edward Island, in eastern Nova Scotia including Cape Breton, and in central and western areas of Nova Scotia, also, although settlement took place in less sprawling fashion than in New Brunswick, lack of means of transportation resulting from the rugged character of the coastline led to the emergence of communities equally isolated in character even though, in some cases, large centres of population were located within a few miles. The Maritime rural frontier was pushed back as roads were built and towns grew but it remained an important factor in the social life of the country.

At the same time, the growth of towns, with the expansion of shipbuilding and trade, was producing a new type of frontier population, a floating labour force dependent upon upward swings of the business cycle for opportunities of employment. Wealth increased in the towns but the increase in wealth was accompanied by an increase in poverty and poor working-class districts emerged alongside of high-class residential districts. Such conditions in the towns were considerably aggravated with the industrial revolution of the last half of the nineteenth century but they had developed even long before 1850 to the point where their effects were felt upon the general social life of the community. In Halifax and Saint John, in particular, slum areas made their appearance early in the century. The populations of such areas were as little a part of the social order of the wider community as the backwoods populations of the new rural settlements.

The growth of religious sects after 1820 was closely related to these developments taking place in the Maritime community. Points of disturbance in religious organization coincided with points of disturbance in the social order. It was in the interior of New Brunswick, in Prince Edward Island, in the isolated areas of Nova Scotia, and in Halifax and Saint John that the new religious sectarian movements flourished.

The older Baptist and Methodist evangelical churches became increasingly less able to meet the needs of the socially marginal populations of such areas. They had become too socially conscious, too absorbed in the affairs of the secular community; too much, that is to say, worldly churches seeking to attract the support of all classes of the community. Efforts to gain a position of influence and prestige had forced a close identification with the more powerful social and political interests in the larger centres of population and such identification led these churches to become a part of the metropolitan structure of trade, politics, and culture. As a result, their work in outlying areas of the country, or in the poorer districts of the towns, assumed the character of a special service rather than constituting the primary purpose of their existence. Denominationalism broke down in such areas as a part of a traditional social and cultural order being imposed from outside.

It was the new religious sects which provided the socially detached elements of the population with a means of entering into some sort of group life. Differing little in character from the Newlight and Methodist movements of a half century earlier, they possessed all the advantages of the religious group which could attract into the ministry men of great zeal and religious conviction and which could place the whole emphasis in its religious appeal upon the elementary problem of man's salvation. The fact that all kinds of people with different sorts of religious belief found their way into these movements was significant as indicating the importance of their role as forces of social reorganization. In the case particularly of the Free Baptists, few demands were placed upon the individual as a condition of his entrance into religious fellowship other than that of the conviction of having secured faith; even the name "Free" taken by this movement was suggestive of its nature as a protest against the strict organizational and doctrinal controls which the regular Baptist churches sought to impose. The smaller Baptist and Methodist sects, such as the Scotch Baptists and Bible Christians, imposed more strict conditions upon membership in the group but they were conditions which were laid down by the group itself; their resistance to outside controls was even more strongly expressed. In a very real sense, all of the religious sects which grew up in the Maritime Provinces after 1820 were movements of local preachers. It was in the activities of local preachers that the most effective check to denominationalism was to be found.

In Canada as in the Maritime Provinces after 1820 developments leading to a greater denominational accommodation of religious groups in the community were checked by the growth of new movements of

religious sectarianism. Social pressures resulting from the growth of population, the rise of towns, the increase of wealth, the spread of education, and the strengthening of political organizations had led to a shift away from an evangelistic position on the part of those Methodist and Baptist religious movements which had grown up in the early years of the nineteenth century, but efforts to build up powerful denominational organizations could be carried only so far in face of the strong sectarian spirit which persisted within the Methodist and Baptist membership bodies; where denied means of expression within the regular denominational organization, this spirit found expression within new religious movements. Thus the further denominational accommodation was carried, the greater was the sectarian activity outside the formal religious bodies. The establishment of the Wesleyan Methodist Church in 1832 and the organization of the Canada Baptist Missionary Society in 1837 led directly to the rise of new Methodist and Baptist sects.

The union of the Canada and English Wesleyan Conferences in 1832 resulted in the break of a number of local preachers in Upper Canada and the organization of a separate church—the Methodist Episcopal Church of Canada. The new religious movement grew with great rapidity with the defection from the main body of a number of preachers and a large number of members. Regular Wesleyan-Methodist societies were disorganized and a substantial decline in membership took place. Ferguson, on the Waterloo circuit during the year 1833-4, found the work considerably weakened by the emergence of the rival party. "This was," he wrote in his journal, "a year of turmoil, agitation and strife from first to last. Some of the local preachers became dissatisfied, and scattered the seeds of discord and litigation wherever they could. The union was their theme, etc. . . . Many were led astray, and lost their piety, and others became luke warm and negligent of duty."[33] Towards the close of the year, Ferguson related, some of the local preachers and exhorters left the church, followed by some of the members; "this was the beginning of sorrows." The next year, on the Sidney circuit, Ferguson again noted the effects of the Episcopal disruption. "I wept, prayed, and visited the people," he wrote, "and entreated them on my knees to follow after holiness, to watch and pray lest they should fall into the temptation. In the meantime the party continued their opposition. . . . Friendship was almost entirely forgotten, neigh-

[33]The University of Toronto, Victoria University Library, The Journal of the Rev. George Ferguson, A Minister of the W. Methodist Church in Canada, copied from the original, p. 144.

bour was arrayed against neighbour, family against family, and the members of families against each other. Even the school children quarelled and fought with each other denouncing each others parents as Wesleyans and Episcopals."³⁴ To bring an end to the conflict, Ferguson called the societies together and asked those members not satisfied with the church to signify by standing up; "in the course of a few weeks," he admitted, "about two hundred left our church."³⁵ The next year Ferguson returned to the Sidney circuit where the state of the church remained unsatisfactory. "The Episcopals," he wrote, "continued their opposition and with increased vehemence. . . . They [two of their preachers] commenced protracted meetings, and continued them from place to place during most of the year, aided by the officials."³⁶ Of his work on the Prescott and Augusta circuit in 1836-7, Ferguson wrote: "The Episcopal party had commenced operations there, aided and abetted by Philander Smith, once a chairman among us, and who possessed a great deal of influence on that Circuit, and adjacent country."³⁷

Evidence of the effects of the Episcopal defection came from a number of other sources. "Mr. Lalor told us to-day," Proudfoot wrote, March 24, 1833, while at Bayham, "that the Methodists hold 2 days' meetings in rivalship to one another. If the Episcopal Methodists announce a protracted meeting then the Wesleyans will announce one the same day a week before it and vice versa. What fellows!"³⁸ From Hallowell, October 25, 1834, John Ryerson, the presiding elder, wrote to his brother Egerton of the extent of the schism in the Bay of Quinte District. "The work of schism," he admitted, "has been purty extencive on some parts of this District. There have left and been expelled on the Waterloo Ct. 150, on the Bay of Quinty 40, in Belleville 47, Sidney 50, on Cobourg 32, making in all 320."³⁹ The addition of 170 members left a net loss of 150. The *Christian Guardian* published an extract from the Reverend Alva Adams, Merrickville, August 25, 1836, regarding the state of religion on the Rideau circuit: "Misrepresentations and palpable falsehoods," part of the extract read, "that have been industriously circulated in relation to the proceedings of the Conference and the character of our Ministers—together with the unwearied public

³⁴*Ibid.*, p. 147.
³⁵*Ibid.*, p. 148.
³⁶*Ibid.*, p. 149.
³⁷*Ibid.*, p. 150.
³⁸"Proudfoot Papers" (*Papers and Records*, Ontario Historical Society, vol. **XXVI**, 1930, p. 512).
³⁹C. B. Sissons, *Egerton Ryerson, His Life and Letters* (Toronto, 1937), vol. **I**, p. 242.

and clandestine efforts of schismatics, have been injurious to religion and the prosperity of our Zion."[40] From Nepean, September 9, 1836, the Reverend E. Healey, chairman of the Augusta district, wrote: "The professed Episcopals have been trying to do us harm, but I believe it will fall upon their own heads in the end."[41] The total membership of the Wesleyan-Methodist Church in Canada declined by 1,109 in 1834.[42] That defections continued to take place was indicated by the report in 1837 that 283 members had been lost to the Episcopal Church.[43]

Growth of Episcopal Methodist influence in the country was accompanied by the growth in influence of the smaller English Methodist churches. In July, 1829, William Lawson, a local preacher from England, began preaching in the market square of York to a few Primitive Methodists from Yorkshire who had settled in the town, and the next year the Primitive Methodist Conference in England appointed a regular missionary—the Reverend R. Watkins—to the country.[44] By 1832 the Primitive Methodist membership had grown to 132 and the Canadian Mission was placed under the care of the Hull circuit.[45] Additional missionaries were sent out as the work expanded, and circuits were organized; by 1845 there were ten travelling preachers and seventy-nine local preachers in the country, serving the seven circuits of Toronto, Brampton, Etobicoke, Markham, Whitby and Reach, Niagara Falls, and Brantford.[46] In 1842 the Canadian Mission was organized as a district, and in 1854 the work was divided into two districts and placed under the charge of a Canadian Conference.[47] The year after the appointment of the first Primitive Methodist missionary to Canada, the Bible Christian Conference in England appointed a missionary to the country. The work of the Bible Christians expanded slowly, but considerable influence came to be exerted by their missionaries, particularly in the district of Cornwall. In 1837 another Methodist group commenced missionary operations in the country when the Reverend John Addyman arrived in Montreal as the representative of the New Connexion Conference in England. In the Eastern Townships, the missionaries of the New Connexion Conference achieved particular success; new fields were opened up

[40]*Christian Guardian*, Sept. 7, 1836.
[41]*Ibid.*, Sept. 21, 1836.
[42]See Sissons, *Egerton Ryerson*, vol. I, p. 237.
[43]*Minutes of the Annual Conferences of the Wesleyan-Methodist Church of Canada, from 1824 to 1845 Inclusive* (Toronto, 1846), p. 171.
[44]Mrs. R. P. Hopper, *Old-Time Primitive Methodism in Canada* (Toronto, 1904), p. 21.
[45]*Ibid.*, p. 26.
[46]*Ibid.*, p. 60.
[47]*Ibid.*, p. 156.

and, in addition, societies which had been formed some six years earlier by preachers of the Protestant Methodist Church in the United States but which had been left without support were brought under their control.[48] With the recruitment of additional missionaries, the work was extended into Upper Canada, and here a union was effected with the church which had been founded by Ryan to give rise to the Canadian Wesleyan Methodist New Connexion Church. By 1846 the Church had a total of thirty-four missionaries and fifty-nine local preachers in the country serving a membership of 3,201.[49]

The new Methodist sects added to their following at the expense of the Wesleyan Methodist Church. "About this time," Carroll wrote of the work on the Toronto circuit in 1830-1, "Primitive Methodist ministers from England began to bid for the patronage of those of Methodist proclivities in that Circuit. Some who had belonged to them in the old country returned to their first love; and some that had not, joined them."[50] In Toronto also, later, the Methodist New Connexion Church gained a substantial following, largely at the expense of the Wesleyan Methodist Church. "Our introduction into Toronto," the Reverend H. O. Crofts stated on the occasion of laying the corner-stone of a new chapel in the city, "was wholly unlooked for on my part. A number of intelligent and respectable men, who, it appears, had for some time held more enlarged views of church government than the majority of those with whom they were associated; and finding, from causes which I shall not enumerate, that they could not be happy where they then were, painful as it must have been to them, resolved to leave that Connexion, and seek a home in some other Church, whose economy of church government was more in unison with their views and feelings."[51] Invited to Toronto to form them into a church, Croft quickly succeeded in establishing a strong cause in the city; in other parts of the country, more particularly in the Eastern Townships, the work of the New Connexion missionaries also cut into the following of the Wesleyan Methodists.

The union of Canadian and English Methodism in 1832 was followed not only by the schism of the Episcopal Methodists and the growth of the smaller English Methodist sects, but by growing conflict within the Wesleyan Methodist Church itself and the eventual dissolution of the union. The fact that the union, instead of bringing the gains

---

[48]See the *Methodist New Connexion Magazine and Evangelical Repository for the Year 1838.*
[49]*Christian Messenger*, Oct., 1846.
[50]John Carroll, *Case and His Cotemporaries, or the Canadian Itinerants' Memorial* (Toronto, 1867-77), vol. III, p. 297.
[51]*Christian Messenger*, Oct., 1846.

anticipated, resulted in an actual decline of membership had much to do with the growing restlessness respecting the terms of the agreement of 1832. Dissatisfaction was evident almost immediately after the agreement was effected. The British Wesleyans in Upper Canada welcomed in 1832 the prospect of again being able to participate in religious services conducted by missionaries from England, and were disappointed when union with the Canadian Conference limited the field in which Wesleyan missionary work was carried on. "There seems," Benjamin Slight, Wesleyan missionary, wrote of his arrival in Kingston, July 27, 1834, "a great interest excited in us amongst the people. There is still a party who remain opposed to the union, and many British Methodists who have settled in U.C. are far from being reconciled to Canadian Methodism, many of whom wish the M.M. Come had sent missionaries according to their first intentions."[52] The bitter complaints of John Ryerson, writing from Hallowell, of the failure to gain the support of the British Methodists in Kingston—made more ironical by the part he had played in bringing about the union—revealed the wide cleavage between the two groups. "There is no union & no prospect of any," he wrote of the situation in Kingston, November 7, 1833, "between the two congregations, so long as Mr. Hetherington remains there. The bitterness of his feallings beggers all discription & he is doing all he can to excite the same kind of fealing in the minds of others & then publish abroad how much their members are opposed to the *Union*."[53] Later in the month, John Ryerson again wrote: "I fear more from the opposition of the Missionary party to the *union* than what I do from any other quarter; if Mr. Stinson should become disaffected towards the *union* or our church & suspitions should be excited at home & should the connection there from *any* consideration undertake to retain Kingston & York, we shall be compleatly ruined."[54] One year later the situation in Kingston had improved little. "Mr. S[tinson] told me," John Ryerson wrote, October 25, 1834, "that he considered that I had no charge of them [the members in Kingston] & he had so informed his people. To be sure he taulks about *union* etc. but what does he mean by that purty term, which I have long since been sick of hearing. Why the *union* he means is that our congregation shall be unighted to them."[55] By this time John Ryerson had become completely disillusioned respecting the benefits of union. "One thing," he wrote

[52]University of Toronto, Victoria University Library, The Journal of Benjamin Slight, Missionary, Appointed by the Wesleyan Missionary Committee, London, to Upper Canada, 1834-1857, vol. I, p. 34.
[53]Sissons, *Egerton Ryerson*, vol. I, pp. 188-9.
[54]*Ibid.*, pp. 212-13.
[55]*Ibid.*, p. 243.

in a postscript to the letter quoted from above, "I have to console myself with is that in advocating *union* I was sincear & thought it would be for the best, but every result of it thus far has been dizasterous & gloomy without a single *iota* of any thing growing out of it that is beneficial to us."[56] The shift of the diplomatically skilful Egerton Ryerson to Kingston resulted in effecting a union of the two parties,[57] but difficulties remained in other areas of the country. From Toronto, John Ryerson, in a letter January 2, 1837, complained that the Wesleyan preachers were working for their own gain—"Indeed," he wrote, "so far from the book agents or the English preachers who have been, or are, in this country trying to assist us in any way, their principle objects appears to be, to *flease* us & git all out of us they can."[58] In nearby Hamilton, William Ryerson was equally embittered by the way the union was working out. "To say the whole in one sentence," he wrote, May 18, 1837, "The Union works *badly, very badly, for us,* and I am sick, in my very soul sick of it. I wish, most heartily wish, it had never taken place. O how deeply I regret that I ever had any hand in bring it about; the only consolation I can feel on this subject is that in the part that I unfortunately took in the affair I acted conscientiously."[59]

Dissatisfaction was not entirely confined to one side. Stinson, the superintendent of missions, charged, probably with some justification, that the Canadian Methodists were responsible for the prolonged conflict between the two parties in Kingston. "But it is not very likely," he wrote, November 21, 1834, "that much union can exist, while persons are allowed to remain in the other society who have acted & continue to act most dishonourably to our members & while some of the Preachers of this District tell our leading members that 'There are *two* English missionaries in the Canada Conference now but that they will get rid of them as soon as possible'."[60] Opposition became particularly strong to the control by the Canadian ministers of the editorial policy of the *Christian Guardian*, and the conflict between the two parties became entangled in issues of colonial politics. The remarks of the Reverend Benjamin Slight, one year after the dissolution of the union in 1841, provide some indication of the feeling among the English Wesleyans.

For some time [he wrote in his journal, August 7, 1842] there have been rumours abroad concerning another Union to be attempted between the Canadian and the British Conferences. This, as was the late Union, is promoted by the Canadians.

---

[56]*Ibid.*, p. 244.
[57]*Ibid.*, p. 269.
[58]*Ibid.*, p. 367.
[59]*Ibid.*, p. 376.
[60]*Ibid.*, p. 245.

I hold sentiments entirely repugnant to anything of the kind; at least, if it were not of an entirely different character, to the last. We suffered enough from that. I see no prospect, considering the spirit and feelings, both of Preachers and People, for any thing like peace and prosperity.[61]

Dissolution of the union was inevitable in terms of the opposing interests brought together in 1832. Both parties in effect wanted all the advantages of union without any of its disadvantages. English Wesleyanism looked upon the Canadian field as properly falling under its control and only accepted the union as a means of accomplishing this object. Canadian Methodism, on its part, sought through union to secure the support of the growing Wesleyan constituency without sacrificing control to an outside ecclesiastical body. Among the great body of members, as distinct from the preachers, the fundamental conflict between English Wesleyanism and American Methodism persisted, whether formal union existed or not. The moment union came to an end, the division between the two parties once more openly asserted itself. "In consequence of some misunderstandings," Ferguson wrote in his journal, "and diversity of opinion, a state of things had arisen rendering a separate position imperitive on the Canada Conference. A number of Preachers disconnected themselves and united with the English Conference."[62] Among the preachers who left the Canadian Conference was William Case, one of the early founders of the movement in Canada. Wesleyan societies were quickly re-organized in Toronto and Kingston, and, although no society had existed in Hamilton before the union, one was formed there.[63] The effects of the division were immediately apparent in Toronto. "When I ascended the pulpit for the first time," Egerton Ryerson wrote of his return from England to his church in Toronto, "the pews in the body of the church, which had been occupied by those who had seceded, were empty, and there were scattered hearers, here and there, in the other pews and in the gallery."[64] In Hamilton, the membership of the Methodist society dropped from one hundred and forty-four to sixty-eight. "We would here remark," a correspondent in the *Christian Guardian*, however, pointed out, "that the secession has been confined *exclusively* to the town; not an individual member in Dundas, where we have three flourishing Classes, nor in the other parts of the Circuit, where we have twenty Classes more, has left us and joined the English Missionary Society."[65] From other sections of the province, reports provided some indication of the

[61]Journal of Benjamin Slight, vol. II, p. 27.
[62]The Journal of the Rev. George Ferguson, p. 158.
[63]*Christian Guardian*, Dec. 9, 1840.
[64]Sissons, *Egerton Ryerson*, vol. I, p. 559.
[65]*Christian Guardian*, Dec. 23, 1840.

extent of the defections to the Wesleyan party. "Our Circuit," Peter Kerr wrote from Beachville, March 10, 1841, "has been visited and revisited by some who 'have gone out from us,' and are now labouring to *destroy* what they once strove to *establish*—the *peace* and *unity* of the Body. These unwelcome visitors have been but too successful in their work of schism and 'mission' of discord. *Congregations, Classes,* and Families have been divided!"[66] On May 10, 1841, Egerton Ryerson wrote generally of the situation resulting from the Wesleyanite defection: "The agents of the London Comttee. have not injured our Societies generally although the scenes of schism which have & are exhibited in many places are sickening & disgraceful."[67]

Recognition on the part of both parties of the heavy price being paid in open denominational conflict led to the re-union of the Canadian and English Conferences in 1847, but differences between the two parties persisted for some years. Although greater care was taken to secure the rights of the various interests, the union nevertheless immediately aroused considerable opposition on the part of the British Methodists in the country. "When Mr. Gundy," the biographer of the Wesleyan missionary wrote, "returned to Brock after the union, there was no little excitement among the Methodists. He found nearly the whole community in arms against the conference, and so far was this spirit carried, that those who were British Methodists refused to allow the conference preacher to occupy the churches which they themselves had built, and which they were resolved should be appropriated to their own use, and consequently they closed them, only to be opened to whomsoever they would."[68] In other parts of the country, strong feelings of dislike for Canadian Methodist leaders persisted among the British Wesleyans. "We reached London," the Reverend E. O. Sallows, a Wesleyan minister, wrote in his journal, June 20, 1848, "and stayed with Whitehouse's people, who were extremely thankful. They were members of the British Wesleyans. Their minds had been very much grieved on account serious prejudices existing with those persons of former Canada Conference against them and their Ministers (Missionaries). They were grieved about Mr. Botterall being removed, being a Missionary."[69] The next year, January 20, 1849, while stationed near Chatham, Sallows wrote: "We proceeded

---

[66]*Ibid.,* Mar. 10, 1841.

[67]Sissons, *Egerton Ryerson,* vol. I, p. 575.

[68]Rev. John Kay, *Biography of the Rev. William Gundy, For Twenty Years a Minister of the Methodist New Connexion Church in Canada* (Toronto, 1871), p. 81. Gundy came out to Canada as a missionary of the British Wesleyan Conference but broke from the Church in 1849 and attached himself to the Methodist New Connexion Church.

[69]University of Toronto, Victoria University Library, Journal of Rev. E. Sallows, 1848-1849, no pag.

as far as Mersea St. . . . I am sorry the Union has not been working well here others are out of the church."[70] Deeply-rooted prejudices lingered in the minds of the older generation particularly and served for some time to disturb the inner unity of the Wesleyan-Methodist Church, although the union this time proved successful in that the conflicts of the opposing interests were submerged behind the facade of denominational harmony. Vested interests of office and of membership increasingly asserted themselves to secure the apparent solidarity of the Church in face of internal disturbing influences.

Conflict within the Baptist movement resulting from the establishment of the English connection developed in much the same fashion as within the Methodist movement. Two of the five Baptist Associations in Upper Canada refused to support the Canada Baptist Missionary Society, and organization of a rival missionary body—the Western Canada Baptist Home Mission Society—in connection with the American Baptist Home Mission Society sharpened the division between the two groups and what amounted to a general schism within the Baptist body occurred. Rival religious journals soon made their appearance, and editorial writers and correspondents vied with one another in attempting to justify their particular point of view. The doctrinal issue became one of the right of the local church to permit unbaptized members into full fellowship. The English Baptists tended to hold open communion views, the American Baptists were strict communionists. Though questions of doctrine and discipline remained entirely under the control of the local churches, and the Canada Baptist Missionary Society included churches which practised closed as well as open communion, the strict Baptists refused to support the Society because of the open communion views of its officers. The Reverend John Gilmour wrote to a friend in England about 1840:

> Their extremely exclusive views prevent me from being able to co-operate with them for they not only refuse all fellowship with paedo Baptists but with all Baptists who hold the principles of free communion—tho' I am a Baptist they would not allow me to have fellowship with them—of this in their official communication with us when attempting to affect a Union of action in Missionary and educational operation they distinctly informed us—They would work with us only on condition that we would relinquish our views on the subject of communion. Now our Society contains churches both open and close communion in their views . . . .
>
> I sincerely wish our Brethren in the Upper Province tho' strict were not so strict— I do not see why close and open communion Baptists should not be able to co-operate in educational and Missionary exertions.[71]

---

[70]*Ibid.*
[71]McMaster University Library, Baptist Historical Collection, Correspondence of John Gilmour.

The effects of the schism were evident in the history of various local Baptist churches. "Few churches," the historian of the churches belonging to the Ottawa Baptist Association wrote in 1865, "were more fiercely or insiduously assailed than the Church in Chatham in her infant state. The faction that did not join were in open hostility to the elder brethren, or secretly tampering with the young and inexperienced." Although the Church succeeded in remaining in existence, a number of its members were led astray and some were forced to withdraw.[72] Other churches in the Ottawa Association faced even greater difficulties. The church of Clarence was formed on close communion principles, but became open in 1835, receiving paedo Baptists not only to occasional fellowship but into full membership. "Murmuring immediately began," to quote again from the same source, "and although the parties withdrew, the disaffection remained. Mr. Edwards [the minister] was blamed, and a dispute arising about some land the Church was brought to ruin. The Church lay desolate nine years, without the regular ministrations of the Word, and without Church fellowship."[73] Similarly, when the open communion church of St. Andrews, in 1837, secured the services of Edwards for half his time through an arrangement with the close communion church of Chatham, growing dissatisfaction resulted eventually in the withdrawal of many of the members and their union with the Congregationalists, and from 1843 until 1848 no Baptist church existed.[74] A similar arrangement between the churches of St. Andrews and Dalesville, the latter being close communion, in 1838 ended in failure, and the two churches eventually were forced to separate, Dalesville church securing a pastor of its own.[75] In the Ottawa Association, the effects of the schism were most felt in the Montreal church; here the strength of both English and American Baptists led to a sharp division within the membership body. The difficulties faced by the Church were related by the historian of the churches of the Ottawa Baptist Association:

The subject of communion agitated the Church at this time. When Mr. Rice became Pastor in 1837, the Church restricted her communion to baptized believers; several at this time left the church, which accounts for the reduction. . . .

In June, 1840, Mr. John Girdwood accepted the pastorate; the Church grew and flourished under his care . . . . In 1847, the Church had well nigh doubled, when a lamentable secession took place. Many able and influential persons withdrew and formed another Church. This was felt throughout the Churches of the Association,

[72]*Minutes of the Thirtieth Annual Meeting of the Ottawa Baptist Association, 1865* (Montreal, 1865), p. 17.
[73]*Ibid.*, pp. 21-2.
[74]*Ibid.*, pp. 27-8.
[75]G. F. Calder, *Historical Sketch of Dalesville Baptist Church* (no place of publication, about 1925), no pag.

and, we think, hastened the downfall of the Canada Baptist Missionary Society, and Baptist College. Disaffection towards Mr. Girdwood's ministrations, and possibly nationality, and the subject of communion, were among the causes which led to this disastrous result. Mr. Girdwood resigned May 25, 1850. Dr. Cramp, of the Baptist College, Montreal, occupied the pulpit till November, when Mr. Spaulding became Pastor. The Church began to recover . . . . In 1852 Mr. Spaulding resigned, and was succeeded by Dr. Church, but he resigned in 1853. Mr. Little was called to the pastorate, and remained two years. He withdrew, a number followed him and formed themselves into another Church. The Church was now reduced by these lamentable divisions and other causes to about the same number it had twenty years before.[76]

In other parts of the country, the widening break between open and close communionists led to bitter conflict between members within the local churches and, in a number of cases, in separation and the organization of rival churches. "In 1844 Rev. Jas. Campbell, formerly pastor of a church in Toronto," an account of the history of the Cheltenham Baptist church reads, "formed a church at Cheltenham, under the principles of open communion. . . . At the end of four years a division took place on the question of communion and the regular Baptists withdrew and united as a church under Hugh Reid."[77] In the annual report of the Malahide and Aylmer Baptist Church in 1885, reference was made, in a historical sketch of the church, to the difficulties faced over the communion question. "Charity would induce us to pass over," the church historian wrote, "a portion of the church's history just here, suffice it to say, that as the result of an unhappy division in the church, for 9 years ('48 to '57), there existed two churches of the same faith and order holding meetings at the same hour and almost within a stone's throw of each other."[78] In the Guelph church, the appointment of a new pastor, December 1, 1855, led to a division and the loss of a number of members. "Serious differences of opinion," the historical account reads, "on questions of doctrine existed between the pastor and some of the more prominent members of the church. This resulted in the exclusion of David Savage, the faithful evangelist of the church in its early days, and the loss of many valuable members who withdrew out of sympathy with him."[79] Although the Reverend William Marsh succeeded in maintaining the unity of his church in Markham, he faced considerable difficulty in preventing conflict on the question of communion Two entries in his diary read:

[76]*Minutes of the Thirtieth Annual Meeting of the Ottawa Baptist Association, 1865,* pp. 24-5.
    [77]McMaster University Library, Baptist Historical Collection, Gwendolyn Campbell, "History of Cheltenham Baptist Church."
    [78]*Annual Report of the Malahide and Aylmer Baptist Church, 1885* (Aylmer, 1886), p. 4.
    [79]Rev. B. W. Merrill, *Historical Sketch of the First Baptist Church, Guelph* (Guelph, about 1903), pp. 7-8.

Wednesday, Feb. 28, 1844—attended a Church meeting for the purpose of discussing the terms of Communion altho we were not agreed yet the meeting was interesting to some.

Monday, March 4, 1844—. . . their is nothing I have met with for many years which has Caused me so much grief as the little Contention in the Church in relation to the terms of Communion—if I could with a Clear conscience in the sight of God Confess I was wrong I would Certainly do it—but at present I Cannot do so without sinning against God and I dare not do that even if it should be for the furtherance of the Cause.[80]

Other instances were not lacking of bitter local church conflicts which led to division and the organization of separate churches. Such local schisms gained significance in relation to efforts to develop a unified Baptist denominational body. Organization of the Canada Baptist Union offered a means of strengthening Baptist leadership in the country, but fundamental differences between various Baptist groups inevitably were forced into the open with the shift towards more centralized control. Failure of the Canada Baptist Missionary Society to gain the support of a large proportion of the Baptist churches led eventually to its dissolution and to the collapse of the Baptist College in Montreal. The dissolution of the Society weakened the position of the Canada Baptist Union, and encouraged efforts upon the part of the Regular Baptists in the country to bring the various churches holding to close communion views together in one central body. Organization of a Regular Baptist Union of Canada in 1845 precluded any immediate prospect of unity within the Baptist body as a whole. Only those churches conforming to the principle of close communion were permitted into the union.[81]

Conflict within the Wesleyan Methodist Church and the Canada Baptist Union, and the rise after 1832 of new Methodist and Baptist sects or groups, effectively checked efforts to build up stable denominational organizations within the community. The Methodists and Baptists were more disunited in 1850 than they had been in 1830. Tendencies towards denominational accommodation had been sharply arrested by the rise of new sectarian movements;

This growth of new sectarian movements from within the Methodist and Baptist religious bodies was accompanied by the growth of movements from outside. The period 1830-50 was characterized by an intensification of sectarian activity through the spread into the country of new evangelistic or "heretical" religious groups which cut sharply into

[80]McMaster University, Baptist Historical Collection, Diary of Wm. Marsh, March, 1843-January, 1845. MSS.
[81]*Minutes of the Convention of Associational Delegates Convened at St. George's, 6th and 7th Sept., 1848, to Effect a Union of the Regular Baptists of Canada* (London, C.W.).

the following of the older Methodist and Baptist denominations. One of the earliest of such groups was the Campbellites or Disciples of Christ.

The Campbellites had been attached to the Baptist denomination for a number of years, and baptism by immersion was one of their accepted principles. Inevitably, as a result, they attracted the support of many good Baptists, and particularly Scotch Baptists who held very similar doctrines. Historically, a close relationship existed between the views of the Haldanes in Scotland and of the Campbells in the United States, and, while the Disciples of Christ developed in the United States as a distinctly separate movement out of Presbyterianism, the Haldane influence was evident in the nature of their religious teachings.[82] The result was that even well informed Baptists experienced some difficulty in distinguishing between Campbellites and Scotch Baptists. It would be expected, therefore, that many Scotch Baptists would be influenced by Campbellite teachings without being aware of the fact that such teachings were contrary to Baptist principles. This was particularly true of the Scotch Baptists in western Upper Canada who, more isolated than their fellow-brethren in the Ottawa Valley, were dependent upon the services of whatever preachers made their appearance. The preaching of Campbellite evangelists, and the dissemination of Campbellite literature, led to the considerable infusion of Disciples' teachings. Local prophets emerged who, through a change in convictions, endorsed the Disciples' cause and promoted the organization of Disciples' churches.

The gradual evolution of the first Disciples church in Eramosa, as related by R. Butchart in *Old Everton*, provides an illustration of the nature of the shift of attachments of the Scotch Baptists. The church was originally a Scotch Baptist church, but very early many of its members began "preaching advanced views." Sometime about 1825, Elder James Black, who had been acting as a minister in Aldborough but who had had differences with his congregation because of his views, settled in the township of Nassagawaya and carried on preaching activities which extended into Eramosa. By this time Black was busy studying the writings of the Campbells, and during the first two years of his preaching in Eramosa "he and his hearers were going through the difficult process of re-learning their religious convictions."[83] The final shift of the Eramosa church into the ranks of the Disciples of

[82]See W. E. Garrison, *Religion Follows the Frontier, A History of the Disciples of Christ* (New York and London, 1931), chap. IV.
[83]Reuben Butchart, *Old Everton and the Pioneer Movement among the Disciples of Christ in Eramose Township from 1830* (Toronto, 1941), p. 5.

Christ came in 1831 or 1832 largely as a result of the visit of a Disciples' evangelist. About the same time, the church in Nassagawaya also shifted from Scotch Baptist to Disciples of Christ.

A number of other Disciples of Christ churches grew out of churches which originally had been Scotch Baptist.[84] The shift of attachments indicated a failure of the main Baptist body to promote sufficiently rapidly processes of assimilation. The considerable differences which separated the Scotch Baptists from the larger Baptist body were exploited by the Disciples of Christ to their advantage. The lack of any statistics relating to denominational membership meant that there were no means of estimating the extent of the loss to the Baptist cause. The growing strength of the Disciples' movement, however, was some indication of its success in drawing off Baptist support.

In a more subtle fashion, the Campbellite "heresy" made its influence felt upon many of the Baptist churches without resulting in open separation. Local preachers, usually of Scotch Baptist origin, engaged in the propagation of religious teachings which embodied a mixture of Campbellite and Baptist doctrines. The effect of this was to strengthen principles of the sect among Baptists and to weaken the supports of denominational organization. The editor of the *Christian Observer* wrote in February, 1852:

We have received a private communication from a brother in the western part of the Province, in which he informs us that in the region where he resides and labours as a minister there are individuals calling themselves Disciples, professing Baptist principles; and yet teaching erroneous doctrines. "They repudiate all ministers as not being necessary, and contrary to the gospel. They deny the existence of the Holy Spirit, as a person in the Trinity; and say the Spirit is in the Word, that Jesus Christ is not God equal with the Father," &c. It is really matter of wonder that such teachers should in a land of Bibles obtain a second hearing; but it is still a patent truth that men have itching ears . . . .

Because the errorists referred to above, practice immersion, they are said to hold Baptist principles. As well might it be affirmed of Romanists that they are Presbyterians, because they practise sprinkling. We have not so learned Christ.

We cannot close this article without, in common justice to the denomination called Disciples, saying that so far as we understand their sentiments they do not harmonize with the errors noted above.[85]

The confusion between Baptist and Campbellite doctrines not only led to a weakening of church discipline on the fringe of the Baptist body but resulted in strains within the higher councils of the denomination. Scotch Baptist influence gained in strength in such areas as Toronto, and the effects of its influence were increasingly felt with the growing control of the

[84]See collection of Master of Arts theses, McMaster University Library.
[85]*Christian Observer*, vol. II, Feb., 1852.

Scots over the publishing industry. The editor of the Toronto *Examiner*, Francis Hincks, was a Scotch Baptist, and the Toronto Baptist church, and the Baptist religious journal published in Toronto, the *Christian Observer*, shifted increasingly in the direction of Scotch Baptist principles. It was probably through the confusion of such principles with the principles of the Campbellites that the editor of the American Baptist publication—the *New York Recorder*—was led to charge that the *Christian Observer* and the recently organized Regular Baptist Missionary Society of Canada were promoting Campbellite heresies.[86] The question at issue was the practice of weekly communion which, the editor of the *Observer* pointed out, in answering the charges of the *Recorder*, came from the old country rather than through Campbellite influence.[87] The seriousness of the charges led to the appointment of a special committee by the Regular Baptist Missionary Society to examine the facts and make them known to the public. The Committee reported on January 14, 1852. Part of its report read:

Our Society is represented by Mr. Cleghorn [in the *New York Recorder*] as an open-communion Campbellite movement. We pronounce this a reckless slander. The Society is just as far removed from open-communionism and Campbellism, as is any missionary body of Baptists on the continent . . . .

But we are Campbellites! Not one of us, "from the least to the greatest." It is sickening to the soul to correct such perversity. None of us believe that every, or *any* member of a church has a right to "break bread." The brethren of Toronto believe that the ordinances of the Gospel are committed to the churches. Not to the eldership, or the brethren, as such, but to the *church* that the ordination of the Pastor leaves him the only authorized administrator of the ordinance of the Supper in the body. They further believe, that the Church is thoroughly independent—that, under Christ, its head, it is the source of all authority ecclesiastic—that here the pastor derives his authority—that when they are destitute of a Pastor, they have a right to appoint a brother to preside in the Pastor's place—a right to conduct the work of discipline, to receive and exclude members, and to attend to the ordinances. Now, whether this be in accordance with primitive practice or not, we all know that it is no part of "Campbellism."[88]

If the statement in reply to the charges of the *New York Recorder* be accepted as substantially correct, the necessity of making such a reply indicated nevertheless the considerable difficulty faced in clearly defining Baptist doctrinal beliefs so as to avoid the infusion of teachings of an heretical character. The independence of the churches rendered ineffectual attempts to maintain the "purity" of Baptist doctrines. The Campbellite heresy thus was able to extend a considerable distance without leading to any formal division within the Baptist body.

[86]*Ibid.*, vol. I, Oct., 1851.
[87]*Ibid.*, Nov., 1851.
[88]*Ibid.*, vol. II, Feb., 1852.

Because of its distinctive appeal to people with a Baptist background, the Disciples of Christ movement had little noticeable effect upon the fortunes of the Methodist Church,[89] but a number of other evangelical religious movements grew up after 1830 which drew off Methodist members. Of these, the one which stood in closest relationship to Methodism was that of Irvingism, a movement which in Canada developed under the influence of one who because of his family connection emphasized the importance of the break from the Methodist Church. Visiting England in 1831, the Reverend George Ryerson made the acquaintance of the Reverend Edward Irving and became one of his disciples. Three years later Irvingism was introduced into Canada with effects unfavourable particularly to the Methodist cause. Carroll wrote of the Conference year 1834-5:

> There was one other element of mischief, not yet noticed, by which a large number of very worthy members were lost in Kingston and Toronto, and, perhaps, some other places. This was Irvingism, sown by two gentlemen from England, one of whom was a Canadian and had been a preacher in connection with the Conference, who had visited the Province the year before. They came disclaiming any intention of making a party, through which they were very unguardedly allowed an entrance into the Methodist pulpits in both the towns above indicated, whence many became leavened with their doctrine.[90]

The movement grew sufficiently rapidly to cause considerable uneasiness in Methodist circles. John Ryerson wrote from Toronto, September 25, 1836:

> Caird [the Irvingite preacher] & Co are now here. Patrick, Vaux & Webb have joined them. I think however that their race is purty nigh run, & that they will get very few more, if any. I am told that most of their performances are truly disgusting & that thinking people are turning from them with fealings of the warmest disaprobation: this is maddening the Irvinites & with no sparing hand they are dealing damnation round the land upon the heads of all who *dare* to call in question their *Apostolical authority.*[91]

On January 2, 1837, John Ryerson again wrote from Toronto: "There are five Irvinite preachers here & four in Kingston. George is here. I have little communication with them. I have never heard any of them preach. I wish you [Egerton] would write some account of them for

[89]In backwoods farm areas, however, the movement did cut into the Methodist following. "During my second year on the Collingwood mission," the Reverend Joseph Hilts wrote, "I held a series of evangelistic services in that place. I was aware that in the vicinity there were some of the Campbellites or Disciples. But I thought that by judicious management it was possible to avoid coming in collision with them. But in this I was mistaken." J. H. Hilts, *Experiences of a Backwoods Preacher* (Toronto, 1887), p. 145.

[90]Carroll, *Case and His Cotemporaries,* vol. III, p. 485.

[91]Sissons, *Egerton Ryerson,* vol. I, p. 360.

the *Guardian* & send it out. Patrick, Vaux, & about 10 more Methodists have joined them; a good many Church people have falled in with them—Receiver General Dunn, Small, etc. etc."[92]

At the end of the Conference year 1836-7, the Church reported a loss of fifteen members to the Irvingites, no great loss in terms of total numbers but one of some significance in that the movement by then had come to the end of its rapid expansion. The losses were almost wholly confined to the larger centres of population and in this fact they assumed even greater significance. The Irvingite movement was an urban movement; Methodism was thus attacked not in the rural frontier where it had distinct advantages but in those areas where its establishment was essential to its future progress.

The Mormon movement entered the country the same time as the Irvingite movement, and like the latter grew rapidly for a few years. Inroads were made upon the following of the evangelical churches. "Some of the victims of this [Irvingite] delusion," Carroll wrote, "became an easy prey to a still worse one, with which it had some features in common, and which, about the same time, began to be propagated throughout the country. We refer to Mormonism, by the seductions of which many most interesting persons and families became ruinously entangled during the next [1835-6] and several following years. In some places whole classes were broken up by this hateful epidemic."[93] The Wesleyan-Methodist Conference in 1837 reported a loss of fifty-two members to the Mormons. Ferguson wrote of his work on the Matilda circuit in 1839-40:

> The "Mormons" had annoyed us considerably, and had induced some of our people to embrace their vagaries and to set out for the "Promised land." Br. N[ankeville] combatted them in public with success, and showed them to the public in their true colors. They were at last defeated and their designs frustrated . . . .
> In consequence of the strict disciplinary course we pursued, and the efforts of the Episcopals and Mormons and others we experienced a decrease of forty-two.[94]

Much more widespread and disorganizing was the adventist movement promoted by Miller which spread throughout the country after 1842. The Millerites did not become a church but gained a large following made up of the members of various churches; in this way they were particularly difficult to combat. They assumed the character of an "heretical" movement. Given to extravagances in the character of its

[92]*Ibid.*, p. 369.
[93]Carroll, *Case and His Cotemporaries*, vol. III, p. 486.
[94]Journal of the Rev. George Ferguson, pp. 156-7. Mormonism was considered a sufficiently serious threat to the Baptist churches to secure some attention in Baptist religious publications. See, for instance, *The Register*, vol. II, Jan. 12, 1843.

religious beliefs and in its form of religious expression, the movement appealed particularly to those who had come under the influence of evangelical religion. "The believers in Miller's theory," the Toronto *Examiner* reported, "have lately erected a large wooden structure for worship in the north part of the city, which is said to be crowded with hearers from day to day, and no small excitement has been created by a succession of preachers from the United States."[95] A traveller in Upper Canada, on a hunting trip in the Ottawa Valley, had occasion to meet with one of the Millerite prophets. He wrote:

On our return expedition up stream we found ourselves necessitated, for lack of sufficient physical force to prosecute our journey, to accept the voluntary assistance of a solitary stranger, who we accidentally picked up, wending his way along the bank of the river towards Bytown, for the express purpose, he afterwards contended, of propagating the undeniable doctrines of the true faith. This benign promulgator of the gospel, (who very quickly discovered himself to be no less a personage than an American citizen fresh from Cape Cod, Massachusetts, where, he was proud to acknowledge, he had been both born and raised) gave us to understand, that he was an independent Millerite, or true believer in the proximate appearance of the second advent . . . .

Having received a cordial invitation to attend a course of lectures which he proposed giving, for the particular benefit of the good people of Bytown, indiscriminately, I made it a duty of especial importance, to present myself in person the first evening of his spiritual outpourings, and was not a little surprised to find, after having listened attentively to him for five and twenty minutes, that there was not less than a congregation of four hundred people. . . . In the estimation of many then present, I do firmly believe, he brought his arguments to bear with such force, as to make very considerable progress . . . . His lecture lasted for about qne hour, and might have continued for double that space of time, had not some of the more rational tradesmen of the neighborhood . . . came in a body consonant, and threatened instant destruction upon the head of the false prophet, if he did not immediately close his discourse and leave the town.[96]

The excitement aroused in a Millerite meeting in Picton was described in the *Church*, the religious publication of the Church of England May, 1843:

On Friday night between the hour of 11 and 12, a "midnight cry" of an appalling kind was uttered by the fair ones of Picton who had met in St. John's Hall to hear the Millerite Prophet Deverell. He had bid them an affectionate farewell, believing he would never see them again till after the Resurrection which would take place in 1843, when some wicked boys fired a train of gunpowder which they had laid around the building. A universal cry of "Lord Save Us" resounded on all sides and some fainted.[97]

---

[95]Quoted in *The Register*, vol. III, Mar. 14, 1844.
[96]C.H.C., *It Blows, It Snows; A Winter's Rambles through Canada* (Dublin, 1846), pp. 39-43.
[97]Quoted "One Hundred Years Ago" (*Church Messenger of Canada*, July, 1943).

The Bishop of Montreal wrote of the Millerite influence in Shefford County and other parts of the Eastern Townships:

The pillar of the cause in this neighbourhood is a tin-smith of Waterloo Village, formerly a soldier in the British army, and now enjoying a pension. Another great preacher of the same doctrine in the township is a man who, eighteen months ago, ran off with a neighbour's wife . . . .

In the meetings of the Millerites, persons acted upon by the vehement proclamations of close approaching judgment, enforced by the expedients usual in such cases for goading the human mind, fall into what are technically called, *the struggles*, and roll on the floor of the meeting-house, striking out their limbs with an excessive violence; all which is understood to be an act of devotion in behalf of some unconverted individual, who is immediately sent for, if not present, that he may witness the process designed for his benefit. Females are thus prompted to exhibit themselves, and I was credibly assured, that at Hatley two young girls were thus in the *struggles*, the objects of their intercessions being two of the troopers quartered in the village. Revolting as such scenes may appear, yet when mixed up with the awful realities of future judgment, they take a prodigious effect, in the wilder and more sequestered parts of the country, upon a large portion of the popular mind; and while, in some instances, they are coupled with blasphemy and crime, in many more with gross inconsistency on the part of persons who cling in heart to their worldly interests, in others still with the danger of consequent unbelief upon the failure of the Miller prophecies within the time, . . . there are other cases in which men, thoroughly persuaded of the immediate dissolution of all things, have forborne from making those provisions and preparations for another season, upon which, when it comes, their families must depend.[98]

The Methodists were particularly affected by the Millerite heresy. "Thousands in our country," a correspondent in the *Christian Guardian* wrote, April 1, 1843, "are deceived by this sophistry, and are expecting the end of the world some time during the present year. . . . Many members of our Church, I most deeply regret to learn, are carried away by these delusions; hundreds are relinquishing their business."[99] The Reverend George Ferguson wrote:

It was truly gratifying to witness the progress of the good work . . . . But Satan was not idle . . . . Although he assumed the garb of an "angel of light," and imposed himself on the unsuspecting and the innocent, in the name of "Millerism" and "end of the world" preachers, he nevertheless continually sought "whom he might devour." He found some who fell an easy prey to his wiles. In Beverly, Echlin's Settlement, the society was much injured by this new fanaticism. The leader who had been useful in the place, was carried away, and became "an-end-of-the-world" lecturer. The excitement was very great in this place, and the evils have ever since been felt in the class.

---

[98] *A Journal of Visitation to a Part of the Diocese of Quebec, by the Lord Bishop of Montreal, in the Spring of 1843* (3rd. ed., London, 1846), pp. 39, 76-7.
[99] *Christian Guardian*, Apr. 19, 1843.

In another part of Beverly . . . the Millerites came and commenced their work. When we came to the place we found the people in a most horrible state of dread and alarm.[100]

Kay wrote of the work of the Reverend William Gundy as a Wesleyan preacher in 1844: "During his stay on the Pickering circuit, he found the sect known as Millerites, greatly agitating the people with their premillenarian views. The whole country was inflamed to a wonderful degree of excitement on account of the declared speedy coming of the Son of Man to set up his kingdom, and begin his thousand years' reign on the earth. Mr. Gundy had often to combat their unscriptural and pernicious doctrines. This he felt it his duty to do on several occasions."[101]

In the Eastern Townships, the Wesleyan missionary, Benjamin Slight faced increasing difficulty in holding the Methodist societies together, partly as a result of the disorganizing influence of the Millerite movement. "I found this Circuit," he wrote, June 1, 1846, shortly after his arrival on the Compton circuit, "in the utmost degree of prostration, perhaps some part of it may be imputed to the deleterious influences of Millerism. There was only one class which met in the whole Circuit."[102] At the end of one year on the circuit, Slight undertook to appraise the various factors which contributed to the weakness of the Methodist cause in the area. Millerism was placed third on the list. "It would be hard to calculate," he wrote, "the unfavourable effects of Millerism has had upon the interests of real piety; and the apathy which has followed this pernicious system."[103]

The Methodist Episcopal Church as well as the Wesleyan Methodist was seriously weakened by the Millerite movement. "This was a year of trial and persecution," the Reverend Schuyler Stewart wrote of his work on the London circuit in 1845. "One-fourth of the members of the Church were affected with Millerism, and with all my prudence and caution our church suffered a considerable loss."[104] The *Canada Christian Advocate*, the official journal of the Church, expressed considerable concern respecting the progress of Millerism. In the issue of June 19, 1845, a correspondent wrote:

Brighton Circuit has suffered some little from the effects of *Millerism*. A few have left the Church, or, as *they say* escaped from Babylon. The unhallowed fruits of

[100]Journal of the Rev. George Ferguson, p. 184.
[101]Kay, *Biography of the Rev. William Gundy*, pp. 77-8.
[102]Journal of Benjamin Slight, vol. II, p. 73.
[103]*Ibid.*, vol. II, no pag.
[104]*Interesting Sketches and Incidents in the Life of Rev. Schuyler Stewart* (Hamilton, 1882), pp. 29-30.

Millerism, are now making their appearance in every place where these vagaries have been countenanced . . . . It is full time that persons who hold such opinions as those alluded to, should escape from the Church or be expelled from her communion. We were of the opinion from the first, that the line of demarcation should have been drawn between "Methodism" and "Millerism."[105]

The problem was as much one of preventing the infusion of Millenarian doctrines among Methodist followers as one of checking defections from the Church. The *Canada Christian Advocate* wrote editorially, October 2, 1845:

We have been led to these reflections from the fact, that the Minutes of both Annual Conferences show a lamentable decrease in the numbers of our Church members the past year. The principal cause of this decrease, in our judgment is, the effects of Millerism . . . .

Some two or three years since, a few of our local preachers fell in with Miller's views of the Second Advent, and commenced preaching that the world would be burned up in a few months . . . . These lecturers went out *as Methodists* declaring that Millerism was true, and that they knew that the world would be destroyed at their set time. This state of things caused great fear among many people and caused numbers to join the [Methodist Episcopal] Church, who after the excitement was over, and time had proved Millerism false left the Church to pursue their old practices.

When the leaders in this delusion saw that their predictions had failed, they resolved at all hazards, to raise a party, and in order to accomplish this, declared that the Christian Churches were all in Babylon, and that the saints, (that is all who were Millerites) should come out of her, or be destroyed . . . . About the time they commenced teaching these, with other absurd dogmas, they formed what they called the "Second Advent Bands," and soon proclaimed their release from Babylon, as they call the Church.

Now we do not regret that people holding such opinions should leave the Church, but we do deeply regret that those local Preachers who commenced sowing the seeds of error, were not called to an account, and cured, or expelled from the connexion before so many of the societies were corrupted by them.

It may be said that they would have continued to lecture even if they had been expelled. That may be true, but then they would not have had the authority of the Church for their proceedings . . . . Perhaps the most of them have left. We regret, however, to learn that one or two Circuits in the west, is in a state of excitement . . . .

It is not, however, those who have publicly professed faith in Millerism, and who have left, or who have been excluded from the Church, who have altogether caused the decrease. The excitement has had a bad effect upon the public mind, and has caused a reaction in the religious feeling of great numbers, who had been much excited.[106]

The Baptists were little less affected than the Methodists by the Millerite heresy. With them as with the Methodists the problem was not only one of checking defections from the Church but also of preventing the infusion of Millerite doctrines in Baptist teachings. The

[105]*Canada Christian Advocate*, June 19, 1845.
[106]*Ibid.*, Oct. 2, 1845.

spread of the Millerite influence resulted in a violent reaction which was often disastrous to the religious cause. "It is to be devoutly desired," the editor of the *Register* wrote of the situation in the Eastern Townships, "that the feverish and unwarrantable excitement which has been so prevalent in that region of late, may not be succeeded by an absolute indifference to religion itself. Such a reaction is, in our opinion, greatly to be feared."[107] The Reverend William Marsh, Baptist preacher in Whitby, wrote in his diary, March 21, 1843: "rode to Clark met a Crowded assembly of anxious hearers—greate excitement has been Created here by the Millerites I have some fears that this excitement will prove injurious to the Cause of vital piety every person almost in some neighborhoods is now profesing religion but fear that with many it is spurious has its foundation only in fright and will soon pass off the Land."[108]

Millenarian views inevitably made a strong appeal among those sections of the population which had become agitated about the problem of religious salvation. The movement represented an extreme expression of the sectarian spirit. The war it waged upon church forms, and its effect in leading to a breakdown of all denominational loyalties, were a natural result of the application of the evangelical view that nothing mattered but salvation. The appeal was made the more urgent through acceptance of the Millenarian doctrine of the imminent coming. The other-worldliness of the Millerite sect found dramatic expression in the doctrine that the end of the world was at hand.

Millerism constituted the most formidable, but at the same time the most short-lived, of the various movements which grew up after 1832 to challenge the claims of denominationalism in the Canadian community. Its rapid growth was a reflection of the instability which was still characteristic of much of religious life in the Canadian society. The evangelical religious denomination, represented by the Wesleyan Methodist Church and the Canada Baptist Union, grew out of demands making for a closer accommodation of the religious organization to the secular order; denominationalism was a product of the increasing claims of social status within the community. At the same time, however, the frontier persisted as an important force in the Canadian society. New developments gave rise to new social masses; status relationships broke down in face of social disturbances which upset the established order. Promotion of settlement by the Canada Company led to the opening up of the Huron Tract and to the emergence of pioneer communities around such centres as Goderich. In the central part of the

[107]*The Register*, vol. II, June 22, 1843.
[108]Diary of Rev. Wm. Marsh.

province of Canada West farm population crept northward about Lake Simcoe and Georgian Bay, while, further east, it spread up the Ottawa Valley, north of Peterborough and, in the Eastern Townships, into areas which had not earlier been penetrated by the pioneer. Absence of roads, the distance from large centres of population, and the difficulties attendant upon clearing the land and establishing homes led to a social isolation not greatly different from what had prevailed in the early settled areas during the pioneer period; the railway had not yet developed to link isolated communities with the town and the city.

The problem of serving these isolated areas was one which religious organization could not escape. The future prosperity of any church to a considerable degree still depended upon staking claims to the support of the new frontier populations. Competition for such support led to an elaboration of denominational machinery and to desperate efforts to be first in the field. Social pressures, however, forcing greater accommodation to the older and more mature society limited the effectiveness of efforts to serve the new frontier areas and led to the emergence of new evangelistic movements free of the vested interests of denominational officialdom and a class conscious membership body. In the case of both the Methodist and Baptist churches the effect of the frontier influence was to wreck attempts to secure denominational solidarity and to raise up new Methodist and Baptist sects which took a lead in the work of religious evangelization.

Difficulties faced by the Wesleyan Methodist Church in maintaining harmony between the Canadian and English Methodists, and rapid growth of new Methodist sects in the country, were an indication that conditions which had earlier called forth the evangelical movement had not disappeared. The problem of serving the backwoods population remained a problem of religious organization. The evangelical appeal still had a strong attraction in rural sections of the country. Inevitably, therefore, efforts of the Wesleyans to moderate the appeal of the Church led to conflict between them and the Canadian preachers. Even more, the shift of the Wesleyan Methodist Church to a conservative position emphasized the advantages of the smaller Methodist sects in maintaining the evangelical tradition. This was particularly evident in the schism led by the local preachers which resulted in the formation of the Methodist Episcopal Church. The local preachers were farthest removed from social influences which favoured a conservative religious appeal and as a result they were the most reluctant to accept the lead of the Wesleyans in abandoning the use of revivalist methods.

Within what backwoods communities remained, about Georgian Bay in the Bruce peninsula and along the shore of Lake Huron, the

Methodist Episcopal itinerant preachers continued for some years after 1830 to engage in evangelistic work little different from the work which had been carried on by Methodist itinerants in the early decades of the century. This church made a conscious effort to maintain the principles of the early Methodist Church in America. It was organized on an episcopal basis, relied heavily upon itinerant and local preachers, and maintained direction over its work through a system of annual and general conferences. Revivalism and camp meetings were kept to the front as means of extending the Church's influence. In the work, for instance, of the Reverend Joseph Hilts in the Georgian Bay district the evangelical character of the Methodist Episcopal Church was evident.

Hilts came up out of the pioneer population in much the same fashion as the early Methodist itinerants. He began as a school teacher and later turned to preaching as a career. In carrying on his work of evangelization he pushed back with the pushing back of settlement in the country. His task was that of gaining new converts for the cause of Methodism rather than that of consolidating the position of the Church. As a consequence, primary emphasis was placed upon promoting revivals of religion, among people who were not of the Methodist faith as well as among people who were.[109] In addition to protracted meetings, Hilts relied upon camp meetings in arousing among the population an interest in religious values, and some of the camp meetings in which he participated were probably as spectacular as the great meetings which had been held a quarter or half century earlier in the Bay of Quinte, Yonge Street, and Niagara districts.[110]

There was little that was new in the revivalist and camp meetings held by the Episcopal Methodists. Their significance lay in the fact that in the new backwoods settlements conditions of religious life were little different from conditions found in older settlements a half century earlier. The Methodist Episcopal Church maintained its frontier influence by maintaining principles of religious organization which had been largely abandoned by other evangelical churches such as the Wesleyan Methodist. The revivalist and camp meeting, discredited in older-settled areas of the country, still made a strong appeal to the population of the new pioneer districts.

None of the other Methodist churches was perhaps as active as the Methodist Episcopal Church in the backwoods settlements after 1830. The other secessionist Methodist churches—the Primitive Methodists, Bible Christians, and the Methodist New Connexion—were old-

---

[109]See Hilts, *Experiences of a Backwoods Preacher,* pp. 122-5.
[110]See *ibid.,* pp. 100-1, 104, 109-10.

country churches which never secured a strong hold in rural districts. Nevertheless, in certain parts of the country these churches carried on successful evangelistic work. Camp-meetings, attracting as many as two or three thousand, were held by the Primitive Methodists in rural communities of Canada West, and, while they were probably more orderly than those described by the Reverend Joseph Hilts, they retained something of the character of the "old-time camp meeting."[111] It was, however, among the floating population of the towns rather than among the backwoods population of the country that the other secessionist Methodist churches were most active. Their experience as a frontier church in England was largely an experience of serving the new industrial frontiers. Methodist New Connexion preachers were pioneers in carrying on religious services in the gaols of the towns.[112] The Primitive Methodists, lacking the money to build handsome churches, resorted to street-preaching among the new urban "social masses." An effort was made, in particular, to reach the population in the new working-class districts largely deprived of the regular services of religion. Excerpts from the journal of the Reverend Edward Barrass, Primitive Methodist missionary in Toronto, afford an indication of the nature of such work:

Monday, 23rd [May, 1853]. . . . In the evening, preached in the open air, in Caroline-street. This is a part of the city which has been much neglected of late years by the religious portion of the community. It is situated at the east end, which is the oldest part of the city. Many of the inhabitants are Roman Catholics, and others are most dissolute and wicked. The attendance was numerous, and good attention was paid to the word spoken . . . .

Thursday, 26th . . . . In the evening had the pleasure of preaching in the open air, in Elizabeth-street . . . . The attendance was numerous and well-behaved. There were several blacks in the congregation, who seemed to take a deep interest in the service. Have reason to think that open-air worship will be productive of great good in this street. It is in the north end of the city, where the labouring population is great.

Friday, 27th . . . . In the evening stood forth near the Custom-house, where, after singing the first hymn, we were surrounded with an attentive auditory, to whom I preached with good liberty; after which we adjourned to the chapel, and terminated our proceedings with an excellent prayer-meeting.

Thursday, June 2nd.—After a course of visiting, preached out of doors, in Elizabeth-street, to a larger audience than last week. Held a prayer-meeting in a friend's house immediately afterwards. The people crowded in very fast . . . .

Sabbath, 5th.—A day of much speaking . . . . At three, stood forth under the canopy of heaven, near the Custom-house, and preached with power to several hundred

---

[111]See, for instance, the description by the Reverend Edward Barrass of a Primitive Methodist camp meeting in the Toronto district in 1854. *Primitive Methodist Magazine*, 1854, pp. 624-5.

[112]See *Life and Labours of Rev. Wm. McClure* (Toronto, 1872).

persons, among whom, it is said, were several Romanists. Great attention was paid to the word preached.[113]

The work of the Primitive Methodist Church during the year 1853 in those working-class areas of Toronto which hitherto had been neglected was reviewed by the Reverend Edward Barass in a report made public in February, 1854. He wrote: "We held open-air services in the streets of Toronto as long as the weather permitted. Being obliged to suspend open-air worship until the return of the spring, we have done what we could to secure rooms in which to preach in the northern and eastern parts of the city, but have not succeeded according to our wishes; so that, for some time to come, we shall labour at considerable disadvantage."[114]

The techniques employed by the Methodist Episcopal Church or by the smaller Methodist sects in appealing to the new backwoods population or to the new working masses of the towns provided them with distinct advantages in competition with the Wesleyan Methodist Church. The more formal Methodist body increasingly demonstrated its incapacity to reach out and serve the marginal social groups of the Canadian community. Emphasis had shifted too strongly to efforts to consolidate the position of the Church in the more settled parts of the country or in the better residential areas of the towns.

Influences of a more generally social character tended also to weaken the position of the Wesleyan Methodist Church in appealing to the backwoods population or to the working masses of the towns. In becoming increasingly the church of the successful classes in the community, it had ceased to serve the needs of the unsuccessful. The new Methodist sects were, on the other hand, movements of the dispossessed; they grew very largely in terms of the support of the social outcasts of the colonial society. "The Episcopals," the wife of John Ryerson wrote in 1835 of the situation in Hallowell, "are doing nothing in these parts but taking the rubbish from our church."[115] The view of Mrs. Ryerson was probably well founded but its implication was one not entirely to the credit of the church of which she was a member; in the same sense the earlier Methodist movement out of which the Ryersons had grown had developed in terms of the support of the "rubbish." The newer religious movements, as the earlier movement, gained their strength by avoiding an appeal to the respectable and socially well established. They inherited, in part at least, the claim of Methodism to serve as

[113]*Primitive Methodist Magazine*, Oct., 1853.
[114]*Ibid.*, Feb., 1854, p. 115.
[115]Sissons, *Egerton Ryerson*, vol. I, p. 271.

the religious agent of the poor and ignorant of the community without social status.

Again, the increasing identification of the Wesleyan Methodist Church with the interests of Empire limited increasingly its influence among those elements of the population which were becoming more Canadian conscious or which, at any rate, had no strong sense of attachment to the Empire. The Methodist Episcopal Church was distinctively a Canadian church; most of its preachers were people born and raised in the country. It was not the Canadianism of this Church, however, but its lack of identification with any nationalist interests which constituted its strength; within its appeal the principle of the religious sect of separating off from worldly affairs was restored. The same was true of the English Methodist sects. Their appeal was largely to people of British origin but people who had no feeling of having a stake in the Empire; they were humble folk who sought for more intimate and more exclusive loyalties within the religious group.

The Wesleyan leadership within the Wesleyan Methodist Church, on the other hand, resulted in the increasing intrusion of the issue of imperial relations into the councils of the Church. The effects of this were most evident in the failure to maintain the union agreement of 1832 and in the dissolution of the union in 1840. As Canadian feeling developed among one element in the Church membership, the strong British feeling of the other element led to a growing conflict. "He was intensely British," Senator John Macdonald wrote of John P. Hetherington, the second superintendent of the church in Toronto, "and was greatly opposed to the Union."[116] Of the congregation of the Wesleyan St. George Street church in Toronto after the dissolution of the union in 1840, Macdonald wrote: "Whatever else they were, they were intensely British, and as between themselves and the Canadian Methodists worshipping in the Newgate Street Church there was no intercourse, I fear there was no friendly feeling."[117] A correspondent wrote in the *Christian Guardian* of the causes leading to the secession of British Methodists in Hamilton upon the dissolution of the union in 1840:

Much speculation, we have reason to believe, has obtained concerning the *cause* of the secession in Hamilton—it being well known that most of the brethren who have withdrawn were hitherto unwavering in their attachment to the Wesleyan Methodist Church in Canada. As far as we have had an opportunity of learning, we are of opinion that the brethren in question have not left us "in disgust with the proceedings

---

[116]"Recollections of British Wesleyanism in Toronto" (*Methodist Magazine*, vol. XXIX, Jan. to June, 1889, p. 526).

[117]*Ibid.*, p. 151.

of the late Special Conference"; nor because, as a Conference, we have departed from or abandoned the lofty and holy principles of Wesleyan Methodism. The cause of their secession appears to assume a national aspect. Converted through the agency of Methodist Ministers in Great Britain; connected with that Body there for many years; the predilections consequent thereon; all united, seem, in their view, to be a sufficient reason to justify them in the adoption of their present course.[118]

The growing conflict within the Wesleyan Methodist Church between the British and Canadian elements was simply one more demonstration of the price which had to be paid in abandoning the evangelical position of a complete separation from worldly interests. Enlistment of the support of nationalist or imperialist interests greatly strengthened the Church's denominational position but weakened it in appealing to those people whose sole interest was the cause of religious salvation. The new Methodist evangelical movements, by avoiding any identification with the issue of imperial relations and concentrating upon the simple message of religious salvation, were able much more effectively to serve as religious agencies of social reorganization.

The effects of the intrusion of worldly affairs into religious councils were particularly apparent in the increasing identification of the Church with political interests in the community and in the consequent increase of religious conflict as a result of political differences. It was such political differences within the Wesleyan Methodist Church, among other influences, which led to the dissolution of the union agreement in 1840. The break of the Canadian Methodist leaders with the Radical party made possible union in 1832, but not all the Canadian preachers fell in line with the shift of political alignments. A petition in 1833 signed by five ministers travelling in the Niagara District strongly deplored the new policy of the *Christian Guardian* in supporting the Conservative position,[119] while John Ryerson, one of those who took the lead in bringing about the break with Radicalism in 1832, was forced to admit, in a letter to his brother Egerton, November 15, 1833, that as a result of the break there was considerable dissatisfaction among certain sections of the membership body. Of the work of the Church in the Hallowell district he wrote:

Your article on the Political Parties of England has created much excitement; through these parts, the only good that can result from it is the breaking up of the Union which has hithertofor existed between us & the Radicles. Were it not for this I should much regret its appearance, but we had got so closely linked with those fellows in one way or another that we cannot expect to get rid of them with out

---

[118]*Christian Guardian*, Dec. 23, 1840.
[119]Sissons, *Egerton Ryerson*, vol. I, pp. 214-16.

fealling the shock & perhaps it may as well come now as any time. . . . To disengage ourselves entirely from them is a work of no little difficulty. We have a host of Radicles in our Church—I am sorry to say it but it is so.[120]

Although John Ryerson was able to boast that Wesleyan Methodist support played an important part in bringing about the Tory victory in 1836, many of the members of the Church, and some of the preachers remained faithful to the Radical cause. "In addition to our other difficulties," George Ferguson wrote of his work on the Sydney circuit, "the election for this Country came on, and brought with it even [more] than the usual excitement. A number were radicals and they had also a great influence over some of our people."[121]

The rebellion, the next year, though intensifying the conservatism of the Wesleyans, placed a sharp check upon the shift of the Canadian Methodists to a conservative position. There was a limit beyond which even the most anti-radical of the Canadian Methodists were not prepared to go. In the *Christian Guardian*, April 18, 1838, W. M. Harvard, the Wesleyan president of the Church, published a communication to the ministers in which he stated that no man who was not disposed to be a good subject of the state could be admitted to the sacrament of the Church. To make certain this was the case, the circuit preachers were instructed to go through the class papers of the societies under their care, "noticing every individual name, in order to be fully satisfied of the Christian loyalty of all who may be returned as members of our Church to the ensuing Conference." If there was a single individual for whose loyalty the preacher could not conscientiously answer to his brethren, Harvard continued, he should not be included in the return of the membership but should become a subject of church discipline. Narrowly defining the meaning of the term "loyalty" with reference to the events of the rebellion, Harvard's "bull" aroused such a storm of indignation that it was necessary for Egerton Ryerson to rush into print setting forth a somewhat more liberal conception of what was involved in the duty of loyalty.[122] "It appears from accounts from all parts," William Ryerson wrote to his brother Egerton, May 4, 1838, "that Mr. Harvard's Presidential *Bull* meets with universal disapprobation or contempt, or both of them. Wherever information has reached us there is one universal expression of surprise & disgust from both preachers & people."[123] On the Prescott and Augusta circuit,

[120]*Ibid.*, pp. 210-11.
[121]Journal of the Rev. George Ferguson, p. 150. See Sissons, *Egerton Ryerson*, vol. I, pp. 350-1, for a discussion of the part played by the Methodists in the election of 1836.
[122]*Christian Guardian*, May 9, 1838.
[123]Sissons, *Egerton Ryerson*, vol. I, p. 459.

George Ferguson faced considerable difficulty in stemming the dissatisfaction of the members. "Mr. Harvard's letter in the Guardian, on
loyalty," he wrote, "directing each Superintendent to ask the members
of our Church individually whether they were loyal subjects, created
great excitement among our people. Dr. Ryerson's rider to the letter
came in the time of need, and had a salutary effect."[124] The society in
one place, Ferguson went on to say, had agreed that if he asked such a
question they would all leave the Church; Ferguson refused to ask the
question.

The Harvard communication revealed that, however far the Canadian
Methodists had moved in the direction of conservatism, they could
not fully share the views held by the English Wesleyans. Egerton
Ryerson's spirited plea for a more tolerant attitude to those who had
been convicted of participating in the rebellion represented a shift
back to a more liberal position.[125] On the other hand, the Wesleyan
leaders became increasingly aggressive in the championship of principles
which they had earlier moderated as a means of securing the success
of the union. As early as 1837, their attitude to the clergy reserves
question was made clear. "We might find a slice of the loaf," Harvard
wrote to Egerton Ryerson in England, "highly helpful for our Parsonage
houses, Supernumerary Preachers, and students for the ministry at
Cobourg. . . . In this matter you can help us at the Colonial Office,
and I should be unutterably vexed to be disinherited of our just ground
of expectation."[126] The Wesleyan leaders failed to carry the Conference
which met this year with them in support of a policy of sharing in the
clergy reserves, with effects evident in the widening of the breach
between the two parties. "The sittings of this Conference," the Reverend
Benjamin Slight wrote in his journal, "have been far from pleasing.
Many of the transactions were evidently intended in opposition to
English Methodism, especially a series of resolutions against 'religious
grants'."[127] The letter of John Ryerson, March 17, 1838, to his brother,
Egerton, provides some indication of the increasing differences between
the Canadian Methodists and English Wesleyans with respect to
political questions:

Never did high Churchism take such rapid strides towards undisputed *domination*
in this country as it is now taking, & never were the prospects of the friends of
Civil & Religious liberty so gloomy & desperate as they now are; & Harvard &
Evans love to have it so . . . . On the subject of the Governor's dispach relative to

---

[124]Journal of the Rev. George Ferguson, p. 153.
[125]See Sissons, *Egerton Ryerson*, vol. I, chap. XII.
[126]*Ibid.*, p. 379.
[127]Journal of Benjamin Slight, vol. I, p. 133.

the Indians & the whole Indian affare, the clergy land question & the house riseing without doing anything about settling it, etc., etc., the *Guardian* remains basely & survily *silent*, while it is filling up its colloms with war stories true, false, & with every species of ribaldry against the American Government etc., for the purpose of pleasing some 2 or 3 dosen high church Aristochrats who have lately become subscribers to the *Guardian*, while our faithful people are dayly becoming more & more alienated from us, & more & more pained & distressed with the *war* like high church character of our *official organ* & of the anti-christian influence which its present *cours* has on the community . . . . It is a great blessing that Mckenzey & Radicalism are down, but we are in immediate danger of being brought under the domination of a military & high church *oligarchy*, which would be equally bad if not infinitely worse.[128]

The conflict which had become clearly defined by 1838 took the next two years to work itself out. The break between the Canadian and English Methodists was inevitable in terms of the opposing views of the two parties with respect to political questions. How far the Wesleyans were prepared to go in support of "high church" views was made evident in a communication to the governor, January 3, 1840, signed by Stinson and Richey, the president of the Conference and the superintendent of the Toronto District respectively, in which the view was expressed that no objection was taken to the claim of the Church of England of being "the Established Church" of all the British colonies and that the Methodist share of the clergy reserves grant should be given to the Wesleyan Methodists connected with the British Wesleyan Conference.[129] The increasing strength of the Canadian Methodists within the Conference, evident in 1838 and 1839, provided an obstacle to the assertion of Wesleyan views which accounted for the decision of the English Conference in 1840 to bring an end to the union.

The dissolution of the union in 1840, however, did not free the Church from its close relationship to colonial politics and parties. With the removal of Wesleyan control over the Conference, the Canadian leaders were subjected to the same sort of influences which had led to their break from radicalism in 1832. The rebuff suffered by the Canadian Church at the hands of the English Conference in 1840 had greatly increased the prestige of Egerton Ryerson within the Church and in the country at large. Ryerson, by 1840, was approaching the stature of an "elder statesman"; his leadership brought increased respectability to the Methodist Church and increased political influence to the Methodist body. His advice was sought by—not forced upon—the colonial government; the tendering of such advice inevitably involved the strengthening of the ties of the Church with the state. Methodism

[128]Sissons, *Egerton Ryerson*, vol. I, pp. 433-4.
[129]*Ibid.*, p. 535.

moved rapidly, under the influence of Ryerson, from the position of the free church to that of the Canadian territorial church. A vested interest in the state became a determining factor in Church policy.

The most important element within such a vested interest was that of the financial position of the Methodist college. Difficulties in financing the college had been one of the decisive influences in bringing about the union with the English Conference in 1832, and such difficulties, with the break from the Conference in 1840, led to an increasing dependence upon the state. The anxiety of the Methodist leaders to secure means of support for the college resulted in their acceptance of the principle that the clergy reserves fund should be divided among the various denominations. The report of Egerton Ryerson of a conversation which he had with Strachan, then Bishop of Toronto, on a trip from Kingston to Toronto was significant. Ryerson wrote in the *Christian Guardian*, February 21, 1842:

> Conversation took place on several important topics, on scarcely any of which did I see reason to differ from the Bishop. He spoke of the importance to us of our getting our College at Cobourg *endowed*—that an annual grant was an insufficient dependence—that as the Clergy Reserve Question had been settled by law, we had as much right to a portion of the Clergy lands as the Church of England—that as we did not desire Government support for our Ministers, we ought to get our proportion appropriated to the College, as religious education was clearly within the provisions of the Clergy Reserve Act. Valuable suggestions, for which I thanked his Lordship.[130]

In acting upon the suggestion of the Lord Bishop of Toronto, the Wesleyan Methodist Church of Canada placed itself in a position little different from that which had been favoured by the British Wesleyans. The opposing views of church and sect respecting the relationship of religious bodies to the state were made clear with the emergence of the bitterly controversial issue of government support of King's College. The endowment by the government of a college controlled by the Church of England was strenuously opposed by the Methodist body as a whole, but when the question came up as to the disposal of the university funds sharp differences appeared between the various Methodist groups. The Wesleyan Methodist Church favoured the division of the funds as a means of securing the endowment of its own college; the Methodist Episcopal Church took its stand in favour of the principles of the free church. "When the editor of the *Guardian*," the *Canada Christian Advocate* wrote editorially, February 12, 1846, "speaks of the Methodists of Canada, being favourable to any government grants for sectarian and religious purposes, he does the members

[130]*Christian Guardian*, Feb. 23, 1842.

and friends of the M. E. Church in Canada great injustice. Let him qualify his expression, and say the Wesleyan Methodists of Canada, and then the public will understand it properly."[131] Two weeks later the journal of the Methodist Episcopal Church returned to the attack in denouncing the *Christian Guardian* for proposing to divide the spoils with the Church of England, and urging as an alternative the establishment of a non-denominational college.[132] The next month, the editor reviewed the whole matter in making clear the position of the Church which he represented. The editorial read in part:

Why should the people be deprived of their rights, to please John Toronto and Egerton Ryerson, and a few of those who belong to the same communities? The manoeuvring and grasping of such men, have done more towards depriving the Province of peace and justice, than any other cause which has ever been in operation in the country; and in order to inflict another act of injustice upon the people, such leaders would have the College funds divided, so that themselves and a few of their adherents may have an ample share of the spoils . . . .

In conclusion, we beg leave to say to the Legislature, that if they have resolved to decide this matter contrary to the expressed wishes of the people, and to divide the funds, so as to gratify certain communities, at the expense of the people at large, the members, and those friendly to the Methodist Episcopal Church,—so far as we have been able to ascertain—would wish to be distinctly understood, as having no interest, or sympathy with Mr. Ryerson, or those few who favour his views on the University Question. He speaks the sentiments, we believe, of but a very lean minority of the Methodists of Canada. Indeed, we doubt whether a majority of the *members of his own body*, coincide with him in opinion upon this question.[133]

Efforts to advance the interests of the Wesleyan Methodist Church forced the leaders further and further into colonial politics, and championship of, in effect, principles of religious privilege led to the strengthening of the alignment with the conservative cause. The active support given by Egerton Ryerson to Governor Metcalfe in the election of 1844 brought Methodism back to the position it had taken in 1836. Dissatisfaction within the Church with such political activity was not lacking, and the break of a number of members in Toronto in 1845 and their shift of support to the Methodist New Connexion Church was indicative of the persistence of more liberal views within the membership body. The opposition to Ryerson found expression in the formation of the *Toronto Periodical Journal or Wesleyan Methodist* which devoted its editorial columns largely to the question of the relationship of the Methodists to politics. "It is unnecessary to conceal," the editor wrote in announcing the appearance of the first issue, "that the occasion which calls this journal into existence, is that of the recent interference

[131]*Canada Christian Advocate*, Feb. 12, 1846.
[132]*Ibid.*, Feb. 26, 1846.
[133]*Ibid.*, Mar. 26, 1846.

of the Rev. Egerton Ryerson, a prominent member of the Methodist Conference, in political controversy to such an extent as to raise the greatest apprehension of a division in the church, as well as of an immediate separation of affection, of those who have so long been happily united in the doctrines and discipline of that church."[134] In the June issue the editor wrote: "It is now seen that neither Dr. Ryerson nor the Conference have any political principles, but those expressed in the words since so familiar, 'We support the party which will give us the most.' . . . It is impossible now to deny, that the Wesleyan Methodist Church has been converted, to a certain extent, into a political engine, for the service of either party, whose ascendancy it could contribute to secure, with a view of receiving Government support in return."[135]

In the August number, in explaining to the public why it had been decided to renew the contract with the publisher for the publication of the journal for another six months, the editor wrote:

The occasion of issuing the journal in question at the first, was the exposure to the members of the church and the public of the recognition and practice of a principle by the leading members of the Conference, by which the political influence of the whole body,—the writings of its ministers, and the influence of the *Christian Guardian* were all devoted to the service of the Government, in order to receive in return Government aid to the Victoria College and to the missions. The proof of this is clearly expressed and concentrated in these remarkable words, so often quoted by us, spoken by the present President of the Conference:—"Before the elections come on we will put out our FEELER, and the party that will take us up, or give us most, shall have our support." This principle was carried fully into practice, in the issue of Dr. Ryerson's writings, the circulation of which was clandestinely aided by the *Guardian* office.

In so doing, the leaders of the Conference have departed from the undeniable principles of a purely evangelical community, as well as from the spirit of the Methodist institutions. They have allied their church, in some sense, to the state.[136]

However justified Ryerson and the other leaders of the Church may have been in the course of action which they followed, the effect inevitably was to weaken the evangelical influence of Methodism. That is not to say that all the ministers of the Church ceased to interest themselves in the evangelical cause and became something of petty politicians. Active participation in politics was confined very largely to the hierarchy. It was the hierarchy, however, which increasingly spoke for the Church in public; the development of the religious newspaper was partly responsible for increasing the general influence of the Church leaders. Through the increasing influence which they came

[134]*Toronto Periodical Journal or Wesleyan Methodist*, Jan., 1845.
[135]*Ibid.*, June, 1845.
[136]*Ibid.*, Aug., 1845.

to exert, by means of lobbying and propaganda, such leaders developed a considerable sense of public responsibility. Egerton Ryerson earned his reputation as a public statesman. A close examination of the part played by the Wesleyan Methodist Church in the promotion of various causes through pressure exerted upon the state would probably justify the conclusion that on the whole it enjoyed very able leadership, but such a conclusion would be largely beside the point. Denominational vested interests—good or bad—forced the Church into close working relationships with the state. Whether it was a matter of securing increased financial assistance for the college, or a law prohibiting certain activities on the Sabbath, the effect in the end was much the same. The Church found itself dependent upon the state; it sought, in turn, to secure control over the state. The fact that the state was no longer feudal in character changed in outward form the nature of the relationship which became established. Land lost its importance in securing the economic position of the state church; tax exemptions and government subsidies, however, emphasized the fact that state aid was not wholly abandoned. On the other side, while the Church no longer obtained a voice in the management of the state through direct representation, lobbying and propaganda provided it with even more effective means of exerting its influence.

Such developments were not peculiar to the Wesleyan Methodist Church, but they proceeded much further in the case of this Church than in the case of some of the other churches, for instance, the Baptist. The reason lay largely in the fact that the Wesleyan Methodist leaders were without any strong liberal philosophy which would have led them to resist tendencies towards a greater dependence upon the state. English Wesleyanism inherited the political philosophy of its parent church, while Methodism on the American frontier developed the philosophy of the religious sect which opposed any tie with the state. In Canada, the Methodist movement was torn between these two opposing philosophies. Within the new Methodist Episcopal Church formed in 1832 the spirit of the sect persisted strongly. Within Wesleyan Methodism, liberal principles had a much weaker hold and the Church as a result moved much more quickly over to a position where it was brought into close relationship with the state. In the end, it was forced to compromise principles of religious liberty in face of the increasing urgency of the need to strengthen the supports of denominational organization. Efforts to enforce the religious view upon the outside society, with respect, for instance, to the matter of temperance, led it in one way or another to seek the support of the state. The principle

of separation from the world was abandoned—inevitably in face of the complexities of the new social order—and in its place was accepted the principle of the territorial church. The price paid was loss of evangelical influence to the new Methodist sects.

If records were available, a detailed investigation of the conflicts which took place in the Baptist churches after 1837 would probably reveal that they had much the same sort of basis as that which underlay the conflicts within Methodism. Doctrinal issues were kept to the fore, and the opposition of the Western Baptists to the Canada Baptist Missionary Society was interpreted as one to the open communion views of the Society. Fundamentally, however, the opposition sprang from the underlying conflict between the sect and church forms of religious organization. The revolt of the western Baptists was a revolt against the authority of the Church. It was a movement of local preachers in opposition to the growing claims of a professional ministry. English Baptist leadership had resulted in drawing the denomination into much closer working relationships with the community. The effect was evident in the weakening of the Baptist evangelical appeal, in the growing class consciousness of the movement, and in the closer identification of Baptist interests with political interests and with the interests of empire. Within those churches which broke from the Society, the spirit of the religious sect found expression. Reliance continued to be placed very largely upon the work of local preachers, the appeal remained highly evangelical, and complete separation from worldly interests was emphasized.

The western Baptist churches possessed advantages in extending the teachings of religion into marginal areas of society similar to those possessed by the Methodist Episcopal Church of Canada and by the smaller English Methodist sects. It was a weakness of the general Baptist position that much less support was drawn from the population of the settled areas of the country than in the case of the Methodists. The result was that the schisms within the churches after 1837 were much more disastrous to the cause of Baptist denominationalism than similar schisms were to the cause of Methodist denominationalism. In Montreal and in a few other parts of the country Baptist churches had succeeded in attracting the support of substantial classes of the community, but the overwhelming majority of the Baptist following was located in fringe areas of the country. Efforts thus to bring about a greater denominational accommodation met with stiff resistance, and when compromise proved impossible schism virtually wrecked the denominational organization. The Wesleyan Methodist Church, and the Methodist

college, survived the schisms and divisions which gave rise to a number of new Methodist churches. The Baptist schisms brought about the immediate collapse of the Baptist college and the eventual disintegration of the Canada Baptist Missionary Society and the Canada Baptist Union.

The breakdown of denominationalism secured still greater emphasis in the rise of new sects outside the Methodist and Baptist faiths. These movements grew up even more than the new Methodist and Baptist sects on the social fringes of the community; they represented an extreme form of religious sectarianism, attracting the support of the least socially and emotionally stable of the population. For the most part, they were not backwoods religious movements. They were a product of the social disorganization resulting from rural depopulation and the growth of towns rather than of that resulting from new rural settlement. Their growth thus reflected the emergence of new points of social disturbance in the Canadian community with commercial expansion, the rise of a floating town population, and agricultural depression. It was from among the marginal social elements of the population in the older-settled rural districts and in the towns that these sects gained a substantial part of their following. The Great Revival of the West had come to an end in Canada; the growth of such "queer" sects as the Irvingites, Mormons, and Millerites marked the final end of the great waves of religious revival which had been sweeping over the rural country-side of Central Canada and the Maritime Provinces for a half or three-quarters of a century. After 1860 it was not these parts of the country but the growing city and the expanding western prairies which offered the most fertile field for the promotion of the evangelical religious cause.

CHAPTER SEVEN

Rise of the Territorial Church

1860-1885

T H E rise of the new religious sects in the Maritimes and Canada in the period 1837-60 was indicative of a failure of church leaders to establish sufficiently strong denominational supports of religious organization. Social influences leading to a greater accommodation of religious to secular life were offset by social influences leading to a greater emphasis upon the other worldliness of the religious appeal. The rural frontier continued as an important force in the social life of New Brunswick and Canada West, and conditions of social disturbance were reflected in the disorganization of religious life. In neither the Maritimes nor Canada was religious organization much more stable in 1860 than it had been at the height of the Great Awakening or Great Revival.

The rural frontier did not cease to exist after 1860 but it became a much less important factor in the development of the Maritimes and Central Canada, and the passing of the rural frontier was reflected in the passing of the rural religious sect and the assertion of the dominance of the church idea in religious organization. Influences, largely associated with commercial expansion and the growth of towns, which had led to a strengthening of denominationalism in religious life before 1860, became very much more important after 1860 with the almost complete disappearance of unoccupied agricultural land and with the growth of industrial towns. The sect retreated with the retreat of the frontiersman, and the Canadian territorial church emerged with the emergence of the Canadian political federation. Church union, like political union, emphasized the urgency of problems making necessary a greater institutional consolidation.

The union of the various Presbyterian religious bodies into the one united Presbyterian Church of Canada, and the modifications in organization which led to the formation of the Church of England in Canada, were indicative of the growing strength of Canadian national interests in the leadership of the older traditional churches in the country. Overseas influences weakened as these churches became more closely

identified with the new Canadian Dominion, and, in the case of the Presbyterian Church, divisions which had been inherited from the old world disappeared in face of the demands for a more united effort. Empire gave way to nation as the primary political basis of denominational attachments.

Similar developments were evident within the Methodist and Baptist churches. The end of agricultural expansion, and the emphasis within Canadian national policy upon industrial production for the home market, were closely related to efforts to consolidate and strengthen the denominational organization of the evangelical religious movements. The sect spirit weakened with the growing maturity of community life, and nationalist interests asserted an increasing influence with the coming to an end of expansion into new areas of economic development. The rural sect grew into the town church, and denominationalism became more closely identified with the territorial interests of nation. Out of such developments, there emerged the united Methodist Church of Canada and the Baptist Conventions of the Maritimes and Central Canada.

In the case of Methodism, particularly, developments leading to church union and to a closer identification with the community proceeded rapidly after 1860. The Wesleyan Methodist Church took the lead, but the smaller Methodist churches were increasingly subjected to social influences which forced them into line with the parent body. Beginning as movements of protest against the emphasis upon denominationalism within the Wesleyan Methodist Church, these separatist Methodist groups became themselves increasingly denominationally conscious. Changes in the Canadian community structure after 1860 made impossible adherence to the principles of the other-worldly religious sect.

These changes first made their effects felt within the rural society which had constituted the most important area of sectarian activity. In many of the country districts of the Maritimes and Central Canada a declining population after 1860 imposed strains upon religious organization which made necessary radical adjustments in Methodist techniques and appeal. The difficulties faced by the Primitive Methodists were indicative of the effects of rural population changes upon the development of a religious movement which lacked strong denominational supports in the secular community. The Primitive Methodists were largely localized in terms of their following and influence; churches became organized only in those areas where a number of adherents had settled. With no strong central organization, the Primitive Methodist churches were not in a position to follow up members when they moved

from one part of the country to another. The result was that in areas of declining population the cause weakened while in areas of increasing population there were no compensating gains; the highly organized denominations enjoyed an advantage in attracting the support of people who had moved to the larger centres of population. "Removals to other parts of the province," the Reverend Edward Barrass wrote respecting the Church's work in 1854, "had been so vast that we could not report much progress. Stations on the frontiers in Canada are subject to great losses, by reason of people removing to the west and north, as soon as they are in circumstances to take up land for themselves. . . . Scores and hundreds of members have been lost to our community, and have cast in their lot with others, while not a few have been lost to the Church of Christ altogether."[1] In April, 1855, the Primitive Methodist preacher in Brampton wrote: "The chief obstacles to our Connexional prosperity are the migratory habits of the people, and lack of preachers. Many societies are reduced, and often broken up through removals."[2] The editor of the *Primitive Methodist Magazine* gave expression to the same view: "At present," he wrote, "the work is suffering for want of more men, and our members are removing by scores, into townships where we have no societies, and we are without the means of reaching them."[3] The problem of a declining rural population became steadily greater during the two decades after 1860; few rural communities in any of the Canadian provinces escaped the effects of the drift of the population to the United States or, to a lesser extent, into the larger industrial towns and cities. Churches, as a result, built in small country towns became only partly filled with worshippers, and overhead costs bore increasingly heavily upon remaining members. "The past six months," the Primitive Methodist preacher in Brantford wrote in 1873, "have brought reverses and trial; family after family left the town, taking away teachers from our school, scholars from our classes, and members from the society, and all of them have gone beyond the reach of the P.M. Church, while we have not received a single member from any other station or from abroad since we came here."[4]

The changing rural population structure led to adjustments within the Methodist evangelical churches which resulted in the end in the loss of what had been the most distinctive attributes of Methodism. In 1873 the Primitive Methodist Conference, by legislative action,

---

[1]*Primitive Methodist Magazine*, Feb., 1854.
[2]*Ibid.*, July, 1855.
[3]*Ibid.*, May, 1855; see, also, Mrs. R. P. Hopper, *Old-Time Primitive Methodism in Canada* (Toronto, 1904), pp. 93-4.
[4]*Christian Journal*, Jan. 31, 1873.

virtually did away with the itinerant system within the church and the system of conference appointments. The period of the minister's stay on one station was extended from three to five years although he was left free to move before the expiration of that period. At the same time, the ministerial invitation system was adopted and the Conference agreed not to interfere with appointments unless there were pressing reasons for so doing.[5] Changes of a similar character were gradually introduced by the other Methodist churches. The disappearance of the frontier, or rather the retreat of the frontier out of the reach of churches situated in central or eastern Canada, made obsolete methods which had been developed to serve communities with a rapidly growing population. On the other hand, a declining population emphasized the importance of strengthening the local congregational organization.

Emphasis in the rural church shifted to consolidation; to the elaboration of techniques for the preservation of what support the church still enjoyed. Union, in the end, was forced upon Methodism to assure the preservation of such support.

In the towns, as well, the changing ecological basis of community organization forced adjustments in religious life. Here, the growth of wealth, and the development of residential districts, emphasized the need for properly appointed and permanent places of worship. Reliance upon private homes—or barns or open fields—as centres of worship became increasingly less satisfactory as population became more concentrated. Very early, the Methodists had undertaken to erect meeting houses or chapels, but these crudely constructed places of worship soon proved unsuitable in the larger towns and cities. The growing demand for large church edifices raised new problems of finance within the church. Dependence had been placed upon co-operative labour and local materials but this was not possible in the construction of buildings costing thousands of dollars. Union of the Canadian and English Conferences strengthened the financial basis of the Wesleyan Methodist Church and made possible the support of a programme of church building, but difficulties were faced by the smaller Methodist churches. Depending upon the support of the less wealthy of the Methodist following, and with a membership severely limited through competition between Methodist groups, these churches found themselves increasingly in a weakened position in the larger centres of population. "Though some good has been effected," the editor of the journal of the Methodist New Connexion wrote of Montreal in 1845, "yet much more, we doubt not, would have been

[5]*Ibid.*, Aug. 15, 1873.

accomplished, had our body possessed a suitable place of worship. Numbers during the last four years have left the Society and gone to other churches solely on the ground of our not having a chapel and their not having the permanent prospect of a home amongst us."[6] In the same year the editor of the journal of the Methodist Episcopal Church wrote:

> No doubt our readers will have observed that where comfortable houses of worship have been erected, for the accommodation and comfort of those who desire to hear the glad tidings of salvation by our ministry, the congregations are large, respectable and *permanent*. On the other hand, where we have no places of worship, or those which are inferior, and uncomfortable, our hearers have generally dwindled down, to be few more than the society, and consequently, we have not the same opportunity for being useful. The building of Churches gives permanency to the cause. This is particularly the case in towns and villages.[7]

The problem of securing proper church accommodation in the city became a major theme of religious editors during the third quarter of the century. The problem was felt particularly keenly by the Primitive Methodists who depended largely upon the support of the poorer elements of the population. Competition with other religious groups forced them to shift from street preaching to the holding of services in attractive houses of worship. "There are difficulties to contend with in this town," a correspondent wrote in the Primitive Methodist journal from Stratford in 1875. "Large churches and finer buildings have attractions we cannot present to the public."[8] In the large cities, such difficulties were even greater. A Primitive Methodist preacher wrote from Montreal in 1875: "*And now for the Church. . . . We must* have one, and a good one, too, by some means. Fashion is everything in Montreal, and all seems to be drawn into its giddy stream. All other denominations have splendid churches, and the multitues flock to them. The Hall we have, though comfortable, is far below par. On this account the people beat shy of it. Even those who were formerly Primitive Methodists look askance upon it."[9]

Later in the year the attention of readers of the Primitive Methodist journal was again called to the problem of church building in Montreal. A correspondent wrote: "Our greatest need is a church. . . . Popery has her gorgeously decorated temples, looking proudly down upon us from every quarter, while among Protestants there is a tremendous competition as to who shall rival her. Talk as we will about God meeting

[6]*Christian Messenger*, Sept., 1845.
[7]*Canada Christian Advocate*, Jan. 23, 1845.
[8]*Christian Journal*, May 14, 1875.
[9]*Ibid.*, Jan. 1, 1875.

us in the humble cot, let it be borne in mind that the difficulty in these days is to get people there to meet with Him."[10]

The need for new church buildings was a reflection of the growing population of the larger towns and of growing wealth. It was also a reflection of the shift of well-to-do elements of the urban population to better residential districts. The problem of the down-town church emerged with the expansion of the business district, and competition between the churches increased the urgency of abandoning places of worship in areas becoming socially undesirable, and building in areas where people of wealth and social standing were situated. A Primitive Methodist preacher wrote from Brantford in 1873:

> If we are ever to have a self-sustaining society in Brantford we must have a new church in a better part of the town. Our present building is too small and too uninviting for a rising place like this . . . . Situated as we are on one side of the town, with a gambling den on one side of us and a whiskey shop on the other, we must be a burden [upon the Missionary Committee] as in the past. We have the will to build, but we lack the means; and yet we cannot stay where we are if the Primitive Methodist Church is to become a power for good.[11]

Increasing overhead costs in church building intensified the financial problem of the smaller Methodist churches and led them to search for a solution through church union. "In my opinion," a correspondent wrote in the Primitive Methodist journal in 1873, "a union of all the Methodist bodies means larger colleges, a better educated ministry, larger churches, shorter journies for the preachers, larger journies for the people, more power and more pay for the clergy."[12] The growing debt of the Methodist churches became a particularly heavy burden as the economic depression of the eighteen-seventies extended into the eighteen-eighties. The business man gained in influence within the councils of the church, and demands for further financial assistance led to growing support of the union cause. Union in effect was the price which had to be paid to secure the expansion of credit necessary to meet the heavy carrying charges resulting from debts through church building. The dominant drive within Methodism after about 1870 was that of strengthening its competitive position in the growing cities. This meant bigger and better churches, and bigger and better churches meant in the end church union. The success ultimately achieved in the field of church building was indicative of the gains secured through the consolidation of church finances. The editor of the *Methodist Magazine* wrote in 1889:

[10]*Ibid.*, Aug. 6, 1875.
[11]*Ibid.*, Jan. 31, 1873.
[12]*Ibid.*, May 2, 1873.

The growth of Methodism in the great cities is a very important factor in its general prosperity. The cities are centres of influence and power. They are in large degree the strategic points in the country. The religious denomination which most largely holds the cities will largely hold the country . . . .

Few cities in the world compare with Toronto, Hamilton, London, Kingston, Ottawa, Montreal, St. John and Halifax, for the number and excellence and religious earnestness of its Methodist Churches. Montreal now possesses the noblest Methodist Church in the world. In Toronto the growth of Methodism has more than kept pace with the phenomenal growth of the city. The new Sherbourne Street Church, McCaul Street, Carlton Street, Bathurst Street, Dundas Street, St. Paul's, Trinity, and Spadina Avenue, Churches, all recently enlarged or opened or now approaching completion, and others already projected, are evidences of great material prosperity.[13]

The changing ecological pattern of the Canadian community weakened the rural basis in the organization of Methodism and led to the union of the various Methodist churches and to the reliance upon a settled professional ministry and permanent place of religious worship, strategically situated in the better residential areas of the city. The church structure symbolized the much closer metropolitan ties of the Methodist denomination. The effects were evident in the gradual disappearance of methods of organization and techniques of appeal which had been developed to meet the religious needs of a rural frontier population.

The decline of lay preaching and of the camp meeting was symptomatic of demands placed upon religious organization in serving the new urban society. Methodism had grown up through the work of the lay preacher and the influence exerted by the camp meeting and both of these agencies of religious propagation had proved highly effective in the rural frontier society; as the Wesleyan Methodist Church came to rely upon them less, they were employed with good effect by the smaller Methodist churches. With the increasing emphasis upon securing the support of the urban population, the lay preacher and the camp meeting came to have a much more limited usefulness, to the smaller Methodist churches as well as to the larger body.

The position of the lay preacher in particular was weakened after 1860. In an editorial on the decline of lay preaching, the Primitive Methodist journal pointed out that the number of Primitive Methodist local preachers in the country was steadily declining while the number of regular preachers was increasing. "With our rapidly increasing population," he wrote, "and the extensive worldlymindedness and irreligion prevailing, is it not necessary that this worthy class of laborers should be kept up? Are not the Young Men's Christian Associations of to-day, in holding open air and other evangelistic meetings, doing a work which has been neglected by the Churches, but which more

[13] *Methodist Magazine*, vol. XXIX, Jan. to June, 1889 (Toronto and Halifax), p. 472.

properly belongs to them, especially to the Methodist Churches."[14] The increasing importance of the city pulpit in the work of the Church led to neglect of the sort of work for which local preachers were particularly suited. The editor of the *Christian Guardian* in 1885 set forward very clearly the reasons for the decline of lay preaching:

The sphere of local preachers has been steadily becoming more limited; and in most cities and towns this branch of our working force is gradually dying out. Our local preachers there are generally the product of other places . . . .

There have been, in cities and towns, changes in the shape of the work and a development of the pastorate that have been steadily closing up the openings for local preacher's work—that is as regulars and stated pulpit supplies. When every congregation in a city is thoroughly supplied with ministers specially chosen for assumed adaptation to these positions, there is really no preaching work left for local preachers, except as an occasional supply . . . . As long as other churches are supplied with the ablest preachers that can be secured, it is not reasonable to suppose that men with less educational advantages, who would have only brief snatches of time taken from daily work, to prepare for the pulpit, could successfully compete at such great disadvantages with more thoroughly trained men, and keep up the interest essential to success.[15]

More significant, as indicating an increasing shift from a rural to an urban appeal, was the decline of the old-time camp meeting. The smaller Methodist churches had been more successful than the Wesleyan Methodist Church in keeping alive this form of religious meeting, but, by the eighteen-seventies, even these churches could boast of few successful camp meetings. The editor of the *Primitive Methodist* journal wrote in 1872: "Are we as a community doing our duty in the matter of open air worship? For some reason or other processions and open air preaching are fallen very sadly into disuse. . . . So far as we remember, there was but one regular Primitive Methodist camp-meeting last year in our work in this Dominion. . . . There is one central camp-meeting announced for the Toronto District this year. We have heard of no other."[16]

The Methodist camp meeting disappeared as an institution of the rural backwoods and developed as an urban religious gathering closely associated with the growing tourist trade. Summer resorts were chosen as centres for the holding of such meetings, and religious worship was brought into close relationship to the recreational needs of urban inhabitants. Grimsby park became one of the chief centres for the holding of camp meetings. The *Canadian Methodist Magazine* reported in 1877: "These 'feasts of tabernacles' have been numerous this season.

[14]*Christian Journal*, Feb. 19, 1875.
[15]*Christian Guardian*, July 8, 1885.
[16]*Christian Journal*, July 26, 1872.

Grimsby grounds were well utilized, not merely for a camp-meeting, but also conventions were held for local preachers, class leaders, and Sunday-school teachers. Some sessions were also devoted to the advocacy of temperance. Excursions from Toronto, Hamilton, and other places were matters of daily occurrence so that the population often amounted to thousands."[17] Two years later, the *Canadian Methodist Magazine* again reported: "The camp-meeting season has been greatly enjoyed by many of our people. A few of them were real old-fashioned 'feasts of tabernacles.' Some of our Indian missions have been favoured with these peculiar services. Grimsby and Thousand Island Park have been visited by such as could spare the time and means to enable them to enjoy a few days sojourn in those healthy retreats."[18]

In Nova Scotia, where the old-time camp meeting had never developed, the "tourist meeting" made its appearance. "Our friends in the east," the *Canadian Methodist Magazine* reported in 1876, "are becoming more interested in camp-meetings. Associations are being formed with a view to secure sites, and erect suitable buildings."[19] In 1887 the same magazine reported: "The Methodists in Nova Scotia have for several years held a camp-meeting at Berwick."[20]

Reliance upon the attendance of urban tourists created new problems of order in the carrying on of camp meetings. "Some are afraid," the *Canadian Methodist Magazine* admitted in 1877, "that the camp-meeting grounds may become places of mere summer resort rather than of religious gatherings. The crowds at Chautauqua and the Thousand Island Park have far exceeded former years, which necessarily increases the responsibility of those in charge of the meetings; for, while it is right to secure pecuniary returns for investments made, it is of more importance that the meetings should give an impetus to Church work."[21] When reporting, two years later, upon the success of the new type of camp meeting, the magazine found it necessary to turn again to the charge made against it. "Complaints are freely made," the concluding section of the item on camp meetings read, "that those summer resorts tend greatly to promote Sabbath desecration, but, we are glad to learn, that Chautauqua, Cazenovia, Round Lake, Ocean Grove, and the above mentioned places, closed their gates against Sabbath excursionists. Camp-meetings cannot be pronounced a universal good where they lead to Sabbath desecration."[22] Inevitably, the close association of the

[17]*Canadian Methodist Magazine*, vol. VI, Sept. to Dec., 1877, pp. 381-2.
[18]*Ibid.*, vol. X, July to Dec., 1879, pp. 382-3.
[19]*Ibid.*, vol. IV, July to Dec., 1876, p. 473.
[20]*Ibid.*, vol. XXVI, July to Dec., 1887, p. 285.
[21]*Ibid.*, vol. VI, Sept. to Dec., 1877, p. 382.
[22]*Ibid.*, vol. X, July to Dec. 1879, p. 383.

camp meeting with the tourist trade led to its increasing secularization. However vigorous the efforts may have been to keep the religious to the fore front, the natural attractions of the summer resort were such as to weaken any strong religious interest. The excitement which the old-time camp meeting had relied upon could hardly be aroused among a population enjoying boating, fishing, swimming, and other forms of recreation at the lakeside. The profane inevitably intruded upon the sacred.

This was of less significance than the shift in the class appeal of the camp meeting. The summer resort attracted an urban rather than a rural population, and the location of camp meetings in such resorts meant that they ceased thereby to serve the rural population, particularly the rural population of the backwoods. On the other hand, they did not come to serve the new working masses of the urban community; the poor worker and his family spent little time at summer resorts, even if excursion rates were offered by the railroads. The summer resort attracted members of the middle class, the urban *bourgeoisie*, and, as a result, the camp meeting became increasingly an urban middle class institution. As such, it assumed a radically different character. Emphasis shifted from crude revivalist methods to the delivery of carefully prepared sermons; it was the "big men" in the church who were invited to address the camp meeting; the local exhorter or self-appointed evangelist was seldom given a place upon the programme.

The declining importance of lay preaching and the camp meeting reflected underlying changes in the character of the Methodist religious appeal. Revivalist methods were gradually abandoned, first in the larger urban churches and later in the smaller churches in towns and in the country. More popular sermons, or sermons displaying a greater familiarity with broad questions of social or academic interest, crowded out the simple sermon with its emphasis upon the problem of religious salvation. The *Committee on the State of the Church* reported to the Methodist Conference in 1878: "The questions force themselves upon our attention,—Is there the requisite degree of consecration to God and His service among our ministry? Has it not sometimes been difficult to find readily, suitable volunteers for our more remote and trying fields of labour? While our ministry is increasing in culture and acceptability to the refined, is it quite as powerful as of old in the awakening and conversion of the outcast and degraded?"[23]

Revivalism became increasingly something which was turned to on particular occasions or in seasons convenient for the holding of

[23]*Journal of Proceedings of the Second General Conference of the Methodist Church of Canada, 1878* (Toronto, 1878), p. 290.

revival meetings. It ceased as the dominant method of Methodism in all places and at all times. The obsolescence of revivalist techniques was almost as evident within the smaller Methodist churches as within the Wesleyan Methodist Church. The editor of the *Primitive Methodist* journal wrote in 1872: "Can any one given a good reason why, as soon as winter leaves us, revival efforts cease? Somehow or other, revivals have come to be associated with frost and snow. . . . Is it the will of God that souls should be saved only in winter? . . . In the winter, we usually work and believe for revivalistic blessings. The same blessings would be given all the year round if we worked and believed for them. Is it not, therefore, because we are not using the right means that we do not see sinners saved at seasons other than winter?"[24]

Social pressures, outside and within the Church, forced the change in the character of the Methodist appeal which involved the gradual abandonment of revivalist techniques. Commercial and industrial expansion, the growth of cities, the spread of education, and the improvement of means of communication with the outside world led to a deterioration among the population generally of evangelical religious values and to a strengthening of worldly attitudes and outlook. Secularism constituted a direct threat to the position of the more evangelical churches in the community. The Conference of the Wesleyan Methodist Church addressed its members in 1852:

In these days this cause [of God] has to contend, not only against the various forms of wickedness in the world, and the opinions by which nominal Christians make void the word of God, but also against systems of superficial philosophy, by which half enlightened men seek to substitute the partial views of perverted reason for the blessed truths of the Gospel. Satan, who has hitherto held the ungodly in a state of heedless slumber, now that they are awakened by the alarms and calls of God's word, presents himself to them as an angel of light, and seeks to enlist them in his active service. The unconverted in many places are no longer careless respecting the cause of God, but by various forms of error are striving to pervert its principles, or to destroy its influence.[25]

Four years later, the Conference of the Wesleyan Methodist Church returned to the problem presented by the growth of attitudes of hostility to religion. Part of its address read:

Never was the path of the ungodly more beset with snares. Never was the selfishness of some men more facilitated to its devices than now. And the construction of great works, and advance in prices, create a buoyancy in the Colonial mind unfavourable to religious prudence and steadiness. The influx. and cheap dissemination of pernicious literature are prolific of error and vanity. The popular cry for advance

[24]*Christian Journal*, Apr. 8, 1872.
[25]*The Minutes of the Annual Conferences of the Wesleyan Methodist Church in Canada, 1846 to 1857* (Toronto, 1863), pp. 203-4.

is productive of a state of thought and feeling which, unless vigilantly guarded, are opposed to a steady approval of things tried, safe, and necessary.[26]

Values associated with the pecuniary, material culture and based upon the precepts of science and philosophy rather than upon the dogmas of religion gained in strength during the last half of the century and provided an increasing threat to the naive evangelical teachings of Methodism. "The ambition to acquire wealth," the Toronto Annual Conference of the Methodist Church of Canada addressed its members in 1882, "has become all-absorbing, and pervades all classes of society. . . . The spirit of reckless speculation has kindled the fires of an unrestrained avarice, which devours and destroys the spirit of simple piety, and issues in utter shipwreck of faith and of a good conscience."[27] In the same year the London Annual Conference found fit to address its members in even stronger terms:

> There is much in the tendencies of our times that is hostile to spiritual religion, against which it is our duty to guard you. There is a headstrong and infatuated desire for wealth, a daring spirit of business speculation, and an inordinate disposition to self-pleasing. The progress of the country in wealth, and the facilities afforded for obtaining individual gratification and enjoyment have their peril. Indulgences in worldly pleasure, fondness of dress and outward adorning, gender indolence, sloth, luxury, inordinate earthly affection in all its forms, destroy all spiritual sympathies and aspirations, and are fatal to a life of faith in Christ.[28]

To some extent, Methodism could protect its following from the influence of the more dangerous currents of social thought, but to an increasing extent it was forced to accommodate its own teachings to these currents. Methodists engaged in business or entered the professions, acquired wealth and turned to the enjoyment of comforts and luxuries. One prominent Methodist sent his daughter to a private dancing school! Asceticism, which had proved an important influence in paving the way to success, lost its hold once success had been achieved. The successful Methodist ceased to conform in terms of the simple principles and practices of the religious sect, and it was the successful Methodist who dominated the outlook of the Church as a whole. The Methodist body became a worldly body as worldliness permeated the thinking of leaders and followers alike. Few Methodists were prepared to pay the price of appearing conspicuous in the eyes of their fellowmen; conspicuousness was something, on the other hand

[26]*Ibid.*, p. 370.

[27]*Minutes of the Proceedings of the Toronto Annual Conference of the Methodist Church of Canada, 1882* (Toronto, 1882), p. 160.

[28]*Journal of the Proceedings of the London Annual Conference of the Methodist Church of Canada, 1882* (Toronto, 1882), p. 188.

which the sectarian had deliberately sought. "One great hindrance," the Primitive Methodist Church addressed its members in 1875, "to spirituality today is conformity to the world. Dress like the world; talk like the world; dissemble like the world; mix with the world; dance with the world; play with the world; join with the world in foolish amusements; go to the theatre and opera with the world; marry with the world; and the great majority of professors who do thus are in great danger of finally going to hell with the world."[29] The chief evidence of such conformity to the world, the church leaders pointed out, was the failure of Primitive Methodists to faithfully attend class meetings. Spokesmen of the Methodist Church of Canada had much the same thing to say. "Is there not occasional evidence," a committee of the Church reported in 1878, "of a growing spirit of worldliness and enervating self-indulgence among our people?—an undue conformity to the world, in tastes and sympathies, in forms of recreation, and modes of business?" Hence, the Committee went on to say, "the means of grace more especially calculated to encourage inward scrutiny and sympathy, such as the class and prayer-meetings, are either neglected altogether, or relegated to a secondary place."[30] In 1884 the editor of the *Christian Guardian* wrote: "The increase in wealth and social position of many of our people, though something that may be a means of greater influence, may also become a snare, producing a worldly spirit. We have known some instances, in which Methodists who had increased in wealth caught the spirit and adopted the practices of worldly and irreligious persons, whom they met in the relations of social life, and gradually sank to their level, till they finally withdrew from the Methodist Church, to find greater freedom from religious restraint somewhere else."[31]

The weakening of the hold of asceticism reflected changes in the educational and social standing of Methodists. The conflict between religion and science became one of the main pre-occupations of people of philosophical interest during the last half of the nineteenth century, and neither the class-room of Victoria University nor the pulpit of the Methodist Church could entirely escape concern with this problem. Modernism crept into the religious teachings of Methodism; science and biblical criticism forced upon thinking Methodists a more rational interpretation of the gospel message. The almost exclusive reliance upon

[29]*Christian Journal*, Aug. 20, 1875.
[30]*Journal of Proceedings of the Second General Conference of the Methodist Church of Canada, 1878*, p. 291.
[31]*Christian Guardian*, July 9, 1884.

a university educated ministry meant that the pulpit took a lead in weakening the foundations of religious fundamentalism. Though probably the majority of the members of the Church clung to the simple faith of their fore-fathers, it became increasingly difficult to find ministers who shared such a faith. The Methodist religious appeal gave expression more and more to the views of the man of education even though he remained one of a minority within the Church; competition of the Church with secular agencies emphasized the advantages of education in leadership. That was evident, for instance, in the changing character of the religious press, faced with the growing competition of the city daily and the weekly and monthly periodical. Emphasis here as in the pulpit shifted away from a purely religious message, and the appeal was made more to the literary, philosophical, and political interests of the readers.

Such developments, of course, proceeded much more rapidly within the Wesleyan Methodist than within the smaller Methodist churches, but they became increasingly characteristic of the Methodist body as a whole. Methodism, whatever branch it represented, became more and more the church of the well-to-do and successful. That is not to say that all of its members were rich or even in comfortable circumstances, but those upon whom the Church came increasingly to depend for support were people of wealth and social standing. Church building, the maintenance of colleges, and missionary work required large financial contributions, and the Church's dependence upon those who were able to freely contribute led to an increasing effort to establish claims to respectability. The Methodist city church emerged as a church of fashion, and seating arrangements, and the locations of church buildings in the community, as well as the character of the service reflected the growing class consciousness of church leadership. As early as 1873 a correspondent in the Primitive Methodist journal felt called upon to give voice to the feeling that the Church was no longer a church of the poor but had become a church of the rich:

The poor to whom the Gospel is to be preached are crowded back against the walls, beneath the galleries, under the rafters, out into the vestibule and into the street . . . . This whole theory of fashionable worship is unchristianlike, unmanlike, discourteous, even cruel to the stranger and outcast.

The times demand a Sabbath service that has something better to show than rhetoric, cadence, kid gloves, chignon and cologne . . . . We are too fastidious, too careful. Our churches and ourselves are too elegant and delicate. There is too much niceness all around. Let the soft velvet of church aisle carpets be worn threadbare by the tread of rough men's feet; let the varnish of pews and altars be made dim by the pressure of the common crowds . . . .

Trouble arises from the fact that the Gospel is surrounded by the large contributions of the pew rather than by the small contributions of the many. Here is where caste crowds itself into the church.[32]

With the increase in the number of the rich and fashionable in the Church, institutional segregation along class lines became characteristic of Methodism. Where one church building served the whole community, segregation was secured through the seating arrangement; in the more populous urban communities, churches serving well-to-do residential areas became sharply set off from churches serving working-class or transitional areas. The effect was to make the Church more socially inclusive—a place was provided in the institutional framework for the rich and the poor—but in becoming more socially inclusive the Church lost the social cohesiveness which was characteristic of the sect. It was no longer the poor man's church, the church which gave him a feeling of distinctiveness; a feeling, that is to say of belonging to something distinctively his own. In becoming a church of the community, Methodism ceased to be a church of the social masses.

The change was strikingly evident in the relationship of the Methodist body to politics. The break from the position of the religious sect had led by 1836 to the active participation in politics of those Methodists belonging to the Wesleyan Methodist Church, and, although large sections of the membership body did not fall in line, considerable success was achieved in securing united action in the elections of 1836 and 1844. By 1880, in contrast, the Methodists were in no sense a united political body. Although deplored by many, such a development was inevitable in view of the wide differences in the economic and social standing of the various members of the Church. The Church was forced to become non-political, with respect to controversial party issues, if it was to avoid the danger of antagonizing large sections of its membership body. W. J. Robertson wrote of the change which had taken place:

A full explanation could not be given of the political influence of Methodists without taking into consideration the attitude the majority of the body took during a critical period in our Canadian struggle for responsible government . . . .

Without wishing to be understood as endorsing this serious charge, we cannot but admit that the action of Egerton Ryerson on two important occasions, influenced the Methodists largely, and led to a temporary triumph of the party opposed to responsible government. Rightly or wrongly, we gained the unenviable reputation of being the satellites of a Methodist dictation, who used us to serve his own purposes; although, to the writer's own knowledge, there were staunch Methodists who were in bitter hostility to Dr. Ryerson for his efforts on behalf of Sir Charles Metcalfe.

---

[32]*Christian Journal*, Feb. 14, 1873.

That day of subserviency to a Methodist Pope has gone forever. No man now in the Methodist body can dictate or mould her politics. Methodists are divided in their politics, the same as other denominations.[33]

The weakening of the denominational influence of Methodism in politics, however, was accompanied by the strengthening of the political influence of the Methodist ministers in the large city pulpits. Here the appeal was not to the whole Methodist membership body but to particular classes which found representation in these particular churches. The city pulpit served as something of a public platform. The remarks of the prominent minister were reported in the daily newspaper, and his influence extended beyond that of the congregation he served. In pronouncing upon matters of politics, he enjoyed a strong moral position. People who did not attend his church—often did not attend regularly any church—were influenced by his views because, in their judgment, he was a "good" man. The result was that urban ministers were likely to be drawn into the field of politics; issues such as prohibition provided a justification for the advocacy of certain lines of political action. Of such participation in the Ontario provincial election of 1886, a "layman" felt called upon to write to the *Christian Guardian*:

If you will allow me as an humble layman of the Methodist Church, I wish to enter a strong protest against the course of those of our Ministers who have taken a prominent part in the recent election contest in Ontario. If those of one political stripe do this, those of the other political stripe will be sure to follow their example. It seems to me that our clergy have shown great wisdom for a good many years past in keeping aloof from political contests, and if they now are going to become active politicians, it can only have the effect of ultimately producing division among our people, and of weakening all our denominational interests. I have heard politicians of both sides agree that it was unwise for our ministers, especially those in prominent positions in our Church, to enter into the bitter strife of politics on either side.[34]

With a great deal more invective, the *Dominion Churchman* wrote of the part played by Methodist ministers in the Toronto municipal election of 1888:

The Methodist ministers in Toronto gave up preaching what they call "the Gospel" to go into political stumping in their pulpits. They determined to decide who should be mayor of Toronto. They poured abuse most malignantly slanderous on all who preferred another candidate; they sought to frighten any such citizen into obedience to their commands by fixing upon him a foul stigma, by attempting to destroy his character. No Romish priest ever sought by fouler means to bull doze his flock than those used by the Methodist ministers in Toronto to drive their sheep and all citizens who were cowards into slavish subservience to their mandate. One preacher wound up a sermon by imploring the audience to "believe on the Lord Jesus Christ

[33]*Christian Guardian*, May 27, 1885.
[34]*Ibid.*, Jan. 5, 1887.

and vote for ————!" One injunction being equal in obligation to the other! Sunday after Sunday this profanation of the Sabbath has gone on; persons by name who differ with these Papistical-minded persons have been slandered in their pulpits. Even one of our clergy was weak and foolish enough to catch this municipal politics fever; but they and the Presbyterians and some others did not so desecrate their pulpits nor insult their flocks. What is the result? The candidate favored by Methodists got 7,050 votes against 10,076 recorded against him. The by-laws for restraining the liquor traffic were thrown out; Mr. Howland's two years' rule was condemned at every point by enormous majorities. Thus that extreme, violent, rash policy, so favored by the intemperate temperance party, has helped to discredit and to very seriously hamper and damage the cause of moral reformation, by identifying it with "Methodist priestcraft" and a policy of slander and falsehood.[35]

Influences which led to a broadening of the appeal from the urban church pulpit inevitably led to the discussion from the pulpit of questions of politics. The pulpit became less a religious rostrum and more of a rostrum for the expression of the economic, social, and political views of the particular minister. The effect was to vastly increase the social standing, influence, and prestige of the minister within the community at large. Methodism, as it became more a church of prominent ministers, struck roots much deeper in the Canadian society. The minister built up a public following, but it was a following no longer confined to a body of peculiar folk known as Methodists. Sectarian lines weakened with the development of channels of communication through the city pulpit.

The union of the various Methodist churches in 1884 was a culmination of developments which had set in in 1832 and had continued throughout the fifty-year period before union. After 1860, developments leading in the direction of closer identification with the Canadian community became particularly strong. The disappearance of free agricultural land, and the growth of manufacturing, forced Methodism into much closer alignment with nationalist interests. Separatist forces springing out of the frontier social situation weakened as the frontier assumed increasingly less importance in the Canadian society, and metropolitanism became a more dominant force in economic, political, and religious organization alike. Union of the Methodist churches took place five years after the adoption of the National Policy of tariff protection and one year before the completion of the Canadian Pacific Railway. Interests which dominated in pushing through the National Policy dominated in pushing through church union. From a narrow economic point of view, union greatly strengthened the credit position of the Methodist Church which enabled it to meet the financial demands of expansion during the next quarter century. From a more general point of view, the Church through union seized all the advantages of a

[35]Quoted *ibid.*, Feb. 8, 1888.

closer alignment with the new powerful forces of nationalism and industrial capitalism. The period almost immediately after 1885 witnessed the rapid development of the Canadian community through the expansion of industrial manufacturing and the opening up of the west. The new Methodist Church of Canada developed in close relationship to the new Canadian nation.

In adjusting to the conditions of an urban-industrial society, the Baptist Church had much farther to go than the Methodist Church and its adjustment by 1885 as a result was much less complete. In Canada, the break between the Regular and Open Communion Baptists, and the organization of the Regular Baptist Union, emphasized the close rural ties of the Baptist churches. The vast majority of Regular Baptists were rural people. Few Baptist preachers were without close contact with the rural community. By virtue of the fact that the Baptist principle of church autonomy weakened denominational organization, the Baptist ministers located in the larger cities, in contrast with the urban Methodist ministers, enjoyed little more prestige than their fellow-preachers in the country and consequently they were not able to exert a dominant influence in determining the general outlook and appeal of the Baptist churches. The rural churches, vastly in the majority, maintained a stubborn independence in resisting any lead from the urban churches. The weakness of home missionary organizations and of Baptist educational institutions reflected the strength of the rural influence and of the principle of church autonomy.

Within the Baptist Church, as a result, the spirit of the evangelistic sect remained strong long after 1860. A large proportion of the Baptist membership continued for some time to be drawn from the more isolated of the rural population, most of the preachers remained men of little education, and the form of local church government fostered a social exclusiveness which served to support attitudes of religious sectarianism. Accounts of church revivals appearing in the *Canadian Baptist* provide evidence of the importance attached to the Church's task of evangelization. The methods employed revealed little that was new in organization and appeal—the Baptists continued to avoid the exhibitionist tactics which had earlier been employed by the Methodists—but the increasing strengthening of the preaching staff made possible more intensive evangelistic work, and through such work the Baptist Church remained an important social reorganizing influence in the backwoods farm settlements of New Brunswick and Central Canada. The local church served as an effective focus of community life; religion was kept to the forefront as a dominant interest of individual and collective effort. In a way unequalled perhaps by any other denomination, the Baptist

Church aroused feelings of group loyalty which resulted in the emergence of a distinctive group character.

Yet, however close its ties with the rural community had been, the Baptist Church could not escape the influence of developments after 1860 which emphasized the importance of new economic, political, and cultural forces in the Canadian society. The increasing mobility of urban life, and the steady depopulation of rural areas, imposed demands upon the Church which could not be met so long as the attitude of the Baptist was the attitude of the sectarian. The new Canadian society was an expensive society in which to operate, and growing financial obligations called for more effective means of encouraging contributions. At the same time, population mobility made necessary a greater centralization of effort than that which had been acceptable within the Baptist denomination. The ecclesiastical and financial autonomy of the local churches proved a serious obstacle to successful adjustment to the conditions of an urban-capitalist society.

The first challenge to the principle of local church autonomy came out of the necessity of developing home missions. Traditionally, the missionary idea was opposed to Baptist ecclesiastical policy—local congregations were expected to provide and exercise complete control over their own preachers—and the conflict between the missionary interest and the interest of local church autonomy emerged as one of the crucial issues in Baptist denominational development, in the United States as well as in Canada. Opposition to missionary efforts was reflected in the unwillingness of Baptists to contribute to missionary funds. "This morning," William Davies wrote of the church in Toronto, May 6, 1855, "we had a collection for the Home Mission to the Back Settlements and I was astonished at the meanness of the people. We sit at the Bottom of the Chapel & when the Plate reach'd us there was not a ¼ in it, mostly coppers."[36] Constant complaints in the columns of the *Canadian Baptist* of the illiberality of church members in supporting home missions suggest that Davies's experience of the meanness of the people was in no way exceptional.[37] The Baptist did not like giving money to the Church and he disliked even more giving money to an outside religious body such as a missionary society; the latter in particular assumed in his eyes the character of ecclesiastical taxation. Reluctance to make financial contributions in support of

---

[36] *Letters of William Davies, Toronto, 1854-1861.* Edited with introduction and notes by William Sherwood Fox (Toronto, 1945), p. 43.
[37] "We recently saw a tabular statement made by a Presbyterian minister," the editor of the *Canadian Baptist* wrote in 1873, "in which he represents the Baptists as the lowest but one of all the denominations in Canada in their support of Home Missions." *Canadian Baptist*, May 22, 1873.

home missions thus was an expression of deeply rooted prejudices against any sort of centralized denominational authority.

Growing financial support of missionary activities after 1860 was indicative of the weakening of Baptist sectarian attitudes and of the increasing influence within the denomination of people with money. In the end, the strengthening of the missionary interest led to fundamental changes in Baptist polity and organization. The missionary society quickly acquired something of the character of a centralized governing body exercising authority over the whole denomination. Though control nominally remained with the local churches, the building up of missionary funds enabled the missionary society to carry on enterprises on its own. The appointment of special missionary evangelists led to the growth of a body of ministers distinct from those preachers attached to particular churches; on occasion, the function of ordination —the most jealously guarded of the prerogatives of the local church— was performed under the direction of the missionary society. The union of Baptist missionary organizations of the Maritime Provinces and Central Canada was indicative of a considerable break from the principle of local church autonomy. Such union, nominally having to do only with missionary work, represented in very real fashion a movement towards greater denominational union, paralleling the movement which culminated in the Methodist union of 1884.

The effect of the growing missionary interest within the Baptist Church was evident not only in the development of powerful missionary organizations but in the development of new attitudes generally with respect to the qualifications and status of the ministry. Closer control over the appointment of missionaries made possible a raising of standards which reacted upon the appointment of ministers in the local churches. Recognition of the disadvantages of depending upon preachers who were badly trained and often had little understanding of Baptist doctrines, led to a growing demand for more centralized control of ministerial appointments. In three successive issues, in 1875, the *Canadian Baptist* drew attention to some of the shortcomings of the Baptist practice of leaving the local churches free to secure the services of whatever preacher they saw fit. "With all due deference to the brethren in our churches," a communication in the issue of November 11 read in part, "I think they are not sufficiently careful in regard to those whom they receive into the ministry—in regard to those whom they encourage to study for the ministry, and in regard to those whom they ordain to the pastorate. How many do the churches ordain whom they scarcely know—men, strangers in the country, without suitable testimonials or credentials—men, who came to us from other denominations, who

know nothing of our doctrines, or church order."[38] The next week, the editor himself turned to a consideration of the problem. "Among the many needed reforms at the present day," he wrote in introduction to a lengthy communication, "no one is more needed than a reformation of the present method of calling pastors. The present system is full of mischief and disaster and should be at once abolished."[39] One result of the system, in the eyes of the editor, was conflict within local churches growing out of disagreement in the choice of candidates. Another result was the check which it placed upon raising the educational qualifications and social status of the ministry. In an editorial in the issue of November 25 of the *Canadian Baptist* the whole problem of building up a stronger ministry was reviewed:

> It may be asked why are there so many destitute churches? We beg to call special attention to what we conceive to be the true explanation. Because Baptists, as we have already intimated, are, in their origin less dependent upon a ministry technically so called, than any other denomination. They spring up spontaneously, wherever the Bible is circulated and read; and they are mostly obliged to be satisfied with such leaders or speakers, as are found on the ground, and as the destitution of the people forces into the foreground .... Many of the churches, originating in the way indicated in this paper, have overlooked the necessity of providing a properly prepared ministry for the work of Christ, hence they do nothing for this all important object .... The early preachers who labored for them, almost without exception, pursued some secular calling, and hence received little or nothing for preaching to the churches. In this way the people never had the grace of benevolence exercised among them, and hence they have not learned to give generously for anything .... What is the state of things in Ontario and Quebec? The large majority of the churches have as yet given nothing at all for ministerial education .... *As a general rule, it discourages or kills one generation of good ministers to make these churches efficient.*[40]

The growing need of developing a professional ministry was closely related to the growing need for better church buildings. Both needs grew out of changing conditions in the Canadian community structure, and efforts to meet them led to fundamental changes in the character of the Baptist denominational organization and in the Baptist religious appeal. Though the Baptist Church was much slower than the Methodist Church in becoming an urban denomination, the growth of towns and cities after 1860 forced upon it a greater attention to the needs of the work in such areas. In particular, the problem of church building, as in the case of the Methodist churches, came to the fore. Churches which had been built in the towns during the early years of settlement often proved to be badly located with the growth of residential districts, while the drift of population from the country to the town left the

[38]*Ibid.*, Nov. 11, 1875.
[39]*Ibid.*, Nov. 18, 1875.
[40]*Ibid.*, Nov. 25, 1875.

country churches depleted of members while there were lacking in the towns churches to take care of the growing population. "We have Churches," a correspondent wrote of the situation in Toronto in 1872, "in the centre, the north, and in the east, but none in the west, or north-western part of the City, and it is in the quarter last named, where we have no footing, that the largest accessions to our populations are being made."[41] The rapid growth of new residential areas in Toronto, and the deterioration of the older parts of the city, presented the Baptists with a serious problem as a result of the location of their principal church on Lombard (Bond), or what had earlier been called March or Stanley, Street. The Reverend R. A. Fyfe wrote:

At that time [1832], the street had indeed been laid out but there were scarcely any buildings on it and no one could have predicted that it would not become one of the very best streets in the city. But such was not to be its favored destiny . . . . Miserable houses sprang up all around it, and what is still worse, many of them were inhabited by the most vicious and miserable kind of people, so that the whole street became extremely unsavory in every sense of that term . . . . The surroundings of the church were constantly growing worse, so that the last part of their sojourn there was worse than the first. Often on Sabbath evening a policeman was asked to patrol the sidewalk in front of March Street Church, to keep down the uproar which the children and others would thoughtlessly make in the neighborhood.[42]

The change in the location of the Baptist church in Toronto made it possible to serve more effectively the better residential area of the city, but other areas were left without places of worship. In 1875 a correspondent wrote to the *Canadian Baptist*:

A very large section of Toronto is destitute of Baptist churches. As it is, the city is only in a measure fringed with Baptist churches. In a few months the Central or Bond street church will be uprooted and transplanted to the corner of Jarvis and Gerrard streets, leaving an unoccupied area of by far the largest and most populous portion of Toronto.

A church is needed either in the lower part of St. John's Ward or that of St. Andrew's Ward. Another is needed in the vicinity of the Western Market; another at Brockton; another on Wellesley street, near the Cemetary, and still another on the east side of the Don.[43]

In the other cities, the Baptists faced the same problem of church building. The need of a suitable place of worship in Ottawa, the Dominion capital, particularly aroused the concern of church leaders anxious to enhance the social standing and prestige of the denomination. Of the cause here, the editor of the *Canadian Baptist* wrote in 1873:

Does not the fact that Ottawa is one of the most important centres of influence within the bounds of the two Conventions, give the small and struggling cause

---

[41]*Ibid.*, June 27, 1872.
[42]Quoted J. E. Wells, *Life and Labors of Robert Alex. Fyfe* (Toronto, n.d.), pp. 164-5.
[43]*Canadian Baptist*, July 22, 1875.

there a Special Claim upon the assistance and sympathy of the denomination as such? The Baptists in Ottawa are opposed by wealth, fashion, tradition and superstition—as well as the prevalence and aggressiveness of other denominations. With their present chapel, which neither in size nor appearance is fitted for the peculiar wants of a growing city, they are placed under a further disadvantage causing an almost insuperable barrier to their occupying that position of influence and respectability which humanly speaking is essential to their further progress.[44]

From Montreal, Winnipeg, Belleville, and most of the other growing towns or cities of the country came appeals for assistance in the building of better churches.[45] The demand for more handsome places of worship, situated in good residential districts, reflected underlying changes taking place in the social status of the Baptist membership body and, more particularly, of Baptist leaders. The increase in the number of members of the Church who were men of money and social influence— one of the deacons of the church in Toronto in 1856, according to William Davies, was reputed to be worth £250,000[46]—made it possible to secure financial support for an ambitious programme of church building, while the financial obligations assumed in carrying out such a programme made for a greater dependence upon the assistance of the more wealthy members. The Jarvis Street church, erected in 1875, cost the denomination $97,000, all but $5,000 of which was contributed in advance by members of the congregation.[47] In other cities, similar sums were expended on church building; in 1875, the St. Catherine Street church in Montreal had been completed at a cost of $60,000, while the Olivet church in Montreal was under construction at an estimated cost of $40,000 and the Chatham church at an estimated cost of at least $17,000.[48] The increasing overhead costs of providing the services of religion led to fundamental changes in the character of such services. William Davies wrote of the influences at work within the denomination which led to the construction of the Jarvis Street church, June 15, 1876:

There has been built in this city recently a large Baptist Chapel [Jarvis Street Baptist Church], gothic, brown stone, spire pointing upward if not heavenward,

---

[44]*Ibid.*, Oct. 30, 1873.

[45]"Our greatest trouble next to the want of another Missionary," a communication in 1873 from Manitoba read, "is, we think, a suitable House of Worship, more especially in the city of Winnipeg. The city is growing rapidly. . . . Here the Roman Catholics, the Church of England, the Presbyterians and the Wesleyans, have good substantial and comfortable Church edifices; while the Baptists have been under the disagreeable necessity of worshipping in a school house of a very poor description formerly, but latterly, in a small upper room." *Canadian Baptist*, Dec. 25, 1873.

[46]"He," Davies wrote of the deacon, January 13, 1856, "is one of the most wealthy merchants in the city. He is said to be worth £250,000, but he is very obstinate & self will'd & likes to lead the minister by the nose." *Letters of William Davies, Toronto, 1854-1861*, p. 63.

[47]*Canadian Baptist*, Dec. 9, 1875.

[48]*Ibid.*, June 10, 1875.

marble bapistry &c &c cost $100,000 & odd, & the organ $7000 besides, & I believe
it is all paid for, but it has been built regardless of the needs of the city. This congregation were in a part of the city (Bond Street) which was thickly populated but
they had an old fashioned building. One of the members, a M.L.C., say a Senator,
very wealthy, married an American, natural result they soon had an American
minister, then this new building also American, then the Lady & the minister lay
their heads together & get a professional singer a sort of *prima donna* & she is paid
$300.00 per year and many are very much hurt about it. It has been sanctioned
by a large majority & the result will be I expect that some of their best people will
leave. This building was erected to the N.E. of its former site which has left the
S.W. part of the city without any Baptist church, while they have gone into a district
that was pretty well served. There appears to have been a spirit of centralization &
aggrandizement abt. it which is hateful.[49]

Throughout many parts of the country, long after 1875, Baptists
retained much of their simple piety and devoutness—the rural ties of
the Church remained strong—but, as in the case of the Methodist
Church, control within the denomination shifted to the more socially
influential members and preachers situated within the larger cities.
The drive to secure better educated ministers and more handsome
places of worship found support among those elements of the membership body which were keenly aware of the social disadvantages under
which they suffered by being attached to the Baptist Church. The
movement to increase the social respectability of the Church grew out
of the movement to increase the social respectability of the new
bourgeoisie class growing up in the Canadian towns and cities. Baptists,
like Methodists, found their way in increasing numbers into business
and the professions, and new class values led to fundamental adjustments within religious organization as in the wider secular organization
of the community.

Professionalization of the ministry, and the construction of new
church buildings, were outward manifestations of underlying changes
in the attitudes and outlook of church members. Bigger and more
beautiful church buildings were indicative of the increasing material
prosperity of Baptists, but there was no corresponding increase in
spirituality. Success among the Baptists as among the Methodists led
inevitably to a break away from the simple virtues cultivated by the
religious sect. The Reverend E. W. Dadson complained in 1893: "We
are getting famous church edifices of late. In the cities and important
towns we vie with any denomination in beauty and convenience of
architecture, in the attractiveness of our services, and in the enthusiasm
and devotedness of the membership. And the danger may exist that,
instead of thought being directed away to the things that are spiritual

[49]*Letters of William Davies, Toronto, 1854-1861*, p. 135.

and eternal, it may find its satisfaction in contemplating those that are seen and temporal."[50]

Much of the simplicity of the Baptist church meeting was necessarily lost when Baptist forms of church organization were transferred from the rural to the urban community. Personal gave way to impersonal relationships, and the spirit of brotherly fellowship within the Church weakened. Complaints that members passed on the street without recognizing one another and that young men and women married outside the Church with the unconverted were suggestive of the ways in which Church controls broke down within the urban situation.[51] The very conditions of urban life—the extreme mobility of the population—made difficult the effective disciplining of Church members.

Deviations from accepted patterns of behaviour were accompanied by deviations from accepted patterns of thought. Baptists within the urban environment could scarcely escape the influence of new currents of thought associated with the development of science and the growth of capitalism. A greater worldliness became characteristic of many Baptists. The editor of the *Canadian Baptist* wrote in November, 1873: "The spiritual condition of many of our churches is a subject that calls for earnest and devout enquiry. In many of them but little religious life is to be seen, and not much noble enthusiasm for Christ and his cause. Prayer-meetings are thinly attended, and conversions are infrequent. We fear that a spirit of indifference has fallen upon many, and that pastors and people are in danger of being overcome by a spirit of lethargy."[52]

The next month the editor wrote:

One of the chief dangers to the cause of Christ in our age and country is the spirit of worldliness, which so widely prevails . . . .

Probably in a less degree than other denominations, have Baptists been affected by the gain-seeking spirit of the times in which we live. The great majority of them have been always poor, or at least in comparatively humble circumstances. Some, however, have become "rich and increased in goods," and the usual effects of wealth have flowed in upon them. With worldly prosperity have come refinement and fashion, and a struggle for social eminence and influence. Even among the churches, the spirit of worldliness is gradually diffusing itself. It brings in its train a fondness for outward display, and a heartless formality, which mar the beauty and paralyze the energies of the churches of Christ.[53]

---

[50]Jones H. Farmer, *E. W. Dadson* (Toronto, 1902), p. 283.
[51]See *Canadian Baptist*, June 20, 1872 and Nov. 28, 1872.
[52]*Ibid.*, Nov. 20, 1873.
[53]*Ibid.*, Dec. 18, 1873. "Whatever I am to do with my prayer-meeting," Dadson wrote from Grafton, May 26, 1874, "is a mystery to me. It is as bad as ever. Nobody will do anything. They tell me they want more urging. I tell them I will not urge them. So there we sit and look at each other." Farmer, *E. W. Dadson*, p. 226.

The weakening of the sectarian spirit within the Baptist membership body inevitably led to a weakening of the evangelical appeal of the Baptist Church. The minister could only hold his following, in the larger urban churches, if he adapted his message to their tastes; the fact that the urban minister was educated and socially prominent meant that he himself was unlikely to favour a reliance upon the crude methods of the revivalist. Thus, by imperceptible degrees, the Baptist Church assumed the character of the more traditional churches in the community. Revivalism became something confined to churches in outlying parts of the country or something which was turned to on special occasions. The revivalist in the urban church was a specialist; one who was called upon for the particular purpose of promoting a revival. The Reverend E. W. Dadson wrote: "It often comes to pass that the entire work of the Church is overtaken by an unaccountable spirit of dulness. Then the pastor thinks is the time for unusual action, and he takes his Bible and reads, not 'do the work of an evangelist,' but 'send for an evangelist.' The evangelist is sent for, with the usual results, viz.: Great blessing in the ingathering of souls, in many cases we frankly admit; but just as generally loss of power to pastor and church, from the fact of allowing someone else to take their crown."[54]

The increasing dependence upon professional evangelists was simply one indication of a growing shift within the Baptist Church away from the methods and principles of the religious sect. Much the same sort of developments took place as within the Methodist Church, if they took place more slowly and less uniformly; the strong spirit of congregational autonomy served to check the carrying through of any general programme of reorganization under denominational direction. It was within particular churches rather than within the denomination as a whole that the change to a more socially accommodative position occurred. Increasingly, however, the churches in which this change was the most marked were the churches which through their situation in the larger urban centres exerted the greatest influence in the denomination. The Baptist denomination came to be represented to a considerable extent by the great metropolitan churches; the ministers of these churches spoke for the denomination because they were the ones who could make themselves heard. It was in this way that the Baptist denomination came to assume its position in the Canadian community as one of the great, and respected, national churches.

By 1885 the transition of the evangelical church, as represented by the Methodist and Baptist movements, from the position of serving

[54]Farmer, *E. W. Dadson*, p. 174.

primarily as the church of the rural frontier to the position of serving primarily as the church of the urban community had become almost complete. In the twenty-five-year period before 1885 the rural areas of Central and Eastern Canada steadily lost in population, while the urban areas steadily grew. Inevitably, therefore, churches which had grown up in the rural areas were forced to become increasingly dependent upon the support of the population of urban areas.

This transition from the position of the rural to that of the urban church involved a fundamental change in the social basis of religious organization. The urban population from which support was drawn was of a different social class from that of the rural population from which support had been drawn. The transition was one from a church of the rural masses to a church of the urban classes. Only to a slight extent did the rural churches extend into the urban community through support in the lower social levels of the population. It is true that the first Baptist church in Toronto was a Negro church, but rapid growth of the Baptist cause in the city came through the support of successful English and Scottish business men who had immigrated to the country with capital and engaged in trade or industry. Thus the evangelical church, in extending into the urban community, quickly lost many of those attributes which had been characteristic of it as the church of the poor and down-trodden. It developed out of the sect into the church.

Extension into the urban community not only strengthened class lines within the evangelical church but brought it into closer contact with political and nationalist forces associated with the rising metropolis. Some of the more prominent leaders within the Methodist and Baptist churches emerged as influential figures in the national life of the country. A Scotch Baptist became Prime Minister of Canada in 1874. Powerful vested interests of trade, transportation, manufacturing, and banking made their influence felt within the councils of the Church. The drive to secure higher tariffs, and the promotion of railway ventures, had far-reaching repercussions upon Church policy. To some extent, Big Business bought out the churches; to a much greater extent, Big Business made its influence felt upon church life simply by virtue of the fact that it represented everything for which the metropolis stood. The church which identified itself with the urban, metropolitan community could not escape the effects of metropolitan forces of expansion and nationalism. The evangelical church emerged as the church of nation with the loss of its strong ties with the rural society and the establishment of strong ties with the urban society.

Although economic, political, and cultural developments in the Canadian community after 1860 strongly supported developments

in religious organization leading to a greater emphasis upon denominationalism, the sect spirit as a force in religious life did not completely disappear. Denominationalism greatly extended its hold, but here and there on the periphery of the religious community challenges to denominationalism found expression in the rise of new sectarian movements. The stability of religious organization implied the acceptance of the conditions of the secular society; on the outer fringes of that society there were still to be found after 1860 areas in which religious separatism—the drive to separate through spiritual fellowship from the secular world—developed strongly.

To some extent, the sectarian spirit found expression in movements which grew up from within the regular religious denominations. This was particularly true of the Baptists. By 1860 the Methodist Church had built a sufficiently powerful denominational organization to check local divisions among adherents but the Baptist Church continued to be faced with the problem of congregational conflicts which led to separations and the organization of different religious bodies bearing the Baptist name. In some cases, these separations grew out of disagreements over the choice of a pastor, while in other cases, doctrinal differences or differences with respect to Church policy provided the apparent cause. The weakness of denominational vested interests made it easy for Baptists to break away and organize a new church. Reports appearing in the *Canadian Baptist* on the state of Baptist work in various parts of the country suggest that divisions in local churches took place frequently.

Many of these divisions were of no great significance, but some of them grew out of fundamental differences making their appearance within the Baptist denomination. This was often true even though the question in dispute seemed to have been a simple matter of Church policy. Thus Davies in 1857 wrote of a division within the Baptist church in Toronto: "I don't know if I told you a few months ago some of the folks wanted an organ and it was carried. 5 or 6 of the minority were so incensed about it that they left and enlisted under the Banner of the City Missionary, one of their number, and met in a bdg for worship every Sunday."[55] The dispute spoken of by Davies was essentially one growing out of the conflict between the sect and church idea of religious organization; the new Baptist church, of which Davies himself soon became a member, developed in protest against tendencies towards an emphasis upon formality and show which had already become evident in the Bond Street church by 1857 and which later

[55]*Letters of William Davies, Toronto, 1854-1861*, p. 87.

led to the move to Jarvis Street where the handsomely constructed church housed an organ costing $7,000. In many other cases, the conflicts which developed within local Baptist churches revealed similarly an underlying restlessness or dissatisfaction growing out of a feeling of opposition to the shift away from the simple principles and practices of the religious sect. The spirit of religious separatism remained strong among large elements of the Baptist membership body, and efforts to strengthen the social supports of denominational organization as a result met with stiff resistance which on occasion led to division and the formation of independent Baptist churches.

It was outside rather than within the regular religious denominations, however, that the spirit of religious separatism found fullest expression. Although no great evangelical religious movement attracting mass support grew up in Canada in the period 1860-85, there was probably no earlier period in Canadian religious history which produced as many different sects. Some of these sects were purely local in character and gained no following outside the area in which they developed, while some had a more scattered following but one which was extremely restricted in terms of the sort of people they attracted.[56] The "queer" sect developed with the growth in importance of printing which made possible the distribution of tracts setting forth all kinds of mystical religious doctrines, but wide deviations from accepted religious teachings could make no general appeal. The real challenge to religious denominationalism came from those sects which taught fundamentally the same Christian doctrines as taught by the larger denominations. Of such sects, a number grew up in Canada after 1860.

It was sometime after the middle of the century, for instance, that the Christadelphians appear to have got their start in Canada. A division in the East Zorra 16th Line Baptist church occurred in 1859 as a result of the spread of the teachings of this sect, and growth of Christadelphian influence was evident throughout the surrounding countryside. "They took hold of many," an account of the history of the East Zorra church read, "and wrought much evil in the neighborhood generally, as well as among the different churches. Many public debates took place and the matter became widely spread and the party increased in numbers and in influence for a time."[57] Occasional references to other sects provide some indication of the variety of religious forms which made their appearance in the Canadian community. The Mormons,

[56]See, for instance, Marchioness of Dufferin and Ava, *My Canadian Journal,* *1872-8* (London, 1891), p. 138.
[57]McMaster University, Baptist Historical Collection, I. Beardsall, "History of the East Zorra 16th Line Baptist Church," manuscript, p. 10.

for instance, were active during the eighteen-sixties in Lambton, Middlesex, and adjoining counties where they attracted a considerable following.[58] A Thomasite preacher was engaged in holding meetings in Owen Sound in the spring of 1872.[59] The Congregation of Christ had grown to sufficient strength by 1883 to attract notice in the columns of the *Christian Canadian*.[60] The first Brethren Church made its appearance at least as early as 1868.

Of these various movements, the one which attracted greatest notice was that of Brethrenism. Closely related to the Baptists—and particularly the Scotch Baptists—in doctrinal teachings and church policy, the Brethren gained their greatest support in areas settled predominantly by people of the Baptist faith, but growth of the movement was general in the years 1870-85. Records of the establishment of particular Brethren churches provide some indication of the rapid spread of Brethren influence.

In 1868, for instance, a division resulted in the Clarence Baptist Church when Plymouth Brethren teachings secured a foothold through the participation in a local revival of a party of military officers camped nearby; two of this party, Lord Cecil and a Captain Dunlop, took an active part in the religious meetings, and exerted their influence in favour of the Plymouth Brethren cause. The Reverend C. C. McLaurin wrote in his history of the Clarence church:

> In the midst of this work, Captain Dunlop and Lord Cecil resigned their military positions in order to give themselves entirely to Christian work. Lord Cecil had money by which they could be supported. When they reached Ottawa they became identified with the Plymouth Brethren. They returned to Clarence, and found sympathizers not only among the converts but the older members. They met in the town hall, across the road from the church, for "breaking bread," as they termed the Lord's Supper. It meant a serious split in the church.[61]

The growth of Brethren churches in other parts of the country occurred in somewhat similar fashion. In 1873, a United Brethren church was organized in Thorold through the exertions of two evangelists from the United States.[62] The same year, the Plymouth Brethren invaded the town of Fergus where, before a meeting house was built, services were carried on in what was called the Fireman's Hall.[63] Again in the same year the Primitive Methodist preacher on the Plympton mission had occasion to call attention to the spread of Plymouth Brethren teachings. "There

[58]*History of the County of Middlesex* (Toronto, 1889), p. 68.
[59]*Canadian Baptist*, Apr. 18, 1872.
[60]*Christian Guardian*, May 9, 1883.
[61]Rev. C. C. McLaurin, *My Old Home Church in Rural Ontario* (Edmonton, 1937), pp. 88-9.
[62]Margaret H. Wetherell, *Jubilee History of Thorold* (Thorold, 1897-8), p. 150.
[63]Hugh Templin, *Fergus, the Story of a Little Town* (Fergus, 1933), pp. 258-9.

was quite an excitement," he wrote, "at our Tenth Line appointment caused by the preaching of two men who styled themselves Evangelists. Better known in this part, however, by the name of Derbyites, or Plymouthites, who obtained liberty to hold forth their poisonous dogmas in the church where our people have held divine service for fourteen years."[64] Two years later, the Christian Brethren secured a sufficiently strong foothold in Elora to take over the Baptist church and force the regular Baptists out. The preamble to a resolution passed at a meeting of Baptist members, June 27, 1875, calling for a council of delegates from sister churches to inquire into the state of affairs in the Elora church, was suggestive of the way in which the influence of Brethren teachings led to division and separation. The preamble of the resolution read in part:

> Whereas, for some months past certain persons who formally were members of the regular Baptist Church of Elora, but who now repudiate that name, have, with the aid of other persons who have associated themselves with them, subverted the order of divine worship in this place, denouncing all Christian sects and denominations as anti-Christian and unscriptural; and calling themselves Christian Brethren, and have practised the breaking of bread in the Lord's Supper in the absence of an ordained minister of the Baptist denomination, repudiating ordination as necessary, or the necessity of having a settled pastor and contributing to his temporal support, and in many other ways having proclaimed views contrary to those held by the regular Baptist church of Elora.[65]

When the special missionary, the Reverend James Coutts, a month or so later, was sent to Elora in an effort to restore order, he found the Brethren party in possession of the church building and he was obliged to meet with the Baptists in a public hall. "In compliance with the request of the Board," he wrote, "I visited Fergus and Elora, but found things in a very sad state. I found a number of those who had been leaders in the church denouncing all christian sects and denominations as anti-christian and unscriptural and refusing to call themselves Baptists. These parties claim the right to hold the church property and refused me the liberty of preaching in the chapel."[66] The growth of Brethren influence in Fergus and Elora made its effects felt in neighbouring areas, and in the First Baptist Church of Guelph a similar division occurred between the regular members and those with Brethren sympathies. "About this time," the historian of the church wrote, probably of 1875, "the Plymouth Brethren, who had already caused disastrous division in the church at Elora, began to make their influence felt in Guelph. As a result, several members withdrew from

[64]*Christian Journal*, Oct. 30, 1873.
[65]*Canadian Baptist*, July 8, 1875.
[66]*Ibid.*, July 29, 1875.

the church, including Benjamin Law, the treasurer, and also a deacon and a trustee, and Wm. Collins, another deacon who had served the church as its clerk since 1859."[67]

Although Brethrenism in Canada never assumed the proportions of a major religious movement, it grew to such strength as to constitute a serious challenge to the formal institutions of religion. In the methods and tactics which it employed, the principles of the sect found militant expression. The way the movement grew up in the country reflected its strong sectarian character. There was no organized campaign of evangelization; rather it was insisted that organization was of no importance and that acceptance of Brethren teachings did not require the establishment of a Brethren church. The result was that the movement often secured a strong hold upon the thinking of certain elements of the regular church followings long before any division and the organization of a Brethren church took place. Hence records of the growth of Brethren churches in the country provide an imperfect measure of the growth in influence of the movement. Brethrenism extended far beyond the reach of any formal Brethren organization.

It was this gradual infiltration of "heretical" beliefs in the thinking of regular church members which made the Brethren movement so difficult to check. Brethren evangelists were often, to outward appearances, good Methodists or good Baptists, and any attempt on the part of church leaders to prevent them giving free expression to their views took on the character of ecclesiastical or clerical dictation. Failure, on the other hand, to take a strong stand against such influences led to the steady strengthening of Brethren ideas and to the eventual dissolution of the Church when the differences in views became clearly evident. The editor of the *Christian Guardian* wrote in 1885: "The GUARDIAN has from time to time, directed attention to current forms of error in the teaching of popular evangelists, both in Canada and Britain. These errors have been popularly known as 'Plymouthism'; because most of them were prominently put forward by the Plymouth Brethren. But as the Plymouth Brethren have no fixed creed, and no proper Church organization, many find it convenient to repudiate all connection with the Plymouth Brethren while they really hold and teach those unscriptural theories."[68] Two years later the same editor wrote with specific reference to the work of Plymouth Brethren evangelists: "Their whole manner of work is stealthy and uncandid. They open their mission plausibly, and generally conceal their most objectionable

[67]Rev. B. W. Merrill, *Historical Sketch of the First Baptist Church, Guelph* (Guelph, 1903), p. 11.
[68]*Christian Guardian*, Apr. 8, 1885.

teaching at first. They live by proselyting from the protestant Churches instead of going out into the unconverted world and gathering souls for Christ. In many places they have brought about dissension and strife, where brotherly relations had formerly prevailed."[69]

The methods employed by the Plymouth Brethren were described at greater length in a communication to the *Christian Guardian* the same year by a correspondent signing himself "Watchman":

> My brief experience in church work in different localities has taught me that we cannot be too watchful against the encroachments of Plymouthism wherever we may dwell. Particularly is this the case in places newly opened up, and where there is a steady growth of population. In such places, people having in many instances but one house of worship, are naturally drawn toward each other, and denominational lines are somewhat effaced. Under these circumstances, the "Brethren" always alive to their own interests ofttime set on foot some plausible scheme of Christian work professedly seeking to bring together all Christians on one common platform, while concealing their real motives of proselytism. . . . .
>
> In some cases they worm themselves into the churches, and particularly Sabbath schools and Bible-classes, where they can exercise their influence and stealthily introduce their pernicious teachings. In times of revival effort they show themselves, and, where they are not altogether lacking in discretion, merely pray or speak as they have opportunity; but a close observer will detect their Plymouthism in the marked absence of confession of sin in the use of the pet phrase "The finished work of Christ," and in great emphasis on the "believe theory." Should a minister of any denomination be so unwise as to ask one of these to fill his pulpit there may be mild allusions to "the dispensations of law and of grace" and warnings against "doing anything" to secure personal salvation.[70]

Such tactics of boring from within the regular denominations accounted for much of the success of Brethren evangelical efforts. The Brethren evangelists built up within the churches a following sympathetic to their views before openly attacking the teachings of the churches. Once Brethren views caught hold, conflict and division were inevitable as a result of the clash of religious principles. The whole influence of the movement was directed against the claims of denominationalism. Like all religious sectarians, the Brethren attacked such principles of denominational organization as the payment of ministers; thus the spread of their teachings threatened the very foundations of denominational order. Denominationalism, in effect, constituted a system of protecting the vested interests of a professional ministry; it constituted a means of securing to certain specially qualified persons the right to perform such religious functions as dispensing the sacraments. It was the claim to this right which was particularly threatened by Brethren teachings. Where Brethren views gained

[69]*Ibid.*, Feb. 2, 1887.
[70]*Ibid.*, May 2, 1888.

acceptance, congregational order was imperiled by the weakening of the authority of the minister, and in the end the whole system of denominational church government was placed in jeopardy. "In the course of our pastoral work," the Reverend R. Strachan wrote in 1885 from Midland, "we have often had that system of religious teaching known as 'Plymouthism,' or 'Bretherenism,' so forcibly pressed upon our attention by the course which its advocates have pursued in propagating it, that we have been compelled to take a decided stand against it. The ministers in this part of the country have had more or less trouble on account of it."[71] Another Methodist minister, the Reverend W. Henderson, wrote the same year of the Plymouth Brethren: "They have come to a small village on an adjacent circuit, and spend seven days and nights of the week in ridiculing our church members and slandering the ministers. . . . They would cure sectarianism by launching, at the expense of the Churches, the most narrow and bitter sect yet known."[72] Recognition of the dangers inherent in Brethren teaching was given even clearer expression in a communication to the *Canadian Baptist* in 1872 in the form of an open letter to Lord Cecil.

May it please your Lordship, bear with a sincere Christian man, who felt and rejoiced not a little, when he heard of your self-denial, public profession of the Gospel, and fervent zeal for the salvation of men. Still I am sorry to find that yourself and fellow-officers, have been led aside to Plymouthism, in the name of Union, while undoubtedly it is the strictest of all the sects.

Lately whilst travelling in the East, I was told by pious and intelligent witnesses, that you, to a large congregation in Ottawa city, exclaimed, "Men, leave your clergy, and save your souls." . . .

How shall we reconcile all this profession of union, and charity with your conduct at Thurso, asking baptism of Rev. John Ross at 1 o'clock, p.m., and after the ordinance was administered, crossing the river, and preaching that evening on the other side, and denouncing the pastor and all the body for bigotry and division? . . .

Look at the assumption, and spiritual pride shown by Dunlop and Turner, at the Thurso meetings. The ministers who baptized them were there day and night, and other ministers of reputation from a distance, but were not called upon to take part; they were everything themselves, and others nothing . . . . Still in a few days, in sight of the chapel, they formed one of their own, did their best to tear the church in which they were baptized to pieces. I was there a few months after this, and found this faction near the chapel, few in number, with an ignorant boy their chief speaker . . . .

Finally, I object most seriously, to the preaching of the whole party, in labouring to keep the mind of their converts from looking to God for any help till their conversion is complete . . . . This is the crusade against formality run mad . . . .

[71]*Ibid.*, Feb. 4, 1885.
[72]*Ibid.*, May 27, 1885.

Their cry against sects makes their own the more unreasonable, calling it a union, and making it a division.[73]

The inroads made by the Brethren churches upon the following of the regular denominations reflected a general problem of religious organization where professional standards could not be maintained among those engaged in preaching and where the soundness of religious doctrines could not be assured in religious publications. "Heretical" teachings were spread through the activities of preachers not professionally qualified for the clerical office and through the circulation of religious tracts published by unorthodox religious bodies. The advances made by education in Canada in the third quarter of the century provided some protection against the spread of religious heresies; there was a growing appreciation of the advantages of a learned ministry and there was a growing tendency to read and accept the views of established church journals. On the other hand, the increase in the number of people who could read and felt themselves informed made the task of the religious "crank" much easier in disseminating his views. With education, the public acquired an almost insatiable appetite for speeches, and there was no effective way of exercising any control over those who might occupy the public platform; almost anyone with a capacity to speak and with ideas sufficiently novel could attract a sizeable audience in the small towns and rural areas. At the same time, the spread of reading habits greatly increased the importance of the printing industry and made it possible for almost any group to make its views known through the publication of pamphlets, tracts, or booklets. While such papers as the *Christian Guardian* served as self-appointed censors of religious publications, the effect mostly was to advertise the censored material. An increasing body of literature setting forth all sorts of strange ideas and doctrines found its way into the hands of the reading public after about 1860. It was through the utilization of the printing industry that the new religious sects like the Plymouth Brethren secured such a strong hold.

This greater mobility of ideas resulting from improved means of communication made its effects felt in the weakening of the position of established institutional systems such as religious denominationalism in the Canadian community after 1860. It was in those areas in which institutional controls could not be easily maintained that the greatest break from the established religious order took place. The sect grew up in rural districts and small towns which were being increasingly neglected by churches anxious to strengthen their position in the larger

[73]*Canadian Baptist,* Oct. 3, 1872.

urban centres. In these peripheral areas of the Canadian society means of communication were sufficiently developed to make possible the spread in influence of new religious movements while vested interests of office and social status were not sufficiently strong to make effective the checks exercised by denominationalism upon the development of deviant forms of religious belief.

However, the character of the religious sectarian movements which grew up in the years 1860-85 reflected the limitations of sectarian activity in the social situation which developed at this time. For the most part, these movements were heretical rather than evangelical. Their growth depended upon the advocacy of peculiar religious doctrines rather than upon evangelization with the result that they concentrated upon gaining support more from among the membership of the regular churches than from among the "unchurched masses". This emphasis upon doctrinal peculiarities made them in some respects a greater threat to the regular churches; their proselytizing activities led to a serious drain upon church followings. On the other hand, these sects by such an emphasis had a limited field of expansion. By failing to carry on work of evangelization, they exerted little influence among those elements of the population which did not attend church services and which had fallen away from religious influences. Their chief significance seems to have been as a "nuisance value" in religious organization. They developed no new techniques of religious revivalism and generally did not contribute to a strengthening of religious interests. They were in many respects parasitical in character, living off the churches rather than extending the boundaries of religious influence.

The reason lay largely in the limited field in which religious organization could expand. The completion of the Grand Trunk Railway in 1859 marked the passing of the backwoods community in Canada and the rise of the industrial town; the next twenty-five years, until the completion of the Canadian Pacific Railway in 1885, was a period of uncertain development which witnessed no spectacular economic changes. Here and there, it is true, from Cape Breton to Vancouver Island, there were to be found areas of new economic activity and population growth. In Nova Scotia, coal mining and the iron industry assumed increasing importance in economic life; in north-eastern New Brunswick and in Muskoka and the Georgian Bay districts new backwoods communities emerged associated with lumbering and farming; along the lake-shore of Ontario industrial towns grew to such importance as to attract a few working-class immigrants from overseas; to the north, about Lake Superior, small beginnings were made in the mining of iron; further west, in the Red River Valley, the establishment of

steamboat and rail connections with Minneapolis led to growing immigration and the expansion of wheat farming; while, on the Pacific Coast, a booming if unstable mining society took its rise with the sudden discovery of gold. These developments produced the Canadian frontier of 1860-85. Industrial unrest, evident on occasion in mass demonstrations and rioting, political dissatisfaction which in the West found expression in armed rebellion, and social restlessness leading to class and ethnic conflicts, family disorganization, and crime were the consequences of underlying disturbances in the social structure resulting from population movements and the development of new kinds of economic activity in the Canadian community after 1860. Disorganization in religious life was closely related to other forms of social disorganization.

Yet, in contrast with the rapid economic expansion of the United States after 1860, the economic development of Canada was slow and sporadic. The great population movements of the continent passed Canada very largely by, and, indeed, in most areas of the country, population moved out rather than in, to participate in expanding economic enterprises in the United States. Fishermen and farmers of Nova Scotia abandoned their native province to seek their fortune in New England; farmer-lumbermen in New Brunswick crossed the border into Maine and proceeded westward to the lumbering centres in Michigan and, later, Wisconsin; rural French Canadians moved down into Vermont, New Hampshire, and Massachusetts to provide the labouring force of the new textile mills; Ontario farmers sold out their holdings to join in the movement into the western American prairies; even in British Columbia, with the passing of boom conditions in the mining industry, the movement of population tended to be one across the border into new American mining areas.[74] The introduction of iron and steel marked the end of the wooden ship and the dominance of Nova Scotia in world trade, while the Pre-Cambrian Shield placed a formidable barrier to western expansion so long as free land was available in the United States. The Galt tariff of 1859 and the National Policy of 1879 gave expression to the needs of economic interests coming increasingly to depend upon the exploitation of a limited home market. Canada, in the period 1860-85, lacked a frontier in any real sense. Emphasis shifted from expansion into new areas of economic development to the consolidation of the position of economic interests in areas already long opened up.

This closing of the Canadian frontier after 1860 made its effects

[74]See M. L. Hansen, *The Mingling of the Canadian and American Peoples.* Completed and prepared for publication by J. B. Brebner (New Haven, 1940).

clearly felt in the development of religious organization. In no area of Canadian life were sectarian religious movements able to secure a strong foot-hold. Few great manufacturing enterprises, employing large numbers of workers, developed, with the result that the new industrial town was little different in character from the country town out of which it had grown; until urban working masses appeared, there was little scope for the activities of urban religious sects. In the country, a declining population, and long settlement, tended to a conservatism and emphasis on order which similarly restricted sectarian activity. Only on the Pacific Coast, where the discovery of gold resulted in a mass influx of population, did conditions of extreme social disorganization develop, and here the character of the population was such as to discourage any interest in forms of religious experimentation. The mining population of Vancouver Island and British Columbia was predominantly male, and new religious movements found little support in a body of deeply held religious beliefs; the family system was too weak to support any strong religious response to the social demands of the mining frontier. Rather, the discontents and social dissatisfactions of the population found expression in movements of a purely secular character.

The limitations placed upon sectarian activity in Canada after 1860 afford an explanation of the character of the sects which did develop. The social base of the Canadian community was too narrow to support any great evangelical crusade such as had taken place earlier with the Great Awakening in the Maritimes and the Great Revival of Upper Canada. The evangelical religious sect depended upon reaching out and gaining support from the great "unchurched masses"; no such masses were produced by the developments which took place in Canada after 1860. As a result, the new religious sects were dependent largely upon living off the older churches. It was for this reason that they assumed largely the character of heretical religious movements.

The great weight of social influences operating in the Canadian community after 1860 favoured developments in religious organization in the direction of church union. Competition became keener as the market became more restricted, and the wastes of competition forced a greater consolidation of effort as a means of cutting down overhead costs. Business factors played a more important part in church policies as the expenses of maintaining religious establishments increased, and the growing financial resources of the larger churches provided them with effective means of squeezing out new religious groups which lacked any support from business. In communities growing slowly

through increase of population, the possession of large and handsome buildings secured the dominance of the church. It was only when the population grew away from the church building that such dominance was really threatened. Until 1885 the religious sect could do little more than engage in sniping from the flanks; after 1885, it was able to launch a frontal attack upon the main positions of denominationalism.

CHAPTER EIGHT

The Great Revival of the City

1885-1900

IN 1884 the Methodist Church of Canada came into being as a result of the union of the Canada Methodist, Methodist Episcopal, Primitive Methodist, and Bible Christian churches. The date gains significance in relationship to two other developments in Canadian religious life. In 1886, two years after the union, a Methodist evangelist by the name of Ralph Horner refused to accept an appointment from the Montreal Conference as a circuit pastor, a break which was to lead nine years later to the organization of the separate Holiness Movement Church, while in 1883, one year before the union, the first branch of the Salvation Army in Canada was organized in London, Ontario, the beginnings of a movement which was to develop as a dominant religious force in the Canadian urban community during the next fifteen years. Union in 1884 marked the culmination of fifty years effort to secure the denominational consolidation of Methodist forces in the country, but no sooner was union attained than many of its gains were lost through the breaking off of large sections of the Methodist membership body with the rise of new evangelical religious sects. The Holiness Movement Church and the Salvation Army grew up in direct response to the challenges of denominationalism in Canadian religious life. It was no mere accident of history that their rise corresponded so closely in time with the union of the Methodist churches.

His own reminiscences, though lacking in such details as dates and place-names, provide a revealing account of the character of Horner's evangelical labours which led the Montreal Conference of the Methodist Church finally in 1895 to drop his name from its roll of ministers.[1] What Horner set in motion first was a great evangelical crusade, a revivalist movement within the Church. What he created in the end was a distinctive creed and a distinctive church. Horner began as a holiness preacher, teaching the doctrine of entire sanctification; he finished by denying the authority of the Church to which he belonged

---

[1]*Ralph C. Horner, Evangelist: Reminiscences from His Own Pen*, published by Mrs. A. E. Horner (Brockville, n. d.).

and by organizing his followers as a separate religious group. In terms of the general development of western Christianity, the movement he founded was simply one of several holiness movements which grew up about the same time in Great Britain and the United States. In Canada, from the beginning, his work became closely associated with that of the Canada Holiness Association, a non-denominational organization which sought to promote the holiness idea, chiefly by means of conventions.

Converted in 1872 at a Methodist camp meeting near his home in the neighbourhood of Renfrew, Horner soon felt the call to preach, and in various parts of his local community he began to conduct religious services and to engage in revivalist exercises. After a year of special evangelistic work, at home and, during the winter, in the lumber camps, he entered Renfrew High School on the understanding that he would be accepted by the Methodist Conference as a regular evangelist. Constantly preaching throughout his high school career, in 1882 he was received on trial for the Methodist ministry, and from 1883 to 1885 he was a student at Victoria University in Cobourg. Here there was no cooling of his enthusiasm for evangelical work. Within the university he was instrumental in organizing holiness meetings among the students, and the spirit of revival thus promoted extended throughout the town; during the summer months, he was engaged in revivalist preaching in the country. Considerable success attended his labours. "I spent the summer in special evangelism," he wrote, of the first summer he was out, "and God gave me a flaming revival in every place where I labored. If I remained three weeks in a home, every person in it would be converted. There was no exception to this. I would ask God to give them to me, and then go to work to lead them to Jesus. The hard, wicked, profane people were the same to me as the respectable and moral."[2]

In 1886, after a year at the National School of Oratory and Elocution at Philadelphia, Horner was appointed by the Montreal Conference to circuit work as a pastor, but he refused to accept the appointment and turned to the work of special evangelism. Though connected with the Church for another nine years, the religious movement which he founded might be considered as having taken its rise in this year with his failure to conform to the Conference instructions. From 1886 onwards, Horner engaged in revivalist work almost wholly on his own, building up about himself a following which had little connection with the regular membership body of the Church. Though ordained the next year, and given permission to engage in special evangelism, he continued

[2]*Ibid.*, pp. 55-6.

to pay no attention to the rules or regulations of his Church. The places where he preached were of his own choosing. "God opened the door for me for special evangelism," he wrote, "that I was not depending on either the President or the Committee. In the first place where I labored, God sent a cyclone of conviction, conversion and entire sanctification. It was said that there were only two men for a number of miles that were not led to the Saviour. Roman Catholics, Episcopalians, Baptists and Methodists were all alike. They bowed together at the same penitent form."[3]

Henceforth, Horner was constantly engaged in revivalist preaching. His influence grew as his power as a preacher developed and more people began to hear of him. His year in Philadelphia studying oratory and elocution probably stood him in good stead, but he appears as a man naturally endowed with the capacity to sway great masses and to arouse a high state of emotional excitement. There were probably few tricks of the revivalist he did not learn. At the same time, the holiness appeal in itself was such as to lead to the expression of strong emotional feelings. Though his own account of his revivalist work was probably highly coloured, the fact that he was viewed by the church authorities as a seriously disturbing influence offers support to the claims which he set forth respecting the success attending his work. "God poured out His Spirit on every field on which I labored," he wrote of the work during the year 1887-8, "and many were converted and entirely sanctified."[4] Of his work during the next year, he wrote: "In some places the people were brought under such strong conviction of sin that they had to die or seek salvation. The devil tore some and made them foam at the mouth before he would come out of them. There were some terrible scenes under extraordinary manifestations of power."[5]

The whole account of his work penned by himself is a tiresome repetition of the results of almost hundreds of revivalist meetings which he held in the years leading up to his break from the Church in 1895. Reports of some of these meetings can be accepted as typical. Of one meeting in the year 1887-8, he wrote:

God manifested His power mightily under my preaching, so that the people commenced to fall under the power of God. God sent cyclones of power and fire, and the people became so hungry for it that they could not be induced to go home without it. God poured out His Spirit on them in every service. One night I went to my room at twelve o'clock and had supper; returned to the service at one o'clock

[3] *Ibid.*, p. 78.
[4] *Ibid.*, p. 79.
[5] *Ibid.*, p. 91.

and it was still going on as I had left it, without any leader. The people fell by the score under the power of God. Some laughed, some cried, but most of them lay as if they were dead. As soon as they were able to creep on the floor, they reached their friends and cried to God for them. They had such power with God and over men, that those whom they prayed for would fall over at once. It was an easy matter to count sixty or seventy under the power of God on the floor. I left the service about half-past one without any leader. I never knew what time the service closed.[6]

Of a meeting the next year, he wrote· "A number became so hungry for entire holiness of heart that they ran to the penitent form, and cried for deliverance from inbred sin. Cyclones of converting and sanctifying power swept over the place. It was refreshing to see those who had been opposing much lying on the floor under the power of God. God saved, sanctified and anointed people by the score. The minister's wife was so overpowered by the Spirit of God that he had to get a carriage to take her home. She shouted, 'Glory to Jesus!' all the way through the village."[7] Attracting crowds which no longer could be accommodated in church buildings, Horner secured a large tent, and henceforth, during the summer months, he, and a number of fellow-preachers or assistants, proceeded from place to place holding tent meetings. With the increase in the number of people taking part, religious excitement was heightened and more extreme forms of religious hysteria manifested themselves. "The night that the camp meeting closed," he wrote of one such meeting, "I felt that a cyclone of power was coming, and I knew that the people would fall under it . . . . I drove them out in great haste, and as soon as they were out in the woods, they fell in every direction."[8] Of another meeting, he wrote: "I preached a few sermons and they commenced to run to each other to be reconciled. The power of God fell upon them, and they ran over the seats, praising God with joyful lips. God opened the heavens, and many fell under His power and lay for hours. In one of the evening services the minister in charge of the circuit fell to the ground under the power of God, and lay until two in the morning. Sometimes he lay as dead, and at others he shouted very loudly."[9]

When the weather became too cold for holding meetings in the tent, church buildings again were brought into use. The spirit of religious revival continued strong no matter where the people were gathered together. "In every service," Horner wrote of the first winter after his introduction of tent meetings, "the power of God fell on the people

[6]*Ibid.*, pp. 81-2.
[7]*Ibid.*, p. 90.
[8]*Ibid.*, p. 102.
[9]*Ibid.*, p. 103.

and they sank to the floor under it. Some lay as if dead."[10] Though the physical exercises of Horner's revivalist meetings usually assumed the form of falling to the floor, at times physical manifestations of religious feelings appeared in even more extreme forms. "When she commenced to pray," he wrote of an Episcopalian woman who went to the penitent form to seek salvation, "the devil put all her joints out of place, and her mouth seemed to be twisted back to her ear. She was a horrid sight."[11] Of a revival later in the same wintei, he wrote:

> The next campaign was on the adjoining circuit. Some of the people who were in a pentecostal flame came over to help me. It seemed as if the revival commenced in a minute. It swept over the whole community. Those who attended the services lost all the powers of resistance. They were overwhelmed by the spirit of conviction and the power of God to save. Saints and sinners alike fell under the power of God. Some lost all their physical strength by the billows of heaven that rolled over them. We had four services each day. We went to the first one in the morning by lamplight. Some would fall under the power of God in the early morning service and lie in the church all day. God was glorified in the salvation and sanctification of scores of people. Whole families were reached and lay on the floor side by side under the converting and sanctifying power of God. The old and young alike were moved, and rushed to the penitent form and cried for mercy.[12]

Succeeding pages of Horner's reminiscences were taken up largely with similar accounts of his revivalist labours. At no time was there any attempt on his part to indicate how many people actually were brought under the influence of his preaching. That his hearers throughout the Ottawa Valley area came to be numbered in the thousands would seem almost certain, but not even Horner himself could have had any definite idea of the size of his real following. Many came to hear him without being greatly influenced by his preaching, while others may never have heard him and yet come to have been counted among his followers. Horner before 1895 was the leader of a movement and not the builder of a church; his influence was something which spread out without leading immediately to the organization of a separate religious group.

His relationship to his co-workers was equally as casual as his relationship to his followers. The names of those who worked with him were never indicated. General references to ministers on various circuits would suggest that he secured their co-operation; apparently he established closest working relationships with the Reverends J. B. Saunders, J. V. MacDowell, A. A. Radley, J. E. Robson, Thomas McAmmond, D. T. Cummings, R. Easson, J. Ferguson, and J. H. Stewart.[13] In

[10]*Ibid.*, p. 104.
[11]*Ibid.*, p. 105.
[12]*Ibid.*, p. 107.
[13]*Ibid.*, p. xiv.

carrying on his tent meetings he employed a number of assistants; some of them may have been trained by himself. How important was this work of others in the revivalist movement in which he took part cannot be certainly known; with the egotism of the prophet, Horner in his account of the movement was inclined to take most of the credit for its growth to himself. Allowing for such exaggeration, however, growing out of a sense of self importance, it would seem that he did come quickly to play a dominant role in what developed into a great evangelical crusade. The character of the man made close co-operation with others almost certainly difficult; his effectiveness as a revivalist preacher won for him his own following and, in the end, his own body of disciples. His expulsion from the Church, in itself, implied that much of the influence he exerted was personal in character.

Inevitably, his work quickly came in conflict with that of the Church to which he nominally belonged. Horner, like all evangelists, had little interest in the denominational attachments of the people to whom he preached; Episcopalians, Presbyterians, Baptists, and Roman Catholics were invited to the penitent bench along with good Methodists. He built up a following outside as well as within the Church, and the effect of this was to weaken denominational attachments among those within the Church. He made good Christians but bad Methodists out of his converts. From the point of view of the church authorities, too many of his followers became Hornerites and ceased to be Methodists.

This break from the regular Methodist body probably would have taken place even if Horner had attempted to prevent it; the Methodist Church could not contain within itself a revivalist movement such as that which he had set in motion. The break, however, was precipitated by Horner's own actions in defying the authority of the Church. From the beginning, Horner refused to go where he was told or to consult with his superiors about his work. He secured his financial independence by refusing to hand over or even report the amount of money he collected. If he co-operated with those ministers who worked with him, he was prepared to wage bitter warfare upon those ministers who offered him resistance; he invaded local churches without any invitation from the pastors in charge and, at times, competed directly with regular Methodist services.

Even more serious, from the point of view of church government, Horner refused to conform to the accepted practices of the Methodist religious service. Church leaders had become much too rational in their outlook to accept as genuine the wild exhibitions of religious feelings which occurred at Horner's revivalist meetings; the rationalist, with little understanding of the psychological force of mass suggestion, was

forced to conclude that such physical manifestations of religious faith as falling on the floor or "speaking in tongues" were fraudulent in character. The Methodist Church, dependent upon the support of rational men, had no other choice but to condemn physical exercises in religious services. Its quarrel with Horner was not because such exercises occurred in his services but because he refused to take a stand in opposition to them. He was too good a publicist not to recognize their value in strengthening the emotional attachments of his followers and in making his cause known.

Opposition to his preaching early made itself felt on the part of various Methodist ministers who were brought into close contact with his work. With the air of the persecuted man, Horner constantly in his reminiscences referred to the difficulties he met with through the hostile attitude of the stationed ministers. "At the next place where I conducted services," he wrote of one of his early preaching appointments, "the preacher opposed me much; but it did not hinder the work."[14] Of a revival sometime later he wrote: "It went on until there was a change of pastors. The new pastor commenced to oppose physical manifestations and noise. He would ridicule the people concerning their manner of praying and the joyful way in which they praised God. The people were left without any instructions, and were abused for being 'fools and fanatics'."[15] On the next circuit similar opposition was met with. "The pastor," he wrote, "opposed the work and got up the spirit of rivalry in the place, so that it became difficult for him to keep up one prayer meeting each week."[16] Later in the same year, he wrote of his work in the city, probably either Montreal or Ottawa: "It was somewhat amusing to see the look of the city preacher when the people would fall to the floor under the power of God. Opposition to noise and physical manifestation was rising very rapidly. Some of the preachers were discussing it wherever a few of them met; it was the topic of the hour. Some concluded that I unconsciously exercised much mesmeric power. . . . I was looked upon by a good many of the ministerial Conference as an unsafe man to have labor on their circuits."[17] On another occasion, he wrote in similar fashion of the opposition which he met with from the stationed ministers: "The revival flame was more than some of the ministers of the church could endure. When the power of God would fall upon the people, and fifty of them would commence to pray at once, the heavens would come down and formalists

[14]*Ibid.*, p. 70.
[15]*Ibid.*, pp. 82-3.
[16]*Ibid.*, pp. 83-4.
[17]*Ibid.*, pp. 87-8.

would be terrified. It was more than a preacher who wished to be popular could endure. The Christians who were aiming to build up a fashionable, popular society had no use for such demonstrative services."[18]

Numerous other references to ministerial opposition serve to indicate the extent of the break which was taking place within the Church. Horner steadily pulled away from his fellow Methodist preachers, and he pulled away with him many of the regular Methodist following. From the point of view of the stationed ministers, he became a dangerous man to work with and a dangerous man to work against. Whatever attitude they took, the work of the Church was likely to suffer. Thus the problem quickly became one which required the official intervention of the Church. In the end, the disrupting effect of his work could be checked only by his expulsion.

Early efforts of local church officials to discipline Horner met with little success. When he began to use a large tent for carrying on revivalist services the district chairman forbade him to continue, but he disregarded the order.[19] Other such injunctions were met with a similar stubborn attitude of independence. The Montreal Conference was forced to take action. In 1893 the report of the Committee on Evangelistic Work was wholly taken up with the problem created by Horner in the Church. The report read in part:

We find first that the financial report of Rev. R. C. Horner presented to the Conference was, according to Mr. Horner's own statement, only partial, representing merely the net surplus after all expenses had been paid, such as moving the tent, salary of singer, board and other expenses. As to the general benefits of these evangelistic efforts, we find that, although we are assured that souls have been converted and believers sanctified, yet the results, spiritual and financial, have as a rule been sadly disappointing.

We find that there have been serious irregularities in the prosecution of our evangelistic work, especially in the following particulars, viz.: In the mode of conducting prayer and enquiry meetings, in which the people were permitted and sometimes encouraged to pray aloud simultaneously, tending to confusion and disorder.

We find that physical manifestations, not calculated to commend our common Christianity to the hearts and consciences of men, but tending rather to bring it into disrepute, such as prostration, ecstasy, immoderate laughter, etc., are common; and we judge that sufficient effort is not exerted towards their restraint and control. . . .

We find that a censorious spirit is exhibited leading to unkind criticism and condemnation of both ministers and members of our Church, who do not see their way clear to adopt the methods referred to above; and we further find that a spirit

---

[18]*Ibid.*, pp. 90-1.
[19]*Ibid.*, p. 95.

of disloyalty to our Church and her institutions is a very painful and frequent outcome.[20]

Because of these serious faults on the part of Horner and his fellow evangelists, the Committee recommended that no evangelist be appointed by the Conference for the following year and that in future all evangelists before being accepted be examined as to character, doctrine, and methods and that none not thus accredited be employed by the quarterly boards. The next year, in face of a charge from the Perth District meeting that Horner was holding services and collecting moneys on some of the circuits without consulting the superintendent in charge,[21] the Montreal Conference resolved that no evangelist would be permitted to conduct evangelistic services on any circuit without the concurrence of the superintendent in charge. "We desire," the Conference resolution went on to read, "in the clearest way to affirm our conviction that all Evangelists in our Church must be subject to the authorities of the Church, and conform to our usual customs."[22]

The action of the Conference, however, did little to check Horner's evangelistic labours. He wrote:

> When we reached the city where we were to have the special services, the ministers had sent to press the resolution of the Conference Special Committee that no chairman of a district should allow me to labor on his district, because I did not go to the circuit assigned me by Conference, and do pastoral work. The resolution was used against me all year. It did not deprive me of work, but it kept many away from the services and produced prejudice against me in the minds of many people. . . . We were not allowed in the church, but were kept down in the basement, which was dark, cold and dreary.[23]

Of later in the year he wrote: "We did not remain long in this place, but moved over to another church. The chairman of the district was using all his influence to keep us out of the churches. He was endeavoring to respect the wishes of the Conference Special Committee which had recommended that no chairman would allow me on his district."[24]

It was significant that, as the doors of the Church were closed against him, Horner came to employ the plural pronoun more and more in reference to the work in which he was engaged. The action of the Church tended to sharpen the line setting off Horner's followers— and his disciples—from the regular members and ministers of the

[20]*Minutes of the Proceedings of the Montreal Annual Conference of the Methodist Church, 1893* (Toronto, 1893), pp. 72-3.
[21]*Christian Guardian*, June 6, 1894.
[22]*Minutes of the Proceedings of the Montreal Annual Conference of the Methodist Church, 1894* (Toronto, 1894), p. 100.
[23]*Ralph C. Horner, Evangelist: Reminiscences from His Own Pen*, pp. 125-6.
[24]*Ibid.*, p. 129.

Church. The movement of which Horner was leader began to assume the definite form of a separate church. People rallied about him in protest against what appeared to be high handed action on the part of the church officials. His followers found themselves forced to worship apart from the regular church members; it was a simple step from this to acquire separate places of worship. In 1894 a group of Horner's followers, or at any rate of people "supposed to be a good deal under his influence," purchased the Concession Street Baptist church in Ottawa and began using it as a centre for holiness meetings. In these meetings when in Ottawa, Horner was the leading spirit. Although he denied that the work was his or that he intended to form a new religious body, the action of his followers virtually constituted a schism from the Methodist denomination.[25] The Concession Street church immedi tely developed as the headquarters of Horner's movement; it soon became the headquarters of his church. In 1895 the Montreal Conference moved to formally expel him from the Methodist body. It reported:

For several years past what has become known as the Horner Movement has been a source of grave solicitude to the Church. We have deemed it prudent to exercise the greatest forbearance towards those who have been unhappily involved in it, in the earnest hope that they would see the falseness and unscripturalness of some of the practices into which they have fallen.

With much prayer and great patience the Church has borne with these, using every means which could be devised to save to the Church and to Christ those who had been thus misled. But in the case of some we regret to say that all these means have failed, and, to preserve the Church from disintegration and reproach, as well as to enable it to perform with as little hindrance as possible its God-given mission to spread scriptural holiness throughout the land, we have found it necessary to depose from the ministry of the Church the chief mover in the said disruption.[26]

The action of the Conference involved more than the expulsion of one recalcitrant minister from the Church. It was naturally hoped that many who had associated themselves with Horner would break with him once he ceased to be a minister in good standing and a number almost certainly did. But his prestige had become so great that he no longer was dependent for his influence upon any connection with the Methodist Church. By 1895 he had built up his own personal following and the loyalty of that following was if anything strengthened by the action of expelling him. The rapid growth of the Holiness Movement Church in the next few years was a measure of the influence which he had come to exercise as an evangelical preacher.

[25]See *Christian Guardian*, May 30, 1894.
[26]*Minutes of the Proceedings of the Montreal Annual Conference of the Methodist Church, 1895* (Toronto, 1895), p. 64.

It was also a measure of the strength of holiness sentiments among large elements of the Canadian population and of the failure of Methodism in its appeal to capitalize upon the holiness idea. In 1894—one year before the expulsion of Horner—the Guelph Conference of the Methodist Church deposed the Reverend Nelson Burns, the president —and prophet—of the Canada Holiness Association, from the ministry,[27] and the action virtually involved a complete break with the holiness movement. Henceforth Methodist ministers participating in holiness conventions were looked on as suspect by church authorities; holiness followers were pulled off into sects distinctively holiness in character. Many of them turned to the support of the Holiness Movement Church. Still more attached themselves to the Salvation Army.

The first Canadian branch of the Salvation Army was organized in London, Ontario, in 1883 on the initiative of some British clerical workers who had been brought in contact with Army teachings before

[27]*Christian Guardian*, June 6 and June 13, 1894. The Canada Holiness Association had developed in close relationship to the Methodist Church, but the character of the Association's leadership, and its peculiar interpretation of the holiness doctrine, raised problems very early of serious concern to Methodist church leaders. Lengthy communications which filled up long columns in the *Christian Guardian* were an indication of growing differences of opinion regarding the validity of the holiness approach which eventually forced the Church officially to disown any connection with the Association.

"We shall not discuss," one communication to the *Christian Guardian* in 1885 read, "the wisdom or the unwisdom of the origin and working of the Canada Holiness Association, or the fallibility or infallibility of the officers of the same. The fact is, here are some brethren of the Methodist Church sincerely banded together for the promotion of holiness. If their methods and teachings are right, we ought as a Church to co-operate with them and help to make the movement universal in the land. If the methods are not wise and the teachings erroneous, then as ministers and people we the more earnestly ought to throw our influence into the work, and by the aid of our counsels assist to direct this work in the right direction. On no account can we afford to look on indifferently, or coldly criticise the Association." *Ibid.*, Oct. 14, 1885.

The conservative position within the Church came to be represented by the editor of the *Christian Guardian* and by the more prominent ministers in the city churches, and the radical position by the more evangelically-minded ministers most closely associated with the Reverend Mr. Burns. A communication in the *Christian Guardian* in 1888 from the Reverend T. S. Linscott, while in qualified defence of Burns, was indicative of the growing opposition to him within the Church which finally led to his deposition from the ministry in 1894.

"For weal or for woe," the communication read in part, "Rev. N. Burns is undoubtedly the modern champion of. this special teaching. . . . If he is a fanatic, there is most decidedly 'method in his madness.'. . .

"All the leading lights in the Holiness movement are against him, either because they misunderstood him, or that they believe a contrary doctrine, or both combined. When such undoubted biblical scholars, and saintly men, as Dr. Asa Mahan, Dr. Steele, Dr. Wm. McDonald, Dr. Asbury Lowrey, the Editor of the Christian Guardian, and others, antagonize his doctrine, it takes no inconsiderable amount of courage to stand alone, and keep on the even tenor of his way. . . . This by no means proves his teaching to be sound. and on the other hand no person should condemn his special theory because of the opposition. Personally, I believe great good will come out of this movement, although it is surrounded by great dangers." *Ibid.*, Apr. 12, 1888.

settling in the country. Organization in Toronto followed quickly, and, with help from Great Britain and the United States, the work expanded rapidly throughout the country. Toronto became the headquarters of the Army in Canada, and growth of the movement here was particularly striking in the years immediately after 1883. "The Salvation Army," the editor of the *Christian Guardian* wrote, February 6, 1884, "is still prosecuting its work in this city vigorously. The meetings held at the Barracks, in the west end of the city, are largely attended, and there can be no doubt that many are reached by this instrumentality that would not otherwise be touched."[28] Seating 1,500 people, the barracks at this time were unable to accommodate the crowds seeking to attend the Sunday services.[29] By 1886 larger buildings had been provided. "The visit of Mr. Ballantyne Booth, a son of 'General' Booth," the editor of the *Christian Guardian* wrote May 5, 1886, "and the opening of their new hall in this city, have given a new impulse to the work of the Salvation Army. The new hall at the corner of James and Albert Streets is a very commodious building, with a reported seating capacity of 2,500."[30] With the growth of the cause in Toronto the work was strengthened throughout the province. The movement spread with almost phenomenal rapidity. The editor of the *Christian Guardian* wrote, April 16, 1884: "In Canada, they labored for some time, at several central points without very marked success. But during the last year the Army has made its influence felt all over the country. Not only in the large towns, but also in many villages, they have made a considerable impression, and been very successful."[31]

Weekly reports in the Canadian issue of the *War Cry* provide some indication of the rapidity with which the Army established its cause in various centres. In the issue of November 1, 1884, for instance, reports were received from the following local corps established in Ontario: Belleville, Lindsay, Uxbridge, Oshawa, Whitby, Stouffville, and Orono and Newcastle in the Kingston Division; Strathroy, Dresden, Norwich, Lucan, Woodstock, Petrolea, Wallaceburg, London City, Seaforth, and Simcoe in the London Division; Cedar Dale, Flamboro, Hespeler, Omemee, Bath, Wyoming, and Otterville in the London Outposts; Lippincott Street (Toronto), Parkdale, Preston, Dundas, Welland, Riverside (Toronto), Thorold, Guelph, Toronto, Brantford, Brampton, and Yorkville in the Toronto Division; Owen Sound, Barrie, Stroud, Orillia, Newmarket, Collingwood, Stayner and New Lowell,

[28]*Ibid.*, Feb. 6, 1884.
[29]*Canadian Methodist Magazine,* vol. XIX, Jan. to June, 1884, p. 371.
[30]*Christian Guardian,* May 5, 1886.
[31]*Ibid.*, Apr. 16, 1884.

and Aurora in the Barrie Division; and Clinton, Brussels, and Palmerston in the Palmerston Division.[32] References to the establishment of the Army in particular places suggest something of the sensation which it created with its first appearance in the field. "The Salvation Army," the historian of the County of Middlesex wrote in 1889, ". . . is one of the latest additions to religious forms. Only a few years ago the members were buffetted about or imprisoned, but their perseverance won for them tolerance, and to-day the Army preach and sing in the market place as well as in their barracks—the members pleased with their worship and the people amused with it."[33] The historian of the County of Welland wrote in similar vein: "The 'Salvation Army' has created sufficient commotion in town to merit mention in our history. The Army invaded Welland on Sunday, April 20, 1884. For some time it flourished like a green bay tree, as many as eighty members being in the march at one time."[34] The author of the *Lady with the Other Lamp*, Mrs. Dean, wrote of the Army's invasion of Guelph:

Early in the year 1885 mysterious posters appeared on the walls and flaming hand bills in the stores of Guelph! They bore dramatic legends, "Blood and Fire," an "Army would open fire" on the city on the 9th of March. . . .

There was much curiosity—more unfavourable criticism. . . .

To this new movement were applied such terms as "travelling tinkers," "Travesty on religion", "fanaticism", and many other epithets. But by the 9th of March there was a good deal of interest and expectation in the breasts of the Guelph citizens. When the little group of queerly attired young people stood in St. George's Square and began to sing . . . there was a huge, excited crowd. . . . Many comments, not complimentary, were passed. . . .

The simple preaching by earnest, consecrated, young girls created a great sensation intermingled with curiosity, criticism, censure and appreciation. The drill hall was packed every night. . . . The whole city was stirred. Many notorious characters were converted.[35]

Squair wrote of the establishment of the Army cause in Bowmanville:

The first preacher in Bowmanville was Captain Ada Hind, who held her first service on the Market Square, on March 16, 1884. Captain Hind was an attractive young lady, bright and intelligent, who spoke well and persuasively. She had a good deal of success, and soon gathered around her a group of converts of considerable size. She spent a second term in Bowmanville in 1886. . . . The Bowmanville corps grew rapidly, and soon was able to erect a Hall in King Street, which still (1926) stands there. . . .

In the early days of the Bowmanville corps the Army held services in neighbouring

[32]*The War Cry*, Toronto, Nov. 1, 1884.
[33]*History of the County of Middlesex* (Toronto, 1889), p. 68.
[34]*History of the County of Welland* (Welland, 1887), p. 401.
[35]*The Lady with the Other Lamp: The Story of Blanche Read Johnston*. As told to Mary Morgan Dean (Toronto, 1919), pp. 30-2.

villages, such as Newcastle and Orono, but no permanent establishment was made in these places.[36]

For some time after 1883 most of the local corps of the Army were to be found in Ontario; it was to this province that the great majority of British workmen were immigrating in the latter decades of the century and, with their old country contacts with the Army, British workmen provided the earliest support of the movement in Canada. The influence of the Army gradually spread, however, into the neighbouring province of Quebec and into the Maritime Provinces. On January 3, 1885, the *War Cry* heralded the establishment of the Army cause in Montreal:

BOMBARDMENT OF MONTREAL

Meetings all the week a great success. Tremendous crowds. Hall far too small packed to the doors every night. Twenty-one prisoners. Hallelujah!

Opposition to the Army provided something of a set-back but served to advertise its meetings and bring it to the greater attention of the public, and the Army following grew rapidly in Montreal during the next few years. The success achieved in the Maritime Provinces was little less spectacular, and along the south shore of Nova Scotia and in New Brunswick the movement secured a strong hold. Areas where Free Baptist influence had been strong provided particularly favourable ground for the dissemination of Salvation Army teachings.[37]

By 1890 the Army was ready to extend its work into Western Canada. The movement became nation-wide in its appeal. The high peak in the growth of its influence was reached about the closing years of the century. By this time there were few centres in Canada of any considerable size where local corps had not been organized. In the larger cities, throughout the working-class districts, the movement had secured almost a dominant position in religious life.

This rapid growth of Army influence was not to be measured simply in terms of numbers of members or numbers of local corps. The Army developed on the wave of a great evangelical revival which swept across the country and which gained particular strength in the large urban centres. There occurred within the period 1885-1900 a religious movement which might well be described as the Great Revival of the City. It was the Salvation Army which capitalized most fully on the growing tide of fundamentalist religious thinking during this period. The reaction to religious denominationalism, the sect spirit in religious

[36]John Squair, *The Townships of Darlington and Clarke* (Toronto, 1927), pp. 327-8.
[37]E. M. Saunders, *History of the Baptists of the Maritime Provinces* (Halifax, 1902), p. 406.

organization, found fullest and most complete expression in its appeal and teachings.

With its peculiar and sensational methods, the Salvation Army developed in sharp conflict to the traditional order of Canadian society. Deeply entrenched social institutions, both secular and religious, met with a formidable challenge in its teachings. The saloon was an obvious point of attack, but the saloon was not alone among the accepted institutions of society subjected to violent onslaught. Nothing considered detrimental to the cause of evangelical religion escaped. Army workers made no nice distinction between what was considered the province of religious interest and what was not. There was no place, whether the saloon, the billiard parlor, or, indeed, the brothel, where the individual could take shelter from the scrutiny of Salvationists concerned about the state of his soul.

The violence of the opposition which developed to the Salvation Army was a reflection of the extent to which it interfered with the normal life of the community. Opposition to its methods quickly expressed itself. Its employment of the city streets for preaching and parades forced the intervention of the law, and, where public feeling was strong, legal prosecution was undertaken. In London, Ontario, where the work of the Army in Canada began, the city authorities sought to prohibit public religious demonstrations. Arrests of the leaders led to the imposition of fines although public sympathy was sufficiently great to check the exercise of too stern measures.[38] Almost every municipality faced the problem of deciding how far to go in using the law to check those practices of the Army considered undesirable.[39] In some centres, public sympathy served to temper the attitude of the authorities of law, while in some other centres, legal disabilities were supported by mob violence. "Accompanied by two Soldiers," Colonel Jack Addie wrote of his assumption of the command of an Outpost formed in 1883 in a town near Dundas, "I rode over with a horse and 'rig.' A howling mob received us and threatened to tar and feather the Captain. Missiles were thrown after us."[40]

In the province of Quebec public feeling against the Army was particularly strong, and persecution was faced by early workers in the field. The account of the establishment of the cause in Montreal

[38]*The War Cry*, various numbers.

[39]Squair, in his history of the townships of Darlington and Clarke, found in the Minutes of the Municipal Council of the Village of Newcastle, under the date June 15, 1885, the following reference to the Army: "Correspondence Received,—From Lieut. Beaver of the Salvation Army, accepting the conditions of the Council respecting the rent of Hall and to cease beating of Drums, &c., on the Sabbath. Filed." Squair, *The Townships of Darlington and Clarke*, p. 328.

[40]*The War Cry*, Aug. 19, 1939.

provides some indication of the difficulties which were faced as well as the success which was achieved. The work here was undertaken by Staff Captain Madden accompanied by Captain Eva Lewis, Lieutenant Low, and Cadets Murray and Yerex. After a meeting at ten o'clock in Weber Hall for half an hour of prayer, Madden and Lewis led the march into the city streets. Opposition was immediately encountered. "As we entered the street," Madden wrote, "we found thousands of people, the chief and a force of thirty police awaiting our arrival. All faces were turned towards us, as we pressed our way through the crowd some scoffed, some laughed, some cheered, and now and then one would whisper God bless you. . . . We had not gone far before the chief gave the signal and the police surrounded us and made the arrest." Bailed out by a number of wealthy friends, the officers proceeded to hold an afternoon meeting in Weber Hall, and, on leaving, enjoyed police protection. At the evening meeting, violence again flared up. "At night, we met early at our Barracks," Madden's account continued, "but the crowd was there before us, and the whole street was again filled, and it was with great difficulty that we got into the hall. As soon as the door was open the place was jammed, and more were disappointed by not getting in than those who gained admittance. We proceeded with the meeting in the usual way until the roughs became uncontrollable. After several seats had been broken, and the windows smashed, they took their departure from the hall to follow us home. Having no protection at night they handled us quite roughly."[41] Persecution developed among the Army evangelists a feeling of martyrdom and increased their zealousness in prosecuting the work of proselytization, and violent clashes continued to occur between them and members of the Roman Catholic community. The *Christian Guardian* wrote of the opposition encountered in the city of Quebec: "Another brutal and unprovoked attack was made last week upon the Salvation Army in the city of Quebec. In connection with a large representative gathering of the Army people a procession paraded the streets in the usual manner. They were molesting nobody. They were fiercely assailed with rocks and stones, and several were severely injured. The onslaught was protracted for a considerable time."[42]

Attacks upon the Army were to some extent simply an expression of the dislike by certain elements of the population of that which was strange and unfamiliar, but such attacks sprang also from annoyance with the interference of the Army with personal habits and conduct. The Salvationists were highly aggressive in carrying on the task of reclaiming

[41]*Ibid.*, Jan. 3, 1885.
[42]*Christian Guardian*, Aug. 31, 1887.

the sinner; intrepid female workers marched into saloons or took their stand at the doorways, while army processions were held in districts settled predominantly by Roman Catholics or in areas where leisure-minded citizens sought the freedom and quiet of out-of-doors. The authorities of the law were torn between protecting the rights of individual freedom and the rights of religious freedom; when sufficient respect was not paid to the right of the individual to conduct himself as he saw fit without interference from religious enthusiasts intent upon his conversion, mob violence often resulted. Thus legal persecution of the religious sect found some justification in protecting the individual from religious persecution, and, where such protection was not provided, the individual was forced to resort to direct means of retaliation. In Quebec, where the teachings of the Salvation Army were highly offensive to people of the Roman Catholic faith, the principle of religious freedom was subjected to the severest strain.

In time, mass demonstrations in opposition to the Army disappeared. As the population became more familiar with its methods, and more appreciative of the sort of work it was doing, there was a growing inclination to accept it, and antagonism gave way to a feeling of silent amusement or of respect. At the same time, the Army workers, with greater experience, came to make themselves less objectionable by more careful observance of the rights of others. Ties of friendship brought the movement into closer relationship with the community.

Underlying the popular dislike of the Army, however, were deep-seated attitudes of hostility on the part of church leaders in the community. So long as the work of the Army did not interfere with established denominational relationships, such church leaders could stand solidly behind the principle of religious freedom, but as its influence spread and it developed into a rival religious body opposition stiffened. The nature of the discussion which took place at the semi-annual meeting of the Western Association of the Congregational Union, held at London the last week of March, 1884, was revealing of the growing feeling of hostility to the Army with its invasion of local communities and interference with the work of local churches. The meeting was reported in the columns of the *Christian Guardian*. The report read in part:

Rev. Mr. Hughes, of Paris, opened up a lively discussion on the merits and demerits of the Salvation Army. He claimed the Army, by attracting away the young people, was sapping and mining the foundations of the Church. Something should be done to keep the young within their own fold. He thought the Army ought to be left severely alone. Mr. McGregor said the Army had invaded Guelph, some two weeks since, and had progressed rapidly. . . . It could not be gainsaid that they did preach Christ but whether they preached him in all his fulness was another question. They

had certainly reclaimed some of the worst cases. Mr. Packard, of Stratford, thought there must be something wrong if they could not succeed in attracting these young people as well as the Salvation Army. Rev. Mr. Allworth thought a minister could not be expected to dress himself up and go around the streets beating a drum. In large cities they are all right. There was work for them to do, but they ought to keep out of small towns. Rev. Mr. Fuller reported the Army in a very unfavourable state in Brantford. It was encouraging immorality, and young boys and girls were found on the street at all hours of the day and night. Rev. Mr. Alexander, of Hamilton, said in that city the Army had got hold of men who had been reduced to the lowest depths of degradation, still he thought it injured the Sunday-schools. Rev. Dr. Hall said he did not believe there was any religion about the Salvation Army. In Kingston sacred things were turned into a jest. The barracks were nightly turned into a dancing hall, where they held what they called free-and-easy meetings. One soldier would get up with his head near the ceiling and remark that he was never so near God before, and then they would all laugh. He had attended two meetings,.and at neither had the Bible been produced. He said the whole thing was a farce. It was an institution of the devil. No wonder gross immoralities were charged and were allowed to stand against the leaders of the Army. It was a movement antagonistic to the Church of Christ. Neither John Wesley nor any of the other conspicuous evangelists had started out by attacking the regular ministry. He did not think it was a movement of God. He thought it would be found to have done much harm instead of good. Mr. Edgar, of Hamilton, differed with Dr. Hall. He had no sympathy with the way the Salvation Army did their work, but he thought they did some good. Rev. Gordon Smith followed in a similar strain to that of Dr. Hall, after which the matter was dropped.[43]

In the methods it employed, the Army challenged the whole basis of the religious service of the established churches. Reliance upon stated places of worship, a professional ministry, and a ritual however simple were accepted practices of the church. An effort was made to maintain a sense of dignity and decorum, in the relationships of the minister to the public and in the behaviour of those participating in the act of religious worship. The professional status of the minister, and the social standing of the congregation in the community, depended upon ridding religion of any appearance of being ridiculous and of being of exclusive concern to "queer" people. By various kinds of institutional safeguards, the religious service was made acceptable to rationally minded individuals. Thus hostility to the Salvation Army on the part of the church leaders derived in part from strong vested interests in traditional religious practices. The emphasis within Army teachings upon a free expression of religious feelings, and the willingness of Army workers to resort to any method however spectacular as a means of attracting attention, threatened to destroy the "good name" of religion and to bring it into disrepute. Religion was pulled out of the control of established denominations and made something, in the eyes of church

[43]*Ibid.*, Apr. 2, 1884.

leaders, which was vulgar and cheap. The editor of the *Christian Guardian* wrote of the Army, April 16, 1884: "Their methods are roughly demonstrative and sensational. While this style may arrest and suit a certain class of minds, it has grave drawbacks. It introduces a sort of coarse ritualism, which certainly is not adapted to promote refinement or good taste. It creates a taste for this rough and irreverent style of worship. . . . There is also a danger of estimating the spiritual power and results of a service by the amount of outward noisy display, which may be got up easily enough, with little deep feeling or real spiritual power."[44] The next year the same editor wrote of the methods employed by the Army: "They depend too largely on noisy parades and claptrap methods, which have no moral element in them, to keep up the interest in their cause. . . . They encourage and practice, by act and speech, coarseness and vulgarity, that has no tendency to promote piety. . . . In pushing to the front ignorant and coarse people who are forward, there is a tendency to make persons of very limited religious knowledge and experience assume airs of superior wisdom and sanctity, to which they have really no just claim."[45]

What the Church in effect objected to was the kind of religious revival which the Army promoted. Among those brought under the influence of Army teachings, the prerogative of judging spiritual worth shifted from the institution to the convert. Religion was made popular in the sense that the understanding of its mysteries was not confined to the select few. Such a conception struck at the basis of authority within the Church. Like all religious sects, the Army attacked directly the claims and pretensions of a professional ministry. In doing thus, it attacked the whole system of ecclesiastical control which had grown up within the Church. The Church could not meet the Army on its own ground. The relationship was not one of competition between rival religious bodies; competition gave way to a fundamental conflict between types of religious organization, that of the church and the sect. The loss of members by the churches to the Salvation Army represented not a shift of denominational attachments but a strengthening of a spirit of religious fellowship hostile to the whole position of religious denominationalism. "They have promoted," the editor of the *Christian Guardian* wrote, "a narrow and intensely sectarian spirit, which prompts the 'soldiers' to unduly glorify the Army and disparage the work of the churches. In many Canadian villages, of limited population, they have by their sensational methods drawn away the

---

[44]*Ibid.*, Apr. 16, 1884.
[45]*Ibid.*, Mar. 4, 1885.

young of the different congregations, and weakened and disorganized the work of the Churches."[46]

It was the Methodist Church which felt most fully the effects of Salvation Army influence upon religious organization. The Army had grown up in Great Britain through a schism from the New Connection Methodist Church, and its doctrinal teachings—and, indeed, its methods—were very similar to those of Methodism. The rise of the Army in Canada took place at a particularly critical period in the development of the Methodist Church, coinciding in time almost exactly with the union of 1884. The Army was able to capitalize to the full upon the dissatisfactions among many Methodists with the act of union. Much of its early support was drawn from people who had belonged to one of the smaller Methodist churches but who were not prepared to attach themselves to the larger denominational body. The editor of the *Christian Guardian* wrote, April 16, 1884:

It is certainly a serious fact that, at a time when much has been sacrificed to unite the resources and put an end to the rivalries of Methodism, practically another Methodist denomination is being organized in this country. In cities there may be work enough to justify their special mission; but in the country villages there is a fair prospect that the waste of resources and the divisions of people of the same faith, which we thought we had brought to an end, is going to be kept up. In these places, the Army draws its recruits largely from Methodist congregations, which of course are proportionately weakened. Go into any Army fellowship meeting, and you will find the bulk of those who speak are either Methodists, or people who have had a Methodist training.[47]

Another correspondent wrote more generally the next year respecting the effects of the Salvation Army upon the work of the Church:

I wish to say a few words of the Army and their work, and its results in towns and villages and rural sections. Having visited several districts outside my own since last Conference, east, west and north, I have had the opportunity to form a wide and more or less correct observation of this work and its effect; and I deeply regret to say the result of their work is evil, serious and many-sided evil. In some places they are an element of disunion and division. The union [that is of the various Methodist churches] in all cases was not immediate or without feeling and friction, and in several instances the Army has stepped in just at the moment of unrest, and widened or prolonged the division. In some cases they have been allowed to purchase or rent an unused Methodist church. . . . In this way the Army has meanly striven to divide families and sections, where they should have allowed the Church to heal her own difficulties and meet her own unrest in the spirit of conciliation and forbearance and mutual concession. . . . Then it has been the studied aim of the Army to cast doubt on the goodness, and zeal, and purity, and power, and usefulness,

---

[46]*Ibid.*, Mar. 4, 1885.
[47]*Ibid.*, Apr. 16, 1884.

and humility, and essential Christlikeness of the Church. Wherever they can sneer at the Christian ministry, or pour contempt on the experience of church members, or insinuate the utter lack of power in the Church, they are eager to do so. Through vanity and self-display and self-exaltation, they try to make themselves out something supremely excellent, and the Churches supremely nothing. And there are some weak, but good people whom they have grievously unsettled in that way.[48]

Some of the gains of Methodist Church union were lost with the rise of the Salvation Army. Complaints of the shift of many Methodists to the ranks of the Army were not without a basis in fact. Two such Methodists were the Reverend John Pinch and a Mr. Meader, the former an ordained minister and the latter a local preacher in the Bible Christian Church in Bowmanville.[49] The vast majority of Salvation Army recruits, however, were not drawn from the Methodist Church following nor from the following of any of the regular churches in the community. Rather the Army gained its chief support from that section of the population which had no definite denominational attachments; from what church leaders liked to call the "unchurched masses." "There were also many gathered in," Squair wrote of the growth of the Army in Bowmanville, "who had been living outside the influence of any church."[50] W. H. Howland, as a result of a visit to an Army meeting in Toronto, came to a similar conclusion; "he was also struck," his view was reported in the *Christian Guardian*, "with the number of the 'non-church attending class' present."[51] Church spokesmen themselves, though anxious to emphasize the bad effects of Army influence, were forced to admit that much of its support came from a class of people which lay beyond the reach of the Church. "They succeed in drawing to their services," the editor of the *Christian Guardian* wrote of the Army in 1884, "a class of rough and careless persons who rarely attend any religious service."[52] The next year he wrote in similar vein: "We believe the Salvationists have reached and rescued a great many sinners, who seemed beyond the reach of ordinary church agencies."[53]

The Canadian city grew rapidly after about 1885 and much of its population was recruited from outside. The chief task of religious organization thus became one of capturing the support of people who found themselves within a new social setting, in many cases far away from their old home community and past associates. Traditional religious attachments broke down and new ones had to be formed if religion were to maintain its hold. It was just here that the established churches

[48]*Ibid.*, Apr. 18, 1885.
[49]Squair, *Townships of Darlington and Clarke*, p. 327.
[50]*Ibid.*
[51]*Christian Guardian*, Feb. 6, 1884.
[52]*Ibid.*, Apr. 16, 1884.
[53]*Ibid.*, Mar. 4, 1885.

experienced their greatest losses to such religious movements as the
Sa'vation Army. The Army broke outside the bounds of the traditional
religious constituency. It brought the teachings of religion to those who
had no religion, and made them a part of its organization. The success
it achieved as a rapidly growing religious movement—and the success
similarly achieved by Horner's Holiness Movement Church—was one
which derived largely from an influence exerted among the social masses
of the urban community.

After 1885, with the completion of the Canadian Pacific Railway
and the end of the long economic depression, developments were set
underway in Canada which ushered in the industrial era. The exploitation of the mineral resources of central British Columbia, the Klondike
gold-rush, and the pushing of agricultural settlement across the border
from the United States into Western Canada supported industrial
developments in Ontario, Quebec, and Cape Breton, and made possible
mass movements of population from overseas into the Canadian community. The industrial city emerged with its smoking factory chimneys
and solid blocks of working-class dwellings to become a dominant
form of community life in Canada.

The problems of Canadian social organization became increasingly
problems of urban industrialism. New social groups emerged—urban
industrial workers—and new social demands made their appearance
which imposed strains upon a social system which had developed in
terms of very different social demands. The intense social disorganization
evident in the transitional areas of the city (the slums) threw into bold
relief the sort of problems associated with increasing population
mobility and the dominant drive of the pecuniary motive. The segregation within the city of various ethnic groups represented strenuous
efforts to maintain the conditions of a folk culture, but powerful
economic and social forces broke down the traditional ties of neighbourhood and local group and threw up floating masses of people without
any definite social attachments and with no clearly defined social
purposes. The problem of the new Canadian urban society was a problem
of developing a distinctive community consciousness. To secure such a
development there were lacking effective agencies of collective effort.

The weakness of various forms of social organization reflected difficulties of adjustment to new conditions of economic and social life.
The background of the population, the dominance of individualistic
pecuniary motives, and the overpowering effects of a new physical
environment, evident, for instance, with respect to housing, tended
to a deterioration of cultural values and to the growth of an attitude of
cultural indifference. Among the new working masses of the urban

community such a break from a traditional cultural system was particularly evident. Long hours of work, the drabness of home life, and the excitements of the city street led to a coarseness of conduct and a feeling of disrespect for traditional forms of behaviour which made its effects felt in cultural life. The saloon grew up as the focus of social activity of the economically and socially dispossessed of the urban community. Crude forms of recreation provided the means of relaxation from work and the cares of the home. The higher values of life lost meaning within a situation dominated by the values of industrial capitalism. The new rich became rich through exploiting the poor, and the poor had little appreciation of the values underlying a social order of rank in which the upper class commanded a position of prestige and worth simply through the possession of wealth. Social inequalities became greater as the values of equality became stronger, and motives of individual gain or survival crowded out motives of social responsibility and service. Acceptance of social obligations was particularly avoided by those sections of the urban population which placed an exaggerated value upon money or pleasure-seeking.

If adjustment to the new conditions of urban social life proceeded slowly on the individual level, it proceeded even more slowly on the institutional level. Leadership, largely sheltered from the effects of industrial urbanization, promoted policies and activities within group organization which went little way in meeting the needs of an industrial urban population. In general terms, the people who held positions of responsibility or influence in the Canadian city of 1890 were people with a rural background and their thinking as a result tended to be in terms of the needs of a rural society. This was evident, for instance, in the family where the parents thought in terms of the conditions of rural social life. It was also evident in such fields of group activity as city government and the organization of political parties. The effects of this failure of the institutions of the secular society to adjust to the conditions of urban life were most felt among those sections of the population brought most rudely in contact with these conditions—the industrial working masses. It was here that there developed what in effect was something of a social vacuum in the community; a body of people standing outside and not really a part of society.

The weakness of secular values—and of secular organization—within the new urban industrial environment emphasized the importance of religious organization as an agency of social solidarity, and the rise of new religious movements such as the Hornerites and the Salvation Army indicated the failure of the traditional organization of religion to effectively act as such an agency of social solidarity. Out of the

limitations of the social and political organization of the city there developed the urban saloon and boss rule, and out of the limitations of the religious organization of the city there developed the new religious sect. The breakdown of denominationalism and the growth of religious sectarianism after 1885 was revealing of a social situation in which the church foim of religious organization no longer effectively met the needs of the population. It was in the limitations of traditional religious denominationalism that the chief explanation was to be found for the rapid growth of new sectarian religious movements. Such limitations were evident in the activities of all the religious denominations in Canada which attempted to serve the urban community. They can be most clearly seen in the case of the Methodist Church.

The failure of the Methodist Church after 1885 was not a failure to grow with the growth of the city nor was it a failure to gain in influence in the social life of the urban community. The building of handsome places of worship, the employment of highly learned—and, in some cases, highly paid—ministers, the increasing reliance upon prominent citizens in the organization of Sunday school and missionary work, and the growing participation of the pulpit in political discussion greatly strengthened the position of the Church as a social institution of the Canadian city. In 1886 the editor of the *Christian Guardian* could boast that in the twenty-seven largest cities and towns in Canada "Methodism has now a larger aggregate population than any other Protestant Church except the Anglican, and its growth is the most rapid."[54] And, in 1889, a correspondent to the same journal could write: "Methodistically, Toronto is perhaps the most remarkable city in the world. The influence of Methodism is felt in all the moral, social, educational, and political concerns of the community. Our members occupy prominent and influential places in the various professions, and in every department of commercial life. They fill many offices. The number of persons attending our churches is greater than that attending those of any other denomination. We have twenty-eight churches."[55]

But this growth of Methodist influence was by no means even throughout the urban community. The Church gained in support in the better residential areas of the city; it came to be made up of people who enjoyed economic and social security. Among the members of St. James Methodist Church in Montreal in 1890 was A. O. Dawson, vice-president and managing director of Canadian Cottons and among the members of Sherbourne Street Methodist Church in Toronto in the same year

[54]*Ibid.*, Aug. 18, 1886.
[55]*Ibid.*, May 29, 1889.

were H. H. Fudger, the president of the Robert Simpson Company, and J. W., later Sir Joseph, Flavelle. There were, it is true, the poor among the Methodist membership but they were the poor who were least affected by industrialism. The Church, that is to say, tended to draw its support from the folk or the classes of the urban community. The people who belonged to it were those able to maintain their traditional attachments within the urban setting.

Among the social masses of the city the influence of Methodism declined. It steadily ceased to serve as the church of the economically and socially dispossessed. This fact was recognized by the church leaders themselves. The editor of the *Canadian Methodist Magazine* wrote in 1886:

> One element in the success of Methodism has been the flexibility of its mode of operation, its power of adaptation to varying circumstances. . . . . It is especially adapted to the lowly and poor. . . . . It is to be feared that to some degree it has lost the hold that it once had upon this class. In the great cities it has developed a highly organized Church life, and has attracted many of the refined and wealthy classes. Whether rightly or wrongly, the idea is sometimes entertained among the poor that they are not as welcome in our elegant modern churches as they were in the quaint, old-fashioned, homely meeting-houses of an earlier day.[56]

The problem of winning the support of the urban masses was a concern of the Church which found increasing expression in the columns of the *Christian Guardian*. In 1888 the editor wrote:

> Are our Churches doing their full duty to the irreligious class in our cities and towns? Is our own Church giving the attention it ought to give to this important department of evangelistic work? No doubt our people have evinced great liberality and zeal in erecting handsome and commodious churches to meet the wants of the growing population in our cities and large towns. . . . But no one who fully knows the condition of our chief cities, would say that this covers the Church's whole duty, or meets the wants of our whole city population. To put up a costly church in a central locality and rent pews at a high price to those who want them and are able and willing to pay for them, and then leave all outside sinners who cannot do this to their fate, is certainly not the whole duty of the Christian people of a community to the irreligious poor, who may be only too willing to stay away from all church services. A church with all its seats rented and occupied, and little or no room for strangers, is not in a good shape for doing aggressive evangelistic work, and should not manifest any jealousy if some city mission or other evangelistic agency is set to work to reach and save those who are not being reached by the ordinary agencies of the churches.[57]

The next year a correspondent wrote to the *Guardian* in very similar vein:

> Are we doing our whole duty to the masses? We are building large and beautiful

---

[56]*Canadian Methodist Magazine*, vol. XXIV, July to Dec., 1886, p. 285.
[57]*Christian Guardian*, Sept. 12, 1888.

churches and filling them with the better class of the people; but what about the lower class of the poor, which is the most difficult to reach? . . . . There is no ignoring the fact that we cannot get the rich and the poor to mingle in our fine churches any more than the iron and clay in the feet of the great image of Daniel's vision. . . . Take as illustration such a large and rapidly growing city as Toronto. Churches are no sooner built than they have to be enlarged or rebuilt to accommodate the worshippers; and yet, outside all this is a vast population of from forty to fifty thousand who go to no church.[58]

A growing division between rich and poor inevitably developed in urban society on social grounds. The emergence of exclusive, as over against working-class, residential districts led to a physical separation of the two social groups within the city. The stratification within the social structure—in social clubs, education, and the like—accentuated the stratification secured within the ecological framework of the community. It was natural that these differences in social class would find expression in religious organization. Methodism, attracting more and more the support of the well-to-do classes, drew itself apart from the poorer classes in the city. "One of the most common," the editor of the *Christian Guardian* admitted, "of the unfavourable criticisms on the mission of the Church is that it has become largely the institution of the wealthy and respectable class, neglecting the poor and vicious class, and leaving them to suffer and sin outside of its pale."[59] On another occasion, the editor wrote:

It is unfortunate that anything in the conduct of Christians should help to create the impression that the religion of the Bible permits undue class feeling or undue class distinctions. We suppose that, in many instances, there is something in the appearance of fashionable and wealthy congregations which lends support to the criticisms of unchurched people. By some, the pew-rent system is considered directly promotive of a monopoly of church standing and advantages by the wealthier portion of society. By others, the grandeur and cost of church edifices are associated with the luxury of the rich, and an aversion to attendance at religious services results from the disparity of condition between rich and poor.[60]

Class conflicts which found expression within the Church were closely related to economic conflicts emerging out of an order of industrial capitalism. Economic exploitation which accompanied the introduction of the factory system led to dissatisfactions and feelings of unrest among industrial workers which found expression in strikes, occasional riots, and in the development of a working-class philosophy, while threats to capitalist enterprise from working-class movements led to strike-breaking efforts upon the part of employers and to combination.

[58]*Ibid.*, Dec. 4, 1889.
[59]*Ibid.*, Sept. 17, 1884.
[60]*Ibid.*, Apr. 18, 1888.

The attempt of Methodism to accommodate itself to this situation of violent economic change and conflict constituted one of the major problems of church leadership towards the close of the century.

It was perhaps inevitable, bearing in mind the impatience of the population generally at the time with the problem of labour, that the Church should commit itself to a policy which would arouse the antagonism of the working class. Methodist leaders strenuously sought to avoid placing the Church in opposition to labour. Methodist religious publications expressed their sympathy for the cause of the working man and appealed to employers to improve working conditions. Social justice became a popular note in the editorial and pulpit message. But such an appeal had little relationship to reality as seen by the working man concerned with strengthening his bargaining position through the organization of trade unions. The Methodist appeal, giving expression to the individualist philosophy of a natural harmony of interests of social classes, attacked directly and indirectly the economic and social assumptions of working-class philosophy. To the Methodist apologist of the capitalist system, class differences reflected differences in the contributions made by different groups to economic welfare; the poor were poor because they made less effort to improve themselves than the rich. The editor of the *Christian Guardian* wrote in 1884:

Classes must exist to some extent as long as there are different degrees of thrift, intellect, and religious education in a community. It is no cause for complaint against the Church that she adapts her services and instruction to the wants of these different classes of hearers. It would be a defect if it were not so. It is shown that a large proportion of the antagonism to the Church, by what are called the lower classes, is the outcome of a communistic feeling of the poor and suffering against the rich and respectable as a class, without regard to their religion or Church. It is to some extent the outcome of the feeling of the unsuccessful and needy against those who are successful and comfortable.[61]

Three years later, the editor wrote again: "Why are some people rich and others poor? As a general rule, because some people, or their parents, were more intelligent, energetic and industrious than others. There may be cases where men have become rich by wrong doing, or a stroke of good fortune, and cases where persons have been reduced to poverty by some inevitable causes; but these are the exceptions to the general rule."[62]

In editorial after editorial during the late eighteen-eighties or early eighteen-nineties the *Christian Guardian* launched out in attack upon the principles of the anti-poverty league, the single-taxers, and socialists.

[61]*Ibid.*, Sept. 17, 1884.
[62]*Ibid.*, May 11, 1887.

Much more important, from the point of view of labour support, was the attitude to strikes. It was about the strike that the fundamental issue of the position of labour in the capitalist system grew up, and Methodist Church leaders were slow to realize the importance of the striking power to the whole labour position. Generally, in both the *Christian Guardian* and the *Canadian Methodist Magazine* the strike was condemned as harmful, not only to society but to the workers themselves. "A strike, even when successful in its object," the editor of the *Canadian Methodist Magazine* wrote, "is always an unhappy means of accomplishing that object. It causes a feeling of estrangement and irritation between those whose interests are identical and whose prosperity must be mutual."[63] Too often, it was argued, strikes resulted from the improvidence of the workers rather than from any real grievances of labour. "Even when in receipt of large wages," the editor of the same Methodist publication wrote, "they often recklessly squander their earnings and lay up nothing for a rainy day, and many through intemperate habits will only work about one half of this time. Nothing but acquiring habits of saving and self-restraint will permanently benefit this improvident class."[64] Similar opposition to "The Eight Hour Movement," on the grounds that the workers would not wisely use their leisure, reflected an attitude which was not likely to gain for the Church any sympathetic support from labour.[65]

The predominantly rural background of the membership, and the long history of the Church in Canada as a rural church, had much to do with the failure of Methodism to effectively appeal to labour. The conception of work as a virtue and of leisure as a temptation to sin persisted strongly in the thinking of Methodists and made difficult an adjustment to the conditions of an industrial-capitalist order. The puritan outlook of persons of rural background was little different from the individualistic outlook of capitalist employers, and, whereas Methodist membership continued largely to be of rural origin, leadership passed to the capitalist classes of the urban community. The increasing influence exerted by employers of labour within the councils of the Church made more difficult the development of a positive appeal to the working-class population of the cities.

To some extent the problem faced by the Methodist Church in appealing to labour was a problem of religious organization in general. Industrial working conditions, in contrast with conditions of farm work, tended to a weakening of religious values. The social philosophy of

[63]*Canadian Methodist Magazine*, vol. XXIII, Jan. to June, 1886, p. 281.
[64]*Ibid.*, p. 280.
[65]*Ibid.*, p. 565.

industrial labour lent little support to a religious outlook; while most farm leaders were intensely religious, trade-union leaders were indifferent if not hostile to religion. The farm leader built his social philosophy upon a system of ethics; the philosophy of trade-unionism grew out of the rational principles of an industrial technology and the theoretical findings of the social sciences. The result was that the secular organization of labour carried with it a direct threat to the religious ethos. Working-class support of the Church dropped off not because of dissatisfaction with the form of religious organization but because of an indifference to the religious appeal. The editor of the *Christian Guardian* sensed something of this when he wrote in 1888: "It cannot be denied that narrow views of religion, speculatively considered, have caused many of the workingmen to reject Christianity. It is reasonable to believe that their rejection of it is more due to narrow and one-sided thought than any moral revulsion against its practical efficiency and influence. In the midst of their doubts and perplexities, Secularism has appeared on the scene and has claimed a peculiar friendship for the honest toiler, who, despairing of hope and rest in a future world, desires to secure the greatest amount of happiness in this."[66]

Only a small proportion of the working population of the city, however, was being drawn into trade-union organization. The great bulk of urban workers, unskilled and transient, lacked any sort of working-class philosophy or any consciousness even of being a part of a distinct working class. They constituted the masses of the urban community. Lacking permanent jobs, permanent homes, or permanent neighbourhood attachments, they had few strong loyalties and little sense of social responsibility. For them, mobility, rather than residence apart from their fellow-men, made for a considerable social isolation. The transient working-class family, moving from one part of the city to another or from city to city, was little less isolated than the unmarried and homeless worker. Family ties were not sufficiently strong to take the place of social ties forged through occupational and neighbourhood associations. The result was that these elements of the population participated little in the group life of the community at large. They withdrew into forms of association interstitial in character—gangs, associations of the saloon, and ephemeral groupings based upon the casual contacts of the street, the rooming house, or street-corner store. The break from the group life of the community was particularly evident in the withdrawal from religious associations. Abandonment of the practice of street preaching, as employed by the early Primitive Methodist

[66]*Christian Guardian*, Feb. 22, 1888.

preachers, and reliance upon services held in imposing places of worship, cut the Church off from the floating masses of the urban community. The problem faced by the Methodist Church in the latter decades of the nineteenth century was not simply one growing out of social differences between the rich and poor of the city. It was one resulting from a new kind of social mobility in the community for which the machinery of the Church was not adapted. Itinerancy had afforded a means of serving the scattered settlers of the rural frontier; street-preaching was the peculiar method adapted to serving the urban masses. Methodism, leading in the employment of itinerant methods, was slow to introduce the practice of street-preaching.

The price paid was the loss of support of the highly mobile masses of the urban community. "Methodism," the editor of the *Canadian Methodist Magazine* wrote in 1884, "has an as yet unfilled mission in our great cities. She must reach, as she does not now reach, the lapsed, the churchless, Christless masses. She must go not only to those who need her, but to those who need her most. If the people will not come to the preaching of the Gospel, we must take the gospel to them."[67] The next year the editor wrote: "There are classes in the cities whom it is difficult, if not impossible, to reach through the regular church agencies. There are multitudes who almost never enter a church door."[68] "It is in vain," the same editor admitted on another occasion, "that we erect handsome buildings and conduct decorous services if we do not reach the unchurched masses."[69]

The problem of reaching the transient population of the city was accentuated by the movement of people from one city to another. Persons who might otherwise have continued to support the Church dropped out simply because they were forced, through taking up residence in another city, to break their old religious associations and were not prepared to make an effort to form new associations in a strange setting. Such people often shifted their attachments from religious to secular organizations because participation in secular organizations involved less effort, or they became a part of "the masses" without definite attachments. In reporting that the total removals from the Methodist Church during the four previous years numbered 127,637, of whom only 13,623 could be accounted for through death, the editor of the *Methodist Magazine and Review* wrote in 1898: "Amid the changes of residence, made more frequent by the depression of the times, a considerable number may have gone to enrich the sister Methodism of the United States, or other

[67]*Canadian Methodist Magazine*, vol. XX, July to Dec. 1884, p. 276.
[68]*Ibid.*, vol. XXII, July to Dec. 1885, p. 376.
[69]*Methodist Magazine and Review*, vol. LI, Jan. to June, 1900, p. 287.

Churches of this country. But a very large leakage has occurred to those who, moving from place to place, have allowed their membership to lapse either through not receiving or not presenting certificates of church standing. Especially is this true of the membership in the towns and cities. In some churches much more than half of the entire membership is changed during the quadrennium."[70]

The effects of increasing population mobility were felt particularly in those areas of church activity where industries had a large turn-over of labour or were seasonal in character or subject to sudden shut-downs with a change in the market situation. But it was not only the mobility of the working class which weakened the position of the Church. Mobility was a characteristic of the urban population as a whole, and ties of family and neighbourhood upon which religious attachments depended were steadily weakened. Methodism had abandoned the methods of the sect where the recruitment of members depended upon drawing in people from the outside through the conversion process. It had come to rely upon the techniques of the church, seeking to perpetuate itself from generation to generation. The Sunday school developed as the chief means of keeping within the Church the new generation, but mobility rendered it increasingly less effective in securing this end. Mobility was greatest in that very age group within which the maintenance of religious attachments depended upon the shift of loyalties from the Sunday school to the Church. A growing gap developed between the membership of the Sunday school and the membership of the Church; many of those who had been faithful adherents of the one were lost to the other through the development of new interests outside the field of religion. The editor of the *Christian Guardian* admitted in 1900:

> The relation of young men to the Church has been brought prominently before us once more. Some strong words have been said of the Church's failure to hold the boys who have grown up in our Sunday-schools, and of reaching the young men who are found in our larger industrial centres. It is true that many of the boys of our Sunday-school, when they reach a certain age, leave the school, and are lost to the church. . . . The truth of the matter seems to be that the young men of today are much like all other mortals. They are human, and many are succumbing to the temptations of the world, the flesh and the devil, which, in our cities, beset them very early in life, and so fill their hours from early morning to late at night with such a whirl of excitement and enticements to folly that almost every day sees boys who have been bravely fighting the battle for manhood, falling victims to one sin or another.[71]

---

[70]*Ibid.*, vol. XLVIII, July to Dec., 1898, p. 282.
[71]*Christian Guardian*, July 4, 1900.

In the same year, W. J. Robertson, in a feature article in the *Christian Guardian*, wrote:

> If we look over Protestant Canada, we must observe an alarming state of affairs. What is most noticeable is the absence from our religious services of men. In our cities from three-fifths to three-quarters of the congregations are women and children. The prayer-meetings have a still smaller representation of men, while the leagues and Christian Endeavor Societies are almost deserted by young men. Along with this indifference to church affairs goes a growing disregard of Sabbath Day observance, and a general neglect of religious instruction. It is a fact that our young people are growing up very ignorant of the Bible, in fact, of all religious literature.[72]

Mobility imposed demands upon church organization which could only be met by the development of new techniques and methods. The house of worship was designed to meet the needs of a settled population; it did not effectively serve a floating population which had no strong local community or neighbourhood attachments. For the masses of the urban community the street became the centre of social life, and it was here that religious teachings had to be brought if they were to have any influence. Religious organization, that is to say, had to adapt itself to the ecology of the urban community. In failing to do so, Methodism paid the price of the loss of support of the more mobile elements of the population.

The problem, however, was not simply one of mobility. The churches had to do more than reach the urban population; they had to attract support through their religious appeal. A half century of effort to build itself into a denomination had led in Methodism not only to an emphasis upon the construction of large church edifices but to an emphasis upon a wordly pulpit appeal. The Methodist minister ostensibly preached to all classes in the community but his preaching was directed more and more to the fashionable, sophisticated elements of the population. The Church by 1885 had lost much of its evangelical drive; the preacher no longer waged the relentless war upon sin which the early revivalists had done (too many of the influential members of his congregation were likely to have been guilty of the sort of sins against which he would have had to preach). The polished and studied sermon took the place of the passionate exhortation calling upon man to repent and seek forgiveness. The effect was to make the pulpit much more popular. But it lost some of its force as a spiritually reorganizing agency among the "little people" of the city who were looking for direction and comfort and a means of securing new ties and attachments. The social problem of the masses was one of developing a new consciousness of group life,

[72]*Ibid.*, Aug. 1, 1900.

of being made to feel that they were a part of something. For them the formal sermons delivered from the Methodist church pulpits could have little meaning. What was wanted was the direct, elementary appeal of the evangelist. A correspondent wrote in the columns of the *Christian Guardian*:

> Our own church reported a few additions by letter, about as many as have left us or died, but only just five by profession of faith. . . . We naturally ask. Why this spiritual stagnation? Why this "lost power?". . . . I am not going to disparage the ability of our ministry. I believe the Methodist Church possesses a large proportion of able and devoted men. But are they employing their great talents and gifts to the best advantage? Is there not a disposition to preach "great" sermons? Deep sermons, eloquent sermons, sermons that please the hearers without disturbing their consciences? It used to be said that the early Methodist pioneers preached from Sinai too much; that, now, such preaching would be considered harsh and distasteful. But such preaching roused the consciences of sinners, and led them to cry out for mercy, and many were added to the church daily. These were men of power. . . . I fear we have left Sinai altogether, and gone to the other extreme, and our congregations are handled with kid gloves, fearing lest some one's feelings would be hurt if their sins were denounced. . . .
>
> Let us look at some of the methods employed to "draw" congregations, instead of the plain, simple truths of the Gospel. The Saturday evening papers give us such silly pulpit topics as, "Where are we at?" "Was Jonah swallowed by the whale?" "The marriageable young man and woman," etc. Then, popular singers from New York and other places are brought here and held before the public as the "great attraction." The question of the spiritual fitness to sing the songs of Zion for a Christian congregation is not considered.[73]

If churches were to be filled with the sort of people financially able to maintain them, the pulpit appeal had to be one directed toward the higher social levels of the population. Revivalism and the large church edifice were incompatibles. The former attracted the support of the poor, the latter required the support of the rich. Thus neither the ecological nor cultural needs of the urban community could be met effectively by a church relying upon regular religious services carried on in stated places of worship. Methodism in becoming a religion of the church—or temple—ceased to be a religion of the city streets. It became increasingly dependent upon the settled residents of the community, upon the people who enjoyed a sense of status and security. Thus it ceased to be a religion which served as a revitalizing or reorganizing influence in the community among those people who lacked a sense of status or security.

The break of the Methodist Church from the Canada Holiness Association was indicative of its inability to align itself with any strong

[73]*Ibid.*, May 20, 1900.

revivalist religious force in the community. The holiness doctrine became "too hot" for Methodism. The Church no longer could afford to make a single appeal; it had to be all things to all men. That was inherent in the character of the church as distinguished from that of the sect. So long as the holiness appeal could be contained within the religious teachings of Methodism it presented no danger, but the holiness advocates tended—inevitably in view of the nature of the doctrine— to place an exclusive emphasis upon the holiness idea, and out of such an exclusive emphasis there emerged the spirit of the sect. Methodism could give only a limited support to the holiness appeal if it was to retain its character as a church. In the end, it was forced to surrender leadership to the new holiness sects such as the Holiness Movement Church and the Salvation Army.

To some extent, an effort was made by the Church to maintain a revivalist influence through the development, or employment, of special evangelistic agencies which, while not a regular part of the church organization, were sufficiently under its control to be doctrinally safe. Various such agencies grew up during the last decades of the century. One of the most important was that of a body of professional evangelists.

The professional evangelist made his appearance in the United States about the eighteen-seventies and soon came to constitute a powerful force in religious life. Though not connected with any church, and unordained, the professional evangelist worked within rather than outside the regular churches. He thus gained his influence not by building up a special following of his own or by developing a peculiar set of doctrinal teachings but by making a special kind of appeal to regular church followings. In this way, the more successful of such evangelists were able to gain a hearing among hundreds of thousands of people without interfering with the work of the Church. Many of the American evangelists engaged in tours outside the country; their work became especially important in Great Britain. An increasing number visited Canada after about 1880.

By far the most widely known of the professional evangelists who visited Canada was Dwight L. Moody who came to Toronto and carried on religious services over the three days of December 3-4-5, 1884. His meetings secured front-page publicity in the *Toronto Globe.* "Mr. Moody's visit to Toronto," the *Christian Guardian* reported, "in connection with the Christian convention last week, attracted more widespread interest than any similar event in the religious history of this city. . . . Great excitement and anxiety to hear him prevailed in nearly

all the congregations of the city."[74] The editor of the *Canadian Methodist Magazine* wrote:

> The recent Christian Convention in this city, under the management of the distinguished evangelist, Dwight L. Moody, was an occasion of very great interest. We have never seen the whole city and surrounding country so stirred as by this great religious gathering. At every one of the nine services the spacious Metropolitan Church was crowded to its utmost capacity. As early as half-past seven in the morning people began to gather at the gates, though the meeting did not begin till ten o'clock. At least twenty-five thousand persons, or half of the adult population of the city, must have heard him, and over-flow meetings were held besides.[75]

Two years later the "Georgia evangelists," Sam Jones and Sam Small, came to Toronto and revivalist services were held in two different places in the city extending over a period of about three weeks. More emotional in their appeal than Moody, they succeeded in arousing among their congregations a high state of religious excitement and something of the character of an "old-time religious revival" took place. "On Sunday night," the *Christian Guardian* reported of one of the early meetings held by the evangelists, "the rink was packed with men in every part and hundreds had to go away. It was a wonderful sight. There was a large proportion of the unconverted classes. The sermon was thrilling and powerful."[76] One week later the *Guardian* wrote:

> No such numbers ever before attended any religious services in Toronto. Not only has the Mutual Street Rink been packed night after night with an eager congregation, estimated at from four to five thousand persons, but the Metropolitan Church has been well filled at the same hour . . . . The discourses of both evangelists have been very earnest and pointed appeals to the conscience. . . .
>
> After the sermon there is an after meeting, at which penitent sinners are invited forward for prayer and instruction respecting the way of salvation by faith. Mr. Jones closes his sermon every night by an appeal to all who desire to be saved and are willing to come out on the Lord's side to stand up. Persons rise in all parts of the house in response to these appeals, and at every meeting a large number profess to have found peace through believing on Christ.[77]

At the end of the next week the *Guardian* was able to report even greater success with respect to the work of the two evangelists: "During the last week the tide of religious interest, in connection with the labors of 'the Georgia evangelists,' has steadily risen higher and higher. The congregations have been simply immense, and the numbers who have given evidence of a purpose to lead a new life unprecedentedly large.

[74]*Ibid.*, Dec. 10, 1884.
[75]*Canadian Methodist Magazine*, vol. XXI, Jan. to June, 1885, p. 75.
[76]*Christian Guardian*, Oct. 13, 1886.
[77]*Ibid.*, Oct. 20, 1886.

The simple fact that night after night both the Mutual Street Rink and the Metropolitan Church have been crowded at the same hour is very significant. This means that in spite of all other attractions and distractions, over 6,000 people were present at these week evening religious services."[78] Two months later Sam Jones returned to Toronto for a shorter visit. Again, great crowds gathered to hear him. The *Christian Guardian* reported: "Every place where he has spoken has been crammed to overflowing. At Yorkville, on Saturday evening, he preached to a crowded house. On Sunday he preached in Carlton Street Church in the morning, in the Metropolitan in the afternoon, and in Elm Street in the evening. At each service the building was packed long before the hour of service, and hundreds were compelled to go away without being able to gain admission."[79] The next Spring Jones again showed up in Toronto where, in the words of the *Christian Guardian*, "he received an enthusiastic welcome."[80]

In succeeding years various other evangelists found occasion to carry on evangelistic campaigns in Canada. Usually these evangelists travelled in pairs, one preaching and one singing. Churches were used when found suitable, but services were often carried on in public halls or in rinks. Non-denominationalism was emphasized by the practice of preaching in the churches of different denominations or outside the churches altogether.

Unquestionably, the larger religious denominations, including the Methodist, gained something from the work of the professional evangelists. Religious interests among regular church followers were quickened and attendance upon religious services increased. Even more important was the influence of the work among people who were not regular church followers. In meetings held by the evangelists, particularly in such places as the skating rink, there were in attendance persons who had dropped away completely from services of the Church. "While the majority of the audiences," the *Christian Guardian* wrote of the meetings of Jones and Small, "have been persons who attend some of the Methodist churches of the city, at every service there were hundreds who do not belong to Methodist congregations, and many who do not attend any church."[81] The real test of the success of the work of the professional evangelists, from the point of view of the Church, was the extent to which these people became regular church adherents. Some of them probably did, but the vast majority lost interest in

[78]*Ibid.*, Oct. 27, 1886.
[79]*Ibid.*, Dec. 15, 1886.
[80]*Ibid.*, Mar. 9, 1887.
[81]*Ibid.*, Oct. 27, 1886.

religious matters once the evangelists left (or became caught up in the work of the newer religious sects). The Church lacked effective means of following up the work of the evangelists and maintaining the attachments of those who had been attracted by the revivalist preaching. "These Rink services," the *Christian Guardian* admitted, "have been vigorously followed up in all the Methodist Churches of the city with a good degree of success. But it was not easy to secure the attendance of the same people who were drawn to the Rink by the attraction of Sam Jones. This, however, is a difficulty which is felt in the case of all popular evangelists. The people, attracted by the preaching of a strange evangelist, are in danger of losing interest when he passes away; especially if the impressions made have not led to actual conversion."[82]

The limitation of the value of the work of the professional evangelists to the regular churches derived simply from the fact that they had no effective means of containing the religious interest which had been aroused. The non-church goer who found himself taking part in revivalist services in the rink or public hall did not easily go from there to attend regular religious services. Social and cultural influences which had previously made him indifferent to the appeal of religion continued to operate as strongly as ever. Revivalism created the urge to enter into religious fellowship, but it was an urge which could not be easily satisfied within the formal organization of the Church. It was for this reason that revivalism was seldom successful in establishing enduring religious attachments except where it led directly to the formation of a new religious sect. To some extent, as a result, the effect of the preaching of the professional evangelists was to strengthen new sectarian movements in the community and thereby to weaken the position of the regular churches. Where the evangelists preached to people who were faithful church goers, their influence was largely that of strengthening the institutional supports of religious organization; they were particularly successful in arousing a willingness to make financial contributions to the Church.

Closely related to the work of the professional evangelists was that of the special evangelists, a body of regularly ordained ministers set apart by the Church to carry on evangelical preaching. The development of such a body in the first instance was forced upon the Church as a means of offsetting the influence of self-appointed evangelists who were carrying on preaching activities throughout the country. The problem presented by these preachers was that of bringing their

[82] *Ibid.*, Nov. 10, 1886.

work under control. The self-appointed evangelist might serve the interests of the Church, but there was no way of making certain. Too often personal ambitions to build up a following, or peculiar doctrinal interpretations, led to the expounding of views or the employment of methods unacceptable to the Church. Where such evangelists were given a free hand, their influence was strongly established before the differences were recognized. The result was serious discord and very often division. It was in this way that the Plymouth Brethren cause became established in many centres, and it was as a means of offsetting the influence of Brethren evangelists that Methodist Church leaders were led as early as 1875 to urge the appointment within the Church of a number of special evangelists. "As a Church," the editor of the *Canadian Methodist Magazine* wrote in this year, "we lack one very important element of strength, in not having certain men—possessed of the required' qualifications—especially set apart for Evangelistic labour amongst us. The most of those who have laboured in that capacity in this country have been so tinctured with Plymouthism and other heresies, sometimes avowed, and sometimes disguised under orthodox names, that a strong prejudice exists amongst our people against this class of workers, which, however, would not obtain with any having the sanction of our own Church."[83]

In succeeding years the problem grew in urgency as religious life became more disorganized. With religious attachments in a state of flux, almost anyone could set himself up as a preacher of the gospel, claiming somewhat vaguely a connection with this or that church. Public halls could be rented, as commercial printing houses could be hired to print, and there was no easy means of controlling the growing flood of religious oratory or of religious literature. The editor of the *Christian Guardian* wrote in 1883 in support of the view that the Church should have its own specially appointed evangelists:

There is hardly a Methodist church in any of our cities or towns that has not at one time or other enjoyed the services of some evangelist, who gave himself specially to the promotion of revival work. Sometimes these were Methodists and sometimes they were not. One is led to wonder that a kind of work, so much in harmony with the genius and spirit of Methodism, has not been more fully recognized and provided for in different branches of the Methodist family. . . .

One great advantage of authorizing and appointing evangelists of our own Church is that it will take away the temptation to employ self-appointed evangelists, about whose personal character and doctrinal soundness little is known. If evangelists are to be employed at all, it would be better to be able to employ those whom we know to be loyal to our Church, and sound in the faith.[84]

---

[83]*Canadian Methodist Magazine*, vol. I, Jan. to June, 1875, p. 271.
[84]*Christian Guardian*, Aug. 22, 1883.

In 1884 the first of the Conference evangelists were appointed by the Church. Ralph Horner was soon to rank among their number. The evangelists were regularly ordained ministers who, instead of being stationed, engaged in preaching throughout the country wherever the opportunity for conducting revivalist services offered itself. Engaged in a special kind of work, they developed a special kind of method. They were under no strong obligation to conform to the conventions of the pulpit. Often they travelled in pairs, one preaching and the other singing. The length of their visit in any particular place was determined largely by their success in promoting a spirit of religious revival.

Among the earlier of such evangelists, the team of Crossley and Hunter attracted the most attention. Reports of their work provide some indication of the growing reliance placed upon such evangelists in the carrying on of revivalist services. "A few days ago," the *Christian Guardian* reported in April, 1887, "evangelistic services were commenced in Port Hope under the direction of Messrs. Crossley and Hunter. The largest churches are thronged with multitudes."[85] During the summer and autumn of 1887, successful revivals were reported from Picton, Cobourg, Windsor, and other places as a result of the work of the same evangelists.[86] In November of this year Toronto was visited, and in the early part of the next year Ottawa; here the evangelists proved particularly successful in their revivalist labours. "This work at Ottawa," the editor of the *Christian Guardian* wrote, "is perhaps the most extraordinary revival that has been seen in this generation in Canada."[87] In the spring of 1888 Belleville was visited. "The revival services of Messrs. Crossley and Hunter at Belleville," the *Christian Guardian* reported, "have produced a profound effect. So widespread are the interest and religious feeling manifested that balls have been stopped and the engagements of theatrical troupes cancelled owing to the sparse attendance and lack of interest taken in them."[88]

Reports in succeeding years of the work of Crossley and Hunter and of other special evangelists were of much the same character. The work grew in terms of the number of evangelists employed. A report in the *Christian Guardian*, March 21, 1900, provides some indication of its importance within the organization of the Church. At the time, Crossley and Hunter were engaged in revivalist services in Elm Street church in Toronto. The previous week they had been engaged in similar services in Sheddon; here evangelists Kennedy and

[85]*Ibid.*, Apr. 13, 1887.
[86]*Ibid.*, Nov. 9, 1887.
[87]*Ibid.*, Feb. 29, 1888.
[88]*Ibid.*, Apr. 11, 1888.

Whyte were expected to continue the work. These evangelists were then carrying on revivalist services in Dorchester. In Hamilton Road church, London, a series of evangelistic meetings under the leadership of Evangelist Collycott had just drawn to a close. In Dundas Centre church in London the local pastor was being assisted by Evangelist McHardy, while in Oakwood church a series of evangelistic meetings had been carried on for two weeks under the direction of the Caldwell Brothers, one preaching and the other singing. In Fenelon Falls, Evangelist Frank J. Hill, in co-operation with the stationed minister, was engaged in revivalist services.[89]

The preaching of the special evangelists undoubtedly did something to strengthen the work of the individual Methodist churches. They could be called in at certain seasons of the year when the regular work of the Church tended to lag, and they became particularly important in the launching of financial campaigns, an undertaking often embarrassing to the stationed minister dependent upon such campaigns for his salary. In the smaller churches in the country, where able ministers could not be secured, their work assumed considerable importance. Here, the problem was not simply one of keeping the church from going dead, but one of avoiding violent upheavals resulting from the visits of self-appointed evangelists. The Church was forced to maintain, as it had been forced to establish, a body of special evangelists to protect its following from the influence of evangelists outside its supervision or control.[90]

In terms of the general religious problem of the community, however, the special evangelists did little more than the professional evangelists to extend the influence of the Church beyond the regular membership body. Their preaching was carried on from the church pulpit and it reached few who were not regular church attendants. The revivals which they promoted tended to assume a stereotyped character; while they preached more people attended church but they were not people

[89]*Ibid.*, Mar. 21, 1900.

[90]In 1890 a correspondent wrote to the *Christian Guardian*:
"The existence in our midst of an apparently ever-increasing number of 'evangelists,' both male and female, calls for serious inquiry as to whereunto this thing shall grow, and what shall be the attitude of the Church towards it.

"We may as well at once face the fact that the evangelist is here, whether to stay or not is another question. Being here, what shall we do with him, extend a welcome, or oppose and endeavor to suppress him? Surely it would seem to be our wisdom to take advantage of this new agency and direct it to the best ends.

"But at present we are in a somewhat dangerous position. As things stand, almost anyone who takes the notion may thrust himself out into this work, and without authority or control wander around the country claiming to be an evangelist and expecting the sympathy and co-operation of ministers and people wherever they happen to drop down." *Christian Guardian*, Apr. 23, 1890.

who had withdrawn very far from regular church activity. Certainly, the revivals of religion associated with the work of these evangelists, reported at frequent intervals in the columns of the *Christian Guardian*, were in no sense revivals of religion among the great unchurched masses of the community. Only where the evangelist broke outside the bounds of the Church, as in the case of Ralph Horner, did he build up any great influence among those who were not already a part of the traditional organization of religion.

The failure of the special evangelists to serve as an effective evangelical agency within the Church resulted not only from the fact that their work was carried on from the church pulpit but from the fact that they were unable to utilize the services of lay workers. They had all the weaknesses of professional ministers. What was needed, if the Church were to reach the highly mobile classes within the city, was a body of workers prepared to go out on to the city streets, into the homes of the poor and into the public meeting places of the common man. The need of maintaining his professional dignity, in itself, made it difficult for the minister to to do this (he could scarcely permit himself to be seen admonishing the prostitute at the door of the brothel). Even if the professional evangelists had been prepared to do such work, they were too few in numbers to do anything worthwhile. The work was such as to require an army of workers, and such an army could only be built up by drawing upon lay volunteers. The success achieved by the Salvation Army demonstrated what could be done in this regard. The competition of the Army forced Methodist Church leaders to consider the advisability of developing a similar type of organization. A correspondent wrote to the *Christian Guardian* in 1883 of the Salvation Army:

> As regards the attitude of other Churches towards this extraordinary organization, I do not wish to say anything, but I think it is well worth while to ask, what position should we Methodists adopt in regard to it. It cannot, I think, be gainsayed, that the whole genius of the thing is Methodistic. Its founder is, or was, a Methodist minister, its doctrines are the same as those of our Church, and in very many of its practices also, such as fellowship meetings, the free use of "lay" agency and open-air preaching, it is working upon lines with which we are perfectly familiar. . . .
>
> I have been asked almost in a spirit of rebuke, "Cannot we do the same work?" I believe, sir, that we can and ought. I have had personal experience of the same kind of work in the Old Country, and I know well that there is a certain class in every city and town who never cross the threshold of our church doors, and who never will hear the Gospel unless you take it to them.
>
> There are hundreds of young men and women throughout Methodism abundantly able for this work. It is a work which can only be done as an adjunct to our present ordinary methods, and it is a work which we as a Church could do far more effectively, and without descending to the extravagances with which it is now accompanied. . . .

Sir, I have no lack of loyalty to the Church to which I owe, under God, the bliss of conversion, and many other blessings, but here is a sphere of labor, which, while preeminently hers at first, seems to have lapsed under the growth of respectability which is too much the bane of all denominations.[91]

The same view was expressed three years later by another correspondent, the Reverend John Weir of Halifax, in answering the question of whether the Church needed a "Salvation Army" branch. He wrote:

The Church already provides for its equivalent. . . . From her local preachers, exhorters and class-leaders, male and female, she can, with slight disturbance of the present Discipline, call out an army of lay agents and station them in every city, village and lumbering centre within the bounds of the General Conference to do the same work as the Salvation Army. . . . Popular and attractive vocal and instrumental music, with bright, crisp, varied, common-sense religious exercises can be readily furnished by Methodist workers, and these powerfully used by the Holy Spirit in moving the heart. Plain houses for such services should be occupied, apart from the churches as at present constituted. It goes without saying that there is a class even in the smaller towns whom nothing will induce to enter the regular edifices. We may make our churches as free as we like; the regular congregation may surrender the building to the masses for the freest possible use on Sunday evenings; exercises may be varied and popularized ad infinitum, and yet there is a people who will not come in. . . . Something irregular is in order to reach an irregular people. If we cannot "compel them to come in" through the church, let us impel them through some other places; and once converted to God, the church will become their natural home. We possess the engine. Set it going, and we have the equivalent of a Salvation Army branch.[92]

It was out of the growing recognition of the need of developing some such activity within the Church that there grew the Gospel Band movement. The origin of the first gospel band was described in the columns of the *Christian Guardian*:

Humanly speaking the Band was accidentally formed. For months a series of cottage prayer-meetings had been held in West Belleville, and there it was decided to pay a visit to Bro. Herrington's friends over the bay, and hold three services in one of our churches on the Sabbath. A sleighload went, accompanied with several members of the Salvation Army. . . . The visit was repeated to a neighboring church on the next Sabbath. . . . It was evident the Lord was leading us, for invitations at once poured in from various churches for a day's visit. In order to systematically go to work, the "Hallelujah Band" was formed. We appointed three brethren as officers, and also a treasurer and a manager. In the morning we hold a holiness meeting, when we preach sanctification. We wage war on all bad habits, particularly the using of liquor and tobacco, and we also fight worldliness. In the afternoon and evening our meetings have but one aim—to win souls. We have short testimonies, interspersed with very hearty singing, enlivened with several tambourines, then a

---

[91]*Ibid.*, Aug. 22, 1883.
[92]*Ibid.*, Dec. 22, 1886.

Scripture reading, and then a prayer-meeting, during which seekers are invited to the penitent form. We pray for souls, work for souls and expect to see souls saved.[93]

The organization of the gospel bands was closely modelled upon that of the Salvation Army Corps. Although direction of the work was assumed by special Conference evangelists, the bands themselves were simply groups of laymen who joined together and undertook specially chosen tasks of evangelization. The influence of the Salvation Army in promoting such a development was freely admitted. One correspondent wrote to the *Christian Guardian*:

The Salvation Army came to our country none too soon. Though they doubtless overestimated their strength, and do not even yet manifest much loyalty to the Christian Churches, yet their efforts to save the masses have stirred up the Churches to form "Gospel Bands." By these I think we can do the work they are doing, without the bad results that often follow. Since local preachers are very few, and the people demand good and systematic preaching, we cannot afford to dispense with Christian workers. By many outside the Church the ministry is regarded in a conventional light. The minister is regarded as a paid professional man. But if a company of Christian workers go out with their pastor to sing, pray, and witness for Christ, his anxiety is removed and his heart encouraged. . . .

Conference evangelists are doing a good work, but few places can secure them We have plenty of material on all our fields, which, if utilized, can help on the work of revival.[94]

The gospel band movement quickly developed to become a regular feature of the Church's work. The Petrolia Band, under the leadership of the Reverend David Savage, assumed particular importance. Savage had most of the qualities of the highly successful evangelist, and, through the organization of tent and camp meetings, he was able to build the Petrolia Band into a powerful evangelistic agency. It came to assume in itself almost the character of a religious movement. A correspondent wrote to the *Christian Guardian* in October, 1884:

This general movement of the people towards salvation appears to be the result of God's blessing upon the organization of the Church into working bands. They are frequently called by the people "Hallelujah Bands," employing an appellative invented, I think, in Belleville, but they do not themselves adopt the name, but call themselves simply "The Bands." They are composed of persons fourteen years of age, at least, who are clearly saved now, and can give a clear account of their conversion, and of "how a work of grace discovers itself when it is in the heart of a man," who do not touch intoxicants nor tobacco, and are willing to work and witness for Christ at any time and in any place under the direction of their leaders. There is no fanaticism about this plan of operation. It is not an excrescence upon the Church's fair form. It is just what ought to exist in every circuit and every church in

93*Ibid.*, May 14, 1884.
94*Ibid.*, Mar. 25, 1885.

Methodism—an organization of happy and willing Christians to work in concert for the salvation of lost men.[95]

Savage himself wrote the next month of the work of the Petrolia Band:

> The leaders of this movement in the West are so busy making history that they have little or no time to write it. A few hurried jottings may, however, help some of your readers to an inside view of the work. It still spreads—thank God. The points touched are left with the several pastors to report. Next week, the Petrolia workers will occupy some six localities simultaneously, in companies of from two to four at each place. This arrangement, however, is only allowed where a local "Band" is available to support the more experienced workers. . . .
> Comparatively few children have been saved in this movement. Young men and women, married people of all ages up to even eighty, the substantial, solid yeomanry of some of the rural sections, artisans, and business men of the villages are among the converts. The most notorious sinners of a locality are frequently included . . . .
> The workers are consecrated. We want none others. The Methodist doctrine of holiness is kept to the front. I believe this to be the secret of power in the "Band" movement.[96]

The movement gained in popularity the next year. The editor of the *Canadian Methodist Magazine* wrote: "The remarkable successes which have attended the labours of Bro. Savage's bands in the west, and of the Belleville and other bands in the east, show the adaptation of those special methods to the necessities of the times. . . . It is certainly much better to employ the energies of lay workers—of whom there is a great reserve force in Methodism—under the direction and oversight of the Church, than to let them be employed without its oversight and beyond its control."[97] A Methodist minister, the Reverend S. J. Hunter, wrote to the *Christian Guardian* the same year:

> After having had the Rev. David Savage and one of his Bands at the Centenary Church for ten days, I wish to point out a few things that commend the movement. First, as Mr. Savage is one of our own ministers, we have a guarantee for correct teaching. Second, the methods employed are all in the line of our time-honored usage, with an entire absence of those questionable excrescences and financial schemes that have marked and marred some evangelistic movements. Third, the Band-workers are simple-minded, humble, consecrated young men and women, who implicitly trust God and have passion for soul-saving. Fourth, Christian testimony is kept prominently before the people, stimulating all to this duty as a means of impressing the unsaved and encouraging the timid and young of the Church.[98]

---

[95]*Ibid.*, Oct. 1, 1884.
[96]*Ibid.*, Nov. 26, 1884.
[97]*Canadian Methodist Magazine*, vol. XXII, July to Dec., 1885, p. 376.
[98]*Christian Guardian*, Nov. 4, 1885.

Two years later, another correspondent, the Reverend W. W. Sparling, wrote to the *Christian Guardian:*

> The Church has entered upon a new era in her methods of work, which is not a new departure but a revival of the old plan of the early days of Methodism. There hardly ever was a time when there was such a demand for lay-workers or when there was such a force in the field as now. The peculiarity of the times seems to have created the very necessity for this demand. And while every pastor does indeed fulfil the command "Do the work of an evangelist," yet owing to the peculiarity of his work as a pastor he cannot enter fully into the work of an evangelist. . . .
>
> The Methodists are not the only denomination who are utilizing this factor in Church work. The Episcopalians have their "Church Army," the Presbyterians and Baptists have their evangelists lay and clerical. Of course caution is necessary as to the character of the persons thus employed. I confess I have my prejudices on this point, but they have all been sent to the winds as I have read of and witnessed the successful labors of these godly men and women.[99]

So long as interest in the movement could be maintained, the Church secured through its gospel bands an effective evangelistic agency for carrying on work among the masses of the urban community. The strength of the bands lay in their employment of young men and women, devoutly religious, who were prepared to throw themselves wholly into the task of spreading the evangelical message of salvation. The band worker had few of the inhibitions of the minister anxious to maintain his professional status in the community. He was prepared to go anywhere and to employ whatever methods seemed suitable to gain a favourable hearing. To the most zealous of the workers, the movement assumed the character of a great evangelical crusade.

Yet in spite of the intense earnestness which was characteristic of the early band workers, the movement quickly weakened and soon virtually disappeared. It is true that the Reverend David Savage for some years remained a prominent evangelist within the Methodist Church, but his work became largely dissociated from that of the gospel band movement. It was easy for Savage, with his gifts as a

---

[99]*Ibid.,* Nov. 9, 1887.

Of the gospel band movement in New Brunswick, the *Canadian Methodist Magazine* wrote in 1887: "One of the finest examples of the success of these aggressive methods that we know is the Band Workers' Association of St. John, N.B. It is thus described by Brother Brewer, pastor of the Centenary Church: 'In all great centres there is a large portion of the population that is seemingly beyond the reach of ordinary church agencies, and this city is no exception to the rule. To reach these classes praying bands have been organized, halls have been secured, and services have been held in the churches.' One of the first places secured was a dance-hall on one of the worst streets in the city. Here a mission service was begun and many lost ones were reclaimed and many souls saved. Open air preaching, house-to-house visitation, tract distribution, and various forms of personal persuasion have been employed to bring men and women to Christ, and God's blessing has abundantly rested upon these efforts. Several of the city churches, we believe, have combined in this band work. The movement has spread to other places." Vol. XXVI, July to Dec., 1887, p. 375.

popular preacher, to establish a reputation as a great evangelist, but it was much more difficult to direct the sort of work which the bands were called into being to do. Interest in such work weakened on the part of Savage and other church leaders, and the weakening of their interest was followed by the weakening of interest of the workers themselves. By 1890, or earlier, all mention of gospel band work had disappeared from the columns of the *Christian Guardian.*

The weakness of the gospel band movement lay in the nature of its relationship to the Church. The gospel bands attempted to do the work of the sect while remaining a part of the Church; in the end, they possessed neither the strengths of the one nor the other. Developing not as a regular but as an irregular feature of church activity, they lacked the denominational supports of regular church work. On the other hand, they had none of the strength deriving from the spirit of the religious sect. The bands could not build up a loyalty separate from the loyalty to the Church; if they had, they would have been forced out of the Church as, indeed, the Salvation Army had been. The person attracted by the work of the gospel band had in a sense nothing to join. It had no distinctive organization, creed, or set of doctrines. It was simply an agency of the Church employed for a certain purpose. It had no prophet and developed no following. The result was that there was no basis on which to build an enduring interest. Had the gospel band movement been able to develop a loyalty similar to that developed within the religious order of the Catholic Church it might conceivably have survived, but Protestant religious organization was unfavourable to a system of religious orders. The movement could only survive by becoming an integral part of Methodist denominational organization or by growing into a separate religious sect. Failing to develop in either direction, it disappeared as a distinctive form of religious activity.

Of a more enduring character was the Epworth League movement which grew up in effect on the wreckage of the gospel band movement. From the beginning, the Epworth League movement developed under the close direction of the Church. It was made an integral part of the denominational organization. The intention in this case was to develop not an agency to reach out among the unchurched masses but an agency to strengthen the attachments of young people already within the Church. The Epworth League was designed to close the gap between the Sunday school and the Church as a means of checking the heavy loss of support of young people to more aggressive evangelistic religious bodies or to secular agencies. "Other associations of young people," the editor of the *Methodist Magazine* wrote in explanation of the founding

of the Epworth League, in 1889, "were springing up amongst us, excellent in their way, but owing no allegiance to Methodism, and in no way under the control of our Church, either as to the courses of prescribed reading, or general management, and having their affiliated relations in a foreign land. . . . It is not a good thing for young people to think that they must leave the Church of their fathers for helpful religious association and religious enjoyment. . . . The newly-formed Epworth League was found to furnish just the nucleus of what seemed required for our needs.[100] The League grew rapidly during the early years after its founding. Reports in the *Christian Guardian* indicate a steady advance in membership until about 1900. As early as 1889 the editor of the *Guardian* was able to write: "The Epworth League movement is awakening great interest throughout the entire country, as evidenced by hundreds of letters of inquiry from all parts—from Newfoundland to British Columbia. Already a considerable number of branches have been established in Toronto, Hamilton, London, Ottawa, Peterboro', Ingersoll, St. Catharines, St. John, N.B., and elsewhere, and others are forming each week."[101]

The work carried on by the Epworth League, and by such other organizations as the Christian Endeavour Society, was undoubtedly of value to the Church. The rapid growth of the urban community imposed heavy demands upon young people through the failure to build up institutions—recreational and cultural as well as religious—to take care of their needs, and the development within the Church of young people's societies was the recognition of the necessity of taking a lead in this respect if the church were to hold its own with commercialized forms of recreation and with rival evangelistic religious agencies. The Methodist young peoples' societies were intended to be strictly religious in character; the primary emphasis was placed upon the evangelical message of salvation. Reports of early activities of the League indicate that the religious interest among the membership was strong. This was particularly true among the students of Victoria College where a number of religious revivals were promoted under the influence of League activities.

But the heavy hand of the Church checked any tendency towards a too great emphasis upon revivalist methods. The Epworth League was a religious movement within a denominational system. Controlled by the leaders of the Church, it could not develop the drive which would have made it into an aggressive evangelistic agency within the com-

[100]*Methodist Magazine*, vol. XXX, July to Dec., 1889, p. 561.
[101] *Christian Guardian*, Dec. 18, 1889.

munity; to have developed such a drive would have endangered its relationship to the Church. The result was that it remained eminently respectable in character but lost much of its evangelical zeal. It developed into an association stressing social and cultural activities; its teachings were those of a parlor rather than of a street-corner religion. As such it became an instrument of consolidation in the denominational organization of the Church rather than an instrument of religious expansion. It achieved little success in extending the influence of religion to those masses of young people in the city who had no close contact with the Church, nor was it wholly successful in maintaining the religious attachments of those young people brought up within the Church. In discussing the problem of reaching the young men of the city, at a meeting of the Toronto Social Union, January 18, 1900, the remarks of Mr. Alfred W. Briggs were reported as follows in the *Christian Guardian*:

Of these young men who cause anxiety, the average of the class go regularly to Sunday-school for years, but unfortunately have passed through untouched by the leaven of righteousness, and at seventeen or eighteen find themselves too old for Sunday-school, and out of sympathy with the average League meeting. Where do these young men go? It is too well known that they meet with their fellows to indulge in amusements that are not always innocent. . . . A few are attracted by the literary and social aspects of the Leagues, but they are comparatively few. To reach or hold these young men, the Methodist Church is making no general organized effort.[102]

In the same year the editor of the *Christian Guardian* wrote:

To meet the wants of young men and women there have been innumerable devices. Intellects were burnished by the old spelling-matches and debating clubs; sobriety was encouraged by the temperance societies; and the young people were trained for Christian work in praying bands. From these have evolved the Christian Endeavour Society, the Epworth League, and kindred denominational organizations, with their different literary, social, temperance and religious departments. The constitution of the League is a splendid piece of legislation, but its organization has not been as carefully fostered as that of the Sunday-school. Wherever the young people have had the advice and co-operation of sympathetic pastors and intelligent church officials, the leagues have prospered, but these cases have not been as many as they ought to have been, and the young people, being left to their own devices, have suffered as much from lack of advice and sympathy from men who ought to have given it, as from the errors of ignorance and the temptations of social enjoyment.[103]

In the end, sharp class lines shut off such organizations as the Epworth League from the great masses of the urban community. One of the conditions of the acceptance of the League was its claim to respectability.

[102]*Ibid.*, Jan. 4, 1900.
[103]*Ibid.*, July 4, 1900.

It was a society made up of "nice young people," the sons and daughters of respectable church-going folk. This very character of the League meant that it could not attract the support of the socially marginal classes of the community. Had a number of the social outcasts actually joined the League it would immediately have lost the support of the "respectable" members of the Church; they could not have permitted their sons and daughters to have associated with such people even in a religious organization. Thus inevitably the Epworth League displayed all the weaknesses of the established religious denomination; made up of people with status it could not serve as an effective social reorganizing influence among people who lacked status. It developed as simply one of many similar types of organization which came to make up the urban church with its far-flung denominational organization.

By 1900 the Methodist Church was in a stronger position to serve the urban community than it had been in 1885. It had learned much in the intervening fifteen years. Up until about 1885 there had been little effort within Methodism to adapt its organization or appeal to the needs of the socially marginal elements of the urban population. The record after 1885 was one of continuous experimentation, and some measure of success was achieved. The work of the professional evangelists, the building up of a body of special evangelists, and the development of such lay organizations as gospel bands and Epworth Leagues did contribute something to strengthening the influence of the Church in the community. Even more, the growth of such activities was an indication of a change in the attitudes of church leaders. The fact that something was tried meant at least that there was a recognition of the problem.

But the problem grew more rapidly than the efforts of the Church to meet it. The failure of the Church derived from the fact that what it did always was done too late and never was carried far enough. Denominational influences within the Church were too strong to permit any radical departure from accepted methods or appeals. It was only when the Church was forced to do something to meet the competition of more aggressive evangelistic religious sects that it acted, and when it did there was always a sharp brake placed upon anything which threatened the denominational position of the Church in the community. Unorthodox preachers like Nelson Burns and Ralph Horner had to be expelled from the Church when their work threatened to disturb traditional denominational relationships. Efforts to develop a type of organization similar to that of the Salvation Army inevitably failed because of the necessity of maintaining conformity to accepted practices of the Church. Activities promoted by the Church necessarily were

subject to its control and became a regular feature of its work, if not abandoned. Such activities thus lent support to the denominational system and ceased to have any importance as a reorganizing social influence outside the system. They became means, that is to say, of securing the status of those who were a part of the denominational organization rather than a means of developing a sense of status on the part of those outside. The latter role was one which the religious sect, such as the Holiness Movement Church or Salvation Army, was in a much better position to perform.

Horner's break from the Methodist Church offered a striking demonstration of the failure of a denominational religious system to adapt itself to the needs of the socially marginal elements of the population in the community. Horner began simply as an evangelist within the Church, but his work gained significance with his refusal to accept its controls. His independence made it possible for him to employ whatever methods he saw fit and to build up about himself his own distinctive following. His highly emotional appeal won for him a hearing; his assumption of the air of a prophet secured the attachments of those to whom he preached. Long before 1895 the Horner movement assumed many of the characteristics of the separate religious sect. This was made evident in Horner's own reminiscences. In the account of his work during the early years of his preaching almost the whole attention is given to the excitements of revival meetings, but in the account of his work during the later years much greater regard is paid to the development among his followers of the spirit of the primitive church. Disavowal of all luxuries and ornaments and acceptance of tithing as an obligation to God became hall-marks of the saved man. The "stripping room" developed alongside the penitent bench as an important feature of the conversion process, while tithing became one of the chief bases of group organization. There grew up a special loyalty, special duties, and a feeling of oneness among Horner's followers. There developed a consciousness of being of the "spiritual elect." "The conversions and sanctifications," Horner wrote respecting one of his revivalist campaigns, "were very clear in this place. Some who were much conformed to the world had to enter the stripping room as soon as they were converted to God, in order to advance in the Christian life. There were two women who each had about one hundred and fifty dollars worth of gold ornaments and dress accordingly. They entered the stripping room at Mt. Horeb, and went on into the promised land. They were entirely sanctified and commenced to tithe their income."[104] On another occasion, Horner wrote in speaking of the results of a revivalist meeting: "They went to

[104]*Ralph C. Horner, Evangelist: Reminiscences from His Own Pen*, pp. 127-8.

the penitent form and were delivered. It was a great cross to them to enter the stripping room until they were humbled before God. They removed their ornaments and appeared in plain attire. It is hard for proud people to see that more than the simplest plainness is in bad taste."[105]

There were few of Horner's followers who had ornaments of any great value to strip off before receiving the experience of entire sanctification, and this fact was significant in the emphasis upon asceticism. By disavowing such luxuries which they had not the means of enjoying, the humble folk who attached themselves to Horner broke through those distinctions which set them off from the more fortunate classes. Plainness which was the lot of the common man became an attribute of godliness; it was thus that the sect could create a consciousness of worth on the part of those who became caught up within it. It would not be possible to determine accurately what sort of people became attached to the movement led by Horner. Some of them may have been, as he suggested, people of social standing in the community, but certainly they must have been exceptional. The fact that the movement developed its greatest strength in the Ottawa Valley is in itself suggestive. Horner appealed to the lumbermen, to isolated farm families, and to those residents of such cities as Ottawa and Montreal who had no great feeling of security in the urban environment. The movement gained its support on the fringes of the rural society and within the transitional areas of the city. Later growth of the Holiness Movement Church also was among such social classes of the community.

The loss suffered by the Methodist Church with Horner's break in 1895 was an indication of the strength of the movement as an agency of religious evangelization. In terms of the general religious organization of the Canadian community, however, the Horner movement had much less significance than the Salvation Army. The really important problem of religious organization in Canada after 1885 was that of reaching the urban masses and it was the Army which demonstrated in its clearest forms the sort of methods and appeals which were required in meeting this problem. The Army had grown in Britain out of urban conditions of life and in Canada its greatest success was achieved in urban rather than rural areas.

The advantages enjoyed by the Army quickly became evident in competition with the traditional churches of the community. Growth of membership in itself was no clear measure of the success which it achieved; it was not a matter of how many but who were brought

[105] *Ibid.*, p. 129.

under its influence. The Army succeeded in a way that the traditional churches did not in attracting the support of the foot-loose elements of the urban population. The appeal of the Army was a mass appeal. At the same time, it was a peculiarly individual appeal. The Army reached those who needed to be reached if religion were to serve as an important socially reorganizing influence in the urban community. "Some most notorious drunkards and evil livers," the editor of the *Canadian Methodist Magazine* admitted, "have been transformed into active Christian workers by the agency of the army. It attracts many whom it seems impossible to reach by the more decorous services of our Churches. Discount as one may the extravagances and grotesquenesses of the services there is ample testimony of their beneficent effect."[106]

The methods employed by the Salvation Army made it possible for it to gain the support of foot-loose elements of the urban population. Street preaching was revived as a regular feature of religious work, and the combination of street preaching with parades, led by brass bands, provided an effective means of attracting attention. Crowds were gathered together on street corners, in public parks and other open spaces, and, when a sufficient state of religious enthusiasm had been aroused, the following was paraded to the barracks where a revivalist meeting took place. At no point did the Army impose any serious obstacle to the participation of the individual in the religious service. He could easily join the crowds on the street and depart if he saw fit. Similarly, the act of entering the house of worship was made easy. The Army sought to provide religious services in the sort of places in which people who had not been accustomed to attend churches felt at home; thus the simplicity of the barracks and the employment, at times, of public halls which had been used for other purposes (in East London, William Booth found it an advantage to convert taverns into Army meeting places).[107] Within the religious service itself, an emphasis was placed upon the free movement of individuals. The lack of decorum in Army meetings served to develop a feeling of homeliness and ease, in sharp contrast to the stiff formality which characterized the church religious service. A meeting in Kingston was described by a visiting Methodist missionary:

The audience room would seat about six hundred persons. Noticeable on the white-painted brick walls were well-designed Scripture mottoes, as—"Salvation is free," "The blood of Jesus Christ cleanseth from all sin," "Now," etc., etc. Upon a raised platform in front sat several of the young, middle-aged, and old, whom we

---

[106]*Canadian Methodist Magazine*, vol. XIX, Jan. to June, 1884, p. 371.
[107]See Harold Begbie, *Life of William Booth* (2 vols., London, 1920).

might designate as Salvationists, though nothing in dress or demeanor distinguished them from other decent people. Presently in came marching a number of young men and women, the former with red woollen jackets and black caps marked "Salvation Army," the latter in plain black and scoop bonnets, also marked. These, just returning from their parade with big drum, kettle drum, cornet, tambourines, and triangle, were followed by quite a few of all sorts, attracted hither by this means. The captain, a vigorous young man, with voice somewhat husky, opened the service with a spirited song. It and several other songs in succession were most heartily sung by all, and intensified by the drum-beating, tambourine-playing, elbow-swinging, and body-swaying, almost dancing with joy as their emotions were thus aroused. In the mean-time, two young women, one a mulatto, moved slowly about the congregation selling the WAR CRY, at three cents a copy. The singing continued about twenty minutes, and ended in a "wave offering," when all on the platform rose to their feet, and in simple chorus sang and waved their handkerchiefs, while many in the audience, seeing the force of the idea, responded with equal enthusiasm, even waving the WAR CRY in their desire to bless the sound of Jesus' name.[108]

The centralized organization of the Army, like that of Methodism a century earlier, resulted in the highly effective prosecution of the work of evangelization. Military discipline became a central feature of Army organization, and while the autocratic character of the leadership led eventually to internal dispute and schism it constituted an element of strength in the early years of the Army's growth. Extension of the work into new areas was undertaken with all the careful planning of a military campaign, and employment of such military terms as "invading," "assaulting," and "laying siege" suggested the considerable reliance upon military tactics. Reports from workers in the field assumed the character of military *communiqués*, and orders from headquarters were designed to stiffen morale and to secure objectives which had been decided upon in terms of a general plan of campaign.

The movement was not only an army, it was also a religious order. The property rights of the worker were surrendered to the organization: he lived in an Army residence, was clothed and fed by the Army, and any earnings were turned over to Army headquarters. The financial dependency of the worker assured obedience to Army orders and conformity to Army principles. On the other hand, the financial security provided by such an arrangement made enlistment in Army ranks highly attractive. The sort of people who were recruited as workers tended to be down-and-outs—the social outcasts of the community—who welcomed the economic as well as emotional security provided by the Army. Their enthusiasm for the Cause substituted for any individual desire for gain or self-aggrandizement. The discipline of the soldier and the devoutness of the ascetic combined to build up among workers a strong feeling of group loyalty and attachment to the leaders.

[108]*Christian Guardian*, Aug. 12, 1885.

The emphasis placed by the Army upon the reclamation of the individual—the drunkard, criminal, prostitute, and wastrel—led to practical results which could be demonstrated and dramatized. The sudden reformation of the individual assumed something of the character of the religious miracle, and reports of such a reformation—written up in a highly coloured manner—provided effective advertising. The work of the Army among the down-and-outs of the city won for it the affection of those who did not feel welcome in the houses of worship of the more richly endowed religious denominations and the sympathy of those who had a philanthropic interest in the welfare of the less fortunate elements of the population. The Salvation Army developed as the poor man's church; it was the church of those who had few claims to respectability and who were often morally as well as economically and socially something of outcasts in the community. The Army worker had no hesitation in stopping to minister to the drunkard, ex-criminal, or prostitute on the street; the Army hostel was always open to those who needed food or clothing. Philanthropic activities came to constitute an important part of the Army's work. Primarily, however, the force of its appeal lay in its emphasis upon the simple message of the gospel. The Army grew up with all the enthusiasm of the new religious sect. It was prepared to encourage the most extravagant forms of religious expression if the object were secured of gaining converts to the cause. It was in this evangelical character of the movement that lay its strength as a religious movement of the masses. "Such exclamations of praise," a correspondent wrote to the *Christian Guardian* in describing a Salvation Army meeting, "caused no nervous shock, or look of surprise, no vulgar stare or indignant frown of offended 'upper ten,' or what in the Lower Province is styled 'codfish' aristocracy, who, to a large extent, control Churches, hamper the usefulness of the minister, and reduce religious vitality to a minimum."[109]

Efforts of the older churches in the community to adopt some of the methods of the Salvation Army were an indication of their effectiveness in dealing with the problems of city life. But the success of the Army, in the end, was not due to any particular methods it employed. The strength of the Army lay in the fact that it was an exclusive religious sect. It expanded through its appeal to a particular social class in the community. However much the older churches may have employed its methods, they were unable to make the sort of single appeal which was characteristic of the Army. To the down-trodden, foot-loose of the urban community the Salvation Army was their church; they were the Army. Within the traditional church, in contrast, if such people were

[109]*Ibid.*

accepted at all, they were accepted simply as one element of the church membership, and an element which was usually considered to require "special treatment." Whatever the traditional churches did for the urban masses the fact of social distinction was emphasized; these people were treated as on a different social level. In the Army, they were of the "elect"; social differentiation disappeared in the emphasis upon spiritual values of worth.

That is not to say that the Army did not attract, as all religious sects do, a certain number of people from the better social classes of the community. In particular cases, no easy explanation could be offered for enlistment in Army ranks. In spirit, nevertheless, the Army was distinctively a lower-class movement; more accurately, it might be described as a classless movement. It developed within the social interstice between the societies of the folk and the classes. There seems little reason to believe that it attracted any great support from the organized working class in the urban community or from those pockets in the urban society where folk ties remained strong. It would be false to conclude from this that it was only the shiftless, the good-for-nothings who came to the support of the Army. Rather, the Army membership tended to be made up predominantly of honest, hard-working people who, in background and thinking, retained a strong attachment to religious values. But these people, at the same time, lacked a sense of social, and often economic, security. Many had come from country districts, others from overseas; all of them were strangers in a strange environment. Class or folk ties had been broken in face of the new conditions of urban life. It was in this sense that they were of the social masses.

The Canadian urban community, towards the close of the nineteenth century, was essentially a first-generation community. Few of the people in Montreal, Toronto, Hamilton, or other Canadian cities at this time had been born and raised in the community in which they were then living; many of them had come to the city from rural districts. The fundamental problem of the urban society was that of absorbing this strange population, and in meeting such a problem there was little effective leadership. The traditional institutions—of government, law and order, recreation, education—which sought to extend their control into the urban community were institutions which had grown up to meet the needs of a much more simple society. The failure of such institutional endeavours was evident in the growth of new forms of group life directed against the welfare of the larger society— the saloon, the gang, and the brothel, for instance. Efforts of the moral reformer to suppress such centres of social life inevitably ended in

failure or resulted in the promotion of new forms of group activity
often more vicious in character. Traditional social organization adapted
itself to urban conditions too slowly to meet some of the more urgent
social needs of the population.

That was particularly true of religious organization. The very fact
that the churches were churches, that is to say established religious
institutions, meant that they were not able to meet the needs of people
who found themselves outside the established social order. The existence
of the church implied a body of members and leaders, and members
and leaders were people with status. Status was something to protect
and could only be protected by protecting the integrity of the church.
Thus there was an unbridgeable gulf between the church and those
sections of the population which had no status position in the community. In particular cases a church could, by dissociating itself to
some extent from the denomination as a whole and from an established
membership body, build up a new following from among the social
masses of the urban community; thus the down-town church sought to
turn itself into a social centre of the nearby residents. Such developments,
however, could only extend a certain distance because the loyalty which
was established was one which could not reach beyond the local church
and pastor. They tended to become sectarian islands in the larger
denominational sea.

The task of developing among the unattached masses of the urban
community a sense of belonging to something—the task of creating
a new social consciousness—was one for which the religious sect was
pre-eminently suited. The sect did not attempt to suppress the saloon—
or the brothel—by urging upon legislative bodies prohibitory action.
The church was prepared to drive the drunkard out of the saloon on
to the streets; the Salvation Army marched him from the saloon to
the meeting barracks. In the sect, the individual was given something
of which he could become a part; he was made to feel important and
as if the movement were his. It did not much matter what particular
form of appeal was employed; indeed, the appeal did not even have
to be religious. But the religious appeal possessed a great advantage
in terms of the background of the population which had to be reached.
That population was little given given to philosophical speculation
or to an interest in public or social questions. Outside the home and
work-shop, its universe of discourse was largely religious. Religion
appealed to deeply rooted values of life. It provided a context in which
the various activities of the individual could find meaning.

In addition, the religious interest could develop as perhaps no other
interest could a dynamic propagandist force. The people who sought

to spread religious teachings were stirred by a zeal and devotion seldom characteristic of propagandists of philosophical, social, or political views. The religious appeal could be spectacular and persistent, and it tended to be such when made by the evangelical sect: thus the advantage of the sect over the church and in competition with secular agencies. Religious fanaticism produced a leadership of irresistible force. It also produced a following of stubborn devotion.

In the long run, perhaps, the effect of the influence of such a movement as the Salvation Army was to arrest the development of a stable urban order. People's attentions were diverted from the real problems of an industrial society; the Army following tended to be held in a state of political and economic illiteracy. The effect was particularly evident in retarding the development of working-class organizations. It may be questioned, however, whether stable secular institutions would have developed much greater strength if the Salvation Army had not emerged. Another form of fanaticism almost certainly would have grown up in the place of the religious. The sort of people to whom the Army appealed in the Canadian city in the closing years of the past century were the sort of people looking for a form of social participation on the most elementary level. The task of social building required building from the bottom, and it was on the bottom that the Army built strongly and securely.

CHAPTER NINE

Church and Sect in the Modern Community

B A R R A C K S still standing in many towns and villages, most of them built before 1900, provide some indication of the rapidity with which the Salvation Army movement grew after 1883. The same buildings, however, long since abandoned or converted to other uses, also suggest that such growth early came to an end and in later years Army influence greatly declined. The high peak in the growth of the movement was reached about the turn of the century. Development since was steadily in the direction of a limitation of the field of evangelical work and a strengthening of organization. Like other religious movements before it, the Army was forced away from the position of the religious sect in seeking a closer accommodation with the community. Its passing as a great evangelical force marked the end of one more chapter in the religious development of Canada.

Growing up as a highly evangelistic religious movement, success had tended to be measured in the early years of the Army's development in terms of the number of places occupied and the number of persons converted. Like that of all evangelists, the Salvationists' thinking had been dominated by the consciousness of the souls still to be saved, and this restless search for the wicked and damned had given to their work its distinctive character; an intense concern for the fate of the unsaved had accounted for their tremendous zeal and endurance in advancing the cause which they served. The urge to spread ever further the message of religious salvation, however, if it had constituted one of the important reasons for the success of the Salvationists' work, also came to constitute one of the important reasons for its ultimate failure. It led inevitably to an impatience with the slow and laborious task of building up a permanent organization. The result was that many of those people drawn into the Army ranks were later lost to the movement through the failure to follow up the early work of evangelization. In several centres, the work was allowed to lapse after one or two visits.[1] In other centres, the chief result of the Salvationists' labours

[1] A Methodist minister wrote in the *Christian Guardian*, June 4, 1884: "A branch of that Army started opposition services to a most successful revival meeting in

was to strengthen the following of the established churches or that of secular institutions.

The decision to withdraw from areas where sufficient support was not secured to maintain a strong local organization was one made by Headquarters in the interests of the larger movement. It reflected the viewpoint of a leadership concerned with problems of administration and finance in opposition to the viewpoint of the evangelist concerned only with saving souls.[2] Necessarily, as the Army grew, greater attention had to be paid to building up a distinctive following loyal to the movement as a whole. Those served by the Army had to be taxed for its support. This meant an increasing emphasis upon organization and financing at the cost in the end of abandoning much of the evangelical work of the movement.

The shift in emphasis did not come about without bitter internal conflict which on a number of occasions led to open division and the organization of rival armies. The fact that International Headquarters were located in London intensified the feeling of distance between the Army leaders and the workers in the field, and opposition to centralized control found support in the view that the interests of the local movement were being sacrificed in the interests of an organization outside the country. In the United States, where resentment against the autocratic control exercised by a headquarters outside the country developed particularly strongly, two major schisms within the movement occurred. Sometime in the early eighteen-eighties Commissioner Thomas E. Moore, in refusing to accept his recall by International Headquarters, withdrew and carried with him nine-tenths of the Army in America; the original movement had to be built up from the ground.[3] Again, in 1896, Commander and Mrs. Ballington Booth, as a result of differences with International Headquarters, were forced to relinquish their command

---

this village. The Church made a compromise, and in a short time gave way. Some sixty professed faith in Christ at meetings conducted by the Army, which lasted about a month. The Army then left, and as far as I can learn not one of that sixty united with any Church in the place. The Army came back, held one meeting; left because it would not pay."

[2]P. W. Philpott, who had been an active Army evangelist, wrote in 1892: "I could not close my eyes to the fact that scores of towns and villages, once held by the Army as strongholds, in which they declared they would remain until the Judgment Day, are now long since closed and the Army work discontinued. Four and a half years ago I had charge of what was then the Palmerston Division, consisting of twenty-two corps; to-day thirteen of these places are no longer known as Army stations. Many other places have been closed in the various divisions during the last two years, and it seems to me that a greater number of the remaining small places will be similarly dealt with." P. W. Philpott and A. W. Roffe, *New Light: Containing a Full Account of the Recent Salvation Army Troubles in Canada* (Toronto, 1892), p. 32.

[3]F. G. Beardsley, *The History of American Revivals* (New York, 1912), p. 303.

of the American wing of the Army,,and under their leadership a new movement was organized called the "Volunteers of America" with a less autocratic form of government and working along lines slightly divergent from those of the parent movement; the new Army seriously weakened the position of the old.[4]

In Canada, local Army leadership was much too dependent upon outside support to go far in breaking with International Headquarters. The close political connection favoured the maintenance of close religious connections with the old country; the Army following in the country was largely recruited from among people who had recently immigrated from Britain. Nevertheless, a restlessness in the ranks of the Canadian Army was early evident. Independent armies grew up in various parts of the country under the leadership of men who had been officers in the regular Army; Mary Morgan Dean wrote of one such army in Windsor at the time Mrs. Johnston, then Captain Goodall, was sent there to take charge of regular army work, probably towards the close of the eighteen-eighties: "A seceder's Army was flourishing, and when the Captain had gathered around her little company, a large crowd of listeners, the band of the other Army would play right past her meeting by the river and carry off her crowd."[5] While most of these independent army movements were short-lived and gained little influence outside the local areas in which they grew up, one in 1891, associated with the name of P. W. Philpott, was to result in a major division in Canadian army ranks.

The defection of 1891 gained importance first from the number of prominent officers involved and second from the amount of publicity it secured. The conflict which ensued assumed something of the character of a public scandal, offering an opportunity to critics to prove many of the charges they had made against the Army.[6] Philpott had been converted by the Army in Dresden, Ontario, and came to Toronto Headquarters as an officer. Influential in evangelical and administrative work, he was in a strong position to lead a local movement of protest against the autocratic control exercised by International Headquarters. Demoted and eventually forced to resign, he carried with him out of the Army hundreds of other officers; the whole of the Richmond Street corps, according to his own statement, separated.[7] Although he declined the offer to head a rival organization, he and many of the other officers

[4]*Ibid.*, p. 305.

[5]Mary Morgan Dean, *The Lady with the Other Lamp, The Story of Blanche Read Johnston* (Toronto, 1919), pp. 72-3.

[6]See, for instance, T. H. Huxley, *Social Diseases and Worse Remedies* (London, 1891), pp. 77-80, 83-9, 92-9.

[7]Private Interview. See also Philpott and Roffe, *New Light.*

who had broken away began what were called "Mission Churches" in a number of Canadian cities. The defection dealt a serious blow to the unity of the Army in Canada.

Fundamental differences in viewpoint and outlook underlay the conflict which led to Philpott's break in 1891. The charges and counter-charges made by the opposing parties tended in the end to obscure the real issue in dispute. Once the break occurred, personal feelings made reconciliation difficult, but the clash of personalities was secondary to the clash of two opposed conceptions of the position of the Army in the community. Herbert H. Booth, representing International Headquarters, was concerned with building the movement into a permanent religious organization with its own distinctive following; Philpott, with the interests of the evangelist, was concerned with saving souls wherever they might be found with little regard to denominational lines.[8] The one view reflected the spirit of the church, the other the spirit of the religious sect. Although the Army suffered a serious loss of support from the defection, in the end it gained greatly in terms of building up a strong organization. Like all evangelical sects, it had to rid itself of some of those very attributes which had accounted for its early success if it were to survive. People like Philpott brought strength to the movement but were also a seriously disturbing influence. The evangelist was one who could not accept direction from above; the condition of Army success depended upon such direction. The movement had grown up around the Booth family and, though the Booths may have abused their position of authority, it was through their close direction that it gained its enormous strength. The solution to the problem of the unlimited power exercised by the leadership came in the end not through abandoning centralized control but through developing within the organization a more responsible form of government.

[8]"That the Army," Philpott and Roffe charged in 1892, "has been converted by its leaders from a *means* to an *end* is evident from the fact that all the administration for some years past has been enacted for the building up of a separate organization. The Army no longer professes to be the friend and auxiliary of the churches, but has declared its open antagonism to them by forbidding its soldiers to attend church services without *special permission*, while its officers are strictly prohibited from taking part in church revivals. . . .

"No doubt the unprecedented success that accompanied the Army's first operations, has in one sense, been a bane to them and has tended, indirectly, to produce the sad state of affairs that now exists; for the moment that the leaders began to attribute the result to the *Army methods*, that moment the spirit of God began to withdraw His power. It will be admitted by all that the success achieved through the Army was not due to its *methods*, for many of these are obnoxious to modern taste, but it was due to the fact that they *preached the pure and simple gospel and sought to glorify God*, who declares in His word that He will not give His glory unto another. The whole point may be summed up in one sentence: *The glorification of the Army has produced a spiritual decline in the work*." *Ibid.*, pp. 111-12.

By 1914 the Salvation Army in Canada had changed radically in character. By then it had ceased to be a movement of the social masses. Where the typical Salvationist had been a reformed drunkard, ex-criminal, or ex-prostitute, he now became a person of some social standing with a particular competence as a religious teacher and social welfare worker. A sharp division developed between the Salvationists, on the one hand, and those being saved, on the other. A greater attention came to be paid to the educational qualifications, social position, and personality of those enlisted in officers' ranks; the rise of Mrs. Johnston to a position of leadership within the movement was indicative of advantages which she possessed in the way of a reputation for respectability.[9] Establishment of a training school to equip young men and women for positions of responsibility and leadership marked the final passing of the old type Salvationist and the emergence of the professional Salvation Army worker.

The change in the character of Army leadership was closely related to the change in the general position of the Army within the community. The movement developed into a sort of social welfare organization. Rescue work among such groups as ex-convicts, drunkards, prostitutes, and unmarried mothers led to the establishment of special homes and institutions, and the management of these came to command a greater share of attention of Army leaders. Recognition of the value of the work done won for the Army a greater measure of public good-will, while the increasing financial costs of the work, in turn, forced the Army to seek greater support from the public. The War of 1914-18 only hastened a development already well underway before 1914. Its war work secured the reputation of the Army as a patriotic organization and strengthened ties with the community which had been established through its social welfare work. Once the support of the community had been secured it could not be easily abandoned. Strong vested interests operated to check any shift back to the separatist position of the religious sect.

If Horner's Holiness Movement Church had continued to grow it also would have been forced away from the position of the religious sect in an effort to establish a more permanent form of organization. Indeed, the secession of Horner in 1916, and his organization of a new religious body called the Standard Church of America, were indicative of increasing strains within the movement as a result of the conflicting claims of the interest in organization and the interest in evangelization. Lacking outside support, however, the Holiness Movement Church

[9]Dean, *The Lady with the Other Lamp*, p. 178.

was unable to develop sufficient strength to build itself into a formal religious denomination. It only survived by becoming caught up within the new Holiness-Pentecostal movements which spread into the country after the turn of the century.

The Great Revival after 1885 had grown out of the social situation produced by industrialization and urban growth; it had developed as a religious movement of the new working masses of the cities and towns. Its chief support had come from that section of the Canadian urban population consisting of recent immigrants from Great Britain or of people who had migrated from rural areas. By 1914 this population had become a second-generation urban population. The industrial community had come to depend increasingly upon the European continent rather than upon Britain or rural Canada for its supply of labour. Sharp ethnic differences set the new working population off from the old, and it was from the old working population, the population which had come to have a stake in the community, that movements such as the Salvation Army derived most of their support.

What happened, fundamentally, was that the section of the population upon which the Salvation Army depended for its following became *proletarianized.* Two decades or more of residence in an urban industrial society had developed by 1914 a working-class consciousness. The worker had come to acquire a sense of status as a worker. The effect was to greatly restrict the area of influence of such an evangelistic religious movement as the Salvation Army; the claims of a working-class philosophy were opposed to the claims of an evangelical religion. Thus much of the mass support of the Army was lost, and emphasis shifted from evangelization to social service. Leadership and financial support came increasingly to be drawn from the middle classes, the work confined to providing for the needs—material as well as spiritual—of the socially unfortunate classes.

The growing class consciousness of the urban working population was closely related to more general changes taking place in the Canadian urban-industrial social order. Developments in education, improvements in means of transportation, the growing importance of the daily newspaper, the rise in living standards with the upward swing of the business cycle after 1896, the widening knowledge of the world with the South African War, the Klondike gold-rush, and the opening of the West, and the establishment of a greater variety of recreational and cultural institutions made for an enrichment of Canadian urban social life and a stronger community spirit. The belief in biological and social evolution gained in popularity, and the new optimism generated by scientific teachings found support in developments in Big Business.

Faith in the idea of human progress undermined the faiths of religious fundamentalism.

At the same time, the community became increasingly self-conscious with regard to such social ills as poverty, bad housing, illiteracy, juvenile delinquency, crime, prostitution, and alcoholism. The voice of the social reformer found a wider hearing, and social problems came to be thought of as something to be legislated out of existence. This shift from a concern about the shortcomings of the individual to a concern about the shortcomings of society, weakened the religious appeal with its emphasis upon human sin. Efforts on the part of the churches to take a lead in formulating a programme of social reform were paralleled by efforts on the part of the Salvation Army to develop more systematic methods of social service. An impatience with purely spiritual remedies increased with the spread of the new social gospel and the gospel of Science.

The defection from the Methodist Church of a number of socially minded ministers, and the establishment of "Peoples' Churches" in several centres in Western Canada, were an indication of the growing dissatisfaction with any sort of fundamentalist religious approach in the years immediately after the close of the Great War of 1914-18. The war resulted in what was perhaps the first real intellectual awakening in Canada's history. It also resulted in the enormous strengthening of business interests in the country. The increase in the power of the state, the strengthening of business monopoly, the intensification of labour conflict, and the rise of militant farmer organizations were an assertion of strong secular forces in the life of the Canadian community. The period 1920-30 was one characterized by a general drift away from religious values, evident in the weakening of puritan mores, the secularization of the Sabbath, the declining influence of the bible, the falling off of church attendance, and the increasing neglect of family prayers. Union of the Methodist, Presbyterian, and Congregational churches in 1925 was a reflection of the growing dominance of secular values associated with Politics and Big Business.

Yet the number and variety of religious sects in the Canadian community today would suggest that among large sections of the population secular systems of thought at no time secured a strong hold. Even in those areas where the break from religious fundamentalism seemed most complete, as in Western Canada, the appeal of secular movements was one of enduring attractiveness to only a small proportion of the total population. Rational methods of solving human problems were eagerly sought so long as the solution appeared within easy reach. When drought and the collapse of wheat prices shook the foundations

of the Western rural society, and man no longer seemed to have any rational control over his fate, the simple faiths of religion secured a new hold. The phenomenal spread of religious sects in Saskatchewan and Alberta after 1930 was a manifestation of a growing disillusionment on the part of the population with the sort of rationalist appeal which had been made by political parties and farmer organizations. In other parts of Canada the shift back to fundamentalist religious beliefs was little less pronounced. Mass immigration, industrialization, war, and depression led to a weakening of traditional social relationships and social values throughout the Canadian community, and the breakdown of secular forms of organization in various areas of social life increased dependence upon religious forms. After 1930 a general reaction to the trend towards secularism became increasingly evident. The amount of space devoted to the advertisement of evangelistic religious services on the church pages of all the Canadian city dailies today offers some indication of the strength of the new revival of religion.

This study is not concerned with the religious movements which have grown up in Canada since 1900. Here it is only necessary to emphasize that there is nothing about them which is fundamentally different from earlier movements. New methods and new techniques, it is true, have been developed. The radio and the printing press have been discovered as powerful agencies of mass religious propaganda. Community supported bible colleges, many of them located in isolated country towns and villages, have been developed as highly effective agencies for the recruiting and training of a large body of zealous evangelical workers and preachers. Business practices in church organization, such as the employment of trained secretaries and the establishment of elaborate filing systems, have been increasingly adopted as means of adding to the efficiency of church government. Though reacting violently against modernism in religious teaching, the sect of today recognizes fully the value of modern techniques of business organization and also of salesmanship; large neon signs, streamer banners, and sensational newspaper advertisements have become accepted means of selling religion to the public. Finally, in ways undreamed of by religious evangelists of an earlier age, new techniques have been discovered of raising vast sums of money, and of doing it without having to render to any responsible authority an accounting of where such sums have come from or how they were disbursed.

But the development of such new methods and techniques has not fundamentally altered the character of the religious sect. Its underlying appeal, its social role, remains the same. It still emphasizes in its teachings the simple, unchanging truths of the gospel. It still gains its

following because it meets certain basic social needs of people which are not being met by the church or by secular agencies in the community. Today, as in the past, the support of the religious sect comes from that section of the population which has lost a sense of belonging to any settled society. It remains a movement of the socially unattached, of the foot-loose of the community.

The religious development of Canada throughout the period 1760 to the present day offers a convincing demonstration of the importance of the religious interest in securing a sense of social solidarity, of *society*. The religious institution as an integral part of the whole institutional complex of the community served as one of the means of entering into social relationships and of becoming a part of a recognized group life. As such, it has been subject to all the influences determining the form of organization of social relationships. Changes in the basic community structure affected inevitably the network of relationships and the complex of values built up around the religious interest. New social demands forced adjustments in the religious institution, and out of this process of adjustment there emerged that pattern of development which has been described here in terms of the conflict between the church and sect forms of religious organization. The new religious movement, the religious sect, offered an important means of securing the adjustment of the religious institution to new social conditions. It served to maintain the religious interest as an effective basis of social organization in areas of change where traditional systems of social control, including that of the church, were breaking down.

It remains only to emphasize in the way of conclusion the close relationship of the development of religious organization to the development of other forms of social organization in the community. The religious interest at no time stood alone as a socially reorganizing force. Alongside the religious movement, and out of much the same social situations, there have developed movements devoted to such causes as the reform of the economic system, political organization, the administration of justice, and the practice of medicine. In the development of the community, the monetary crank, the political rebel, the vigilante leader, and the medical quack have played a role at various times very similar to that of the religious prophet. The new social movement, whatever the form it assumed, developed as a protest against constituted authority, or, more specifically, against the claims to authority of a special class of officials or functionaries in society— clergymen, bankers, politicians, judges, licensed medical practitioners, and such. The making of such a protest involved the search for new sources of authority and the establishment of new grounds of loyalty.

Appeal to the voice of the masses provided the political rebel with a means of undermining the privileged position of the professional politician as effective as appeal to the call of God the religious prophet of undermining the privileged position of the professional church minister. Similarly, conversion offered a means not only of building up a religious loyalty but of building up a loyalty to the cause of economic or political reform, the reform of the administration of justice or of the practice of medicine. The charismatic influence of the unlicensed doctor who claimed miraculous powers in the cure of physical ills was little different from the charismatic influence of the self-appointed religious teacher who claimed miraculous powers in the cure of spiritual ills; the devotion of the following of the one was scarcely less fanatical than the devotion of the other.

In terms of their social role, the significance of these various kinds of social movements lay in their securing a feeling of fellowship and status on the part of people who had lost a sense of belonging to any organized society. This was as true of movements devoted to the reform of the economic system, the political system, the administration of justice, or the practice of medicine as of movements devoted to religious reform. It was much the same sort of people, for instance, who sought relief for their physical ailments from unlicensed medical doctors as sought relief for their spiritual wants from untrained religious teachers; similar social factors operated to shut people off from the services of the professionally recognized physician and church minister: the distrust of the educated man (a distrust rooted deeply in the attitudes of a large section of the population), the feeling of awkwardness in the presence (in the physician's reception office or in the house of worship) of people of a higher social class, the very inertia or timidity of gaining access to the imposing sorts of places where the services of medicine or religion were dispensed. This study has sought to reveal how great were the limitations of the church in attracting the support of large sections of the population at various times; few church leaders have ever been prepared to admit the real strength of the opposition to the formal services of religion. In other areas of social life similarly, to an extent seldom recognized, the formal social institution has been faced with considerable lack of support in the attitudes and mores of the population. A study of the institution of medicine, for instance, would probably reveal that the feeling of trust in the professional medical practitioner, assumed to be general, is actually confined very largely to the upper social classes of the community. The same, it seems safe to suggest, would be found to be true of such institutions as banking, the party system, and the administration of justice.

It would be beyond the scope of this study to go further in seeking to establish a parallel between developments in religious organization and developments in other areas of social life. Here attention was necessarily confined to movements within the organization of religion. Study of the development of religious organization, however, points the way to the study of the whole complex of social development. The pattern of development of social movements generally probably would be found to conform closely to the pattern of development of religious movements. Indeed, the conception of religious development elaborated here in terms of the conflict between the church and sect might well offer suggestive leads in the study of other types of social movements and institutions.

Index

Aberhart, William, xi

Acadia University, 251-3

Acadians, evacuation of, 3-4

Addie, Colonel Jack, 382

Addyman, Rev. John, 294

Adolphustown: Methodists in, 94, 97; camp meeting in, 153-4

Agreement of 1818, between Methodist Episcopal Church and Wesleyan Conference, 201, 203

Alberta, new religious sects in, 432

Alder, Rev. Robert, 203, 274

Allan, Rev. Daniel, 215

Alline, Henry, xi, 18-29, 32-3, 36-7, 46, 55, 84, 174-5, 176, 177, 181-2, 187-90, 261, 278

Allinites, 183

American Baptist churches, 204

American Baptist Home Mission Society, 300

American Baptists, in Canada, 224, 300

American influence: on religious developments in Maritimes, 46; on Presbyterian Church, 137; on Methodist movement, 160-2; on religious developments in Canada, 165-6

American Methodists, in Canada, 199-201

American preachers, 84-5

American Presbyterian Church, 100-1, 136-7, 161: organization of in Montreal with Methodists, 201; conflict within, 205; weaknesses of, 231

American Protestant Church, 198

American Revolutionary War, 31-2, 35-6; and Newlight movement, 39; and religious movements in Quebec, 44; effect of in Nova Scotia, 45, 87; and failure Nova Scotia to secure Wesleyan missionaries, 55; and growth of settlement in Canada, 90

Amherst, Baptist Church of, 55; Methodists in, 55-6, 62, 181-2

Amherstburg, Methodist Church in, 160, 267

Anabaptists, 65, 104

Ancaster Circuit, of Methodist Church, 94, 96; camp meeting in, 211

Andrews, Rev. Mr., 68

Annapolis: Church of England in, 5, 10; preaching of Henry Alline in, 18; Congregational Church in, 29; Baptist Church in, 54; Methodist preaching in, 56, 193, 196; state of the Church of England in, 64-5, 77

Annapolis Valley: preaching of Henry Alline in, 19; Methodists in, 239

Annual Conference, Methodist Church in Canada, 202

Ansley, Thomas, 247

Anti-burgher Synod, 138

Antiburghers, 79, 138

Antigonish, Baptist Church in, 234

Antinomian preacher, 184

Antinomianism, and Newlight movement, 181, 184, 189

Anti-poverty league, and Methodist Church, 394

Archdeacon of York, 203

Argyle: Congregational Church in, 11, 12, 15, 16; Newlight movement in, 26, 48, 54; Church of England in, 66; Newlight Church in, 178, 180; Free Christian Church in, 280

Army, influence of: in Quebec, 41; in Canada, 92-3

Arnold, Rev. Oliver, 68

Asbury, Bishop Francis, 198

Asceticism: and Congregationalism, 13-14; and Newlightism, 37-8; of Methodists, 85-6, 159-60, 266-7; weakening of among Methodists, 340; and Holiness Movement Church, 417-18

Ashley, William W., 285

Associate Synod, of Presbyterian Church, 134, 138

Augusta: Church of England in, 104, 110-11; Baptist Church in, 226

CHURCH AND SECT IN CANADA